Consumers in Europe

2009 edition

Europe Direct is a service to help you find answers to your questions about the European Union

Freephone number (*):

00 800 6 7 8 9 10 11

(*) Certain mobile telephone operators do not allow access to 00 800 numbers or these calls may be billed.

More information on the European Union is available on the Internet (http://europa.eu).

Luxembourg: Office for Official Publications of the European Communities, 2009

ISBN 978-92-79-11362-8
ISSN 1831-4023
doi 10.2785/29257
Cat. No. KS-DY-09-001-EN-C

Theme: General and regional statistics
Collection: Statistical books

Printed in Belgium

PRINTED ON WHITE CHLORINE-FREE PAPER

FOREWORD

In the current difficult economic climate, the needs of Europe's citizens must be a top priority, and so policies must be oriented towards its citizens and towards the benefits they can deliver for them. In the two years since European Consumer Policy became the exclusive responsibility of a single European Commissioner, the policy focus has shifted, and increasingly aims for better outcomes for consumers and citizens. Consumer policy has brought the consumer to the heart of the market. It has worked to empower consumers through accurate information and market transparency, to enhance their welfare and to protect them from risks and threats. Consumer Policy is not just helping to build the internal market, it is also building a European consumer market – with better access, more choice, the possibility to compare products and prices, and increased quality and safety. In an increasingly globalised economy, a market, which responds to consumer demands helps contribute to an innovative and competitive economy.

We believe that confident, informed and empowered consumers are the powerhouse of economic evolution. EUROSTAT has stepped up its efforts to meet the rising demand for statistical information with clear, accessible data in the belief that it would further encourage the engagement of users such as nongovernmental organisations, stakeholder and lobby groups in the political process. Furthermore, it recognises the need to step up coordinated European action to fight the economic crisis through harmonised and comparable information. However, producing information is not enough. In recent years it has been recognised that a special effort has to be made to communicate this information better.

Keeping this in mind, a joint venture between EUROSTAT and DG SANCO Consumer Affairs resulted in producing an interesting and worthwhile string of publications entitled "Consumers in Europe". Using the wealth of information in EUROSTAT and also complimenting this through other sources, this fourth edition gives an overview of the single market from the consumer's perspective, and covers 12 specific sectors (including food and beverages; clothing and footwear; housing, electricity, gas and other fuels).

The aim of the fourth edition is to bring together the most relevant and useful data for the evaluation and development of consumer policy, not only as a tool for policy-makers, but also for those interested in end-markets and consumer affairs. This data will not only help deliver better consumer policy, it will be used to argue the consumer case in other policy areas too so that consumer interests are built into all EU policies. Much of the data that has been used feeds into the Consumer Markets Scoreboard, which aims at informing on the malfunctioning of markets from a consumer perspective. Thus the data contribute to monitoring outcomes in the Single Market and to make European Union policy in this area more responsive to the expectations and concerns of consumers.

Citizens are more aware than ever of the policies that shape their environment. We hope that these facts and figures reflect the serious approach we take when developing and shaping that policy and that it will contribute to enhanced consumer confidence which has never been more important.

Mrs. Meglena Kuneva
Commissioner for Consumer Protection

Mr. Joaquín Almunia
Commissioner for Eurostat

ABSTRACT

The 2009 edition of Consumers in Europe presents a comprehensive set of data and related information concerning consumer markets and consumer protection issues within the European Union. The aim of the publication is to bring together the most relevant and useful information for the evaluation and development of consumer policy, not only as a tool for policy-makers, but also for those interested in end-markets and consumer affairs, such as representative organisations, public authorities, or suppliers of goods and services. Much of the data that has been used will feed into the consumer markets scoreboard which has been designed to monitor outcomes in the single market and to make European Union policy in this area more responsive to the expectations and concerns of consumers.

The publication starts with an overview of the single market from the consumer's perspective, presenting a profile of European consumers and the retail network, as well as issues relating to access and choice, before looking at key indicators for consumption and prices. The overview also presents information on consumer satisfaction, the quality and safety of goods and services, as well consumer representation and protection.

The remainder of the publication is devoted to 12 specific consumer markets (for example, food and non-alcoholic beverages, housing, transport, or recreation and culture); each chapter covers one top-level heading within the classification of individual consumption by purpose (COICOP), the main classification used to provide detailed data on consumer prices, price levels and consumption expenditure. The chapters are structured in a similar manner to the overview, in an attempt to present harmonised data and a range of key indicators that may be compared across the publication.

Project management:

This publication has been financed by the Directorate-General for Health and Consumers of the European Commission, led by unit B1 responsible for consumer markets (acting Head of Unit, David Mair). The project has been managed by Eurostat (the statistical office of the European Communities), led by unit F3 responsible for living conditions and social protection statistics (Head of Unit, Anne Clemenceau). The opinions expressed are those of the individual authors alone and do not necessarily reflect the position of the European Commission.

Co-ordination:

Peter-Paul Borg
BECH D2/704
Eurostat – statistical office of the European Communities
Bâtiment Joseph Bech
Rue Alphonse Weicker, 5
L-2721 Luxembourg (Kirchberg)
peter-paul.borg@ec.europa.eu

Marie-Luise Altmutter
Directorate-General for Health and Consumers
European Commission
marie-luise.altmutter@ec.europa.eu

Data compilation, production and desktop publishing:

INFORMA sarl (informa@informa.lu)
Giovanni Albertone, Simon Allen, Edward Cook, Andrew Redpath

Data extraction:

The statistical data presented were extracted during the summer of 2008 and represent data availability at that time. The accompanying text was drafted during the autumn months of 2008. Some specific data was not available until a later date, namely: a consumer protection survey carried out by Eurobarometer and a retail satisfaction survey (both published in October 2008).

For more information, please consult:

Directorate-General for Health and Consumers: http://ec.europa.eu/consumers/index_en.htm

Eurostat: http://ec.europa.eu/eurostat

Copyright of photographs

TABLE OF CONTENTS

Introduction

A reader's guide 6
Structure of publication 6
Data coverage 6
Basic concepts: main data sources 8

Consumer policy 11
Consumer policy strategy 2007-2013 11
Consumer protection 12

Part A: Overview

I. CONSUMER PROFILE 16
Consumers and consumption in the economy 16
People and households 18
Time-use 25
Income levels and income distribution 28
Consumption or savings? 33
Credit, ability to pay and indebtedness 34
Consumer confidence 38

II. RETAILING AND ADVERTISING 40
In-store retailing 41
Out-of-store sales 46
E-commerce 50
Cross-border sales to consumers 55
Advertising 58

III. ACCESS, CHOICE AND SWITCHING 60
Access and choice 60
Switching 63

IV. CONSUMPTION 65
Ownership 65
Frequency of purchase 67
Structure of consumption expenditure 68
Expenditure patterns of different population groups 75

V. PRICES AND INDIRECT TAXES 87
Price inflation 87
Price levels 93
Indirect taxes 98

VI. CONSUMER SATISFACTION AND COMPLAINTS 100
Satisfaction 100
Complaints 104

VII. QUALITY AND SAFETY 109
Quality 109
Safety 113

VIII. EXTERNALITIES 119
Environment 119
Waste 121

IX. CONSUMER REPRESENTATION AND PROTECTION 123
Representation 123
Protection 125

Part B: Consumer markets

1. Food and non-alcoholic beverages 131
1.1 Access, choice 132
1.2 Consumption 138
1.3 Prices 147
1.4 Consumer satisfaction 152
1.5 Quality and safety 153
1.6 Externalities 160
2. Alcoholic beverages and tobacco 163
2.1 Access and choice 164
2.2 Consumption 164
2.3 Prices 170
2.4 Safety 172
2.5 Externalities 174
3. Clothing and footwear 177
3.1 Access and choice 178
3.2 Consumption 181
3.3 Prices 184
3.4 Consumer satisfaction and complaints 186
3.5 Quality 187
4. Housing, water, electricity, gas and other fuels 189
4.1 Access, choice and switching 191
4.2 Consumption 195
4.3 Prices 205
4.4 Consumer satisfaction and complaints 211
4.5 Quality 219
4.6 Externalities: environment 220
5. Furnishings, household equipment and maintenance 223
5.1 Access and choice 224
5.2 Consumption 227
5.3 Prices 232
5.4 Consumer satisfaction and complaints 235
5.5 Quality 237
6. Health 239
6.1 Access and choice 241
6.2 Consumption 245
6.3 Prices 250
6.4 Consumer satisfaction 252
7. Transport 255
7.1 Access and choice 256
7.2 Consumption 262
7.3 Prices 267
7.4 Consumer satisfaction and complaints 271
7.5 Quality and safety 275
7.6 Externalities 280

8. Communications 281
8.1 Access, choice and switching 282
8.2 Consumption 288
8.3 Prices 293
8.4 Consumer satisfaction and complaints 299
8.5 Quality 301
8.6 Externalities: health 302
9. Recreation and culture 303
9.1 Access and choice 304
9.2 Consumption 307
9.3 Prices 311
9.4 Consumer satisfaction 313
9.5 Quality 315
10. Education 317
10.1 Access and choice 319
10.2 Consumption 322
10.3 Prices 332
10.4 Consumer satisfaction 333
10.5 Quality 334
11. Restaurants and hotels 337
11.1 Access and choice 338
11.2 Consumption 339
11.3 Prices 342
11.4 Quality 344
12. Miscellaneous goods and services 345
12A. Personal products, social care and other services 346
12A.1 Consumption 346
12A.2 Prices 350
12B Insurance and financial services 352
12B.1 Access, choice and switching 353
12B.2 Consumption 355
12B.3 Prices 357
Part C: Methodology
Annex 363
Data sources 364
Classifications 370
Abbreviations 372

A READER'S GUIDE

The 2009 edition of Consumers in Europe presents a comprehensive set of data and related information concerning consumer markets and consumer protection issues within the European Union. The aim of the publication is to bring together the most relevant and useful information for the evaluation and development of consumer policy, not only as a tool for policy-makers, but also for those interested in end-markets and consumer affairs, such as representative organisations, public authorities, or suppliers of goods and services. Much of the data that has been used will feed into the consumer markets scoreboard which has been designed to monitor outcomes in the single market and to make European Union policy in this area more responsive to the expectations and concerns of consumers.

Structure of the publication

The publication starts with an overview of the single market from the consumer's perspective, presenting a profile of European consumers and the retail network, as well as issues relating to access and choice, before looking at key indicators for consumption and prices. The overview also presents information on consumer satisfaction, the quality and safety of goods and services, as well consumer representation and protection.

The remainder of the publication is devoted to 12 specific consumer markets (food and non-alcoholic beverages; alcoholic beverages and tobacco; clothing and footwear; housing, water, electricity, gas and other fuels; furnishings, household equipment and maintenance; health; transport; communications; recreation and culture; education; hotels, cafés and restaurants; miscellaneous goods and services); each of these covers one top-level heading within the classification of individual consumption by purpose (COICOP) the main classification used to provide detailed data on consumer prices, price levels and consumption expenditure. The chapters are structured in a similar manner to the overview, in an attempt to present harmonised data and a range of key indicators that may be compared across the publication. As such, each chapter is structured, subject to data availability, with information relating to: access, choice and switching; consumption; prices; consumer satisfaction and complaints; quality and safety; and externalities.

The methodological information at the end of the publication covers the main data sources, classifications, as well as a list of statistical symbols, abbreviations and acronyms employed. A brief summary of the key methodological concepts is provided below for those readers who wish to explore the publication immediately.

Data coverage

Classification of individual consumption by purpose (COICOP)

Much of the official data presented in this publication has been compiled using the classification of individual consumption by purpose (COICOP). An extract of the classification is provided at the end of the publication; otherwise, a full listing can be obtained from the United Nations' website at http://unstats.un.org/unsd/cr/registry/regcst.asp?Cl=5&Lg=1.

COICOP is structured hierarchically in three levels. The chapter headings within Part B of this publication have been aligned on the Division level of COICOP (level 1), while more detailed information is provided within each chapter. While the COICOP classification officially has three levels of detail, certain Eurostat data sets have been extended to include more detailed data at a fourth level for some consumption items.

Geographical entities

This publication presents information for the 27 Member States of the European Union (EU-27), as well as the individual Member States. The EU-27 aggregate is only provided when information for all of the countries is available, or if an estimate has been made for missing information. Any partial totals that are created are footnoted with respect to the missing components.

The order of the Member States in tables generally follows their order of protocol; in other words, the alphabetical order of the countries' names in their respective languages; in some graphs the data are ranked in descending order according to the values of a particular indicator or other criteria.

Time-series for geographical aggregates are based on a consistent set of countries for the whole of the time period shown (unless otherwise indicated). In other words, although the EU has only had 27 Member States since the start of 2007, the time-series for EU-27 generally refer to the sum or an average of all 27 countries for the whole of the period presented, as if all 27 Member States had historically been part of the European Union.

When available, information is also presented for the candidate countries of Croatia, the former Yugoslav Republic of Macedonia and Turkey, for EFTA countries, as well as Japan and the United States. In the event that non-member countries did not provide data, then these have been excluded from tables and graphs; however, the full set of 27 Member States is generally maintained in tables even when data are not available, with footnotes being added to graphs when country information is missing or only partially available. In the event that a reference year is not available for a particular country, then efforts have been made to fill tables and graphs with previous reference years (again these exceptions are footnoted).

Monetary values

Monetary values are generally expressed in terms of euro (EUR). The data have been converted using average exchange rates prevailing for the year in question. The conversion of data expressed in national currencies to a common currency facilitates comparisons; however, fluctuations in currency markets may be responsible for at least some of the movements identified when observing the evolution of a time-series in euro terms.

Economic and Monetary Union (EMU) consists of three stages co-ordinating economic policy and culminating with the adoption of the euro. At the time of writing, 15 of the EU Member States – Belgium, Germany, Ireland, Greece, Spain, France, Cyprus, Italy, Luxembourg, Malta, the Netherlands, Austria, Portugal, Slovenia, and Finland – have so far entered the third stage, adopting the euro as their common currency. All EMU members are eligible to adopt the euro, but Denmark and the United Kingdom have opted to remain outside the euro, Slovakia is expected to join at the beginning of 2009, while Bulgaria, the Czech Republic, Estonia, Hungary, Latvia, Lithuania, Poland, Romania and Sweden have no target date for joining.

Technically, time-series information prior to 1 January 1999 should be denominated in ECU terms. However, given that the conversion rate was ECU 1 = EUR 1, for practical purposes this publication denotes all such values in euro terms.

While most of the monetary data presented in this publication are denominated in euro terms, some are presented in terms of purchasing power standards (PPS); expenditure data in PPS terms have been converted into a common currency using purchasing power parities (PPPs) that reflect the purchasing power (based on price levels for similar products) of each currency, rather than using market exchange rates. PPS data therefore facilitate a comparison between economies with different price levels for comparable products. PPS data are intended for cross-country comparisons rather than temporal comparisons as the relative price levels between countries change over time.

Timeframe

The statistical data presented were extracted during the summer of 2008 and represent data availability at that time. The accompanying text was drafted during the autumn months of 2008. Some specific data was not available until a later date, namely: a consumer protection survey carried out by Eurobarometer and a retail satisfaction survey (both published in October 2008).

Note that the data are generally presented for the latest years for which information is available. Longer time-series or alternative reference periods may well be available when consulting Eurostat's online databases (see below).

Additional or fresher information

The simplest way of accessing Eurostat's broad range of statistical information is through the Eurostat website (http://ec.europa.eu/eurostat). The website is updated daily and provides direct access to the latest and most comprehensive statistical information available on the European Union; the information published (including data, PDF publications and methodological information) is free of charge and often provided in German, English and French.

The most important statistical indicators are presented on the Eurostat website in the form of 'main tables'. These can be found by clicking on the link provided on the Eurostat homepage. The data navigation tree presents information divided into nine statistical themes that are used to classify data by topic. The main tables are stored under the first heading in the data tree. They generally present information for a single indicator, with European geographic aggregates and data for the Member States on the y-axis (down the screen) and time on the x-axis (across the screen).

More detailed statistics and larger volumes of data can be downloaded from Eurostat's databases, which are found under the second node of the data explorer tree. These allow the user to download a whole table or to extract a tailor-made selection of data, refining the criteria for one or more of the dimensions that make-up the data set in question. The database codes, which are provided as part of the information in the source under tables and figures, can be used as a search criteria on the Eurostat website (for example, 'hbs_exp_t121') to obtain direct access to these databases.

Detailed meta-data using the Special Data Dissemination Standard (SDDS) format (established by the International Monetary Fund) are presented for each official data source on the Eurostat website under the heading of 'Methodology', or alternatively from the data explorer tree by clicking on an icon (▣) presented next to the main data nodes.

Non-official data sources

While the majority of the information presented comes from official statistical sources (Eurostat, other Directorate-Generals of the European Commission, or international organisations such as the OECD or UN), in some cases data has been compiled from alternative sources.

Particular care should be taken when comparing or interpreting the data from non-official sources, as information on the data production methods may not be available and data may not be harmonised, while the coverage of the data may also not be fully representative. Each table and figure in the publication has a source included.

Data symbols

Statistical data are often accompanied by additional information in the form of statistical symbols (also called 'flags') to indicate missing information or some other meta-data. In this publication, the use of statistical symbols has been restricted to a minimum. The following symbols have been included:

Italic value is a forecast, provisional data, or an estimate and is therefore likely to change;
: not available, confidential or unreliable value;
– not applicable or zero by default.

Breaks in series are indicated in the footnotes provided under each table and figure.

A full list of statistical symbols, abbreviations and acronyms is provided at the end of the publication.

Basic concepts: main data sources

Household budget survey (HBS)

The household budget survey (HBS) describes the level and the structure of household expenditure. HBS focus on consumption expenditure, and within the national context its primary use is to calculate the weights that are used in the compilation of consumer price indices (CPIs); the HBS may also be used in the compilation of national accounts.

Within the EU context, the HBS provides a picture of consumption expenditure patterns of private households across all Member States, broken down by a variety of socio-economic household characteristics such as the employment status of the main reference person, their income, their age, the number of active persons living in the household, the type of household, the location of the household (rural or urban), or the main source of income of the household. Information is available at a detailed level using the classification of individual consumption by purpose (COICOP), with as many as 233 headings (including aggregates at higher levels of detail) which cover a wide range of products and services.

HBS data are confined to the population residing in private households: in other words, the survey excludes collective or institutional households (such as convents, hospitals, old persons' homes, prisons, or military barracks), as well as persons without a fixed place of residence. While the main statistical unit for data collection is the household (defined as 'a social unit which shares household expenses or daily needs, in addition to having a common residence'), the HBS also identifies the head of the household, as their personal characteristics are often used as the basis to classify information on socio-economic characteristics. The head of the household is normally the person who contributes the most income (the main earner).

In order to allow household expenditures to be compared between households of different sizes, household expenditures can be expressed per adult equivalent. These figures take economies of scale into account, and assign a coefficient of 1 to the first adult, 0.5 to other persons aged 14 and over, and 0.3 to children aged less than 14.

A household's internal production (for own consumption) constitutes a non-monetary component of consumption; Eurostat guidelines encourage such production to be included within the HBS. Internal production should ideally be valued at retail prices, as if the product had been bought in a shop. Examples of internal production include own production of food (by a farming household, or in a vegetable garden or allotment), or withdrawals from stocks for own-use (for example, in the case of retailers). HBS data should also reflect benefits in kind provided by employers in exchange for work done.

National accounts final consumption expenditure

National accounts are compiled in accordance with the European system of national and regional accounts (ESA 1995). In national accounts, final consumption expenditure consists of expenditure incurred by resident institutional units on goods or services that are used for the direct satisfaction of individual needs or wants or the collective needs of members of the community; such expenditure may take place on the domestic territory or abroad.

Final consumption expenditure of households is primarily made-up of goods and services purchased in the market, but also includes consumption of household production for own final use, such as the services of owner-occupied dwellings, or goods and services received as income in kind by employees. Household final consumption expenditure excludes social transfers in kind (like expenditures initially incurred by households but subsequently reimbursed by social security, for example, medical expenses), as well as intermediate consumption and gross capital formation, items treated as acquisitions of a non-produced asset (in particular the purchase of land), payments by households which are regarded as taxes (including for example, licences for transport vehicles, or licences to hunt, shoot or fish), payments to non-profit institutions serving households (NPISHs, for example, trade unions, professional societies, consumers' associations, churches, social, cultural, recreational and sports clubs), and voluntary transfers in cash or in kind by households to charities, relief and aid organisations.

Price level indices (PLIs)

With the introduction of the euro, prices within those Member States that share a common currency are said to be more transparent, as it is relatively simple for consumers to compare the price of items across borders. From an economic point of view, the price of a given good within the single market should not differ significantly depending on geographic location, beyond differences that may be explained by transport costs or tax differences. When comparing prices between euro area countries and non euro area countries, the most common way to compare prices of products and services between countries is to use an exchange rate to convert the prices to the same denomination. However, such comparisons (both within the euro area and within the EU) do not give an ideal picture of the actual price levels.

Purchasing power parities (PPPs) are a type of exchange rate constructed to take account of the price level differences between countries; they are more suitable for making international price and expenditure comparisons. PPPs can be used as currency conversion rates that convert expenditures or prices expressed in national currencies into an artificial common currency, the purchasing power standard (PPS), eliminating price level differences across countries. Data denominated in PPS terms show how many currency units a given quantity of goods and services will cost in different countries.

Price level indices can be constructed from this PPS data, by aggregating price comparisons over a large number of goods and services. Eurostat produces data for comparative price level indices with respect to the EU average (given the index value 100 by convention) using the COICOP classification. If the price level index is higher than 100, then the country concerned is relatively expensive compared with the EU average and vice-versa.

The coefficient of variation of the price level indices of the Member States can be used as a measure of price convergence. If the coefficient of variation for the EU decreases over time, then national price levels in the Member States are converging. The coefficient of variation is calculated as the ratio of the standard deviation to the arithmetic mean of the price level indices for the individual Member States.

Harmonised indices of consumer prices (HICPs)

While consumers are likely to be most interested in comparisons of current prices of goods and services, they are also interested in price changes over time – changes in the price of goods and services are usually referred to as inflation. All other things being equal, price inflation concerning consumer goods and services indicates a loss (gain if there is deflation) of living standards due to price changes.

HICPs are economic indicators constructed to measure the changes over time in the price of consumer goods and services acquired by households. They are calculated according to a harmonised approach and a single set of definitions, providing an official measure of consumer price inflation for the purposes of monetary policy and assessing inflation convergence as required under the Maastricht criteria.

HICPs are presented with a common reference year, which is currently 2005=100. Normally the indices are used to create percentage changes that show price increases (decreases) for the period in question. HICPs cover practically every good and service that may be purchased by households; price changes for owner occupied housing are, however, not yet collected. The different goods and services are classified according to the COICOP and at its most disaggregated level, Eurostat publishes around 100 sub-indices: these allow users, including consumers, to follow the price developments of certain categories of products, for example petrol or food. The all-items (overall, total or headline) index of consumer prices shows the price development of a very wide range of consumer goods and services and is one of the most well-known economic statistics among the general public.

Price stability is one of the primary objectives of the European Central Bank (ECB), with changes in the all-items consumer price index for the euro area used as a prime indicator for monetary policy management in the euro area. The ECB has defined price stability as an annual increase in the harmonised index of consumer prices (HICP) for the euro area of close to but below 2 % (over the medium-term).

Eurobarometer

Eurobarometer is a source that presents opinion polls that have been conducted by and for the Public Opinion Analysis sector of the European Commission. Since 1973, the European Commission has been monitoring the evolution of public opinion in the Member States, thus helping the preparation of texts, decision-making and the evaluation of its work. While initially a regular, twice-yearly, public opinion survey, Eurobarometer studies have since broadened their scope to cover a range of topics, such as citizenship, enlargement, social situations, health, culture, information technology, the environment, the euro, or agriculture. Some of these address consumer issues and these have, where relevant and relatively recent, been used within this publication. Note that Eurobarometer surveys are opinion polls based on subjective responses.

For more information:

http://ec.europa.eu/public_opinion/index_en.htm

CONSUMER POLICY

Many of the almost 500 million people living in the European Union (EU) may well imagine that they will lead safe, healthy and full lives. Promoting consumers' rights, prosperity, their health and well-being are core values of the EU. More specifically, within the European Commission, the Directorate-General for Health and Consumers aims to:

- empower consumers;
- protect and improve human health;
- ensure food is safe and wholesome;
- protect the health of animals and plants;
- promote the humane treatment of animals.

The policies and laws for which the Directorate-General for Health and Consumers are responsible touch the everyday lives of Europe's population, playing an important role in trying to ensure that food and other consumer goods sold in the EU are safe, that the EU's internal market works for the benefit of consumers, and that the population's health is protected and improved.

EU consumer policy strategy

The internal market has played a central role in European economic development and most commentators agree that it has stimulated the level of trade between Member States and delivered tangible benefits to European consumers. The initial policy focus for developing the internal market was based on the premise of free trade across borders. This approach has been criticised in some quarters, and more recent policy developments have tended to reflect the increasing importance of social and environmental considerations too, with, for example, the consumer being placed at the heart of further developments of the internal market [1].The European Commission has three main objectives concerning consumers:

- to empower EU consumers so they make more informed choices and thus boost competition and competitiveness;
- to enhance EU consumers' welfare in terms of price, choice, quality, diversity, affordability and safety;
- to protect consumers effectively from the serious risks and threats that they cannot tackle as individuals.

The European Commission's aim is to achieve a more integrated and more effective internal market by 2013 such that consumers from each Member State have an equally high level of confidence in products, traders, selling methods, as well as consumer protection – no matter where they decide to make their purchases within the EU. The European Commission aims to ensure that consumer markets should be competitive, open, transparent and fair, while products and services that are available in European markets should be safe. Furthermore, it seeks to guarantee consumers access to essential services at affordable prices, while promoting market access for traders, especially small and medium-sized enterprises (SMEs). These policies are outlined in a recent Communication from the European Commission to the Council, the European Parliament and the European Economic and Social Committee on 'EU Consumer Policy strategy 2007-2013' [2] which presents an agenda for policy developments.

It is therefore hoped that EU consumer policy will interact more closely with other policies, both at an EU level, as well as through pursuing closer co-operation with the Member States. To some degree this marks a continuation of existing policy, for example, legislative changes that have been made in the interest of consumers concerning guarantees of product safety or adapting market structures and encouraging competition within telecommunications and energy markets.

To attain the objectives above, the European Commission intends to monitor EU consumer policy through a set of tools and indicators to assess how consumer markets are functioning, in order to identify areas of market failure. This assessment of consumer markets will be based on a range of measures, including:

- switching;
- price levels;
- satisfaction;
- complaints;
- safety.

These headings have been used to organise the material that is presented for each of the consumer markets analysed in Part B of this publication, where they are supplemented by data on consumption patterns (in value and volume terms), information on price changes, and information relating to access, choice and quality.

For more information on policy developments:

http://ec.europa.eu/consumers/strategy/index_en.htm

(2) 'EU Consumer Policy strategy 2007-2013 empowering consumers, enhancing their welfare, effectively protecting them', COM(2007) 99 final of 13 March 2008.

(1) 'A Single Market for Citizens', COM(2007) 60 of 21 February 2007.

Monitoring consumer outcomes in the single market: the consumer markets scoreboard

A Communication from the European Commission [3] highlights the importance of monitoring and evaluation of the internal market in terms of outcomes for citizens. This Communication recognises that the internal market is not exclusively an economic project, whereby consumer interests are solely defined in terms of efficiency. Rather, it states that 'citizens expect single market policy to deliver socially acceptable outcomes, sometimes at the expense of economic efficiency'. It also draws attention to the principle of affordable access to certain essential services of general interest (SGIs), vital for economic and social inclusion, which should be guaranteed to all, no matter where they live. The Communication reflects on consumer outcomes in terms of other non-economic criteria such as health, the environment, or safety, and argues that areas such as these sometimes require regulation in order to protect consumers.

(3) 'Monitoring consumer outcomes in the single market: the Consumer Markets Scoreboard', COM(2008) 31 final of 29 January 2008.

In addition to monitoring markets, the scoreboard is also designed to assess the integration of EU consumer markets and can be used to benchmark national conditions. The scoreboard is divided into three different dimensions:

- the first looks at the performance of consumer markets, and may be used to identify problem areas for further analysis;
- the second concerns the degree of integration within retail markets, in light of the European Commission's strategic objective of making consumers and retailers as confident to shop across borders as in their home countries by 2013;
- the final dimension relates to national markets as regards enforcement, information, education, and redress – benchmarking the consumer policy systems and institutions of individual Member States.

For more information on the consumer markets scoreboard:

http://ec.europa.eu/consumers/strategy/facts_en.htm

Consumer protection

Community legislation aims to protect consumers through rules and regulations that provide important guarantees to consumers, in terms of their rights, their protection and their redress. These laws are designed to:

- allow consumers to buy what they want, where they want;
- enable consumers to take back/send back any goods that do not work;
- let consumers benefit from high safety standards for food and other consumer goods;
- enable consumers to know what they are eating;
- ensure that contracts are fair to consumers;
- allow consumers to change their mind as regards a purchase;
- make it easier for consumers to compare prices;
- ensure that consumers are not misled;
- protect consumers while they are on holiday;
- provide effective redress for cross-border disputes.

In some of the Member States, Community law forms the cornerstone of national consumer protection systems. Existing EU consumer rules and regulations are often based on the principle of 'minimum harmonisation', with legislation designed to explicitly recognise the right of Member States to add stricter rules. Many of the areas alluded to in the list above are covered in a general nature in Part A of this publication, while market-specific information is provided within Part B.

The strength and influence of consumer representation movements varies considerably across the EU. The European Commission supports national consumer organisations, in particular from the Member States that have joined the EU since 2004, in the belief that a strong consumer movement at a national level is essential both to a strong EU consumer movement and to well-functioning national markets. At the same time, the European Commission has instigated a series of information campaigns among those Member States that have joined the EU since 2004, designed to raise awareness around consumer rights and the role of consumer NGO's.

At a European level, the European Commission co-finances and manages the European Consumer Centres Network (ECC-Net) which aims to promote consumer confidence, advise citizens on their rights, and provide redress in cross-border cases; the European Commission aims to establish such centres in each of the Member States. In addition, there are two umbrella organisations that are eligible for receiving Community funding to help them carry out their activities: the European Association for the Coordination of Consumer Representation in Standardisation (ANEC) which represents and defends consumer interests in the process of standardisation and certification (http://www.anec.eu), and the European Consumers' Organisation (BEUC) which aims to defend and promote the interests of European consumers as purchasers or users of goods and services (http://www.beuc.org).

For more information on ECC-Net:

http://ec.europa.eu/consumers/redress_cons/index_en.htm

Overview

CONSUMER PROFILE

Consumers and consumption in the economy

The economic cycle can have an important impact on consumption patterns, with expenditure usually rising during periods of economic upturn. When an economy is booming, there is often an upturn in the consumption of luxury goods and consumer durables. Consumers have the potential to be a motor for European competitiveness, if they seek out the best offers (particularly, if this is done regardless of national borders), rewarding the EU's best and most innovative businesses. Indeed, consumer spending is often cited as a key driver for growth and economic integration.

In contrast, during periods of recession, disposable income is reduced and consumer confidence usually falls. A slowdown or contraction in economic activity often results in fewer luxury purchases being made, for example, lower sales of jewellery, holidays abroad, or other big-ticket purchases (such as cars or furniture). Consumption of items such as these is often postponed or deferred until there is evidence of an upturn in economic fortunes, with many consumers holding back their purchases. Alternatively, during times of recession or slow economic growth, some households may choose to downsize, for example, selling a second car or moving to cheaper accommodation.

While general patterns of consumption across a whole economy may reflect economic fortunes, income is clearly a key determinant in explaining expenditure patterns at the level of each household. In other words, the rich are generally more likely to spend more than those who are less well off, although they are also likely to save more. The relationship between an individual's income and their standard of living is often complicated by the fact that the majority of people do not live alone, and therefore income generated and spent by a household may be influenced by both the composition and size of the household. For example, two adults both working with no children are likely to have more disposable income at the end of the month than a single parent working part-time living with two children and an elderly parent (income levels and distribution are covered in more detail later in Section A1).

A national accounts perspective

Within national accounts there are three classes of final consumer: individuals, non-profit institutions serving households (NPISH) and government; consumption attributed to enterprises is considered as intermediate, in the sense that it is used as an input in the production of other goods and services.

Figure 1.1: Final consumption expenditure of households, 2007
(% of GDP)

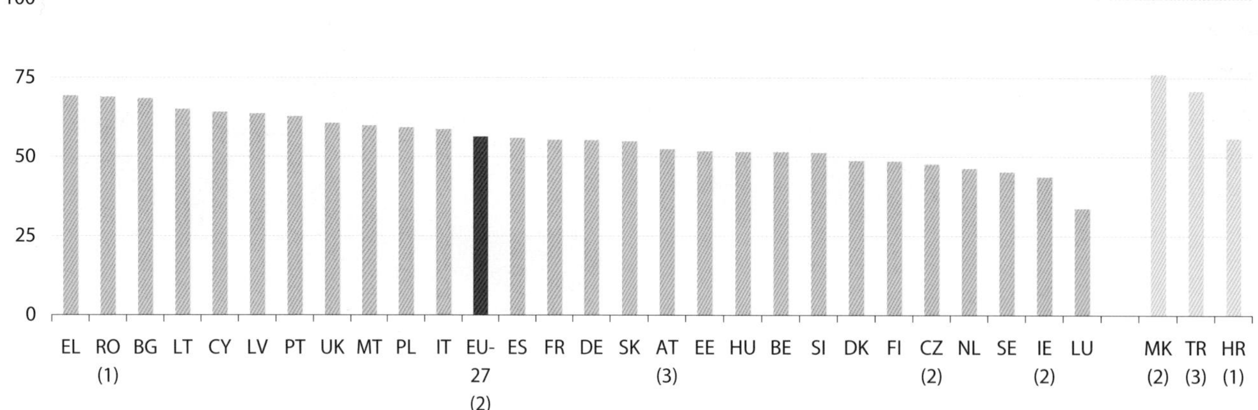

(1) 2006, forecast.
(2) Forecast.
(3) 2006.

Source: Eurostat, GDP and main components (nama_gdp_c)

Final consumption expenditure of households was estimated to account for 56.4 % of the EU-27's GDP in 2007. The relative importance of consumers (based on this measure) ranged from 69.3 % of GDP in Greece to 33.6 % of GDP in Luxembourg, with final household consumption expenditure tending to account for a higher proportion of GDP among those Member States that joined the EU in 2004 or 2007; if final household consumption expenditure accounts for a high share of GDP, this implies that the size of government activity is relatively low.

The developments of economic output and consumption expenditure were closely related over the period 1995 to 2007, as EU-27 GDP per inhabitant rose, on average, by 4.5 % per annum compared with a 4.4 % increase in final consumption expenditure of households and non-profit institutions serving households; in a similar vein, the final consumption expenditure of general government also rose, on average, by 4.5 % each year.

Figure 1.2: GDP, 2007
(per inhabitant)

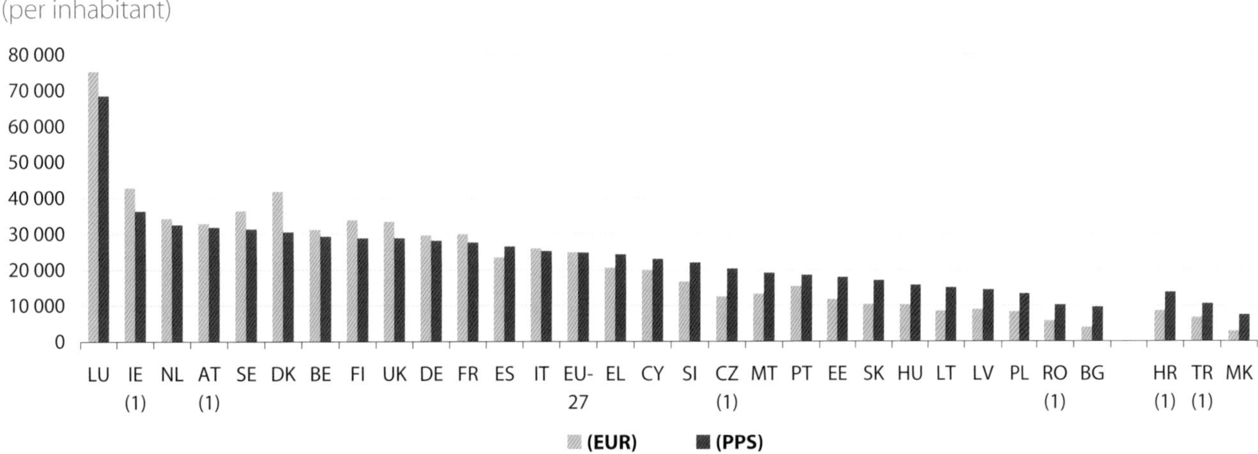

(1) Forecasts.

Source: Eurostat, GDP and main components (nama_gdp_c)

Figure 1.3: GDP and final consumption expenditure, EU-27
(EUR per inhabitant)

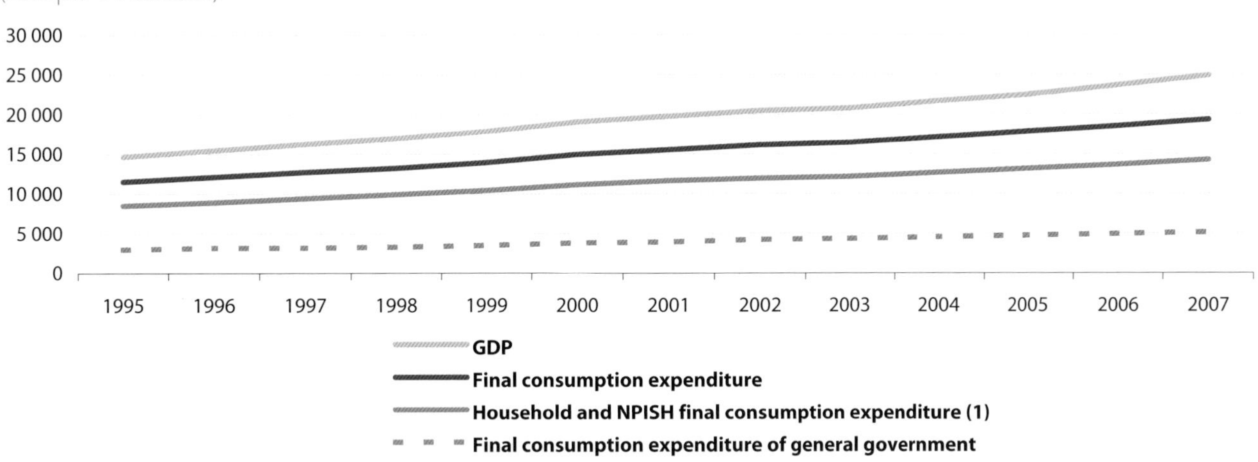

(1) NPISH: non-profit institutions serving households.

Source: Eurostat, GDP and main components (nama_gdp_c)

One measure that may be used to determine the 'openness' of an economy is the share of imports relative to GDP. Imports of goods and services accounted for 39.7 % of GDP in 2007 within the EU-27. This ratio rose to 141.9 % in Luxembourg, while at the other end of the scale France imported goods and services valued at just 28.4 % of its GDP. Generally, this indicator is strongly related to the size of an economy, as larger countries generally produce a broader range of goods and services and therefore (at least have the potential to) supply their own domestic demand, while smaller countries will need to import a wider range of goods and services, as many of these will not be produced within their own territory. As such, consumers in smaller countries are, a priori, more likely to purchase goods and services from abroad.

People and households

The EU-27's population reached 495.1 million inhabitants in 2007. There is a wide disparity in the number of persons living in each Member State, ranging from 82.3 million in Germany (16.6 % of the EU-27 total) to less than a million inhabitants in each of Malta, Luxembourg and Cyprus (no more than 0.2 % of the EU-27 total). Six Member States together accounted for just over 70 % of the EU-27's population in 2007 (Germany, France, the United Kingdom, Italy, Spain and Poland).

The principal urban area in most countries is usually centred on the capital city, while rural areas that are less densely populated tend to be found towards the extremities of each country, although this pattern is less evident in Germany,

Figure 1.4: Imports of goods and services, 2007
(% of GDP)

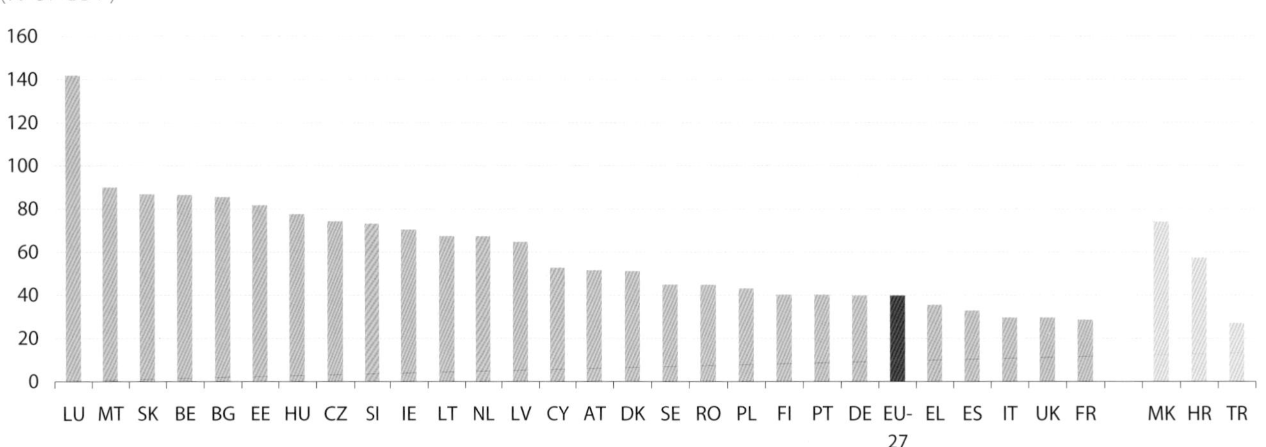

Source: Eurostat, GDP and main components (nama_gdp_c)

Figure 1.5: Population on 1 January, 2007
(millions)

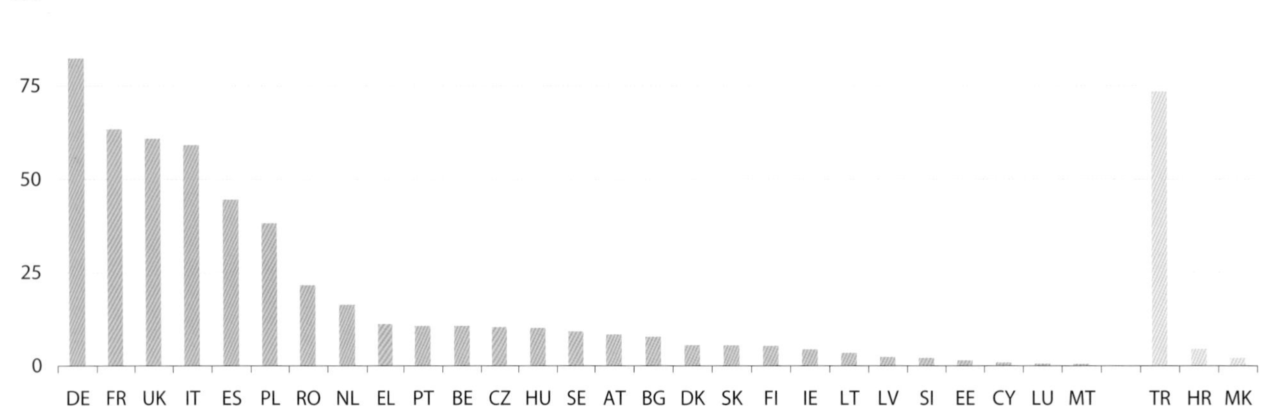

Source: Eurostat, Population by sex and age on 1 January of each year (demo_pjan)

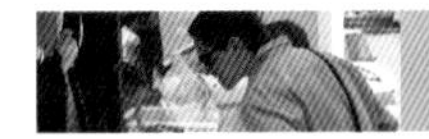

Italy and the Netherlands. The spread of the population within a country plays an important role in influencing (among others) the distribution of retail outlets, the construction and upkeep of energy, communication and transport networks, or the provision of other services of general interest (SGIs).

Changes in the demographic structure of the EU's population also affect the pattern of consumption. An ageing population suggests that an increasing share of consumption will be accounted for by the elderly. This pattern is observed across most of Europe and is driven by a range of factors, including lower birth rates, the so-called baby-boom generation reaching retirement age, and

Map 1.1: Population density, 2006 (1)
(inhabitants per km^2)

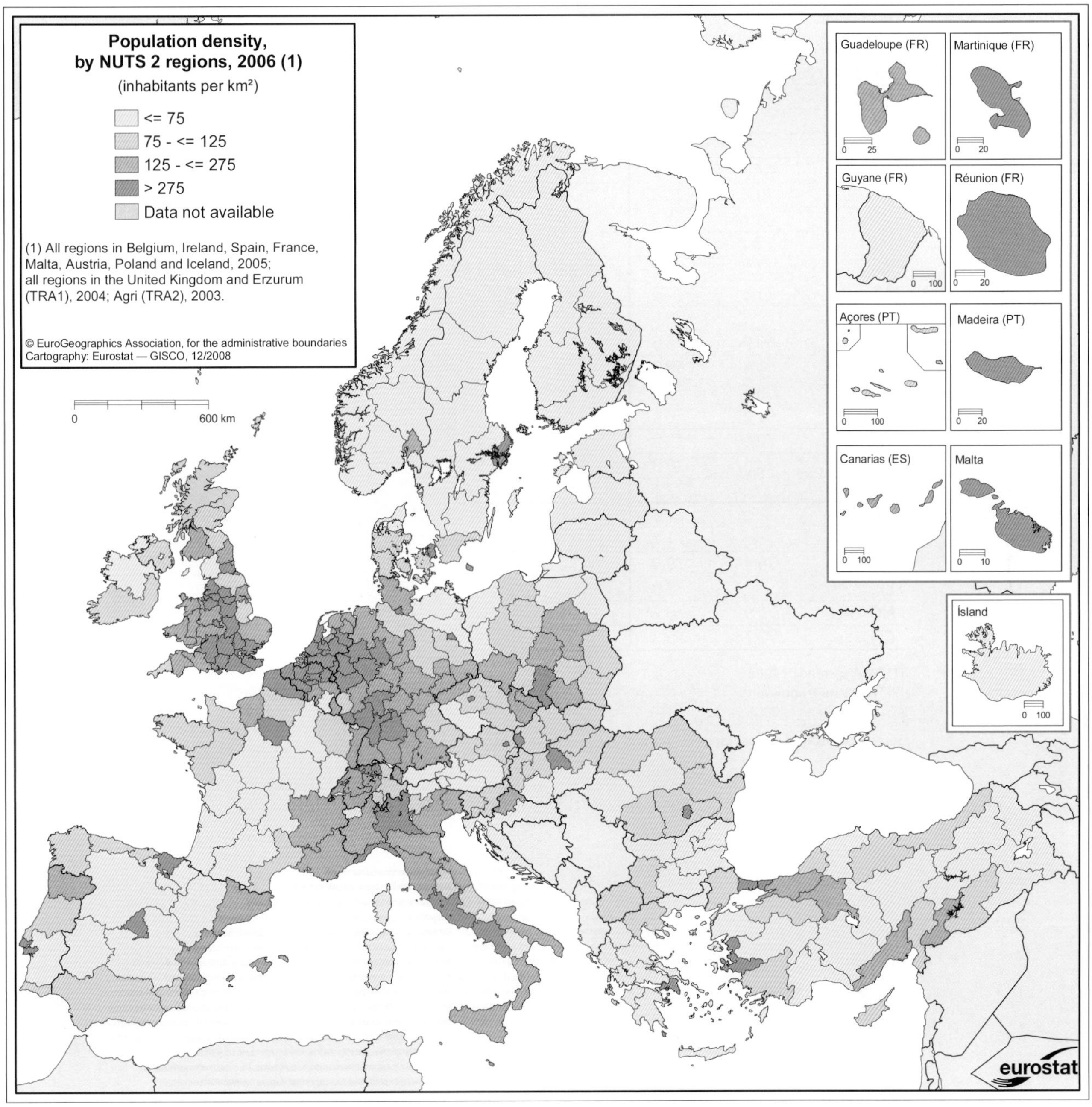
Population density,
by NUTS 2 regions, 2006 (1)
(inhabitants per km²)
<= 75
75 - <= 125
125 - <= 275
> 275
Data not available
(1) All regions in Belgium, Ireland, Spain, France, Malta, Austria, Poland and Iceland, 2005; all regions in the United Kingdom and Erzurum (TRA1), 2004; Agri (TRA2), 2003.
© EuroGeographics Association, for the administrative boundaries
Cartography: Eurostat — GISCO, 12/2008
0
600 km
Guadeloupe (FR)
Martinique (FR)
Guyane (FR)
Réunion (FR)
Açores (PT)
Madeira (PT)
Canarias (ES)
Malta
Ísland
eurostat

Source: Eurostat, regional population densities (reg_d3dens)

Table 1.1: Life expectancy
(years)

	Male		Female	
	1986	2006	1986	2006
EU-27 (1)	:	75.2	:	81.5
BE	71.4	76.6	78.2	82.3
BG	68.5	69.2	74.8	76.3
CZ	67.5	73.5	74.7	79.9
DK	71.8	76.1	77.7	80.7
DE	71.4	77.2	77.7	82.4
EE	:	67.4	:	78.6
IE	70.8	77.3	76.4	82.1
EL	74.1	77.2	78.8	81.9
ES	73.4	77.7	79.9	84.4
FR (2)	71.6	77.4	79.8	84.4
IT (1)	72.6	77.9	79.1	83.8
CY	:	78.8	:	82.4
LV	:	65.4	:	76.3
LT	67.8	65.3	76.4	77.0
LU	70.7	76.8	78.7	81.9
HU	65.3	69.2	73.3	77.8
MT	:	77.0	:	81.9
NL	73.1	77.7	79.7	82.0
AT	71.0	77.2	77.8	82.8
PL	:	70.9	:	79.7
PT	69.9	75.5	76.8	82.3
RO	66.8	69.2	72.8	76.2
SI	68.4	74.5	76.4	82.0
SK	67.2	70.4	75.1	78.4
FI	70.6	75.9	78.9	83.1
SE	74.0	78.8	80.2	83.1
UK (3)	:	77.1	:	81.1
HR	:	72.5	:	79.3
MK	:	71.7	:	76.2
IS	75.4	79.5	80.7	82.9
LI	:	78.9	:	83.1
NO	72.9	78.2	80.0	82.9
CH	73.7	79.2	80.5	84.2

(1) 2004, instead of 2006.
(2) France métropolitaine.
(3) 2005, instead of 2006.

Source: Eurostat, life expectancy by sex and age (demo_mlexpec)

an increase in life expectancy – all of which contribute to older generations accounting for a larger proportion of the total population.

There were 83.8 million persons aged 65 or over in the EU-27 on 1 January 2007, equivalent to almost 17 % of the total population. With the relative importance of these older generations forecast to continue growing until at least the middle of the century, it is likely that there will be significant changes in the structure/composition of consumption, as demand for goods and services like health or social services is likely to expand rapidly, while the older generations are less likely to embrace the purchase of new technologies.

At the other end of the age range, children also constitute an important consumer market, and it is nowadays commonplace for children (usually indirectly through their parents) to pay a mobile telephone bill, to spend considerable sums of money on electronic games, or to dress in the latest fashions.

Figure 1.6: Population breakdown by gender and age on 1 January, 2007
(millions)

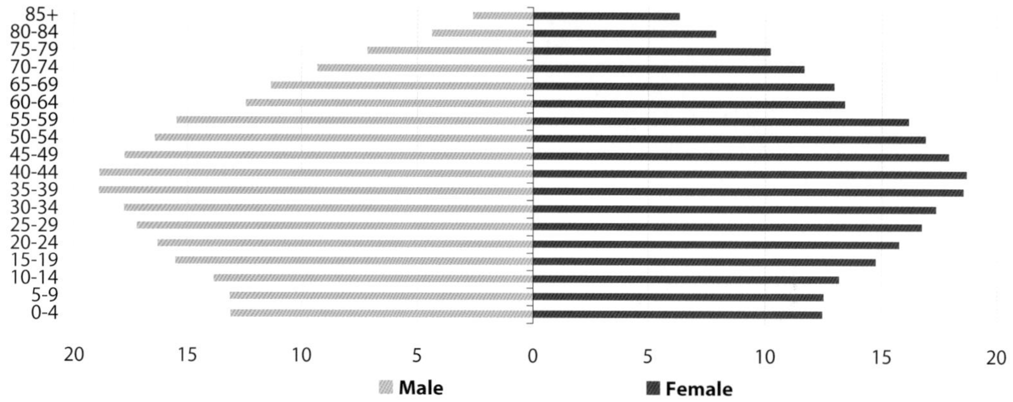

Source: Eurostat, population by sex and age on 1 January of each year (demo_pjan)

In between the younger and the older generations are those of working age (classified here as persons aged 15-64). Age dependency ratios are often used to gauge the relative importance of this segment of the population: they measure the proportion of younger and older persons who are 'dependent' upon those of working age. By summing young and old-age dependency ratios, the overall dependency on those of working age was 48.6 % in the EU-27 at the start of 2007; in other words, for approximately every two persons of working age there was a 'dependent' child or older person. Dependency ratios across the EU ranged from a high of 53.4 % in France to a low of 38.9 % in Slovakia.

Table 1.2: Population structure, 1 January
(%)

	Aged 0-14 years old (as % of total population)		Aged 65 years and over (as a % of total population)		Young-age dependency ratio (population aged 0-14 compared with those 15-64)		Old-age dependency ratio (population aged 65 and over compared with those 15-64)	
	1997	2007	1997	2007	1997	2007	1997	2007
EU-27	17.9	15.8	15.1	16.9	26.7	23.5	22.5	25.2
BE	17.8	17.0	16.3	17.1	27.0	25.8	24.7	25.9
BG	17.2	13.4	15.3	17.3	25.6	19.4	22.7	24.9
CZ	17.9	14.4	13.5	14.4	26.0	20.2	19.6	20.2
DK	17.8	18.6	15.0	15.3	26.4	28.2	22.4	23.2
DE	16.1	13.9	15.7	19.8	23.6	21.0	23.0	29.9
EE	20.0	14.9	14.1	17.1	30.4	21.9	21.5	25.1
IE	23.2	20.3	11.4	11.1	35.5	29.7	17.4	16.2
EL	16.8	14.3	15.6	18.6	24.8	21.3	23.0	27.6
ES	15.9	14.5	15.8	16.7	23.3	21.1	23.2	24.2
FR	19.4	18.6	15.3	16.2	29.8	28.4	23.5	24.9
IT	14.5	14.1	17.2	19.9	21.3	21.3	25.2	30.2
CY	24.3	17.9	11.1	12.3	37.6	25.7	17.1	17.6
LV	20.0	14.0	14.1	17.1	30.3	20.2	21.4	24.8
LT	21.4	15.9	12.8	15.6	32.5	23.2	19.5	22.7
LU	18.6	18.3	14.2	14.0	27.7	27.1	21.2	20.7
HU	17.7	15.2	14.5	15.9	26.1	22.1	21.3	23.2
MT	21.7	16.7	11.6	13.8	32.5	24.0	17.4	19.8
NL	18.4	18.1	13.4	14.5	26.9	26.8	19.6	21.5
AT	17.7	15.6	15.3	16.9	26.3	23.1	22.8	25.0
PL	21.9	15.8	11.5	13.4	32.8	22.3	17.2	19.0
PT	17.1	15.5	15.3	17.3	25.3	23.0	22.6	25.6
RO	20.0	15.4	12.6	14.9	29.7	22.1	18.6	21.3
SI	17.5	14.0	12.9	15.9	25.2	19.9	18.5	22.7
SK	21.7	16.1	11.1	11.9	32.2	22.4	16.5	16.5
FI	18.9	17.1	14.5	16.5	28.3	25.7	21.7	24.8
SE	18.8	17.0	17.4	17.4	29.5	25.9	27.4	26.4
UK	19.4	17.6	15.9	16.0	29.9	26.5	24.5	24.1
HR	19.9	15.6	12.3	17.1	29.3	23.2	18.2	25.4
MK	24.1	18.9	9.0	11.2	36.0	27.1	13.4	16.0
TR	31.2	27.9	5.1	6.6	48.9	42.2	8.0	10.1
IS (1)	24.0	21.8	11.5	11.7	37.2	32.8	17.8	17.6
LI	18.8	17.1	10.3	11.9	26.5	24.0	14.6	16.8
NO	19.7	19.4	15.8	14.6	30.5	29.3	24.5	22.2
CH	17.7	15.8	14.9	16.2	26.2	23.1	22.1	23.8

(1) 2006 instead of 2007.

Source: Eurostat, population structure indicators on 1 January (demo_pjanind)

Table 1.3: Activity rates by gender, persons aged 15-64 years old
(%)

	Male		Female	
	1987	2007	1987	2007
EU (1)	80.3	77.6	51.1	63.3
BE	72.4	73.6	45.5	60.4
BG	:	70.6	:	62.1
CZ	:	78.1	:	61.5
DK	85.5	83.9	76.5	76.4
DE	81.3	81.8	52.7	70.1
EE	:	77.5	:	68.7
IE	80.8	81.4	41.0	63.3
EL	78.6	79.1	41.1	54.9
ES	77.9	81.4	37.1	61.4
FR	78.1	74.9	57.6	65.6
IT	77.9	74.4	41.7	50.7
CY	:	82.9	:	65.4
LV	:	77.6	:	68.3
LT	:	71.0	:	65.0
LU	79.9	75.0	43.5	58.9
HU	:	69.0	:	55.1
MT	:	78.9	:	39.9
NL	79.7	84.6	49.3	72.2
AT	:	81.7	:	67.8
PL	:	70.0	:	56.5
PT	82.1	79.4	55.0	68.8
RO	:	70.1	:	56.0
SI	:	75.8	:	66.6
SK	:	75.9	:	60.8
FI	:	77.2	:	73.8
SE	:	81.4	:	76.8
UK	86.0	81.9	63.0	68.9
HR	:	70.4	:	56.4
TR	:	74.4	:	26.1
IS (2)	:	90.5	:	83.4
NO	:	81.6	:	75.9
CH	:	88.2	:	75.0

(1) Moving EU aggregate based on membership (EC-12 for 1987, EU-27 for 2007).
(2) 2006 instead of 2007.

Source: Eurostat, population structure indicators on 1 January (lfsa_argan)

While dependency ratios give some idea of the structure of a population, it is important to bear in mind that they are based purely on age class data and do not take account of whether those of working age are actually in employment or not. Some people choose not to work, while others (for example, single parents) may find it difficult to balance family responsibilities with a career and struggle to hold down a job, and others (unemployed) may not be able to find employment.

During recent decades there has been a considerable increase in the number of women entering the labour market, such that the activity rate of women aged 15-64 (those employed and those seeking work as a proportion of the total female population of the same age) climbed by 12.2 percentage points between 1987 and 2007 to reach 63.3 % in the EU-27, still some way behind the corresponding rate for men (77.6 %). Across the Member States there were wide disparities, with Denmark, Germany, the Netherlands, Finland and Sweden all reporting activity rates of more than 70 % for women, while at the other end of the range female activity rates were 39.9 % in Malta, 50.7 % in Italy, and 54.9 % in Greece. With higher proportions of the female population in the labour force, it is likely that women will continue to become more financially independent and as such, it can be imagined that consumption patterns may change somewhat to reflect this trend.

Care responsibilities taken on by women (primarily for children, but also for relatives or friends) are thought to play a significant role in explaining lower female activity rates. In 2005, some 4.4 % of women in the EU-27 said they would like to work more (and reduce their caring time), compared with just 2.0 % of men.

Figure 1.7: Activity rates by gender, persons aged 15-64 years old, EU (1)
(%)

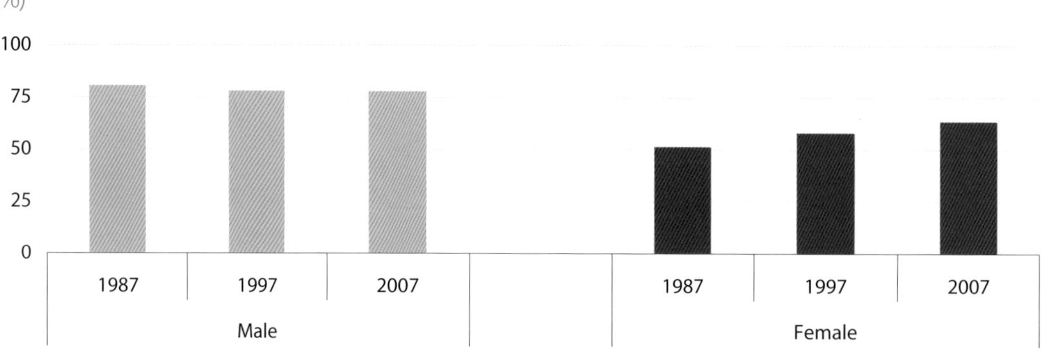

(1) Moving EU aggregate based on membership (EC-12 for 1987, EU-15 for 1997, EU-27 for 2007).

Source: Eurostat, activity rates by sex, age groups and nationality (lfsa_argan)

The reduction in the size of the average household (in terms of the number of persons) is, at least in part, linked to the ageing population, as older generations increasingly live their final years alone (as opposed to sharing a house with their off-spring or other family members). Average household size is also affected, among others, by factors such as the reduction in birth rates, less importance being attached to the family unit, higher divorce rates and young adults choosing to live away from home. There are nevertheless considerable differences between countries (often on the basis of a north/south split). A higher proportion of persons live alone in the northern countries, while the family unit is often more robust in southern countries (be it children continuing to live with their parents through university and after they have started work, or older generations being cared for by their offspring).

Figure 1.8: Persons wishing to change the organisation of their working life and care responsibilities, EU-27, 2005
(% of population aged 15-64)

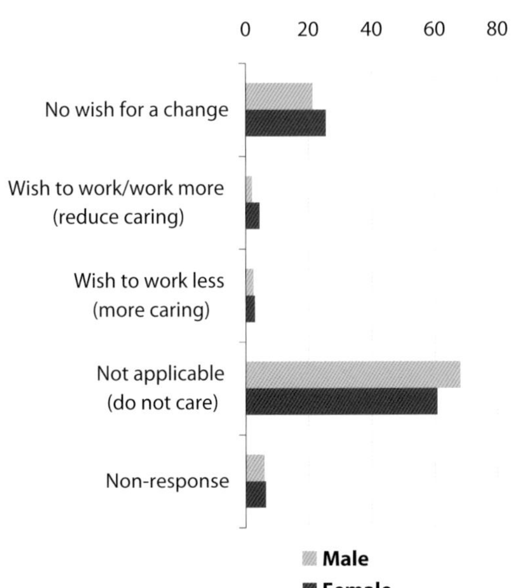

Source: Eurostat, number of persons wishing to change the organisation of their working life and care responsibilities (lfso_05changp)

Table 1.4: Activity rates by gender and marital status, persons aged 15-64 years old, EU-27
(%)

	Male		Female	
	2000	2007	2000	2007
Total	77.1	77.6	60.1	63.3
Single persons	67.0	68.6	57.4	60.4
Married persons	84.0	84.7	61.3	64.5
Widowed persons	55.5	57.7	41.1	44.4
Divorced persons	79.7	81.0	73.4	75.2

Source: Eurostat, activity rates by sex, age groups and marital status (lfst_argams)

Table 1.5: Households, breakdown by type of dwelling, 2006
(% of all dwellings)

	Detached	Semi-detached or terraced	Flat in building with <10 dwellings	Flat in building with =>10 dwellings	Other building
BE	35.3	38.3	17.9	7.5	1.0
BG	:	:	:	:	:
CZ	33.9	9.2	13.7	42.5	0.7
DK	48.2	13.3	7.6	29.7	1.2
DE	22.4	12.1	39.7	23.7	2.0
EE	26.2	3.5	8.8	60.4	1.1
IE	40.2	55.3	2.0	2.1	0.4
EL	35.2	10.0	35.4	19.4	0.1
ES	18.9	17.9	19.0	44.0	0.2
FR	40.7	19.0	15.1	24.8	0.3
IT	23.9	19.5	25.1	27.0	4.6
CY	46.4	27.4	15.2	8.6	2.4
LV	23.3	5.6	10.0	60.8	0.3
LT	30.1	8.9	7.0	53.8	0.1
LU	35.8	30.5	22.3	9.9	1.6
HU	56.5	10.0	4.5	28.6	0.5
MT	3.2	51.3	44.2	1.0	0.3
NL	13.7	54.8	6.2	19.6	5.6
AT	38.5	12.8	16.2	31.5	1.0
PL	39.1	4.6	11.7	44.3	0.3
PT	40.7	24.4	18.5	15.9	0.5
RO	:	:	:	:	:
SI	65.8	3.8	8.0	22.1	0.3
SK	49.7	1.7	4.9	43.6	0.1
FI	37.6	18.9	2.4	40.4	0.7
SE	41.9	8.0	11.8	36.9	1.5
UK	23.0	58.2	11.4	7.1	0.2
IS	31.2	15.9	16.6	34.3	2.0
NO	58.9	18.7	2.0	6.4	14.1

Source: Eurostat, EU-SILC cross sectional 2006 data

Table 1.6: Households, breakdown by type of tenure, 2006
(% of all dwellings)

	Owner	Tenant paying rent at market rate (1)	Accomm. is rented at a reduced rate (2)	Accomm. is provided free (3)
BE	67.7	22.4	7.7	2.2
BG	:	:	:	:
CZ	71.5	5.3	19.7	3.5
DK	57.8	42.2	:	:
DE	43.0	46.6	7.1	3.3
EE	84.9	4.5	1.8	8.8
IE	77.3	9.1	12.3	1.3
EL	72.5	20.4	1.3	5.8
ES	82.5	7.3	3.1	7.1
FR	59.0	21.0	15.8	4.2
IT	71.9	12.8	5.4	9.9
CY	66.5	12.6	1.2	19.7
LV	80.8	6.9	7.9	4.3
LT	90.9	1.4	1.3	6.4
LU	70.4	20.9	4.8	4.0
HU	85.9	3.6	3.6	6.9
MT	76.3	3.4	17.0	3.3
NL	55.5	44.1	:	0.4
AT	51.5	33.2	6.9	8.4
PL	55.7	3.8	1.3	39.2
PT	74.2	10.0	7.1	8.7
RO	:	:	:	:
SI	83.1	4.8	1.3	10.7
SK	89.3	8.8	0.6	1.4
FI	67.2	12.4	19.4	1.0
SE	60.9	37.4	1.3	:
UK	69.4	15.7	13.6	1.2
IS	82.2	16.9	:	0.9
NO	77.6	15.0	4.4	2.6

(1) Lithuania, unreliable.
(2) Cyprus and Slovakia, unreliable.
(3) The Netherlands and Iceland, unreliable.

Source: Eurostat, EU-SILC cross sectional 2006 data

Changes in how and with whom people live have considerable implications for the location, type and size of housing that people can afford to live in. The traditional stock of housing in a country is not always suited to the rapidly changing demographic make-up of society. For example, in countries where there is a large stock of detached and semi-detached dwellings, there may be a lack of smaller houses or flats/apartments that are more suited to single persons or single parent families.

Housing forms one of the most important expenditure items of household budgets. The purchase of a house or flat is normally the biggest purchase that home-owners make in their lives, while those who choose to rent are also likely to spend a considerable part of their income on housing; it should be noted that the purchase of real estate itself is not considered as consumption expenditure.

In 2006, Germany was the only Member State to report that less than half (43 %) of its households were living in owner-occupied accommodation. Owner occupation rates rose to upwards of 90 % in Lithuania and to more than 80 % in the two other Baltic States, Spain, Hungary, Slovenia and Slovakia. The highest proportion of tenants paying rent was found in Germany (46.6 %), while upwards of 40 % of households rented in the Netherlands and Denmark too.

Time-use

Time-use surveys fill a number of gaps in the statistical information available in the social domain, as they can be used to unveil differences between women and men that can be related to their position in labour markets, their participation in education, cultural activities, or other spheres of life. In particular, time-use surveys provide valuable information on the possibilities of reconciling professional and family life – statistics that deal with the division of gainful (paid) and domestic work. Information on voluntary work, care, mobility and leisure time can also be produced from time-use surveys. The analysis of time-use data is of growing relevance to policy makers who are interested in learning about the evolution of the organisation of time in society and its economic implications.

The information presented covers the time spent per person per day on a particular activity (averaged over the course of a whole year). The most important category is that of sleep, which generally accounts for just over eight hours per day. This is usually followed by time spent at work, after which the differences between the genders become more apparent, with women tending to spend considerably more time on domestic chores and caring for children, while men tend to spend more time watching television, playing sports or using a computer. Women spend, on average, about ten minutes more per day shopping, with the highest average time spent shopping being recorded in France (41 minutes per day), followed by the United Kingdom (39 minutes).

Table 1.7: Number of rooms available to the household, 2006 (1)
(rooms)

	1	2	3	4	5	6	7	8+
BE	1.8	5.5	13.1	20.4	23.4	17.1	8.8	9.9
BG	:	:	:	:	:	:	:	:
CZ	8.4	28.0	37.0	16.3	6.2	2.7	0.8	:
DK	4.6	18.4	22.4	24.6	15.9	7.0	3.6	2.6
DE	4.5	21.9	30.3	20.9	11.8	6.0	2.5	2.0
EE	14.4	35.8	31.1	10.7	5.0	2.1	0.6	:
IE	0.6	2.8	4.9	12.6	30.4	21.6	14.4	10.7
EL	4.3	20.2	43.5	25.1	5.5	1.1	:	:
ES	0.3	1.3	6.8	20.9	40.6	20.6	5.6	4.0
FR	4.8	12.3	23.3	26.6	19.7	8.3	3.1	2.0
IT	3.2	17.9	37.5	26.3	9.7	3.3	1.0	:
CY	:	1.8	6.7	14.4	24.5	30.4	14.1	7.8
LV	16.4	41.7	27.9	9.4	3.2	0.9	:	:
LT	15.0	37.8	31.5	9.1	5.0	1.2	0.3	:
LU	4.0	10.5	17.4	19.7	20.7	12.9	7.4	:
HU	12.0	40.1	33.2	10.0	3.5	1.0	:	:
MT	:	1.1	5.3	18.0	27.6	23.3	11.4	10.6
NL	1.6	5.5	12.9	26.3	31.5	14.1	4.8	3.6
AT	5.4	20.2	27.9	20.3	12.5	7.4	3.2	3.0
PL	13.4	35.3	29.1	11.1	6.2	2.9	1.1	:
PT	1.0	6.1	28.4	38.9	15.1	6.3	2.4	:
RO	:	:	:	:	:	:	:	:
SI	9.3	28.1	33.0	18.1	7.1	2.7	0.8	:
SK	12.3	21.6	40.6	14.5	7.1	2.8	0.8	:
FI	7.9	13.2	22.5	21.7	18.0	9.5	3.9	3.3
SE	8.6	20.3	21.6	19.1	14.9	8.2	4.1	2.5
UK	0.7	9.2	22.0	30.1	20.1	10.5	4.5	2.5
IS	2.5	13.0	23.8	25.8	19.4	8.6	3.6	2.3
NO	3.7	15.5	20.7	22.0	17.1	11.5	5.5	3.0

(1) A room is defined as a space of a housing unit of at least $4m^2$ such as normal bedrooms, dining rooms, living rooms and habitable cellars and attics with a height of over 2 metres and accessible from inside the unit. Kitchens are not counted unless the cooking facilities are in a room used for other purposes; thus for example, kitchen-cum-dining room is included as one room in the count of rooms. The following space of a housing unit does not count as rooms: bathrooms, toilets, corridors, utility rooms and lobbies. Verandas, lounges and conservatories only count if they are used all year round. A room used solely for business use is excluded, but is included if shared between private and business use. 1 room: Ireland, Spain, the Netherlands, Portugal, the United Kingdom and Iceland, unreliable. 2 rooms: Malta, unreliable. 6 rooms: Latvia, unreliable. 7 rooms: Lithuania and Slovakia, unreliable.

Source: Eurostat, EU-SILC cross sectional 2006 data

Table 1.8a: Time-use, population aged 20-74 years old (1)
(hours:minutes per day)

	BE	BG	DE	EE	ES	FR	IT	LV
Male								
Sleep	08:15	09:08	08:08	08:24	08:36	08:45	08:17	08:35
Eating	01:49	02:07	01:43	01:19	01:47	02:18	01:57	01:33
Other personal care	00:42	00:39	00:49	00:52	00:48	00:41	01:02	00:37
Main and second job	03:05	03:27	03:21	04:20	04:17	03:46	04:11	04:55
Food preparation	00:22	00:15	00:16	00:21	00:19	00:16	00:11	00:16
Dish washing	00:10	00:05	00:08	00:06	00:04	00:08	00:05	00:04
Cleaning dwelling	00:08	00:06	00:11	00:09	00:07	00:11	00:09	00:06
Laundry	00:01	00:01	00:02	00:01	00:01	00:01	00:00	00:01
Ironing	00:01	00:00	00:01	00:00	00:00	00:01	00:00	00:00
Gardening	00:19	00:36	00:17	00:16	00:09	00:18	00:16	00:17
Shopping and services	00:24	00:13	00:29	00:20	00:19	00:30	00:22	00:12
Entertainment and culture	00:10	00:01	00:14	00:05	00:07	00:05	00:06	00:05
Walking and hiking	00:12	00:16	00:13	00:10	00:39	00:20	00:23	00:12
Other sports, outdoor activities	00:15	00:10	00:15	00:13	00:14	00:17	00:15	00:19
Computer and video games	00:05	00:00	00:05	00:01	00:02	:	00:02	00:02
Other computing	00:22	00:01	00:16	00:02	00:09	00:07	00:07	00:03
Reading books	00:06	00:06	00:06	00:14	00:04	00:01	00:04	00:09
Other reading	00:22	00:15	00:31	00:23	00:13	00:22	00:17	00:17
TV and video	02:35	02:41	01:58	02:29	02:00	02:08	01:52	02:18
Travel to/from work	00:25	00:23	00:27	00:28	00:31	00:24	00:32	00:37
Travel related to shopping	00:16	00:12	00:16	00:13	00:07	:	00:12	00:12
Travel related to leisure	00:15	00:21	00:34	00:22	00:28	:	00:36	00:26
Other	03:41	02:57	03:40	03:12	02:59	03:21	03:04	02:44
Female								
Sleep	08:34	09:07	08:15	08:26	08:32	08:55	08:19	08:44
Eating	01:50	01:55	01:46	01:12	01:44	02:11	01:52	01:26
Other personal care	00:47	00:36	00:56	00:53	00:49	00:46	01:01	00:43
Main and second job	01:52	02:33	01:53	03:02	02:05	02:16	01:50	03:26
Food preparation	00:57	01:37	00:49	01:19	01:20	01:01	01:19	01:06
Dish washing	00:20	00:36	00:21	00:25	00:29	00:25	00:35	00:22
Cleaning dwelling	00:26	00:31	00:39	00:34	00:50	00:58	01:24	00:27
Laundry	00:09	00:19	00:13	00:14	00:11	00:07	00:10	00:09
Ironing	00:19	00:06	00:10	00:07	00:12	00:15	00:20	00:03
Gardening	00:10	00:24	00:13	00:19	00:03	00:09	00:06	00:20
Shopping and services	00:33	00:16	00:38	00:29	00:35	00:41	00:36	00:21
Entertainment and culture	00:11	00:01	00:14	00:04	00:06	00:05	00:04	00:04
Walking and hiking	00:11	00:14	00:15	00:10	00:32	00:17	00:17	00:15
Other sports, outdoor activities	00:07	00:03	00:12	00:05	00:06	00:06	00:06	00:06
Computer and video games	00:02	00:00	00:02	00:00	00:00	:	00:00	00:00
Other computing	00:09	00:00	00:06	00:01	00:03	00:02	00:02	00:01
Reading books	00:08	00:10	00:08	00:17	00:04	00:01	00:06	00:13
Other reading	00:16	00:06	00:30	00:20	00:08	00:22	00:10	00:16
TV and video	02:13	02:14	01:40	02:06	01:46	01:55	01:29	01:55
Travel to/from work	00:15	00:17	00:13	00:20	00:18	00:15	00:15	00:24
Travel related to shopping	00:18	00:14	00:19	00:16	00:12	:	00:17	00:20
Travel related to leisure	00:16	00:13	00:33	00:18	00:24	:	00:27	00:23
Other	03:57	02:28	03:55	03:03	03:31	03:13	03:15	02:56

(1) Data only shown for those countries participating in the survey; all remaining Member States, not available.

Source: Harmonised European Time Use Survey [online database version 2.0]; created 2005-2007 by Statistics Finland and Statistics Sweden [reference date 2007-10-01]; (https://www.testh2.scb.se/tus/tus/)

Table 1.8b: Time-use, population aged 20-74 years old (1)
(hours:minutes per day)

	LT	PL	SI	FI	SE	UK	NO
Male							
Sleep	08:28	08:21	08:18	08:22	08:01	08:18	07:56
Eating	01:32	01:33	01:33	01:23	01:32	01:24	01:25
Other personal care	00:53	00:50	00:40	00:38	00:39	00:41	00:45
Main and second job	04:43	03:58	03:49	03:46	04:00	04:06	04:03
Food preparation	00:20	00:25	00:16	00:21	00:25	00:26	00:25
Dish washing	00:04	00:06	00:04	00:04	00:10	00:09	00:08
Cleaning dwelling	00:10	00:09	00:08	00:08	00:15	00:11	00:14
Laundry	00:01	00:01	00:00	00:02	00:03	00:02	00:02
Ironing	00:00	00:01	00:00	00:00	00:01	00:02	00:00
Gardening	00:11	00:12	00:32	00:06	00:12	00:12	00:10
Shopping and services	00:13	00:21	00:16	00:26	00:22	00:24	00:21
Entertainment and culture	00:01	00:02	00:05	00:06	00:05	00:07	00:07
Walking and hiking	00:08	00:13	00:19	00:12	00:09	00:04	00:13
Other sports, outdoor activities	00:13	00:12	00:17	00:25	00:23	00:14	00:20
Computer and video games	00:03	00:06	00:01	00:04	00:04	00:04	00:03
Other computing	00:05	00:05	00:06	00:06	00:13	00:10	00:10
Reading books	00:05	00:07	00:04	00:09	00:09	00:05	00:07
Other reading	00:18	00:14	00:19	00:35	00:21	00:21	00:26
TV and video	02:36	02:34	02:12	02:25	01:58	02:37	02:06
Travel to/from work	00:28	00:23	00:21	00:18	00:23	00:29	00:26
Travel related to shopping	00:13	00:14	00:11	00:11	00:16	00:16	00:13
Travel related to leisure	00:23	00:27	00:28	00:33	00:37	00:36	00:36
Other	02:52	03:26	04:01	03:40	03:42	03:02	03:44
Female							
Sleep	08:35	08:35	08:25	08:32	08:11	08:27	08:10
Eating	01:26	01:34	01:26	01:19	01:36	01:26	01:20
Other personal care	00:56	00:54	00:41	00:47	00:52	00:50	00:56
Main and second job	03:29	02:14	02:39	02:32	02:47	02:21	02:37
Food preparation	01:18	01:30	01:24	00:55	00:50	00:59	00:51
Dish washing	00:22	00:29	00:28	00:15	00:21	00:18	00:21
Cleaning dwelling	00:38	00:34	00:39	00:26	00:30	00:38	00:33
Laundry	00:11	00:14	00:09	00:13	00:12	00:11	00:11
Ironing	00:04	00:07	00:16	00:05	00:05	00:11	00:04
Gardening	00:15	00:10	00:25	00:08	00:10	00:07	00:09
Shopping and services	00:21	00:30	00:21	00:32	00:29	00:39	00:27
Entertainment and culture	00:02	00:02	00:04	00:05	00:06	00:06	00:06
Walking and hiking	00:08	00:12	00:18	00:13	00:13	00:03	00:13
Other sports, outdoor activities	00:05	00:04	00:08	00:15	00:13	00:07	00:14
Computer and video games	00:00	00:01	00:00	00:01	00:01	00:01	00:01
Other computing	00:02	00:02	00:02	00:02	00:06	00:04	00:05
Reading books	00:10	00:13	00:09	00:14	00:13	00:07	00:11
Other reading	00:13	00:12	00:14	00:33	00:21	00:18	00:28
TV and video	01:59	02:03	01:44	02:02	01:40	02:09	01:39
Travel to/from work	00:20	00:14	00:16	00:14	00:17	00:17	00:18
Travel related to shopping	00:19	00:19	00:14	00:14	00:17	00:22	00:14
Travel related to leisure	00:19	00:25	00:23	00:31	00:35	00:34	00:33
Other	02:48	03:22	03:35	03:52	03:55	03:45	04:19

(1) Data are taken from national time use surveys (TUS) conducted between 1998 and 2004 and refer to men and women aged 20 to 74 years; data only shown for those countries participating in the survey; all remaining Member States, not available.

Source: Harmonised European Time Use Survey [online database version 2.0]; created 2005-2007 by Statistics Finland and Statistics Sweden [reference date 2007-10-01]; (https://www.testh2.scb.se/tus/tus/)

Income levels and income distribution

Within the context of this publication, income distribution refers to individuals and households (as opposed to its distribution between factors of production). Governments may try to create more inclusive societies through the re-distribution of income, either through macro-economic expansion that puts more people into work, or through compensatory policies (taxes and social benefits) that adjust for discrepancies in income distribution.

As noted above, income is clearly a key determinant in explaining consumption expenditure patterns. In order to take account of the different sizes and compositions of households, statistics on income levels can be adjusted to an 'equivalised income': where members of a household are given weights, with 1 given to the first adult in a household, 0.5 to each remaining adult, and 0.33 to each child; the 'equivalised size' of a household is the sum of these weights. The 'equivalised income' of a household and each of its members can then be calculated by summing the income of each member of the household and dividing by the equivalised size, allowing comparisons to be made between household units of different sizes and structures.

Wages from paid employment are generally the main source of income for most households – this is particularly true among those who are relatively rich, whereas social transfers can be the main source of income among households with lower incomes. In the EU-27 in 2005, average gross annual earnings in industry and services of full-time employees in enterprises with 10 or more employees were almost EUR 29 000, ranging from EUR 48 307 in Denmark (two thirds more than the EU-27 average) to EUR 2 195 in Bulgaria (7.6 % of the EU-27 average).

Figure 1.9: Average gross annual earnings in industry and services of full-time employees in enterprises with 10 or more employees, 2006 (1)
(EUR)

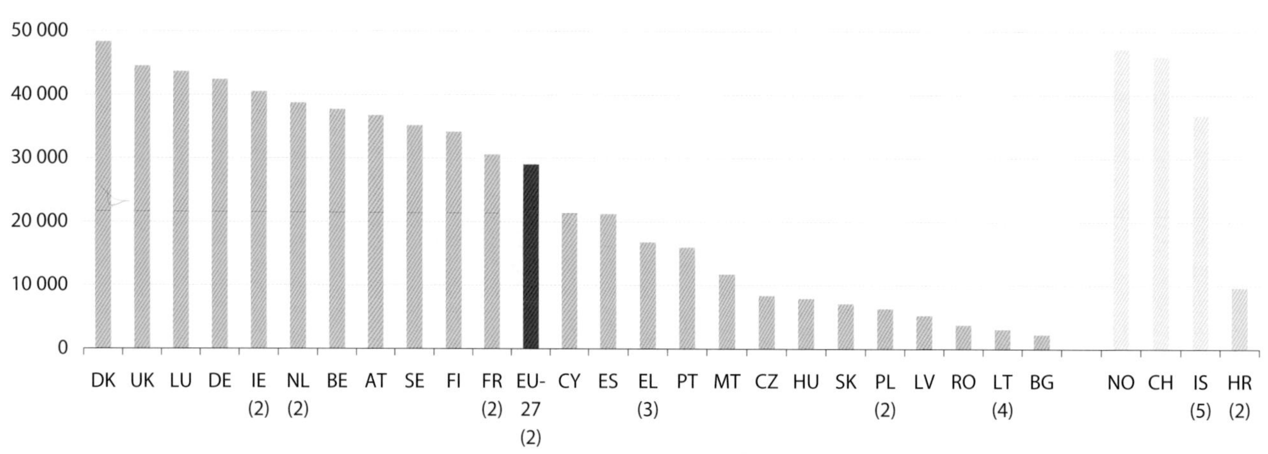

(1) Estonia, Italy and Slovenia, not available.
(2) 2005.
(3) 2003.
(4) 1999.
(5) 2002.

Source: Eurostat, earnings (tec00030)

Map 1.2: Disposable income at NUTS level 2, 2005 (1)
(EUR per inhabitant)

Disposable income, by NUTS 2 regions, 2005 (1)
(EUR per inhabitant)

- <= 10 000
- 10 000 - <= 15 000
- 15 000 - <= 17 500
- > 17 500
- Data not available

(1) All regions in Italy and Norway, 2004; Italy, provisional.

© EuroGeographics Association, for the administrative boundaries
Cartography: Eurostat — GISCO, 12/2008

0 600 km

Guadeloupe (FR) 0 25
Martinique (FR) 0 20
Guyane (FR) 0 100
Réunion (FR) 0 20
Açores (PT) 0 100
Madeira (PT) 0 20
Canarias (ES) 0 100
Malta 0 10
Ísland 0 100

eurostat

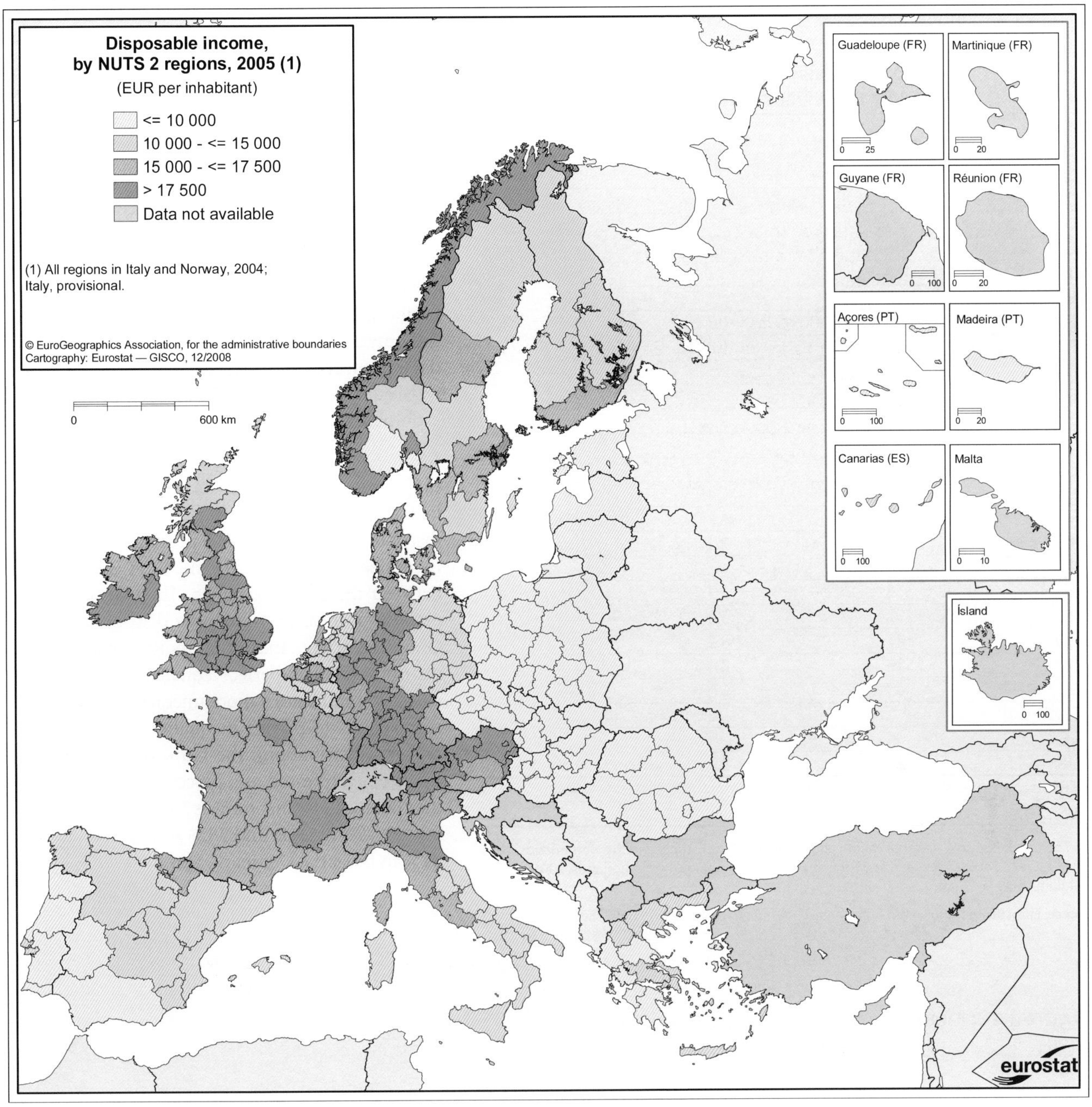

Source: Eurostat, household accounts - ESA95 (reg_ehh2inc)

Table 1.9: Minimum wages, industry and services

	Monthly minimum wage, first half 2008 (EUR)	Full-time employees earning the minimum wage, 2007 (%) (1)	Minimum monthly wage as proportion of average monthly earnings, 2007 (%) (2)
BE	1 310	:	46.4
BG	113	12.4	42.6
CZ	304	2.3	39.7
DK	:	:	:
DE	:	:	:
EE	278	4.8	33.2
IE	1 462	3.3	43.0
EL	681	:	:
ES	700	0.7	42.1
FR	1 280	9.0	:
IT	:	:	:
CY	:	:	:
LV	229	9.2	31.5
LT	232	7.0	33.5
LU	1 570	11.0	50.5
HU	273	2.4	35.4
MT	612	4.2	51.9
NL	1 335	2.2	45.5
AT	:	:	:
PL	313	2.3	36.1
PT	497	5.5	41.6
RO	141	8.2	35.7
SI	539	3.4	44.2
SK	243	1.6	46.6
FI	:	:	:
SE	:	:	:
UK	1 223	2.0	38.2
TR	354	:	:
US	696	1.3	33.6

(1) The Czech Republic, Ireland, Poland and Romania, 2006; Estonia and the Netherlands, 2005.
(2) The Czech Republic, Poland and Romania, 2006; Estonia and the Netherlands, 2005; Belgium, 2002.

Source: Eurostat, earnings (earn_minw_cur, earn_minw_pc and earn_minw_avg)

Some governments try to ensure a certain standard of living by fixing a minimum wage, while others try to effect a redistribution of income by applying different tax rates – in particular, lower or zero rates for lower incomes. In the first half of 2008, minimum wages ranged from EUR 1 570 per month in Luxembourg to EUR 113 in Bulgaria.

The ratio of the minimum wage compared with average gross earnings in industry and services provides one indication of income equality. In the Baltic Member States, the minimum monthly wage equated to approximately one third of average monthly earnings. At the other end of the range, Malta (51.9 %) and Luxembourg (50.5 %) were the only Member States (among those for which data are available) to report that their minimum wage equated to more than half the average level of monthly earnings.

Income distribution across society could (in theory) range from an equal distribution, where everyone had the same income, to a completely unequal distribution, where only one person was earning all the money; in practise, the situation is somewhere between these two extremes. The Gini coefficient provides a measure of income distribution: a low Gini coefficient indicates more equal income distribution (0 is perfect equality), while a high coefficient indicates a more unequal distribution (1 corresponds to perfect inequality or a completely unequal distribution); the Gini index is the Gini coefficient expressed as a percentage. In the EU-25 the Gini index for income was 30 % in 2006, ranging from 39 % in Latvia and 38 % in Portugal down to 24 % in Bulgaria, Denmark, Slovenia and Sweden.

Figure 1.10: Inequality of income distribution: Gini index, 2006 (1)
(%)

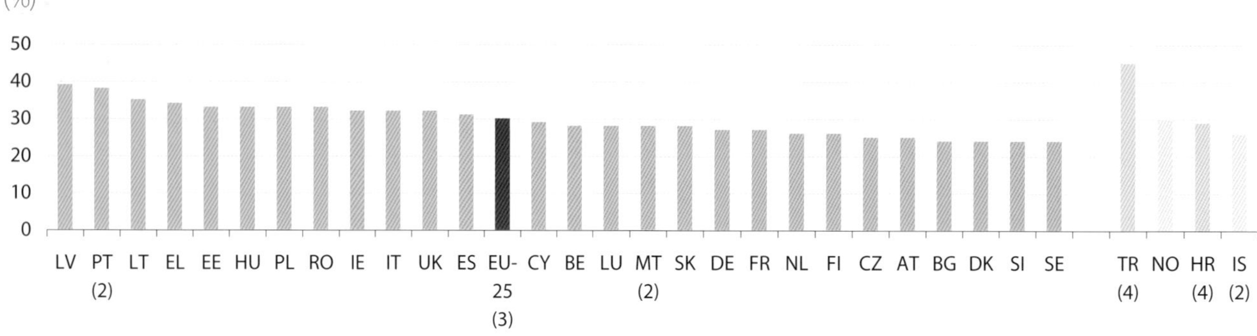

(1) The Gini index is a measure of statistical dispersion: a low Gini coefficient indicates more equal income or wealth distribution, while a high Gini coefficient indicates more unequal distribution (0 corresponds to perfect equality and 1 corresponds to perfect inequality); the Gini index is the Gini coefficient expressed as a percentage.
(2) Provisional.
(3) Estimate.
(4) 2003.

Source: Eurostat, income distribution and monetary poverty (ilc_sic)

The S80/S20 income quintile share ratio is an alternative measure of income distribution, derived as the ratio of total income received by the 20 % of the population with the highest income (the top quintile) compared with that received by the 20 % of the population with the lowest income (bottom quintile). In the EU-25 this ratio stood at 4.8 in 2006; in other words the top 20 % had an annual income that was 4.8 times as high as that for the lowest 20 % of earners. The distribution of the Member States around the EU average was similar to that recorded for the Gini coefficient, ranging from a high of 7.9 in Latvia and more than 6 in Portugal, Lithuania and Greece, down to 3.4 in Denmark and Slovenia.

Figure 1.11: Inequality of income distribution: S80/S20 income quintile share ratio, 2006 (1)

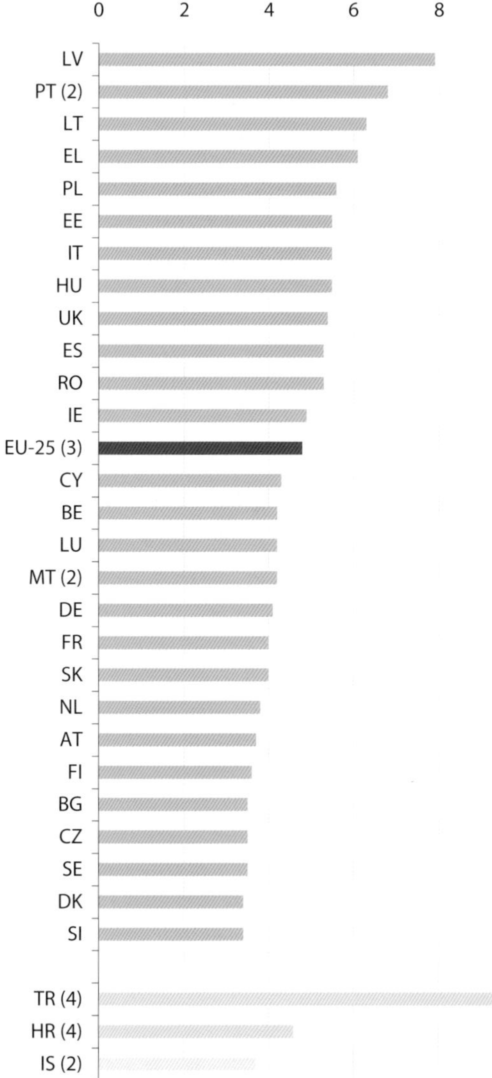

(1) Ratio of total income received by the 20 % of the country's population with the highest income (top quintile) to that received by the 20 % of the country's population with the lowest income (lowest quintile); income must be understood as equivalised disposable income.
(2) Provisional.
(3) Estimate.
(4) 2003.

Source: Eurostat, income distribution and monetary poverty (ilc_pns)

Table 1.10: Tax rates on low wage earners, 2006 (%)

	Tax wedge on labour costs (1)	Unem-ployment trap (2)	Low wage trap: single person without children (3)	Low wage trap: one-earner married couple with two children (3)
EU-27	40.1	75.4	47.4	62.2
BE	49.2	83.0	58.0	46.0
BG	31.1	74.3	16.2	19.2
CZ	40.1	63.0	31.0	53.0
DK	39.3	91.0	82.0	92.0
DE	47.4	75.0	51.0	79.0
EE	38.4	64.0	25.0	19.0
IE	16.3	76.0	53.0	77.0
EL	35.4	59.0	19.0	16.0
ES	35.9	80.0	26.0	17.0
FR	44.5	81.0	35.0	56.0
IT	41.5	71.0	33.0	-12.0
CY	11.9	62.0	6.0	93.0
LV	41.8	88.0	32.0	100.0
LT	40.6	78.7	30.0	52.2
LU	30.6	88.0	51.0	110.0
HU	42.9	78.0	31.0	54.0
MT	18.4	61.7	17.9	8.3
NL	40.6	86.0	70.0	77.0
AT	43.5	67.0	37.0	64.0
PL	42.5	82.0	66.0	78.0
PT	31.7	81.0	20.0	78.0
RO	42.2	70.5	30.3	19.4
SI	41.2	94.1	67.5	72.6
SK	35.6	44.0	24.0	29.0
FI	38.9	76.0	61.0	100.0
SE	46.0	87.0	55.0	89.0
UK	30.4	68.0	58.0	85.0
TR	42.0	:	:	:
IS	23.6	82.0	39.0	67.0
NO	34.3	75.0	37.0	84.0
CH	26.9	:	:	:
JP	:	59.0	20.0	93.0
US	26.4	70.0	32.0	42.0

(1) Income tax on gross wage earnings plus the employee's and the employer's social security contributions, expressed as a percentage of the total labour costs; single persons without children earning 67 % of the average wage in industry and services.
(2) Percentage of gross earnings which is taxed away through higher tax and social security contributions and the withdrawal of unemployment and other benefits when an unemployed person returns to employment; single persons without children earning 67 % of the average wage in industry and services.
(3) Percentage of gross earnings which is taxed away through the combined effects of income taxes, social security contributions and any withdrawal of benefits when gross earnings increase from 33 % to 67 % of the average wage in industry and services.

Source: Eurostat, net earnings and tax rates (earn_nt_taxwedge, earn_nt_unemtrp and earn_nt_lowwtrp)

Income distribution in the EU-27 is generally skewed in favour of men, as there was, on average, a 15 % difference between average gross hourly earnings of male and female paid employees (when measured as a percentage of average gross hourly earnings of men) in 2006. Gender pay gaps existed in each of the Member States, ranging from a high of 25 % in Estonia (2005) to just 3 % in Malta.

The relative median income ratio compares the median income of those aged 65 or more with that of persons aged less than 65. Given that most persons aged 65 or over no longer work, it is not surprising to find that their median income was usually below that of the younger generations; within the EU-25 the ratio was 0.85 in 2006. Poland was the only Member State where the median income of those aged 65 or more was higher than that of persons aged less than 65 (1.07).

A related measure is the aggregate replacement ratio, which is defined as the ratio of income from pensions for persons aged between 65 and 74 years compared with income from work for persons aged between 50 and 59 years. This stood at 0.51 for the EU-25 in 2006, with highs of 0.65 in Luxembourg and Austria, while Ireland (0.35) and Cyprus (0.28) closed the ranking; note that this indicator can be affected not only by the level of pensions and incomes in each country, but also by the rate of early retirement among those aged 50 to 59.

Figure 1.12: Gender pay gap in unadjusted form, employees aged 16-64 working at least 15 hours per week, 2006
(difference between average gross hourly earnings of male paid employees and of female paid employees as a percentage of average gross hourly earnings of male paid employees)

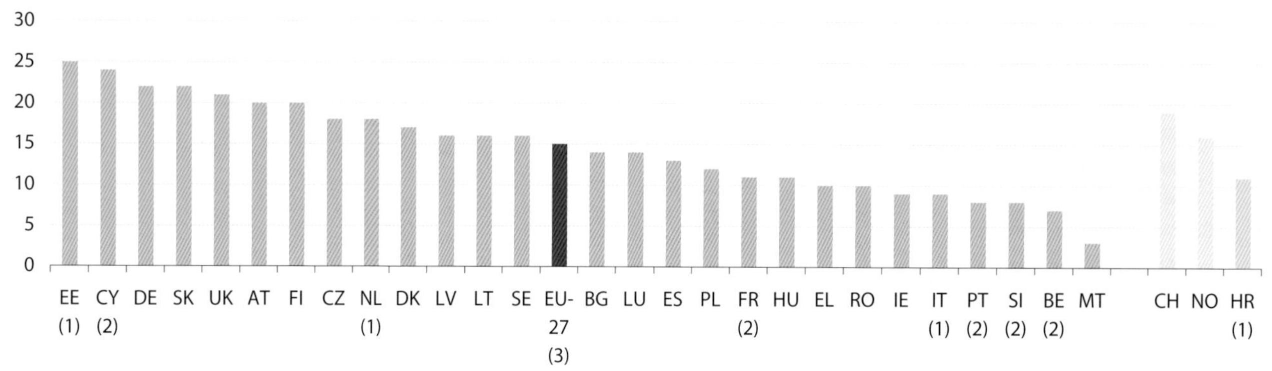

(1) 2005.
(2) Provisional.
(3) Estimate.

Source: Eurostat, gross earnings - annual data (earn_gr_gpg)

Figure 1.13: Relative median income ratio, 2006 (1)

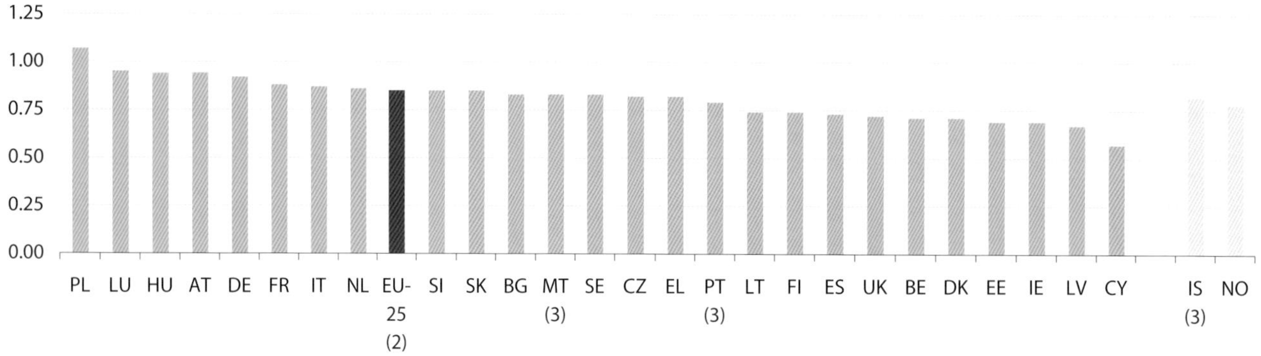

(1) Persons aged 65 years and over compared with persons aged less than 65 years; Romania, not available.
(2) Estimate.
(3) Provisional.

Source: Eurostat, income and living conditions (ilc_ov7a)

Figure 1.14: Aggregate replacement ratio, 2006 (1)

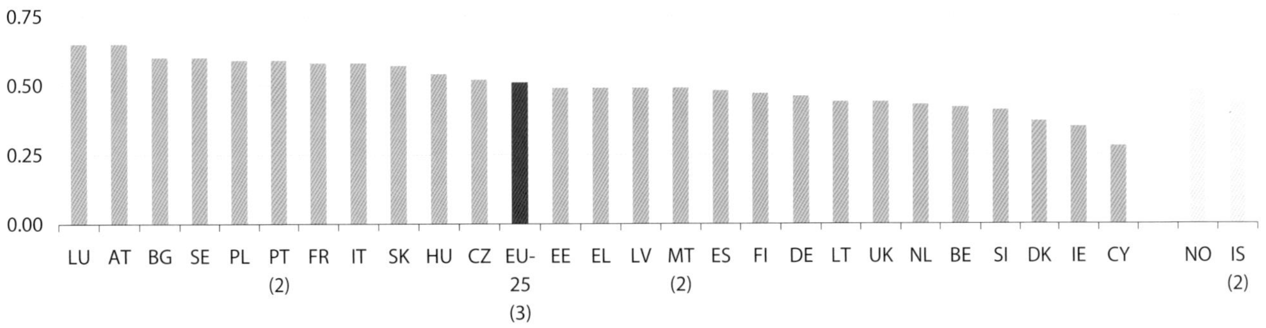

(1) Ratio of income from pensions of persons aged between 65 and 74 years compared with income from work of persons aged between 50 and 59 years; Romania, not available.
(2) Provisional.
(3) Estimate.

Source: Eurostat, income distribution and monetary poverty (ilc_pns)

Consumption or savings?

Consumers often save with a particular goal in mind: for example, the purchase of a house, a car, a holiday or retirement; savings in this light may be seen as deferred or postponed consumption. Savings can also be made in order to smooth income fluctuations and to have some security – for example, to have some money available in case of illness, unemployment or retirement.

As with consumption expenditure, the capacity to save depends primarily on income: those with more money are generally more likely to be able to save something at the end of the month. However, the willingness to save also varies between individuals: some people are more prudent, while others tend to live from day-to-day. Otherwise, demographics, the inflation rate, interest rates, the performance of financial markets, or national tax regimes are all factors that can influence, to some degree, the rate of saving.

Net disposable income ranged from upwards of EUR 30 000 per inhabitant in Denmark, Sweden and Ireland in 2007, to less than EUR 10 000 in the majority of the Member States that joined the EU in 2004 or 2007 (Cyprus and Slovenia were exceptions, while no data are available for Malta or Romania).

The (net) savings ratio is defined as net savings divided by net disposable income; net savings are the part of net disposable income that is not spent as final consumption expenditure. As such, the savings ratio will increase when disposable income grows at a faster pace than consumption expenditure. The savings ratio may be negative if

Table 1.11: Income and savings, 2007
(EUR per inhabitant)

	Net disposable income	Net saving	Saving as a share of disposable income (%)
EU-15	24 700	2 000	8.1
BE	26 400	3 100	11.7
BG	3 200	0	0.0
CZ (1)	9 500	1 000	10.5
DK	34 800	3 300	9.5
DE	25 200	3 200	12.7
EE	9 500	1 400	14.7
IE (1)	31 500	4 300	13.7
EL	17 600	-300	-1.7
ES	18 900	1 300	6.9
FR	25 500	1 800	7.1
IT	21 400	1 000	4.7
CY	29 500	:	:
LV	7 400	0	0.0
LT	7 200	400	5.6
LU	:	:	:
HU (2)	7 100	300	4.2
MT	:	:	:
NL	29 300	4 700	16.0
AT (1)	27 400	3 800	13.9
PL (1)	6 900	600	8.7
PT	12 300	-700	-5.7
RO	:	:	:
SI	13 700	2 000	14.6
SK	8 000	500	6.3
FI	28 700	4 400	15.3
SE	32 100	5 800	18.1
UK	29 300	1 000	3.4
IS	38 300	-500	-1.3
NO	52 400	15 400	29.4
CH (1)	35 500	7 900	22.3
JP (1)	19 900	1 900	9.5

(1) Forecasts.
(2) 2006.

Source: Eurostat, income, saving and net lending/net borrowing - current prices (nama_inc_c)

Figure 1.15: Consumer attitudes to making major purchases or savings and interest rates, EU-27
(seasonally adjusted balance, left-hand scale; %, right-hand scale)

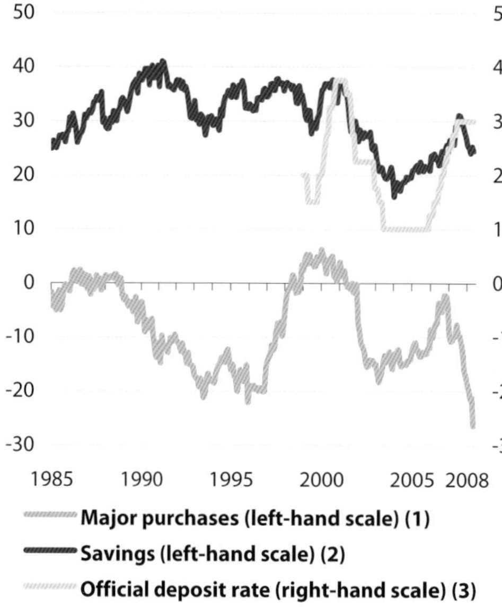

(1) In view of the general economic situation, do you think that now is the right moment for people to make major purchases such as furniture, electrical/electronic devices, etc.?
(2) Which of these statements best describes the current financial situation of your household (saving a lot, saving a little, just managing to make ends meet on our income, having to draw on our savings, running into debt)?
(3) Moving euro area aggregate based on membership (EA-11 up to 2000, EA-12 up to 2006, EA-13 up to 2007, EA-15 from 2008); series starts in 1999.

Source: Eurostat and Directorate-General for Economic and Financial Affairs, business and consumer surveys and interest rates (bsco_m and irt_cb_a)

expenditure exceeds income, which may occur when people run down their savings or incur debt. Savings ratios have fallen in many countries in recent decades, perhaps as a result of credit becoming more easily accessible. The financial crisis in the second half of 2008 may have reversed this trend and, at the time of writing, it is already apparent that many consumers face difficulties in obtaining mortgages or loans.

In 2007, the highest savings ratios within the EU were recorded in Sweden, the Netherlands and Finland (all above 15 %). On the other hand, there was no net saving in Bulgaria or Latvia, and households in Greece (-1.7 %) and Portugal (-5.7 %) were spending more than their income.

Credit, ability to pay and indebtedness

Prior to the credit crisis in the second half of 2008, it was relatively easy for most consumers to access credit, as retailers and lenders made a range of different payment methods available, allowing consumers a high degree of flexibility to make purchases. As such, it was commonplace for consumers to turn to credit in order to satisfy their desire to purchase new goods, such as a new car or a piece of furniture, rather than deferring purchases until they had enough money to pay for them outright. At the time of writing, it remains to be seen how the credit crisis will affect the liquidity of markets and whether it will be as easy for consumers to borrow money in the future.

The development of banking and payment networks, financial markets, and various technological advances all contribute to change the way that consumers purchase goods. This can be witnessed in terms of both the number of bank cards issued and the number of automated teller machines (ATMs) available to customers. It is technically easy for the majority of consumers to pay for goods and services, whether they happen to be doing their shopping in a retail store, on-line or by mail. However, the ease of making payments and the availability of credit carries risks, as witnessed by the crisis in the second half

of 2008. It would appear likely that in the future, credit, at least for a period, will be less easily accessible. Furthermore, with growing fears of a recession, it is likely that the number of people who face difficulties in paying back mortgages, loans or other forms of debt will increase.

According to the European Central Bank (ECB), there were just over 715 million bank cards issued in the EU-27 (excluding Denmark) in 2006, while more than 360 thousand ATMs were available across the whole of the EU-27.

The most common payment instrument in the majority of the Member States that joined the EU in 2004 or 2007 was generally the credit transfer, which accounted for more than seven out of every ten transactions in Hungary, Romania and Poland. In most of the EU-15 Member States the bank card was generally the most common method of payment, accounting for more than six out of every ten transactions in Portugal, Denmark and Sweden. The use of direct debit as a payment instrument was particularly high (above 40 % of all transactions) in Spain and Germany. There were wide disparities in the use of cheques across the Member States: a majority of transactions in Malta were conducted using cheques, and they were also the most important payment method in Cyprus, and remained relatively important in France (25.6 % of all transactions), Ireland and Greece (both around 20 %). In contrast, cheques accounted for less than 1 % of all transactions in 16 of the remaining Member States.

While increased European integration in the form of the internal market and the single currency may help explain, at least in part, the convergence of interest rates during the past decade, consumer credit remained almost twice as expensive in Portugal (12.2 %) as in Finland (6.3 %) in 2007. It is interesting to note that the two countries reporting negative savings rates, Portugal and Greece, also reported the highest consumer credit rates (among those for which data are available). According to Eurofinas, the majority (56 %) of consumer credit loans in 2006 (in terms of value) were granted for personal consumption, while almost one third (31 %) were for vehicle finance, and the remainder (13 %) for mortgages.

Table 1.12: Access to the banking network and payment instruments, 2006

	Number of cards issued (million)	Number of terminals - ATMs (1 000)	Payment instruments (% of total volume of transactions)			
			Credit transfers	Direct debit	Cards	Cheques
BE	16.61	13.94	42.5	11.7	40.3	0.7
BG	6.02	3.66	68.2	1.6	30.2	0.0
CZ	8.19	3.28	52.9	34.8	10.9	0.0
DK	:	3.09	21.6	14.2	62.6	1.6
DE	120.17	53.89	42.2	42.8	14.2	0.6
EE	1.62	0.92	39.7	7.1	53.1	0.0
IE	8.25	3.31	27.6	18.0	33.8	20.6
EL	15.14	6.74	20.0	11.2	49.0	19.0
ES	74.31	58.45	14.5	44.7	35.7	3.5
FR	94.05	47.82	17.5	18.3	37.6	25.6
IT	70.87	43.69	29.6	13.3	34.3	12.6
CY	0.86	0.52	14.8	15.9	32.3	37.0
LV	2.07	0.95	63.7	2.2	34.1	0.0
LT	3.54	1.15	52.1	3.9	43.5	0.2
LU	1.07	0.44	48.3	10.1	38.5	0.3
HU	8.22	3.81	76.7	9.3	13.8	0.0
MT	0.51	0.16	17.2	3.1	27.0	52.8
NL	31.44	8.11	32.7	27.2	36.3	0.0
AT	9.35	7.99	47.5	35.7	15.2	0.3
PL	23.85	9.94	71.3	1.1	27.5	0.0
PT	17.64	14.69	10.1	11.3	63.6	15.0
RO	9.18	6.04	75.7	10.6	9.5	4.0
SI	3.14	1.52	54.9	12.6	32.2	0.3
SK	4.32	2.00	66.8	16.1	17.0	0.0
FI	6.26	3.28	42.5	5.1	52.3	0.0
SE	13.89	2.81	29.2	10.0	60.7	0.1
UK	164.64	60.47	21.2	19.8	46.6	12.3

(1) 2004.

Source: European Central Bank (sdw.ecb.int)

Figure 1.16: Convergence of interest rates, coefficient of variation for housing loans to households (1)

(%)

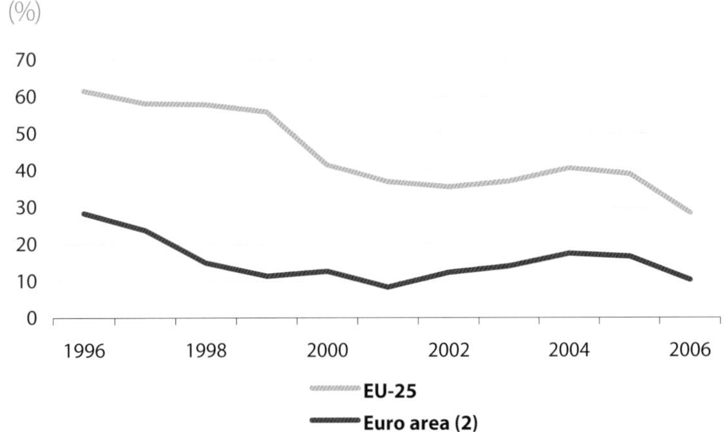

(1) Estimates.

(2) Moving euro area aggregate based on membership (EA-11 up to 2000, EA-12 up to 2006).

Source: Eurostat, convergence of interest rates - annual data (irt_cvg_a)

Figure 1.17: Consumer credit rate, 2007 (1)
(%)

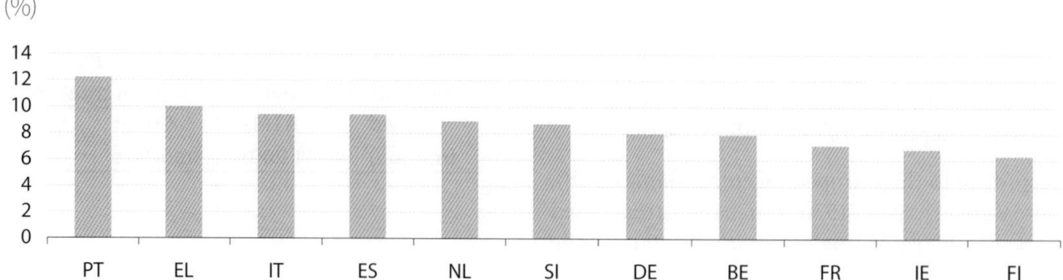

(1) Information presented for those Member States with data available.

Source: European Central Bank (sdw.ecb.int)

Table 1.13: Ability to pay, 2006
(% of households)

	Arrears on mortgage or rent payments (1)		Arrears on utility bills (2)		Arrears on hire purchase or other loans (3)		Capacity to face unexpected expenses (4)	
	Yes (5)	No	Yes (6)	No	Yes (7)	No	Yes	No
BE	2.6	58.9	4.4	93.0	1.7	33.1	76.9	23.0
BG	:	:	:	:	:	:	:	:
CZ	4.0	55.9	5.0	93.8	2.4	20.3	58.7	41.3
DK	2.0	98.0	2.8	97.2	3.5	96.5	71.7	26.9
DE	2.1	94.6	4.5	94.1	2.3	95.9	58.1	41.3
EE	0.8	14.7	5.7	94.1	1.1	21.8	69.2	30.8
IE	3.6	44.5	6.0	90.5	2.4	68.0	60.6	39.2
EL	5.3	24.1	26.3	72.5	10.1	26.3	66.9	33.1
ES	2.1	35.1	2.6	74.4	1.5	20.7	68.7	31.2
FR	5.2	59.7	6.0	93.9	2.5	42.7	65.7	34.0
IT	3.2	28.0	9.3	90.7	2.2	14.4	71.6	28.4
CY	6.8	27.5	9.0	89.1	11.4	38.6	55.1	44.9
LV	3.0	29.3	12.6	85.2	1.6	28.7	27.6	72.4
LT	0.5	5.1	12.9	86.7	1.4	18.2	38.9	61.1
LU	1.0	61.6	1.6	95.6	0.7	54.6	81.7	18.1
HU	1.9	17.8	12.9	86.1	2.1	15.2	46.5	52.9
MT	1.3	33.6	5.9	94.0	0.8	11.0	68.0	32.0
NL	2.9	96.5	2.7	97.2	1.3	13.4	74.0	25.6
AT	1.4	57.8	1.6	98.3	1.1	10.4	72.0	27.5
PL	1.8	7.9	17.5	78.3	4.4	24.8	42.0	58.0
PT	2.0	40.4	4.5	90.9	1.0	36.9	81.8	18.2
RO	:	:	:	:	:	:	:	:
SI	1.6	6.2	10.4	88.7	3.9	30.0	54.3	45.5
SK	4.6	57.5	5.9	93.3	2.3	48.8	48.7	51.1
FI	4.6	59.1	4.0	95.6	2.2	37.8	65.4	33.4
SE	3.5	85.3	4.1	91.7	3.5	49.5	83.3	14.9
UK	4.0	64.4	0.2	99.8	2.4	97.5	71.1	28.7
NO	6.1	72.6	6.5	84.3	3.8	31.2	70.8	28.6
IS	6.1	72.9	5.0	93.5	6.3	40.2	66.0	32.0

(1) In arrears at any time in the last 12 months; figures do not sum to 100 % as some households are outright owners or live in rent free accommodation.
(2) In arrears at any time in the last 12 months; figures do not sum to 100 % as some households do not pay utility bills.
(3) In arrears at any time in the last 12 months; figures do not sum to 100 % as some households have no hire purchase instalments or other loan payments.
(4) Capacity for household to face a financial expense without asking for financial help from anybody, debiting their account within one month, while not affecting their ability to pay for existing debts in the same manner as before the unexpected expense was borne.
(5) Estonia, Lithuania and Malta, unreliable.
(6) The United Kingdom, unreliable.
(7) Malta, Austria and Portugal, unreliable.

Source: Eurostat, EU-SILC cross-sectional 2006 data

Figure 1.18: Breakdown of consumer credit by product, EU, 2006 (1)
(share of value of new loans granted, EUR million)

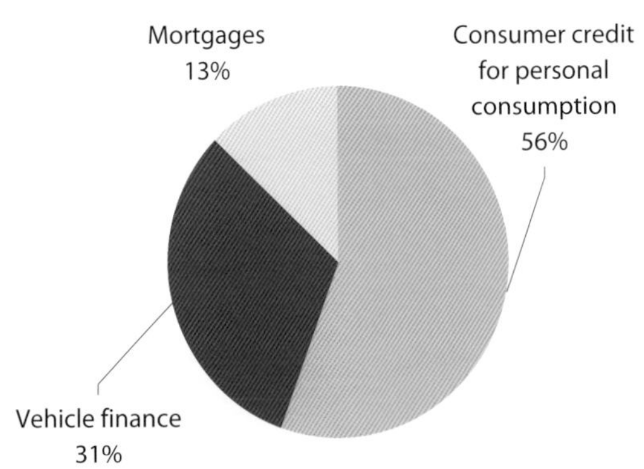

(1) Eurofinas currently represents 16 Member Associations in 15 countries, and more than 1 000 finance houses, captive companies, specialised and universal banks.

Source: Eurofinas, facts and figures (www.eurofinas.org)

With consumers using a variety of credit facilities, some households face considerable difficulties in balancing their accounts at the end of the month. Eurostat statistics on income and living conditions (EU-SILC) for 2006 show that as many as 6.8 % of households in Cyprus were in arrears on mortgage or rent payments, and upwards of 5 % of households in Greece and France. In a similar vein, more than 10 % of households in Latvia, Lithuania, Hungary and Slovenia were in arrears for paying their utility bills, a share that rose to 17.5 % in Poland and 26.3 % in Greece. A similar picture emerged concerning hire purchase instalments or other loans, where more than 10 % of Greek and Cypriot households were in arrears, the next highest proportion being 4.4 % in Poland.

An alternative measure for studying whether households are living within their means is to look at the capacity of households to face unexpected financial expenses, defined for this purpose as being able to meet an expense without asking for financial help from anybody, debiting an account within one month, while not affecting the ability to pay for existing debts in the same manner as before the unexpected expense was borne. Upwards of four out of every five households in Luxembourg, Portugal and Sweden reported that they were able to cope with such an unexpected financial expense in 2006, while less than half of all households in Latvia, Lithuania, Hungary, Poland and Slovakia were able to do so.

Figure 1.19: Difficulty paying the bills at the end of the month, capital cities, 2006 (1)
(index, 0-100)

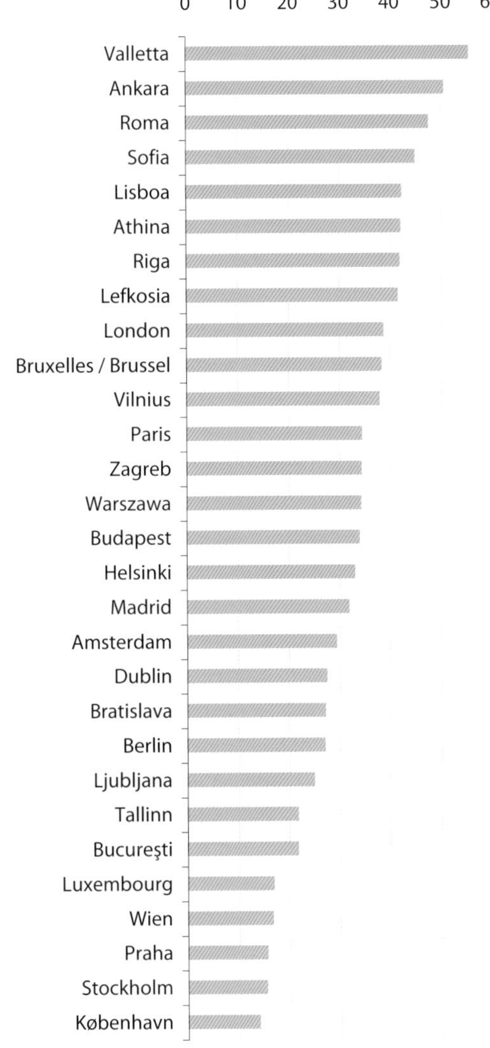

(1) 0: no difficulty; 100: always have difficulty.

Source: Eurostat, perception survey results (urb_percep)

Consumer confidence

The choice of whether to spend or save money is, in part, related to consumer confidence – in particular, the outlook that consumers have for the evolution of the general economic situation during the coming months. Consumer confidence can be measured in terms of the expected and actual evolution of a range of different indicators. For example, when questioned about their expectations for the evolution of prices during the next 12 months, consumers in the EU-27 were generally quite accurate, although actual price changes tended to vary more than consumers anticipated.

When questioned about future expectations for the financial situation of their own household, EU-27 consumers have, since 1985, been consistently slightly more optimistic than the actual reality of their situation, as measured by the change in their financial position during the previous 12 months. Nevertheless, when asked whether they thought they would be likely to make a major purchase in the coming 12 months, a balance of -20.9 was recorded for the EU-27 in May 2008. Using this measure, there were particularly low levels of consumer confidence in Greece, Hungary and Portugal, where the balance fell below -40 in each case. Given the current economic situation and the reverberations of the credit crisis, it is likely that consumer confidence has subsequently fallen much lower.

Table 1.14: Consumer opinion, May 2008
(seasonally adjusted, balance, -100 to 100)

	Price trends over the next 12 months (1)	Major purchases over the next 12 months (2)	Consumer confi-dence (3)
EU-27	30.8	-20.9	-13.6
BE	20.5	-16.9	-7.8
BG	54.2	-15.2	-29.5
CZ	36.7	-7.9	-5.9
DK	22.5	-2.9	3.7
DE	36.1	-29.6	-4.2
EE	37.3	-17.4	-19.2
IE	:	:	:
EL	59.0	-33.2	-43.8
ES	27.4	-35.6	-30.5
FR	19.8	-8.0	-18.2
IT	6.6	-12.9	-19.5
CY	47.1	-1.3	-30.6
LV	48.9	-5.7	-22.9
LT	57.5	16.2	-14.9
LU	35.5	-17.2	1.7
HU	68.5	-50.0	-49.5
MT	50.3	0.3	-17.5
NL	48.8	-12.4	1.4
AT	37.4	-24.4	1.6
PL	40.8	-1.2	-1.0
PT	55.1	-13.5	-48.0
RO (4)	56.9	-29.0	-13.8
SI	31.2	-9.4	-20.7
SK	68.7	-19.1	-14.0
FI	44.7	-12.7	12.0
SE	41.2	-10.9	7.1
UK	32.7	-28.1	-14.6

(1) By comparison with the past 12 months, how do you expect that consumer prices will develop in the next 12 months?
(2) Compared to the past 12 months, do you expect to spend more or less money on major purchases (furniture, electrical/electronic devices, etc.) over the next 12 months?
(3) Arithmetic average of the balances (in percentage points) of the answers to the questions on the financial situation of households, the general economic situation, unemployment expectations (with inverted sign) and savings, all over the next 12 months.
(4) April 2008.

Source: Directorate-General for Economic and Financial Affairs, business and consumer surveys (bsco_m)

Figure 1.20: Consumer opinion, EU-27, May of each year
(seasonally adjusted, balance, -100 to 100)

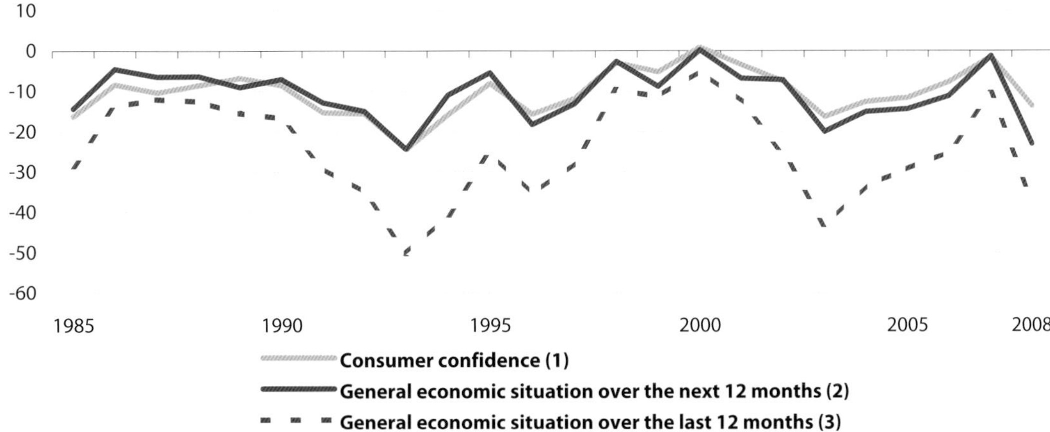

(1) Arithmetic average of the balances (in percentage points) of the answers to the questions on the financial situation of households, the general economic situation, unemployment expectations (with inverted sign) and savings, all over the next 12 months.
(2) How do you expect the general economic situation in this country to develop over the next 12 months?
(3) How do you think the general economic situation in the country has changed over the past 12 months?

Source: Directorate-General for Economic and Financial Affairs, business and consumer surveys (bsco_m)

Figure 1.21: Consumer opinion, EU-27, May of each year
(seasonally adjusted, balance, -100 to 100)

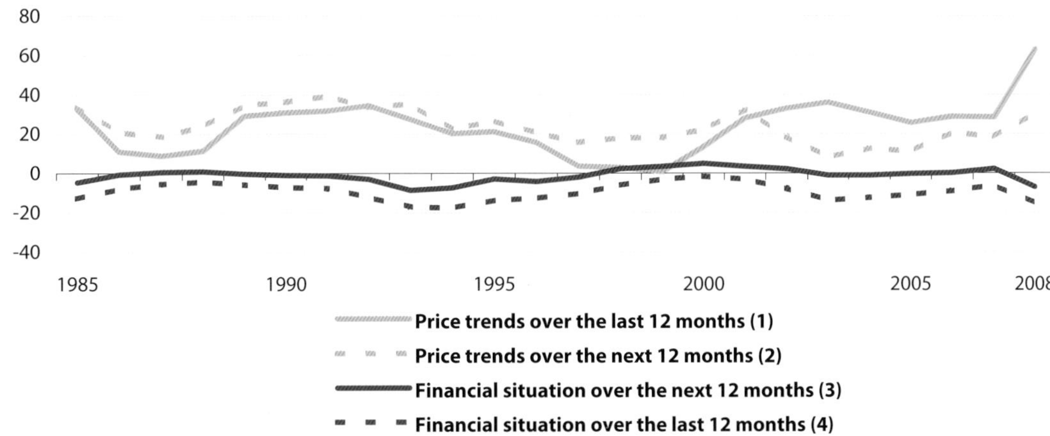

(1) How do you think that consumer prices have developed over the last 12 months?
(2) By comparison with the past 12 months, how do you expect that consumer prices will develop in the next 12 months?
(3) How do you expect the financial position of your household to change over the next 12 months?
(4) How has the financial situation of your household changed over the last 12 months?

Source: Directorate-General for Economic and Financial Affairs, business and consumer surveys (bsco_m)

RETAILING AND ADVERTISING

Retailing acts as an interface that brings together manufacturers and consumers, providing access to a wide range of products and services. The existence of a single European market gives consumers considerable choice, as well as opportunities to find cheaper goods and services in other Member States. The level of choice has been extended further by developments within the retail sector, as shoppers within the EU can choose to purchase goods in-store, out-of-store, on the Internet, cross-border, or through a variety of other formats such as direct selling or timeshare.

Table 1.15a: Shop opening hours

	Weekdays	Saturdays	Sundays and public holidays
BE	05.00-20.00: working days; 05.00-21.00: Fridays and working days before public holiday	05.00-20.00	All retail stores: 05.00-12.00; furniture or gardening shops: 40 Sundays/year 05.00-20.00; food chains with less than 5 employees, butcher's, baker's, newsagents, flower shops, shops in tourist areas: 05.00-20.00
BG	:	:	:
CZ	No restrictions	No restrictions	No restrictions
DK	Closed between 00.00-06.00 Monday; else no restrictions	No restrictions until 17.00; closed thereafter	In principle closed with some exceptions
DE	00.00-24.00 except in Rhineland-Palatinate, Saxony 06.00-22.00 and Saarland-Bavaria 06.00-20.00	00.00-24.00 except in Mecklenburg-Western Pomerania 06.00-22.00, Rhineland-Palatinate, Saxony 06.00-22.00, Saarland 06.00-20.00, Saxony - Anhalt, Thuringia 0.00-20.00	In principle closed with some limited exceptions
EE	No restrictions	No restrictions	No restrictions
IE	No restrictions on opening; alcohol may not be sold before 07.30	No restrictions on opening; alcohol may not be sold before 07.30	Alcohol may not be sold until 12.30; alcohol may not be sold on Christmas Day and Good Friday
EL	05:00-21:00	05-20:00	All shops are closed, except e.g. petrol stations, restaurants, bars, pastry shops, photo shops, florists, antiquaries
ES	Legislation defined at regional level; no restrictions	Legislation defined at regional level; no restrictions	Legislation defined at regional level; opening is allowed for at least 12 Sundays/public holidays per year
FR	No restrictions	No restrictions	In principle shops can be open on Sundays but employees are not allowed to work; there are numerous permanent and temporary exceptions
IT	07.00-22.00 (with a maximum of 13 opening hours per day)	07.00-22.00 (with a maximum of 13 opening hours per day)	In principle closed; exceptions for certain types of shops (e.g. bakeries and flower shops) and for tourist areas; in total, shops can open on Sundays 8 times a year and are generally open all Sundays of December
CY	1 April-31 October shops close: Mon, Tue, Thu at 20:30, Wed at 14:00, Fri at 21:30; opening hours vary according to the nature of the shop 07:00-09:00; winter period: Mon, Tue, Thu close at 19:00, Wed at 14:00, Fri at 20:00	1 April-31 October shops close at 17:00; winter period shops close at 15:00; during the summer, special provisions for shops within designated tourist areas, open until 22:00	All the shops are obliged to stay closed between 14:00-17:00 from 15 June to 31 August
LV	No restrictions	No restrictions	No restrictions
LT	No restrictions	No restrictions	No restrictions

Source: EuroCommerce (updated September 2007)

No matter where a consumer decides to shop for their goods and services, they are protected by the same rules and regulations as in their home country throughout the EU. Indeed, independent of the country of purchase, choice of retailer or type of retail format, European consumers should expect (although they may not always be aware) their purchases to be covered by a basic set of principles whereby Community law imposes obligations on retailers to ensure that minimum protection rights are adhered to.

While most commentators would agree that the creation of the internal market and the liberalisation of services have resulted in increased choice and downward pressure on prices to the general benefit of consumers, there are areas (particularly as regards services) where legislative safeguards continue to perform a role when markets do not work adequately, for example, policy makers try to ensure that affordable and universal access is granted to services of general interest (such as energy services or postal services).

In-store retailing

During recent years, most Member States have liberalised their in-store opening hours. Many countries have virtually no restrictions on shop opening hours during the week or on Saturdays, while opening times on Sundays and public holidays tend to remain restricted.

Table 1.15b: Shop opening hours

	Weekdays	Saturdays	Sundays and public holidays
LU	06.00 - 20.00; once per week shops can close at 21.00	06.00-18.00; these hours also apply to days which precede public holidays	06.00-13.00
HU	Opening hours decided by the trader; in Budapest and suburbs Mayor's Office have the right to regulate hours from 06:00-22:00	Open up to 14:00 or 16:00	Generally closed; 24 December open up to 14:00; exceptions for restaurants; hotels, flower shops, gasoline stations and confectionary outlets
MT	:	:	:
NL	06.00-22.00	06.00-22.00	In principle, closed; local governments can allow Sunday opening (max. 12 Sundays per year); they can also permit Sunday opening for tourist areas; exceptions for shops in petrol stations and hospitals
AT	06.00 - 19.30	06.00 - 17.00; 4 Saturdays before Christmas until 18.00	Exemptions for tourist areas
PL	:	:	:
PT	06.00-24.00	06.00-24.00	Opening of hypermarkets is limited to 08.00-13.00 from January to October (in November and December: 06.00-24.00)
RO	:	:	:
SI	No restrictions	No restrictions	Shops are not allowed to open on Sundays and on national holidays; exceptions: shops with fast moving consumer goods, sales premises up to 200 m^2, petrol stations, tourist centres
SK	No restrictions	No restrictions	No restrictions
FI	07.00-21.00	07.00-18.00	12.00-21.00 in May, June, July, August, November and December
SE	No restrictions	No restrictions	No restrictions
UK	No restrictions	No restrictions	Small shops (not more than 280 m^2) can open freely; larger shops may open for any six continuous hours between 10:00 and 18.00; larger shops may not open on Easter Sunday or on Christmas Day

Source: EuroCommerce (updated September 2007)

The number of retail outlets varies considerably between Member States, reflecting to some degree differences in lifestyles and patterns of shopping. In northern and eastern Europe there is generally a relatively low density of retail units per inhabitant, in contrast to much higher numbers in southern Europe. For example, there was an average of about 50 local retail units per 10 000 inhabitants in 2004 in the United Kingdom, which was one third of the density of local units in Spain, or a quarter of the density in Portugal (both 2005). These figures suggest that retail units in northern Europe were, on average, relatively large in size, and that a higher proportion of shoppers chose to visit large supermarkets, hypermarkets, or out-of-town retail parks and shopping centres in northern Europe. Such trends may be a result of easier transport access, free parking (allowing a large volume of goods to be bought that can be easily loaded into a car), and

Map 1.3: Number of local units, retail trade, 2005 (1)
(per 10 000 inhabitants)

Number of local units in retail trade, by NUTS 2 regions, 2005 (1)
(per 10 000 inhabitants)

<= 60
60 - <= 90
90 - <= 140
> 140
Data not available

(1) All regions in the United Kingdom: number of inhabitants, 2004.

© EuroGeographics Association, for the administrative boundaries
Cartography: Eurostat — GISCO, 12/2008

0 600 km

Guadeloupe (FR)
Martinique (FR)
Guyane (FR)
Réunion (FR)
Açores (PT)
Madeira (PT)
Canarias (ES)
Malta
Ísland

eurostat

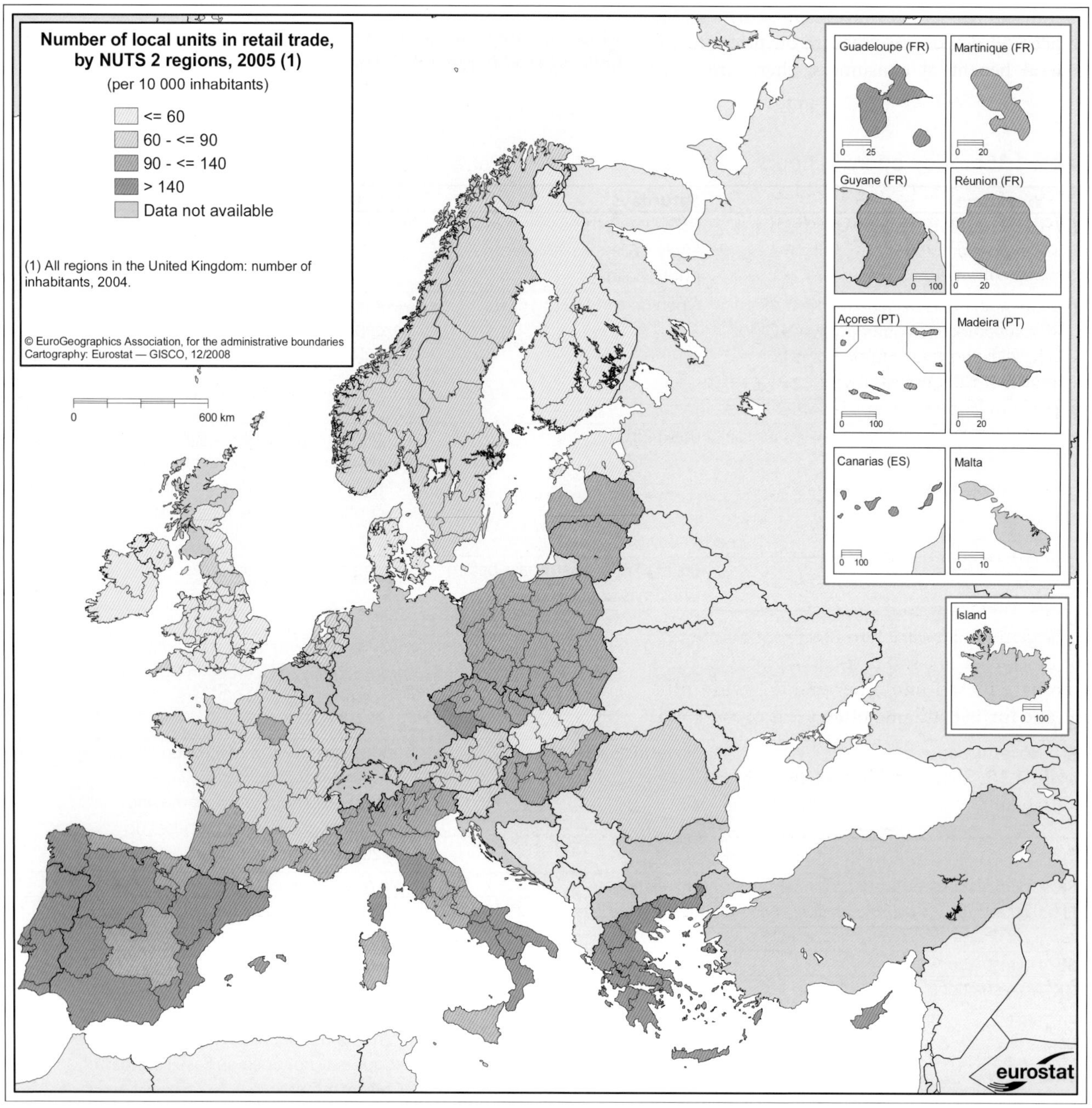

Source: Eurostat, regional structural business statistics and regional demographic statistics (sbs_r_nuts03 and reg_d2jan)

Table 1.16: Largest hypermarkets in Europe, based on total retail sales of food and non-food, 2005
(EUR million)

Company	Country	Sales
Carrefour	FR	74 574
Metro	DE	55 569
Tesco	UK	55 354
Schwarz	DE	36 886
Aldi (1)	DE	36 247
Rewe-Zentral	DE	35 398
Group Auchan	FR	33 100
Edeka Zentrale (1)	DE	31 705
Ahold	NL	29 654
E. Leclerc	FR	35 494

(1) Estimate.

Source: Deloitte, Global powers of retailing, 2007

Table 1.17: Largest department stores in Europe, based on total retail sales, 2005
(EUR million)

Company	Country	Sales
Metro (Galeria Kaufhof)	DE	55 569
El Cortes Inglés	ES	12 695
KarstadQuelle	DE	11 498
Marks & Spencer	UK	11 196
John Lewis Partnership	UK	7 493
LVMH (Le Bon Marché, Samaritaine)	FR	3 651
Groupe Galerie Lafayette	FR	3 632
Debenhams	UK	3 100

Source: Deloitte, Global powers of retailing, 2007

the convenience of having all goods and services under one roof (particularly when the weather is cold or wet). The retail make-up of southern Europe is often characterised by a range of small, local, independent shops. Shopping activity in southern Europe tends to be more frequent (if not daily), with shoppers more likely to visit a range of specialist retailers in town or city centres. The situation in eastern Europe is somewhat different, as some retail markets have yet to reach saturation and hence, local, national and international players continue to seek to establish (or expand) their presence.

National retail markets have traditionally been served by a mixture of local shops and national chains. There has, however, been a growing trend towards the internationalisation of retailing and the emergence of a small group of global retailers who have moved into other markets within the EU and further still into other areas of the world.

This pattern has been particularly prominent for major food and beverage retailers, which have extended the range of products they traditionally offered to include items of clothing, electrical goods, DIY or gardening items. In a similar vein, many non-food retailers (typically department stores) have also expanded the range of products they carry such that many now also have a food section.

There were just over 3.75 million enterprises active within the retail trade sector in the EU-27 in 2005 (note that each enterprise can have a number of different local units/outlets). The retail sector in the EU-27 remains dominated, in terms of numbers of enterprises, by very small enterprises, as more than half (54.6 %) of all retail trade enterprises only employed one person. The relative importance of large enterprises (with 250 or more persons employed) in terms of their contribution to the total turnover or value added of the EU-27's retail trade sector was 46.4 % and 43.1 % respectively in 2005. In contrast, enterprises with only one person employed accounted for 6.1 % of total retail trade turnover and 5.9 % of value added.

Table 1.18: Structural indicators for retail trade, EU-27, 2005
(EUR million)

NACE Rev. 1.1		Number of enterprises (units)	Turnover	Value added at factor cost	Gross operating rate (%)
52	Retail trade, except motor trades	3 758 005	2 126 665	391 802	6.9
52.1	In non-specialised stores (1)	583 194	900 000	130 000	4.1
52.2	Food, beverages, tobacco in specialised stores	508 817	126 891	24 929	9.9
52.3	Pharmaceutical, medical goods, cosmetics	198 233	191 708	40 878	9.6
52.4	Other new goods in specialised stores (2)	1 740 562	:	170 000	8.0
52.5	Second-hand goods in stores	63 852	7 324	1 996	15.2
52.6	Not in stores	524 260	97 781	19 453	9.9
52.7	Repair of personal and household goods	139 082	11 071	4 590	19.9

(1) Estimates, except for number of enterprises; gross operating surplus, 2004.
(2) Estimates, except for number of enterprises.

Source: Eurostat, annual detailed enterprise statistics on trade (sbs_na_3b_tr)

Table 1.19: Relative importance of different retail formats: share in total value added of retail trade, 2005
(% of total)

	Non-specialised stores	of which: Food, beverages or tobacco predominating	of which: Other	Specialised stores	Second-hand goods	Not in stores	Repair
EU-27 (1)	33.2	28.1	5.7	60.2	0.5	5.0	1.2
BE	36.5	34.8	1.7	60.2	0.5	2.1	0.7
BG	29.5	25.6	3.9	63.9	0.8	4.0	1.8
CZ (2)	42.2	:	:	51.6	0.8	3.7	1.8
DK (3)	37.5	26.2	9.6	59.2	0.2	1.1	2.0
DE	31.3	24.5	6.8	59.8	0.4	7.4	1.1
EE	44.2	36.4	7.8	53.0	0.3	1.9	0.6
IE	45.5	39.8	5.7	52.0	0.2	1.3	1.0
EL	26.9	24.0	2.9	65.6	0.1	4.9	2.6
ES	31.3	24.6	6.7	64.4	0.1	3.2	1.0
FR	34.9	33.3	1.6	59.2	0.6	4.2	1.1
IT	23.9	22.4	1.5	67.8	0.1	6.8	1.4
CY	26.9	19.1	7.8	68.7	0.2	2.5	1.7
LV	39.8	33.4	6.4	51.5	2.1	5.5	1.1
LT	41.0	36.3	4.7	48.4	1.4	8.3	1.0
LU	23.5	22.7	0.8	73.0	0.3	2.4	0.8
HU	42.5	36.4	6.1	51.0	0.9	3.4	2.1
MT	:	:	:	:	:	:	:
NL	:	21.9	:	:	0.7	4.9	0.9
AT	27.6	26.1	1.4	69.3	0.3	2.4	0.5
PL	40.4	31.3	9.1	53.1	0.4	5.3	0.9
PT	30.4	27.9	2.5	66.5	0.2	1.8	1.2
RO	40.7	35.4	5.3	51.8	0.7	5.7	1.1
SI	52.0	42.6	9.3	43.1	0.0	3.7	1.2
SK	48.2	15.0	33.2	40.4	0.3	10.8	0.3
FI	46.8	33.8	13.0	50.1	0.4	1.5	1.3
SE	30.6	27.1	3.5	63.1	0.2	4.1	2.0
UK	38.4	28.6	9.8	54.2	1.1	5.2	1.2

(1) Includes rounded estimates based on non-confidential data.
(2) 2004.
(3) 2004 for non-specialised stores.

Source: Eurostat, annual detailed enterprise statistics on trade (sbs_na_3b_tr)

Figure 1.22: Structural indicators for retail trade (NACE 52), breakdown by employment size class (persons employed), EU-27, 2005
(% of total)

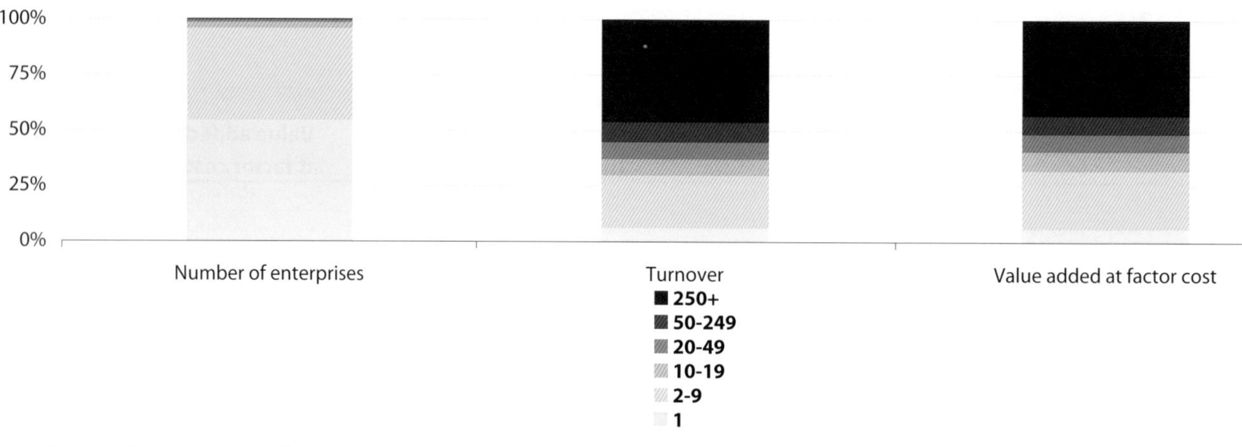

Source: Eurostat, distributive trade broken down by employment size classes (sbs_sc_3ce_tr02)

Table 1.20: Relative importance of different retail formats - specialised stores: share in total value added of retail trade, 2005
(% of total)

	Specialised stores	of which: Food, beverages or tobacco	Pharma-ceuticals, medical goods, cosmetics	Clothing	Footwear & leather goods	Furniture, lighting equip. & household articles n.e.c.	Electrical household appliances, radio & TV	Hardware, paints & glass	Books, news-papers & stationery
EU-27 (1)	60.2	6.4	10.4	10.7	2.2	5.7	3.4	5.5	2.1
BE	60.2	7.5	9.5	10.8	2.4	5.8	3.2	5.4	2.8
BG	63.9	5.4	8.9	5.8	1.8	4.6	5.8	10.2	3.2
CZ (2)	51.6	4.2	7.7	:	:	:	:	:	:
DK	59.2	3.7	6.6	11.4	2.1	7.1	3.9	5.1	1.4
DE	59.8	4.4	14.1	9.7	2.7	7.3	3.6	5.0	2.0
EE	53.0	1.9	5.2	5.9	2.5	6.6	2.6	12.2	2.1
IE	52.0	4.5	8.5	11.5	1.3	3.8	4.9	4.2	1.9
EL	65.6	10.9	8.3	10.8	2.0	3.4	6.0	5.9	1.5
ES	64.4	11.1	9.9	11.1	2.0	6.0	2.8	4.7	1.9
FR	59.2	5.1	13.9	8.3	1.9	5.1	3.3	5.5	2.3
IT	67.8	10.1	11.8	10.4	2.9	6.5	2.5	7.9	2.9
CY	68.7	5.7	3.2	10.6	3.8	9.9	5.2	8.5	1.7
LV	51.5	1.5	8.2	6.4	1.9	2.9	3.4	10.0	2.9
LT	48.4	0.7	11.0	4.7	2.9	2.7	4.6	8.9	2.5
LU	73.0	6.4	10.7	15.2	3.2	7.2	4.1	5.1	2.7
HU	51.0	3.8	15.1	4.9	1.3	3.0	2.5	5.8	3.6
MT	:	:	:	:	:	:	:	:	:
NL	:	5.7	11.4	12.5	2.9	8.3	4.0	7.5	1.7
AT	69.3	6.3	11.1	12.9	3.2	9.3	3.8	6.9	2.7
PL	53.1	8.3	10.4	4.7	1.2	2.9	3.8	1.8	1.8
PT	66.5	6.3	13.5	8.9	1.4	6.0	3.7	6.7	2.0
RO	51.8	5.0	10.7	2.7	1.5	3.4	4.9	4.2	2.9
SI	43.1	1.8	13.8	4.8	1.5	3.8	1.9	3.4	2.5
SK	40.4	2.0	6.5	1.5	1.0	4.4	2.7	5.6	0.9
FI	50.1	4.1	9.4	6.3	0.8	4.3	2.8	8.6	1.5
SE	63.1	5.6	6.3	13.8	2.0	10.3	3.4	6.6	1.4
UK	54.2	5.0	4.9	13.9	1.7	3.6	3.3	4.5	1.9

(1) Includes rounded estimates based on non-confidential data.
(2) 2004.

Source: Eurostat, annual detailed enterprise statistics on trade (sbs_na_3b_tr)

Short-term business statistics provide information on the evolution of sales in the retail trade sector, presented in terms of both value and volume indices. There was a bigger increase in the volume of non-food sales (an average of 2.6 % per annum between 1995 and 2008), compared with food sales (1.7 %). This may be expected, as there was a relatively small increase in the EU's population during the period considered, while there are physiological limits as to how much additional food a particular individual can eat. Nevertheless, with the price of food items rising at a more rapid pace than non-food items between 1995 and 2008, the growth in the value of food sales (3.8 % per annum) outstripped that of non-food sales (3.1 %).

Out-of-store sales

Consumers may choose alternatives to traditional, in-store retailing because of a variety of factors, including: the location of a retail outlet, awkward opening times, lack of choice, or simply not having enough time to go shopping. There has been growth in the range of out-of-store alternatives that give more freedom to consumers to shop in different ways. Some of the most popular forms of out-of-store retailing include e-commerce (which is covered in the next section), mail order, direct selling (for example, door to door), outdoor markets or retailing through petrol stations.

A survey conducted for the European Commission gives some insight into the different forms of sales channels that were used by retailers with

Figure 1.23: Evolution of retail sales, seasonally adjusted, EU-27 (1)
(1995=100)

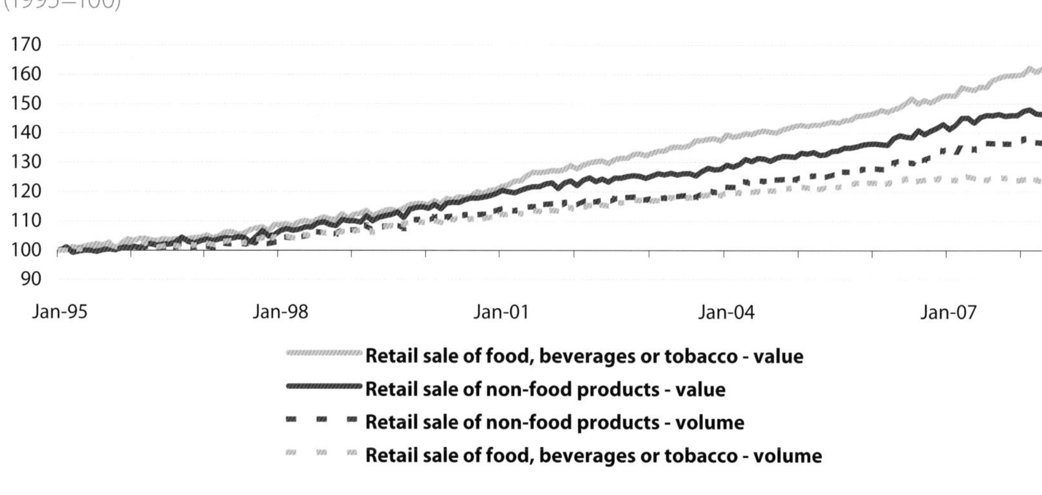

(1) Estimates.

Source: Eurostat, retail trade (NACE Rev.1 52) (ebt_ts_ret)

Figure 1.24: Sales channels used by retailers, EU-25, 2006 (1)
(% of retailers)

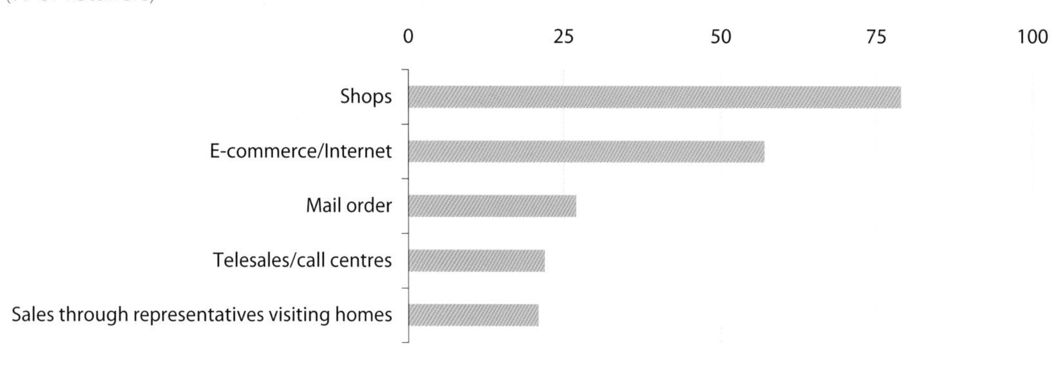

(1) Companies employing 10 or more persons.

Source: 'Business attitudes towards cross-border sales and consumer protection', Flash Eurobarometer 186, European Commission

ten or more persons employed in the EU-25 for 2006 (note that multiple answers were allowed). A large majority (79 %) of the retailers surveyed said that they had shops, while more than half (57 %) also made recourse to e-commerce or the Internet. Just over a quarter (27 %) of the enterprises responding to the survey said they made use of mail order, while slightly more than a fifth said they used telesales (22 %) or direct sales through representatives visiting homes (21 %). It is important to note that this survey only covered relatively large enterprises, as 95.9 % of all retail enterprises in the EU-27 employed less than ten persons in 2005 – and that these smaller enterprises are likely to have made less use of e-commerce, mail order, and other forms of distance selling.

A survey conducted in early 2008 reports that 8 % of retailers sold goods or services to consumers in one or two other EU countries, 6 % of retailers to three to five other EU countries, and 7 % of retailers to six or more countries; some 75 % of retailers had their operations based solely on national markets (while 4 % of respondents were unable to answer the question).

Structural business statistics provide further insight into the structure of out-of-store retailing in 2005. Note that the classification of economic activities, NACE Rev. 1.1, distinguishes between motor trades (Division 50, including wholesale and retail trade as well as repair) and retail trade (Division 52). There were approximately 362 thousand enterprises engaged in retail sales via stalls and markets, compared with 353 thousand enterprises selling (wholesale or retail) motor vehicles, parts and accessories thereof, or automotive fuel, and a further 23 thousand enterprises operating within the mail order sector.

The economic weight (in terms of sales or value added) of the motor trades sector (excluding repair) was considerably larger than the contribution made by either mail order or outdoor markets. Turnover among the motor trades' subsector was valued at EUR 1 125 billion in 2005, with added value of EUR 115 billion. The relatively few mail order enterprises together generated twice the value of sales or value added of outdoor markets. Nevertheless, neither sector was particularly large when looking at their overall contribution to total retail trade activity (excluding motor trades), as mail order enterprises generated just under 2.5 % of sales and value added.

Table 1.21: Structural indicators for out-of-store retailing, EU-27, 2005
(EUR million)

NACE Rev. 1.1		Number of enterprises (units)	Turnover	Value added at factor cost	Gross operating rate (%)
50.1	Motor vehicles	182 520	822 709	81 095	4.5
50.3	Motor vehicle parts & accessories	97 981	124 187	19 964	6.0
50.5	Automotive fuel	72 350	178 261	13 643	4.1
52	Retail trade, except motor trades	3 758 005	2 126 665	391 802	6.9
52.61	Via mail order houses (1)	23 000	50 000	9 000	6.0
52.62	Via stalls and markets (1)	362 000	19 400	4 100	14.1

(1) Estimates.

Source: Eurostat, annual detailed enterprise statistics on trade (sbs_na_3b_tr)

Map 1.4: Number of local units, petrol retailing, 2005 (1)
(per 10 000 inhabitants)

Number of local units in petrol retailing, by NUTS 2 regions, 2005 (1)
(per 10 000 inhabitants)

- <= 1
- 1 - <= 2
- 2 - <= 4
- > 4
- Data not available

(1) All regions in the United Kingdom: number of inhabitants, 2004.

Cartography: Eurostat — GISCO, 12/2008

0 600 km

Guadeloupe (FR) 0 25
Martinique (FR) 0 20
Guyane (FR) 0 100
Réunion (FR) 0 20
Açores (PT) 0 100
Madeira (PT) 0 20
Canarias (ES) 0 100
Malta 0 10
Ísland 0 100

eurostat

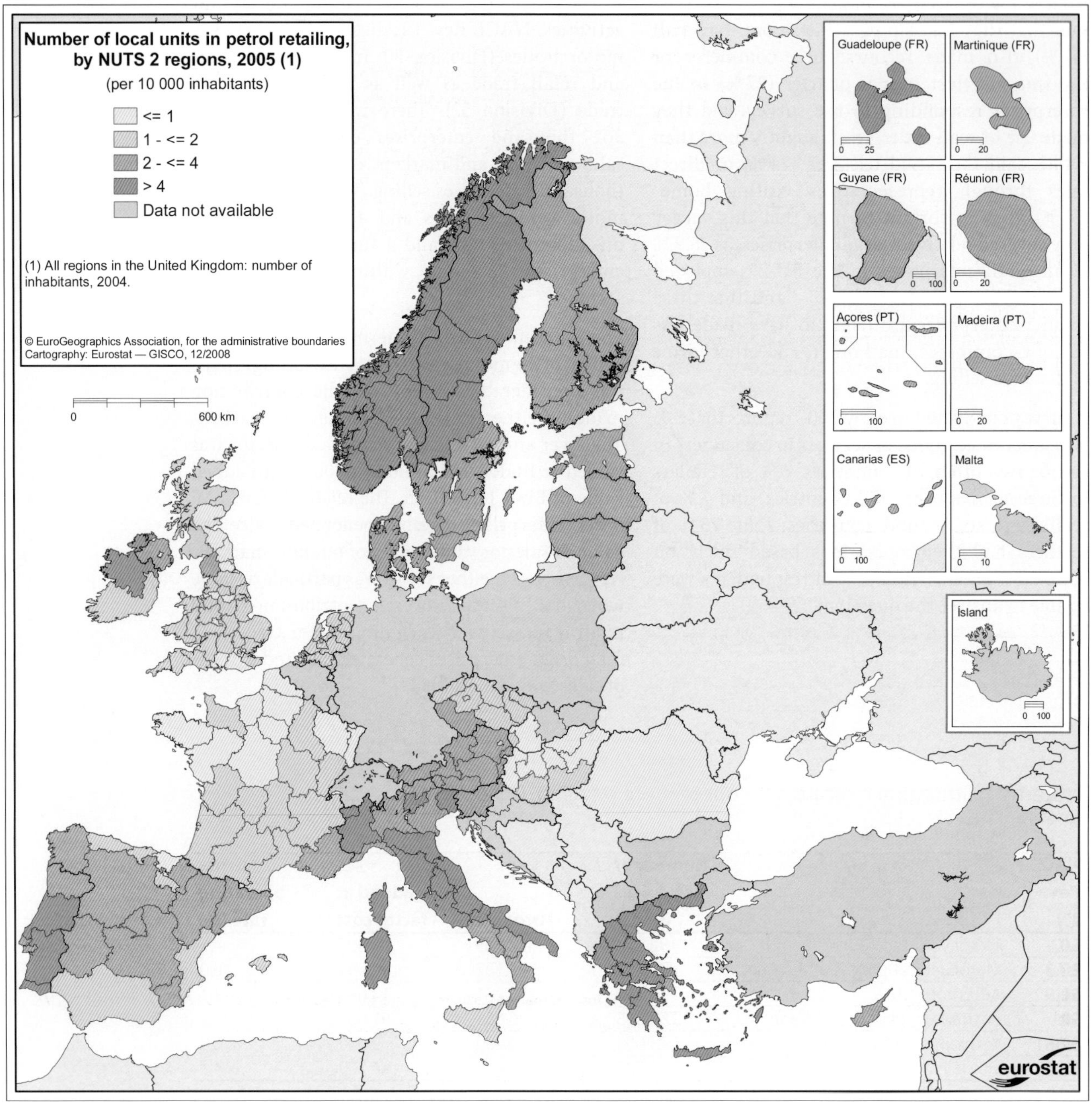

Source: Eurostat, regional structural business statistics and regional demographic statistics (sbs_r_nuts03 and reg_d2jan)

The composition of out-of-store retail networks varies considerably between countries, with more than 40 % of retailers employing ten or more persons using mail order in Austria, Slovenia, Germany and the Czech Republic, while the proportion of retailers (again employing ten or more persons) selling through a representative visiting homes was above 40 % in Slovakia, and higher than 30 % in Luxembourg and Spain.

Direct selling is the marketing of consumer goods and services directly to consumers on a person-to-person basis, generally in their own home (or the home of others). With this type of retailing there is the potential for consumers to benefit as a result of convenience, personal demonstration, and home delivery, while direct selling can also provide a channel of distribution for enterprises with innovative or distinctive products that are (for whatever reason) not afforded space in retail outlets.

According to FEDSA (the Federation of European Direct Selling Associations), direct sales in the EU (excluding Cyprus and Malta) were valued at EUR 9.8 billion in 2007, equivalent to an average of around EUR 20 of direct sales per inhabitant. The most common product categories for direct sales were typically personal or household goods, with cosmetics and personal care items accounting for almost half (47 %) of all sales, followed by household goods and wellness items (both 17 %).

Table 1.22: Sales channels used by retailers, 2006 (1)
(% of retailers)

	Mail order	Sales through representatives visiting homes
EU-25	27	21
BE	8	24
BG	:	:
CZ	40	28
DK	11	14
DE	41	23
EE	13	4
IE	25	23
EL	25	22
ES	31	32
FR	11	18
IT	20	21
CY	27	24
LV	16	18
LT	28	12
LU	21	34
HU	31	22
MT	33	18
NL	12	16
AT	47	26
PL	36	24
PT	32	29
RO	:	:
SI	46	26
SK	29	41
FI	10	6
SE	10	14
UK	29	15
NO	9	8

(1) Companies employing 10 or more persons.

Source: 'Business attitudes towards cross-border sales and consumer protection', Flash Eurobarometer 186, European Commission

Figure 1.25: Direct selling, EU, 2007 (1)
(% share of total value)

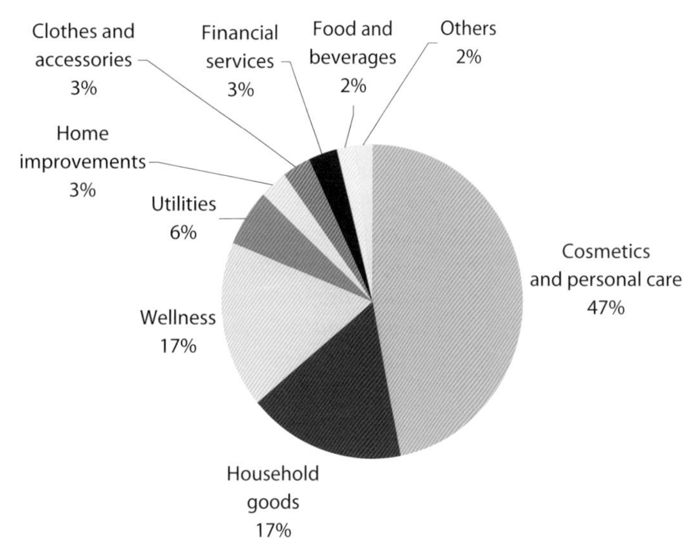

(1) Total EU market (excluding Cyprus and Malta) valued at EUR 9 836 million excluding VAT.

Source: FEDSA (http://www.fedsa.be/main.html)

Table 1.23: Main indicators for the timeshare industry in Europe, 2006

	2006
Number of resorts	1 500
Number of homes/apartments	85 000
Number of bed-nights	70 000 000
Number of families owning weeks	1 450 000
Number of weeks owned	2 500 000
Number of families buying a new timeshare	80 000
Occupancy rate	80%

(1) Estimates.

Source: OTE (Organisation for Timeshare in Europe) - presentation to European Commission (www.ote-info.com)

E-commerce

Information and communications technologies (ICT) are considered one of the main drivers of economic growth, with the potential to transform productivity and knowledge. In order to measure these transformations, there has been a considerable amount of development work to harmonise official statistics. New statistical surveys have been set-up and indicator definitions established. However, with technological change progressing at an ever-quickening pace, it is often necessary to adapt these indicators on a regular basis so that figures take into account new information technology products, the technological means of delivering the Internet, or problems and concerns that households and enterprises face when using the Internet. As of 2002, there have been annual information society surveys conducted by Eurostat, based on surveys of ICT developments in enterprises and among individuals and households.

The basic working definition of e-commerce is based on the OECD guide to measuring the information society, and is defined as:

'the sale or purchase of goods or services, whether between businesses, households, individuals or private organisations, conducted over computer-mediated networks. The goods and services are ordered over those networks, but the payment and the ultimate delivery of the good or service may be conducted on or off-line'.

Many commentators argue that one of the key drivers to productivity gains will be the rolling-out of broadband technologies, which, it is thought, will lead to an increase in the volume of e-commerce, stimulating economic growth and improving consumer welfare through greater choice and price transparency. Future growth in e-commerce will, in part, be based on highly-targeted, niche advertising, with the provision of goods and services increasingly tailored to individual clients; such changes could potentially benefit small and medium-sized enterprises (SMEs), as well as consumers.

On the other hand, the growth in e-commerce could reinforce the 'digital divide' between different segments of the population, such that potential consumer benefits are unlikely to be shared among those who do not own a computer or those without the necessary skills to use a computer or the Internet.

Consumers will only benefit from more choice if enterprises make their goods and services available on the Internet. The latest figures available from the information society survey suggest that 15 % of enterprises in the EU-27 sold goods or services over the Internet (or similar electronic networks) in 2007. This proportion rose considerably as a function of the average size of an enterprise, reaching 31 % for large enterprises employing 250 or more persons.

Figure 1.26: Enterprises selling via the Internet and/or networks other than the Internet, EU-27, 2007 (1)
(% of enterprises having received orders on-line over the last calendar year)

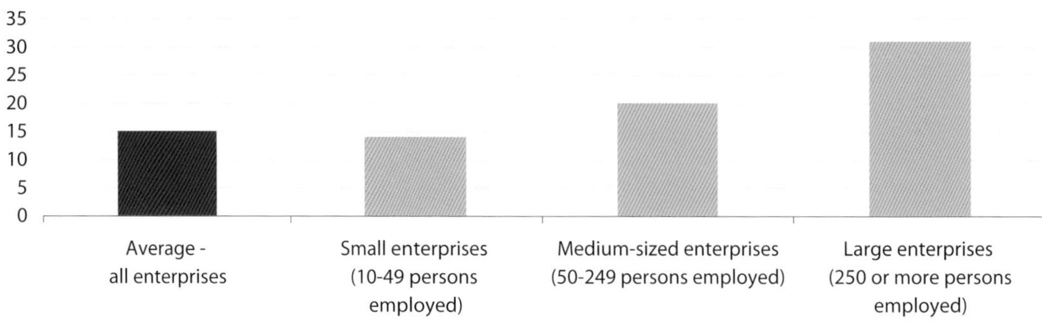

(1) Only enterprises with 10 or more persons employed, at least 1 % of annual turnover being derived from on-line orders, and active in manufacturing, construction or non-financial services are covered.

Source: Eurostat, enterprises selling via Internet and/or networks other than Internet (isoc_ec_esel)

An alternative indicator to measure the relative importance of e-commerce is the share of enterprises' turnover that may be attributed to e-sales. On average, some 4.2 % of enterprise turnover could be attributed to e-commerce within the EU-27 in 2007; note these figures include business to business (B2B), as well as business to consumer sales (B2C). E-commerce was particularly important to enterprises in Ireland, where it accounted for 9.8 % of total sales, with the next highest proportions recorded in the United Kingdom (7.0 %) and Spain (6.2 %).

There was a wide disparity between countries as regards the proportion of persons ordering or selling goods and services over the Internet. On average, some 23 % of individuals in the EU-27 stated that they had ordered goods or services on the Internet during the three-month period prior to the survey in 2007, while 10 % had sold items; this pattern of a higher propensity to order, rather than to sell goods or services, was repeated in each of the Member States.

The use of the Internet for ordering goods or services was generally higher in the northern Member States and in the EU-15 Member States, rising to over 40 % in the United Kingdom, Denmark, the Netherlands and Germany. The proportion of the population ordering goods or services over the Internet was below the EU-27 average for each of the Member States that joined the EU since 2004, as well as in Greece, Portugal, Italy, Spain and Belgium.

Figure 1.27: Enterprise turnover from e-commerce via the Internet, 2007 (1)
(% of total turnover)

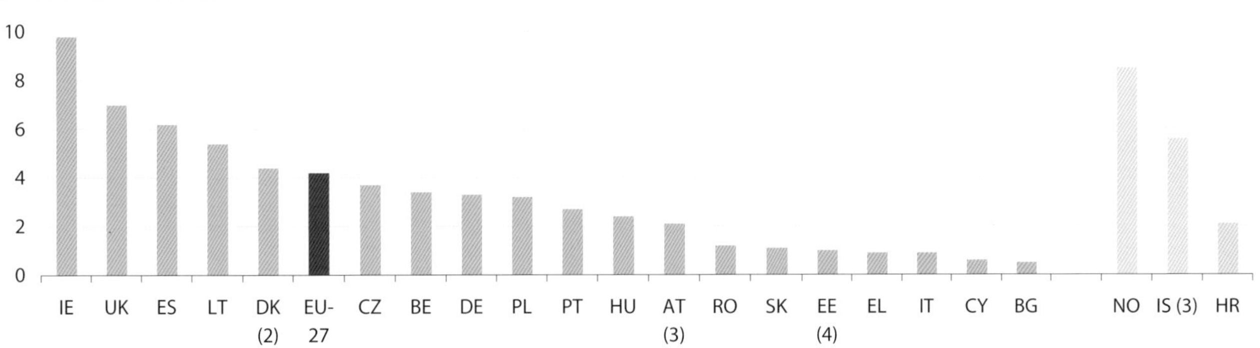

(1) Only enterprises with 10 or more employees are covered; France, Latvia, Luxembourg, Malta, the Netherlands, Slovenia, Finland and Sweden, not available.
(2) 2004.
(3) 2006.
(4) 2005.

Source: Eurostat, structural indicators (strind_t)

Figure 1.28: Internet activities of individuals (for private use), in the three months prior to the survey, 2007
(% of individuals)

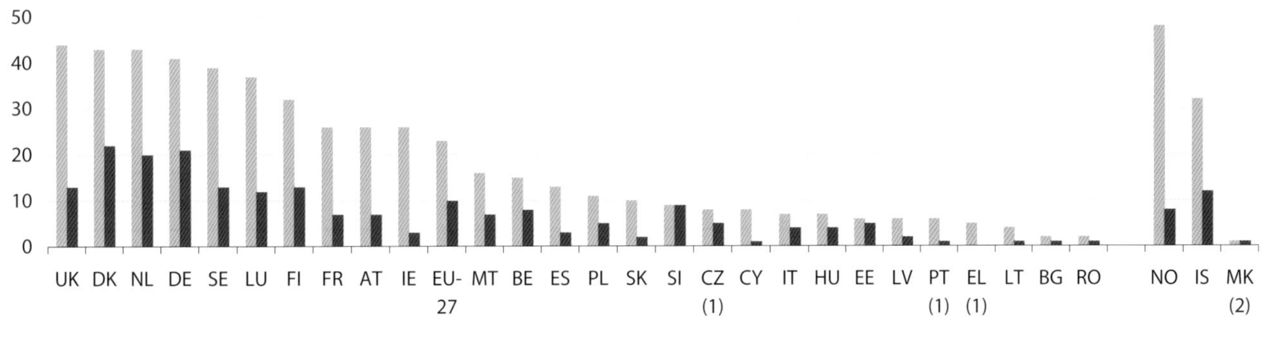

(1) 2006 for selling.
(2) 2006.

Source: Eurostat, Internet purchases by individuals and Internet activities - individuals (isoc_ec_ibuy and isoc_ci_eu_i)

In 2007, fewer than one third (29 %) of the EU-27's population had never made an Internet purchase. Adding this proportion to the 23 % of the population who had not made an order in the three months prior to the survey reveals the sporadic nature of Internet purchases among almost half of the EU population.

Among those who made an Internet order in the year prior to the survey, some of the most commonly purchased items included travel and holiday accommodation, clothes and sports goods, films, music, household goods, or tickets for events (note that some individuals may have bought all of these, while others restricted their Internet purchases to particular goods or services).

Table 1.24: Internet purchases by individuals (for private use) during the last year, 2007
(% of individuals)

		Goods and services ordered over the Internet during the last year								
	Never ordered goods or services	Food/ groceries	House-hold goods (furniture, toys, etc.)	Films/ music	Clothes, sports goods	Software (incl. video games)	Elec. equip-ment (incl. cameras)	Shares/ financial services/ insurance	Travel & holiday accomm.	Tickets for events
EU-27	29	3	10	10	12	7	7	3	13	9
BE	46	1	3	4	4	3	3	1	8	6
BG	32	0	0	1	1	0	0	0	0	0
CZ	36	0	6	2	4	2	7	0	4	5
DK	27	6	9	18	20	16	15	6	27	27
DE	19	5	24	19	25	19	17	5	23	18
EE	57	:	2	2	3	1	1	1	3	5
IE	27	2	3	10	5	5	4	2	20	11
EL	29	0	1	1	1	1	1	0	2	1
ES	36	2	2	2	3	3	3	1	11	6
FR	31	2	14	11	17	6	7	2	14	10
IT	30	0	1	2	2	2	2	1	3	2
CY	32	0	1	2	3	2	2	1	4	1
LV	46	0	2	1	2	1	4	0	2	3
LT	45	0	1	1	1	1	1	1	1	2
LU	29	2	8	18	13	13	10	3	24	18
HU	42	1	1	2	2	2	2	1	3	3
MT	26	0	2	6	5	4	4	1	5	2
NL	27	4	10	13	19	11	13	6	25	18
AT	33	2	7	8	12	5	8	1	8	7
PL	33	3	5	3	6	2	4	:	:	2
PT	33	1	1	2	2	2	2	1	3	2
RO	26	0	0	1	0	1	0	0	0	0
SI	39	2	5	2	5	2	3	1	3	2
SK	44	0	3	3	5	2	3	0	3	2
FI	31	1	10	15	17	9	10	4	26	20
SE	24	2	8	18	17	8	10	10	28	23
UK	21	11	21	27	20	11	11	5	24	18
IS	32	3	8	18	11	15	6	10	40	24
NO	18	2	12	22	21	14	18	10	41	34

Source: Eurostat, Internet purchases by individuals (isoc_ec_ibuy)

Consumers using the Internet are increasingly aware that the medium provides the possibility to gather a wealth of information in advance of making a decision to purchase a good or service. The Internet has the potential to help consumers make more informed choices, for example, by looking at price comparison sites, reading reviews, gathering information on product features, or looking at pictures of holiday resorts and accommodation.

A Eurobarometer survey conducted in early 2008 shows that 36 % of respondents in the EU-27 said that in the 12 months prior to the survey they had used the Internet to compare goods and services from different sellers/providers. There was a wide range in the use of the Internet for this purpose, from upwards of 60 % of respondents in Sweden, the Netherlands and Denmark, down to 15 % or less of the population in Greece, Portugal, Romania and Bulgaria.

According to a survey of individuals aged 15 or more using the Internet either at home or at work, around 50 % of the population in some Member States made Internet searches in March 2008, with the typical user making over 100 unique searches during the month (note that these searches were for any search term). Additional information on search terms concerning consumer electronic products in the run-up to Christmas 2007 shows the high numbers of consumers who made use of the Internet for this purpose.

Table 1.25: Internet searches, selected European countries, March 2008 (1)

	Unique searchers (thousand)	Searches (million)	Average number of searches per searcher
BE	4 575	510	111
DK	2 997	260	87
DE	36 011	3 935	109
IE	1 290	116	90
ES	14 535	1 472	101
FR	26 280	2 955	112
IT	17 562	1 867	106
NL	11 713	1 097	94
AT	3 528	399	113
PT	3 401	437	128
FI	2 653	378	143
SE	5 023	606	121
UK	32 392	4 030	124
NO	2 327	183	79
CH	3 630	401	111

(1) Internet audience of individuals aged 15 or more, using the Internet either at home or work (excluding Internet access from Internet cafés, mobile phones or PDAs).

Source: comScore qSearch (www.comscore.com)

Table 1.26: Average weekly Internet searches for selected gadgets, November 2007 (1)
(searches)

	DE	FR	UK
Nintendo Wii	588 059	556 885	3 758 069
Nintendo DS Lite	753 282	608 705	3 758 069
Apple iPod	1 193 417	663 342	1 650 100
Microsoft Xbox 360	221 635	282 905	918 805
Apple iPhone	697 027	302 743	706 734
Sony Playstation PSP	564 237	780 833	583 394
Apple iPod Nano	246 232	87 236	286 825
Sony Playstation 3	:	80 700	241 703
Nokia N95	340 606	107 451	237 924
Samsung U600	:	102 023	165 032
Sony Playstation 2	195 970	:	:
Apple iPod Touch	298 681	:	:

(1) Survey of 20 different models of games consoles, mobile phones, portable music players during the period 29 October to 18 November 2007; Internet audience of individuals aged 15 or more, using the Internet either at home or work (excluding Internet access from Internet cafés, mobile phones or PDAs).

Source: comScore World Metrix (www.comscore.com)

Figure 1.29: Reasons for not ordering goods or services over the Internet in the last 12 months, EU-27, 2006 (1)
(% of individuals who ordered goods or services over the Internet for private use more than a year ago or who never ordered anything over the Internet)

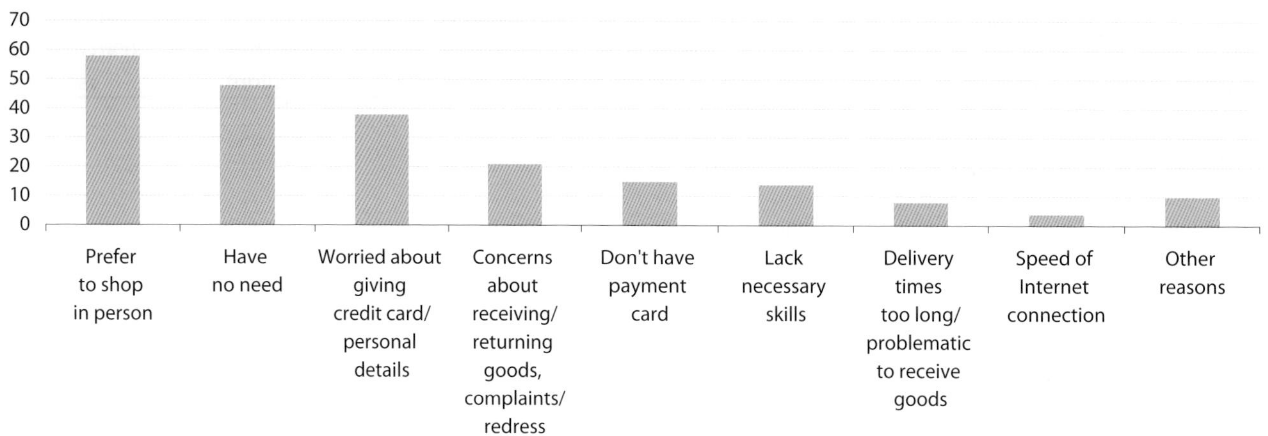

(1) Multiple answers allowed.

Source: Eurostat, perceived barriers to buying/ordering over the Internet (isoc_ec_inb)

Figure 1.30: Consumer complaints and disputes made to ECC-Net regarding on-line marketplaces, Europe, 2007 (1)
(breakdown by type of complaint in % of total)

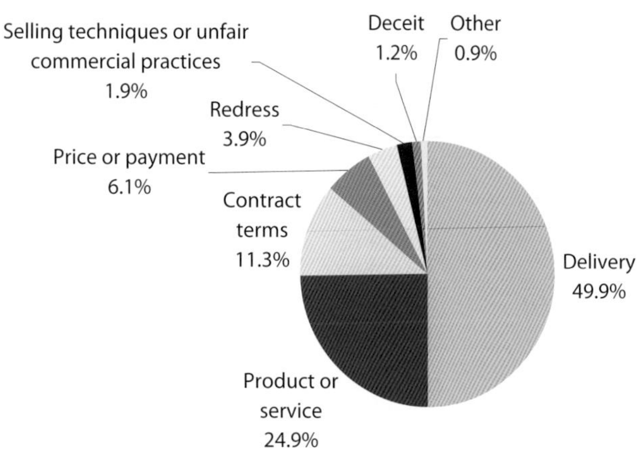

(1) EU-25, Iceland and Norway.

Source: European Online Marketplace: consumer complaints 2007, European Consumer Centres' Network (ECC-Net)

Among those consumers who had never made an Internet purchase, or whose last Internet purchase was more than a year prior to the survey, a majority (58 %) had not used e-commerce in 2006 because they preferred to shop in person, while 48 % of the same sub-population said they had no need to shop using the Internet. Aside from these reasons of simply choosing not to use the Internet, the most important perceived barriers to e-commerce involved concerns over security and safety, as 38 % of respondents were worried about providing credit card details, and 21 % had concerns about receiving/returning or complaining about the goods or services ordered. A smaller proportion cited a lack of access as one reason they did not shop on the Internet, as 15 % of respondents were without a credit card to make on-line payments, while 14 % lacked the necessary computing skills to make an order. Some 8 % of respondents preferred not to make Internet purchases because they thought that delivery times were too long or they found it problematic to arrange for the delivery of goods.

There were more than 1 500 consumer complaints and disputes made to the European consumer centres network (ECC-Net) dealing with e-commerce in 2007. Of these, almost half (49.9 %) concerned problems relating to delivery, one quarter (24.9 %) were related to the product or service, and 11.3 % to the terms of contract; the remaining complaints (including issues relating to the price, consumer redress, selling techniques and commercial practices, or deceit) were relatively infrequent.

Cross-border sales to consumers

Further evidence of the internationalisation of retail networks comes from studies relating to cross-border trade. This form of shopping may be defined as any purchase that is made, in person or via distance shopping, from retailers or providers located in another country. If cross-border trade increases, traditional retailers may increasingly be exposed to competition. Some commentators argue that even a relatively small number of consumers switching to make cross-border purchases could result in established, domestic retailers changing their behaviour (for example, lowering prices, or offering new products or services). As such, the actions of relatively few cross-border shoppers could potentially result in much larger economic gains for a wider cross-section of the population, including those who continue to make their purchases from local or domestic markets.

Within the European context, some of the practical barriers to cross-border trade have been removed following the creation of the internal market, the introduction of the single European currency, and developments regarding on-line shopping. However, only one in four (25 %) Europeans took advantage of the possibility to purchase goods or services from traders in other Member States in early 2008. Geographical location and the close proximity of neighbouring countries can play an important role in determining whether or not a consumer will consider physically crossing a border to go shopping, as witnessed by the 68 % of consumers in Luxembourg (a relatively small country in the middle of the European land mass bordering three other countries) who made a cross-border purchase in 2008. Otherwise,

Table 1.27: Cross-border purchases made in another EU country, 2008
(% of respondents)

	On trips (holiday or business)	Specific trip for shops	Internet	Mail order
EU-27	17	9	7	2
BE	24	14	13	2
BG	5	3	1	0
CZ	24	18	3	2
DK	37	18	23	2
DE	17	11	6	1
EE	29	9	7	8
IE	24	7	16	3
EL	7	3	5	1
ES	11	4	8	2
FR	11	9	9	1
IT	10	5	4	2
CY	27	6	13	1
LV	19	11	5	9
LT	14	4	3	1
LU	36	42	38	18
HU	10	6	1	0
MT	22	10	23	7
NL	36	12	16	2
AT	35	30	19	8
PL	13	9	2	1
PT	6	3	2	0
RO	10	8	1	1
SI	26	27	6	3
SK	15	20	2	2
FI	41	16	14	4
SE	48	16	17	1
UK	28	7	12	2

Source: 'Consumer protection in the Internal Market, 2008', Special Eurobarometer 298, European Commission

Figure 1.31: Persons making at least one cross-border purchase from a seller/provider in another EU country, 2008
(% of respondents)

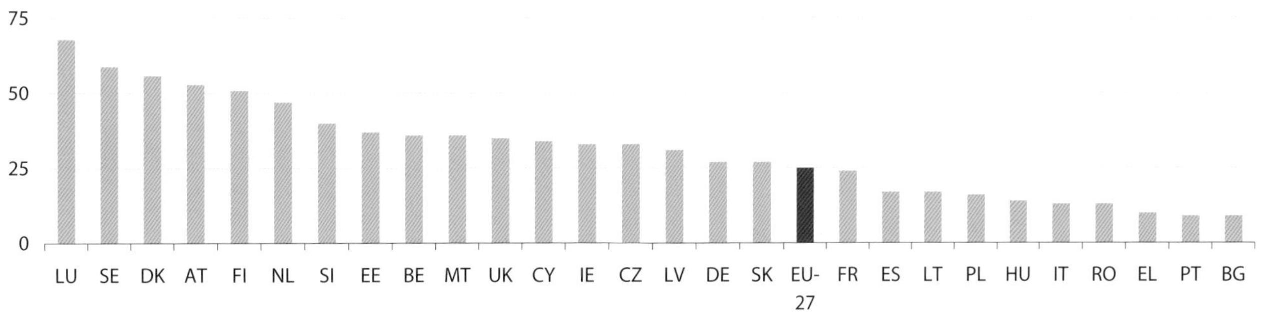

Source: 'Consumer protection in the Internal Market, 2008', Special Eurobarometer 298, European Commission

Figure 1.32: Value of cross-border purchases made from sellers/providers in other EU countries: breakdown by amount spent, EU-27, 2008
(% of respondents who made at least one cross-border purchase)

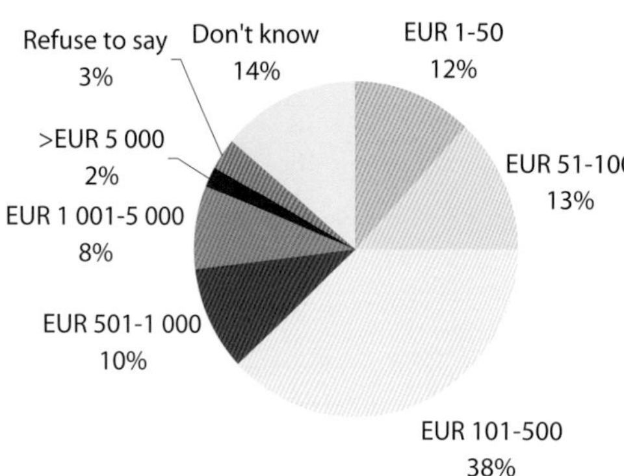

Source: 'Consumer protection in the Internal Market, 2008', Special Eurobarometer 298, European Commission

Figure 1.33: In the last 12 months have you seen or heard adverts which invited you to purchase goods or services in another EU country, EU-27, 2008
(% of respondents)

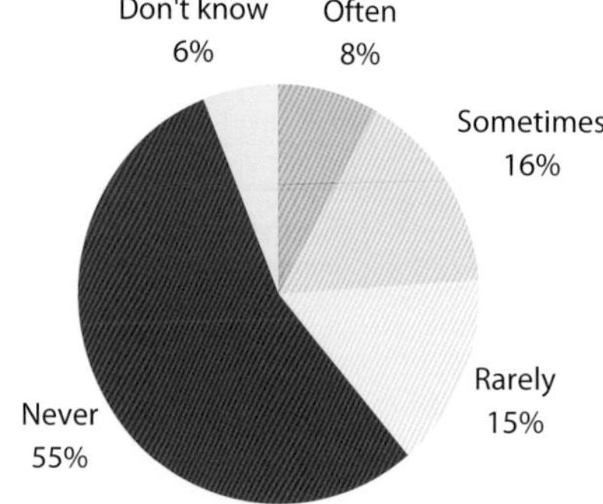

Source: 'Consumer protection in the Internal Market, 2008', Special Eurobarometer 298, European Commission

common language skills are also likely to contribute to the overall awareness of consumers as regards goods, services and offers that may be available in neighbouring Member States. In contrast, those countries at the geographical extremities of Europe tended to report much lower rates of cross-border purchases, such as 10 % of consumers in Greece, or 9 % of consumers in Portugal and Bulgaria.

More than one third (38 %) of the EU-27 consumers who made at least one cross-border purchase during the twelve months prior to the survey in early 2008 spent a total of between EUR 101 and EUR 500. Similar proportions of those who made purchases abroad spent less than EUR 50 (12 %), between EUR 51 and EUR 100 (13 %) and between EUR 501 and EUR 1 000 (10 %), while 2 % of Europeans spent in excess of EUR 5 000 across borders. Among those persons who made at least one cross-border purchase, the average level of spending in the EU-27 was EUR 797, rising to more than EUR 2 000 for consumers from Luxembourg and to more than EUR 3 000 for those from Malta.

Figure 1.34: Average value of cross-border purchases made from sellers/providers in other EU countries, 2008 (1)
(EUR)

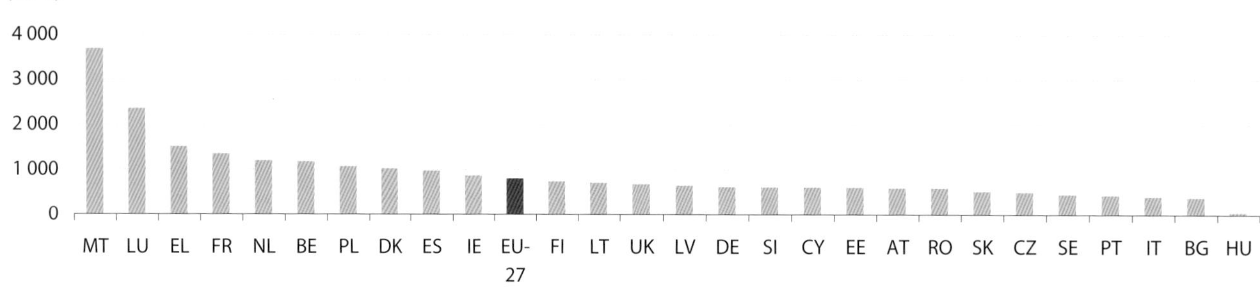

(1) Among those who made cross-border purchases; Greece, Romania, Portugal, Italy, Bulgaria and Hungary, unreliable.

Source: 'Consumer protection in the Internal Market, 2008', Special Eurobarometer 298, European Commission

One barrier that clearly inhibits cross-border trade is language, with only a third (33 %) of people in the EU-27 willing to make a cross-border transaction in another European language in 2008 – a share that rose above 50 % in Luxembourg, the Netherlands, Sweden, Denmark, Malta and Slovenia.

There remain other barriers to cross-border trade, although some of these may be perceptions or prejudices, rather than actual barriers. For example, 36 % of EU-27 inhabitants in 2008 believed that traders located in other Member States were less likely to respect consumer protection laws than those in their own country, while only 6 % were more confident that traders from other countries would respect such laws.

Table 1.28: Consumer confidence in making purchases while on holiday, a shopping trip or business, compared with making purchases from sellers/providers located in home country, 2008 (% of respondents)

	More confident	As confident	Less confident	Don't know
EU-27	6	37	36	21
BE	4	40	46	10
BG	7	21	20	52
CZ	11	49	27	13
DK	4	43	43	10
DE	6	31	46	17
EE	7	34	31	28
IE	3	30	31	36
EL	12	47	41	0
ES	5	42	22	31
FR	9	33	36	22
IT	4	45	29	22
CY	7	31	38	24
LV	6	37	28	29
LT	7	43	19	31
LU	7	34	24	35
HU	3	34	42	21
MT	14	30	27	29
NL	5	52	35	8
AT	5	35	48	12
PL	8	37	31	24
PT	3	41	27	29
RO	11	39	13	37
SI	7	46	31	16
SK	4	40	40	16
FI	4	36	52	8
SE	2	36	53	9
UK	5	32	47	16

Source: 'Consumer protection in the Internal Market, 2008', Special Eurobarometer 298, European Commission

Figure 1.35: Persons who are prepared to purchase goods and services using another EU language, 2008 (% of respondents)

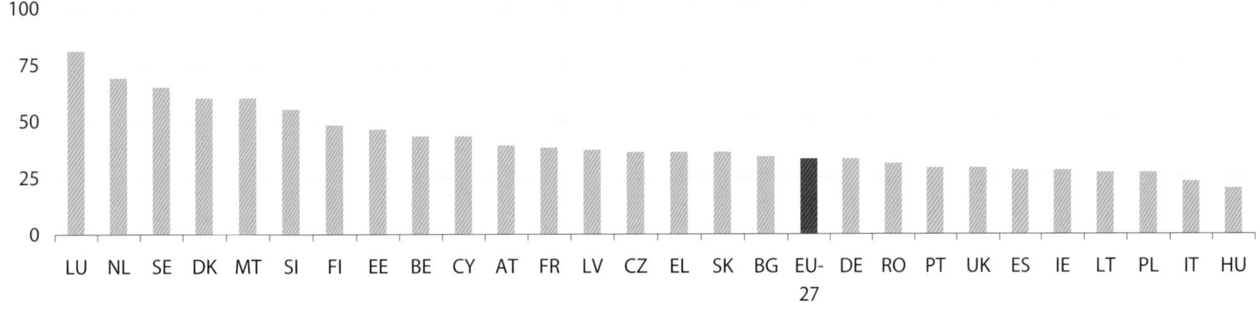

Source: 'Consumer protection in the Internal Market, 2008', Special Eurobarometer 298, European Commission

Advertising

Advertising is used by a wide range of enterprises to shape and influence consumer choice, as well as encourage purchases. There are many different ways that advertising can be classified – for example, a distinction between product and brand marketing, or between regular advertising (to maintain awareness) and a product launch.

Irrespective of the type, the range of delivery media for advertising has progressively expanded, and while television and daily newspapers remain the most popular form of dissemination, there is a movement away from mass media towards target-specific, niche advertising that is linked as closely as possible to consumer profiles (in terms of, for example, age, gender, occupation, and income group). By making such a change, advertisers are weighing up the costs of reaching a large number of consumers against the likelihood that they are targeting the correct audience.

A survey in October 2007 asked Internet users from across the globe whether or not they trusted a range of different advertising media. The results suggest that consumers place more trust in the opinions of fellow consumers and more traditional lines of advertising, such as newspapers, magazines, television and radio advertising, while on-line advertising or text adverts sent to mobile phones were generally distrusted.

Figure 1.36: Trust in different advertising mediums, October 2007 (1)
(% of respondents)

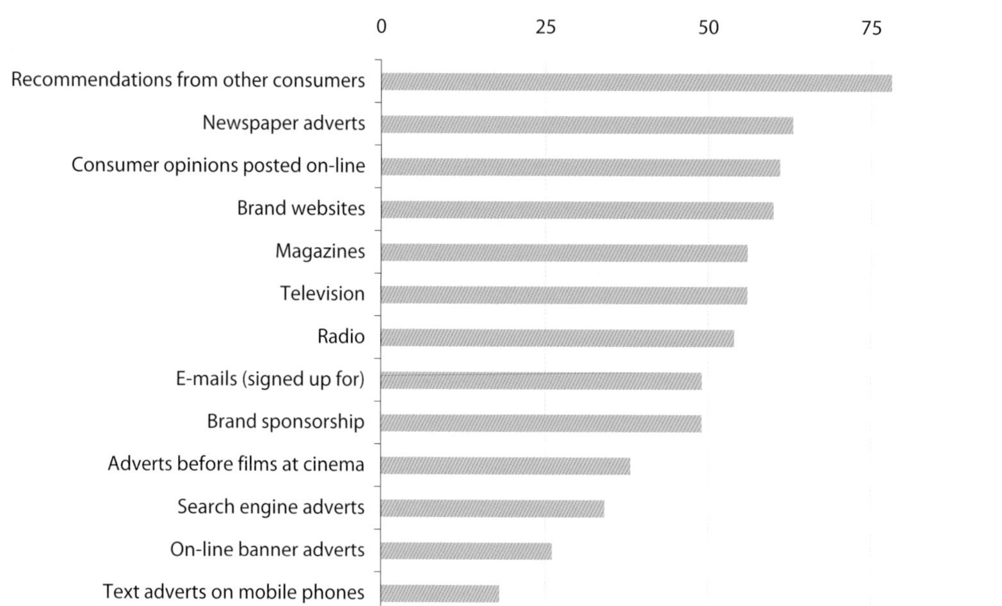

(1) Global survey conducted among 26 486 Internet users in Europe, Asia Pacific, the Americas and the Middle East.

Source: A.C. Nielsen, Trust in advertising (www.acnielsen.com)

The EU has laid down a set of common rules that are applicable across all Member States in order to protect consumers from misleading advertising and its unfair consequences. For this purpose, misleading advertising is defined as any advertising which, in its wording or presentation, deceives or is likely to deceive the consumer. All its features are taken into account, including, information concerning the nature of the product, its availability, composition, price or quantity, results to be expected from its use, or tests that have been carried on it.

Some 42 % of respondents in the EU-27 reported that they had come across misleading or deceptive advertising in the 12 months prior to a European Commission survey that was conducted in early 2008, while more than half (58 %) of those questioned had come across unsolicited commercial advertising (in the form of cold calls, spam e-mail, direct marketing, etc.) during the same period.

Figure 1.37: Misleading and unsolicited advertising, 2008
(% of respondents)

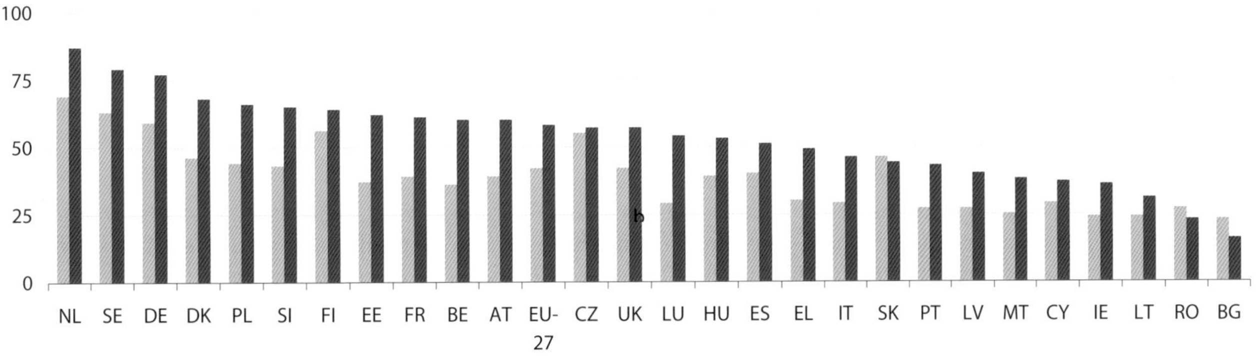

Source: 'Consumer protection in the Internal Market, 2008', Special Eurobarometer 298, European Commission

ACCESS, CHOICE AND SWITCHING

Certain aspects of how markets function are difficult to measure concretely; these intangible elements are often left uncovered by official statistics. However, consumer opinion and perception surveys provide a source of information covering some important determinants of how markets function, asking respondents for their opinions on topics such as branding, advertising, quality, choice, switching, or after-sales service – all of which are thought to play an important role in shaping consumption patterns.

Pricing within product markets is usually based on the cost of production of tangible goods (which is essentially determined by the price of intermediate and labour inputs). In contrast, the intangible market for services is often based more on perceived value (as determined by factors such as timeliness, content, or brand).

The level of market transparency is generally quite high for most product markets and it is relatively easy for consumers to compare goods on a range of criteria (for example, price, quality, or length of a manufacturer's guarantee). If consumers decide to switch goods (buying a different brand of clothes, food, cosmetics or washing-up liquid), there are usually no implications on current or future consumption patterns. Exceptions do exist, for example, those consumers who bought an HD DVD player are 'locked-in' to playing discs using this format, while most shops have since decided to only stock Blu-Ray discs.

In contrast, some services are characterised by monopoly supply, or the need for consumers to have access to a specific network/infrastructure in order to be able to use them, while the liberalisation of service markets is generally less advanced than markets for goods. As such, some service markets remain characterised by a range of barriers, which may explain why, even when choice exists, some consumers exhibit 'sticky behaviour' – in other words, they do not take full advantage of the situation as a rational consumer, but instead refrain from purchasing or switching to substitute services.

Access and choice

Services of general interest cover a range of activities – for example, water, energy, telecommunications, transport, radio and television, postal services, banking, schools, health and social services. The EU works to guarantee that services such as these are made universally available at affordable prices, reflecting a desire to ensure social, economic and territorial cohesion.

A survey conducted in 2006 found that a majority of respondents within the EU-25 experienced easy access to a wide range of services of general interest. For water, postal and fixed telephony services, more than nine out of ten consumers reported easy access. Rail (73 %), gas (72 %) and broadband Internet access (60 %) were the only three services where fewer than three quarters of respondents experienced easy access.

Among the Member States there was a wide range of results, and a number of cases where a majority of consumers reported difficult access to a particular service. The lowest proportion of consumers reporting easy access was consistently registered for either broadband Internet access or for gas services, except in Cyprus and Malta, where there are no gas or rail services.

Four consumer surveys were conducted over the period 2000 to 2006 asking consumers if they faced difficult or no access to a range of services – note that there is a break in series as the composition of the EU aggregate shifts from 15 Member States to 25 Member States. During the period considered, there was a consistent improvement in access to mobile phone services (where those facing difficult or no access almost halved), while the opposite was true for gas services (resulting in almost a quarter of all consumers experiencing difficult or no access by 2006).

Table 1.29: Access to services of general interest, 2006
(% of respondents experiencing easy access)

	Mobile phone	Fixed phone	Broad-band	Elec-tricity	Gas	Water	Local trans-port	Rail	Post	Banks
EU-25	85	91	60	93	72	93	80	73	91	88
BE	89	93	77	96	75	97	84	80	92	94
BG	:	:	:	:	:	:	:	:	:	:
CZ	86	86	53	93	80	93	85	78	92	82
DK	89	90	72	98	38	98	81	74	89	97
DE	88	95	57	97	74	96	84	74	91	94
EE	91	81	53	93	40	82	79	51	93	85
IE	94	93	46	97	51	95	79	62	96	89
EL	94	99	54	99	29	99	95	77	95	92
ES	91	96	72	95	77	94	89	79	95	96
FR	79	91	57	96	76	96	70	71	93	91
IT	72	74	48	76	74	77	69	69	78	70
CY	95	96	62	98	-	98	40	-	93	90
LV	92	77	43	98	56	78	83	59	96	77
LT	86	78	54	96	70	82	88	71	94	84
LU	88	92	65	93	58	96	83	68	91	95
HU	90	87	58	95	90	96	81	71	96	80
MT	91	98	64	97	-	97	80	-	89	89
NL	87	96	77	91	89	92	80	80	94	94
AT	85	90	62	93	69	92	88	80	92	92
PL	88	89	51	97	68	95	84	67	93	84
PT	93	96	63	98	43	96	85	62	94	89
RO	:	:	:	:	:	:	:	:	:	:
SI	90	92	59	98	46	97	70	58	91	91
SK	93	93	48	95	88	93	84	72	92	81
FI	94	81	75	99	11	98	77	71	95	97
SE	89	98	66	96	9	86	66	59	77	87
UK	87	96	71	97	89	97	83	80	96	93

Source: 'Consumers' opinions of services of general interest', Special Eurobarometer 260, European Commission

Figure 1.38: Access to services of general interest over time
(% of respondents experiencing difficult access or no access)

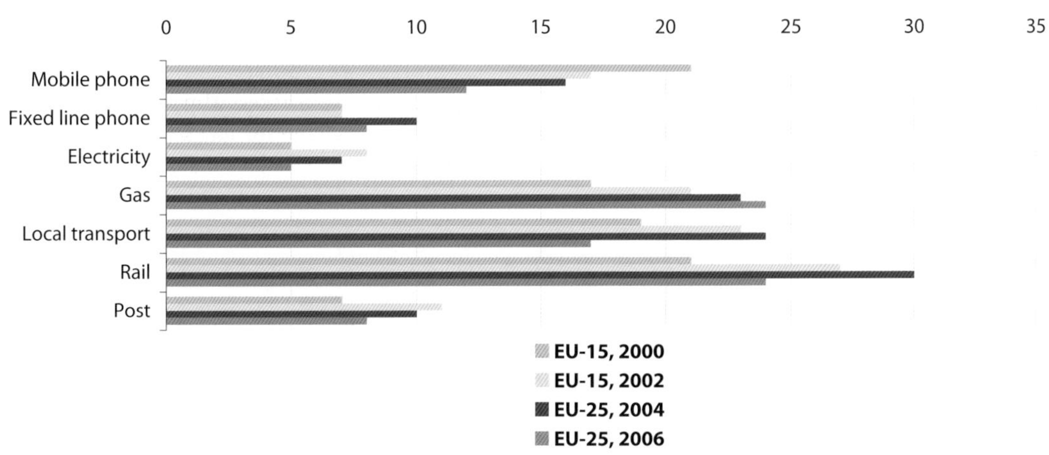

Source: 'Consumers' opinions of services of general interest', Special Eurobarometer 260, European Commission

Economic benefits resulting from the introduction of the single market can be measured, among other indicators, by consumers' perceptions as to changes experienced in the range, the quality, and the price of goods and services. Almost three quarters (73 %) of respondents in the EU-25 in 2006 thought that the introduction of the single market had resulted in an improved range of products and services, compared with 57 % who thought that the quality of products and services had improved, and 50 % who thought that there had been a positive effect on prices. On the other hand, just 9 % of respondents thought that there had been a reduction in the range of products and services on offer, some 17 % that the quality of products had fallen, and 30 % that there had been a negative effect on prices.

A majority of consumers in each Member State agreed that the choice of products imported from other Member States in shops and supermarkets had become better during the ten years through to 2006. Only slightly more than half (53 %) of consumers in Slovenia and in Germany were of this opinion, a share that rose to three quarters or more in Ireland, Finland, Latvia, Sweden and Luxembourg.

Figure 1.39: Selected consumer outcomes resulting from the introduction of the single market, EU-25, 2006
(% of respondents)

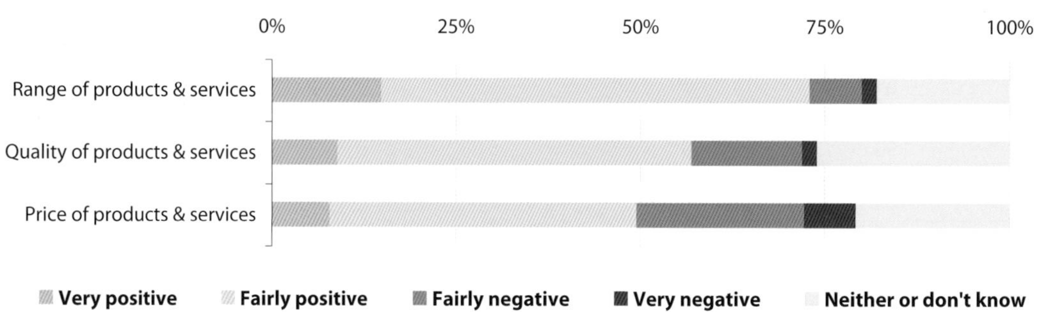

Source: 'Internal market - Opinions and experiences of citizens in EU-25', Special Eurobarometer 254, European Commission

Figure 1.40: Consumers agreeing that the choice of products from other Member States in shops and supermarkets has become better in the last ten years, 2006 (1)
(% of respondents)

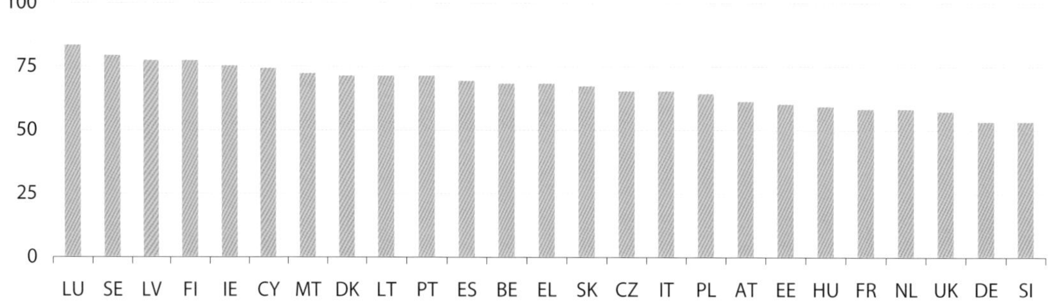

(1) Bulgaria and Romania, not available.

Source: 'Internal market - Opinions and experiences of citizens in EU-25', Special Eurobarometer 254, European Commission

Switching

Consumer switching is considered an important measure as it covers both the range of choice and the ability of consumers to pursue their preferences. Policy in this area is based on the premise that switching is beneficial for the success of market liberalisation concerning services of general interest, as it results in improved efficiency and gains in consumer welfare. Data on switching attitudes exist for a limited number of services of general interest from consumer surveys, covering aspects such as how easy consumers find it to compare offers from different service providers, or the proportion of consumers who switched provider, tried to switch but gave up, or did not try to switch.

A higher proportion of EU-25 respondents to a consumer survey in 2006 agreed that it was easy (compared with difficult) to compare offers relating to four services of general interest. Around half of those questioned thought it was easy to compare offers from fixed phone providers (53 %), banks/financial institutions (53 %) and mobile phone providers (50 %), while a somewhat lower proportion (43 %) thought it was easy to compare offers from Internet service providers. This pattern was generally repeated across Member States, as the lowest rates for ease of comparison were usually recorded for Internet service providers – where this was not the case, consumers faced their greatest difficulty in comparing offers from different mobile phone providers.

Table 1.30: Consumers agreeing that it is very or fairly easy to compare offers from different providers of services of general interest, 2006
(% of respondents)

	Mobile phone	Fixed phone	Internet	Banks/ finance
EU-27	50	53	43	53
BE	40	46	41	54
BG	:	:	:	:
CZ	69	58	51	51
DK	31	36	33	35
DE	39	51	38	62
EE	66	55	53	69
IE	69	61	44	62
EL	75	74	49	69
ES	56	54	47	53
FR	34	45	36	39
IT	52	50	42	44
CY	66	52	38	66
LV	59	42	39	57
LT	60	39	41	51
LU	54	60	47	64
HU	56	50	34	37
MT	73	63	47	74
NL	39	42	44	49
AT	55	58	42	58
PL	62	58	43	51
PT	71	63	44	66
RO	:	:	:	:
SI	70	54	57	68
SK	72	60	38	58
FI	46	34	48	54
SE	27	36	35	47
UK	55	53	54	64

Source: 'Consumers' opinions of services of general interest', Special Eurobarometer 260, European Commission

Figure 1.41: Ease of comparing offers from different providers of services of general interest, EU-25, 2006
(% of respondents)

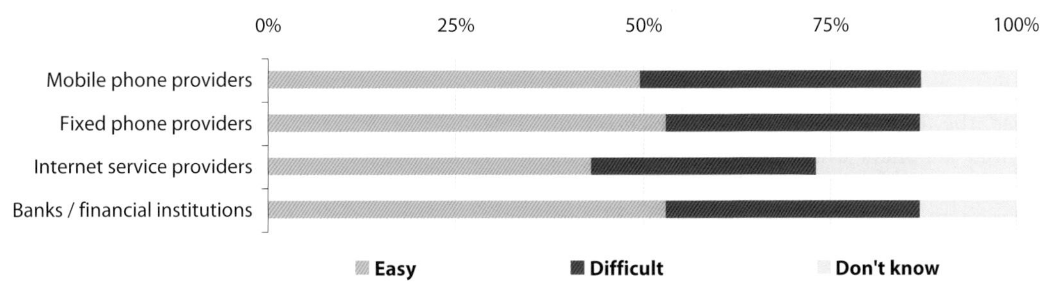

Source: 'Consumers' opinions of services of general interest', Special Eurobarometer 260, European Commission

Table 1.31: Consumer intentions towards switching suppliers, EU-25, 2006
(% of respondents)

	This year I will still use the same supplier	It is easy to change supplier	Buying in another country is possible and interesting	I prefer to deal with a national supplier
Mobile phone	84	78	41	79
Fixed line phone	77	67	28	80
Electricity	85	54	23	81
Gas	87	42	21	78
Water	91	8	14	84
Urban transport	89	32	15	77
Extra-urban transport	88	48	30	75
Air transport	76	87	81	61
Post	94	51	29	83
Banking	90	80	48	83
Insurance	87	77	37	83

Source: IPSOS consumer satisfaction survey, 2007

Even when consumers appear to have a range of affordable alternatives, switching does not guarantee, per se, an efficient market solution, as exit barriers may result in the full costs of switching outweighing potential benefits. Consumers may be obliged to purchase specific equipment, sign fixed duration contracts, or give a lengthy period of notice before being able to switch provider – these types of conditions often 'tie' consumers to an individual service provider and may dissuade them from looking at alternatives.

A consumer satisfaction survey conducted in 2006 tends to give some support to this view, insofar as a majority of EU-25 respondents said that they would stay with their current provider for the next year. The highest proportions who stated they would stay with the same suppliers were registered for postal, water, and banking services (at least 90 %), while fixed line telephony (77 %) and air transport (76 %) were the only services where fewer than 80 % of consumers said they would continue to use the same supplier. The data presented for the ease of changing supplier would appear to reflect, at least to some degree, the degree of competition (or choice of potential suppliers available to consumers), as those markets which still tend to be dominated by a monopoly supplier (such as postal or water services) reported the highest proportion of respondents stating that they intended to use the same supplier.

Table 1.32: Attempts to switch supplier in the last two years, 2006
(% of respondents)

	Mobile phone	Fixed phone	Internet	Bank - current account
EU-25	29	24	25	12
BE	28	27	23	11
BG	:	:	:	:
CZ	21	17	25	13
DK	40	22	27	16
DE	34	25	28	13
EE	26	11	20	7
IE	26	18	12	7
EL	25	12	22	13
ES	23	12	18	10
FR	29	34	30	14
IT	31	28	23	20
CY	14	3	5	10
LV	18	5	12	8
LT	31	4	15	9
LU	26	8	17	9
HU	17	15	17	10
MT	10	6	27	9
NL	37	38	32	9
AT	34	11	19	9
PL	25	21	15	10
PT	7	9	12	5
RO	:	:	:	:
SI	16	4	13	8
SK	15	6	10	14
FI	52	5	21	10
SE	32	42	27	12
UK	30	25	27	9

Source: 'Consumers' opinions of services of general interest', Special Eurobarometer 260, European Commission

CONSUMPTION

Household spending is analysed according to the classification of individual consumption by purpose (COICOP). This allows a harmonised comparison of spending patterns between different countries, or between different socio-economic groups of consumers. The vast majority of the consumption figures are presented in terms of monetary measures, although it is important to remember that some people supplement their monetary expenditure by other forms of non-monetary consumption. These include, for example, growing fruit and vegetables in a garden or on an allotment for own consumption, or benefiting from the use of a company car for personal use; attempts are made to estimate the value of these items in the household budget survey (HBS). In addition, there are a number of services that are provided in the majority of Member States free (or at greatly reduced prices) at the point-of-use by governments (for example, health or education services), and special care needs to be taken when comparing other items with expenditure data in these domains and when comparing expenditure on these items between countries.

This section starts by providing information on the ownership of a range of consumer durable goods and the ability of consumers to afford these. It is followed by information relating to the frequency with which consumers make purchases. The main bulk of this section is focused on providing an overview of consumption expenditure patterns across the EU, looking at the overall level of expenditure, the structure of expenditure, and patterns among different groups of consumers.

Ownership

Eurostat collects information on ownership rates for a range of consumer durables through the survey on income and living conditions (EU-SILC). This shows that households in higher income groups are more likely (than those in the lower income groups) to own a range of different goods, such as a home computer, a washing machine, or a car.

The 94.3 % share of households owning a colour television in Finland was the lowest across the EU-25 Member States in 2006: note that only 1.2 % said they could not afford a television with the remaining 4.5 % making a choice not to own one. Lithuania (2.8 %) and Latvia (2.6 %) recorded the highest proportions of households that could not afford a colour television.

The vast majority of households in the EU also possessed a telephone in 2006, although penetration rates were somewhat lower than for colour televisions. The lowest ownership rates were recorded in Lithuania (89.9 %), Portugal (90.3%) and Latvia (92.2 %); in all three of these countries, upwards of 5 % of households said they could not afford a telephone.

The lowest proportion of households with a washing machine was recorded in Denmark (76.5 %), followed by Latvia (80.3 %) and Lithuania (81.9 %). While only 2.7 % of Danish households reported that they could not afford a washing machine, between 11 % and 12 % of households in Lithuania and Latvia could not afford one.

The proportion of households owning a particular consumer durable is generally lower for consumer durables with higher average prices, as shown by ownership rates for computers or cars. Those countries characterised by relatively higher degrees of income inequality tended to be among those reporting the lowest ownership rates for computers or cars; they also tended to report the highest proportion of households with problems in being able to afford a computer or a car. Ten of the 25 Member States for which data are available for 2006 reported that less than 50 % of households owned a computer, a share that fell to 35.1 % in Greece, and was also below 40 % in Latvia and Lithuania. For cars, the lowest household ownership rate was 41.6 % in Latvia, while the other two Baltic States and Hungary were the only other EU-25 Member States where less than 50 % of households owned a car. More than one in five households in Latvia, Poland, Slovakia and Lithuania were unable to afford a computer, while the same four countries (together with Hungary and Estonia) reported that more than one in five households could not afford a car. At the other end of the scale, the highest ownership rates for computers were registered in the Netherlands, Sweden and Denmark, while car ownership rates were highest in Luxembourg, Cyprus, Slovenia and France.

Table 1.33: Ownership of selected consumer durables, 2006
(% of households)

	Do you have a telephone? (1)		Do you have a colour TV?		Do you have a computer?		Do you have a washing machine?		Do you have a car?	
	Yes	No, cannot afford (2)	Yes	No, cannot afford (3)	Yes	No, cannot afford (4)	Yes	No, cannot afford (5)	Yes	No, cannot afford
BE	99.2	0.4	97.3	0.6	62.0	8.6	89.5	2.9	78.1	8.7
BG	:	:	:	:	:	:	:	:	:	:
CZ	93.7	2.2	97.6	0.5	46.5	12.0	95.5	0.9	61.0	14.5
DK	100.0	0.0	95.3	0.8	74.4	2.9	76.5	2.7	66.4	13.2
DE	99.2	0.4	94.9	0.9	68.3	6.4	95.0	0.8	76.9	7.9
EE	94.5	2.7	97.7	0.9	48.1	17.2	86.3	5.0	48.2	23.4
IE	98.8	0.6	98.8	0.3	56.6	10.6	94.9	1.4	76.1	11.5
EL	98.8	0.8	99.1	0.5	35.1	14.3	94.5	3.2	72.3	11.1
ES	97.7	0.5	99.5	0.1	54.7	9.0	98.6	0.4	76.4	4.8
FR	96.8	0.9	97.0	0.4	54.3	8.2	93.9	1.4	80.6	4.6
IT	94.2	1.5	96.6	0.5	43.5	7.3	96.8	0.8	78.7	3.8
CY	99.3	:	99.5	:	50.6	8.2	95.9	1.5	86.1	2.6
LV	92.2	5.5	96.4	2.6	36.7	28.5	80.3	12.3	41.6	35.7
LT	89.9	6.2	96.1	2.8	38.7	20.6	81.9	11.4	49.4	21.9
LU	99.3	:	98.9	:	65.3	2.4	95.0	0.3	87.2	2.0
HU	93.4	3.8	97.8	1.1	45.8	17.2	90.5	4.3	47.9	24.1
MT	97.0	1.1	98.5	:	52.8	4.6	96.2	:	79.1	3.4
NL	100.0	0.0	98.5	:	80.6	3.1	97.5	:	76.2	8.1
AT	98.7	:	97.2	:	56.6	5.0	95.7	0.9	75.1	6.2
PL	92.4	4.6	96.9	1.7	44.4	24.4	96.2	1.9	50.7	23.7
PT	90.3	5.4	98.4	1.1	43.4	16.2	91.7	4.8	70.9	11.6
RO	:	:	:	:	:	:	:	:	:	:
SI	98.0	0.9	97.0	1.2	56.5	7.7	97.9	0.7	81.1	5.1
SK	94.7	2.7	98.0	1.0	43.1	23.0	96.4	1.5	51.8	29.6
FI	98.8	:	94.3	1.2	63.2	8.4	90.7	2.5	71.7	13.8
SE	99.8	:	94.9	0.7	75.1	2.8	99.1	:	76.1	6.0
UK	99.4	0.2	98.8	:	68.8	5.7	95.3	0.8	77.0	5.3
IS	99.8	:	97.0	:	84.5	1.7	97.8	2.0	91.4	2.9
NO	98.8	:	96.5	0.8	71.6	3.3	96.3	0.6	76.1	6.6

(1) Including mobile phone.
(2) Belgium, Germany, Ireland, Malta, Slovenia and the United Kingdom, unreliable.
(3) Belgium, the Czech Republic, Denmark, Estonia, Ireland, Greece, Spain, France, Portugal, Sweden and Norway, unreliable.
(4) Iceland, unreliable.
(5) Luxembourg, Slovenia, Iceland and Norway, unreliable.

Source: Eurostat, EU-SILC cross-sectional 2006 data

Frequency of purchase

The frequency of purchase is simply defined as the number of times that a person buys a product or service. The nature and price of some products means that they are bought on a far more regular basis (for example, perishable foods) than others (for example, a new car). Retailers and advertisers are particularly interested in identifying those consumers who have a high frequency and value of purchases.

Changes in lifestyle patterns and increasing demands on the efficient use of time mean that there have been changes in the way people do their shopping, the time they spend shopping, and the frequency with which they visit shops. Some differences between Member States have already been alluded to (see Section A2 for more details), insofar as the southern Member States tend to report a much higher retail density of enterprises, while large (often out-of-town) supermarkets/hypermarkets and shopping centres are increasingly the most popular places to go shopping in northern Europe.

A survey conducted in the United Kingdom confirmed that Saturday was the favourite day for shopping. Despite a liberalisation in shop opening hours (leading to later opening and Sunday opening), some 22 % of shopping trips made in the United Kingdom in 2005 were made on a Saturday, with Friday the next most popular day (16 % of trips).

The European time-use survey suggests that, on average, consumers spend between 15 minutes a day in Bulgaria and 36 minutes a day in France to do their shopping. The average time spent was generally higher in EU-15 Member States (for which data are available), while women consistently spent longer than men shopping, probably reflecting both the division of tasks within family life, as well as a higher proportion of women shopping as a recreational activity. The difference between the sexes in terms of time spent shopping peaked at 16 minutes a day in Spain, 15 in the United Kingdom and 14 in Italy.

Figure 1.42: Number of shopping trips by day of the week, United Kingdom, 2005 (1)
(% of total number of trips)

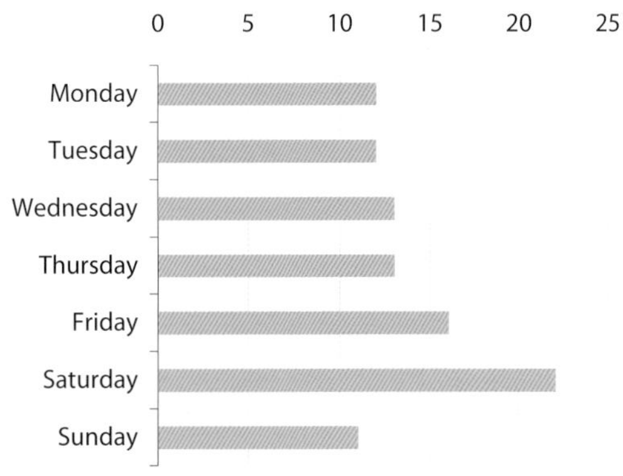

(1) A shopping trip is defined as any trip to the shops, whether or not anything was bought, and even when there was no intention to buy.

Source: Office for National Statistics (UK), National Travel Survey (www.statistics.gov.uk)

Figure 1.43: Time-use for shopping, population aged 20-74 years old (1)
(hours:minutes per day)

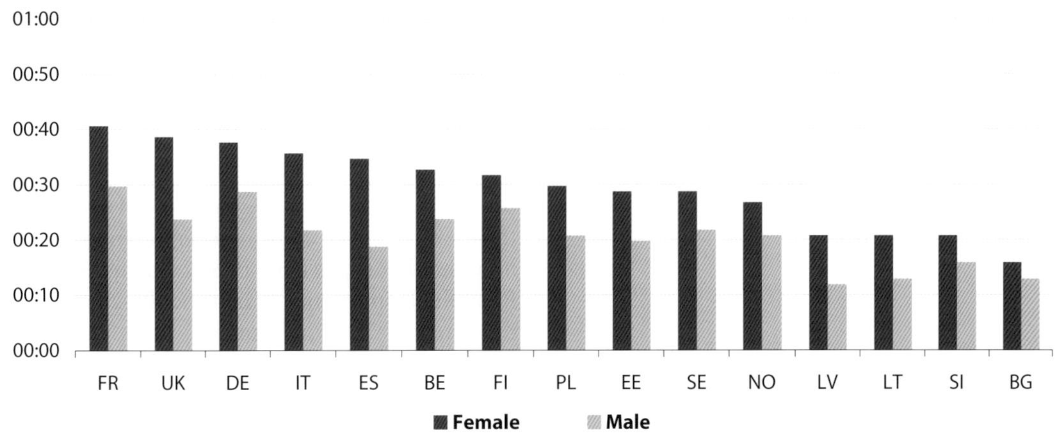

(1) Data only shown for those countries participating in the survey; all remaining Member States, not available.

Source: Harmonised European Time Use Survey [online database version 2.0]; created 2005-2007 by Statistics Finland and Statistics Sweden [reference date 2007-10-01]; (https://www.testh2.scb.se/tus/tus/)

Figure 1.44: Average number of shopping trips per year, by age and gender of shopper, United Kingdom, 2005 (1)
(trips)

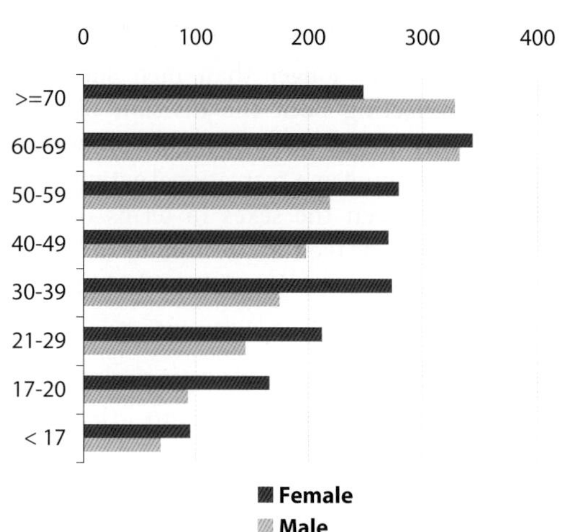

(1) A shopping trip is defined as any trip to the shops, whether or not anything was bought, and even when there was no intention to buy.

Source: Office for National Statistics (UK), National Travel Survey (www.statistics.gov.uk)

The survey of shopping patterns in the United Kingdom confirms this gender imbalance in terms of the average number of shopping trips made by each of the sexes. British women made a higher number of shopping trips than men for each age group, other than for those aged 70 or more. The number of shopping trips made by men rose steadily with age through to the age of retirement, after which it remained stable, while the number of shopping trips made by women reached a plateau by the age of 30, remaining almost unchanged through to the age of 60. The higher number of shopping trips made by people aged 60 or more may be attributed to the additional free-time available to persons in retirement (shopping as a leisure pursuit), as well as their lower reliance on the car resulting in more shopping trips in order to be able to carry the shopping home.

Structure of consumption expenditure

For the purpose of the household budget survey (HBS), total expenditure represents current (consumption) expenditure on goods and services. Consumption expenditure therefore excludes payments which are really savings or investments (for example, life assurance premiums, pension fund contributions, income tax payments, social security contributions, or mortgage capital repayments).

HBS data are often presented in terms of the level of expenditure per household. This is because, although one person may earn all of the money, or one person may buy all of the food, it is likely that the money/food will be divided between different members of each household; as such, consumption of individuals cannot be estimated with reference to the expenditure incurred, rather it is generally assumed to be shared across a household – be that a traditional, family unit, or a group of unrelated persons.

Average consumption expenditure per household in the EU-27 stood at EUR 24 447 in 2005, ranging from a high of EUR 52 754 in Luxembourg to a low of EUR 2 863 in Romania; these figures do not reflect the (sometimes considerable) differences in prices between EU economies. Adjusting to take account of differing purchasing powers, there was still a wide range between the Member States, with the same countries at each end of the ranking; expenditure reached a high of PPS 51 932 in Luxembourg, which was almost 10 times the level recorded in Romania (PPS 5 324). Relatively high expenditure per household (above PPS 30 000) was also recorded in Ireland, Cyprus, the United Kingdom, Greece, Austria and Belgium. Cyprus and Malta were the only Member States that joined the EU since 2004 to record expenditure per household above the EU-27 average, while spending in Slovenia was only slightly below the average. There was a significant gap in the ranking, with nine of the Member States that joined the EU since 2004 recording the lowest levels of consumption expenditure per household, ranging from PPS 12 142 in the Czech Republic (approximately half the EU-27 average) down to PPS 5 324 in Romania.

Table 1.34: Mean consumption expenditure

	Per household				Per adult equivalent			
	(EUR)		(PPS)		(EUR)		(PPS)	
	1994	2005	1994	2005	1994	2005	1994	2005
EU-27 (1)	:	24 447	:	24 655	:	15 190	:	15 218
BE	23 858	31 521	22 716	30 048	14 755	19 754	14 049	18 831
BG	:	3 030	:	7 099	:	1 798	:	4 213
CZ	:	7 146	:	12 142	:	3 837	:	6 520
DK	24 899	33 241	19 185	24 062	16 570	22 378	12 767	16 199
DE	23 231	29 232	20 660	28 501	15 006	19 438	13 345	18 952
EE	:	6 936	:	10 848	:	4 176	:	6 531
IE	19 899	44 909	22 243	36 373	10 060	25 413	11 245	20 583
EL	13 754	27 081	17 701	30 975	7 432	15 205	9 564	17 391
ES	16 404	23 682	19 586	26 028	8 160	12 684	9 742	13 940
FR	24 507	29 632	22 319	27 886	15 084	18 620	13 738	17 523
IT	19 531	28 053	22 807	28 782	10 931	17 215	12 764	17 663
CY	:	30 856	:	34 208	:	15 419	:	17 094
LV	:	5 981	:	10 589	:	3 002	:	5 316
LT	:	5 109	:	9 378	:	3 210	:	5 892
LU	38 777	52 754	38 647	51 932	23 334	33 313	23 255	32 794
HU	:	6 715	:	10 694	:	3 920	:	6 241
MT	:	18 829	:	28 605	:	9 945	:	15 108
NL	21 451	30 360	20 314	29 368	13 762	19 660	13 033	19 018
AT	26 766	30 428	24 322	30 167	15 438	19 511	14 029	19 344
PL	:	6 428	:	10 594	:	3 530	:	5 817
PT	11 333	17 607	16 311	20 869	5 816	9 849	8 371	11 674
RO	:	2 863	:	5 324	:	1 541	:	2 866
SI	:	17 738	:	23 806	:	9 909	:	13 299
SK	:	5 952	:	10 772	:	3 248	:	5 879
FI	18 547	29 705	16 014	24 360	11 906	19 611	10 280	16 082
SE	21 641	29 885	17 994	25 612	14 426	20 320	11 995	17 414
UK	18 433	34 859	20 461	31 959	11 400	21 866	12 654	20 047
HR	:	11 500	:	16 840	:	6 472	:	9 478
NO	:	40 328	:	29 106	:	26 498	:	19 125

(1) Estimates.

Source: Eurostat, mean consumption expenditure by household and per adult equivalent (hbs_exp_t111)

Data based on average household consumption expenditure do not reflect differences in the size and composition of households between countries. An alternative analysis can be done based on consumption expenditure per adult equivalent. Each member of the household is given a weight ranging from 1.0 for the head of the household to 0.3 for children and these are summed to derive a standardised household size in terms of adult equivalents: the household consumption expenditure can then be divided by this standardised household size to determine average expenditure per adult equivalent.

A ranking of average consumption expenditure, in terms of adult equivalents, shows the same countries at the top and bottom of the ranking, from a high of PPS 32 794 in Luxembourg to PPS 2 866 in Romania; as such, consumption expenditure per adult equivalent was 11.4 times as high in Luxembourg as it was in Romania in 2005. While consumption expenditure per household in Cyprus averaged PPS 34 208 (which was 39 % above the EU-27 average), consumption expenditure per adult equivalent averaged PPS 17 094 (only 12 % above the EU-27 average). A similar pattern (although not as pronounced), was observed in some other Mediterranean countries, such as Malta, Spain and Greece, as well as in Ireland. These differences between consumption expenditure levels for households and adult equivalents are likely to result from a higher than average proportion of (extended) families living together in the Mediterranean countries, where a greater level of importance tends to be attached to the family unit. In the case of Ireland, the difference may be attributed to the relatively high proportion of children within the population.

Consumption expenditure analysed per adult equivalent results in Sweden, Denmark, Germany and Finland improving their position relative to the EU-27 average. In Sweden for example, average consumption expenditure per household was around 4 % more than the EU-27 average, whereas average consumption expenditure per adult equivalent was 14 % above the average; these figures reflect a higher proportion of people living alone or in smaller family units in many northern European countries.

Total household consumption expenditure can be broken down using the classification of individual consumption by purpose (COICOP). This hierarchical classification has 12 main expenditure items for private households at its most aggregated level. Information for the EU-27 in 2005 shows that the most important item on the household budget was housing, water, electricity, gas and other fuels, which accounted for PPS 6 936, of which the most important sub-item was rent (or imputed rent). The next largest items were everyday expenditures namely, food and non-alcoholic beverages (PPS 3 594) and transport (PPS 3 078), followed by miscellaneous goods and services (insurance, hairdressers or beauty salons), and recreation and culture; both of these were characterised by people in higher income brackets tending to spend proportionally more of their budget on such items. The overall level of EU-27 expenditure per household on restaurants and hotels; furnishings, household equipment and routine maintenance of the house; as well as clothing and footwear was similar, averaging just over PPS 1 400 for each the three items, while the five remaining goods and services (at the first level of the COICOP) each accounted for less than PPS 1 000 of spending per annum.

Figure 1.45: Mean consumption expenditure, 2005
(% relative to EU-27, based on PPS series)

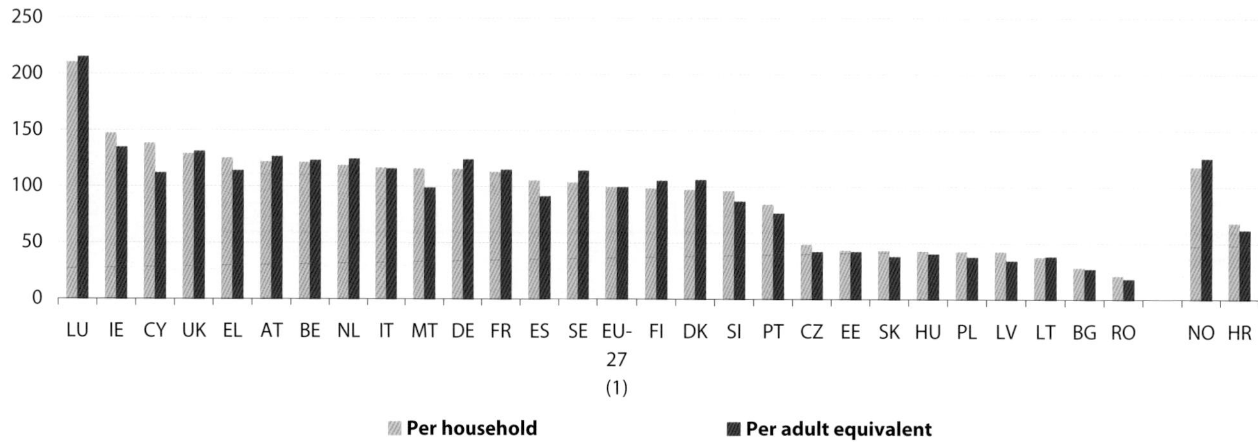

(1) Estimates.

Source: Eurostat, mean consumption expenditure by household and per adult equivalent (hbs_exp_t111)

Table 1.35: Mean consumption expenditure per household, 2005

	EU-27 average (PPS)	Highest	(PPS)	Lowest	(PPS)	Ratio: highest/ lowest
Food & non-alcoholic beverages	3 594	Malta	6 082	Bulgaria	2 238	2.7
Food	3 329	Malta	5 394	Bulgaria	2 143	2.5
Non-alcoholic beverages	282	Malta	688	Bulgaria	96	7.2
Alcoholic beverages, tobacco	560	Ireland	2 032	Poland	262	7.8
Alcoholic beverages	281	Ireland	1 508	Bulgaria	85	17.7
Tobacco (1)	242	Greece	845	Lithuania	123	6.9
Clothing & footwear	1 412	Luxembourg	3 343	Bulgaria	218	15.3
Clothing (1)	934	Luxembourg	2 747	Bulgaria	152	18.1
Footwear including repair	295	Luxembourg	596	Bulgaria	67	8.9
Housing, water, electricity, gas & other fuels	6 936	Luxembourg	15 611	Romania	832	18.8
Actual rentals for housing	3 095	United Kingdom	6 650	Poland	52	127.9
Imputed rentals for housing (2)	5 256	Luxembourg	12 889	Latvia	668	19.3
Maintenance & repair of the dwelling	371	Malta	1 729	Finland	5	345.8
Water supply; misc. serv. relating to dwelling	455	Austria	1 010	Bulgaria	132	7.7
Electricity, gas & other fuels	1 192	Luxembourg	1 894	Malta	502	3.8
Furnishings, househ. equip. & maintenance	1 416	Luxembourg	3 702	Romania	201	18.4
Furniture, furnish., carpets, floor cover.	558	Luxembourg	1 770	Romania	35	50.6
Household textiles	109	Greece	326	Bulgaria	12	27.2
Household appliances	205	Ireland	815	Romania	41	19.9
Glassware, tableware & househ. utensils	90	Greece	223	Romania	9	24.8
Tools & equip. for house & garden	114	Sweden	258	Romania	6	43.0
Goods & services for routine maintenance	336	Luxembourg	909	Bulgaria	82	11.1
Health	796	Greece	1 824	Romania	205	8.9
Medical products, appliances & equip.	428	Luxembourg	801	Romania	168	4.8
Out-patient services	330	Greece	1 196	Romania	28	42.7
Hospital services	39	Greece	265	Netherlands	1	265.0
Transport	3 078	Luxembourg	8 403	Romania	344	24.4
Purchase of vehicles	1 165	Luxembourg	4 954	Bulgaria	37	133.9
Operation of personal transport equip. (1)	1 234	Luxembourg	3 020	Bulgaria	196	15.4
Transport services	325	Malta	673	Romania	93	7.2
Communications	738	Ireland	1 255	Romania	259	4.8
Postal services (1)	16	Malta	42	Romania	0	-
Telephone & telefax equipment (1)	28	Malta	139	Romania	4	34.8
Telephone & telefax services (1)	555	Ireland	1 174	Romania	255	4.6
Recreation & culture	2 187	United Kingdom	3 943	Bulgaria	204	19.3
Audio-vis., photo., info. process. equip. (1)	241	Luxembourg	648	Romania	27	24.0
Oth. durables for recreation & culture (1)	44	Netherlands	231	Romania	0	-
Oth. recreational equip., garden & pets (1)	325	Luxembourg	1 027	Romania	23	44.7
Recreational & cultural services	619	Ireland	1 438	Bulgaria	72	20.0
Newspapers, books & stationery	356	Malta	686	Bulgaria	44	15.6
Package holidays (3)	414	Austria	1 224	Lithuania	20	61.2
Education	238	Cyprus	1 354	Sweden	8	169.3
Pre-primary & primary education (4)	35	Cyprus	203	Estonia	0	-
Secondary education (5)	48	Cyprus	422	Bulgaria	4	105.5
Post-secondary non-tertiary education (6)	16	Ireland	107	Bulgaria	1	107.0
Tertiary education (7)	68	Cyprus	706	Finland	6	117.7
Education not definable by level (8)	44	Netherlands	306	Sweden	1	306.0
Restaurants & hotels	1 417	Luxembourg	4 098	Romania	58	70.7
Catering services (1)	1 035	Luxembourg	3 240	Romania	38	85.3
Accommodation services (1)	178	Luxembourg	858	Latvia	9	95.3
Miscellaneous goods & services	2 291	Netherlands	4 945	Romania	162	30.5
Personal care	615	Luxembourg	1 242	Romania	118	10.5
Personal effects n.e.c. (1)	113	Luxembourg	896	Romania	14	64.0
Social protection (y)	82	Ireland	400	Romania	1	400.0
Insurance	1 159	Netherlands	3 623	Romania	11	329.4
Financial services n.e.c. (9)	31	Netherlands	198	Bulgaria	2	99.0
Other services n.e.c. (1)	191	Finland	1 370	Romania	10	137.0

(1) Germany, not available. (2) Czech Republic, Hungary, Malta and Romania, not available. (3) France, not available. (4) Belgium, Denmark, Germany, Italy, the Netherlands, Finland and Sweden, not available. (5) Belgium, Germany, Italy, the Netherlands and Sweden, not available. (6) Belgium, Denmark, Germany, Estonia, France, Italy, Cyprus, Latvia, Lithuania, Malta, the Netherlands, Portugal, Romania and Finland, not available. (7) Belgium, Germany, Spain, the Netherlands, Slovenia and Sweden, not available. (8) Germany and Romania, not available. (9) Germany and Italy, not available.

Source: Eurostat, mean consumption expenditure by detailed COICOP level (hbs_exp_t121)

A comparison between the highest and lowest levels of spending shows that average household consumption expenditure in Malta was 2.7 times as high as in Bulgaria for food and non-alcoholic beverages, an expenditure item that can be largely regarded as a necessity. This ratio was generally much bigger for other items: for example, spending in Luxembourg was 24.4 times as high as in Romania for transport (purchases of vehicles and running costs), while the ratio for the same two countries for restaurants and hotels stood at 70.7. An even larger ratio was recorded for education services, although it is important to underline that the comparability between countries for education, as well as for health services, may be limited due by the significant differences that exist in terms of the relative importance of free delivery at the point-of-use.

An analysis of the average household spend can be supplemented by information on the structure of expenditure, in other words, the relative importance of each item in the total household budget. Housing, water, electricity, gas and other fuels accounted for more than a quarter (27.7 %) of total household consumption expenditure in the EU-27 in 2005, while food and non-alcoholic beverages (16.8 %) and transport (11.9 %) were the next most important items.

The proportion of the household budget spent on food and non-alcoholic beverages rose to 44.2 % of in Romania and fell to as low as 9.3 % in Luxembourg. The highest share of consumption expenditure on the purchase of alcoholic beverages was recorded in Ireland (4.1 % of total expenditure), while Romania (3.5 %) registered the highest proportion of total expenditure on tobacco. The relative importance of housing, water, electricity, gas and other fuels was highest in Bulgaria (34.7 % of the total budget), while consumers in Malta recorded the highest proportion of expenditure on transport (16.6 %), furnishings and household equipment (10.7 %) and clothing (6.3 %). Portugal registered the highest relative expenditure on health services (6.1 %) and for restaurants and hotels (10.8 %), while consumers in Austria spent more (12.6 %), in relative terms, on recreation and culture than in any other Member State, and Cyprus (4.0 %) had the highest share of spending on education.

The differences in consumption patterns between the Member States displayed a larger variation for those items considered as luxuries, where expenditure depends (at least to some degree) on the ability to afford goods or services. For example, households in Luxembourg spent 9.5 % of their total budget in 2005 on the purchase of vehicles, compared with just 0.5 % in Bulgaria. These figures reflect not just the ability of consumers in Luxembourg to buy a car (Luxembourg is the Member State with the highest car ownership rate), but also the relatively high price paid by consumers in that country for higher-end motor vehicles. In contrast, there was far less variation across the Member States as regards the share of household expenditure that was devoted to the operation of personal transport equipment, or the purchase of transport services. Indeed, the main use of a car, a bus, or a train is usually to make the journey between home and work or home and school, in part explaining why there is less variation between countries.

Table 1.36: Structure of consumption expenditure for households, 2005 (1)

	EU-27 average (‰)	Highest	(‰)	Lowest	(‰)	Ratio: highest/ lowest
Food & non-alcoholic beverages	168	Romania	442	Luxembourg	93	4.8
Food	156	Romania	419	Luxembourg	83	5.0
Non-alcoholic beverages	12	Slovakia	25	Portugal	7	3.6
Alcoholic beverages, tobacco	24	Romania	58	Various	17	3.4
Alcoholic beverages	12	Ireland	41	Cyprus	5	8.2
Tobacco (2)	14	Romania	35	Luxembourg	6	5.8
Clothing & footwear	57	Malta	83	Bulgaria	31	2.7
Clothing (2)	45	Malta	63	Bulgaria	21	3.0
Footwear including repair	13	Lithuania	26	Finland	6	4.3
Housing, water, electricity, gas & other fuels	277	Bulgaria	347	Malta	91	3.8
Actual rentals for housing	45	Sweden	96	Estonia	0	-
Imputed rentals for housing (3)	150	Spain	229	Latvia	57	4.0
Maintenance & repair of the dwelling	15	Malta	60	Finland	0	-
Water supply; misc. serv. relating to dwelling	20	Hungary	48	Malta	5	9.6
Electricity, gas & other fuels	55	Slovakia	159	Malta	18	8.8
Furnishings, househ. equip. & maintenance	55	Malta	107	Bulgaria	30	3.6
Furniture, furnish., carpets, floor cover.	21	Malta	42	Bulgaria	5	8.4
Household textiles	4	Greece	11	Bulgaria	2	5.5
Household appliances	8	Malta	22	Portugal	7	3.1
Glassware, tableware & househ. utensils	4	Greece	7	Bulgaria	2	3.5
Tools & equip. for house & garden	4	Sweden	9	Various	1	9.0
Goods & services for routine maintenance	14	Greece	26	Various	6	4.3
Health	34	Portugal	61	United Kingdom	12	5.1
Medical products, appliances & equip.	19	Lithuania	41	United Kingdom	6	6.8
Out-patient services	13	Greece	39	Various	5	7.8
Hospital services (4)	2	Greece	9	Various	0	-
Transport	119	Malta	166	Bulgaria	50	3.3
Purchase of vehicles	44	Luxembourg	95	Bulgaria	5	19.0
Operation of personal transport equip. (2)	59	Austria	81	Bulgaria	28	2.9
Transport services	14	Malta	24	Various	7	3.4
Communications	32	Hungary	65	Various	22	3.0
Postal services (5)	1	Various	1	Bulgaria	0	-
Telephone & telefax equipment (2)	1	Malta	5	Greece	0	-
Telephone & telefax services (2)	31	Hungary	63	Italy	19	3.3
Recreation & culture	83	Austria	126	Bulgaria	29	4.3
Audio-vis., photo., info. process. equip. (2)	11	Denmark	24	Various	5	4.8
Oth. durables for recreation & culture (6)	2	Various	8	Various	0	-
Oth. recreational equip., garden & pets (2)	15	Denmark	25	Various	4	6.3
Recreational & cultural services	24	Ireland	40	Various	10	4.0
Newspapers, books & stationery	14	Malta	24	Bulgaria	6	4.0
Package holidays (7)	18	Austria	41	Various	2	20.5
Education	10	Cyprus	40	Sweden	0	-
Pre-primary & primary education (8)	2	Various	6	Various	0	-
Secondary education (9)	2	Greece	13	Various	0	-
Post-secondary non-tertiary education (10)	1	Various	3	Various	0	-
Tertiary education (11)	5	Cyprus	21	Various	0	-
Education not definable by level (12)	2	Netherlands	10	Sweden	0	-
Restaurants & hotels	53	Portugal	108	Romania	11	9.8
Catering services (2)	47	Portugal	105	Romania	7	15.0
Accommodation services (2)	8	Italy	17	Various	1	17.0
Miscellaneous goods & services	87	Netherlands	168	Romania	30	5.6
Personal care	25	France	33	Bulgaria	18	1.8
Personal effects n.e.c. (2)	6	Luxembourg	17	Bulgaria	2	8.5
Social protection (13)	4	Denmark	13	Various	0	-
Insurance	42	Netherlands	123	Various	2	61.5
Financial services n.e.c. (14)	2	Netherlands	7	Various	0	-
Other services n.e.c. (2)	9	Finland	56	Various	2	28.0

(1) Czech Republic, not available. (2) Germany, not available. (3) Hungary, Malta and Romania, not available. (4) Slovenia, not available. (5) Germany, Slovenia and Poland, not available. (6) Germany and Poland, not available. (7) France, not available. (8) Belgium, Denmark, Germany, Italy, the Netherlands, Finland and Sweden, not available. (9) Belgium, Germany, Italy, the Netherlands and Sweden, not available. (10) Belgium, Denmark, Germany, Estonia, France, Italy, Cyprus, Latvia, Lithuania, Malta, the Netherlands, Portugal, Romania and Finland, not available. (11) Belgium, Germany, Spain, the Netherlands, Slovenia and Sweden, not available. (12) Germany and Romania, not available. (13) Germany, Italy and Poland, not available. (14) Germany and Italy, not available.

Source: Eurostat, overall structure of consumption expenditure by detailed COICOP level (hbs_exp_t211)

The evolution of consumption expenditure over time presented here is based on an analysis of national accounts data. This shows that alcoholic beverages and tobacco was the only one of the 12 consumption items (at the first level of the COICOP) to register a reduction in its volume (in other words, adjusted for price changes) of consumption between 1995 and 2006 in the EU-27, as consumption fell in each of the last four years for which data are available. The volume of consumption across the remaining 11 items in the COICOP rose between 1995 and 2006. The slowest growth rates were often registered for items characterised as necessities, such as food and non-alcoholic beverages, or housing, water, electricity, gas and other fuels – where demand is generally inelastic (expenditure on these items increases with income, but not as fast as income, so the proportion of expenditure devoted to these items falls over time assuming that income rises). In contrast, the most rapid growth was recorded for communications, where consumption increased by an average of 10.2 % per annum in the EU-27, followed by a 4.4 % per annum increase in the consumption of recreation and culture.

Figure 1.46: Evolution of volume of final consumption expenditure of households by consumption purpose, EU-27 (1)
(1995=100, based on expenditure per inhabitant)

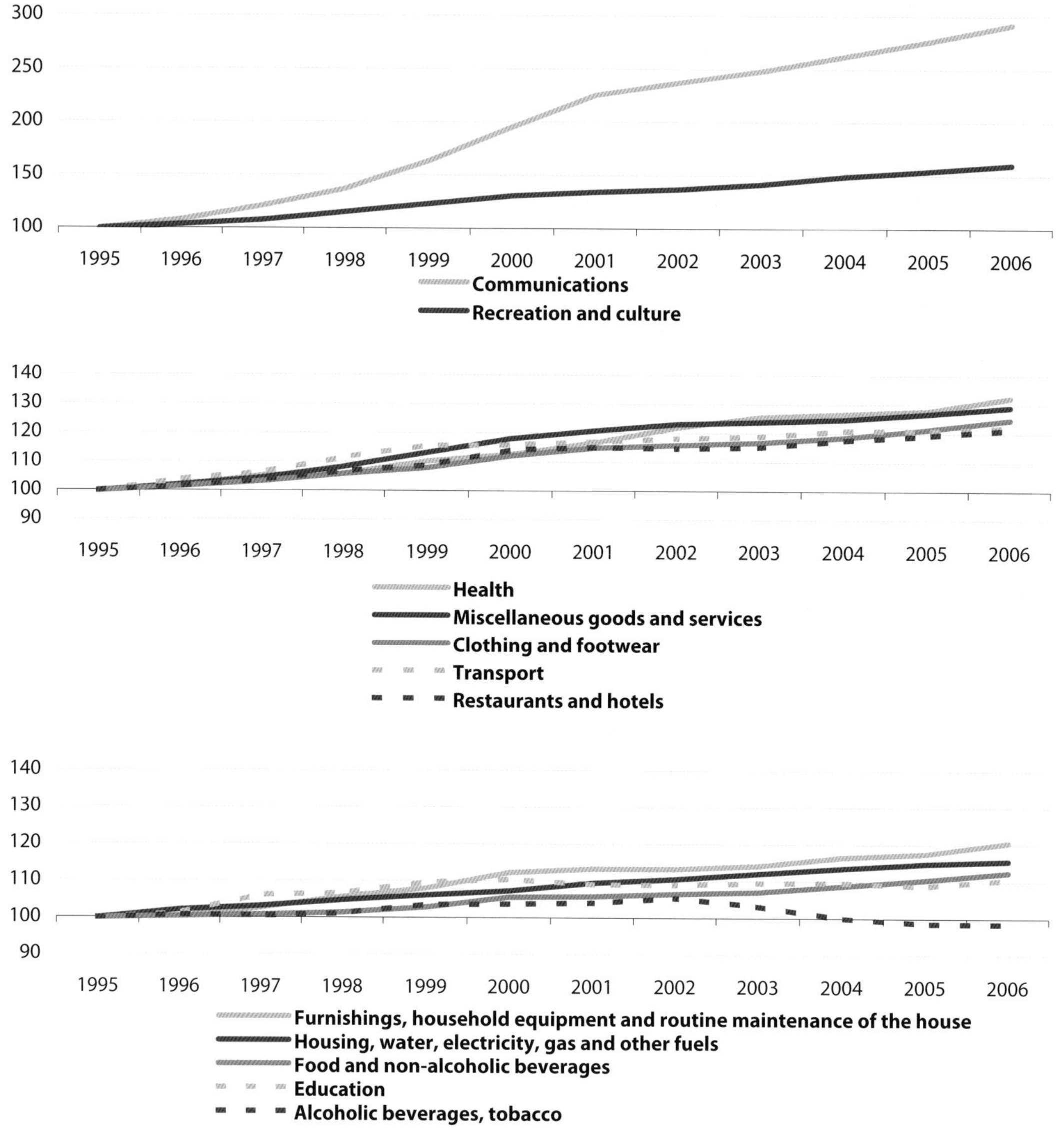

(1) Note: the y-axis of the first graph has a different scale.

Source: Eurostat, final consumption expenditure of households by consumption purpose - volumes (nama_co2_k)

Expenditure patterns of different population groups

Household income

Many of the differences in consumption patterns between and within countries can be related to income. Average consumption expenditure per household broken down by income quintile is an indicator that is derived by ranking all households according to their income and then dividing them into five groups of equal number of households.

The figures show, unsurprisingly, that average spending in the EU-27 in 2005 increased as a function of income – with the expenditure of the fifth quintile (the top 20 % of earners) some 2.8 times as high as that for the lowest income quintile (the bottom 20 % of earners). The ratio of household expenditure between the top and bottom quintiles gives an indication of the distribution of household expenditure, with high ratios – such as those recorded in Luxembourg, Portugal, Italy and Cyprus – indicating a lower degree of equality, while lower values – such as those in the Netherlands, Austria or the Czech Republic – suggesting a more equal distribution of consumption expenditure across society.

Table 1.37: Mean consumption expenditure per household by income quintile, 2005
(PPS)

	Total	1st	2nd	3rd	4th	5th
EU-27 (1)	24 655	14 158	18 731	23 046	28 073	39 262
BE	30 048	18 929	24 998	29 634	34 173	42 461
BG	7 099	3 782	5 395	6 886	8 222	11 209
CZ	12 142	11 142	10 306	10 588	13 199	15 469
DK	24 062	13 395	18 092	24 595	28 854	35 308
DE	28 501	14 388	20 978	26 877	33 216	47 047
EE	10 848	5 561	7 286	8 900	12 741	19 717
IE	36 373	18 272	25 758	37 589	46 345	53 881
EL	30 975	18 617	22 926	27 629	35 673	50 020
ES	26 028	16 874	21 609	25 164	28 816	37 670
FR	27 886	18 069	23 095	27 003	31 243	40 020
IT	28 782	12 667	19 723	25 352	32 163	54 014
CY	34 208	13 676	24 795	34 189	41 065	57 269
LV	10 589	5 875	6 950	9 236	12 361	18 517
LT	9 378	5 009	6 631	8 776	11 004	15 469
LU	51 932	21 139	32 673	44 751	60 862	100 177
HU	10 694	6 743	7 829	9 721	11 712	17 457
MT	28 605	13 683	22 345	29 241	35 077	42 680
NL	29 368	22 694	22 733	27 257	33 047	41 091
AT	30 167	24 766	23 801	28 511	32 398	41 358
PL	10 594	5 315	7 400	9 450	12 186	18 618
PT	20 869	8 375	13 811	18 521	24 493	39 152
RO	5 324	2 828	3 870	4 859	6 112	8 952
SI	23 806	10 588	18 296	22 857	28 822	38 434
SK	10 772	6 984	8 659	10 200	11 671	16 338
FI	24 360	13 085	18 508	23 438	28 640	38 099
SE	25 612	16 571	20 082	25 100	29 252	37 041
UK	31 959	18 941	24 341	29 455	36 638	50 401
HR	16 840	9 324	12 375	16 096	19 767	26 617
NO	29 106	17 596	34 411	35 179	30 788	27 568

(1) Estimates.

Source: Eurostat, mean consumption expenditure by income quintile (hbs_exp_t133)

Figure 1.47: Ratio of mean consumption expenditure per household for the fifth quintile compared with the first quintile, 2005
(ratio, based on PPS series)

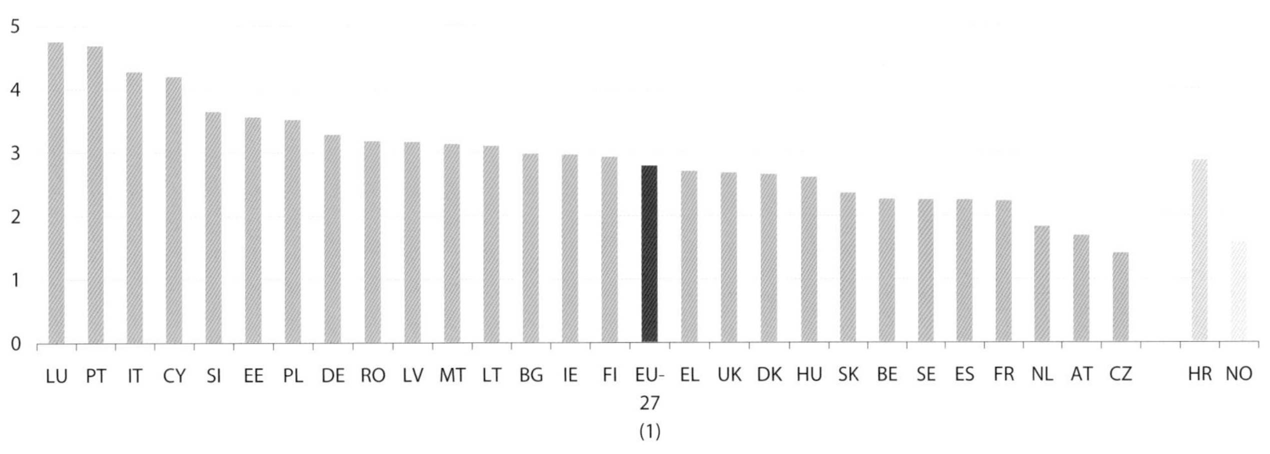

(1) Estimates.

Source: Eurostat, mean consumption expenditure by income quintile (hbs_exp_t133)

Table 1.38: Structure of consumption expenditure per household by income quintile, EU-27, 2005
(‰)

	Total	1st	2nd	3rd	4th	5th
Food & non-alcoholic beverages	168	222	201	184	166	130
Alcoholic beverages, tobacco	24	31	27	25	24	20
Clothing & footwear	57	50	51	55	58	61
Housing, water, electricity, gas & other fuels	277	326	304	287	271	244
Furnishings, househ. equip. & maintenance	55	40	47	50	54	67
Health	34	30	33	32	32	37
Transport	119	81	97	111	121	144
Communications	32	37	35	34	33	30
Recreation & culture	83	64	73	82	87	94
Education	10	7	7	8	10	12
Restaurants & hotels	53	40	45	49	55	62
Miscellaneous goods & services	87	70	78	82	88	99

Source: Eurostat, structure of consumption expenditure by income quintile (hbs_str_t223)

Table 1.39: Mean consumption expenditure per household by number of active persons, 2005
(PPS)

	Total	0	1	2	3+
EU-27 (1)	24 655	17 397	23 206	32 247	37 645
BE	30 048	22 825	26 641	39 966	38 635
BG	7 099	4 901	6 793	8 910	10 055
CZ	12 142	7 197	11 015	16 513	22 373
DK	24 062	16 305	22 205	34 616	25 549
DE	28 501	22 487	25 969	38 606	44 393
EE	10 848	5 749	9 570	15 446	17 348
IE	36 373	19 501	34 137	48 530	62 138
EL	30 975	18 201	31 455	41 813	43 805
ES	26 028	16 756	25 358	31 250	35 048
FR	27 886	20 728	25 118	36 754	39 382
IT	28 782	20 563	28 959	38 842	54 014
CY	34 208	15 688	28 757	43 222	56 177
LV	10 589	5 013	8 990	14 587	17 859
LT	9 378	5 565	8 485	12 697	14 834
LU	51 932	41 436	46 810	66 090	62 353
HU	10 694	7 292	11 125	14 377	15 651
MT	28 605	15 978	27 193	38 329	46 063
NL	29 368	:	:	:	:
AT	30 167	21 872	28 899	38 695	44 086
PL	10 594	7 476	10 104	13 209	13 178
PT	20 869	12 879	19 951	26 509	30 179
RO	5 324	3 289	4 902	6 751	7 183
SI	23 806	14 908	21 751	30 533	31 976
SK	10 772	:	:	:	:
FI	24 360	16 059	23 249	36 280	42 085
SE	25 612	:	:	:	:
UK	31 959	21 255	29 907	40 232	51 517
HR	16 840	10 540	15 686	22 309	25 213
NO	29 106	30 876	24 741	:	44 424

(1) Estimates for total and 3 or more; remaining values are unreliable.

Source: Eurostat, mean consumption expenditure by number of active persons (hbs_exp_t132)

Items considered as necessities – such as food or housing – generally see their relative share of total consumption expenditure fall as a function of income rising. For example, the proportion of total expenditure that was devoted to food and non-alcoholic beverages by the highest income quintile was almost half that recorded by the lowest income quintile in the EU-27; this pattern was repeated for alcoholic beverages and tobacco, and for communications.

In contrast, there are a number of items which are often classified as luxuries, where high-income households tend to spend more than lower income households, both in absolute and relative terms – these include transport (where the top quintile spent a higher proportion of their total expenditure on the purchase of new motor vehicles); furnishings, household equipment and the routine maintenance of the house; education; restaurants and hotels; recreation and culture.

Number of active persons

As might be expected, average household consumption expenditure in the EU-27 in 2005 generally rose as a function of the number of active persons living in the household. It is important to bear in mind that the HBS classifies the highest earner in each household as the first active person or the reference person for that household. This explains, to some degree, why the expenditure of households with three or more active persons is not three times as high as the expenditure of households with only one active person. Another reason may be that economies of scale can be achieved by people who live together in households, by pooling their

incomes, expenditure on items such as housing can become relatively cheaper (as there is no need for each person in a shared house to have their own kitchen, living room, or bathroom). Other consumer durables and many services can also be shared, for example, a car, heating in a living room, or a television license), thereby reducing the degree of expenditure in houses with several active persons.

Given the link that exists with income, it is not surprising to find that households with no economically active persons recorded the lowest average consumption expenditure in each Member State. The level of expenditure among those EU-27 households with three or more active persons was 116 % higher than that recorded by households with no active persons in 2005. The average expenditure of a household with three or more active persons was 62 % higher than that of a household with one active person, and 17 % higher than for a household with two active persons.

This pattern of expenditure increasing as a function of the number of active persons in a household was repeated in the majority of the Member States, although in Denmark, Luxembourg, Belgium and Poland, households with two active persons recorded a higher level of expenditure than those with three or more active persons. This may be the result of factors such as younger persons who have just entered the labour market sharing accommodation. Younger adults are likely to have relatively low income levels (as they are at the start of their working lives), while households with two active persons may often be composed of couples who could be further into their working lives and earning more.

Figure 1.48: Ratio of mean consumption expenditure per household for three or more active persons compared with zero active persons, 2005 (1)
(ratio, based on PPS series)

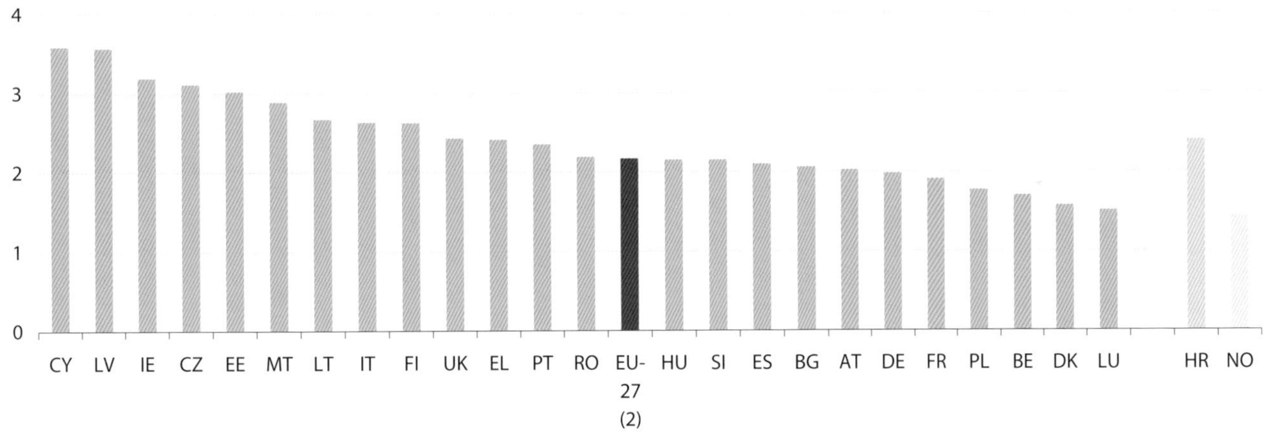

(1) The Netherlands, Slovakia and Sweden, not available.
(2) Estimate; unreliable.

Source: Eurostat, mean consumption expenditure by number of active persons (hbs_exp_t132)

The difference in expenditure between households with zero or one active person was less than 20 % in Luxembourg, Germany and Belgium, but was higher than 70 % in Malta, Greece, Ireland, Latvia and Cyprus; these figures may reflect differences in social benefits and pensions that are made available to the economically inactive.

Households with three or more active persons in the EU-27 spent a higher proportion of their expenditure (than any other type of household) on alcoholic beverages and tobacco; clothing and footwear; transport; communications; restaurants and hotels. In contrast, those households without active persons spent proportionally more on food and non-alcoholic beverages; housing, water, electricity, gas and other fuels; and health services.

Type of household

The analysis can be extended to the composition of each household, not just in terms of the number of active persons, but also its other members. As already shown, household expenditure usually rises as a function of the size and the income of a household, although the relationship is not linear, as economies of scale can often be made by people sharing an abode.

This was reconfirmed when looking at a breakdown of EU-27 expenditure by type of household, with the total budget of two adults living together some 65 % higher than that of a single person in 2005. This ratio was particularly low across the southern Member States of Italy (45 %), Greece, Spain (both 49 %), and Portugal (51 %), where female activity rates are among the lowest in the EU. In contrast, the average expenditure of two adults living together was at least 80 % higher than that of a single person in the Czech Republic, Finland, Latvia, Germany and Estonia.

Table 1.40: Structure of consumption expenditure per household by number of active persons, EU-27, 2005 (1)
(‰)

	Total	0	1	2	3+
Food & non-alcoholic beverages	168	190	169	160	175
Alcoholic beverages, tobacco	24	21	26	25	30
Clothing & footwear	57	41	57	64	65
Housing, water, electricity, gas & other fuels	277	347	281	245	228
Furnishings, househ. equip. & maintenance	55	54	54	58	49
Health	34	53	31	28	28
Transport	119	77	119	138	153
Communications	32	29	34	33	36
Recreation & culture	83	74	82	87	80
Education	10	3	10	13	10
Restaurants & hotels	53	36	54	59	61
Miscellaneous goods & services	87	77	83	91	88

(1) Unreliable.

Source: Eurostat, structure of consumption expenditure by number of active persons (hbs_str_t222)

Table 1.41: Mean consumption expenditure per household by type of household, 2005 (PPS)

	Total	Single person	Single parent with dependent children	2 adults	2 adults with dependent children	3+ adults	3+ adults with dependent children
EU-27 (1)	24 655	14 788	21 323	24 470	31 981	31 957	36 042
BE	30 048	19 341	24 723	30 451	41 583	33 455	40 335
BG	7 099	4 153	7 338	6 286	9 185	9 145	9 971
CZ	12 142	6 401	10 647	12 084	16 493	20 063	21 211
DK (2)	24 062	15 175	19 730	26 891	34 918	36 932	36 203
DE	28 501	17 476	22 685	32 433	38 798	42 036	46 745
EE	10 848	5 703	9 157	10 285	15 494	15 399	16 607
IE	36 373	18 150	24 188	32 203	46 686	51 737	55 071
EL	30 975	16 552	31 720	24 637	41 541	37 984	42 161
ES	26 028	14 266	24 903	21 286	31 132	28 906	34 537
FR	27 886	17 251	24 125	28 059	37 849	34 201	40 311
IT	28 782	18 966	28 008	27 449	35 786	34 875	37 814
CY	34 208	14 242	27 797	22 056	42 836	39 209	55 790
LV	10 589	5 081	8 869	9 527	14 689	13 253	15 804
LT	9 378	5 607	9 215	9 349	12 901	11 856	14 086
LU	51 932	35 071	44 167	53 537	65 721	58 839	74 110
HU	10 694	5 714	10 585	9 979	14 039	13 375	15 254
MT	28 605	14 817	22 767	23 426	32 774	33 765	41 143
NL	29 368	:	:	:	:	:	:
AT	30 167	19 530	28 847	31 384	39 257	39 126	43 053
PL	10 594	6 710	9 427	10 368	12 836	11 904	13 217
PT	20 869	11 338	21 026	17 121	25 926	24 314	27 303
RO	5 324	2 596	4 417	4 524	6 493	6 324	7 032
SI	23 806	12 670	22 359	21 310	29 825	27 446	33 496
SK	10 772	5 541	8 210	9 440	12 251	13 954	14 695
FI	24 360	14 176	21 795	26 776	38 309	31 471	46 864
SE	25 612	16 434	22 036	28 839	35 569	32 728	35 893
UK	31 959	18 927	25 177	32 911	41 200	46 010	50 954
HR (3)	16 840	9 145	16 525	13 879	22 526	21 479	24 945
NO	29 106	17 873	26 459	31 931	41 332	38 254	45 355

(1) Estimates.
(2) Three or more adults and three or more adults with dependent children, unreliable.
(3) Single parent with dependent children, unreliable.

Source: Eurostat, mean consumption expenditure by type of household (hbs_exp_t134)

The presence of dependent children is associated with still higher levels of average household consumption expenditure. When making country comparisons it is important to note that expenditure is not simply a function of the average number of children per household, but also relates to the provision of childcare and whether this is met through social transfers or directly from household expenditure.

Consumption expenditure of a two adult household in the EU-27 was 31 % higher with the additional presence of dependent children. The extent of higher expenditure associated with the presence of dependent children was relatively low in Germany (20 %), Luxembourg, Sweden (both 23 %), Poland (24 %), Austria and the United Kingdom (25 %). At the other end of the scale, two adult households with dependent children in Cyprus reported expenditure that was almost twice as high (94 %) as for those two adult households without children.

The proportion of total household consumption expenditure accounted for by housing, water, electricity, gas and other fuels was considerably

Figure 1.49: Ratio of mean consumption expenditure per household for two adult household with dependent children compared with average for all households, 2005 (1)
(ratio, based on PPS series)

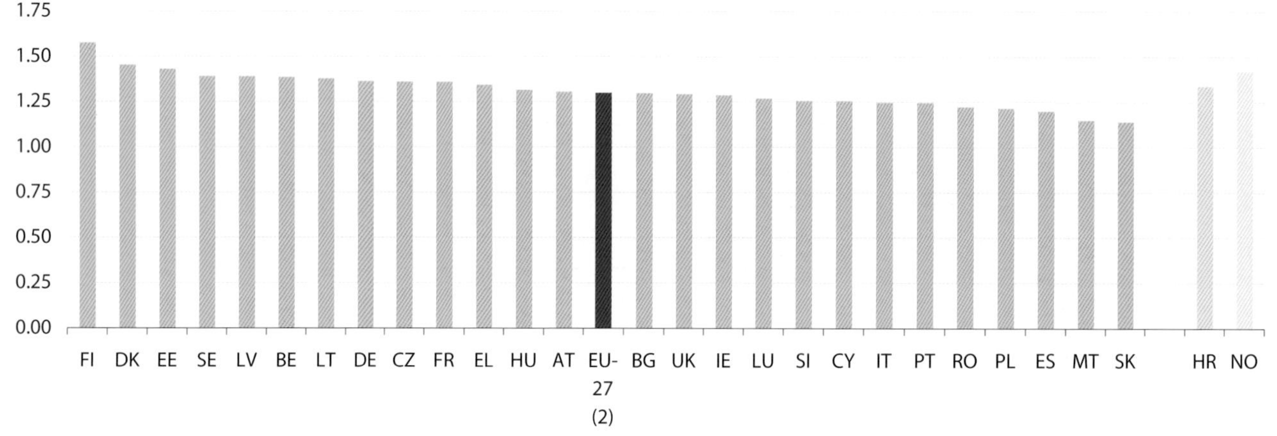

(1) The Netherlands, not available.
(2) Estimates.

Source: Eurostat, mean consumption expenditure by type of household (hbs_exp_t134)

Table 1.42: Structure of consumption expenditure per household by type of household, EU-27, 2005
(‰)

	Total	Single person	Single parent with dependent children	2 adults	2 adults with dependent children	3+ adults	3+ adults with dependent children
Food & non-alcoholic beverages	168	189	203	206	202	222	228
Alcoholic beverages, tobacco	24	20	16	23	19	26	24
Clothing & footwear	57	46	67	49	70	57	63
Housing, water, electricity, gas & other fuels	277	371	293	313	255	273	250
Furnishings, househ. equip. & maintenance	55	49	49	55	58	52	50
Health	34	48	34	55	32	41	35
Transport	119	73	88	101	119	122	130
Communications	32	34	38	31	33	34	35
Recreation & culture	83	58	77	59	74	58	61
Education	10	3	19	3	16	8	15
Restaurants & hotels	53	47	50	38	51	40	41
Miscellaneous goods & services	87	62	69	69	74	78	75

Source: Eurostat, structure of consumption expenditure by type of household (hbs_str_t224)

higher for single persons living alone when compared with larger household units. Indeed, these items accounted for 37.1 % of the total household budget for single persons in the EU-27 in 2005. In contrast, spending on food and non-alcoholic beverages tended to be higher as a proportion of total expenditure among larger households, and the same was true for expenditure on clothing and footwear (which accounted for even greater shares if dependent children were present). A two adult household spent an average 4.9 % of their total budget on clothing and footwear, while the corresponding share for a two adult household with dependent children was 2.1 percentage points higher. Two adult households with dependent children also spent a higher share of their budget on transport (1.8 percentage points higher than the average for a two adult household without children); recreation and culture (1.5 points higher); education; and restaurants and hotels (both 1.3 points higher).

Employment status

Expenditure across households headed by a person working in a non-manual activity or a self-employed person was more than 30 % above the overall EU-27 average in 2005. Households headed by someone in manual work had a total budget that was 3 % higher than the average for all households (which includes information on households headed by unemployed or retired persons).

Table 1.43: Mean consumption expenditure by employment status of the reference person, 2005
(PPS)

	Total	Manual workers in industry & services	Non-manual workers in industry & services	Self-employed	Unem-ployed	Retired
EU-27 (1)	24 655	25 442	32 263	32 621	17 968	20 120
BE	30 048	28 499	36 508	:	16 741	24 012
BG	7 099	8 102	10 205	8 729	5 135	5 051
CZ	12 142	13 090	14 359	14 790	:	7 198
DK	24 062	26 414	30 050	26 282	:	:
DE	28 501	27 655	34 122	41 554	17 943	24 397
EE	10 848	10 675	16 045	15 378	6 986	6 657
IE	36 373	39 927	47 206	41 326	25 837	25 316
EL	30 975	31 449	44 510	39 691	23 926	23 375
ES	26 028	26 525	33 942	29 325	20 128	20 644
FR	27 886	27 287	35 524	35 038	20 078	22 686
IT	28 782	28 766	35 298	36 685	22 135	24 411
CY (2)	34 208	33 701	46 544	37 139	32 342	17 600
LV	10 589	10 589	15 905	13 537	5 735	5 239
LT	9 378	10 143	13 874	9 504	5 596	5 638
LU	51 932	47 073	59 758	66 495	35 441	45 674
HU	10 694	10 942	15 175	15 724	7 440	7 169
MT	28 605	30 198	39 245	34 275	15 156	19 570
NL (2)	29 368	31 269	34 335	41 961	21 112	22 811
AT	30 167	30 627	36 156	39 283	20 025	23 716
PL	10 594	10 271	15 186	12 401	6 504	8 138
PT	20 869	23 991	23 991	25 448	17 124	14 441
RO	5 324	:	:	:	:	:
SI	23 806	22 820	32 299	32 113	12 570	16 331
SK	10 772	11 633	13 924	14 215	6 766	6 741
FI	24 360	25 245	33 075	34 285	13 899	16 961
SE (2)	25 612	25 545	31 083 :		15 233	20 754
UK	31 959	30 938	41 664	41 524	21 575	22 148
HR	16 840	19 742	25 545	18 496	14 578	13 405
NO	29 106	:	:	29 222	19 214	22 121

(1) Estimates; unemployed and retired, unreliable.
(2) Unemployed, unreliable.

Source: Eurostat, mean consumption expenditure by employment status of the reference person (hbs_exp_t131)

Lithuania was the only Member State to report that households headed by a self-employed person spent less, on average, than those headed by a manual worker. Households headed by a non-manual worker spent more, on average, than those headed by a manual worker in every Member State except Portugal (where expenditure levels for these two groups were identical).

Unsurprisingly, households headed by someone in work tended to have higher levels of expenditure than those headed by an unemployed or retired person; this was the case in every Member State. The lowest relative spending among households headed by an unemployed person was recorded in Malta and Slovenia (53 % of the national average), while among households headed by a retired person spending was 49 % of the national average in Latvia. There were relatively high levels of expenditure in Luxembourg, Germany and Italy among households whose reference person was retired, as spending equated to at least 85 % of the national average.

Expenditure patterns among households headed by the unemployed and the retired were skewed in favour of necessities, as these two groups spent a higher proportion of their household budget on food and non-alcoholic beverages; housing, water, electricity, gas and other fuels. Households headed by an unemployed person reported the highest relative expenditure on alcoholic beverages and tobacco, as well as communications, with these items accounting for 3.3 % and 3.8 % of total expenditure (compared with EU-27 averages for all households of 2.4 % and 3.2 %).

Figure 1.50: Ratio of mean consumption expenditure per household for retired reference person compared with average for all households, 2005 (1)
(ratio, based on PPS series)

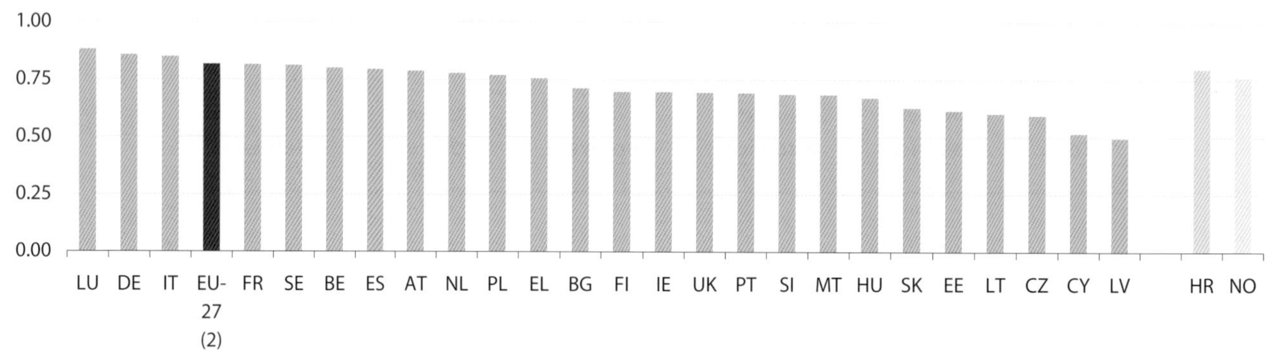

(1) Denmark and Romania, not available.
(2) Estimate; unreliable.

Source: Eurostat, mean consumption expenditure by employment status of the reference person (hbs_exp_t131

Table 1.44: Structure of consumption expenditure by employment status of the reference person, EU-27, 2005
(‰)

	Total	Manual workers in industry & services	Non-manual workers in industry & services	Self-employed	Unem-ployed	Retired
Food & non-alcoholic beverages	168	167	134	152	183	175
Alcoholic beverages, tobacco	24	29	20	21	33	20
Clothing & footwear	57	58	64	61	53	42
Housing, water, electricity, gas & other fuels	277	268	254	254	326	336
Furnishings, househ. equip. & maintenance	55	53	60	57	41	57
Health	34	24	29	27	26	49
Transport	119	136	137	134	99	89
Communications	32	35	33	32	38	27
Recreation & culture	83	84	96	84	69	78
Education	10	8	14	14	10	2
Restaurants & hotels	53	54	63	59	49	40
Miscellaneous goods & services	87	84	96	104	74	83

Source: Eurostat, structure of consumption expenditure by employment status of the reference person (hbs_str_t221)

Age

The information presented on the age breakdown of household consumption expenditure is strongly linked to life-cycle effects concerning incomes. The youngest age groups tend to display the lowest levels of expenditure as they usually receive relatively low incomes at the start of their working life, or are balancing studies and temporary and/or part-time work, or are unemployed (with youth unemployment rates particularly high in a number of Member States).

Income and expenditure tend to rise with age through the working years, such that towards the end of most people's working life their income is near or at its peak. Expenditure subsequently falls off once retirement is taken: the extent of this reduction depends to a large degree upon pension provisions, but also depends on the health of each individual and whether this restricts their capacity to consume a range of goods and services. However, with an ageing population, increasing life expectancy, and a higher number of healthy life years, it is likely that the overall consumption of those aged 60 or more will increase in the coming years.

Consumption expenditure for households whose head was aged less than 30 years was PPS 20 882 in the EU-27 in 2005, some 85 % of the average for all households. Spending was 11 % higher than the overall average among those households where the reference person was aged between 30 and 44 years, rising to 18 % higher when the reference person was aged between 45 and 59 years.

This pattern was generally reproduced across the majority of the EU-15 Member States, other than in Belgium and Finland (where households headed by a person aged between 30 and 44 years spent the most), or Sweden (where the same level of expenditure was recorded for households headed by someone aged 30 to 44 or someone aged 45 to 59). In contrast, expenditure levels for households headed by someone aged less than 30 were often above the national average in those Member States that joined the EU since 2004; some 25 % higher in Latvia, 19 % higher in Bulgaria, 18 % higher in Romania, at least 10 % higher in Cyprus, Lithuania, Hungary and Malta, and up to 10 % higher in Poland, Slovenia and Slovakia. This may reflect a number of different trends, including higher incomes for new jobs (in part, resulting from higher wages in foreign-owned enterprises), a greater variety of goods and services being on offer, a higher degree of brand and product awareness among the younger generations, rapid economic growth, and greater economic prosperity. A similar pattern was observed in Ireland, the only EU-15 Member State to report that households headed by someone aged less than 30 years old spent more (7 %) than the national average.

Table 1.45: Mean consumption expenditure by age of the reference person, 2005
(PPS)

	Total	<30 years	30-44 years	45-59 years	>=60 years
EU-27 (1)	24 655	20 882	27 467	29 018	19 606
BE	30 048	27 820	33 971	32 513	23 965
BG	7 099	8 435	8 922	8 145	5 212
CZ	12 142	11 962	14 551	13 812	8 293
DK	24 062	18 549	27 912	28 828	18 685
DE	28 501	19 121	30 218	34 207	25 428
EE	10 848	10 422	14 039	11 630	7 630
IE	36 373	38 889	42 513	43 039	22 634
EL	30 975	25 747	37 247	39 564	21 543
ES	26 028	23 095	27 928	31 830	20 464
FR	27 886	23 632	31 728	32 181	22 041
IT	28 782	24 955	31 594	34 558	23 405
CY	34 208	38 327	38 559	43 721	19 153
LV	10 589	13 206	12 902	11 723	6 313
LT	9 378	10 537	11 608	10 256	6 193
LU	51 932	44 541	53 941	59 954	43 792
HU	10 694	11 827	12 905	12 680	7 022
MT	28 605	33 060	31 315	34 051	19 483
NL	29 368	22 177	33 447	33 445	22 849
AT	30 167	26 197	33 404	35 516	23 603
PL	10 594	10 627	12 424	11 152	8 270
PT	20 869	20 688	23 750	25 159	14 838
RO	5 324	6 261	5 919	3 685	2 841
SI	23 806	25 230	27 486	26 912	16 322
SK	10 772	11 504	12 589	11 929	6 956
FI	24 360	19 735	30 868	28 184	17 853
SE	25 612	18 665	28 669	28 677	22 985
UK	31 959	28 918	35 742	38 198	24 334
HR	16 840	13 988	21 215	20 691	12 487
NO	29 106	20 637	33 500	32 373	24 566

(1) Estimates.

Source: Eurostat, mean consumption expenditure by age of the reference person (hbs_exp_t135)

Figure 1.51: Ratio of mean consumption expenditure per household for reference person aged 60 years and over compared with average for all households, 2005
(ratio, based on PPS series)

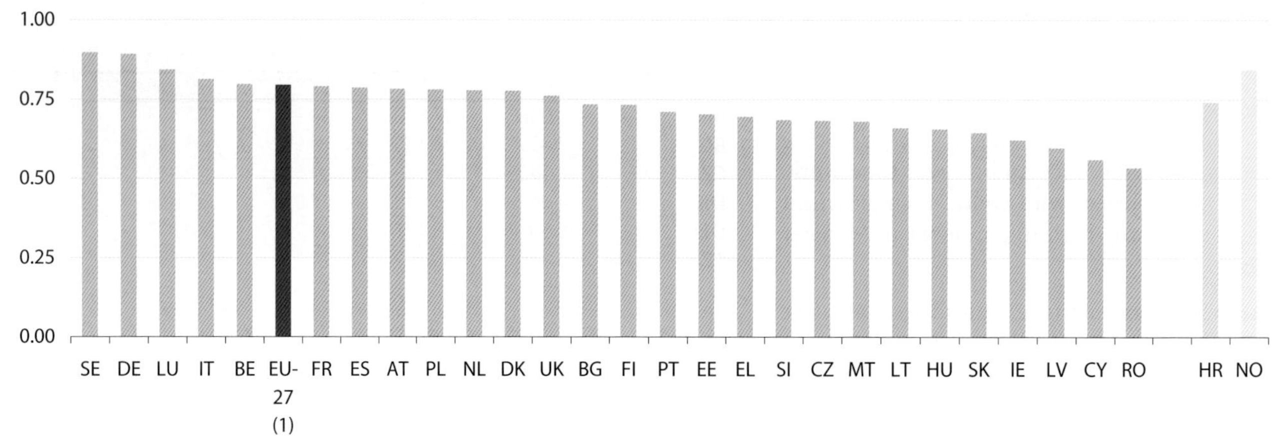

(1) Estimates.

Source: Eurostat, mean consumption expenditure by age of the reference person (hbs_exp_t135)

Table 1.46: Structure of consumption expenditure by age of the reference person, EU-27, 2005
(‰)

	Total	<30 years	30-44 years	45-59 years	>=60 years
Food & non-alcoholic beverages	168	131	143	150	165
Alcoholic beverages, tobacco	24	25	22	24	19
Clothing & footwear	57	56	56	49	36
Housing, water, electricity, gas & other fuels	277	237	226	230	289
Furnishings, househ. equip. & maintenance	55	45	50	48	49
Health	34	18	23	30	46
Transport	119	121	116	114	77
Communications	32	40	32	30	25
Recreation & culture	83	76	81	78	72
Education	10	12	11	10	2
Restaurants & hotels	53	58	52	49	36
Miscellaneous goods & services	87	74	81	80	74

Source: Eurostat, structure of consumption expenditure by age of the reference person (hbs_str_t225)

EU-27 households headed by someone aged less than 30 years old devoted a higher than average proportion of their spending to communications, restaurants and hotels, transport, education, and alcoholic beverages and tobacco. In contrast, a shift in consumption patterns for the older generations resulted in a lower proportion of their budget being spent on transport (in particular, purchases of cars and their associated running costs), clothing and footwear, recreation and culture, or restaurants and hotels. On the other hand, the older generations devoted much higher shares of their total expenditure to health services, as well as water, electricity, gas and other fuels.

Degree of urbanisation

EU-27 households living in densely populated areas (with more than 500 inhabitants per km²) spent 6 % more than households in intermediate areas (100-499 inhabitants per km²), and 9 % more than households in sparsely populated areas (with less than 100 inhabitants per km²) in 2005.

This pattern was prevalent in most of the southern, Mediterranean countries, and most of the Member States that joined the EU since 2004. Higher expenditure in urban areas may, in part, be related to inter-regional economic migratory patterns, for example, from the predominantly rural, agriculture-based, south of Italy to the industrial and service-orientated cities of the north. In Italy, the expenditure of households in densely-populated regions in 2005 was 77 % higher than in intermediate urbanised areas, and 58 % higher than in sparsely populated areas.

Household expenditure in the remaining EU-15 Member States was usually lower in urban areas than it was in intermediate or sparsely populated regions. This may be a result of those with the highest incomes choosing to move away from city centres, in search of an improved quality of life in suburbs or surrounding villages.

Table 1.47: Mean consumption expenditure by degree of urbanisation, 2005
(PPS)

	Total	Densely-populated (500+ inhab./km²)	Intermediate urbanised area (100-499 inhab./km²)	Sparsely populated (<100 inhab./km²)
EU-27 (1)	24 655	25 467	24 039	23 452
BE	30 048	29 337	31 500	27 960
BG	7 099	8 754	7 264	5 743
CZ	12 142	12 628	11 779	11 791
DK	24 062	23 601	24 480	24 278
DE	28 501	27 614	29 918	28 320
EE (2)	10 848	10 816	16 183	10 751
IE	36 373	:	:	:
EL	30 975	32 152	28 408	30 190
ES	26 028	28 147	25 853	22 467
FR	27 886	27 833	25 596	28 610
IT	28 782	28 148	15 905	17 825
CY	34 208	36 428	33 489	30 108
LV (2)	10 589	12 228	15 634	8 950
LT	9 378	11 501	:	7 825
LU	51 932	47 824	56 573	51 787
HU	10 694	11 900	10 448	9 548
MT	28 605	:	28 137	28 659
NL	29 368	:	:	:
AT	30 167	29 197	31 428	30 415
PL	10 594	11 437	10 511	9 666
PT	20 869	23 766	20 748	16 047
RO	5 324	:	:	:
SI	23 806	26 358	23 251	23 035
SK	10 772	11 569	10 517	10 441
FI	24 360	25 914	25 045	23 332
SE	25 612	26 380	27 858	24 732
UK	31 959	31 480	34 206	33 585
HR	16 840	19 424	17 453	14 849
NO	29 106	30 651	29 303	26 520

(1) Estimate for total; remaining data, unreliable.
(2) Unreliable for intermediate urbanised area.

Source: Eurostat, mean consumption expenditure by degree of urbanisation (hbs_exp_t136)

Figure 1.52: Ratio of mean consumption expenditure per household for densely populated areas compared with sparsely populated areas, 2005 (1)
(ratio, based on PPS series)

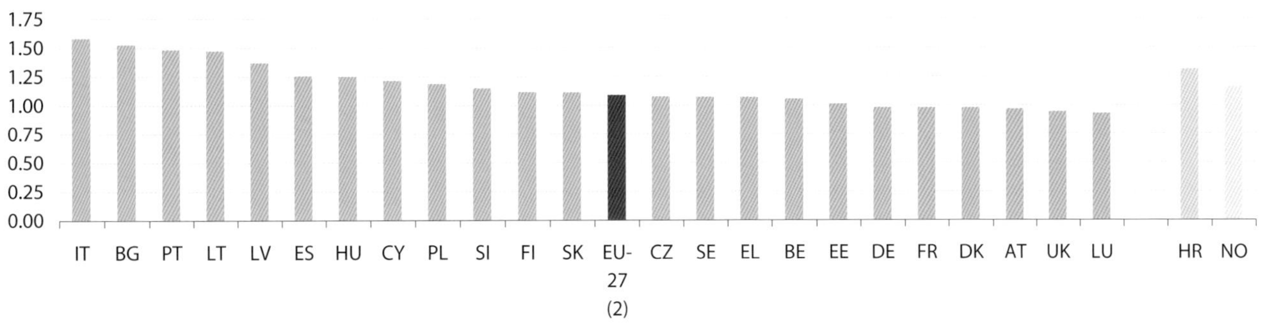

(1) Ireland, Malta, the Netherlands and Romania, not available.
(2) Estimate for total; remaining data, unreliable.

Source: Eurostat, mean consumption expenditure by degree of urbanisation (hbs_exp_t136)

Consumption expenditure may be expected to vary between rural and urban areas as a function of the ease with which consumers can access various goods and services. In rural areas choice may be limited, and retailers might charge more for their goods or services as they face less competition, have a smaller mass of customers, and (in the case of independent shops) may have less bargaining power with producers, suppliers or wholesalers. As a result, some consumers from sparsely populated areas may choose to defer or abandon making specific purchases, while others may prefer to make journeys to urban centres on an irregular basis. People living in rural areas are more likely to produce their own food (and perhaps other products), the value of which may not be completely captured by the household budget survey.

The structure of expenditure by degree of urbanisation shows that people living in sparsely populated areas of the EU-27 spent 16 % more of their budget on food and non-alcoholic beverages than those living in densely-populated urban areas. They also spent a considerably higher proportion of their household budget on transport (possibly travelling longer distances to work or to buy goods and services). In contrast, those living in urban areas devoted higher shares of their total expenditure to education; housing, water, electricity, gas and other fuels; restaurants and hotels; recreation and culture.

Table 1.48: Structure of consumption expenditure by degree of urbanisation, EU-27, 2005 (‰)

	Total	Densely-populated (500+ inhab./km²)	Intermediate urbanised area (100-499 inhab./km²)	Sparsely populated (<100 inhab./km²)
Food & non-alcoholic beverages	168	148	161	172
Alcoholic beverages, tobacco	24	23	23	24
Clothing & footwear	57	55	57	58
Housing, water, electricity, gas & other fuels	277	292	273	264
Furnishings, househ. equip. & maintenance	55	55	57	58
Health	34	35	33	34
Transport	119	117	129	130
Communications	32	33	31	31
Recreation & culture	83	88	85	82
Education	10	10	9	8
Restaurants & hotels	53	56	53	52
Miscellaneous goods & services	87	87	89	85

Source: Eurostat, structure of consumption expenditure by degree of urbanisation (hbs_str_t226)

PRICES AND INDIRECT TAXES

Prices show how much consumers pay for a particular good or service. This section starts with an analysis of price changes for goods and services over time – as measured by harmonised indices of consumer prices (HICPs) that reflect price inflation. The evolution of consumer prices can be used to assess price stability – a key objective for the European Central Bank (ECB).

While consumers may reflect on a loss of living standards as a result of price inflation, they are also interested in comparing specific prices of individual goods and services at a particular moment in time, especially during periods of mixed economic fortunes when they look to tighten their purse strings, as well as when making big-ticket purchases. Price levels can differ between brands, retailers, geographical regions, or countries, and by identifying the best offer available, consumers can potentially make considerable savings and improve their welfare. Price level indices can be used at a more aggregated level to generally compare the cost of living in different cities and countries.

At a practical level, price comparisons of food across the EU have been made easier as EU law requires supermarkets to publish the unit price of a product (how much it costs per kilogram or per litre, for example), to make it easier to compare different offers and to decide which product is the best value for money. In a similar vein, banks and other financial services have to present information on loans and credit to consumers in a standardised way, providing information on the annual percentage rate of interest.

A survey of consumer protection in the internal market conducted in early 2008 for the European Commission shows that price is the most important criteria influencing consumers when they decide which non-food items to buy. When allowed to give up to three different answers, some 75 % of EU-27 consumers cited price as one of the aspects that most frequently influences their choice.

Price inflation

Increases in the overall price of consumer goods and services are usually referred to as inflation, and when expressed in terms of a percentage change as the inflation rate. The inflation rate is used as a leading indicator to determine monetary policy management, with price stability defined by the ECB as an annual increase in the harmonised index of consumer prices for the euro area of close to but below 2 % (over the medium-term). For consumers, the main interest in the inflation rate is that it provides information on how quickly prices are eroding their standard of living, given that incomes remain unchanged.

Compared with historical trends, consumer price indices in the EU have only risen at a moderate pace in the last couple of decades. The EU inflation rate was reduced during the 1990s such that by the end of the decade in 1999 it stood at 1.2 %, after which the pace at which prices were rising quickened somewhat during the period between 2001 and 2007 to reach 2.3 % (note that the EU aggregate is made up of a moving aggregate in terms of its geographical composition, reflecting changes in the membership of the EU). Oil and commodity price increases during 2007 and 2008 saw the inflation rate rise fairly rapidly.

Most of the Member States that joined the EU since 2004 witnessed considerable reductions in their inflation rates on the basis of a comparison between the rates in 1997 and those in 2007, although several recorded a renewed upward trend towards the end of this period. Indeed, Slovakia, Malta and Romania were alone in reporting a reduction in inflation rates between 2006 and 2007, while inflation rates fell in eight of the EU-15 Member States in 2007.

Malta recorded by far the lowest (0.7 %) inflation rate in 2007. The majority of Member States had inflation rates within +/- 0.7 percentage points of the EU-27 average of 2.3 %, although Slovenia, Romania, the three Baltic States, Bulgaria and Hungary, all reported inflation rates that were over 3.0 %, with the highest rate in Latvia (10.1 %).

Table 1.49: All-items harmonised index of consumer prices (inflation rate), annual growth rate
(%)

	1997	1998	1999	2000	2001	2002	2003	2004	2005	2006	2007
EU (1)	1.7	1.3	1.2	1.9	2.2	2.1	2.0	2.0	2.2	2.2	2.3
BE	1.5	0.9	1.1	2.7	2.4	1.6	1.5	1.9	2.5	2.3	1.8
BG	:	18.7	2.6	10.3	7.4	5.8	2.3	6.1	6.0	7.4	7.6
CZ	8.0	9.7	1.8	3.9	4.5	1.4	-0.1	2.6	1.6	2.1	3.0
DK	2.0	1.3	2.1	2.7	2.3	2.4	2.0	0.9	1.7	1.9	1.7
DE	1.5	0.6	0.6	1.4	1.9	1.4	1.0	1.8	1.9	1.8	2.3
EE	9.3	8.8	3.1	3.9	5.6	3.6	1.4	3.0	4.1	4.4	6.7
IE	1.3	2.1	2.5	5.3	4.0	4.7	4.0	2.3	2.2	2.7	2.9
EL	5.4	4.5	2.1	2.9	3.7	3.9	3.4	3.0	3.5	3.3	3.0
ES	1.9	1.8	2.2	3.5	2.8	3.6	3.1	3.1	3.4	3.6	2.8
FR	1.3	0.7	0.6	1.8	1.8	1.9	2.2	2.3	1.9	1.9	1.6
IT	1.9	2.0	1.7	2.6	2.3	2.6	2.8	2.3	2.2	2.2	2.0
CY	3.3	2.3	1.1	4.9	2.0	2.8	4.0	1.9	2.0	2.2	2.2
LV	8.1	4.3	2.1	2.6	2.5	2.0	2.9	6.2	6.9	6.6	10.1
LT	10.3	5.4	1.5	1.1	1.6	0.3	-1.1	1.2	2.7	3.8	5.8
LU	1.4	1.0	1.0	3.8	2.4	2.1	2.5	3.2	3.8	3.0	2.7
HU	18.5	14.2	10.0	10.0	9.1	5.2	4.7	6.8	3.5	4.0	7.9
MT	3.9	3.7	2.3	3.0	2.5	2.6	1.9	2.7	2.5	2.6	0.7
NL	1.9	1.8	2.0	2.3	5.1	3.9	2.2	1.4	1.5	1.7	1.6
AT	1.2	0.8	0.5	2.0	2.3	1.7	1.3	2.0	2.1	1.7	2.2
PL (2)	15.0	11.8	7.2	10.1	5.3	1.9	0.7	3.6	2.2	1.3	2.6
PT	1.9	2.2	2.2	2.8	4.4	3.7	3.3	2.5	2.1	3.0	2.4
RO	154.8	59.1	45.8	45.7	34.5	22.5	15.3	11.9	9.1	6.6	4.9
SI	8.3	7.9	6.1	8.9	8.6	7.5	5.7	3.7	2.5	2.5	3.8
SK	6.0	6.7	10.4	12.2	7.2	3.5	8.4	7.5	2.8	4.3	1.9
FI	1.2	1.3	1.3	2.9	2.7	2.0	1.3	0.1	0.8	1.3	1.6
SE	1.8	1.0	0.5	1.3	2.7	1.9	2.3	1.0	0.8	1.5	1.7
UK	1.8	1.6	1.3	0.8	1.2	1.3	1.4	1.3	2.1	2.3	2.3
TR	85.6	82.1	61.4	53.2	56.8	47.0	25.3	10.1	8.1	9.3	8.8
IS	1.8	1.3	2.1	4.4	6.6	5.3	1.4	2.3	1.4	4.6	3.6
NO	2.6	2.0	2.1	3.0	2.7	0.8	2.0	0.6	1.5	2.5	0.7
CH	:	:	:	:	:	:	:	:	:	1.0	0.8

(1) Moving EU aggregate (EU-15 up to 2004; EU-25 up to 2006; EU-27 for 2007); estimates, 1997 and 1998.
(2) Estimates, 1997 and 1998.

Source: Eurostat, harmonised indices of consumer prices - annual data (prc_hicp_aind)

Figure 1.53: All-items harmonised index of consumer prices (inflation rate), average annual growth rate, 1997-2007
(%)

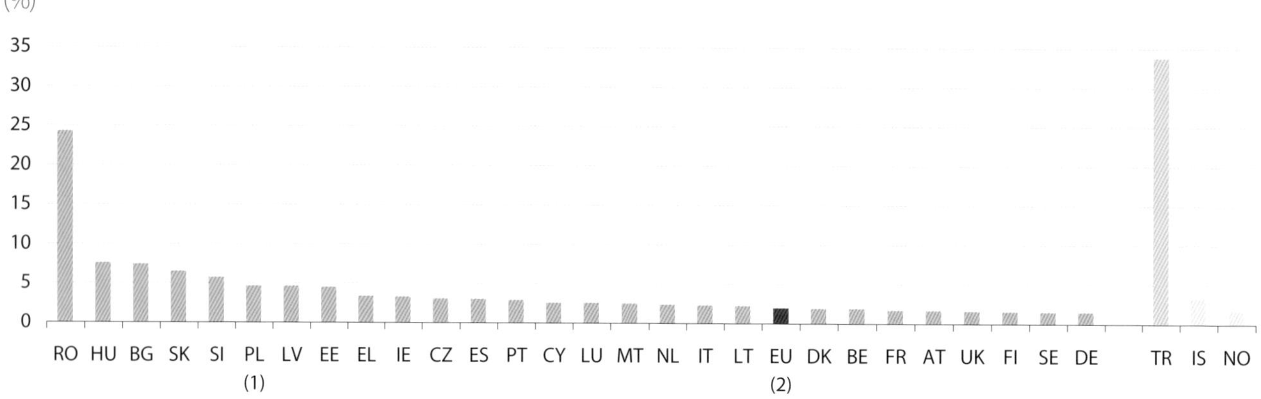

(1) Estimate, 1997.
(2) Moving EU aggregate (EU-15 up to 2004; EU-25 up to 2006; EU-27 for 2007); estimate, 1997.

Source: Eurostat, harmonised indices of consumer prices - annual data (prc_hicp_aind)

Eurostat publishes around 100 HICP sub-indices that allow the overall inflation rate to be broken down into its constituent indices. These cover broad categories of goods and services, for example, the first level of the COICOP (which is used to delineate the individual markets that are used to delineate the chapters in the second half of this publication), as well as more detailed indices for specific goods and services.

Using the first level of the COICOP, the highest price increases in the EU during the period 1996 to 2007 were recorded for education (on average 4.3 % per annum); alcoholic beverages and tobacco (3.7 %); and restaurants and hotels (3.1 %). At the bottom end of the ranking, the price of recreation and culture rose by just 0.4 % per annum, while there was no change in the price of clothing and footwear, while the price of communications fell by 2.4 % per annum. In general terms, relatively high price increases were often recorded for a broad range of non-durable goods and services, which also displayed some of the largest fluctuations in price developments between countries. In contrast, there was less variation in the price evolution of consumer durables between countries, with the price of some goods falling.

Figure 1.54: Evolution of harmonised indices of consumer prices, average annual index, EU (1) (1996=100)

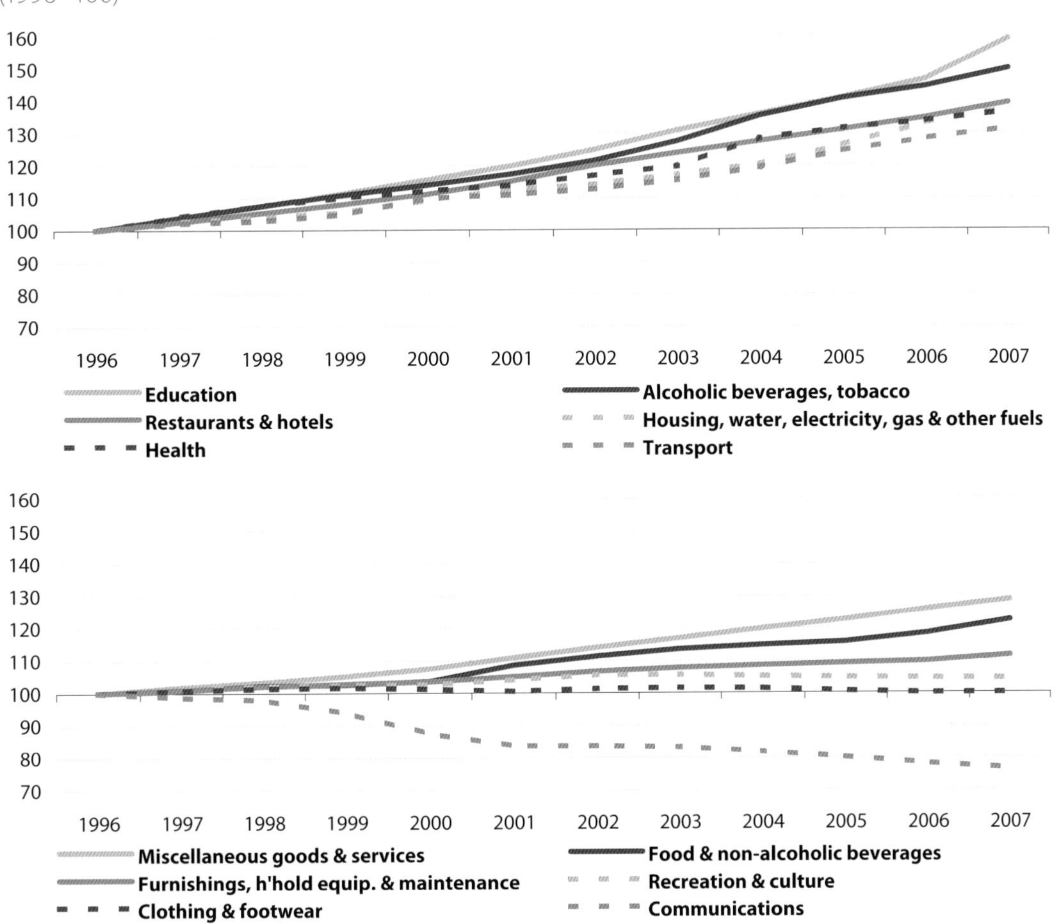

(1) Moving EU aggregate (EU-15 up to 2004; EU-25 up to 2006; EU-27 for 2007); estimates, 1996-1998.

Source: Eurostat, harmonised indices of consumer prices - annual data (prc_hicp_aind)

Table 1.50: Harmonised indices of consumer prices, annual growth rate, EU (1)
(%)

	1997	1998	1999	2000	2001	2002	2003	2004	2005	2006	2007
Total - all items	1.7	1.3	1.2	1.9	2.2	2.1	2.0	2.0	2.2	2.2	2.3
Food & non-alcoholic beverages	0.8	1.4	0.3	1.0	4.7	2.5	1.9	1.1	0.8	2.3	3.5
Alcoholic beverages, tobacco	3.9	3.5	3.2	2.7	3.0	3.5	4.9	6.1	4.0	2.6	3.8
Clothing & footwear	0.8	0.6	0.2	-0.5	-0.7	0.8	0.2	-0.2	-0.8	-0.6	0.1
Housing, water, elec., gas & oth. fuels	2.7	1.2	1.5	3.6	2.9	1.5	2.6	2.7	4.9	5.4	3.3
Furnish., househ. equip. & mainten.	1.0	1.1	0.7	0.6	1.5	1.5	1.0	0.7	0.6	0.6	1.6
Health	4.2	3.3	2.3	1.9	1.6	2.7	2.3	7.1	2.4	1.7	2.2
Transport	2.1	0.7	2.0	4.8	1.0	1.6	2.5	3.2	4.3	3.0	2.5
Communications	-1.3	-0.8	-4.1	-6.8	-4.4	-0.1	-0.5	-1.8	-2.1	-2.5	-2.0
Recreation & culture	1.3	0.8	0.4	0.1	1.4	1.4	0.0	-0.4	-0.3	-0.3	-0.1
Education	3.4	3.9	3.8	3.8	3.7	4.2	4.7	3.8	3.7	4.0	8.6
Restaurants & hotels	2.5	2.7	2.6	2.9	3.6	4.3	3.2	2.9	2.8	2.8	3.4
Miscellaneous goods & services	1.9	1.4	1.8	2.1	3.1	2.8	2.5	2.5	2.3	2.6	2.3

(1) Moving EU aggregate (EU-15 up to 2004; EU-25 up to 2006; EU-27 for 2007); estimates, 1997 and 1998.

Source: Eurostat, harmonised indices of consumer prices - annual data (prc_hicp_aind)

The long-term evolution of prices may be contrasted with more recent events, in particular the volatile evolution of oil and gas prices, and rising food prices, some of which are reflected in the ten highest price increases recorded in the EU between 2006 and 2007 (for example, solid fuels, vegetables, and electricity). A similar analysis for the ten goods and services in the EU where prices fell at their most rapid pace was dominated by consumer durables and semi-durables, and in particular, those related to communications, media and technology (such as computers, telephones, cameras and televisions). This pattern could be observed both in terms of developments (between 1997 and 2007), as well as over a more recent timeframe between 2006 and 2007.

Figure 1.55: Harmonised indices of consumer prices, average annual growth rate, EU, 1997-2007 (1)
(%)

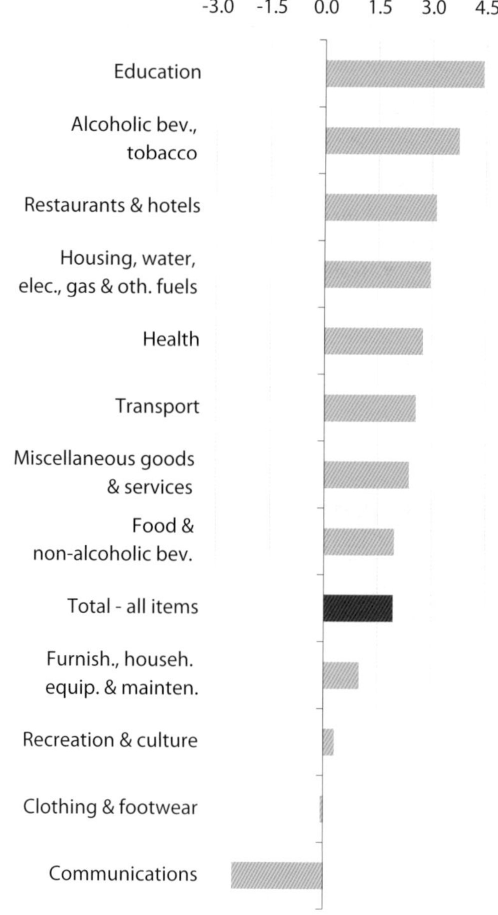

(1) Moving EU aggregate (EU-15 up to 2004; EU-25 up to 2006; EU-27 for 2007); estimates, 1997 and 1998.

Source: Eurostat, harmonised indices of consumer prices - annual data (prc_hicp_aind)

Table 1.51: Harmonised indices of consumer prices, average annual growth rates, EU (1)
(%)

	1997-2002	2002-2007	2006-2007	1997-2007
Total - all items	1.7	2.1	2.3	1.9
Food & non-alcoholic beverages	2.0	1.9	3.5	1.9
Food	2.1	2.0	3.5	2.1
Non-alcoholic beverages	0.4	1.3	2.8	0.8
Alcoholic beverages, tobacco	3.2	4.3	3.8	3.7
Alcoholic beverages	1.2	0.8	1.6	1.0
Tobacco	4.8	6.7	5.4	5.8
Clothing & footwear	0.1	-0.3	0.1	-0.1
Clothing	-0.2	-0.4	-0.1	-0.3
Footwear including repair	1.2	0.2	0.5	0.7
Housing, water, electricity, gas & other fuels	2.1	3.8	3.3	3.0
Actual rentals for housing	1.9	2.2	2.4	2.0
Maintenance & repair of the dwelling	2.3	3.1	4.7	2.7
Water supply; misc. serv. relating to dwelling	2.6	3.6	4.0	3.1
Electricity, gas & other fuels	2.3	5.9	3.6	4.1
Furnishings, househ. equip. & maintenance	1.1	0.9	1.6	1.0
Furniture, furnish., carpets, floor cover.	1.3	1.2	2.0	1.2
Household textiles	0.6	-0.2	-0.1	0.2
Household appliances	-0.5	-1.0	-0.2	-0.7
Glassware, tableware & househ. utensils	1.1	0.8	1.9	1.0
Tools & equip. for house & garden	0.3	0.5	1.5	0.4
Goods & services for routine maintenance	2.2	1.9	2.5	2.1
Health	2.3	3.1	2.2	2.7
Transport	2.0	3.1	2.5	2.5
Purchase of vehicles	0.4	0.8	1.0	0.6
Operation of personal transport equip.	2.7	4.3	3.1	3.5
Transport services	2.8	3.4	3.3	3.1
Communications	-3.3	-1.8	-2.0	-2.5
Postal services (5)	1.5	2.5	2.6	2.0
Telephone & telefax equipment	-5.8	-15.4	-12.6	-10.7
Telephone & telefax services	-4.3	-1.0	-1.0	-2.6
Recreation & culture	0.8	-0.2	-0.1	0.3
Audio-vis., photo., info. process. equip.	-5.9	-8.4	-9.6	-7.2
Oth. durables for recreation & culture	1.7	1.6	1.3	1.6
Oth. recreational equip., garden & pets	0.4	-0.3	0.7	0.1
Recreational & cultural services	2.4	2.7	3.0	2.6
Newspapers, books & stationery	2.4	2.0	2.2	2.2
Package holidays	4.7	1.2	1.9	2.9
Education	3.8	5.0	8.6	4.4
Restaurants & hotels	3.2	3.0	3.4	3.1
Catering services	3.0	3.0	3.5	3.0
Accommodation services	4.1	2.9	2.9	3.5
Miscellaneous goods & services	2.3	2.5	2.3	2.4
Personal care	2.1	1.4	2.0	1.8
Personal effects n.e.c.	0.7	2.2	3.8	1.5
Social protection	:	3.6	2.3	:
Insurance	3.5	2.3	2.7	2.9
Financial services n.e.c.	3.1	2.8	0.0	2.9
Other services n.e.c.	2.6	3.9	3.2	3.2

(1) Moving EU aggregate (EU-15 up to 2004; EU-25 up to 2006; EU-27 for 2007); estimates, 1997.

Source: Eurostat, harmonised indices of consumer prices - annual data (prc_hicp_aind)

Table 1.52: Highest price increases, average annual growth rates, EU (1)
(%)

	1997-2007
Liquid fuels	7.2
Maintenance & repair of other major durables for recreation & culture	6.7
Tobacco	5.8
Gas	5.3
Heat energy	4.5
Education	4.4
Fuels and lubricants for personal transport equipment	4.3
Maintenance and repair of personal transport equipment	3.6
Other imputed rentals	3.6
Accommodation services	3.5
	2006-2007
Maintenance & repair of other major durables for recreation & culture	34.9
Education	8.6
Solid fuels	7.1
Passenger transport by sea and inland waterway	6.6
Tobacco	5.4
Jewellery, clocks and watches	5.4
Vegetables	5.1
Services for the maintenance and repair of the dwelling	5.0
Other insurance	4.9
Electricity	4.7

(1) Moving EU aggregate (EU-15 up to 2004; EU-25 up to 2006; EU-27 for 2007); estimates, 1997; ranking based on the most detailed level of COICOP available.

Source: Eurostat, harmonised indices of consumer prices - annual data (prc_hicp_aind)

Table 1.53: Largest price reductions, average annual rates of change, EU (1)
(%)

	1997-2007
Garments	-0.4
Household appliances	-0.7
Equipment for sport, camping and open-air recreation	-1.0
Recording media	-1.7
Games, toys and hobbies	-1.8
Telephone and telefax services	-2.6
Equip. for the reception, recording & reproduction of sound & pictures	-6.6
Photographic and cinematographic equipment and optical instruments	-8.0
Telephone and telefax equipment	-10.7
Information processing equipment	-16.4
	2006-2007
Passenger transport by air	-0.4
Liquid fuels	-0.6
Equipment for sport, camping and open-air recreation	-0.8
Telephone and telefax services	-1.0
Games, toys and hobbies	-1.5
Recording media	-2.2
Equip. for the reception, recording & reproduction of sound & pictures	-10.7
Telephone and telefax equipment	-12.6
Information processing equipment	-15.4
Photographic and cinematographic equipment and optical instruments	-16.0

(1) Moving EU aggregate (EU-15 up to 2004; EU-25 up to 2006; EU-27 for 2007); estimates, 1997; ranking based on the most detailed level of COICOP available.

Source: Eurostat, harmonised indices of consumer prices - annual data (prc_hicp_aind)

When questioned on their attitudes to price changes, exactly half of all respondents to a survey conducted in 2006 agreed that the single market had had a positive effect on the price of products and services in the EU-25. Around three quarters of those surveyed in Denmark and Sweden agreed there had been a positive effect on prices, while the lowest rates of agreement were reported in Latvia and France, less than four out of every ten people.

Some 39 % of EU-25 respondents to the same survey were aware that different prices existed for the same goods and services in other Member States. This proportion ranged from a high of 76 % in Luxembourg, and between 50 % and 60 % of respondents in Slovakia, Finland, Belgium, the Netherlands and Malta, to lows of less than one third of all respondents in Spain, Italy, the United Kingdom and Hungary.

A regional analysis of consumer price developments in France shows that the price of a particular basket of goods in French supermarkets and hypermarkets rose by between 2.7 % in Lorraine and 4.2 % in Rhône Alpes between April 2007 and April 2008 – the French capital was among a group of three regions that recorded the second highest price increases, while the four regions that recorded the lowest consumer price increases were all situated in the east of the country.

Table 1.54: Consumer attitudes to price changes, 2006
(% of respondents)

	Agree that the single market has had positive effect on price of products and services	Have noticed different prices for the same goods and services between Member States
EU-25	50	39
BE	44	56
BG	:	:
CZ	67	45
DK	75	46
DE	45	41
EE	43	41
IE	67	42
EL	47	49
ES	44	29
FR	39	47
IT	52	31
CY	53	45
LV	31	45
LT	46	37
LU	46	76
HU	49	32
MT	49	51
NL	52	53
AT	42	42
PL	47	36
PT	50	43
RO	:	:
SI	63	40
SK	50	58
FI	56	56
SE	74	44
UK	61	32

Source: 'Internal market - opinions and experiences of citizens in EU-25', Special Eurobarometer 254, European Commission

Price levels

While the euro has increased price transparency, there remain considerable price differences across the whole of the EU for a variety of different goods and services. These may be attributed to a range of influences, including a lack of competition, regulatory frameworks, retail structures, as well as variations in demand and cost structures.

Consumers may be interested in comparing prices, especially when they are on holiday or making cross-border trips. However, the reality of most people's lives means that the opportunity cost of making an extensive comparison of prices is too high, while there is little chance to choose in which country to make other types of purchases. For example, it is difficult to imagine consumers (other than those who live very close to a neighbouring country) making cross-border

Table 1.55: Regional price evolution in supermarkets and hypermarkets, France, April 2007-April 2008
(%)

	Lowest price increases
Lorraine	2.7
Franche-Comté	3.0
Alsace	3.0
Picardie	3.2
Poitou-Charantes	3.2
	Highest price increases
Rhône Alpes	4.2
Auvergne	4.0
Champagne-Ardenne	4.0
Île de France	4.0
Basse-Normandie	3.9

Source: LSA, 15 May 2008 - No. 2045 (www.lsa.fr)

Table 1.56: Industrial countries' effective exchange rates
(1999=100)

	1999	2003	2007
BE/LU	100.0	103.5	106.5
BG	100.0	101.1	100.8
CZ	100.0	116.0	133.2
DK	100.0	103.1	106.2
DE	100.0	104.5	109.3
EE	100.0	100.2	100.2
IE	100.0	104.6	110.7
EL	100.0	103.2	106.2
ES	100.0	104.2	107.2
FR	100.0	104.0	108.0
IT	100.0	104.9	109.3
CY	100.0	99.6	99.9
LV	100.0	97.9	89.6
LT	100.0	123.8	123.9
LU (1)	:	:	:
HU	100.0	100.0	100.8
MT	100.0	100.0	99.3
NL	100.0	103.1	105.7
AT	100.0	102.8	105.8
PL	100.0	96.3	111.9
PT	100.0	102.3	104.8
RO	100.0	43.4	48.8
SI	100.0	83.2	81.1
SK	100.0	106.5	130.9
FI	100.0	104.6	108.7
SE	100.0	100.4	103.1
UK	100.0	98.9	105.5
TR	100.0	26.7	26.1
NO	100.0	107.0	109.5
CH	100.0	109.6	106.6
JP	100.0	96.3	84.8
US	100.0	99.7	86.2

(1) Included with Belgium.

Source: Eurostat, industrial countries' effective exchange rates including new Member States - annual data (ert_eff_ic_a)

price comparisons for perishable goods (a litre of milk), and there is no point in comparing cross-border prices for a range of services which have to be consumed at the point-of-use (a train journey to work, or household rubbish collections). On the other hand, there is the possibility for consumers to make price comparisons for big-ticket items (such as buying new furniture or large household electrical items), comparing different retailers in their home country, extending this to see if it would be economically advantageous to order the item from a neighbouring country, or alternatively trying to find out if it is possible to make the purchase directly from the manufacturer, or over the Internet.

While prices, per se, may remain unchanged in two economies, if the two areas do not share the same currency it is possible that exchange rate movements will affect any price comparison over time. The nominal effective exchange rate measures changes in the value of a currency against a trade-weighted basket of currencies; a rise in the index means a strengthening of the currency. During the period 1999 to 2007 most European countries saw their currencies strengthen, as Romania, Slovenia and Latvia were the only Member States that experienced a significant weakening of their currencies. The change in effective exchange rates on a global level means that during the period 1999 to 2007 it became increasingly attractive for Europeans to purchase items from Japan or the United States.

The index of purchasing power of the euro aims to adjust consumer price indices for movements in euro exchange rates. An increase in the index means that the purchasing power of the euro has fallen.

Table 1.58: Correction coefficients in the capital cities of the European Union, 1 July
(Brussels=100)

	Total		Total excluding rents	
	1996	2006	1996	2006
Bruxelles / Brussels	100	100	100	100
Sofia	:	66	:	63
Praha	:	81	:	73
Kobenhavn	125	139	133	134
Berlin	111	99	107	100
Tallinn	:	80	:	75
Dublin	92	122	93	113
Athinai	86	95	89	92
Madrid	91	100	88	93
Paris	116	117	106	103
Roma	97	111	95	101
Nicosia	:	90	:	97
Riga	:	79	:	72
Vilnius	:	71	:	65
Luxembourg	100	100	100	100
Budapest	:	90	:	79
Valletta	:	85	:	90
Amsterdam	105	112	97	102
Wien	115	108	106	103
Warszaw	:	81	:	74
Lisboa	84	92	80	92
Bucureşti	:	76	:	68
Bratislava	:	81	:	75
Ljubljana	:	88	:	82
Helsinki	117	118	124	113
Stockholm	118	117	121	111
London	115	143	91	110

Source: Eurostat, correction coefficients in the European Union capitals, from 2004 (prc_colc_nat)

Table 1.57: Index of purchasing power of the euro
(1996=100)

	1996	2001	2006
EU-25 (1)	100.0	114.0	122.4
BE	100.0	106.1	116.9
BG	100.0	91.1	117.5
CZ	100.0	132.6	171.8
DK	100.0	109.4	119.3
DE	100.0	103.7	112.1
EE	100.0	131.4	154.6
IE	100.0	116.8	136.6
EL	100.0	107.6	127.5
ES	100.0	109.0	128.4
FR	100.0	105.2	116.4
IT	100.0	112.2	126.5
CY	100.0	117.5	133.5
LV	100.0	151.3	154.5
LT	100.0	171.6	190.5
LU	100.0	107.0	123.5
HU	100.0	134.8	165.7
MT	100.0	132.2	140.3
NL	100.0	110.5	122.7
AT	100.0	104.4	113.8
PL	100.0	148.9	154.4
PT	100.0	111.5	128.8
RO	100.0	174.7	236.7
SI (1)	100.0	115.6	126.9
SK	100.0	135.0	202.9
FI	100.0	107.7	113.7
SE	100.0	99.0	106.7
UK	100.0	139.9	138.6
IS	100.0	113.6	131.1
NO	100.0	115.0	123.8

(1) 2005 instead of 2006.

Source: Eurostat, index of purchasing power of the euro/ECU - annual data (mny_ppe_a)

Figure 1.56: Correction coefficients in the European Union, 1 July 2007
(Belgium=100)

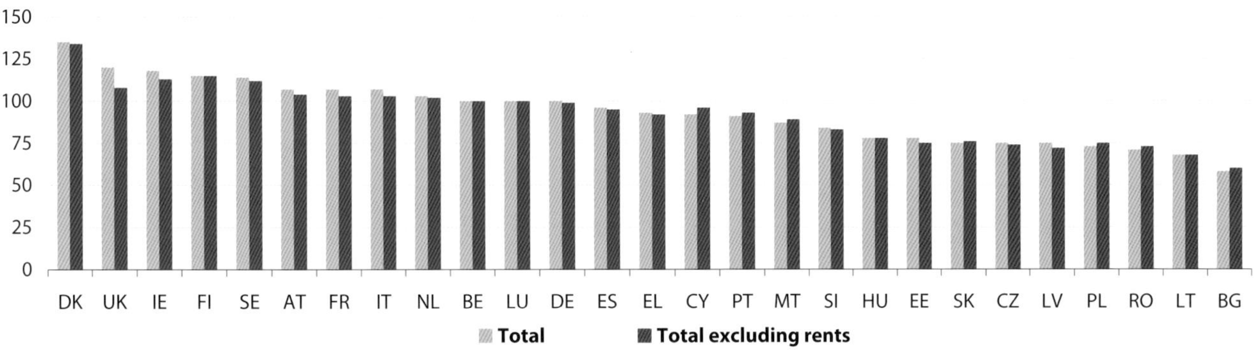

Source: Eurostat, correction coefficients in the European Union, from 2004 (prc_colc_nat)

Correction coefficients are used within the European institutions to ensure equality of purchasing power of salaries and pensions between members of staff. These figures have a more general interest, insofar as they can also be used to gauge where the cost of living is highest/lowest. Note that the data presented refer to a single reference period of July each year and are compared against a base value of Belgium=100. As such, the relative cost of living in Denmark was 35 % higher than in Belgium, while the other Scandinavian Member States, the United Kingdom and Ireland were also relatively expensive places to live in July 2007.

A similar analysis can be performed for capital cities and this shows a similar set of results with the most expensive cities including London, Dublin and the Scandinavian capitals. The cost of housing raised the cost of living in most capital cities (in relation to Brussels), nowhere more so than in London or Paris.

Price comparisons in their simplest form are based on a conversion into a common currency – which has been made easier for many Europeans following the introduction of the euro. However, price level differences can also be measured through the use of indices based on purchasing power rather than exchange rates. The ratio between purchasing power parities (PPPs) and the exchange rate can be calculated for each country, and then this ratio compared with some benchmark, which for the purposes of this publication is the average for the EU-27, which is then given a value = 100. Price level indices that are above 100 indicate relatively expensive countries, while those under 100 show countries that are relatively cheap. Price level indices should only be used to compare the price levels of a particular good or service across countries, and should neither be employed to compare prices across a range of different goods and services, nor to compare prices over time.

Table 1.59: Comparative price levels of final consumption by private households including indirect taxes
(EU-27=100)

	1997	2002	2007
BE (1)	105.8	101.5	105.4
BG	34.0	40.8	46.0
CZ	44.4	57.1	62.6
DK	131.6	133.8	136.9
DE	109.6	106.6	103.2
EE	50.8	60.8	71.3
IE	113.0	125.2	126.0
EL	87.6	80.2	88.6
ES	86.9	84.6	93.0
FR (1)	112.0	103.5	106.7
IT	99.7	102.7	102.9
CY	86.6	89.1	87.7
LV	47.8	57.0	65.0
LT	43.2	54.2	59.7
LU	106.6	102.1	105.1
HU	46.4	57.4	65.7
MT	68.7	74.6	73.2
NL	103.4	102.9	103.1
AT	107.1	103.4	100.0
PL	51.8	61.2	63.4
PT	82.5	86.3	84.6
RO	34.7	43.0	64.7
SI	72.4	74.4	76.9
SK	41.6	44.8	63.0
FI	125.0	123.9	121.4
SE	131.6	121.7	116.4
UK	107.6	117.1	112.3
HR	:	:	69.5
MK	:	:	43.0
TR	:	51.6	72.2
IS	120.8	134.6	146.0
NO	136.6	151.2	137.5
CH	135.8	146.7	125.7
JP (2)	158.8	156.3	109.1
US (2)	100.0	119.7	91.6

(1) Break in series, 2005.
(2) 2006 instead of 2007.

Source: Eurostat, structural indicators (strind_t)

Table 1.60: Comparative price level indices, 2007
(EU-27=100)

	Household final consumption	Consumer goods	of which: Non-durables	Semi-durables	Durables	Consumer services
BE	105.4	104.2	105.5	108.3	99.6	107.4
BG	46.0	65.7	63.5	69.7	75.6	31.8
CZ	62.6	80.4	75.9	94.8	89.3	47.5
DK	136.9	131.4	135.1	117.2	137.3	143.2
DE	103.2	104.1	108.7	101.9	95.2	103.4
EE	71.3	78.6	73.6	93.3	86.2	65.5
IE	126.0	115.7	124.9	97.0	113.0	135.2
EL	88.6	91.7	88.9	100.6	96.6	85.4
ES	93.0	89.6	86.3	95.8	98.8	95.2
FR	106.7	98.3	99.8	96.2	97.9	116.3
IT	102.9	104.4	106.5	102.7	103.0	101.3
CY	87.7	98.0	98.1	98.6	100.0	77.4
LV	65.0	74.5	68.9	94.1	85.3	55.6
LT	59.7	71.6	66.7	85.5	83.3	46.5
LU	105.1	99.8	100.2	104.2	97.4	110.7
HU	65.7	81.1	77.7	91.5	88.1	51.6
MT	73.2	89.5	82.2	99.0	110.2	59.9
NL	103.1	100.1	99.4	100.2	105.5	106.2
AT	100.0	102.3	104.4	102.5	99.1	97.0
PL	63.4	75.6	70.8	92.5	87.4	52.1
PT	84.6	91.9	88.1	92.7	108.7	77.8
RO	64.7	75.3	73.0	86.6	78.4	54.0
SI	63.0	82.4	78.3	94.3	93.5	46.2
SK	76.9	87.2	84.2	99.1	90.4	67.7
FI	121.4	113.9	114.2	113.6	115.7	129.7
SE	116.4	113.4	117.2	117.3	101.0	119.3
UK	112.3	111.4	119.8	100.3	104.3	113.2
HR	69.5	86.6	81.8	103.2	94.8	55.0
MK	43.0	58.6	53.5	69.4	80.2	28.4
TR	72.2	87.1	87.4	79.6	96.2	57.5
IS	146.0	140.6	142.4	148.1	132.8	161.2
NO	137.5	140.5	150.0	128.2	127.5	137.7
CH	125.7	106.6	110.7	105.9	93.2	141.5

Source: Eurostat, price level indices (prc_ppp_ind)

Table 1.61: Comparative price level indices, 2007

	Highest	(EU-27 =100)	Lowest	(EU-27 =100)	Coefficient of variation (%)
Food & non-alcoholic beverages	Denmark	142.4	Bulgaria	61.1	22.0
Alcoholic beverages, tobacco	Ireland	178.2	Lithuania	55.5	35.0
Clothing & footwear	Sweden	121.1	Bulgaria	70.9	10.2
Housing, water, elec., gas & oth. fuels (1)	Denmark	149.2	Bulgaria	28.0	45.1
Furnish., househ. equip. & mainten.	Denmark	119.9	Bulgaria	62.0	18.2
Health (1)	Denmark	152.8	Bulgaria	25.9	43.8
Transport	Denmark	146.0	Bulgaria	57.8	21.7
Communications	Czech Republic	123.6	Cyprus	47.1	18.7
Recreation & culture (1)	Denmark	134.4	Bulgaria	44.4	29.0
Education (1)	Luxembourg	183.9	Bulgaria	14.5	54.9
Restaurants & hotels	Denmark	145.4	Bulgaria	34.4	30.3
Miscellaneous goods & services (1)	Denmark	143.9	Bulgaria	36.7	35.5

(1) 2006.

Source: Eurostat, price level indices (prc_ppp_ind)

The price level indices information presented confirms that consumers living in the Scandinavian countries, Ireland and the United Kingdom face some of the highest prices in Europe, while the cheapest countries are generally those in the east or the south of Europe.

The variation in price levels across the Member States is generally lower for semi-durable and durable goods (clothing and footwear or household equipment) than it is for non-durables (for example, alcoholic beverages and tobacco), while the largest variation in price levels is seen among consumer services. This was particularly the case for regulated services (such as education, health and the utilities), where markets may be protected from competition and prices may be set independently of market conditions.

Across the 12 first level headings of the COICOP, Denmark recorded the highest price level for eight of the categories in 2007, while Bulgaria was the country with the lowest relative prices for ten of the categories. Despite the widespread differences that remain between countries in terms of different price levels, an analysis (based on the coefficient of variation of comparative price level indices for final household consumption) suggests that prices in the EU-27 are gradually converging.

Official statistics are quite weak in terms of providing information on actual prices. It may be hoped that on-going development work will, in the medium-term, give rise to meaningful data that allows the actual price of generic and pan-European branded goods and services to be compared.

In the meantime, a survey conducted in Ireland shows that the price of specific goods and services can vary considerably even between regions of the same country. The comparison made for 79 products and services between Dublin and regional towns and cities shows that in May 2008, the price of a range of food items was somewhat lower in Dublin. On the other hand, the price of a haircut, or an alcoholic drink in a bar in the capital city was considerably higher than elsewhere – providing further evidence that the price of services tends to vary far more than the price of consumer durables (both regionally and internationally).

Figure 1.57: Coefficient of variation of comparative price level index for final household consumption, EU-27
(%)

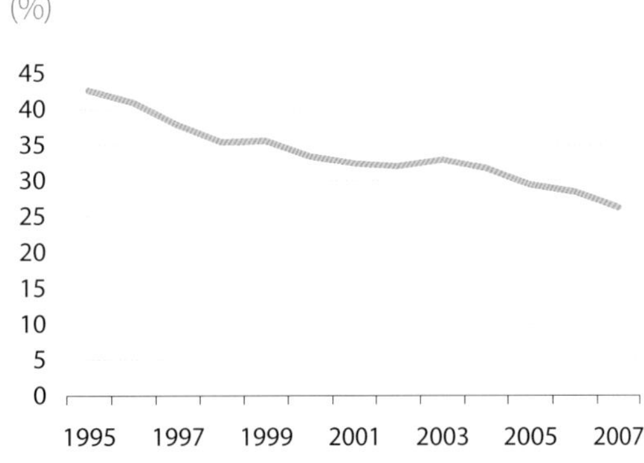

Source: Eurostat, price convergence indicator (prc_ppp_conv)

Table 1.62: Price level comparisons in Ireland between Dublin and outside Dublin, May 2008 (1)

	Unit	Higher average price in Dublin (% difference)
Men wash, cut & blow dry	unit value	44.7
Men dry cut	unit value	34.7
Bacon, best back rashers	1 kg	22.3
Women wash, cut & blow dry	unit value	20.7
Medium uncooked chicken	1 600 g	20.0
Orange juice	1 litre	18.6
Draught lager	1/2 pint	13.8
Draught lager	1 pint	13.4
Draught cider	1 pint	12.8
Pork steak	1 kg	12.3
	Unit	**Lower average price in Dublin (% difference)**
Fillets of plaice	1 kg	-9.5
Flour, white, self-raising	2 kg	-8.4
Round steak	1 kg	-5.9
Lamb, whole leg	1 kg	-5.2
Spaghetti	500 g	-5.1
Milk, fresh, pasteurised full fat	2 litre	-5.0
Bread, white, sliced (large)	800 g	-5.0
Sherry, bottle (take home)	75 cl	-4.7
Cider, can (take home)	500 ml	-4.5
Ham fillet	1 kg	-4.3

(1) Comparison made for 79 products and services between Dublin and regional towns and cities.

Source: Central Statistics Office, Ireland (www.cso.ie/releasespublications/documents/prices/2008/apa_may2008.pdf)

Table 1.63: Internet price comparisons, July 2008 (1)
(EUR)

	Amazon DE	Amazon FR	Amazon UK (2)	Kelkoo	Manufacturer's website (3)
Sony Cyber-shot T300 camera	297.50	285.90	276.75	303.32	379.00
Apple iPod classic 80GB	204.97	215.14	177.26	203.00	217.65
Philips 32PFL5403/12 LCD TV	637.90	838.90	784.46	821.90	:
Coldplay - Viva la Vida... LP	12.30	8.13	7.93	9.48	9.99

(1) All prices include VAT and shipping within country.
(2) Converted at daily exchange rate of EUR 1 = GBP 0.795294713.
(3) Sony online shop for T300, price includes free memory stick; Apple store Luxembourg for iPod; Apple iTunes Luxembourg for Coldplay LP (digital version, not physical product).

Source: various websites, 8 July 2008

Table 1.64: Main indicators for taxes on consumption, 2005

	Taxes on consumption (% of GDP)	of which: VAT (% of GDP)	of which: Excise duties (% of GDP)	Taxes on consumption (% of total taxation)
EU-27	11.1	6.9	2.8	28.1
BE	11.3	7.2	2.4	24.9
BG	18.4	12.4	5.0	51.3
CZ	11.4	7.2	3.7	31.4
DK	16.1	10.0	3.5	31.9
DE	10.1	6.2	2.9	26.1
EE	12.9	8.8	3.8	41.8
IE	11.4	7.7	3.2	37.1
EL	12.0	7.4	2.8	34.9
ES	9.8	6.3	2.4	27.5
FR	11.4	7.4	2.4	25.8
IT	10.1	6.0	2.3	24.8
CY	14.7	9.8	4.1	41.4
LV	12.4	7.9	3.7	42.0
LT	10.9	7.2	3.0	37.9
LU	10.9	5.9	4.3	28.5
HU	14.6	8.4	3.2	37.8
MT	14.4	8.2	3.2	40.9
NL	12.1	7.3	2.5	31.8
AT	12.1	7.9	2.8	28.9
PL	12.2	7.7	4.2	35.8
PT (1)	12.8	8.1	3.2	37.5
RO	12.4	8.1	3.3	44.3
SI	13.9	9.0	3.5	34.5
SK	12.5	8.0	3.7	42.7
FI	13.7	8.7	3.8	31.2
SE	13.1	9.3	3.1	25.5
UK	11.4	6.8	3.2	30.9
NO	10.6	8.0	1.4	23.8

(1) 2004.

Source: 'Taxation trends in the EU', Directorate-General Taxation and Customs Union, European Commission

Indirect taxes

Direct taxes are paid and borne by the taxpayer in the form of income tax, corporation tax, wealth tax and some local taxes. On the other hand, indirect taxes are levied on the consumption of goods or services. They can be applied in a variety of manners, including: as a proportion of the sales price (such as value added tax, VAT); as a fixed amount per unit of consumption (as with most excise duties); or as a flat rate (as with most license fees).

Indirect taxes are generally collected on behalf of governments by manufacturers, wholesalers, or retailers. The two most important indirect taxes (in terms of revenues that are raised) are VAT and excise duties, while other indirect taxes include: stamp duty on the purchase of a house; taxes on entertainment, lotteries and gambling; television license fees; car registration taxes; or environmental levies.

Indirect taxes are often described as being 'regressive'. This is because in contrast to income tax systems, where the marginal and average rates of tax generally rise with income, indirect taxes often result in lower income groups paying relatively more tax. For example, a person who smokes 20 cigarettes a day and earns a relatively low wage will pay a bigger proportion of his/her income in the form of VAT and excise duties than someone who earns a substantially higher salary and also smokes 20 cigarettes a day. Furthermore, any subsequent increase in tax on cigarettes will affect the low-income person proportionally more than the high-income earner.

Indirect taxation is often used by governments to change both the level and pattern of consumption, in particular with the aim of meeting a variety of policy objectives. In the example of taxation on cigarettes, any tax increases may be justified by governments as an attempt to dissuade people from smoking and so reduce the burden on healthcare systems from smoke-related diseases.

The European Commission's Directorate-General for Taxation and Customs Union estimates that consumption taxes accounted for 11.1 % of EU-27 GDP in 2005. The most important share (6.9 % of GDP) was attributed to receipts from VAT, while excise duties accounted for a further 2.8 % of GDP. The relative importance of taxes on consumption varied from 9.8 % of GDP in Spain to 18.4 % of GDP in Bulgaria.

While there is a standard VAT rate in each of the Member States, this is not systematically applied to all goods and services. Rather, some items can be exempt from VAT, while others may have a lower tax rate. Standard VAT rates at the start of January 2008 ranged from 15 % in Cyprus and Luxembourg to 25 % in Denmark and Sweden.

Excise duties are levied on three main consumption items: mineral oils (petrol and diesel), alcoholic drinks, and manufactured tobacco. The nature of excise duties (based on a fixed level per unit of consumption) means government receipts generally remain unchanged when the price of a good or service changes; this is in contrast to VAT. For example, if the price of oil rises on global markets, then VAT receipts from petrol and diesel received by government will increase in proportion to the increase in the pump price, while receipts from excise duties will remain unchanged (given the increase in price does not result from falling demand).

Figure 1.58: Standard VAT rates applied, 1 January 2008
(%)

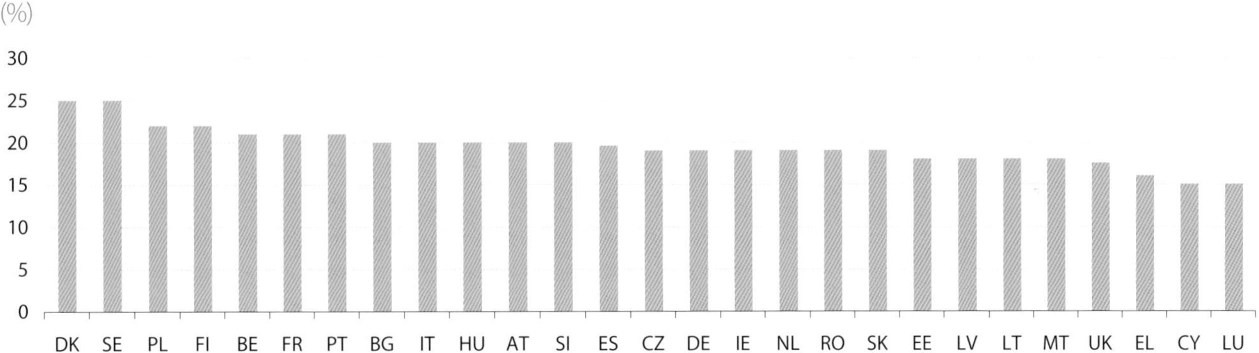

Source: 'Taxation trends in the EU', Directorate-General Taxation and Customs Union, European Commission

CONSUMER SATISFACTION AND COMPLAINTS

Consumer attitudes affect the demand for goods and services. Many aspects can be cited, including: satisfaction, expectations of quality and safety, environmental concerns, fashion, as well as the availability and reliability of the information used by consumers to take consumption decisions.

Satisfaction

Consumer satisfaction depends on a variety of factors: for example, price, quality, the fairness of terms and conditions, or after-sales service. Some intangible aspects relating to satisfaction are difficult to measure through the use of traditional, statistical surveys, and while these are thought to be particularly important for understanding how service markets function, information is largely restricted to evidence from opinion surveys.

Statistics on consumer satisfaction are generally based on surveys of consumer perceptions and expectations, that tend to query whether pre-purchase expectations are matched by the post-purchase experience of using or consuming a good or service. A satisfaction survey held in May 2007 covered 11 services of general interest: gas supply, electricity supply, water distribution, fixed telephony, mobile telephony, urban transport, extra-urban transport, air transport, postal services, retail banking, and insurance services. The following year (August/October 2008) another survey was conducted, focusing on a range of consumer goods, including: fruit and vegetables, meat, non-alcoholic beverages, clothing and footwear, household electrical equipment, motor vehicles, entertainment and leisure goods, and information and communication equipment.

The overall results of both surveys may be summarised by stating that more consumers were generally satisfied with the provision of goods and services than dissatisfied. Among product markets, there was generally less difference in levels of overall satisfaction (either between products or across countries) than for services

Figure 1.59: Consumer satisfaction: to what extent are you satisfied with your supplier, EU (1)
(% of respondents)

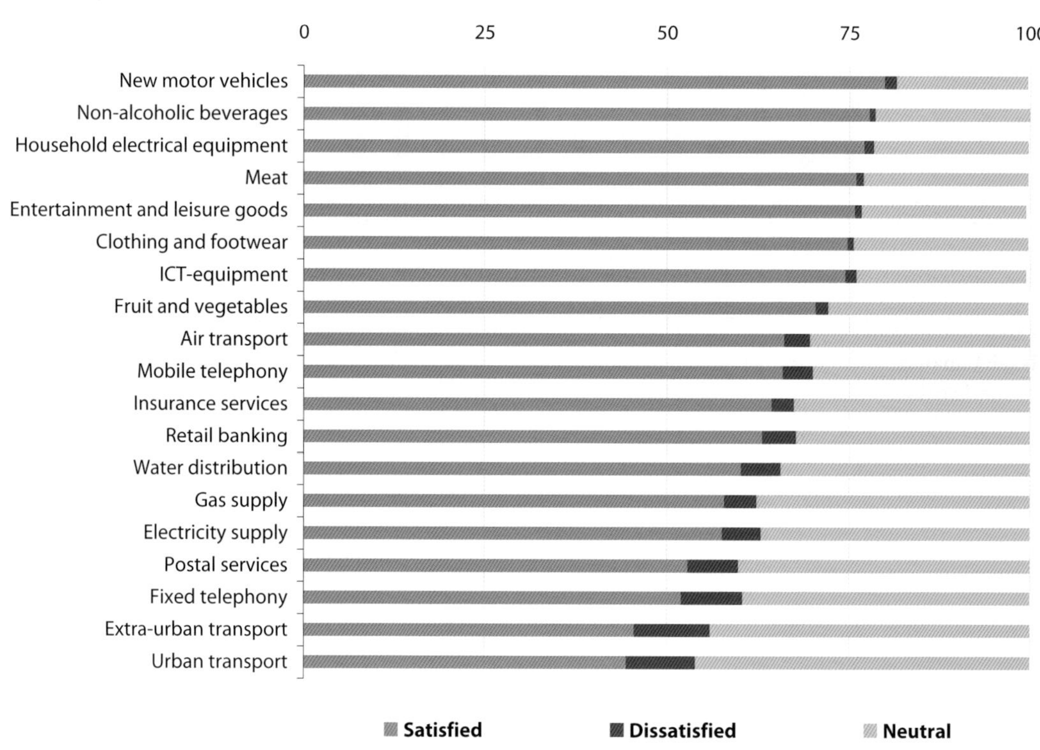

(1) For services of general interest, EU-25, May 2007; for products, EU-27, August/October 2008; respondents who replied do not know or who gave no reply are not shown.

Source: Consumer satisfaction surveys, Directorate-General Health and Consumer Protection, IPSOS INRA for the European Commission

of general interest. However, some countries consistently displayed higher/lower satisfaction and dissatisfaction levels across the different markets, suggesting that cultural differences and expectations may play some role in determining satisfaction. Note more detailed statistics by Member State from these surveys are shown in a number of chapters within Part B of this publication.

Among the services of general interest that were surveyed in 2007, air transport, mobile telephony and insurance services had the highest satisfaction levels across the EU-25, while urban and extra-urban transport were the only services where less than 50 % of consumers were satisfied (note this does not mean the remainder were dissatisfied, as a high proportion of respondents gave a neutral answer – either non-response or do not know). Price was the most important criterion influencing consumers' overall satisfaction for 6 out of the 11 services surveyed.

Table 1.65: Relative weights in overall consumer satisfaction, EU-25, May 2007 (1)
(scale, 0-1)

	Quality	Pricing	Image
Gas supply	0.49	0.20	0.28
Air transport	0.37	0.36	0.35
Urban transport	0.35	0.39	0.52
Water distribution	0.34	0.43	0.37
Extra-urban transport	0.33	0.38	0.53
Postal services	0.33	0.39	0.48
Electricity supply	0.30	0.49	0.32
Mobile telephony	0.28	0.44	0.34
Fixed telephony	0.24	0.46	0.43
Insurance services	0.24	0.52	0.32
Retail banking	0.22	0.47	0.38

(1) Weights are determined by regression coefficients and can have a value ranging from 0 to 1, with 0 meaning that the criteria has no influence on overall consumer satisfaction and 1 meaning that it has total influence.

Source: 'Consumer satisfaction survey', Directorate-General Health and Consumer Protection, IPSOS INRA for the European Commission

Table 1.66: Consumer satisfaction: to what extent are you satisfied with your supplier (1)
(% of respondents)

	EU (2)		EU-15		New Member States that joined EU (3)	
	Satisfied	Dissatisfied	Satisfied	Dissatisfied	Satisfied	Dissatisfied
New motor vehicles	79.9	1.6	79.8	1.4	80.5	2.6
Non-alcoholic beverages	77.8	0.8	77.0	0.7	80.7	0.9
Household elec. equip.	77.1	1.3	75.8	1.2	81.7	1.6
Meat	76.0	1.0	75.4	0.8	78.3	1.7
Entertain. & leisure goods	75.8	0.9	75.5	0.8	77.3	1.4
Clothing & footwear	74.8	0.8	75.4	0.4	72.8	2.0
ICT-equipment	74.5	1.5	73.1	1.5	80.4	1.4
Fruit & vegetables	70.4	1.7	69.0	1.7	76.4	1.9
Air transport	66.1	3.5	65.5	3.6	72.6	3.1
Mobile telephony	65.9	4.1	64.4	4.2	72.8	3.9
Insurance services	64.4	3.0	64.6	2.6	62.9	5.3
Retail banking	63.1	4.6	62.1	4.5	67.9	4.7
Water distribution	60.2	5.4	60.5	4.8	59.1	7.9
Gas supply	57.9	4.4	57.2	4.0	60.9	6.6
Electricity supply	57.6	5.3	56.5	4.9	62.3	6.7
Postal services	52.9	6.9	50.5	6.8	62.7	7.5
Fixed telephony	52.0	8.4	52.1	7.6	51.4	12.6
Extra-urban transport	45.6	10.3	45.3	9.9	47.1	12.0
Urban transport	44.5	9.4	45.2	8.4	40.3	14.7

(1) For services of general interest, May 2007; for products, August/October 2008.
(2) For services of general interest, EU-25; for products, EU-27.
(3) For services of general interest, 10 new Member Sates that joined the EU in 2004; for products, 12 new Member States that joined the EU since 2004.

Source: Consumer satisfaction surveys, Directorate-General Health and Consumer Protection, IPSOS INRA for the European Commission

Figure 1.60: Consumer satisfaction: comparability of prices, EU-27, 2008 (1)
(% of respondents)

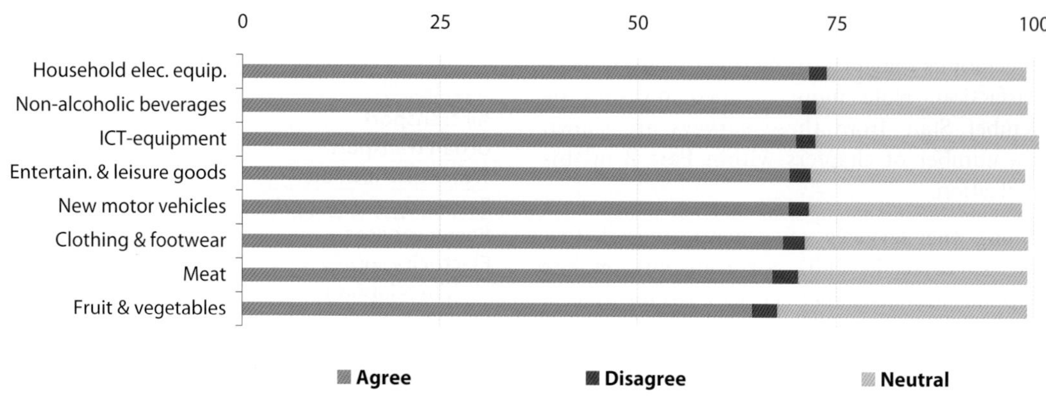

(1) Respondents who replied do not know or who gave no reply are not shown.

Source: Consumer satisfaction survey 2008, Directorate-General Health and Consumer Protection, IPSOS INRA for the European Commission

Figure 1.61: Consumer satisfaction: comparability of quality, EU-27, 2008 (1)
(% of respondents)

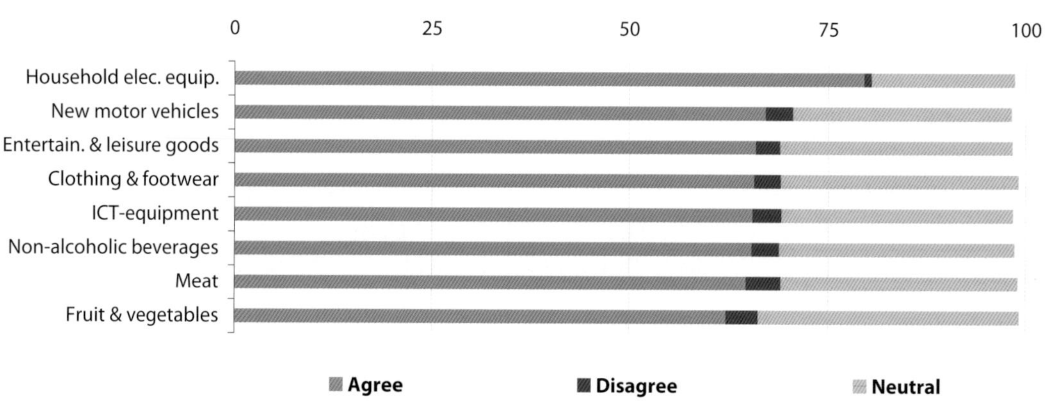

(1) Respondents who replied do not know or who gave no reply are not shown.

Source: Consumer satisfaction survey 2008, Directorate-General Health and Consumer Protection, IPSOS INRA for the European Commission

Product markets were generally characterised by higher levels of satisfaction than services of general interest. Indeed, more than three quarters of all EU-27 consumers in 2008 were satisfied with their suppliers of new motor vehicles, non-alcoholic beverages, household electrical equipment, meat or entertainment and leisure goods.

There were a number of questions in the 2008 satisfaction survey of product markets concerning consumers' views in relation to price, quality and choice. The results show that very few consumers had a negative opinion regarding any of these criteria. For example, among the eight product markets surveyed, the highest proportion of respondents that did not agree that it was easy to compare prices was recorded for meat (3.2 %), followed by fruit and vegetables (3.1 %). In contrast, the proportion of respondents that agreed it was easy to compare prices stood at 64.5 % for fruit and vegetables and at 67.0 % for meat, rising to upwards of 70 % of respondents for household electrical equipment or non-alcoholic beverages.

When asked for their opinion of whether or not it was easy to compare the quality of the same group of eight products, a majority of respondents again agreed. The proportion in agreement was lowest for food and drink products, rising to more than two thirds of all respondents for new motor vehicles, and considerably higher (79.5 %) for household electrical equipment.

Figure 1.62: Consumer satisfaction with choice of retailers, EU-27, 2008 (1)
(% of respondents)

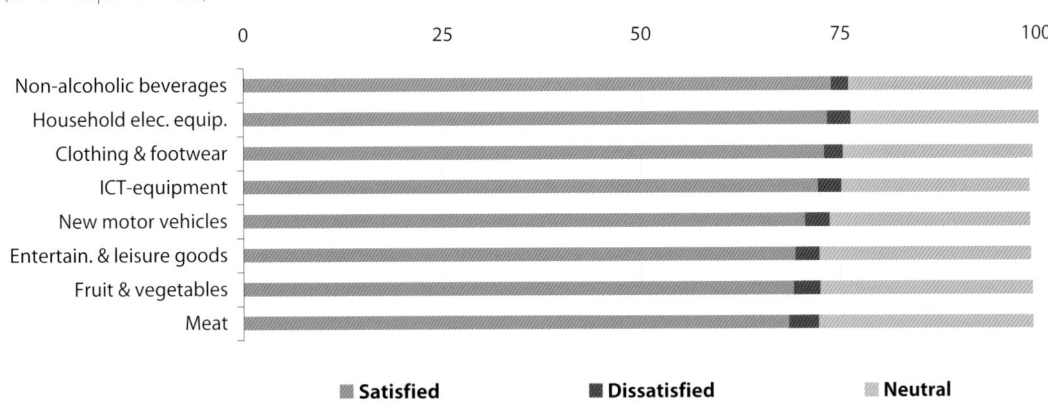

(1) Respondents who replied do not know or who gave no reply are not shown.

Source: Consumer satisfaction survey 2008, Directorate-General Health and Consumer Protection, IPSOS INRA for the European Commission

Figure 1.63: Consumer satisfaction with trustworthiness of retailers to adhere to rules set in place to protect consumers, EU-27, 2008 (1)
(% of respondents)

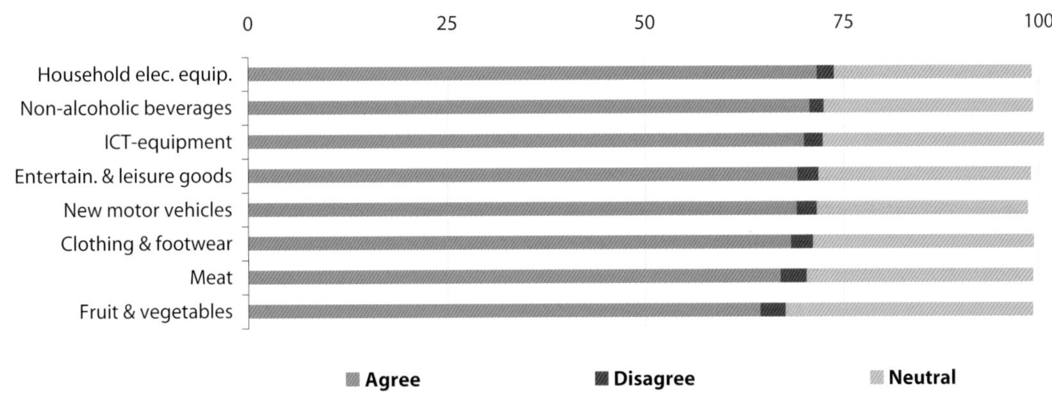

(1) Respondents who replied do not know or who gave no reply are not shown.

Source: Consumer satisfaction survey 2008, Directorate-General Health and Consumer Protection, IPSOS INRA for the European Commission

While price and quality are generally considered as the main motivations behind consumer decision-making, the 2008 satisfaction survey also looked at consumers' satisfaction with their choice of retailer. The results show that more than two thirds of EU-27 respondents were satisfied with the choice of available retailers for each of the eight product markets covered. The lowest levels of satisfaction concerned retail choice in relation to food products, namely, meat and fruit and vegetables.

The same survey questioned consumers on the trustworthiness of retailers and whether retailers adhered to rules put in place to protect consumers. Once again a majority of respondents for all eight product categories agreed that retailers were, in general, trustworthy. The proportion of respondents that disagreed with this question never rose higher than the 4.5 % recorded for retailers of ICT-equipment; this figure was, nevertheless, more than twice the level of disagreement recorded for any of the other products. The highest level of trustworthiness was recorded for meat retailers (69.0 % in agreement), closely followed by retailers of new motor vehicles and household electrical equipment, while this indicator fell to lows of 63.5 % for fruit and vegetable retailers and 62.4 % for retailers of ICT-equipment.

Complaints

Data on consumer complaints have been described as the 'gold standard' for the functioning of consumer markets. Information on the number of consumer complaints (made to enforcement agencies, consumer NGOs, and similar bodies) provides information on where consumer markets might be inefficient or face other forms of restriction.

Complaints data are collected in a heterogeneous way across the Member States, and the European Commission's Directorate-General for Health and Consumers published a consultation document in 2008 seeking the views of complaint handling bodies (among others) on how to move towards a more harmonised system of classifying complaints.

As with satisfaction, the willingness to complain is likely to vary between countries as a function of cultural differences, and may also be related to the perceived likelihood of success of pursuing a complaint. The results of satisfaction surveys conducted in 2007 and 2008 show that consumers faced, on average, more problems regarding services of general interest than they

Figure 1.64: Consumers having experienced problems in the last 12 months, EU (1)
(% of respondents)

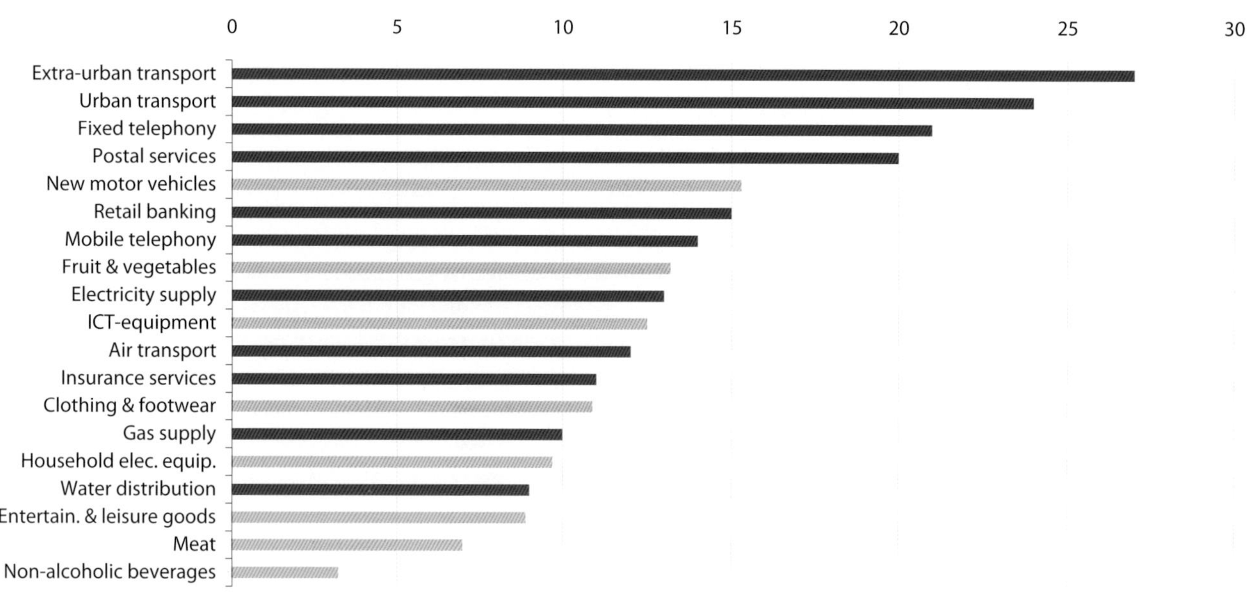

(1) For services of general interest (shaded blue), May 2007; for products (shaded yellow), August/October 2008.

Source: Consumer satisfaction surveys, Directorate-General Health and Consumer Protection, IPSOS INRA for the European Commission

Figure 1.65: Consumer complaints: in the last 12 months, have you made any kind of formal complaint in writing, by telephone or in person, to a seller/provider, 2008
(% responding yes)

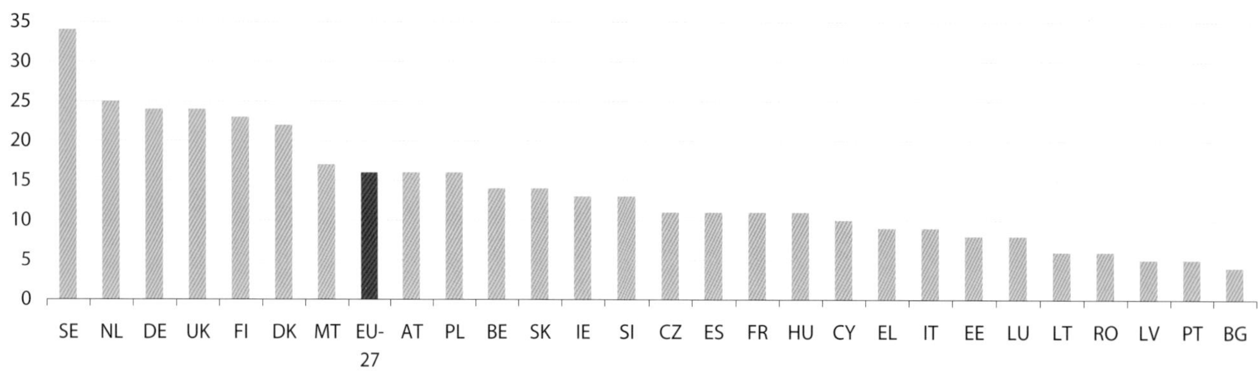

Source: 'Consumer protection in the Internal Market, 2008', Special Eurobarometer 298, European Commission

did concerning products. Among the eight product categories that were surveyed, the highest proportion of problems was reported for new motor vehicle purchases (15 %), whereas for services the highest rate was 27 % for extra-urban transport services. A survey of consumer protection in the internal market conducted in early 2008 for the European Commission reveals that on average 16 % of consumers in the EU-27 made a formal complaint (in writing, by telephone or in person) during the previous 12 month period. More than 20 % of consumers in the northern European countries of Sweden, the Netherlands, Germany, the United Kingdom, Finland and Denmark made a complaint, compared with no more than 8 % in the Baltic Member States, Luxembourg, Romania, Portugal or Bulgaria.

Those who had complained were asked to elaborate on how well they thought their complaint had been dealt with. At the EU-27 level, slightly more than half (51 %) of those complaining agreed that their complaint had been handled well.

It is perhaps surprising to find that 51 % of unsatisfied customers chose not to take any further action despite feeling that their complaint had been dealt with in an unsatisfactorily manner. Among those who chose to continue their action, the most popular option was to seek advice from a consumer organisation (14 %), followed by consulting a solicitor (9 %), bringing the matter to court (4 %) or to arbitration/conciliation (3 %).

Another survey conducted in May and June 2006 revealed that telephone services (both fixed and mobile) and Internet services were among the services of general interest that had the highest levels of complaints. All three of these services reported rates of complaint that were approximately twice those registered for a range of other services of general interest (including utility providers, postal services, retail banking and transport services).

Figure 1.66: Consumer complaints: in general, were you satisfied or not with the way your complaint(s) was (were) dealt with, 2008
(% responding yes)

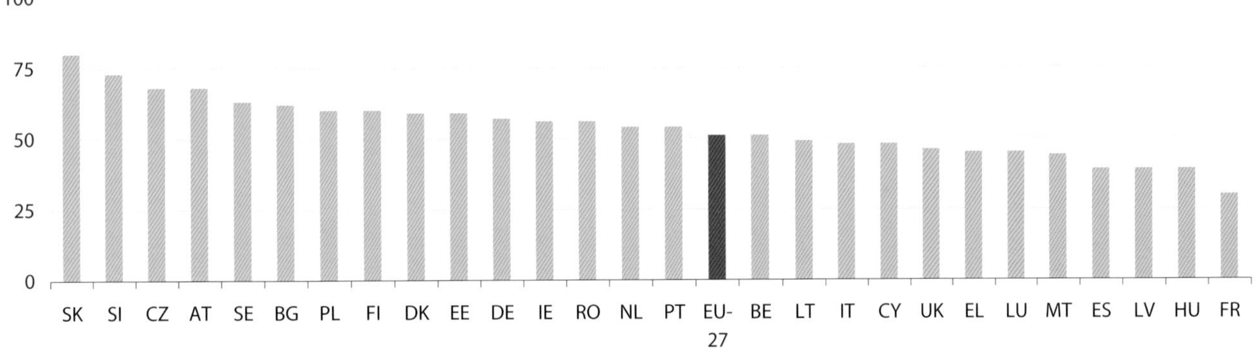

Source: 'Consumer protection in the Internal Market, 2008', Special Eurobarometer 298, European Commission

Figure 1.67: Consumer complaints: what did you do when your complaint(s) was (were) not dealt with in a satisfactory manner, EU-27, 2008
(% of respondents)

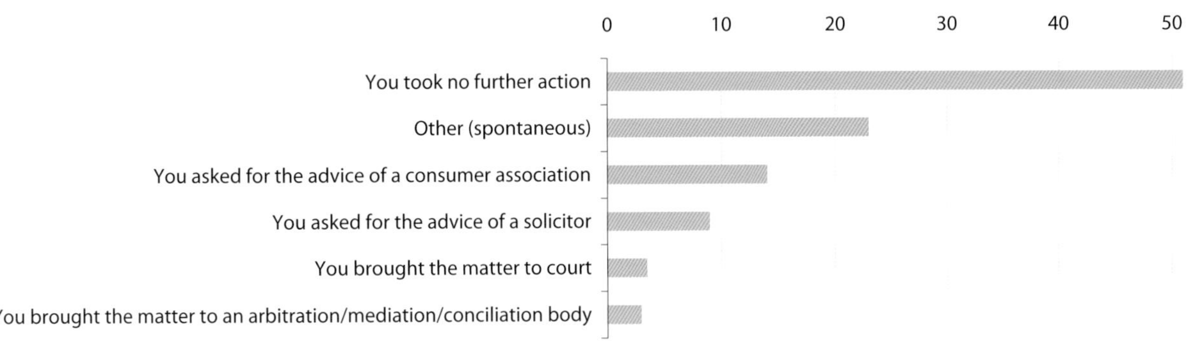

Source: 'Consumer protection in the Internal Market, 2008', Special Eurobarometer 298, European Commission

Table 1.67: Consumer complaints: in the last two years, have you personally made a complaint about any aspect of the following services, May-June 2006
(% responding yes)

	Fixed telephony	Mobile telephony	Internet service provider	Electricity	Gas	Water	Postal service	Rail services: local	Rail services between towns	Retail banking: current account
EU-25	11	12	13	6	5	3	5	4	5	6
BE	9	6	10	5	5	2	5	2	2	3
BG	:	:	:	:	:	:	:	:	:	:
CZ	12	10	11	4	3	3	10	4	1	6
DK	8	14	11	3	4	2	9	6	6	5
DE	14	14	14	8	8	3	6	4	5	7
EE	7	6	15	5	2	4	4	3	2	3
IE	6	7	6	3	4	2	2	2	2	5
EL	6	7	5	4	11	3	2	2	1	4
ES	7	11	10	3	1	2	1	1	1	3
FR	5	6	10	1	1	1	5	3	5	5
IT	20	15	15	7	5	4	6	6	7	9
CY	12	5	7	9	-	5	2	8	-	10
LV	6	5	11	2	0	3	1	1	0	1
LT	4	7	9	3	0	3	1	1	0	1
LU	1	2	2	1	1	0	2	2	1	1
HU	13	9	15	7	6	6	5	5	3	7
MT	8	9	16	10	-	9	3	3	-	7
NL	9	11	19	10	5	2	7	6	12	7
AT	6	15	9	6	4	2	8	3	6	9
PL	14	11	13	3	2	3	4	3	2	4
PT	5	5	12	3	3	2	1	1	1	3
RO	:	:	:	:	:	:	:	:	:	:
SI	2	6	4	1	1	2	2	2	2	3
SK	9	11	8	6	4	5	6	5	1	7
FI	4	16	17	5	0	2	7	4	2	5
SE	19	16	26	14	0	2	8	12	5	5
UK	11	15	14	9	9	4	7	6	7	9

Source: 'Services of general interest', Special Eurobarometer 260, European Commission

Table 1.68: Consumer complaints: how well was your complaint dealt with, May-June 2006
(% responding 'well', as opposed to 'badly')

	Fixed telephony	Mobile telephony	Internet service provider	Electricity	Gas	Water	Postal service	Rail services: local	Rail services between towns	Retail banking: current account
EU-25	52	55	49	49	45	51	52	54	52	50
BE	60	60	52	42	52	57	45	65	70	48
BG	:	:	:	:	:	:	:	:	:	:
CZ	58	61	81	68	70	61	50	44	53	52
DK	57	48	56	65	35	82	56	57	60	57
DE	46	49	37	32	19	32	37	47	19	44
EE	60	64	72	55	75	37	67	43	62	64
IE	47	59	50	52	22	47	57	9	11	47
EL	47	43	37	26	76	32	16	22	14	33
ES	44	51	41	45	51	58	91	75	67	45
FR	43	50	37	38	43	47	52	52	62	49
IT	56	57	51	66	61	76	64	58	52	57
CY	67	60	61	53	-	52	32	42	-	72
LV	49	56	54	65	0	56	66	74	100	60
LT	65	50	78	59	100	36	58	60	0	38
LU	42	24	47	28	100	100	69	0	-	100
HU	57	56	54	50	52	63	74	43	41	51
MT	66	58	53	43	-	45	30	34	-	78
NL	51	46	58	40	34	32	53	43	69	50
AT	49	77	68	64	34	49	45	41	33	46
PL	58	73	87	66	85	58	64	61	71	77
PT	50	42	56	57	69	53	37	49	0	35
RO	:	:	:	:	:	:	:	:	:	:
SI	39	51	58	31	38	52	35	57	32	32
SK	60	65	72	68	63	58	54	43	7	71
FI	62	63	73	56	-	65	62	53	22	67
SE	63	58	62	64	-	83	43	58	58	54
UK	53	58	39	52	48	45	56	59	65	47

Source: 'Services of general interest', Special Eurobarometer 260, European Commission

The European Consumer Centres (ECC) and Consumer Protection Cooperation (CPC) networks provide information relating to the number of cross-border complaints. The ECC data relate to cross-border online transactions for consumer goods and services. In 2007 there were more than 26 000 requests for information, 18 070 simple complaints (which required no follow-up, other than providing advice to the consumer), and 4 759 normal complaints and disputes (which required the subsequent intervention or follow-up of an ECC or the referral of a complaint to an out-of-court scheme or ADR body by an ECC).

Table 1.69: Number of cross-border information requests, complaints, disputes and enforcement requests, Europe, 2007 (1)
(number)

ECC (European Consumer Centres)	
Information requests	26 215
Simple complaints	18 070
Normal complaints & disputes	4 759
CPC (Consumer Protection Cooperation)	
Information requests	52
Enforcement requests	57
Alerts	22

(1) EU-25, Norway and Iceland.

Source: ECC and CPC networks

Table 1.70: Number of cross-border information and enforcement requests, complaints, and disputes, Europe, 2007 (1)
(number)

	ECC: normal complaints & disputes	CPC		
		Information	Enforcement	Alerts
Total	4 759	52	57	22
Food & non-alcoholic beverages	13	1	1	1
Alcoholic beverages, tobacco	22	0	0	0
Clothing & footwear	134	1	0	0
Housing, water, elec., gas & oth. fuels	75	0	0	0
Furnish., househ. equip. & mainten.	334	1	1	0
Health	40	8	11	5
Transport	1 633	8	15	3
Communications	278	0	2	1
Recreation & culture	1 150	8	10	4
Education	17	1	0	0
Restaurants & hotels	508	5	2	1
Miscellaneous goods & services	350	13	9	4
Outside COICOP classification	205	6	6	3

(1) EU-25, Norway and Iceland.

Source: ECC and CPC networks

QUALITY AND SAFETY

Quality

In its traditional sense, the term 'quality' is often used in a narrow sense to describe how a manufactured product conforms to its stated objectives, in other words, quality is measured in terms of defects introduced on manufacturing production lines. However, a broader concept of quality might cover the aspirations of consumers, and consider how a product or service matches up to these. This more subjective definition means that individual consumers can have their own definition of what constitutes a quality product or service, reflected in a move away from supply-side measures that focus on manufacturers' processes (such as total quality management), towards customer-based measures. This shift in focus accompanies the increasing economic importance of services in the global economy. As such, quality may be defined in terms of the customer or end-user experience – how a product was sold, how it was delivered, how it performed, or how well the after-sales service functioned.

While price undoubtedly plays an important role in consumer decision-making processes, the influence of quality may, at least in some cases, be more central. In this respect, quality can be synonymous with safety – for example, edible, wholesome foods, toys that are not dangerous, or airlines that have a good safety record. Quality can also be synonymous with the speed of delivery – for example, transport services (buses or trains) that arrive according to schedule, Internet services being offered at high-speeds, postal services that result in parcels being delivered quickly. However, the more subjective nature of quality extends its impact further, into areas where it is difficult to measure consumers' perceptions or the perceived value that they give a good and service. One area where perceived quality may be particularly important is with respect to designer and branded goods. A survey conducted in November 2005 shows that a relatively small proportion (22 %) of European consumers thought that designer brands were significantly higher quality than standard brands, while three quarters of respondents believed that designer brands were over-priced.

A more recent survey of consumer protection in the internal market conducted in early 2008 for the European Commission reveals that branding plays an important role in consumer's decision-making processes. When asked which factors (up to three responses allowed) played an important role in determining the choice of non-food items that EU-27 consumers purchased, some 49 % of respondents cited the brand as a factor. Branding was generally the third most important factor, behind price and safety, for influencing consumer choice, although in Bulgaria, Estonia, Spain, France, Ireland, Lithuania, Malta, Austria, Poland, Romania, Slovenia and Sweden, the brand was cited by a slightly higher proportion of respondents than safety.

Table 1.71: Perceived quality: to what extent do you agree with the following, November 2005
(% of respondents)

	I buy designer brands	Many people I know buy designer brands	Designer brands are usually over-priced for what they are	Designer brands are significantly higher quality than standard brands
Europe	21	42	75	22
Latin America	24	67	82	39
Asia-Pacific	20	39	79	35
North America	14	41	87	18
Other	20	45	79	34
Global average	21	44	77	28

Source: Global online survey (based on 23 500 consumers in 42 countries), A.C. Nielsen

In order to help consumers make informed choices there are a number of schemes that have been set-up to help identify goods and services adhering to particular ethical principles – for example, fair-trade products, ecologically friendly products, organic produce. Additional information may be found in the opening chapter of Part B, which covers food and non-alcoholic beverages. This includes information relating to quality food products manufactured in specific regions (Protected Designation of Origin (PDO) and Protected Geographical Indication (PGI)).

The eco-label (shown) was introduced in 1992 to help consumers identify greener products and services and may be granted to any product or service except food, drinks, pharmaceutical products or medical appliances. Products that are given the label must be manufactured by the most environmentally friendly procedure possible and their disposal must impose less of a burden on nature than that of conventional products. Furthermore, products that are granted the label must be of high quality, and the label is only awarded if a product is at least as effective as a 'normal' product. A survey conducted at the end of 2006 by Eurobarometer found that only 11 % of consumers in the EU-25 were aware of the meaning of the European eco-label.

Ethical factors are becoming more important in consumers' buying decisions and are often cited by consumers as a safeguard in relation to quality. According to the Fairtrade Labelling Organization (www.fairtrade.net), there was rapid growth in the retail value of fair-trade products between 2006 and 2007, with several national markets doubling in size. The highest value of retail sales of fair-trade products, among those countries for which data are available, was recorded in the United Kingdom, where the fair-trade retail market was estimated to be valued at EUR 704 million in 2007. In contrast, the relative importance of fair-trade sales was particularly low in Italy and Spain.

Figure 1.68: Public perception of eco-label: in your opinion what does this European label mean, EU-25, November-December 2006
(% of respondents)

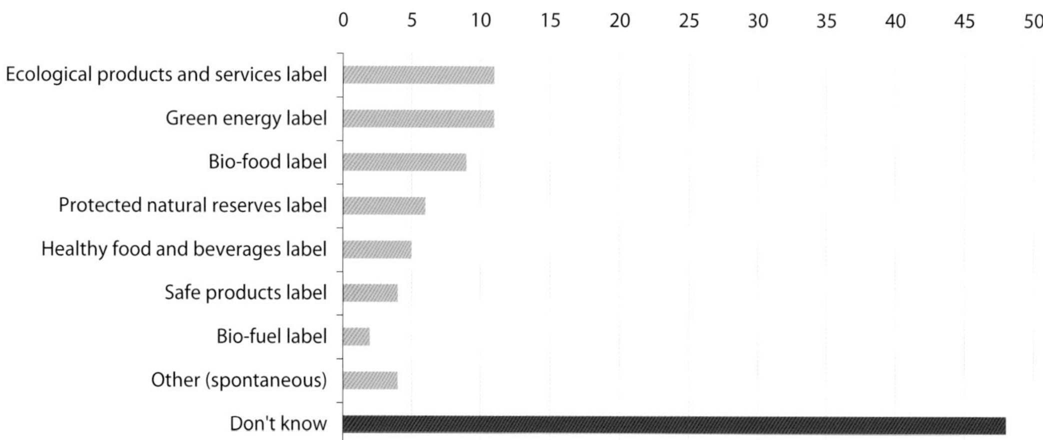

Source: 'Eco-label flower week', Special Eurobarometer 275, European Commission

A recent Eurobarometer survey conducted in early 2008 reveals that 8 % of consumers in the EU-27 stated that ethical considerations were among the three most important aspects that influence their choice of purchase. There was a fairly wide range in values between the Member States, as upwards of 20 % of Swedish and Danish consumers gave importance to ethical considerations, while shares of less than 5 % were recorded in Cyprus, Hungary, Malta Portugal, Romania, Bulgaria and Slovenia.

Fraudulent goods and services are often charged with being of sub-standard quality, either due to inferior materials being used to manufacture them, or because they have lower product safety: they may also be charged with being produced using manufacturing methods that fail to respect rules and regulations concerning labour or environmental regulations.

Table 1.72: Estimated retail value of sales of fair-trade products (1)
(EUR million)

	2006	2007	(% increase)
BE	28	35	25
DK	23	40	71
DE	110	142	29
IE	12	23	101
ES	2	4	105
FR	166	210	27
IT	35	39	13
LU	3	3	14
NL	41	48	16
AT	42	53	27
FI	23	35	54
SE	16	43	166
UK	410	704	72
NO	9	18	110
CH	142	158	11

(1) Information only available for those Member States shown in the table.

Source: Annual report 2007, Fairtrade Labelling Organizations International (www.fairtrade.net)

Table 1.73: Community customs activities concerning counterfeit and piracy: number of cases registered and number of articles seized at EU-25 borders, 2006
(number)

	Number of cases registered	Number of articles seized	Change in number of articles seized, 2005-2006 (%)
Total	37 334	128 631 295	70
Foodstuffs, alcoholic and other drinks	54	1 185 649	-77
Perfumes and cosmetics	1 093	1 676 409	141
Clothing and accessories	24 297	14 361 867	31
Sportswear	3 254	1 210 196	-60
Other clothing (ready to wear)	9 977	4 315 338	1
Clothing accessories (bags, sunglasses...)	11 066	8 793 123	137
Electrical equipment	1 342	2 984 476	-9
Computer equipment (hardware)	543	152 102	-81
CD (audio, games, software), DVD, cassettes	288	15 080 161	55
Watches and jewellery	3 969	943 819	83
Toys and games	678	2 370 894	25
Other	1 682	13 287 274	41
Cigarettes	300	73 920 446	126
Medicines	497	2 711 410	384

Source: Directorate-General Taxation and Customs Union, European Commission (http://ec.europa.eu/taxation_customs/resources/documents/customs/customs_controls/counterfeit_piracy/statistics/counterf_comm_2006_en.pdf)

Figure 1.69: Community customs activities concerning counterfeit and piracy: origin of goods seized at EU-25 borders, 2006
(%)

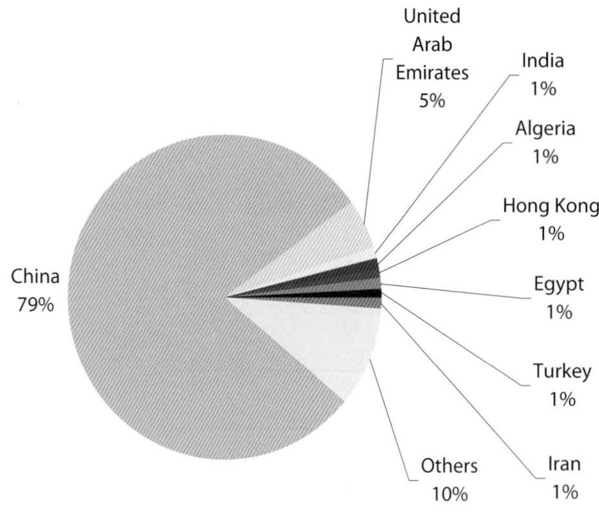

Source: Directorate-General Taxation and Customs Union, European Commission (http://ec.europa.eu/taxation_customs/resources/documents/customs/customs_controls/counterfeit_piracy/statistics/counterf_comm_2006_en.pdf)

The Directorate-General for Taxation and Customs Union of the European Commission is responsible for customs activities and collects information on counterfeit and pirated goods. Their annual report shows that in 2006 there were more than 37 000 cases registered by Community customs officials at EU-25 borders concerning counterfeit and pirated goods, with a total of close to 130 million items being seized. Of these, the most popular items were cigarettes, followed by CDs and DVDs (audio, games or software), and clothing accessories (such as handbags or sunglasses). The most frequent origin of counterfeit goods crossing EU-25 borders in 2006 was China (79 % of all articles seized).

Table 1.74: Community customs activities concerning counterfeit and piracy: share of articles seized at EU-25 borders by origin of provenance, 2006
(%)

	Main origin		Second origin		Third origin	
Foodstuffs, alcoholic and other drinks	Turkey	18	China	17	Singapore	12
Perfumes and cosmetics	China	37	Ukraine	19	Indonesia	17
Clothing and accessories	China	63	India	5	Turkey	3
Sportswear	China	43	Vietnam	13	Switzerland	7
Other clothing (ready to wear)	China	50	India	19	Turkey	9
Clothing accessories (bags, sunglasses…)	China	81	Malaysia	2	Algeria	2
Electrical equipment	China	61	Hong Kong	21	U.A.E.	7
Computer equipment (hardware)	China	47	Spain	17	Hong Kong	15
CD (audio, games, software), DVD, cassettes	China	88	Iran	5	Taiwan	1
Watches and jewellery	China	72	Hong Kong	19	South Korea	2
Toys and games	China	85	Hong Kong	3	Spain	2
Other	China	82	Turkey	3	Hong Kong	2
Cigarettes	China	83	U.A.E.	6	Algeria	2
Medicines	India	31	U.A.E.	31	China	20

Source: Directorate-General Taxation and Customs Union, European Commission (http://ec.europa.eu/taxation_customs/resources/documents/customs/customs_controls/counterfeit_piracy/statistics/counterf_comm_2006_en.pdf)

Safety

In order to protect health and safety, manufacturers and importers are obliged by Community law to ensure that only safe products are made available to consumers for purchase. In other words, products should not present any more than the minimum risk consistent with their use under normal or foreseeable conditions. In order to ensure product safety, manufacturers and importers must take into account: the characteristics of the product, such as its composition, packaging, installation and maintenance requirements; its effect on other products, where it is reasonably foreseeable that it will be used with other products; the presentation of the product, its labelling, and instructions for using and disposing of it; as well as the types of consumers at serious risk when using the product, particularly children or elderly people. Indeed, producers, importers and, in certain circumstances, suppliers of goods and services can be liable for physical injury or material damage if consumers are harmed by defective products.

In addition to these general rules, sectoral provisions have been adopted to cater for the characteristics of specific products, with safety legislation introduced for individual items, such as: foodstuffs, pharmaceutical products, cosmetics, toys, and domestic electrical appliances. A range of European standards exist to help ensure that these products are fit for their purpose, safe, comparable and compatible. European standards are developed by the three organisations: CEN (European committee for standardisation which deals with all sectors except the electro-technology and telecommunications sectors); CENELEC (European committee for electro technical standardisation); and ETSI (European telecommunications standards institute).

Market surveillance authorities are entitled to take a range of measures in relation to defective products, for example, by removing them from sale, or subjecting them to a product recall. There are established systems in place to ensure the exchange of information between Member States if a dangerous product is found. Information is passed via a rapid alert system called 'RAPEX' (rapid alert system for non-food products). The system facilitates cooperation between national and European authorities to track down dangerous products and remove them quickly from the marketplace; a similar rapid alert system is in place for food and feed (RASFF).

As well as market regulation at a national and European level, safety also depends, at least to some degree, on the behaviour and responsibility of individual consumers. Self-regulation to avoid accidents can take a variety of forms: for example, checking that the sell-by date of food has not been exceeded before consuming it; ensuring that a toy with a recommended minimum age cannot be picked up by a younger child; making sure that electrical appliances are kept away from water; or avoiding the excessive consumption of alcohol before driving.

Figure 1.70: Consumers' understanding of safety information: in the last 12 months, have you encountered any difficulties in understanding safety information relating to goods or services, EU-25, February-March 2006
(% of respondents)

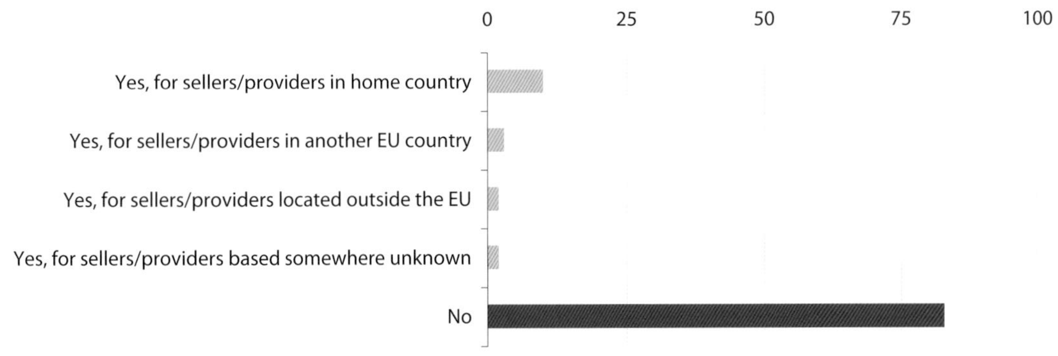

Source: 'Consumer protection in the internal market', Special Eurobarometer 252, European Commission

Figure 1.71: Consumers' understanding of safety information: in the last 12 months, have you encountered any difficulties in understanding safety information relating to goods or services, February-March 2006 (1)
(% of respondents)

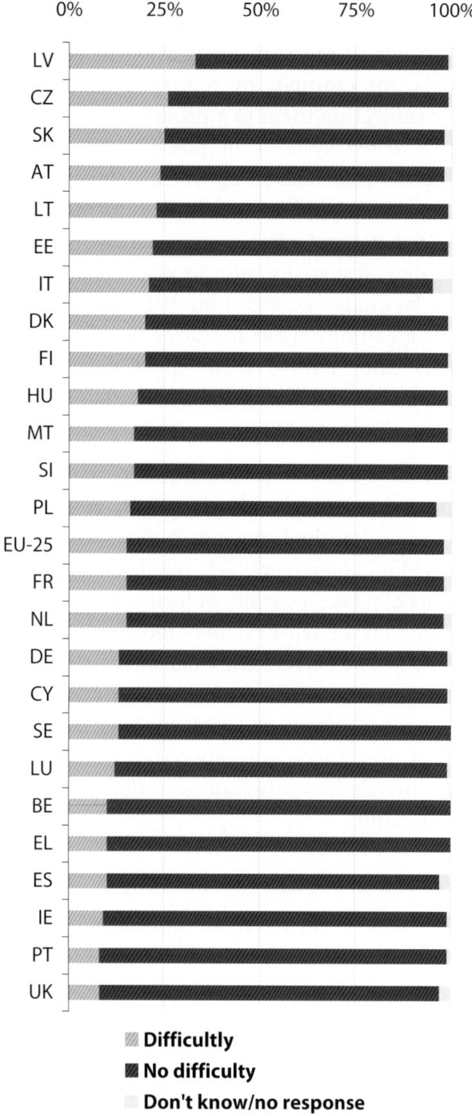

(1) Bulgaria and Romania, not available.

Source: 'Consumer protection in the internal market', Special Eurobarometer 252, European Commission

A Eurobarometer survey conducted in early 2006 asked respondents whether they had encountered any difficulties in understanding safety information relating to goods or services during the previous 12 months. A high proportion (83 %) of persons within the EU-25 replied that they had not experienced any difficulties, while 10 % of respondents faced difficulties for goods or services bought in their own country, 3 % for goods and services bought in another EU-25 country, and 2 % for goods or services bought outside of the EU.

The proportion of people facing difficulties in understanding safety information was equal to or less than 10 % in Belgium, Greece, Spain, Ireland, Portugal and the United Kingdom, rising to around a quarter of all respondents in Austria, Slovakia and the Czech Republic, and reaching a maximum of one third of all respondents in Latvia.

A study of consumer perceptions conducted at the end of 2004 by Eurobarometer suggested that the majority of consumers in the EU-25 felt that a range of services of general interest were safe. Almost nine out of ten (89 %) consumers in the EU-25 felt that their electricity and water supply services were safe, a share that fell to seven out of ten (70 %) consumers when questioned about the safety of mobile telephony or long-distance rail services. It is important to note that there were some quite high levels of non-response; for several of the Member States this could often be explained by the lack of a particular service, for example there are no rail services in Malta, while in several Member States there is either no, or a severely restricted, provision of gas supply.

Table 1.75: Consumers' perception of safety of services of general interest, November 2004 (% of respondents)

	Mobile telephony		Electricity supply		Gas supply		Water supply		Urban transport		Extra-urban rail	
	Safe	Not safe	Safe	Not safe	Safe	Not safe	Safe	Not safe	Safe	Not safe	Safe	Not safe
EU-25	70	17	89	6	74	8	89	5	76	12	70	14
BE	78	16	96	3	75	12	96	2	81	14	83	9
BG	:	:	:	:	:	:	:	:	:	:	:	:
CZ	78	13	87	7	70	21	91	4	73	16	73	17
DK	74	11	96	1	42	2	94	2	71	10	69	7
DE	74	13	91	4	75	7	92	4	80	13	75	16
EE	64	17	81	10	48	6	75	7	58	15	48	7
IE	63	21	94	3	51	7	86	6	75	5	68	4
EL	52	36	80	17	25	20	85	14	74	18	68	16
ES	73	16	86	9	79	10	89	6	85	8	81	7
FR	63	22	93	3	76	3	89	6	70	10	69	11
IT	68	22	80	12	79	13	79	12	63	20	58	21
CY	82	12	92	5	-	-	89	7	47	15	-	-
LV	77	9	93	5	86	6	80	8	83	9	67	6
LT	53	29	82	11	77	11	76	9	72	19	64	12
LU	78	14	94	4	65	7	95	2	76	9	69	10
HU	76	6	92	5	82	9	90	7	70	14	66	9
MT	69	19	88	9	-	-	88	9	65	24	-	-
NL	62	22	88	3	85	4	88	2	73	16	68	21
AT	72	11	88	6	60	6	88	4	69	8	67	9
PL	59	20	86	9	78	13	92	4	76	10	58	20
PT	77	4	88	3	78	7	88	2	73	9	63	5
RO	:	:	:	:	:	:	:	:	:	:	:	:
SI	56	39	73	23	63	21	87	10	80	10	78	6
SK	72	16	87	7	76	15	87	6	71	19	69	15
FI	88	7	96	2	40	10	94	2	83	4	79	2
SE	77	18	89	8	29	17	93	3	80	10	77	9
UK	74	11	96	1	84	2	94	3	85	8	73	15

Source: 'Consumers' opinions on services of general interest', Special Eurobarometer 219, European Commission

Figure 1.72: RAPEX, product notifications concerning safety: by product category, Europe, 2007 (1)
(%)

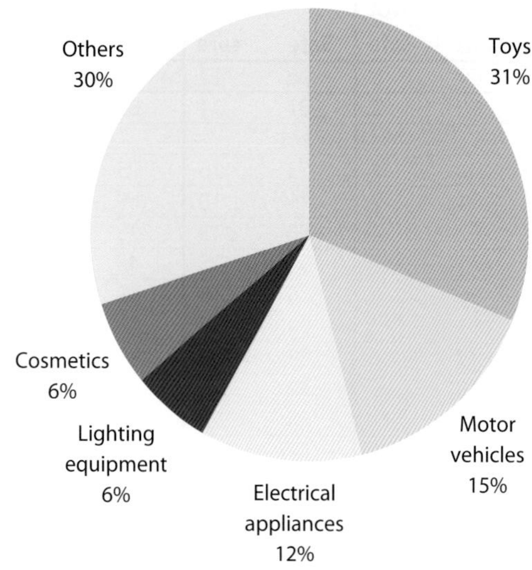

(1) EU-27, Iceland, Liechtenstein and Norway.

Source: Keeping consumers safe, Annual report 2007, RAPEX

A more recent Eurobarometer survey of consumer protection in the internal market carried out in early 2008 shows that some 50 % of EU-27 respondents cited safety as a factor when asked which factors (up to three responses allowed) played an important role in determining purchases of non-food items. Safety was often the second most important criteria for deciding which non-food item to buy behind price.

In the same survey, when asked whether they thought non-food items were safe, 17 % of EU-27 consumers replied that essentially all products are safe, 48 % thought that a small number of items are unsafe, while 18 % said that a significant number are unsafe, the remaining 17 % replied that they either did not know or that it depends on the product in question.

The same survey conducted in early 2008 shows that 2 % of EU-27 consumers said that they personally or an immediate member of their family had suffered an injury or an accident from a defective product during the two years prior to the survey; across the Member States the range of values was from 1 % to 4 %.

Figure 1.73: RAPEX, product notifications concerning safety: by country of notification, 2007 (1)
(% of EU-27)

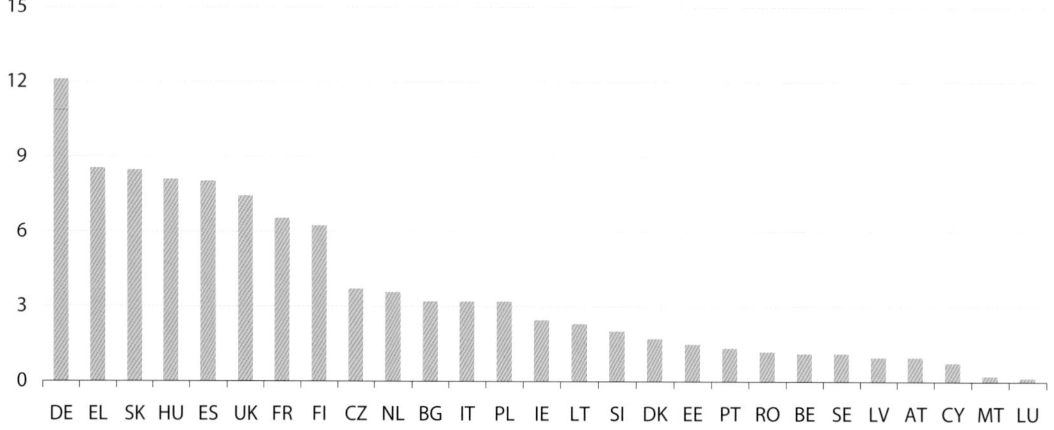

(1) EU-27 notifications, 2007: 1 347.

Source: Keeping consumers safe, Annual report 2007, RAPEX

Aside from consumer surveys, the safety of consumer goods and services can also be measured by statistical information relating to accidents and injuries, as well as information on dangerous products. The RAPEX annual report provides data on the number of dangerous (non-food) consumer product notifications across the EEA. Almost one third (31 %) of these were for toys in 2007, while motor vehicles (15 %) and electrical appliances (12 %) were the only other product categories to account for a double-digit share of total notifications.

Note that the level of product notifications will, at least to some degree, reflect the frequency with which certain goods are checked, and that the data presented gives no indication as to the percentage of notifications in relation to the number of inspections. In a similar vein, the breakdown of notifications between Member States may reflect the size of a country, the number of goods that are checked in each country, or the thoroughness of the checks carried out, and do not necessarily show which countries have a higher proportion of dangerous consumer goods. Just over half (51 %) of all the dangerous product notifications recorded in the EEA in 2007 concerned goods originating from China.

Figure 1.74: RAPEX, product notifications concerning safety: by origin of product, Europe, 2007 (1)
(%)

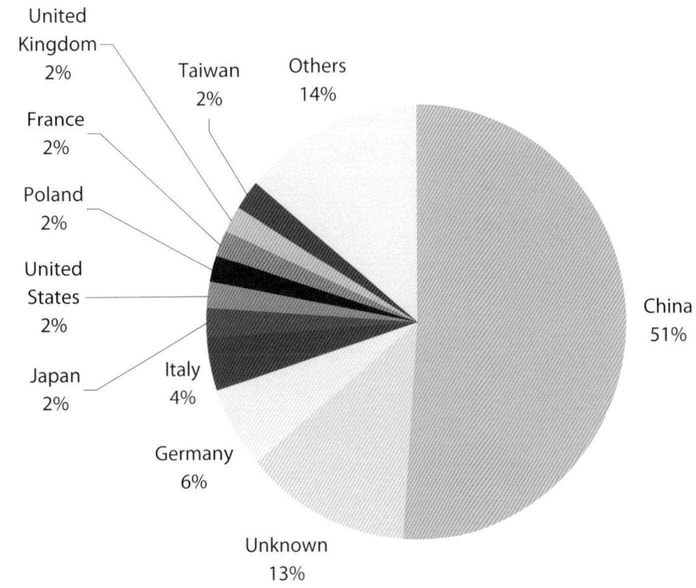

(1) EU-27, Iceland, Liechtenstein and Norway.

Source: Keeping consumers safe, Annual report 2007, RAPEX

Table 1.76: Injuries from all types of accidents: breakdown by product involved in the accident, 2005-2006
(% of all injuries)

	BE	CZ	EE	CY	LV	MT
Building, building component, or related fitting	13.3	13.5	9.3	33.8	14.8	16.3
Land vehicle or means of land transport	9.5	7.3	4.0	10.4	6.8	9.6
Ground surface or surface conformation	17.8	2.9	1.9	2.4	11.3	6.8
Animal, plant, or person	18.6	14.9	0.0	0.0	0.0	0.0
Tool, machine, apparatus mainly work-related	4.5	1.8	2.6	4.6	7.3	7.6
Furniture/furnishing	7.4	3.7	2.7	4.9	3.6	3.9
Utensil or container	4.6	1.3	1.1	6.0	2.9	3.5
Equipment mainly used in sports/recreation	4.2	4.9	0.0	0.0	0.0	0.0
Appliance mainly used in household	1.4	0.9	0.4	3.7	1.1	1.0
Infant or child product	1.2	1.2	0.4	3.0	1.0	0.6
Item mainly for personal use	2.1	0.3	0.3	1.4	0.3	1.2
Hot object/substance n.e.c.	0.3	0.2	0.3	1.9	2.0	0.7
Food, drink	1.8	0.2	0.2	0.3	0.9	1.0
Pharmaceuticals for human use, i.e. drug, medicine	1.0	0.1	0.0	1.7	0.1	0.1
Other non-pharmaceutical chemical substance	0.5	0.1	0.1	1.0	0.4	0.8
Mobile machinery or special purpose vehicle	0.5	0.3	0.4	0.5	0.3	0.2
Fire, flame, smoke	0.2	0.0	0.1	0.2	1.4	0.1
Medical/surgical device	1.4	0.0	0.1	0.2	0.0	0.1
Weapon	0.5	0.3	0.1	0.3	0.1	0.0
Other	9.2	46.1	76.0	23.7	45.7	46.5

Source: All injuries in Europe – pilot data 2005-2006 - Injuries Database

Table 1.77: Consumer products involved in home and leisure accidents, 2005-2006 (1)
(% of all accidents)

	(%)	Most reported injury
All home and leisure accidents		
Bicycle and accessories	3.3	Contusion/bruise
Ball	3.2	Distortion/sprain
Door	2.3	Contusion/bruise
Ski	2.0	Fracture
Chair/bench	2.0	Contusion/bruise
Bed	1.9	Contusion/bruise
Stationary equip. in playground	1.7	Fracture
Rolling sports equipment	1.6	Fracture
Ladder/scaffold	1.3	Fracture
Gymnastic/body-building equip.	1.2	Contusion/bruise
Do-it-yourself accidents		
Ladder/scaffold	11.7	Fracture
Drilling	7.0	Open wound
Sawing	5.3	Open wound
Motor vehicle	3.9	Open wound
Striking/hewing/hammering	3.6	Open wound
Domestic work accidents		
Kitchen utensils (not electric)	10.7	Open wound
Cutlery and tableware	5.0	Open wound
Household machines	4.2	Open wound
Ladder/scaffold	4.2	Fracture
Chair/bench	3.1	Fracture
Play and leisure activities		
Bicycle and accessories	4.9	Contusion/bruise
Stationary equip. in playground	4.3	Fracture
Door	3.1	Contusion/bruise
Rolling sports equipment	2.9	Fracture
Chair/bench	2.7	Contusion/bruise

(1) Based on information for Denmark, France, Austria and Sweden for the period 2003-2005.

Source: Injuries in the European Union, statistics summary 2003-2005, Injuries Database (https://webgate.ec.europa.eu/idb)

A pilot study provides a limited data set with information on the products responsible for injuries and accidents; statistical work in this area is being developed and is currently focused on agreeing a harmonised classification for causes of injuries and accidents.

The data collected so far may be split into two distinct areas, information covering all accidents, and that covering home and leisure accidents. For the former, some of the most often cited products involved in accidents include buildings and their fittings, vehicles, tools and machines, and furniture, while for home and leisure accidents the most common products involved in accidents include bicycles, balls, doors, skis, furniture, ladders and kitchen utensils.

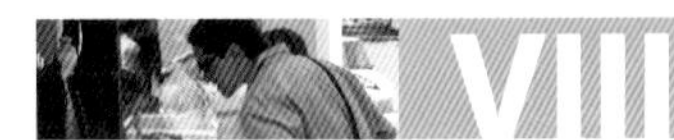

EXTERNALITIES

An externality occurs when an activity causes external costs, or results in external benefits, for a third party. Examples of negative externalities include: a manufacturing enterprise that generates air and water pollution as a by-product; a smoker in an enclosed space; or, a person consuming alcohol and then having a driving accident which injures or kills someone else. Positive externalities can result in benefits for a wider public, for example, cooling water from power stations increasing fish stocks, or a vaccination programme may reduce the risks of contracting a disease – not only for those who receive the vaccination, but also other people who did not receive the vaccination, as the risk of contracting the disease is reduced.

When presented with enough information on the impact of their lifestyle choices, some consumers are empowered to change their consumption patterns, for example, to foster a more sustainable lifestyle or improve their health – often these choices involve positive externalities. On the other hand, other consumers are not willing to give up items that define their way of life, for example: running a car with high fuel consumption, making several short leisure trips by plane each year, or buying fresh fruit all the year around – all of which involve negative externalities.

Governments can influence the behaviour of individuals, for example, by declaring certain actions illegal (smoking in public places), or by changing the tax and subsidy regime to encourage a different pattern of consumption (increasing excise duty on alcohol). Governments can also try to shape consumption patterns by giving information on energy-efficient appliances, or by taxing environmental damage through fuel surcharges or levies on the disposal of household appliances. Another idea currently under consideration in a number of the Member States is carbon trading systems for individuals. This would require individuals to manage their own carbon dioxide emissions, with emissions rights (in the form of carbon credits) being allocated across the population; those who needed to, or wanted to emit more than their allowance would have to buy additional allowances from those who emit less. In a similar vein there are also a number of companies that operate similar, voluntary schemes.

Environment

The level of air pollution within the EU varies considerably between, as well as within, countries. One measure is based on the calculation of average ozone concentrations (during 8 hour periods) from which the highest average each day is recorded: the highest value (in 2005) was recorded in Greece, more than 30 times as high as in Latvia, which had the lowest levels. In terms of particulate matter, the differences between countries were less marked, with the highest level recorded in Italy, just over three times as high as in Ireland.

Table 1.78: Urban population exposure to air pollution, 2005

	Ozone (micrograms per m^3 * day) (1)	Particulate matter (micrograms per m^3) (2)
BE	2 688	30.9
BG	:	:
CZ	5 531	39.8
DK	1 472	23.4
DE	3 323	24.2
EE	1 328	20.7
IE	:	13.8
EL	9 625	41.1
ES	4 089	31.7
FR	4 245	20.4
IT	7 748	42.8
CY	:	:
LV	307	:
LT	5 047	22.9
LU	:	:
HU	5 091	37.7
MT	:	:
NL	1 490	32.0
AT	5 730	28.9
PL	4 022	39.4
PT	3 894	34.8
RO	:	:
SI	6 053	36.4
SK	7 430	33.2
FI	1 692	15.3
SE	2 851	19.5
UK	1 250	23.6
IS	66	19.6
NO	:	18.6

(1) Population weighted annual sum of maximum daily 8-hour mean ozone concentrations above a threshold (70 micrograms of ozone per m^3).
(2) Population weighted annual mean concentration of particulate matter.

Source: Eurostat, Structural indicators (strind_t)

Eurostat's statistics on income and living conditions (EU-SILC) provide information on consumer perceptions in relation to pollution, grime and other environmental problems caused by traffic or industry. Less than 10 % of respondents in Ireland, Austria, Denmark and Sweden were concerned by the pollution, grime or other environmental problems caused by traffic or industry in 2006; this could be contrasted with shares of 31 % in Latvia, rising to a high of almost 40 % in Malta.

A survey conducted across the main European cities reveals that, aside from Luxembourg, a majority of respondents were of the opinion that air pollution was a big problem in their capital city in 2006. A similar pattern was observed for noise pollution, with a majority of respondents agreeing it was a problem in every capital city other than Luxembourg and Stockholm.

Table 1.79: Perception survey results concerning pollution and noise in capital cities, 2006

	Air pollution is a big problem here (synthetic index 0-100)	Summer smog: ozone concentrations exceed 120 microgram/m³ (number of days)	Nitrogen dioxide concentrations exceed 200 microgram/m³ (number of days)	Particulate matter concentrations exceed 50 microgram/m³ (number of days)	Noise is a problem: agree (somewhat+ strongly) (%)
Bruxelles / Brussel	82.2	:	0	15	62.5
Sofia	92.2	:	:	:	79.8
Praha	84.8	19	0	51	77.9
København	74.8	0	0	2	63.2
Berlin	67.8	6	0	17	60.3
Tallinn	69.7	0	0	8	62.4
Dublin	60.2	:	:	:	60.1
Athina	94.6	:	:	:	91.7
Madrid	89.0	28	0	47	85.6
Paris	87.9	11	0	3	75.4
Roma	92.7	48	0	13	81.3
Lefkosia	83.3	5	0	183	79.6
Riga	75.4	0	0	:	61.2
Vilnius	86.7	2	0	19	68.0
Luxembourg	48.1	:	:	:	36.8
Budapest	83.6	11	0	33	81.3
Valletta	94.3	:	:	:	79.8
Amsterdam	78.8	4	0	24	56.2
Wien	52.2	23	0	21	53.8
Warszawa	81.5	8	0	38	78.4
Lisboa	87.4	12	5	55	81.4
Bucureşti	91.2	26	63	147	80.6
Ljubljana	76.5	31	0	88	66.5
Bratislava	73.9	22	0	40	65.6
Helsinki	62.6	4	0	3	53.6
Stockholm	56.4	1	0	3	45.4
London	86.1	3	1	9	76.7
Ankara	53.7	:	:	164	59.2

Source: Eurostat, Perception survey results and data collected for core cities (urb_percep and urb_vcity)

Figure 1.75: Consumer perceptions: do you feel that the pollution, grime or other environmental problems caused by traffic or industry are a problem in your area, 2006 (1)
(% of respondents)

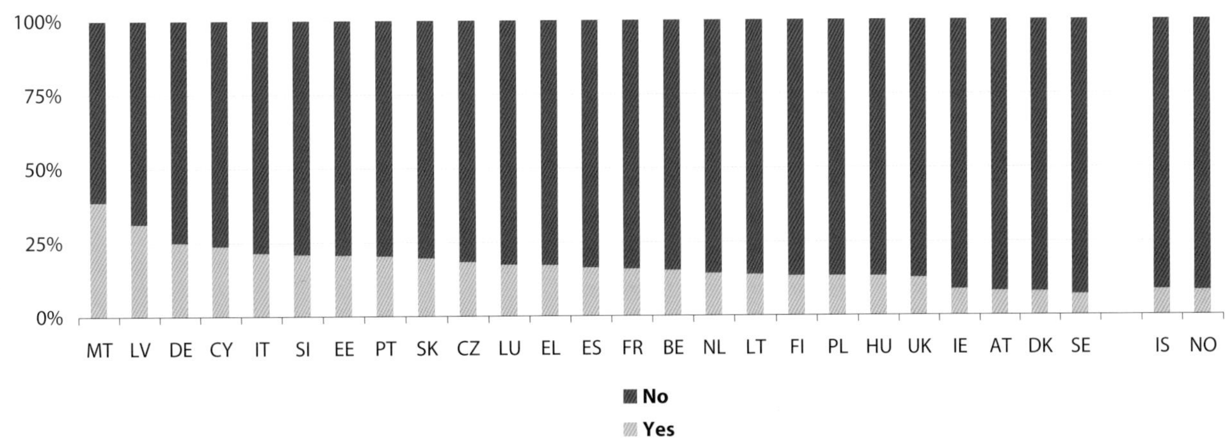

(1) Bulgaria and Romania, not available.

Source: Eurostat, EU-SILC cross sectional 2006 data

Waste

Aside from damage to the environment in terms of pollution, one of the other main by-products of consumption is waste; households are estimated to have accounted for just under 8 % of all the waste generated in the EU-27 in 2004.

Some consumers are highly aware of the implications of their consumption and shopping practices, and consider not only the product but its packaging when making purchases, for example, purchasing loose items rather than pre-packed products, and using their own shopping bags or containers rather than disposable plastic bags. Nevertheless, households continue to produce large quantities of waste, including significant quantities of food that has passed its sell-by date. The extent to which households separate waste also varies, influenced not only by household members' willingness to sort, but also the availability of collection and processing schemes for different waste streams.

On average 517 kg of municipal waste was generated per person in the EU-27 in 2006, ranging from a high of 804 kg in Ireland down to 259 kg in Poland. While some forms of household waste can be reused or recycled, other waste streams need to be treated and disposed of. An average of 213 kg of waste per person was placed in landfill sites in the EU-27 in 2006, while a further 98 kg of waste per person was incinerated.

Table 1.80: Generation of waste from households, 2004

	Household waste (thousand tonnes)	of which: Non-hazardous (%)	Household waste as a proportion of total waste (%)
EU-27 (1)	211 666	99.3	7.7
BE (1)	5 325	93.2	10.1
BG	2 634	100.0	1.0
CZ	2 841	99.2	9.7
DK	2 016	100.0	15.7
DE	38 008	99.3	10.4
EE	402	99.0	1.9
IE	1 702	100.0	6.9
EL (1)	4 213	100.0	14.6
ES	24 410	99.8	15.2
FR (1)	26 432	99.9	6.5
IT	31 150	99.8	22.3
CY	367	100.0	24.1
LV	543	100.0	43.2
LT	602	100.0	11.4
LU	221	99.1	2.7
HU (1)	4 442	100.0	18.0
MT	100	98.0	4.0
NL	9 440	96.9	10.8
AT	3 441	97.8	6.5
PL	6 768	100.0	4.9
PT	4 583	99.7	15.7
RO	3 638	100.0	1.0
SI	661	99.8	11.5
SK	1 475	99.8	13.8
FI	1 164	99.6	1.6
SE	4 079	90.9	3.9
UK	31 007	99.9	8.7
TR (1)	29 225	100.0	49.7
IS	141	100.0	28.2
NO	1 934	99.6	25.9

(1) Estimates.

Source: Eurostat, Generation of waste by economic sector and households (env_wasgen) and population by sex and age on 1 January of each year (demo_pjan)

Figure 1.76: Perception survey results concerning cleanliness of capital cities, 2006
(% of respondents)

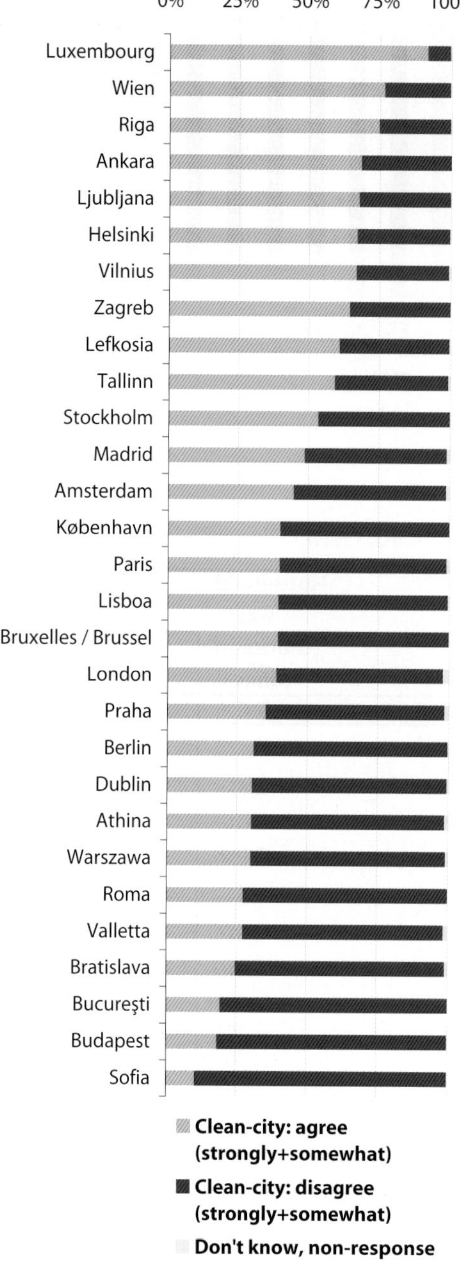

Source: Eurostat, Perception survey results and data collected for core cities (urb_percep and urb_vcity)

A perception survey conducted in 2006 asked respondents whether or not they thought they lived in a 'clean' city. A high proportion (91.6 %) of respondents living in Luxembourg agreed that their city was clean, while around three quarters of the residents of Vienna and Riga also gave positive replies. The other Baltic and Scandinavian capital cities were among those to report a majority of respondents agreeing that their city was clean, as was the case for residents of Ankara, Ljubljana, Zagreb, and Nicosia. At the other end of the ranking, almost nine out of ten (89.6 %) residents in Sofia disagreed with the premise that their city was clean, a share that stood close to eight of ten in Bucharest and Budapest.

Table 1.81: Waste generation and treatment, 2006
(kg per person)

	Municipal waste generated	Municipal waste landfilled	Municipal waste incinerated
EU-27	517	213	98
BE (1)	475	24	155
BG	446	356	0
CZ	296	234	29
DK (1)	737	37	405
DE (1)	566	4	179
EE (1)	466	278	1
IE (1)	804	471	0
EL	443	386	0
ES (1)	583	289	41
FR (1)	553	192	183
IT (1)	548	284	65
CY	745	652	0
LV	411	292	2
LT	390	356	0
LU (1)	702	131	266
HU	468	376	39
MT	652	562	0
NL	625	12	213
AT (1)	617	59	181
PL	259	236	1
PT (1)	435	274	95
RO (1)	385	326	0
SI	432	362	3
SK	301	234	36
FI	488	286	42
SE	497	25	233
UK	588	353	55
TR (1)	434	364	0
IS (1)	534	370	47
NO	793	245	132
CH	715	1	355

(1) Estimates.

Source: Eurostat, Structural indicators (strind_t)

CONSUMER REPRESENTATION AND PROTECTION

Dissatisfied consumers who wish to lodge complaints or seek some form of protection may be deterred from doing so by the fact that they often have to take action as an individual. A recent Eurobarometer survey of consumer protection in the internal market found that 76 % of EU-27 consumers in early 2008 agreed that they would be more willing to defend their rights in court if they could join with other consumers who were complaining about the same thing. Furthermore, individual consumers may lack information, time, knowledge, confidence, or finance to seek protection in the courts or through other forms of redress. As a result, consumer interests are often defended collectively by representative bodies, in a similar vein to employee interests being defended by trades unions, or business interests through trade or business organisations.

Table 1.82: Financial resources of national consumer organisations, 2006 (1)
(EUR thousand)

	Total funding	Average funding per consumer organisation
BE	1 673	112
BG	30	3
CZ	750	75
DK	:	:
DE	:	:
EE	51	10
IE	65	65
EL	250	6
ES	:	:
FR	7 379	224
IT	:	:
CY	:	:
LV	30	30
LT	72	10
LU	830	830
HU	946	38
MT	0	0
NL	438	438
AT	2 235	745
PL	556	111
PT	200	15
RO	40	40
SI	374	62
SK	70	10
FI	521	261
SE	965	321
UK	:	:

Source: national governments, provided to Directorate-General for Health and Consumers, European Commission

Representation

When consumer representative groups work for the benefit of a collective body of consumers, they have the potential to exert significant pressure on businesses and governments. At the same time, many consumer groups play an important role in making consumers aware of their rights. The European Commission believes that the involvement of these organisations is important to develop effective legislation reflecting the needs of all stakeholders.

Consumer organisations have the potential to help consumers make sense of a growing volume of information on a range of increasingly complex goods and services, helping markets function more efficiently, and providing effective representation and protection. Most consumer organisations seek to promote, defend and represent the interests of consumers – generally they provide services, such as information, advice and legal assistance. However, a number also carry out product testing, provide education and training, engage in consumer-based research, or contribute to the development of consumer legislation.

There is a vast array of different consumer organisations across the EU, ranging in size, capacity and goals, often dependent on historical and legal differences between Member States. The financial resources made available to consumer organisations vary considerably, as does the number of organisations that receive public funding. A list of consumers' organisations in each Member State can be found at: http://ec.europa.eu/consumers/cons_org/associations/national/index_en.htm.

It is equally difficult to measure the number of consumers who are represented by these consumer organisations: either in terms of their membership (some require individual, family or household membership, while others do not have any formal membership status); or in terms of the number of cases that are dealt with each year. Generally membership levels are thought to be relatively low, with only a handful of northern European countries reporting in excess of 10 % of their population being members of a consumer representative group.

European Community funding helps the activities of the European Association for the Coordination of Consumer Representation in Standardisation

(ANEC) and the European Consumers' Organisation/Bureau Européen des Unions des Consommateurs (BEUC). ANEC (www.anec.eu) is a voice for European consumers in relation to standardisation and certification, while BEUC (www.beuc.org) defends and promotes the interests of European consumers as purchasers or users of goods and services; note that these pan-European organisations generally represent the views of their national consumer bodies, rather than dealing with queries from individual consumers.

The European Consumer Centres Network (ECC-Net) helps consumers with cross-border disputes and was set up in January 2005 by the European Commission in cooperation with national authorities. These consumer centres give information and advice on problems with shopping across borders and intervene when problems arise. A full listing of ECC-Net offices can be found at: http://ec.europa.eu/consumers/redress/ecc_network/index_en.htm.

A consumer survey conducted by Eurobarometer in 2006 showed that there was a relatively low proportion of European consumers aware of a range of services launched by the European Commission to promote consumer protection and inform citizens of their rights; generally the most well-known services were the ECC-Net and Europe Direct, for which more information may be obtained at: http://ec.europa.eu/europedirect/index_en.htm.

A more recent Eurobarometer survey conducted in early 2008 asked if respondents had heard of the European Consumer Centres (Euroguichets). This showed that, on average, some 15 % of the EU-27 population were aware of the service, which was somewhat higher than the 11 % share recorded for the EU-25 in 2006.

Table 1.83: The European Commission offers the following services to help citizens concerning their rights in the Single Market; which of the following services have you heard of, 2006
(% of respondents, multiple answers possible)

	Your Europe	SOLVIT	Citizens Signpost Service	FIN-NET	Europe Direct	European Consumer Centres (Euro-guichets)	None	Don't know
EU-25	4	2	3	2	6	11	69	9
BE	8	3	2	2	3	13	75	1
BG	:	:	:	:	:	:	:	:
CZ	5	1	6	4	8	16	55	14
DK	3	1	1	2	12	8	73	5
DE	4	1	1	3	6	19	72	3
EE	4	2	1	4	8	9	64	17
IE	9	6	5	2	10	12	57	15
EL	4	2	3	4	1	16	72	3
ES	3	2	6	2	5	8	72	12
FR	3	0	1	2	6	9	76	6
IT	3	4	4	3	3	5	62	18
CY	5	2	9	3	16	18	58	10
LV	3	1	2	3	7	10	66	13
LT	3	2	5	2	3	12	54	24
LU	3	4	1	2	8	19	63	7
HU	4	2	5	1	8	6	66	15
MT	8	5	3	2	10	9	58	19
NL	8	4	2	4	6	6	72	6
AT	6	5	9	2	5	18	50	13
PL	7	2	4	1	5	17	64	9
PT	3	2	2	3	4	9	73	14
RO	:	:	:	:	:	:	:	:
SI	7	4	7	3	6	12	69	5
SK	12	2	7	4	14	17	47	15
FI	10	2	10	5	6	10	65	6
SE	9	2	4	2	16	30	55	2
UK	2	3	2	1	6	6	77	7

Source: 'Internal Market, 2006', Special Eurobarometer 254, European Commission

Protection

Consumer protection extends beyond trying to ensure that goods and services are safe, and covers a range of issues that touch on economic interests, as well as the health and safety. It is considered by policy makers when developing legislation for a range of issues, for example, from food safety to the liberalisation of services of general interest, or from the introduction of the euro to advertising claims.

More specifically, consumer confidence may be expected to increase as a result of consumer protection and consumer rights being upheld. The central theme of most consumer protection legislation is to guarantee that dangerous goods or malicious practices are uncovered and taken off the market as quickly as possible. Consumer protection legislation has been introduced at a pan-European level to cover areas such as unfair commercial practices (Directive 2005/29/EC of the European Parliament and of the Council concerning unfair business-to-consumer commercial practices in the internal market) and consumer protection co-operation (Regulation (EC) No 2006/2004 of the European Parliament and of the Council on co-operation between national authorities responsible for the enforcement of consumer protection laws).

EU consumers have the same basic rights in all Member States, for example, the right: to buy what they want where they want; to expect goods and services to be safe; to return faulty goods; to change their mind after having purchased something; and to have redress in cross-border disputes. If a consumer believes that the law is being broken – for example, fraudulent labelling, misleading advertising, unfair contract terms, the absence of a clear price on goods, or an unsafe product – they can take their complaint to the national authority responsible for monitoring that market, or to a consumers' representative organisation. Often the problems encountered can be resolved by simply complaining to the supplier, manufacturer or distributor directly. Otherwise, out-of-court settlements can be aided by contacting an ombudsman, going to arbitration, or contacting a conciliation organisation. In the event that a dispute cannot be resolved, then a case can be pursued before the courts, although this may involve high costs and considerable delays; in response to this, some Member States have established simplified judicial proceedings that deal more rapidly with small claims.

The European Commission has launched a debate on the need for a collective redress mechanism in the EU. A European group action procedure would allow a number of consumers to bring a case together before a court to obtain compensation for a damage caused by the same trader. It is argued that this could improve competitiveness as a result of changing the way the internal market functions, giving consumers more confidence to shop abroad, facilitating access to justice, minimising litigation costs, reducing discrimination, and being generally advantageous to compliant businesses.

A Eurobarometer survey conducted in early 2008 shows that 54 % of respondents in the EU-27 thought that public authorities protected their consumer rights, while 64 % of respondents agreed that independent consumer organisations protected their rights.

A Eurobarometer survey conducted in 2006 showed that a higher proportion of consumers in the EU-15 Member States agreed that they had adequate consumer protection (57 %), compared with a share of 43 % among the ten Member States that joined the EU in 2004. The

Figure 1.77: To what extent do you trust consumer organisations and public authorities to protect your rights as a consumer, EU-27, 2008
(% of respondents)

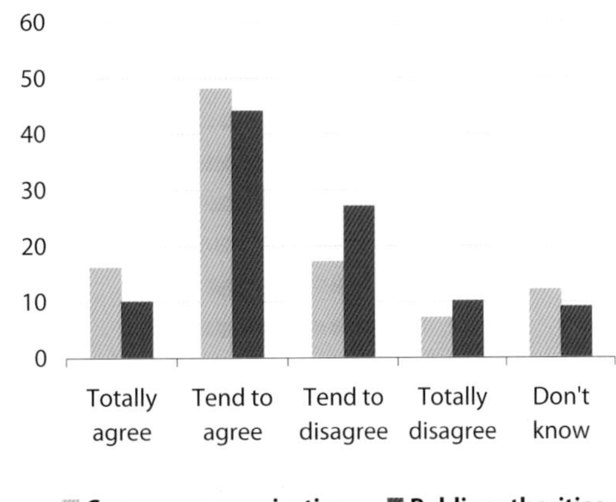

Source: 'Consumer protection in the Internal Market, 2008', Special Eurobarometer 298, European Commission

same question was posed in early 2008 and the results were quite similar. Of the Member States that joined the EU since 2004 (including Bulgaria and Romania), only Cyprus and Malta reported a higher proportion of respondents (compared with the EU-27 average, 51 %) agreeing that they had adequate consumer protection. At least two thirds of consumers in the Netherlands, Denmark, Finland, Sweden and the United Kingdom agreed that they were adequately protected.

When asked if they thought the internal market had increased consumer protection within the EU-25, some 53 % of respondents agreed (compared with 21 % who disagreed). The highest proportion of respondents in agreement was recorded in Slovenia and Cyprus (both 69 %), while all of the other Member States that joined the EU in 2004 also reported shares above the EU-25 average. At the other end of the ranking, less than half of those questioned in Germany, Sweden, France, Austria and the United Kingdom agreed that the internal market had increased consumer protection, while as many as 34 % of respondents in both France and Austria disagreed.

Figure 1.78: To what extent do you agree that you are adequately protected by existing measures to protect consumers, 2008
(% of respondents)

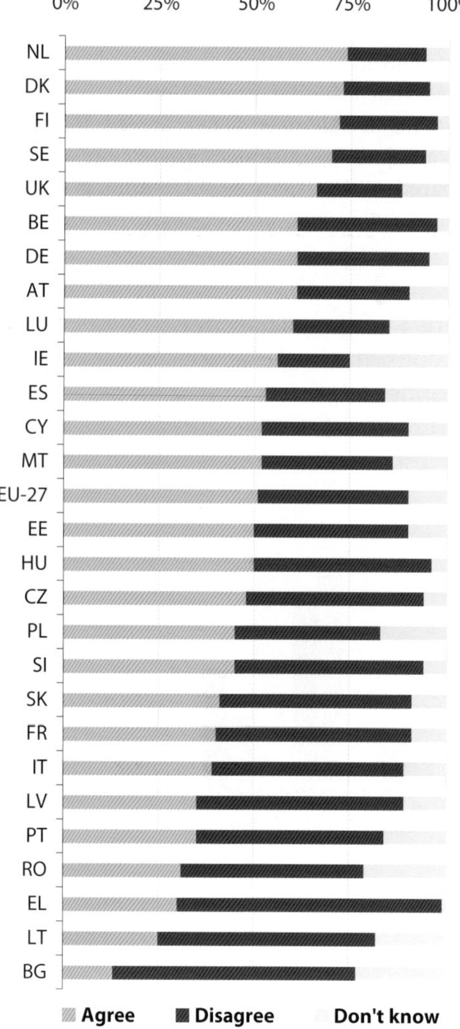

Source: 'Consumer protection in the Internal Market, 2008', Special Eurobarometer 298, European Commission

Figure 1.79: Do you agree or disagree that the internal market rules have increased consumer protection within the European Union, 2006 (1)
(% of respondents)

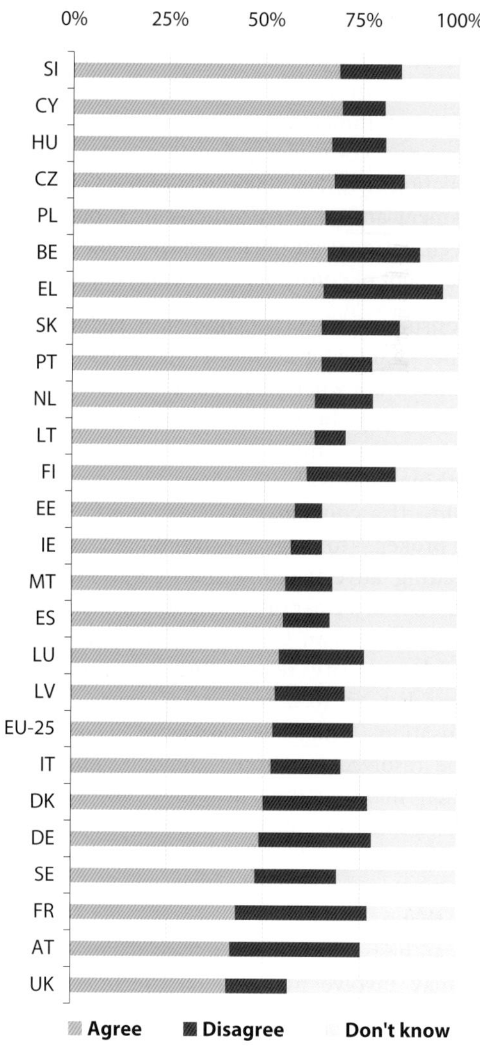

(1) Bulgaria and Romania, not available.

Source: 'Consumer protection in the internal market', Special Eurobarometer 252, European Commission

Almost six out of every ten (59 %) consumers in the EU-27 agreed that sellers and providers of goods and services from their home country respected their consumer rights in 2008. This ratio rose to more than seven out of ten persons in Finland (the highest proportion of consumers in agreement, 88 %), the Benelux countries, Sweden, the United Kingdom and Germany. Of the Member States that joined the EU since 2004, Estonia and Slovenia were the only ones to record a higher proportion of consumers agreeing that their rights were respected by sellers/providers than the EU-27 average; by far the lowest levels were reported in Bulgaria, where only one in five respondents agreed their rights were respected by sellers/providers in 2008.

Some 15 % of EU-25 consumers questioned in 2006 reported that during the previous 12 months they had tried to replace, repair, ask for a price reduction, or cancel a contract within their warranty rights. A similar proportion (15 %) had tried to return a product or cancel a contract within the cooling-off period, after having purchased something by Internet, phone or post in their own country or elsewhere in EU, while 14 % of respondents stated they had tried to return a product or cancel a contract having purchased something from a sales representative.

When asked if they had been unduly coerced or pressurised to purchase something or sign up to a contract, 13 % of EU-25 consumers agreed, while one in ten said they had come across unfair consumer contract terms, particularly in standard contracts or terms and conditions in their own country or elsewhere in EU. It is interesting to note that the proportion of consumers trying to return goods was often relatively high in those countries which also reported a high proportion of consumers agreeing that their rights were respected by sellers and providers of goods and services (Germany, the Netherlands, Finland and Sweden).

Figure 1.80: Do you agree that sellers/providers in your home country respect your rights, 2008
(% of respondents)

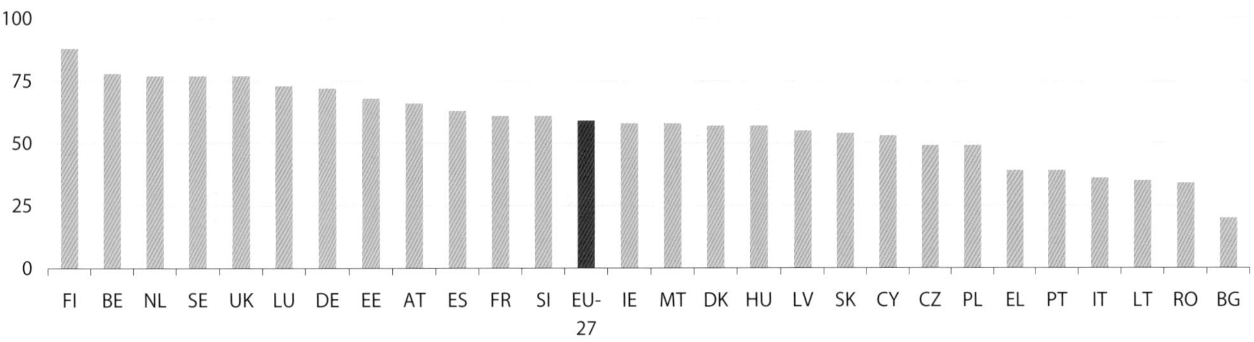

Source: 'Consumer protection in the Internal Market, 2008', Special Eurobarometer 298, European Commission

Table 1.84: Consumers' behaviour with respect to returns and contract terms, during the previous 12 months, 2006
(% of respondents)

	Tried to replace, repair, ask for a price reduction, or cancel a contract within warranty rights	Tried to return a product or cancel a contract within cooling-off period, after having purchased something by Internet, phone or post in own country or elsewhere in EU	Tried to return a product or cancel a contract within cooling-off period, after having purchased something from a sales representative at home or workplace	Were unduly coerced or pressurised to purchase something or sign up to a contract	Came across unfair consumer contract terms, particularly in standard contracts or terms and conditions in own country or elsewhere in EU
EU-25	15	15	14	13	10
BE	13	17	5	13	11
BG	:	:	:	:	:
CZ	32	19	15	16	28
DK	32	9	8	2	8
DE	23	24	13	11	10
EE	15	21	14	13	8
EL	4	5	4	19	4
ES	8	9	15	9	7
FR	10	11	13	16	14
IE	11	11	22	15	9
IT	11	14	24	17	10
CY	4	6	36	7	10
LV	14	13	8	24	7
LT	12	8	7	8	10
LU	12	11	6	10	8
HU	13	10	10	5	12
MT	14	8	3	13	7
NL	24	18	6	7	8
AT	18	18	30	10	12
PL	13	5	7	14	12
PT	6	9	17	9	3
RO	:	:	:	:	:
SI	14	22	21	14	7
SK	23	10	6	14	18
FI	23	24	17	11	12
SE	20	15	8	7	8
UK	17	14	12	15	9

Source: 'Consumer protection in the internal market', Special Eurobarometer 252, European Commission

As regards dispute resolution, in early 2008 some 39 % of respondents in the EU-27 thought that it was easy to resolve disputes with sellers/providers from their own country through out-of-court settlements involving arbitration, mediation or conciliation bodies, while less than a third (30 %) agreed that it was easy to resolve a dispute through the courts.

Table 1.85: Consumers' opinions regarding dispute resolution with sellers/providers from their home country, 2008
(% of respondents)

	Agree they would be more willing to defend their rights in court if they could join with other consumers who were complaining about the same thing	Agree it is easy to resolve disputes through arbitration, mediation or conciliation body	Agree it is easy to resolve disputes through courts
EU-27	76	39	30
BE	86	51	41
BG	48	12	12
CZ	77	25	19
DK	87	47	46
DE	81	43	36
EE	68	33	20
EL	65	36	31
ES	83	43	47
FR	73	29	23
IE	85	46	30
IT	69	27	31
CY	82	50	22
LV	64	32	26
LT	56	23	17
LU	76	48	19
HU	50	34	18
MT	48	31	17
NL	91	57	40
AT	71	38	28
PL	75	35	22
PT	54	19	14
RO	46	29	22
SI	67	40	20
SK	61	17	14
FI	78	47	24
SE	88	45	31
UK	88	52	40

Source: 'Consumer protection in the Internal Market, 2008', Special Eurobarometer 298, European Commission

Food and non-alcoholic beverages

Food and beverages are amongst the most important consumption items, satisfying the basic physiological needs related to hunger and thirst and forming one of the most recurrent expenditure items for the majority of EU households. The EU has great diversity in its food and drink products, and these often form a part of local, regional, or national, cultural identity.

1.1 Access, choice

Alongside own production, households source food and non-alcoholic beverages mainly from the retail network: market stalls, independent retailers (grocers, butchers or bakers), and (inter-) national chains of supermarkets, hypermarkets and discount stores (who often sell a range of products well beyond food and beverages).

The largest food retailers (see Table 1.1) in western and central Europe are, unsurprisingly, from some of the largest Member States, namely Germany, France and the United Kingdom. The absence of large Italian retailers can be explained to a large extent by the relative importance of independent enterprises within Italian retailing, underlined by the low market share of the three largest food retailers in Italy (see Table 1.2). Food retailing concentration, as measured by the market share of the three largest retailers, was particularly high in all of the Nordic countries shown in Table 1.2, and was lowest in the southern EU Member States.

The growing number of large food retail outlets outside of urban centres with dedicated parking facilities and integrated transport infrastructure has generally led to a reduction in the average number of shopping trips that are made for food each week. Indeed, according to a 2008 retail satisfaction survey, more than two thirds (68.6 % and 66.9 %) of European consumers regularly purchased fresh fruit and vegetables or meat at a supermarket or hypermarket, a share that rose to over three quarters (77 %) for non-alcoholic beverages – see Figure 1.1. The next most popular retail format varied according to the product in question, with discount stores used by a relatively high proportion of people shopping for non-alcoholic beverages, butchers by those shopping for meat, and street markets or farm shops by those purchasing fresh fruit and vegetables.

Table 1.1: Western and central Europe: top 30 grocery retailers, 2006

			Market share (%)	Grocery sales (EUR million)
1	Carrefour	FR	6.0	59 732
2	Tesco	UK	4.5	45 117
3	Schwarz Group	DE	3.3	37 294
4	Rewe	DE	3.3	34 036
5	Edeka	DE	2.9	33 029
6	Aldi	DE	2.7	29 603
7	Metro Group	DE	4.7	29 167
8	Ahold (1)	NL	2.1	23 373
9	Auchan	FR	2.8	23 359
10	ITM (Intermarché)	FR	2.2	22 627
11	Casino	FR	2.2	22 225
12	Sainsbury	UK	2.0	20 386
13	Leclerc	FR	2.4	19 788
14	Wal-Mart	US	2.0	18 346
15	Morrisons (2)	UK	1.5	15 478
16	Système U	FR	1.2	13 262
17	Mercadona	ES	0.9	11 793
18	Coop Norden	SE	1.1	11 589
19	Tengelmann	DE	1.4	11 288
20	Coop Italia	IT	0.9	10 034
21	Migros	CH	1.1	8 609
22	Louis Delhaize	BE	0.8	7 247
23	Baugur	IS	0.9	6 999
24	Coop (CH)	CH	0.7	6 832
25	Marks & Spencer (3)	UK	1.0	5 917
26	SOK	FI	0.8	5 546
27	Alliance Boots	UK	0.7	4 811
28	Kesko	FI	0.9	4 721
29	El Corte Inglés	ES	1.5	4 708
30	Co-operative Group	UK	1.1	4 019

(1) Consolidated operations only.
(2) Estimates.
(3) Figures include wholly owned operation in the United Kingdom only.

Source: Planet Retail Ltd - www.planetretail.net

There were quite large differences between countries as regards the most common forms of retail format – with supermarkets and hypermarkets highly frequented in Ireland, the Netherlands and the United Kingdom, whereas discount stores were more often used in Denmark and Germany. Consumers in Greece and Romania favoured street markets or farm shops for purchasing fresh fruit and vegetables, while those in Estonia and Lithuania preferred this retail format for their meat purchases.

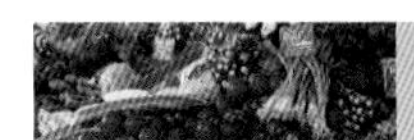

Table 1.2: Concentration of the three largest food retailers, 2004 (1)

	Number 1	Number 2	Number 3	Market share (%)
BE	Carrefour	Delhaize	Colruyt	68
DK	Coop	Dansk supermarket	Supergros	86
DE	Edeka	Rewe	Aldi	55
IE	Tesco	Dunnes	Supervalue	58
EL	Carrefour	Alfa-Beta	Sklavenitis	38
ES	Carrefour	Mercadona	Eroski Group	54
FR	Carrefour	Leclerc/Systu	Intermarché	64
IT	Coop	Conad	Carrefour	27
NL	Ahold	Laurus	Tsm	59
AT	Bml-Rewe	Spar	Hofer-Aldi	68
PT	Sonae	Jmr	Intermarché	47
FI	Kesko	Sok	Tradeka	80
SE	Ica	Axfood	KF	91
UK	Tesco	Sainsbury	Asda	58
NO	Norgesgruppen	Coop	Hakon	83
CH	Migros	Coop	Denner	77

(1) No data available for those Member States not shown.

Source: ACNielsen, 2004 in 'Data & trends of the European food and drink industry, 2007' (CIAA, Confederation of the food and drink industries of the EU)

Figure 1.1: In which of the following places have you or has a member of your household bought the following products the most, EU-27, 2008?
(%)

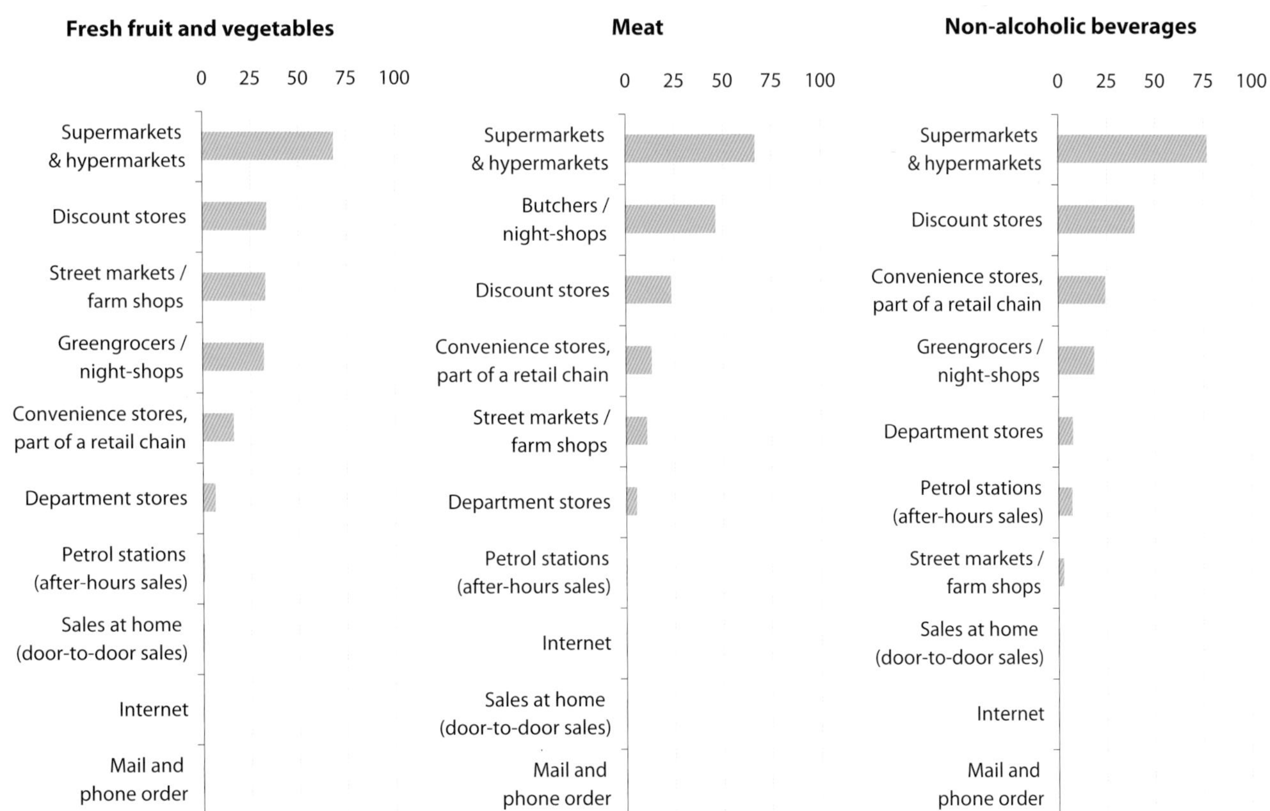

Source: 'Retail satisfaction survey', IPSOS for the European Commission, August/September 2008

Figure 1.2: When you go shopping for food, what would you say are the most important factors that influence your choice, EU-25, September-October 2005
(%, maximum two answers)

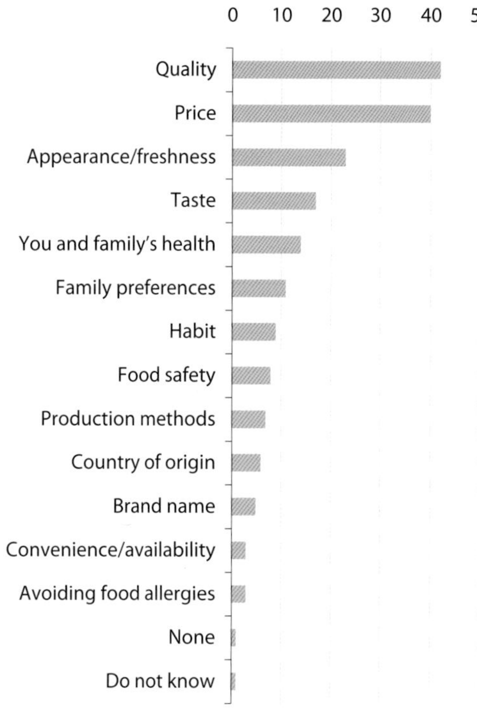

Source: 'Risk issues', Special Eurobarometer 238, European Commission

A Eurobarometer survey carried out in the autumn of 2005 looked in more detail at factors influencing choice when food shopping. By far the two most important factors were price and the broad heading of quality (see Figure 1.2). A number of specific issues related to quality were also considered important, notably freshness, issues relating to family health, and food safety, while taste and family preferences were also mentioned by more than 10 % of respondents. Issues such as production methods, or the food's country of origin were less important, but nevertheless ranked higher than brand names. An analysis by country indicates that price was regarded as important by a greater proportion of respondents in Portugal than in any other Member State, and by the lowest proportion of respondents in Luxembourg and Austria. Quality appeared to be an important factor for a large proportion of respondents in Greece and Cyprus, while only a relatively small proportion of respondents in Poland and the Czech Republic considered it an important factor.

A more recent survey carried out in 2008 focused on a number of product categories, including fresh fruit and vegetables; respondents were asked to rate a variety of factors in relation to their regular retailer. For each of the different criteria, consumers gave generally favourable responses (see Figure 1.3), with the lowest levels of satisfaction recorded with respect to the choice of environmentally-friendly, new or innovative, or ethically produced fruit and vegetables. Given that price and quality are often identified as the most important factors for consumer decision-making, it is interesting to note the apparent similarities in terms of how consumers rate these two categories for fresh fruit and vegetables, meat or non-alcoholic beverages. Consumers in Ireland, Italy and Finland appeared to make the largest distinction in favour of quality, whereas those in Germany, Latvia and Slovakia placed a greater emphasis on price (see Figure 1.4).

Figure 1.3: Fresh fruit and vegetables: consumer satisfaction with various aspects of choice relating to their regular retailer, EU-27, 2008 (1)
(average, 1-10)

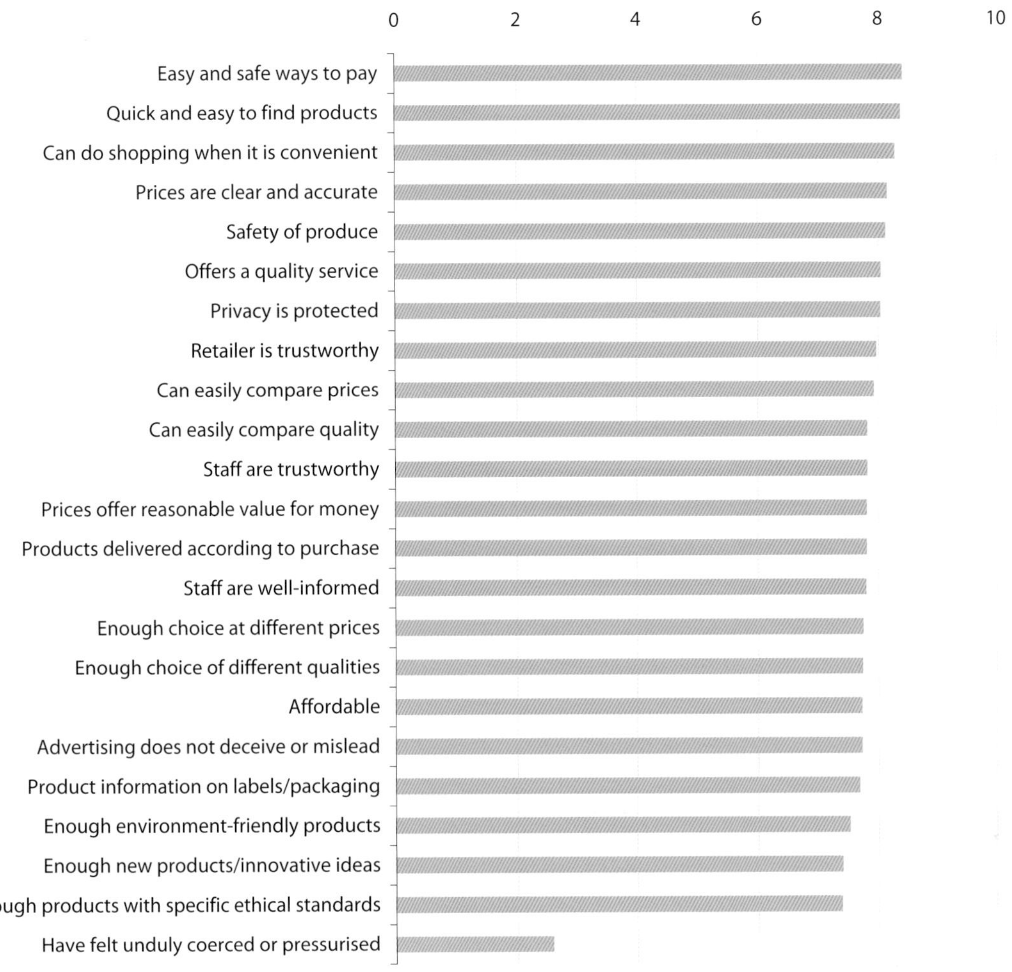

(1) Average on a scale of 1 (not at all in agreement) to 10 (totally in agreement).

Source: 'Retail satisfaction survey', IPSOS for the European Commission, August/September 2008

Figure 1.4: Price and quality: does your regular retailer offer a wide enough choice, 2008? (1)
(average, 1-10)

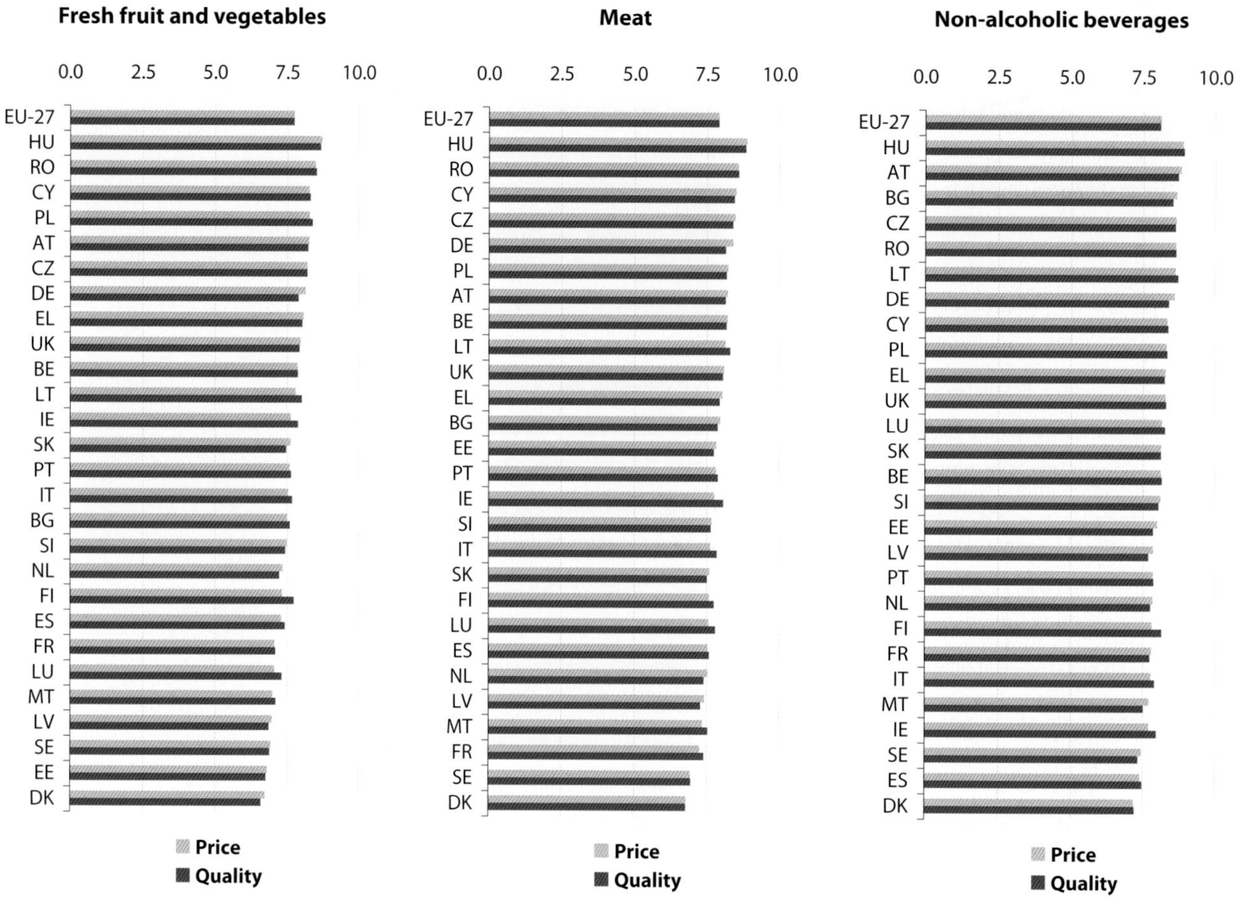

(1) Average on a scale of 1 (totally disagree) to 10 (totally agree).

Source: 'Retail satisfaction survey', IPSOS for the European Commission, August/September 2008

Figure 1.5 concerns one aspect of the combination of price and quality, more specifically looking at value for money and relating this to the availability of own label products. More than half of respondents in all of the countries shown regarded a large selection of such products as indicating good value for money.

British consumers' changing awareness of prices, own brand products, and special food products are presented in Table 1.3. While a majority of consumers regarded price as a more important factor than two years earlier, this increasing price awareness was stronger among women than men. Equally women were more likely than men to be frequent purchasers of own label or economy products. In a similar manner the increased price awareness and likelihood of frequently purchasing own label or economy products was influenced by occupational category, rising from a low among consumers in higher and intermediate managerial, administrative and

Figure 1.5: In deciding what stores offer good value for money, how important is it that the store carries a lot of own label products that are cheaper, January 2008 (1)
(%, very important/somewhat important)

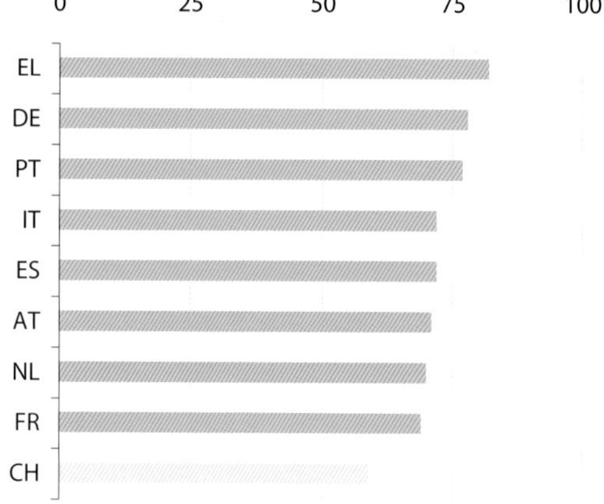

(1) No data available for those Member States not shown.

Source: http://www2.acnielsen.com/reports/documents/Nielsen_GOReport_WEB.pdf

professional positions to a high among those who were semi-skilled and unskilled manual workers, State pensioners, widows, casual or lowest grade workers. About half of the surveyed British consumers reported unchanged levels of spending on special food products (defined here as organic, fair trade or premium product lines) compared with two years earlier, while over one third reported increased spending on such products.

One particular category of special products that has received a lot of attention is organic produce, and it is widely accepted that the market share of organic produce has increased. Eurostat provides data for the vast majority of EU Member States on the prevalence of organic operators, including producers, processors and importers. By far the largest number of organic operators were reported in Italy with 51 000, followed by Greece, Germany and Austria, each with over 20 000 such operators (see Table 1.4).

Table 1.3: Factors influencing consumer choice in food retailing, United Kingdom, December 2006 (1)
(%)

Compared to two years ago to what extent do low prices influence your decision about which supermarket you visit?					
		More important	**No difference**	**Less important**	**Don't know**
Gender	Total	54	40	5	1
	Male	48	46	5	2
	Female	60	34	5	1
Occupational category (2)	AB	44	48	7	1
	C1	50	43	6	1
	C2	55	40	4	1
	DE	67	27	2	3
To what extent do you make a point of buying supermarkets' own brand value/economy food products?					
		Always or often	**Only basic products**	**Don't often or never**	**Don't know**
Gender	Total	44	31	23	1
	Male	42	32	26	1
	Female	47	30	21	2
Occupational category (2)	AB	40	28	31	2
	C1	44	32	23	2
	C2	45	33	21	1
	DE	51	30	18	1
Compared to two years ago, what do you spend on special food products such as organic, fair trade or premium lines?					
		Spend more	**About the same**	**Spend less**	**Don't know**
Gender	Total	34	50	11	6
	Male	33	53	10	5
	Female	35	48	12	6
Occupational category (2)	AB	34	55	9	2
	C1	38	44	11	7
	C2	30	55	11	4
	DE	32	48	12	8

(1) Excluding Northern Ireland.

(2) A: higher managerial/administrative/professional; B: intermediate managerial/administrative/professional; C1: supervisory or clerical and junior managerial/administrative/professional; C2: skilled manual worker; D: semi-skilled and unskilled manual workers; E: State pensioners, widows, casual and lowest grade workers.

Source: prepared on behalf of Retail Week by ICM Research

Table 1.4: Number of registered organic operators, 2006 (1)
(units)

	Operators	Processors	Importers
BE (2)	1 403	625	76
BG (2)	571	73	:
CZ (3)	1 093	192	8
DK (2)	3 584	642	176
DE (2)	23 978	8 052	689
EE	1 187	17	0
IE (2)	1 208	147	13
EL	24 666	1 044	9
ES	18 318	1 973	60
FR (3,4)	16 566	5 802	169
IT	51 065	6 887	208
CY	:	:	:
LV	4 105	38	0
LT	2 370	:	:
LU (4)	110	36	1
HU (5)	1 898	281	15
MT	11	5	0
NL	2 305	998	201
AT (4)	21 455	1 056	138
PL (5)	:	55	:
PT (3,4)	1 660	82	1
RO (2)	3 409	:	:
SK	298	27	2
SI	1 992	115	2
FI	4 315	148	6
SE (3)	3 317	303	121
UK	6 485	1 933	317
NO	2 878	376	32

(1) Provisional.
(2) Includes Eurostat estimates.
(3) Figures might contain double counting as mixed operators could be counted more than once.
(4) 2005.
(5) 2004.

Source: Eurostat, Organic farming (theme5/food/food_act2)

1.2 Consumption

1.2.1 Consumption volume

Table 1.5 provides an analysis, in quantity terms, of consumption of selected food items. Wide disparities exist between the per capita consumption levels of certain food items within the EU, often related to whether or not a product can be supplied locally. For example, the principal consumers of vegetable fats and oils were Greece, Spain and Italy, while meat consumption was high in Denmark.

Among those products for which data are available, the highest variation in consumption levels per capita was recorded for the consumption of dried pulses and the consumption of vegetable fats and oils. For the former, consumers in Malta ate an average of 6.7 kg, which was more than 25 times as much as in Austria (0.25 kg). In Greece, the average consumption of vegetable fats and oils was 48.6 kg per person, which was 18 times as much as in Sweden (2.7 kg).

1.2.2 Frequency and time spent food shopping, preparing and consuming

Just under half (46 %) of respondents to a 2005 Eurobarometer survey in the then 25 EU Member States reported that they always shopped for the food consumed by their household (see Table 1.6), while 7 % reported that they never did any household food shopping. The proportion of persons always food shopping for their household generally ranged from 39 % to 52 %, with the United Kingdom (57 %) above this range, and the Czech Republic (30 %), Slovakia (31 %) and Slovenia (34 %) below. As well as representing divisions of responsibility within a household, these trends may also reflect the proportion of respondents living in households with just one adult. In contrast, 18 % of Maltese respondents said that they never went food shopping for their household, and double digit shares were also recorded in Ireland, France, Spain and Portugal.

Moving from buying to consuming, the European time use survey (see Table 1.7) provides data for 14 Member States and Norway, and indicates the time spent preparing and eating food. In Estonia men and women on average ate for around one and a quarter hours per day, while in France the average was around one hour longer. Generally the average time spent eating did not vary greatly between men and women, the biggest absolute difference being in Bulgaria where men, on

Table 1.5: Gross human apparent consumption of selected food items, latest available year (1)
(kg per inhabitant)

	Cereals (excluding rice)	Rice	Meat	Vegetable fats & oils	Potatoes	Dried pulses	Sugar (equiv. white sugar)
BE	114.9	3.6	:	:	83.1	:	52.3
BG	:	3.9	:	16.4	38.3	5.1	26.0
CZ	128.2	:	:	:	75.1	2.0	:
DK	135.8	1.6	107.0	:	55.1	0.7	55.8
DE	112.7	4.4	87.1	:	63.0	0.6	37.4
EE	75.8	3.0	:	11.9	107.1	0.8	37.6
IE	110.8	7.8	:	:	123.0	0.7	31.8
EL	199.9	4.8	83.1	48.6	93.7	5.7	28.6
ES	101.0	:	122.6	33.3	81.9	5.4	:
FR	109.8	5.5	101.2	15.5	47.0	1.8	36.5
IT	169.2	10.4	90.6	22.5	43.1	1.8	43.6
CY	904.0	:	:	:	:	:	:
LV	112.6	2.1	:	:	147.4	2.2	24.4
LT	109.0	3.1	:	15.1	116.0	2.4	31.7
LU	82.5	:	:	:	79.9	0.3	51.1
HU	167.4	6.1	:	14.0	65.4	2.3	31.2
MT	110.3	9.6	:	17.5	95.3	6.7	34.6
NL	85.5	4.6	:	18.0	:	1.6	27.5
AT	111.6	3.0	98.7	11.8	53.6	0.3	39.0
PL	151.3	2.5	:	6.3	126.3	1.8	37.8
PT	126.7	:	104.8	:	86.8	4.3	30.4
RO	:	3.8	:	15.2	85.6	2.2	28.4
SI	:	:	:	:	:	:	:
SK	182.6	6.3	:	:	60.0	1.8	33.6
FI	:	4.5	72.5	5.0	85.8	1.1	39.1
SE	89.1	6.6	:	2.7	83.4	0.7	39.4
UK	125.6	5.6	83.8	4.7	101.4	2.6	23.7

(1) Mixed reference years, 2004 to 2006.

Source: Eurostat, Gross human apparent consumption of main food items per capita (theme5/food/food_ch_concap)

average, spent an extra 12 minutes per day eating. In contrast, there were large differences between men and women as regards the time spent on food preparation, with Italian women dedicating 7.2 times as much time to this activity as Italian men, while at the other end of the range Swedish and Norwegian women spent about twice as much time as their male compatriots preparing food. Overall Bulgarian women spent the most amount of time preparing food, an average of more than one and a half hours per day.

In terms of the frequency of eating certain types of food, Figure 1.6 ranks countries by the proportion of respondents (to a 2005 Eurobarometer survey) that reported eating meat four or more times per week. Denmark, the Netherlands and Belgium topped the ranking with over three quarters of respondents eating meat at least four times a week, in sharp contrast to Italy where only a quarter of respondents reported eating meat this frequently. In all countries the proportions of respondents eating no meat (defined here as including fish) were less than 5 %, the highest proportions being 4 % in Luxembourg and the United Kingdom.

Table 1.6: Frequency of purchasing food for the household, 2005
(% of respondents)

	Always	Often	Some-times	Hardly ever	Never
EU-25	46	25	14	7	7
BE	48	24	13	10	5
BG	:	:	:	:	:
CZ	30	36	25	7	2
DK	51	28	12	7	2
DE	49	24	15	7	4
EE	45	32	14	5	4
IE	47	14	14	13	12
EL	46	32	16	4	2
ES	45	20	15	8	11
FR	47	30	9	4	11
IT	42	24	18	8	9
CY	45	26	16	6	7
LV	44	33	16	4	3
LT	49	31	14	4	2
LU	52	23	14	6	5
HU	47	27	13	9	5
MT	43	18	15	6	18
NL	48	27	13	6	4
AT	43	23	16	14	3
PL	39	35	13	9	4
PT	44	17	16	12	11
RO	:	:	:	:	:
SK	31	35	22	10	3
SI	34	30	19	13	4
FI	47	32	14	5	3
SE	40	37	15	7	2
UK	57	17	11	6	8

Source: 'Attitudes of consumers towards the welfare of farmed animals', Special Eurobarometer 229, European Commission

Figure 1.6: How often do you eat meat each week, 2005 (1)
(% of respondents)

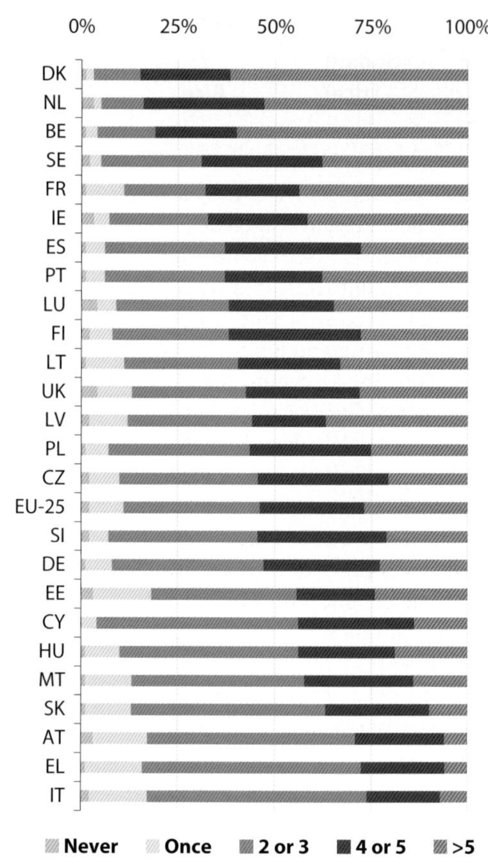

(1) Poultry, beef, pork, fish, etc; Bulgaria and Romania, not available.

Source: 'Attitudes of consumers towards the welfare of farmed animals', Special Eurobarometer 229, European Commission

Table 1.7: Time-use, persons aged 20-74 years, latest available year (1)
(hours:minutes per day)

	Eating		Food preparation		Participation rate for food preparation (%)	
	Males	Females	Males	Females	Males	Females
BE	01:49	01:50	00:22	00:57	55	84
BG	02:07	01:55	00:15	01:37	29	88
DE	01:43	01:46	00:16	00:49	46	80
EE	01:19	01:12	00:21	01:19	46	90
ES	01:47	01:44	00:19	01:20	44	87
FR	02:18	02:11	00:16	01:01	36	83
IT	01:57	01:52	00:11	01:19	28	86
LV	01:33	01:26	00:16	01:06	35	84
LT	01:32	01:26	00:20	01:18	37	90
PL	01:33	01:34	00:25	01:30	57	94
SI	01:33	01:26	00:16	01:24	34	86
FI	01:23	01:19	00:21	00:55	58	86
SE	01:32	01:36	00:25	00:50	64	87
UK	01:24	01:26	00:26	00:59	62	87
NO	01:25	01:20	00:25	00:51	67	88

(1) No data available for those Member States not shown; mixed reference years.

Source: harmonised European time use surveys (https://www.testh2.scb.se/tus/tus/StatMeanMact2.html)

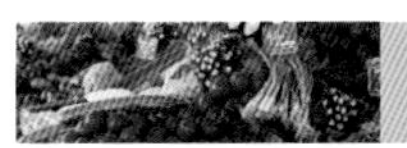

1.2.3 Consumption expenditure

It is important to note that the consumption expenditure data covered in this chapter does not include food or beverages sold for immediate consumption by hotels, restaurants, cafés and bars, nor cooked dishes prepared by restaurants or catering contractors (whether collected by the customer or delivered to the customer's home).

In 2006 annual expenditure on food and non-alcoholic beverages averaged EUR 1 700 per person within the EU-27 (see Table 1.8), with national averages ranging from less than EUR 1 000 per person in the Czech Republic, Estonia, Hungary, Poland, Romania and Slovakia, up to EUR 2 600 per person in Luxembourg. Compared with average expenditure in 2000, the most notable increase was recorded in Greece where the level of expenditure on food and non-alcoholic beverages rose from an average of EUR 1 400 per person to EUR 2 200. Figure 1.7 shows that this situation was due not only to a large increase in the volume of food and non-alcoholic beverages that were purchased, but also to relatively high price increases; there were also considerable increases in the volume of expenditure on food and non-alcoholic beverages in Estonia, Poland and Slovakia.

Table 1.8: Final consumption expenditure of households, food and non-alcoholic beverages: consumption per head
(EUR)

	2000	2006
EU-27	1 400	1 700
BE	1 600	2 000
BG	300	:
CZ	600	900
DK	1 900	:
DE	1 600	1 700
EE	500	900
IE	1 100	1 000
EL	1 400	2 200
ES	1 400	1 800
FR	1 900	2 200
IT	1 900	2 200
CY	1 800	2 200
LV	500	:
LT	700	1 200
LU	2 200	2 600
HU	500	800
MT	1 400	1 400
NL	1 400	1 700
AT	1 700	1 900
PL	700	900
PT	1 300	:
RO (1)	400	900
SI	1 100	1 200
SK	500	800
FI	1 500	1 900
SE	1 700	:
UK	1 600	1 700
TR (1)	900	1 100
IS	2 800	2 800
NO	2 400	:
CH	2 300	2 500

(1) Forecasts.

Source: Eurostat, Final consumption expenditure of households by consumption purpose (theme2/nama/nama_co2_c)

Figure 1.7: Final consumption expenditure of households, food and non-alcoholic beverages: price and volume changes between 2000 and 2006 (1)
(%)

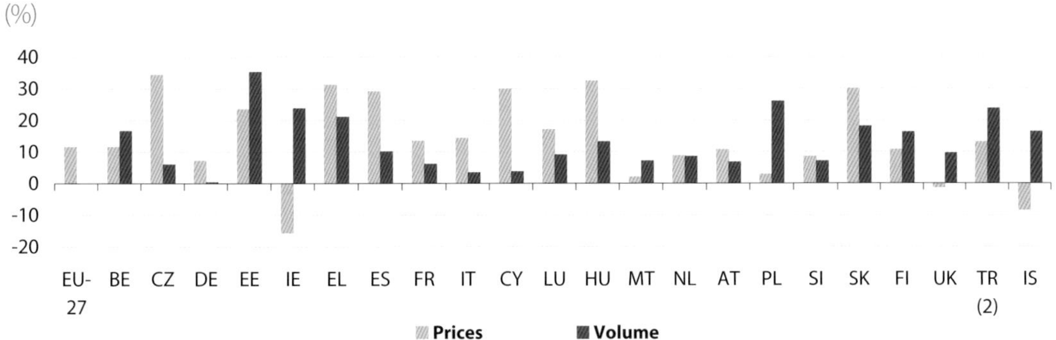

(1) Bulgaria, Denmark, Latvia, Lithuania, Portugal, Romania, Sweden, not available; EU-27: volume, not available.
(2) Forecasts.

Source: Eurostat, Final consumption expenditure of households by consumption purpose (theme2/nama/nama_co2_k and nama_co2_p)

Table 1.9 provides a comparison of expenditure on the same items, based on 2005 household budget survey (HBS) data. Note that this HBS data always takes account of self-production of food and beverages, which may account for a considerable share of household consumption in some countries. The HBS data is presented in PPS rather than in euro (EUR) terms and shows that at comparable price levels, expenditure on food and non-alcoholic beverages within the EU-27 ranged from PPS 2 238 per household in Bulgaria to PPS 5 359 in Italy, with Malta above this range at PPS 6 082. Figure 1.8 shows that there was a considerable range across the Member States in average expenditure per household on different food and non-alcoholic beverage items. Generally the range was greatest for items that account for a large proportion of expenditure, such as meat, or bread and cereals, however there were also large difference in expenditure on some of the smaller items, most notably fish and seafood.

Together food and non-alcoholic beverages accounted for 16.8 % of total household expenditure in the EU-27 in 2005 (see Figure 1.9). This share ranged from around 10 % in the United Kingdom, Sweden and the Netherlands, to over 20 % in many of the Member States that joined the EU in 2004 or 2007. By far the highest share was recorded in Romania, where food and non-alcoholic beverages accounted for 44 % of total household expenditure in 2005 (see Figure 1.10). The share of household expenditure allocated to food and non-alcoholic beverages was generally higher among Member States with a low overall level of average household expenditure (in PPS). Among the Member States with relatively high average household expenditure, several of the Mediterranean Member States reported relatively high proportions of expenditure on food and non-alcoholic beverages, notably Italy, Malta and Spain.

Table 1.9: Mean consumption expenditure per household, food and non-alcoholic beverages, 2005
(PPS)

EU-27	3 594
BE	4 043
BG	2 238
CZ	2 503
DK	2 872
DE	3 185
EE	2 440
IE	4 491
EL	4 801
ES	4 685
FR	3 733
IT	5 359
CY	5 158
LV	3 091
LT	3 166
LU	4 851
HU	2 413
MT	6 082
NL	3 089
AT	3 933
PL	2 704
PT	3 243
RO	2 355
SI	3 966
SK	2 910
FI	3 086
SE	2 913
UK	3 159
HR	4 564
NO	3 402

Source: Eurostat, Household Budget Survey (theme3/hbs/hbs_exp_t121)

Figure 1.8: Mean consumption expenditure per household, food and non-alcoholic beverages, 2005
(PPS, minimum and maximum (vertical lines at end of horizontal line), inter-quartile range containing half of the Member States (box), median (vertical line within box))

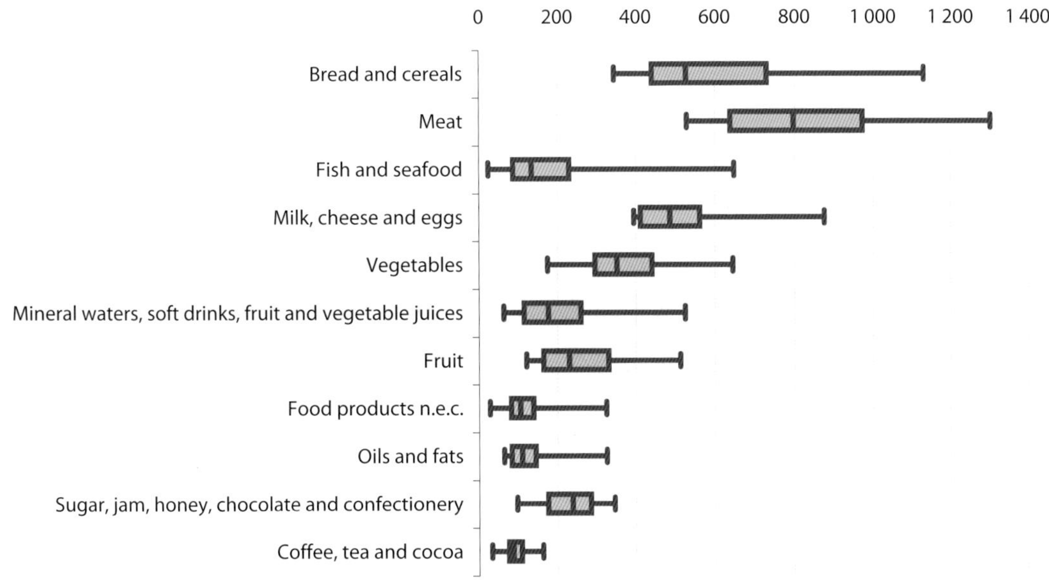

Source: Eurostat, Household Budget Survey (theme3/hbs/hbs_exp_t121)

Figure 1.9: Structure of consumption expenditure: share of food and non-alcoholic beverages in total expenditure, EU-27, 2005
(%)

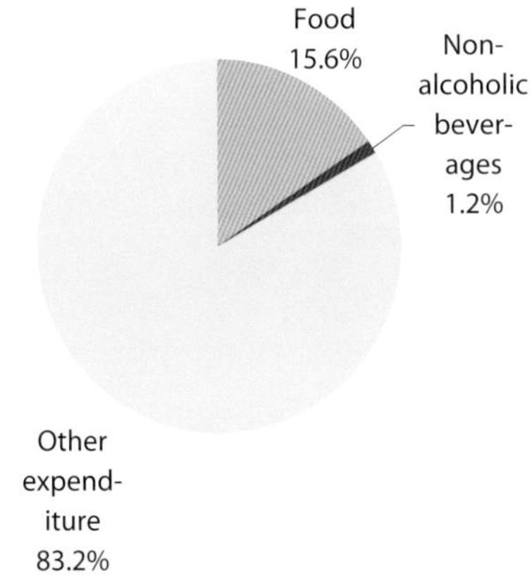

Source: Eurostat, Household Budget Survey (theme3/hbs/hbs_str_t211)

Figure 1.10: Structure of consumption expenditure: share of food and non-alcoholic beverages in total expenditure, 2005 (1)
(%)

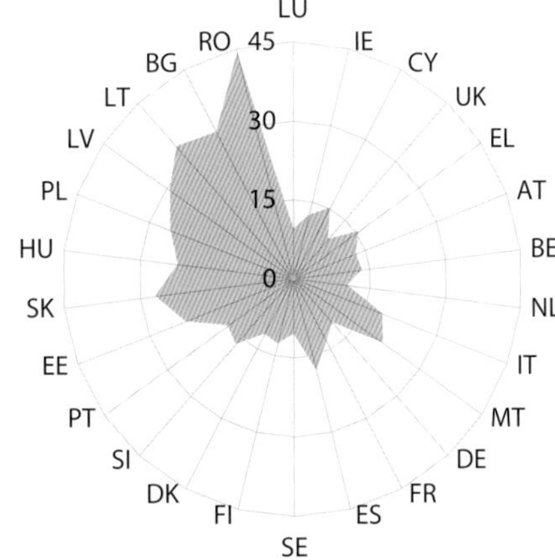

(1) Graph is ranked on overall household consumption per household (PPS); Czech Republic, not available.

Source: Eurostat, Household Budget Survey (theme3/hbs/hbs_str_t211 and hbs_exp_t121)

Figure 1.11: Structure of consumption expenditure: share of food and non-alcoholic beverages in total expenditure, EU-27, 2005
(%)

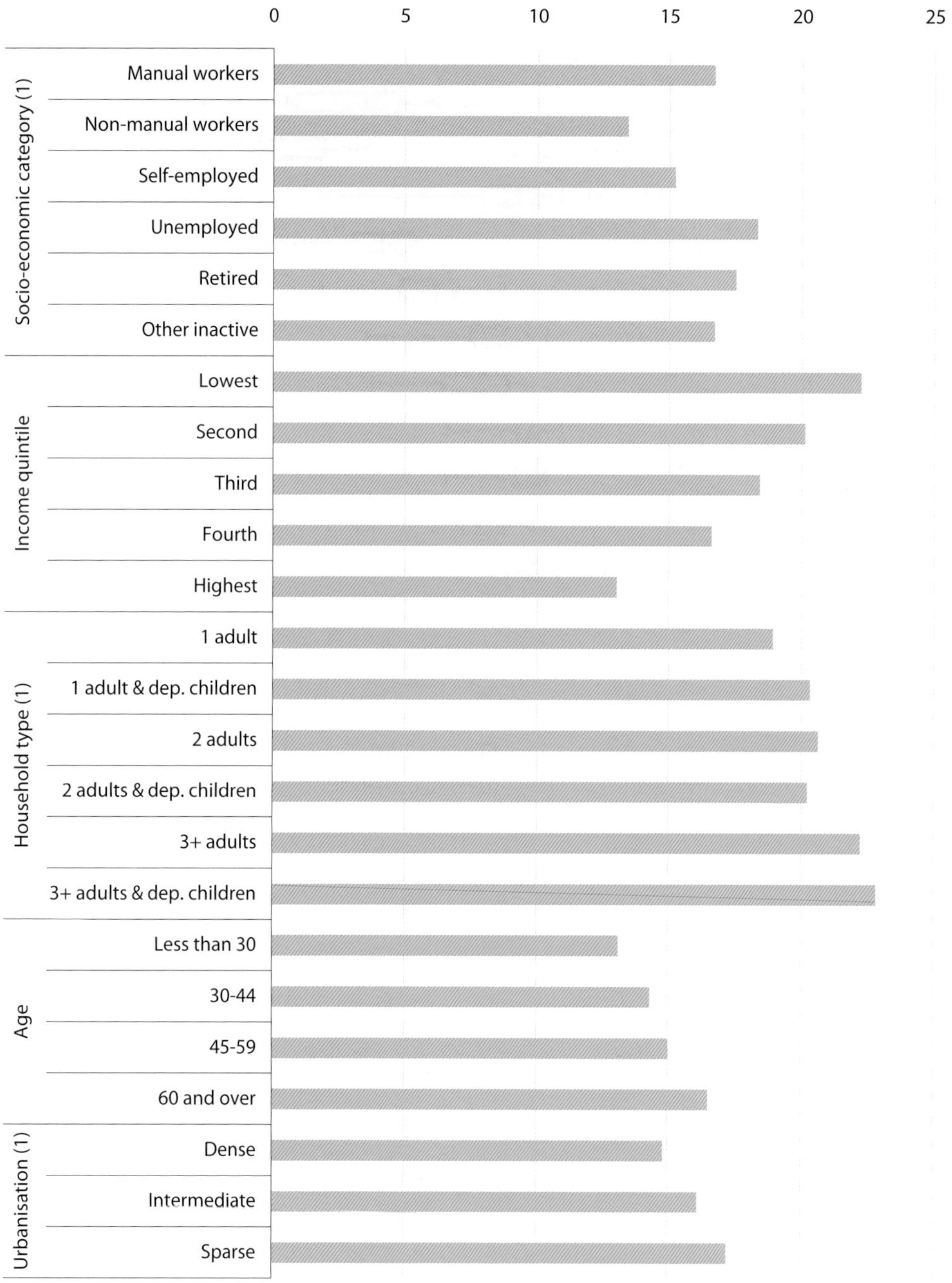

(1) Unreliable.

Source: Eurostat, Household Budget Survey (theme3/hbs/hbs_str_t221, hbs_str_t223, hbs_str_t224, hbs_str_t225, hbs_str_t226)

Figure 1.11 shows the importance of expenditure on food and non-alcoholic beverages for a number of different subgroups of households. As food is a necessity, the share of expenditure on food and non-alcoholic beverages in total expenditure is inversely related to income (spending on food increases disproportionately less than any increase in overall expenditure), and the proportion of household expenditure allocated to food and non-alcoholic beverages was around two thirds higher for households in the lowest income quintile than those in the highest quintile. Equally, households headed by older persons (60 or over) on average committed a higher proportion of their total expenditure to food and non-alcoholic beverages (around one quarter more) than households where the head was less than 30 years old. Furthermore, it is often the case that consumers from the Member States that joined the EU since 2004 spend a higher proportion of their income on food.

As price increases for many food products have risen at a faster rate than inflation (see next section for more details), there has likely been a negative impact on the purchasing power of many disadvantaged households throughout Europe – where the share of food and non-alcoholic beverages has taken an increasing proportion of the family budget for those households with lower incomes (to the detriment of spending on other items that may be considered more as luxuries). It will, however, only be possible to investigate these likely effects in more detail after the next household budget survey is conducted.

Given that there are limits as to how much food people can physiologically eat, after a certain point it is likely that any increase in household income will result in the substitution of one food product/type for another, rather than an increase in the volume of food consumed. Such changes, coupled with changes in lifestyle and the introduction of new products, may lead to a switch in consumption patterns towards items like organic products, frozen foods or convenience foods.

Table 1.10a: Structure of consumption expenditure on food, 2005
(% of consumption expenditure on food and non-alcoholic beverages)

	Food	Bread and cereals	Meat	Fish and sea-food	Milk, cheese and eggs	Oils and fats	Fruit	Vege-tables	Sugar & confec-tionery (1)	Food prod-ucts n.e.c.
EU-27	92.9	18.5	26.8	6.5	16.1	4.2	7.1	11.9	6.0	3.0
BE	89.6	18.5	25.2	5.9	11.9	2.2	6.7	9.6	6.7	3.7
BG	95.9	19.4	23.5	1.9	18.1	4.1	5.7	15.6	5.4	1.9
CZ	:	:	:	:	:	:	:	:	:	:
DK	90.8	16.0	21.8	4.2	14.3	2.5	7.6	10.9	10.9	3.4
DE	90.2	:	:	:	:	:	:	:	:	:
EE	92.4	14.2	24.9	4.4	16.4	3.1	6.2	11.1	7.6	4.4
IE	90.2	21.1	21.1	2.4	11.4	2.4	5.7	11.4	7.3	7.3
EL	94.8	12.3	23.2	7.7	18.1	7.1	7.1	12.3	6.5	1.3
ES	94.4	14.4	26.1	13.9	13.3	3.3	8.9	9.4	3.3	2.2
FR	92.5	19.4	25.4	6.0	14.2	2.2	6.0	9.7	6.0	3.0
IT	95.2	17.7	23.7	9.1	14.5	3.8	9.1	9.7	6.5	1.1
CY	82.1	15.2	17.2	3.3	15.9	2.6	9.3	11.9	4.0	2.0
LV	93.8	13.7	25.7	4.5	16.8	3.4	6.5	13.0	7.5	2.1
LT	94.1	13.3	29.6	5.0	15.1	3.8	5.3	10.9	7.7	2.7
LU	89.2	16.1	23.7	6.5	14.0	2.2	7.5	9.7	6.5	3.2
HU	91.2	14.6	30.1	0.9	16.4	4.4	5.8	9.3	6.2	3.1
MT	88.7	18.8	21.6	5.6	14.6	2.8	8.5	10.8	4.7	2.3
NL	91.4	17.1	21.0	2.9	15.2	2.9	7.6	11.4	6.7	6.7
AT	90.0	18.5	22.3	2.3	14.6	3.1	6.9	9.2	7.7	3.1
PL	92.9	15.7	28.6	2.7	14.5	5.1	5.5	10.6	6.3	3.1
PT	95.5	16.1	24.5	16.1	13.5	4.5	7.7	9.0	3.2	1.3
RO	94.8	19.5	26.7	2.5	17.2	4.1	5.2	14.0	4.3	1.1
SI	91.0	17.4	24.6	2.4	13.8	3.0	9.0	10.8	7.2	4.2
SK	91.1	17.4	25.6	3.0	17.0	5.2	5.2	6.3	8.5	3.0
FI	92.1	17.3	18.1	4.7	17.3	2.4	7.1	9.4	7.9	8.7
SE	92.4	16.2	18.1	5.7	15.2	2.9	7.6	10.5	8.6	3.8
UK	91.9	17.2	22.2	4.0	13.1	2.0	8.1	14.1	6.1	4.0
HR	92.3	14.8	31.0	4.4	14.4	3.7	5.5	10.3	4.8	3.3
NO	89.7	14.5	21.4	6.0	14.5	1.7	7.7	9.4	10.3	5.1

(1) Including also, jam, honey and chocolate.

Source: Eurostat, Household Budget Survey (theme3/hbs/hbs_str_t211)

Table 1.10b: Structure of consumption expenditure on non-alcoholic beverages, 2005
(% of consumption expenditure on food and non-alcoholic beverages)

	Coffee, tea & cocoa	Mineral waters, soft drinks, fruit & vegetable juices
EU-27	3.0	4.8
BE	2.2	8.1
BG	1.6	2.9
CZ	:	:
DK	3.4	5.9
DE	:	:
EE	3.1	4.0
IE	1.6	8.1
EL	1.9	3.9
ES	1.7	4.4
FR	2.2	5.2
IT	2.7	5.4
CY	2.0	7.3
LV	3.8	2.4
LT	3.3	2.7
LU	3.2	8.6
HU	3.1	5.3
MT	2.8	8.5
NL	2.9	5.7
AT	3.1	6.9
PL	3.1	3.9
PT	1.3	3.2
RO	2.7	2.7
SI	3.0	6.0
SK	3.7	5.2
FI	2.4	5.5
SE	2.9	4.8
UK	2.0	6.1
HR	3.3	4.8
NO	2.6	7.7

Source: Eurostat, Household Budget Survey (theme3/hbs/hbs_str_t211)

Figure 1.12: Structure of consumption expenditure on food and non-alcoholic beverages, EU-27, 2005
(%)

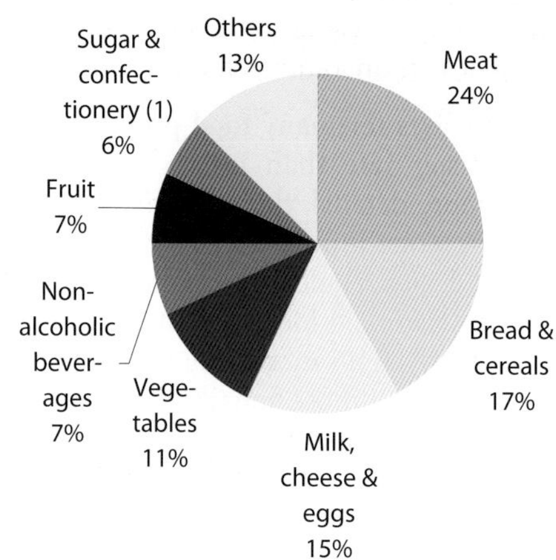

(1) Including also, jam, honey and chocolate.

Source: Eurostat, Household Budget Survey (theme3/hbs/hbs_str_t211)

Meat, bread and cereals, and milk, cheese and eggs collectively accounted for more than half of the total expenditure on food and non-alcoholic beverages in the EU-27 in 2005 (see Figure 1.12), with meat alone representing around one quarter of the total. Among the Member States (see Table 1.10) the share of meat was highest in Hungary (30.1 %) and lowest in Cyprus (17.2 %), Finland and Sweden (both 18.1 %). As noted above, the variation in expenditure on fish and seafood between the Member States was high, and these items accounted for just 0.9 % of expenditure on food and non-alcoholic beverages in land-locked Hungary, compared with 13.9 % in Spain. Such patterns may, at least in part, be linked to geographical location and local supply, although other factors are also likely to play a role, for example, local customs and traditional dishes.

1.3 Prices

1.3.1 Price inflation

The harmonised index of consumer prices for food and non-alcoholic beverages rose in the EU-27 by 22.0 % between 2000 and 2007, equivalent to an average of more than 3.4 % per annum. This was notably higher than the rate of increase recorded for the all-items consumer price index, which gained on average 2.4 % per annum between 2000 and 2007. During this period, the change in prices of food and non-alcoholic beverages varied significantly, ranging from an increase of 6.5 % in 2001 to a low of 1.1 % in 2005 (see Table 1.11), before accelerating again in the two most recent years. In 2007 the highest price increases in the Member States were recorded in Bulgaria and Latvia (both 13.5 %), and increases in excess of 10 % were also recorded in Hungary and Lithuania, as well as in Turkey. The lowest price increase for food and non-alcoholic beverages was recorded in France (1.4 %).

Between 2000 and 2007 the EU-27's consumer price index rose more quickly for food than for non-alcoholic beverages, with the fastest increase recorded for vegetables (4.0 % per annum on average), oils and fats (3.9 %) and fruit (3.8 %). The lowest average price increases between 2000 and 2007 were recorded for coffee, tea and cocoa, at just 1.0 % per annum. Table 1.13 indicates which products recorded the highest and lowest annual average rates of change between 2000 and 2007.

Table 1.11: Harmonised indices of consumer prices, food and non-alcoholic beverages, annual rate of change (1)
(%)

	2000	2001	2002	2003	2004	2005	2006	2007
EU-27	3.9	6.5	2.9	2.0	1.8	1.1	2.4	3.5
BE	0.7	4.5	2.3	1.9	1.1	1.7	2.7	3.9
BG	10.3	6.5	0.0	-1.0	6.7	4.1	5.8	13.5
CZ	1.1	5.1	-2.0	-2.0	3.5	-0.1	0.5	4.4
DK	1.6	3.9	2.2	1.4	-1.0	0.6	2.7	4.5
DE	-0.4	4.5	0.8	-0.1	-0.4	0.4	1.9	2.9
EE	2.4	7.8	3.1	-1.9	4.2	3.6	4.8	9.4
IE	3.1	6.5	3.4	1.4	-0.2	-0.7	1.4	2.8
EL	2.1	5.3	5.8	4.9	0.9	0.8	3.5	2.2
ES	2.3	5.4	4.7	4.1	3.9	3.2	4.2	3.7
FR	2.2	5.5	2.7	2.3	0.5	0.1	1.7	1.4
IT	1.6	4.0	3.6	3.2	2.1	-0.1	1.7	2.9
CY	5.3	4.2	5.8	5.2	3.8	2.4	5.6	4.8
LV	0.7	4.8	3.5	2.6	7.4	9.2	8.2	13.5
LT	-2.4	3.9	-0.8	-3.7	2.2	4.0	6.1	11.1
LU	2.0	4.7	3.9	2.0	1.8	1.7	2.4	3.3
HU	8.9	13.2	4.3	1.4	5.6	1.6	8.2	12.0
MT	1.0	4.0	2.1	2.0	-0.3	1.8	2.2	3.9
NL	0.8	7.1	3.5	1.2	-3.5	-1.2	1.7	1.6
AT	1.6	3.3	1.2	1.5	1.7	1.1	1.5	4.2
PL	9.9	4.6	-0.6	-1.2	6.2	2.1	0.6	4.7
PT	2.1	6.5	1.5	2.3	1.1	-0.6	2.7	2.4
RO	44.0	36.1	18.3	14.6	9.4	6.1	3.8	3.9
SI	5.6	9.1	7.4	4.4	0.1	-1.0	2.3	7.2
SK	5.3	5.5	1.2	3.3	4.9	-0.7	2.0	4.0
FI	1.0	4.4	3.1	0.6	0.8	0.3	1.5	2.1
SE	0.4	3.3	3.5	0.6	-0.2	-0.7	0.8	2.0
UK	-0.5	3.8	0.8	1.2	0.7	1.5	2.5	4.5
TR	46.2	49.9	50.5	27.3	8.5	3.9	7.8	12.4
IS	4.1	6.9	4.1	-2.7	1.0	-2.5	8.0	-1.1
NO	2.0	-1.8	-1.6	3.6	1.8	1.6	1.4	2.5
CH	:	:	:	:	:	:	-0.1	0.5

(1) Hungary (2000), EU-27 and Bulgaria (2000 and 2001), Turkey (2000 to 2003), estimates.

Source: Eurostat, Harmonised indices of consumer prices (theme2/prc/prc_hicp_aind)

Table 1.12: Harmonised indices of consumer prices, annual rate of change, EU-27 (1)
(%)

	2000	2001	2002	2003	2004	2005	2006	2007
Food and non-alcoholic beverages	3.9	6.5	2.9	2.0	1.8	1.1	2.4	3.5
Food	1.9	5.9	3.1	2.1	1.9	1.1	2.4	3.5
Bread and cereals	2.4	4.4	2.7	3.0	3.8	0.6	1.7	4.9
Meat	2.7	8.9	1.2	0.2	2.4	1.8	1.9	2.8
Fish and seafood	3.2	5.5	4.5	2.1	0.7	1.8	4.1	3.1
Milk, cheese and eggs	1.9	5.0	2.9	2.2	2.0	0.5	1.1	4.5
Oils and fats	0.3	0.8	7.7	1.6	4.0	2.0	6.9	0.8
Fruit	0.0	8.2	4.7	4.1	0.5	0.4	1.3	3.7
Vegetables	0.3	5.3	5.9	3.3	-1.8	1.3	5.6	4.4
Sugar, jam, honey, chocolate and confectionery	2.2	2.7	2.4	3.5	3.0	0.8	2.0	1.7
Food products n.e.c.	1.1	3.3	3.0	1.9	0.7	0.3	0.8	1.4
Non-alcoholic beverages	0.1	1.4	0.9	1.1	0.2	0.7	2.4	2.8
Coffee, tea and cocoa	-1.4	-0.5	-0.7	0.1	-1.1	3.1	3.2	2.0
Mineral waters, soft drinks, fruit and vegetable juices	1.0	2.5	1.7	1.6	0.8	-0.3	2.0	3.1

(1) 2000 and 2001, estimates.

Source: Eurostat, Harmonised indices of consumer prices (theme2/prc/prc_hicp_aind)

In most countries the lowest annual average rates of change, often negative, were for coffee, tea and cocoa, while there was a greater variety among the products with the highest price increases, with vegetables, bread and cereals, and fruit the most commonly observed.

While the annual statistics presented in this section show the effects of higher price inflation for a number of food products in late 2006 and 2007, this trend continued into 2008. The European Commission released a Communication titled 'Tackling the challenge of rising food prices: Directions for EU action' on 20 May 2008 [4]. This document provides further background to the price surge that affected several commodities, such as cereals, meat, and dairy products. It states that the transmission of price rises on global commodity markets to consumer prices has been limited by three factors: (i) the appreciation of the euro; (ii) the declining share of agricultural raw materials in food production costs compared with energy and labour costs (mainly due to increased processing), and (iii) the relatively low share of food in total household expenditure.

(4) COM(2008) 321 final; for more information: http://ec.europa.eu/commission_barroso/president/pdf/20080521_document_en.pdf.

Figure 1.13: Harmonised indices of consumer prices, EU-27 (1)
(2005=100)

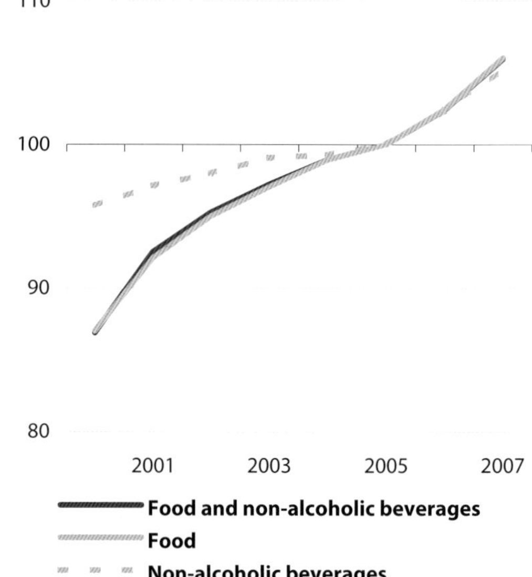

(1) 2000 and 2001, estimates.

Source: Eurostat, Harmonised indices of consumer prices (theme2/prc/prc_hicp_aind)

Table 1.13: Harmonised indices of consumer prices, selected food and non-alcoholic beverage products, annual average rate of change, 2000 to 2007 (1)
(%)

	Lowest annual average change	Change	Highest annual average change	Change
EU-27	Coffee, tea and cocoa	0.9	Vegetables	3.4
BE	Coffee, tea and cocoa	0.7	Bread and cereals	3.4
BG	Coffee, tea and cocoa	1.5	Bread and cereals	6.5
CZ	Coffee, tea and cocoa	-2.4	Bread and cereals	4.2
DK	Coffee, tea and cocoa	-0.3	Mineral waters, soft drinks, fruit & veg. juices	3.3
DE	Coffee, tea and cocoa	0.3	Fish and seafood	3.2
EE	Coffee, tea and cocoa	-0.5	Vegetables	7.8
IE	Mineral waters, soft drinks, fruit & veg. juices	1.4	Milk, cheese and eggs	2.7
EL	Vegetables	1.2	Bread and cereals	4.2
ES	Coffee, tea and cocoa	1.8	Fruit	5.9
FR	Milk, cheese and eggs	1.2	Fruit	3.0
IT	Coffee, tea and cocoa	1.0	Fish and seafood	3.4
CY	Coffee, tea and cocoa	-0.4	Meat	5.9
LV	Coffee, tea and cocoa	2.0	Vegetables	12.7
LT	Coffee, tea and cocoa	-1.5	Fruit	6.1
LU	Coffee, tea and cocoa	1.0	Vegetables	3.9
HU (2)	Coffee, tea and cocoa	1.6	Vegetables	13.0
MT	Milk, cheese and eggs	1.5	Fruit	3.8
NL	Coffee, tea and cocoa	-0.9	Vegetables	3.7
AT	Coffee, tea and cocoa	-0.5	Milk, cheese and eggs	2.7
PL	Mineral waters, soft drinks, fruit & veg. juices	1.0	Bread and cereals	3.4
PT	Coffee, tea and cocoa	-0.5	Vegetables	3.7
RO (2)	Coffee, tea and cocoa	6.1	Vegetables	12.8
SI	Coffee, tea and cocoa	2.3	Bread and cereals	6.0
SK	Coffee, tea and cocoa	-0.7	Bread and cereals	5.3
FI	Coffee, tea and cocoa	-1.2	Fruit	3.9
SE	Coffee, tea and cocoa	-1.7	Fruit	3.6
UK	Food products n.e.c.	0.2	Vegetables	3.3
TR	Coffee, tea and cocoa	17.9	Fruit	25.0
IS	Fruit	-1.5	Fish and seafood	3.9
NO	Coffee, tea and cocoa	-1.0	Oils and fats	2.8

(1) EU-27 and Bulgaria (2000 and 2001), Turkey (2000 to 2003), estimates.
(2) 2001 to 2007.

Source: Eurostat, Harmonised indices of consumer prices (theme2/prc/prc_hicp_aind)

1.3.2 Price levels

The results of the 2006 survey on income and living condition (SILC) indicates that only a small proportion of households in most of the EU-15 Member States could not afford a meal with meat, chicken or fish at least every other day (see Figure 1.14). Among the EU-15 Member States, the highest proportion of households that felt that they could not afford such a meal with this frequency was recorded in Germany.

In general terms, price level indices for 2007 show that food and non-alcoholic beverages were cheaper in the eastern and southern Member States, and were particularly expensive in the Nordic countries. Price levels for food and non-alcoholic beverages in the most expensive Member State, Denmark, were 2.3 times as high as in the least expensive, namely Bulgaria. In Denmark price levels were on average 42 % above the EU-27 average, while in Bulgaria they were 39 % below the EU-27 average. The ratio of most expensive to least expensive Member State was around two for oils and fats, and for milk, cheese and eggs, but reached three for meat and bread and cereals. Bulgaria recorded the lowest price levels for several of the food and non-alcoholic beverage categories shown in Table 1.14, although Lithuania recorded the lowest levels for fish, Poland for milk, cheese and eggs, and the Netherlands for oils and fats. Equally, Denmark was the most expensive Member State for most of the categories, with Cyprus more expensive for milk, cheese and eggs.

Figure 1.14: Capacity of households to afford a meal with meat, chicken, fish (or vegetarian equivalent) every second day, 2006 (1)
(%)

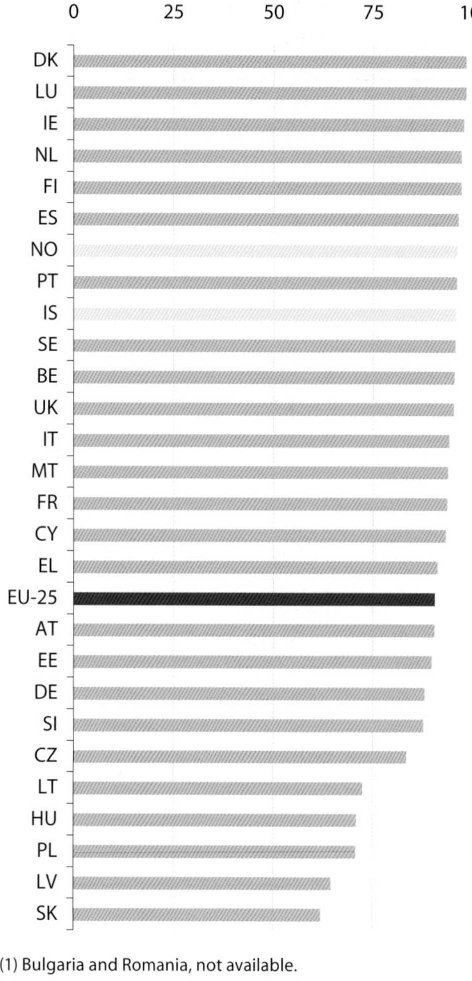

(1) Bulgaria and Romania, not available.

Source: Eurostat, EU-SILC

Figure 1.15: Price level indices, food and non-alcoholic beverages, 2007
(EU-27=100)

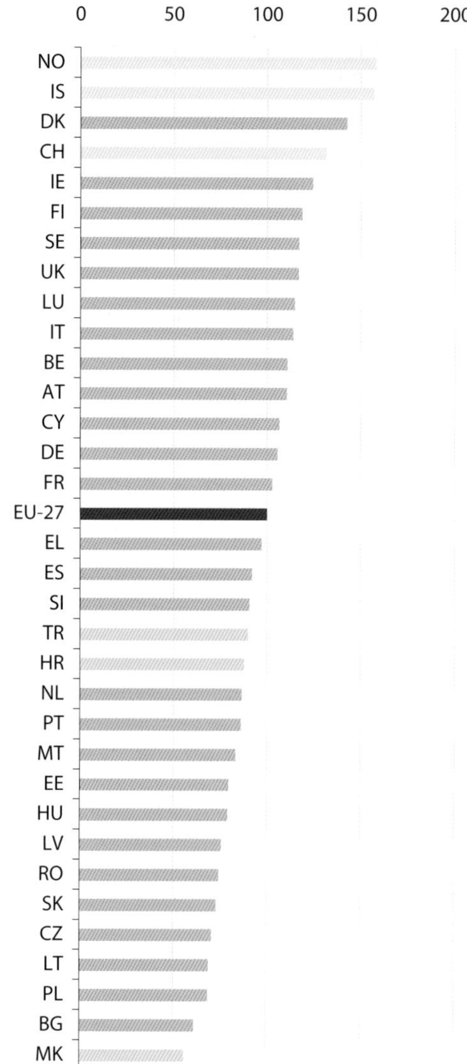

Source: Eurostat, Price level indices (theme2/prc/prc_ppp_ind)

Although Table 1.14 shows disparities in price levels between Member States, Table 1.15 indicates that for food and non-alcoholic beverages as a whole these differences among EU-27 Member States fell between 2000 and 2007, although the coefficient of variation (a measure of relative dispersion) increased for the price of fish. For nearly all of the categories shown in Table 1.15 the price level indices in 2007 were closer (in other words, had a lower coefficient of variation) among the EU-15 Member States than among the EU-27 Member States, with oils and fats an exception to this rule. Within the EU-27 oils and fats had the lowest price dispersion among the Member States, while the highest levels of price dispersion were recorded for meat.

Table 1.14: Price level indices, food and non-alcoholic beverages, 2007 (1)
(EU-27=100)

	Food and non-alcoholic beverages	Food	Bread and cereals	Meat	Fish	Milk, cheese and eggs	Oils and fats	Fruit, vegetables, potatoes	Other food	Non-alcoholic beverages
EU-27	100	100	100	100	100	100	100	100	100	100
BE	111	112	112	123	134	110	113	102	102	102
BG	61	60	51	49	61	93	114	54	70	75
CZ	71	70	66	60	76	84	84	66	84	83
DK	142	139	151	147	140	117	138	132	160	172
DE	106	106	106	118	121	88	96	117	98	102
EE	80	78	78	67	72	86	102	87	85	91
IE	124	124	120	129	123	127	98	129	117	131
EL	97	96	99	92	103	138	109	70	115	117
ES	92	92	113	83	87	97	77	95	101	88
FR	103	105	100	122	103	97	104	106	96	82
IT	114	115	108	119	122	124	112	112	115	107
CY	107	104	110	81	137	139	134	92	124	135
LV	76	74	68	62	72	83	104	81	87	94
LT	69	68	71	53	57	83	103	73	79	83
LU	115	117	120	121	111	112	114	130	105	103
HU	79	79	74	72	81	95	101	73	90	82
MT	83	81	76	69	85	110	101	71	102	108
NL	87	87	87	103	113	77	68	87	78	83
AT	111	112	126	122	113	101	119	107	107	96
PL	69	67	63	55	68	70	88	72	85	87
PT	86	86	95	81	71	104	90	78	107	92
RO	74	73	61	63	87	102	108	72	91	87
SI	91	91	95	85	100	89	109	93	96	89
SK	73	72	65	62	73	82	110	68	96	85
FI	119	118	136	119	109	105	119	125	112	131
SE	117	117	130	132	107	101	119	121	114	115
UK	117	116	106	127	98	119	112	123	111	125
HR	88	86	86	84	85	89	110	77	109	107
MK	56	55	55	52	64	62	87	43	75	66
TR	90	89	77	81	77	130	103	78	112	107
IS	157	157	178	185	112	141	143	145	158	156
NO	158	158	162	184	125	161	160	137	164	162
CH	132	135	130	186	133	116	153	120	122	97

(1) Highest price level index for each product group across the Member States shown in yellow font; lowest index shown in blue font.

Source: Eurostat, Price level indices (theme2/prc/prc_ppp_ind)

Table 1.15: Coefficient of variation for price level indices, food and non-alcoholic beverages
(%)

	EU-15		EU-25		EU-27	
	2000	2007	2000	2007	2000	2007
Food and non-alcoholic beverages	13.9	13.7	26.0	20.6	27.9	22.0
Food	13.8	13.3	26.7	21.0	28.7	22.4
Bread and cereals	15.9	14.9	33.8	24.8	35.9	27.4
Meat	18.1	15.9	32.7	30.2	35.7	32.1
Fish	11.0	15.8	20.9	23.9	22.2	24.6
Milk, cheese and eggs	10.9	14.7	23.4	18.4	23.3	17.8
Oils and fats	13.6	16.8	20.4	15.2	21.5	14.6
Fruits, vegetables, potatoes	21.5	17.8	29.2	23.3	31.2	25.0
Other food	16.0	15.8	24.1	17.0	25.4	17.8
Non-alcoholic beverages	18.1	21.3	22.3	21.4	22.8	21.7

Source: Eurostat, Price level indices (theme2/prc/prc_ppp_ind)

1.4 Consumer satisfaction

A 2005 Eurobarometer survey of the EU-25 Member States looked at consumers perceptions of food, in particular of the risks attached to food consumption. The words most commonly associated with food could be construed as positive ones (see Figure 1.16), namely taste and pleasure, marginally ahead of hunger.

A survey conducted in 2008 shows that consumers were generally satisfied with their regular retailer (usually supermarkets or hypermarkets) for fresh fruit and vegetables, meat or non-alcoholic beverages. Satisfaction levels tended to be lower for fresh vegetables and fruit than the other two products (see Figure 1.17).

Figure 1.16: When thinking about food, what words first come to mind, EU-25, 2005 (1)
(%)

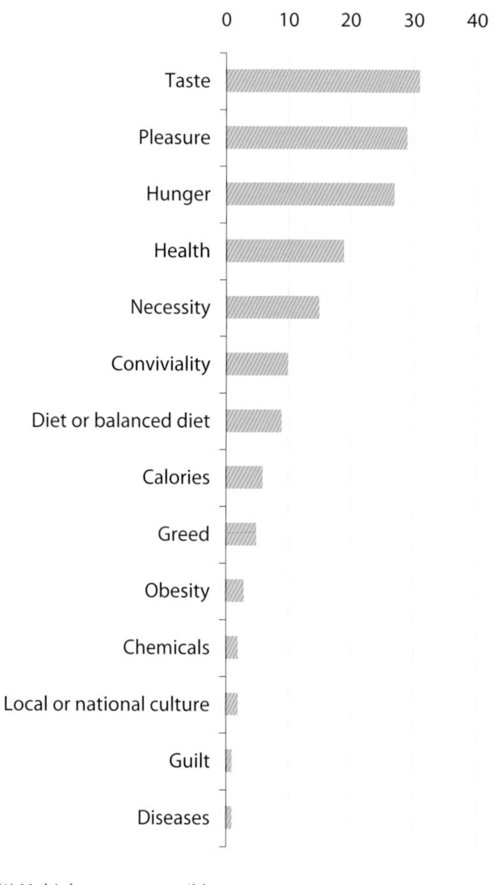

(1) Multiple answers possible.

Source: 'Risk issues', Special Eurobarometer 238, European Commission

Figure 1.17: Overall, to what extent are you satisfied with your regular retailer for the following products, 2008? (1)
(average, 1-10)

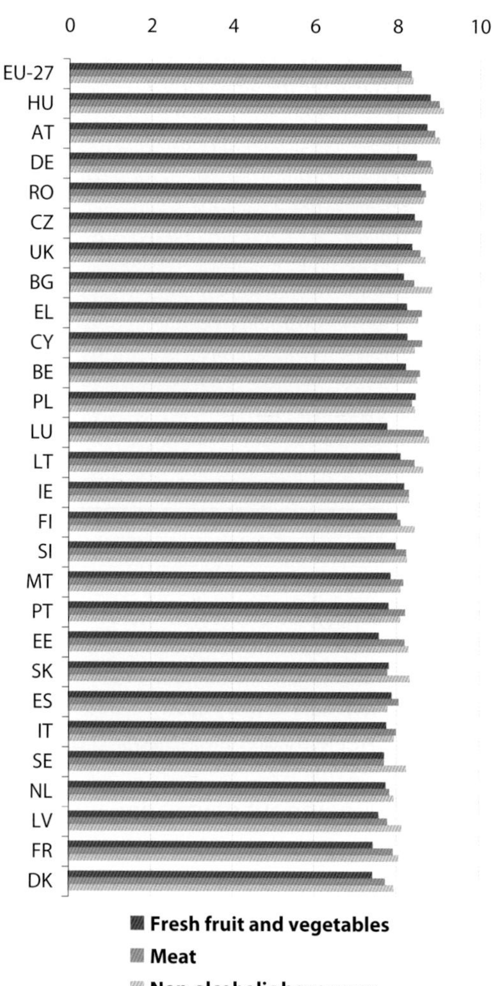

(1) Average on a scale of 1 (not at all satisfied) to 10 (fully satisfied); graph is ranked on the average score for the three different product groups.

Source: 'Retail satisfaction survey', IPSOS for the European Commission, August/September 2008

1.5 Quality and safety

1.5.1 Quality

As shown above, European consumers consider not only price but also quality when purchasing food. The European Union works to safeguard food quality in many ways, concerning food safety and hygiene, labelling and nutritional information, animal and plant health and welfare regulations, as well as restrictions on pesticide residues and food additives.

Specific instruments have been developed to recognise the origin or quality of specific food products. These include rules on the protection of geographical indications (PGI) and designations of the origin of agricultural products and foodstuffs (PDO), as well as rules on certificates of specific character for agricultural products and foodstuffs (TSG). These rules were created in 1992 with the aim to protect specific product names from misuse and imitation and to help consumers by giving them information concerning the specific characteristics of products.

The names of more than 700 products are currently registered as either PDOs or PGIs (see Tables 1.16 and 1.17). Nearly 90 % of these certified products are from the southern Member States of Italy, France, Spain, Portugal and Greece, or Germany. The most recent data indicates that products from Cyprus, Hungary and Slovakia have recently been certified, brining the number of EU Member States with certified products to 21. The main types of products that are certified include crops (fruit, vegetables or cereals), cheese, oils or fats (mainly olive oil), and fresh meat and offal, for each of which there are over one hundred certified products.

Table 1.16: Certified products: Protected Designations of Origin (PDO) and Protected Geographical Indications (PGI), March 2008 (1)
(number)

	Cheese	Meat-based products	Fresh meat & offal	Fish & fish products	Other animal products	Oils & fats	Table olives	Fruit & veg. & cereals	Bread, pastry, cakes etc.	Mineral waters
BE	1	2	-	-	-	1	-	-	1	-
BG	-	-	-	-	-	-	-	-	-	-
CZ	-	-	-	2	-	-	-	2	5	-
DK	2	-	-	-	-	-	-	1	-	-
DE	4	8	3	3	-	1	-	3	4	31
EE	-	-	-	-	-	-	-	-	-	-
IE	1	1	1	1	-	-	-	-	-	-
EL	20	-	-	1	1	26	10	22	1	-
ES	20	10	13	1	3	20		33	7	-
FR	45	4	53	2	6	9	3	26	2	-
IT	33	29	2	-	2	38	2	48	3	-
CY	-	-	-	-	-	-	-	-	1	-
LV	-	-	-	-	-	-	-	-	-	-
LT	-	-	-	-	-	-	-	-	-	-
LU	-	1	-	-	1	1	-	-	-	-
HU	-	1	-	-	-	-	-	-	-	-
MT	-	-	-	-	-	-	-	-	-	-
NL	4	-	-	-	-	-	-	2	-	-
AT	6	2	-	-	-	1	-	3	-	-
PL	2	-	-	-	-	-	-		-	-
PT	12	28	27	-	10	6	1	21	-	-
RO	-	-	-	-	-	-	-	-	-	-
SK	-	-	-	-	-	-	-	-	1	-
SI	-	-	-	-	-	1	-	-	-	-
FI	-	-	-	-	-	-	-	1	-	-
SE	1	-	-	-	-	-	-	-	1	-
UK	12	-	7	3	1	-	-	1	-	-

(1) A PDO covers the term used to describe foodstuffs which are produced, processed and prepared in a given geographical area using recognised know-how; for a PGI the geographical link must occur in at least one of the stages of production, processing or preparation.

Source: Directorate-General for Agriculture and Rural Development, European Commission (http://ec.europa.eu/agriculture/qual/en/1bbab_en.htm)

Table 1.17: Certified products: evolution of the number of products (PDOs and PGIs), EU-27 (number)

	2003	2004	2005	2006	2007	Growth 2003-2007 (%)
Total	607	681	698	712	763	25.7
Fresh meat & offal	88	100	100	100	103	17.0
Meat-based products	65	78	78	79	86	32.3
Cheese	149	153	154	154	161	8.1
Other animal products	17	18	22	23	24	41.2
Fish & fish products	6	9	9	9	12	100.0
Oils and fats	72	86	90	94	104	44.4
Fruit & veg. & cereals	133	153	156	162	175	31.6
Bread, pastry, cakes etc.	12	15	17	18	24	100.0
Other products of Annex I	13	14	17	18	20	53.8
Beers	15	18	18	18	17	13.3
Mineral waters	31	31	31	31	31	0.0
Essential oils	3	3	3	3	3	0.0
Naturals gums and resins	2	2	2	2	2	0.0
Hay	1	1	1	1	1	0.0

Source: Directorate-General for Agriculture and Rural Development, European Commission

Table 1.18: Certified products: Traditional Speciality Guaranteed (TSG), 2007 (1)

Cheese	
IT	Mozzarella
NL	Boerenkaas
SE	Hushållsost
Meat-based products	
ES	Jamón Serrano
SE	Falukorv
Fresh meat (and offal)	
UK	Traditional Farmfresh Turkey
Other products of animal origin (eggs, honey, milk products excluding butter etc.)	
ES	Leche certificada de Granja
Bread, pastry, cakes, confectionery, biscuits and other baker's wares	
ES	Panellets
FI	Kalakukko
FI	Karjalanpiirakka

(1) A TSG does not refer to the origin but highlights traditional character, either in the composition or means of production.

Source: Directorate-General for Agriculture and Rural Development, European Commission (http://ec.europa.eu/agriculture/qual/en/1bbb1_en.htm)

Figure 1.18: What are all the things that come to your mind when thinking about possible problems or risks associated with food, EU-25, 2005 (1)
(%)

(1) Multiple answers possible.

Source: 'Risk issues', Special Eurobarometer 238, European Commission

1.5.2 Safety

From farm to fork

The EU has an integrated approach to food safety, from farm to fork. The main focus of this policy is to protect the health of consumers, animals and plants, while encouraging the diversity of food and beverage products that are on offer within the EU through assuring effective control systems and compliance with EU food safety standards both within the EU and in non-Community countries (as concerns their exports to the EU).

Consumer confidence in relation to food safety issues was undermined by a number of crises in recent years, including outbreaks of BSE, avian flu, and foot and mouth disease. In January 2000, the European Commission released a White Paper on Food Safety [5] which set out plans for a proactive food policy, modernising legislation, reinforcing controls, increasing the capability of the scientific advice system, and making the whole system from farm to fork more transparent. There were three main pillars:

- the creation of a European Food Safety Authority (EFSA);
- to consistently implement a farm to fork approach across all food legislation;
- and to establish a principle that feed and food operators have primary responsibility for food safety, while Member States should ensure surveillance and controls, and the Commission should test the capacities and capabilities of the Member States through audits and inspections.

Food law, as laid down in Regulation 178/2002 [6] aims at ensuring a high level of protection of human life and health, taking into account the protection of animal health and welfare, plant health and the environment. The Regulation establishes the principles of risk analysis, as well as the mechanisms for scientific and technical evaluations undertaken by EFSA. The identification of the origin of feed and food ingredients and food sources is of prime importance for the protection of consumers and in order to facilitate this traceability was identified as a key area for reform. Traceability facilitates the withdrawal of foods and enables consumers to be provided with targeted and accurate information concerning implicated products. Importers are similarly affected as they are required to identify from whom the product was shipped (non-Community suppliers).

(5) 'White paper on food safety', Brussels, 12 January 2000, COM (1999) 719 final. For more information: http://ec.europa.eu/dgs/health_consumer/library/pub/pub06_en.pdf.

(6) Regulation (EC) No 178/2002 of the European Parliament and of the Council of 28 January2002 laying down the general principles and requirements of food law, establishing the European Food Safety Authority and laying down procedures in matters of food safety. For more information: http://eur-lex.europa.eu/pri/en/oj/dat/2002/l_031/l_03120020201en00010024.pdf.

Figure 1.19: Food safety issues: for each of the following, please tell me if you are very worried, fairly worried, not very worried, or not at all worried, EU-25, 2005
(%)

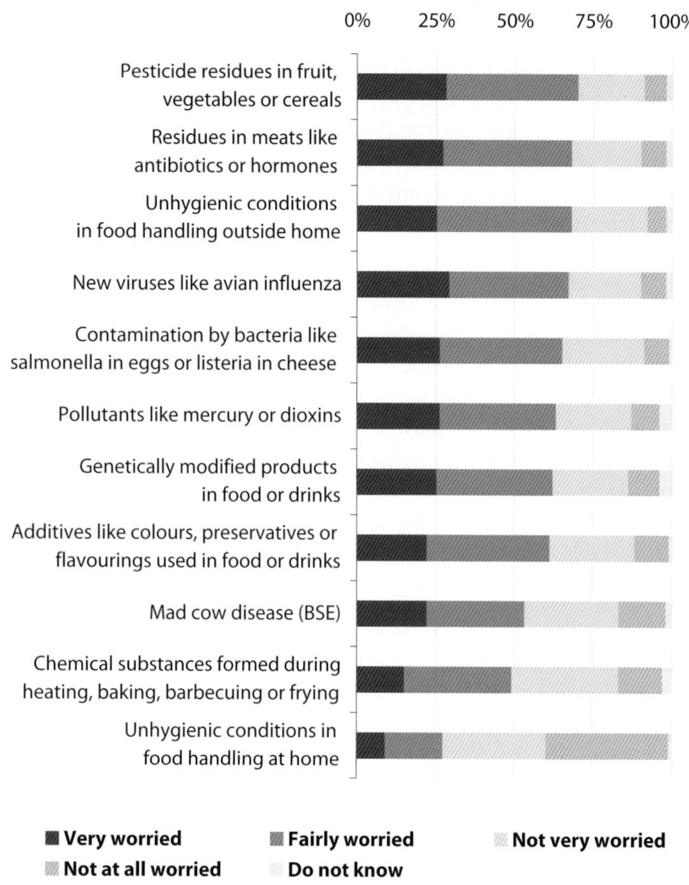

Source: 'Risk issues', Special Eurobarometer 238, European Commission

As such, at all stages of the food production chain, business operators must ensure that food and feed satisfies the requirements of food law and that those requirements are being adhered to. The traceability of food, feed, food-producing animals and all substances incorporated into foodstuffs must be established at all stages. If an operator considers that a food or feed product which has been imported, produced, processed, manufactured or distributed is harmful to human or animal health, steps must be taken immediately to withdraw the product from the market and to inform the competent authorities.

The Rapid Alert System for Food and Feed (RASFF) is a system which has been in place since 1979; its legal basis is also Regulation 178/2002. The purpose of the RASFF is to provide the control authorities with an effective tool for the exchange of information on measures taken to ensure food safety. The RASFF covers all foodstuffs and animal feed and is based on a network that includes the Member States, the European Commission in a management capacity, and EFSA. Information concerning a food-related risk which is disseminated within the rapid alert network must be made available to the general public.

Consumer concerns about food safety range from illness or disease in animals or crops, through chemical treatments or residues, to poor hygiene in food handling. In 2005 a Eurobarometer survey looked at consumers' concerns with risks, including those related to food safety. When focussing on specific risks associated with foods (see Figure 1.18), the most common was food poisoning, which was cited by 16 % of respondents, followed by chemicals, pesticides and toxic substances (14 %) and obesity/overweight (13 %). These issues are studied in more detail later under the headings of safety and health.

Figure 1.19 shows that there were a large range of issues that a majority of consumers were fairly or very worried about, most of all residues in crops and animal products. Notably there were far greater concerns among consumers about unhygienic food handling outside of their own control (during production, processing or distribution, for example) than within their own homes. The same survey noted that just over 60 % of consumers had heard of EU regulations concerning food safety in comparison with 85 % who had heard of EU regulations concerning cigarette health warnings.

A further analysis available from the 2005 Eurobarometer survey on risks presents consumers' awareness through the media of unsafe food and of obesity and insufficient exercise (see Table 1.19). While two thirds (66 %) of consumers were aware of media reporting in the previous month concerning obesity and insufficient exercise only two fifths (40 %) were similarly aware of reports concerning unsafe food.

Table 1.19: Health risks: how recently have you heard or seen something in the media about the following, 2005
(%)

	Obesity and not exercising enough						A certain type of food being unsafe/bad for health					
	This week	In the last month	In the last 6 months	More than 6 months ago	Never	Do not know	This week	In the last month	In the last 6 months	More than 6 months ago	Never	Do not know
EU-25	31	35	17	9	5	3	13	27	24	17	12	7
BE	32	38	20	7	4	0	9	26	32	21	11	1
BG	:	:	:	:	:	:	:	:	:	:	:	:
CZ	22	35	24	11	4	4	8	22	26	19	14	11
DK	60	30	6	1	1	1	10	26	27	16	12	8
DE	26	35	19	13	4	3	9	24	28	25	9	5
EE	30	35	14	5	8	8	8	28	21	8	23	11
IE	31	32	20	8	5	5	10	22	29	19	11	10
EL	15	27	27	22	7	2	9	22	29	24	10	6
ES	31	39	17	4	5	5	11	38	21	9	11	10
FR	32	41	17	5	3	2	9	25	26	19	14	7
IT	27	35	17	9	9	4	26	31	16	9	13	6
CY	33	32	16	8	11	0	15	34	27	13	9	2
LV	26	33	20	8	9	3	11	31	23	15	15	5
LT	24	30	19	9	13	5	6	22	20	14	28	9
LU	30	30	25	7	5	3	11	30	25	16	11	6
HU	38	38	14	5	2	2	13	27	25	15	13	7
MT	34	33	13	11	5	3	14	24	23	16	13	10
NL	56	34	7	2	1	1	10	24	28	24	7	6
AT	14	34	23	10	8	10	9	26	22	15	14	13
PL	20	27	16	23	9	5	6	18	21	21	22	13
PT	26	28	31	9	2	4	13	24	30	15	9	10
RO	:	:	:	:	:	:	:	:	:	:	:	:
SI	30	40	21	5	2	3	11	36	29	12	6	8
SK	22	34	24	11	5	4	7	22	28	20	14	8
FI	49	36	10	3	1	0	16	35	28	13	7	1
SE	50	37	9	3	0	1	23	30	19	15	7	6
UK	43	37	12	2	3	3	18	31	27	10	8	5

Source: 'Risk issues', Special Eurobarometer 238, European Commission

The greatest awareness of media reports relating to unsafe food was in Italy. Some 16 % of respondents across the EU-25 reported permanently changing their eating habits in reaction to the most recent story they had heard about unsafe food (see Figure 1.20), whereas a larger proportion (19 %) reported that they ignored the story. More than half of all respondents either avoided the food for a while or got worried without changing their eating habits. Around 30 % of British, Swedish and Finnish consumers reported ignoring the story while a similar proportion of Polish and Cypriot consumers reported that they had permanently changed their eating habits.

Figure 1.20: How did you react the last time you heard a story about a type of food being unsafe or bad for your health, EU-25, 2005
(%)

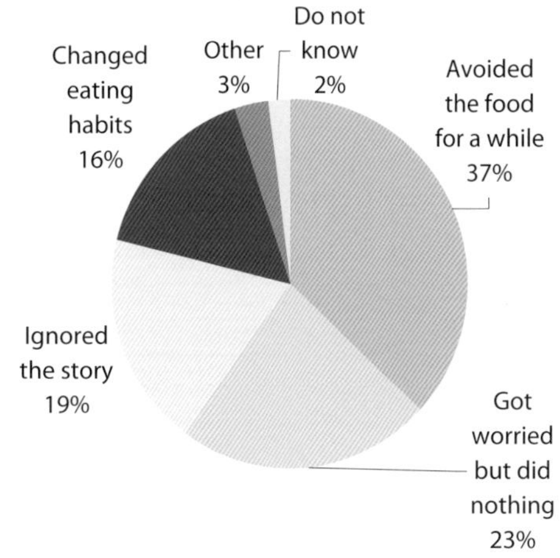

Source: 'Risk issues', Special Eurobarometer 238, European Commission

Table 1.20 provides a ranked list of diseases related to food safety, with the ranking based on a number of factors, such as severity, incidence, and (non-)treatability.

The European Commission is active in the field of food safety and quality to protect consumer health. Attention to food safety and quality are necessary in all stages of the food chain: feed production, primary production, food processing, storage, transportation and distribution, in other words from farm to fork. At the EU level, one of the practical aspects concerning food safety is the rapid alert system for food and feed (RASFF), which is a notification system for concerns about food and drinks (including alcoholic drinks), providing a system for the swift exchange of information between Member States and the coordination of response actions to food safety threats. In 2006 the system was expanded to cover pet food and animal health issues. Figures 1.21 to 1.23 indicate the type of controls that gave rise to notifications, the type of products concerned, and the country of origin of the notification. In 2006, by far the single largest number of notifications concerned nuts and nut products, followed by fruit and vegetables, and fish and fish products. It should be noted that the country making the notification may well be different from the country of origin of the product, especially in the case where the notification results from a border control: in 2006 almost 30 % of notifications concerned products originating from within the EU-27, and just under a tenth (8 % to 9 %) originated from each of China, Turkey, Iran and the United States.

Figure 1.21: Rapid alert system for food and feed products: notifications according to type of control, 2006 (1)
(%)

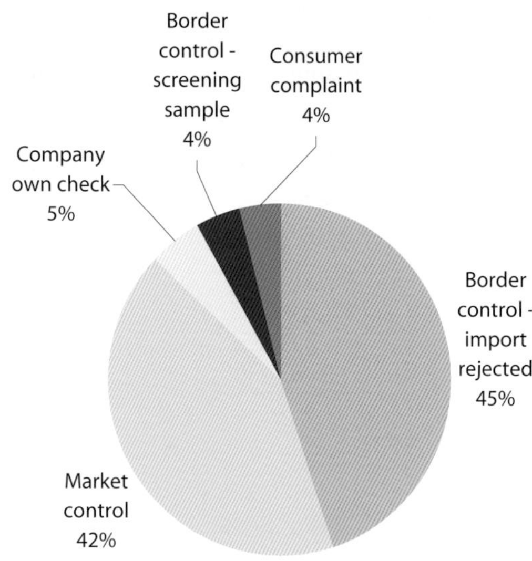

(1) There was a total of 2 923 original notifications made in 2006 (including alerts in relation to wine and other alcoholic drinks).

Source: The Rapid Alert System for Food and Feed (RASFF), Directorate-General Health and Consumers, European Commission

Table 1.20: Inventory of food safety statistics: ranking of the most important diseases, 2007 (1)

	Disease	Category of causing agent	Obligation to report to EU
1	Verotoxigenic E. Coli (VTEC) (Enterohaemorrhagic E. coli)	Bacterium	EFSA, ECDC
2	Salmonella infections other than those due to S. Typhi and S. Paratyphi	Bacterium	EFSA, ECDC
3	Campylobacteriosis (Campylobacter enteritis)	Bacterium	EFSA, ECDC
4	Listeriosis	Bacterium	EFSA, ECDC
5	Variant Creutzfeldt-Jakob disease	Prion	ECDC
6	Viral intestinal infections due to Calicivirus (incl. Norovirus)	Virus	ECDC
7	Rotaviral enteritis	Virus	ECDC
8	Botulism	Toxin (exotoxin)	EFSA, ECDC
9	Acute Hepatitis E	Virus	ECDC
10	Yersiniosis (Enteritis due to Yersinia spp.)	Bacterium	EFSA, ECDC

(1) The importance of each disease is based on a ranking for a range of criteria, including: severity, attributable fraction to food, risk group, incidence, outbreaks, geo scale, non preventability, non treatability, and social impact; EFSA: European Food Safety Authority; ECDC: European Centre for Disease Prevention and Control.

Source: Eurostat task force

Figure 1.22: Rapid alert system for food and feed products: notifications by product category, 2006
(number)

Source: The Rapid Alert System for Food and Feed (RASFF), Directorate-General Health and Consumers, European Commission

Figure 1.23: Rapid alert system for food and feed products: notifications by country, 2006 (1)
(number)

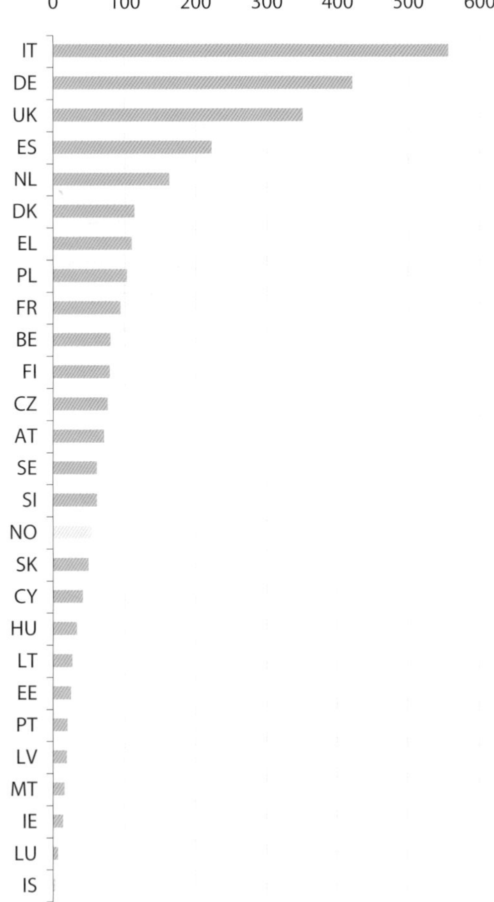

(1) Bulgaria and Romania, not available.

Source: The Rapid Alert System for Food and Feed (RASFF), Directorate-General Health and Consumers, European Commission

1.6 Externalities

1.6.1 Health

Health concerns lie behind many of the safety issues related to food mentioned in the previous point. There are however health issues relating to food that are not directly linked to the inherent safety of the food, but to the level and balance of food consumption. Guideline Daily Amounts (GDAs) are guides for the total amount of energy and nutrients that a typical healthy adult should be eating in a day, including fats, carbohydrates, protein, and fibre, as well as sodium (salt); the GDAs for women are shown in Table 1.21 along with recommended daily allowances (RDAs) for vitamins and minerals. It is hoped that such guidelines, combined with product labelling, can help consumers to understand better how individual products contribute to achieving an overall balanced diet. For any individual, energy and nutrient requirements may be higher or lower than the published GDAs, based on their gender, age, weight, level of physical activity and other factors: GDAs are not strict targets for each individual.

As well as risking nutritional deficiencies, a poor diet (as well as other factors, for example exercise and hereditary factors) may lead to weight problems. Over and above the direct health problems of being overweight or obese, costs arise from the treatment of weight related illnesses. Obesity can also be related to a range of chronic diseases, including diabetes, cancers and heart disease.

The Directorate-General for Health and Consumers is currently considering a number of labelling issues in relation to food and beverages. At the time of writing, there are no common labelling criteria across the EU. Indeed, labelling all of the ingredients in a food product is not compulsory, and the situation can vary considerably from one Member State to another; several countries only require the main ingredients to be labelled, while others have more stringent requirements that may include increasing the size of the ingredients label, placing the label in a prominent position, including a full list of ingredients, or using an easy-to-understand labelling system that promotes healthy living.

Table 1.21: Guideline daily amounts for women, based on an intake of 2 000 kcal

Energy	2 000 kcal (calories)
Total fat	<=70g
Saturated fat	<=20g
Carbohydrates	270g
Total sugars	<=90g
Protein	50g
Fibre	>=25g
Sodium (salt)	<=2.4g (6g)
Vitamin A	800µg
Vitamin D	5µg
Vitamin E	10mg
Vitamin C	60mg
Thiamin	1.4mg
Riboflavin	1.6mg
Niacin	18mg
Vitamin B6	2mg
Folic acid	200µg
Vitamin B12	1µg
Blotin	0.15mg
Pantothenic acid	6mg
Calcium	800mg
Phosphorus	800mg
Iron	14mg
Magnesium	300mg
Zinc	15mg
Iodine	150µg

(1) mg = milligram = 1/1 000 of a gram;
µg = microgram = 1/1 000 000 of a gram.

Source: EUFIC, the European Food Information Council (http://www.eufic.org), Council Directive 90/496/EEC of 24 September 1990 on nutrition labelling for foodstuffs

The issue of labelling is often of concern to consumers, particular, in relation to nutritional health claims that are often made on the packaging of food products or through advertisements. In December 2006, a Regulation on the use of nutrition and health claims for foods was adopted by the Council and Parliament. This Regulation [7] lays down harmonised rules for the use of a specific group of health or nutritional claims (such as 'low fat', 'high fibre' and 'helps lower cholesterol'). This should ensure that claims made on food labels in the EU are clear, accurate and substantiated, while contributing to a higher level of human health protection and healthier lifestyle choices.

(7) Regulation (EC) No 1924/2006 of the European Parliament and of the Council of 20 December 2006 on nutrition and health claims made on foods. For more information: http://eur-lex.europa.eu/LexUriServ/LexUriServ.do?uri=OJ:L:2007:012:0003:0018:EN:PDF.

1.6.2 Animal welfare

A 2005 Eurobarometer survey studied consumer attitudes towards the welfare of farmed animals (see Table 1.22). A small majority (55 %) of respondents across the EU-25 reported that animal welfare/protection does not receive enough importance in national food and agricultural policies, with the highest proportion by far in Greece (73 %). Almost one third of all respondents indicated that they had never considered animal welfare/protection when purchasing meat, a share that climbed to around 50 % in Estonia, Poland, the Czech Republic, Lithuania and Slovakia, while the lowest share by far was recorded in Sweden (10 %). Generally, those countries where a high proportion of respondents did not consider animal welfare/protection when purchasing meat tended to be the same as those where only a small proportion of respondents said that they could easily identify (from labelling) products from animal welfare friendly production systems, and equally they tended to have a large proportion of respondents unwilling to pay extra for products from such systems (the example used in the survey was for chicken's eggs).

For more information

Directorate-General for Health and Consumers – Food safety – from the farm to the fork: http://ec.europa.eu/food/index_en.htm

European Food Safety Authority (EFSA): http://www.efsa.europa.eu

Table 1.22: Animal welfare issues, EU-25, 2005
(%)

	Animal welfare does not receive enough importance in our country's food and agricultural policy	I never consider the welfare/ protection of animals when purchasing meat (poultry, beef, pork, fish, etc.)	For eggs, meat or milk I can easily identify from the label those products sourced from welfare friendly systems	I would not be willing to pay a premium for hen's eggs that are sourced from a welfare friendly system	I rate the welfare/protection of the following farmed animals as very good or fairly good		
					Laying hens	Dairy cows	Pigs
EU-25 (1)	55	32	20	34	32	66	45
BE	54	42	18	34	26	79	46
BG	:	:	:	:	:	:	:
CZ	65	50	3	40	24	63	49
DK	60	19	34	18	20	74	34
DE	54	24	31	26	23	72	43
EE	43	51	6	45	55	62	59
IE	47	32	17	32	32	67	41
EL	73	17	17	29	34	42	28
ES	44	43	7	45	44	52	46
FR	64	39	20	36	23	70	35
IT	53	21	14	45	41	58	51
CY	53	26	13	29	56	58	41
LV	46	40	8	45	33	43	42
LT	58	50	4	53	53	57	55
LU	54	18	42	18	40	77	50
HU	45	42	5	57	38	51	41
MT	44	33	5	37	68	77	62
NL	48	32	41	22	19	83	37
AT	54	16	35	19	25	65	43
PL	49	51	4	32	50	66	47
PT	:	36	8	46	38	46	42
RO	:	:	:	:	:	:	:
SK	62	48	5	57	37	48	30
SI	65	28	17	30	54	71	56
FI	40	34	29	25	41	85	61
SE	54	10	44	15	27	82	49
UK	62	25	26	24	29	74	51

(1) Excluding Portugal for the importance of animal welfare/protection.

Source: 'Attitudes of consumers towards the welfare of farmed animals', Special Eurobarometer 229, European CommissionSource: 'Attitudes of consumers towards the welfare of farmed animals', Special Eurobarometer 229, European Commission

2

Alcoholic beverages and tobacco

Alcohol and tobacco are a major part of the social and cultural fabric of life for many of the EU's citizens. While domestic sales and exports of alcoholic drinks and tobacco provide employment for many EU workers, and excise duties provide tax revenues to governments, the consumption of these goods can also have a number of associated costs; these can be characterised as costs to individuals (such as poor health or death), costs to business (such as lower productivity through absenteeism), costs to society (such as crime and intimidation), or costs to government (such as associated strains on police and healthcare budgets). Any consumption of tobacco will result in harmful health effects, whereas there is some evidence that a limited level of alcohol consumption (in particular of wine) may be a contributing factor in preventing disease, while alcohol abuse is also detrimental to health.

2.1 Access and choice

In most of the Member States there are restrictions on the sale of alcoholic drinks, generally through licensed premises. According to a report on alcohol use in Europe carried out by the Institute of Alcohol Studies on behalf of the European Commission, over one third of Member States (and some regions) limit the hours of sale of alcohol, while others have different restrictions for the days of week. All of the Member States for which information is available (see Table 2.1) prohibit the sale of alcohol to people beneath a certain age in cafés, restaurants, bars or pubs. In most of the Member States, the same age restrictions that apply in these points of sale (generally 16 or 18 years old), also apply to sales of alcohol to young persons in off-premise shops. However, there is a lower age restriction on the sale of alcohol through off-premise shops in Denmark, while in Malta, Luxembourg, Greece and Belgium (beer and wine only) there is no particular age limit for the sale of alcohol within off-premise outlets. In Germany, France (on-premise only), the Netherlands, Austria and Finland (off-premise only), age restrictions on sales of spirits are higher than those for beer or wine.

Restrictions on the sale and availability of tobacco also exist across the EU and are subject to a broad range of different national policies. Nevertheless, Council Recommendation 2003/54/EC of 2 December 2002 underlines a common position on the prevention of smoking and on initiatives to improve tobacco control. Among these are recommendations that prevent: the sale of tobacco products to minors; the accessibility of self-service and vending machines to minors; the sale of individual cigarettes or packages with fewer than 19 cigarettes.

2.2 Consumption

Both tobacco and alcohol consumption can be associated with problems of addiction. The Directorate-General for Health and Consumers estimates that 55 million adults across the EU drink to harmful levels, with some 23 million persons considered as being addicted to alcohol. A range of campaigns and initiatives to draw consumers' attention to the dangers of smoking and alcohol abuse are supported by the European Commission. By way of example, 'HELP: for a life without tobacco' is a programme aimed at reaching out to young non-smokers tempted to start, or those exposed to second-hand smoke, as well as smokers who want to stop.

2.2.1 Consumption volume

According to World Drink Trends, a publication released by the World Health Organisation (WHO), the EU remains the heaviest drinking region in the world. Although the average amount of alcohol (pure alcohol equivalent) that adults drank fell from 15 litres each year in the mid-1970s to about 11 litres by 2004, this is still two and a half times the average for the rest of the world.

There are considerable differences in recorded alcohol consumption among Member States (see Table 2.2); in about half of the Member States, average consumption was above 10 litres of pure alcohol equivalent per adult, but was lowest in Malta (6 litres) and Bulgaria (5.9 litres). In a majority of Member States the largest volume of alcohol was consumed in the form of beer, the highest levels being a little over 9 litres of alcohol per adult per year in the Czech Republic and Ireland. Annual alcohol intake consumed in the form of wine tended to be highest in wine-producing areas, such as France, Italy or Luxembourg. In Cyprus and Latvia, alcohol consumed in the form of spirits was equivalent to 5 and 7 litres of pure alcohol per adult respectively, which was a higher level than for any other type of alcoholic drink in these countries.

Table 2.1: Minimum age limit for the purchase of wine, beer and spirits
(years)

	Beer		Wine		Spirits	
	On-premise	Off-premise	On-premise	Off-premise	On-premise	Off-premise
BE	16	None	16	None	18	18
BG	18	18	18	18	18	18
CZ	18	18	18	18	18	18
DK	18	15	18	15	18	15
DE	16	16	16	16	18	18
EE	18	18	18	18	18	18
IE	18	18	18	18	18	18
EL	17	None	17	None	17	None
ES (1)	16-18	16-18	16-18	16-18	16-18	16-18
FR	16	16	16	16	18	16
IT	16	16	16	16	16	16
CY	:	:	:	:	:	:
LV	18	18	18	18	18	18
LT	18	18	18	18	18	18
LU	16	None	16	None	16	None
HU	18	18	18	18	18	18
MT	16	None	16	None	16	None
NL	16	16	16	16	18	18
AT	16	16	16	16	18	18
PL	18	18	18	18	18	18
PT	16	16	16	16	16	16
RO	18	18	18	18	18	18
SI	18	18	18	18	18	18
SK	18	18	18	18	18	18
FI	18	18	18	18	18	20
SE	18	20	18	20	18	20
UK	18	18	18	18	18	18

(1) Varies by region.

Source: World Health Organisation (www.who.int) and the Alcohol Policy Network co-financed by the European Commission

Binge-drinking

Concerns over binge-drinking can be categorised into two broad areas: those affecting long-term health and those with behavioural consequences that may impact on other members of society. The former include well-documented evidence such as links to increased risk of liver disease, cardio-vascular or mental health problems. Behavioural consequences extend to a variety of areas, including an increased incidence of accidents, violence, poor social behaviour, or unsafe sex, as well as higher levels of absenteeism and lower productivity at work.

There appears to be somewhat of a north-south divide in terms of the occurrence of binge-drinking among 15-16 year-olds (typically single drinking occasions involving more than five alcoholic drinks), aside from relatively low rates of binge-drinking reported in Finland and Sweden (where alcohol is relatively expensive and where more rigorous age restrictions apply to the sale of alcohol). About one third of all 15-16 year-old boys in Denmark, Germany and Ireland (all 31 %) and particularly the Netherlands (37 %) reported binge-drinking at least three times a month, compared with between 13 and 14 % in France or Greece. In general, binge-drinking reported among boys was higher than among girls, but this was not the case in Ireland or the United Kingdom, where the prevalence of binge-drinking among girls was slightly higher.

Within the EU-15 Member States, those countries with the highest proportion of male and female 15-16 year-old binge drinkers tended to be the same as those that reported some of the highest levels of alcohol consumption among adults. This pattern was not repeated in the Member States that joined the EU since 2004, as, for example, relatively low levels of binge-drinking among 15-16 year-olds were recorded in Hungary and the Czech Republic, while these Member States recorded the third and fourth highest levels of adult alcohol consumption in the EU-27.

Table 2.2: Alcoholic beverage consumption per adult (over 15 years old) and youth binge drinking

	Consumption (litres per adult) (1)	of which:			People drinking any alcohol in 2005 (%)		Binge drinking in 15-16 year olds (2)	
		Beer	Wine	Spirits	Male	Female	(% boys)	(% girls)
BE	10.6	5.8	3.1	1.6	88.5	74.3	28	14
BG	5.9	0.5	2.8	2.5	78.2	49.2	26	16
CZ	13.0	9.3	2.2	4.5	89.4	72.8	24	13
DK	11.7	5.9	4.5	1.4	:	:	31	18
DE	12.0	6.9	3.1	2.4	90.1	77.6	31	24
EE	9.0	4.3	:	1.7	83.7	62.7	26	15
IE	13.7	9.0	2.1	2.5	86.6	82.6	31	33
EL	9.0	2.4	4.4	1.9	:	:	14	8
ES	11.7	4.6	3.9	2.8	68.7	44.1	:	:
FR	11.4	2.2	6.6	2.9	:	:	13	7
IT	8.0	1.8	6.1	0.5	89.1	66.5	19	8
CY	11.5	3.8	2.5	5.0	77.0	42.4	17	6
LV	9.6	2.2	0.5	7.2	83.5	72.6	24	18
LT	9.9	4.5	1.1	4.3	94.3	92.4	19	7
LU	15.6	6.3	9.0	2.0	:	:	:	:
HU	13.6	4.3	4.9	4.2	71.5	37.7	12	5
MT	6.0	2.4	3.0	0.9	78.3	56.2	32	19
NL	9.7	4.8	2.6	1.8	91.0	78.3	37	20
AT	11.1	6.6	3.9	1.6	:	:	:	:
PL	8.1	4.8	1.6	1.6	81.6	59.5	17	5
PT	11.5	3.5	5.6	1.7	76.7	40.8	20	10
RO	9.7	4.0	3.0	2.4	68.2	34.2	:	:
SI	6.7	3.8	2.0	1.0	91.0	81.4	23	18
SK	10.4	5.4	1.7	4.3	92.3	83.4	20	12
FI	9.9	4.6	2.4	2.9	83.0	73.4	18	15
SE	6.5	3.3	2.2	1.1	90.6	83.8	18	14
UK	11.8	6.2	2.7	2.2	90.6	85.0	26	29

(1) Mixed reference years: 2003 or 2004, except for Estonia, 2002.
(2) Reference year: 2006 except for Bulgaria, 2003.

Source: World Health Organisation (www.who.int) and Eurostat, Population and social conditions (theme3/hlth/hlth_ls_dk12ma)

Smoking habits

In all of the Member States for which data are available for 2005, a majority of adults were non-smokers. The highest proportion of smokers was recorded in Austria (45.1 %) and Slovakia (44.5 %), while the highest majority of non-smokers (81.3 %) was registered in Portugal. In Greece, Cyprus and the Netherlands, a majority of both men and women who smoked on a daily basis, smoked more than 20 cigarettes each day.

Some individuals face considerable difficulties in reducing the frequency at which they smoke or in giving up their smoking habit altogether. In the 12 months preceding a Eurobarometer survey on attitudes towards smoking, almost one in every three smokers (31 %) in the EU-25 had tried to give up smoking and this proportion rose to nearly 50 % in the United Kingdom. One in every ten attempts to give up smoking in the EU-25 lasted less than a day, while 27 % of those trying to give up sustained their efforts over a period of at least two months. Over the longer-term, attempts made by individuals to give up smoking can succeed, as just over 20 % of the EU-25's adult population described themselves as ex-smokers in 2006.

Table 2.3: Frequency of smoking among adults (over 15 years old), 2005
(% of respondents)

	Non-smoker	Occasional smoker	Daily smoker	Breakdown of male daily cigarette smokers: >20 a day	Breakdown of male daily cigarette smokers: <20 a day	Breakdown of female daily cigarette smokers: >20 a day	Breakdown of female daily cigarette smokers: <20 a day
BE	71.5	4.4	24.1	35.6	64.4	31.5	68.5
BG	59.9	7.8	32.3	18.4	81.6	6.3	93.7
CZ	69.1	6.1	24.9	30.6	69.4	12.5	87.5
DK	63.0	2.9	34.1	39.9	60.1	26.2	73.8
DE	67.5	6.2	26.3	49.6	50.4	31.8	68.2
EE	65.2	1.5	33.3	46.0	54.0	13.7	86.3
IE	73.8	4.3	21.9	53.1	46.9	33.1	66.9
EL	65.4	7.1	27.6	80.3	19.7	59.6	40.4
ES	69.0	2.8	28.1	49.0	51.0	30.4	69.6
FR	73.9	:	26.1	38.5	61.5	27.3	72.7
IT	75.5	:	24.5	41.8	58.2	22.9	77.1
CY	72.3	3.8	23.9	79.2	20.8	51.4	48.6
LV	61.6	5.7	32.7	43.8	56.2	12.2	87.8
LT	61.1	11.6	27.3	37.2	62.8	6.5	93.5
LU	:	:	:	:	:	:	:
HU	66.1	3.4	30.5	62.2	37.8	40.6	59.4
MT	73.8	2.8	23.4	33.2	66.8	11.7	88.3
NL	66.0	5.8	28.2	71.8	28.2	71.4	28.6
AT	54.9	8.8	36.3	17.4	82.6	8.7	91.3
PL	64.4	5.8	29.9	63.8	36.2	38.9	61.1
PT	81.3	2.2	16.4	66.3	33.7	40.1	59.9
RO	69.5	9.6	20.8	46.5	53.5	23.8	76.2
SI	72.4	8.5	19.2	43.3	56.7	13.7	86.3
SK	55.5	9.8	34.6	62.7	37.3	34.0	66.0
FI	77.4	4.5	18.1	46.1	53.9	23.7	76.3
SE	72.0	10.4	17.5	:	:	:	:
UK	73.3	:	26.7	37.1	62.9	26.1	73.9

Source: Eurostat, Population and social conditions (theme3/hlth/hlth_ls_smka and hlth_ls_cgsmka)

2.2.2 Consumption expenditure

Consumption expenditure data presented here excludes alcohol or tobacco sold by hotels, restaurants, cafés and bars for immediate consumption (see Chapter 11 for more information on hotels and restaurants). The average annual expenditure on alcoholic beverages and tobacco across the EU-27 was EUR 500 per person in 2006, the equivalent of 2.4 % of total expenditure. National averages ranged from lows of EUR 100 in Romania and EUR 200 in Slovakia to a high of EUR 2 600 per person in Luxembourg. However, relative to total expenditure the range was reversed, as 1.7 % of the average household budget in Luxembourg was spent on alcoholic beverages and tobacco, a proportion that rose to a high of 5.8 % in Romania.

The relative importance of alcoholic beverages or tobacco in total household expenditure varied considerably, as shown in Figure 2.1 which relates the structure of consumption to purchasing power. In Ireland, 4.1 % of the household budget was spent on alcoholic beverages, which was almost twice as high as the next highest shares reported in Romania (2.3 %) and Lithuania (2.2 %). The highest proportion of household expenditure devoted to tobacco products was recorded in Romania (3.5 %), well above the next highest shares in Greece, Bulgaria and Hungary – all within the range of 2.4 % to 2.7 %.

Across the EU-27, approximately 50 % of expenditure on alcohol and tobacco products was devoted to tobacco, a quarter of the average spend was on wine, and about an eighth each on beer and on spirits (see Table 2.5). By far the highest relative spend on beer was reported in Ireland (41.1 % of the total for alcoholic beverages and tobacco), whereas Belgium and Luxembourg were the only Member States where consumers spent more on wine than on beer, spirits or tobacco products. Expenditure on spirits was relatively high in the Baltic Member States, although tobacco products accounted for a higher proportion of household expenditure in each of these three countries. Indeed, the relative importance of tobacco products was generally high in most countries, and in particular the southern Member States, with tobacco accounting for almost 80 % of expenditure on alcoholic beverages and tobacco in Greece, upwards of 70 % in Cyprus and Malta, and relatively high shares in Spain and Portugal too.

Table 2.4: Final consumption expenditure of households, alcoholic beverages and tobacco: consumption per head
(EUR)

	2000	2006
EU-27	400	500
BE	500	500
BG	0	:
CZ	300	400
DK	700	:
DE	500	500
EE	200	400
IE	800	900
EL	400	600
ES	300	400
FR	400	500
IT	300	400
CY	600	900
LV	200	:
LT	200	300
LU	2 700	2 600
HU	200	400
MT	300	300
NL	400	400
AT	400	500
PL	200	300
PT	300	:
RO (1)	100	100
SI	300	400
SK	100	200
FI	700	800
SE	500	:
UK	700	700
TR (1)	:	:
IS	800	900
NO	800	:
CH	800	800

(1) 2006, forecast.

Source: Eurostat, Final consumption expenditure of households by consumption purpose (theme2/nama/nama_co2_c)

Figure 2.1: Structure of consumption expenditure: share of alcoholic beverages and tobacco in total expenditure, 2005
(%)

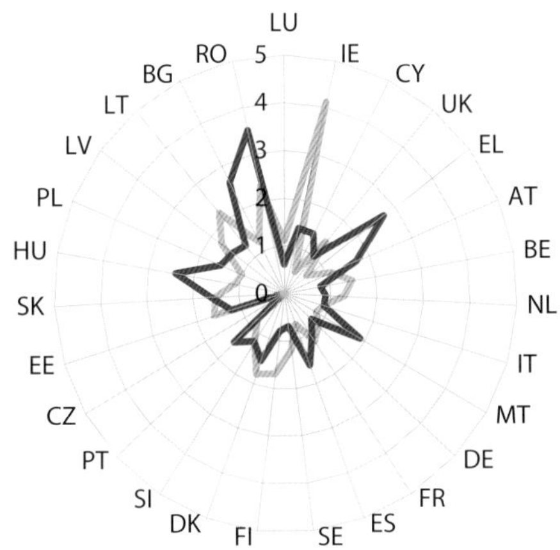

(1) Graph is ranked on overall household consumption per household (PPS); Czech Republic, not available.

Source: Eurostat, Household Budget Survey (theme3/hbs/hbs_str_t211 hbs_exp_t121)

The proportion of total expenditure spent on alcoholic beverages and tobacco decreased steadily as a function of higher incomes for the EU-27. Among socio-economic groups, the share of total expenditure devoted to alcoholic beverages and tobacco was highest among the EU-27's unemployed (3.3 %) and manual workers (2.9 %), when compared with the average expenditure on these items by the self-employed (2.1 %), non-manual workers or the retired (both 2.0 %).

Table 2.5: Structure of consumption expenditure on alcoholic beverages and tobacco, 2005 (1)
(% of total expenditure on alcoholic beverages and tobacco)

	Beer	Wine	Spirits	Tobacco
EU-27	12.5	25.0	12.5	54.2
BE	13.6	45.5	9.1	36.4
BG	13.2	5.3	10.5	68.4
CZ	:	:	:	:
DK	15.2	30.3	9.1	45.5
DE	:	:	:	47.1
EE	17.9	17.9	25.0	42.9
IE	41.1	19.6	14.3	25.0
EL	5.9	5.9	5.9	79.4
ES	8.7	13.0	4.3	69.6
FR	4.3	34.8	13.0	47.8
IT	11.1	33.3	5.6	50.0
CY	10.5	5.3	5.3	73.7
LV	16.1	16.1	22.6	45.2
LT	20.0	14.3	28.6	37.1
LU	11.8	41.2	11.8	35.3
HU	13.9	11.1	5.6	66.7
MT	7.4	14.8	7.4	70.4
NL	14.3	33.3	14.3	42.9
AT	17.9	17.9	3.6	60.7
PL	16.0	8.0	16.0	60.0
PT	4.3	21.7	4.3	65.2
RO	10.3	17.2	12.1	60.3
SI	20.8	25.0	4.2	50.0
SK	16.1	12.9	19.4	51.6
FI	29.2	29.2	12.5	33.3
SE	15.8	36.8	10.5	36.8
UK	12.5	33.3	12.5	41.7
HR	18.2	18.2	3.0	57.6
NO	22.6	22.6	12.9	38.7

(1) Data include estimates and rounding; sum of components does not always sum to 100 %.

Source: Eurostat, Household Budget Survey (theme3/hbs/hbs_str_t211)

2.3 Prices

In many of the Member States, a high proportion of the price paid by consumers for alcoholic beverages and tobacco may be attributed to taxes and duties. The data presented in this section include these taxes and duties, which, to some degree, explain some of the wide-ranging differences in price levels and the evolution of prices over time; more information on taxes and duties is provided at the end of this section.

2.3.1 Price inflation

The harmonised index of consumer prices for alcoholic beverages and tobacco rose overall by 34.1 % across the EU-27 between 2000 and 2007, equivalent to more than 4.3 % per annum on average. This was considerably higher than the rate of increase recorded for the all-items consumer price index during the same period (an average of 2.4 % per annum).

With the exception of 2004, the average annual rate of increase in the price of alcoholic beverages and tobacco across the EU-27 was relatively steady. In contrast, there were a number of countries where there were considerable annual fluctuations, such as Bulgaria and France. The strongest price increases (between 10 % and 15 %) across the Member States in 2007 were recorded in Romania, Latvia and the Czech Republic, with relatively high price increases also recorded in Sweden, Spain and Hungary (see Table 2.6).

By far the most rapid price increases for the EU-27 were recorded for tobacco (where an average increase of 6.5 % per annum was registered over the period 2000 to 2007) – see Figure 2.2. The rate of price increases for wine, beer and spirits averaged 0.9 % to 1.4 % per annum; all of these below the general inflation rate (as measured by the all-items consumer price index). It was therefore unsurprising to find that the highest price increases among the Member States were also recorded for tobacco products. This was the case for all 25 of the Member States for which data are available (no data for Hungary or Romania) for the period 2000 to 2007, with average price increases for tobacco peaking at 19.7 % per annum in Bulgaria and 10.7 % per annum in Slovenia. In contrast, there was downward pressure on the price of some alcoholic beverages between 2000 and 2007.

Figure 2.2: Harmonised indices of consumer prices, EU-27 (2005=100)

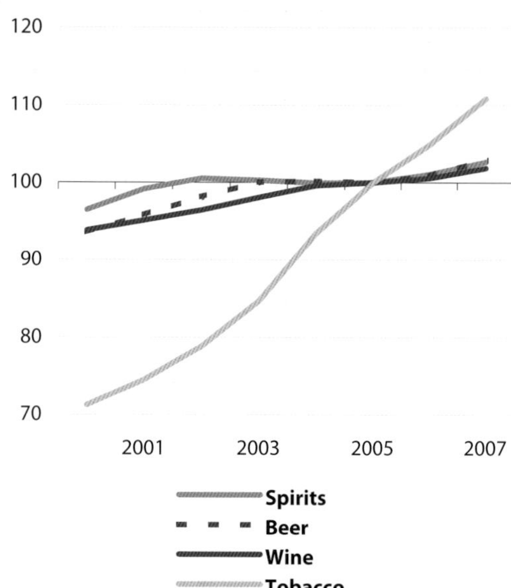

Source: Eurostat, Harmonised indices of consumer prices (theme2/prc/prc_hicp_aind)

Table 2.6: Harmonised indices of consumer prices, alcoholic beverages and tobacco, annual rate of change
(%)

	2000	2001	2002	2003	2004	2005	2006	2007
EU-27	3.8	3.7	4.0	4.8	6.1	4.1	3.2	4.0
BE	1.7	1.9	1.6	4.4	4.8	2.8	1.4	4.4
BG	2.1	0.6	27.0	3.8	26.8	7.7	54.7	0.8
CZ	4.3	3.2	1.9	0.9	3.0	1.4	1.3	10.2
DK	2.4	2.3	0.6	-1.1	-5.0	2.0	0.8	1.7
DE	1.5	1.7	4.0	5.3	6.8	8.5	3.6	3.1
EE	3.3	2.9	1.4	3.0	2.1	4.3	3.5	4.1
IE	12.0	2.5	5.6	9.9	3.5	0.6	1.1	5.4
EL	2.8	7.4	7.0	4.2	4.5	2.2	5.7	6.4
ES	3.1	3.2	5.7	3.4	4.3	5.1	1.8	7.0
FR	3.0	3.2	4.9	8.8	14.3	0.1	0.4	1.9
IT	1.1	2.6	2.1	7.0	7.9	6.8	4.8	3.5
CY	8.5	3.4	9.9	18.0	8.3	0.5	0.9	1.0
LV	6.9	2.7	2.8	1.6	5.0	4.2	8.5	13.6
LT	-9.8	-0.5	1.5	3.3	3.0	0.1	-0.4	5.4
LU	3.1	3.9	5.2	5.7	6.5	6.7	3.4	4.5
HU	10.7	10.3	9.3	11.1	11.6	2.7	4.3	6.9
MT	8.3	4.5	7.6	1.2	13.0	1.8	0.6	0.8
NL	2.8	6.7	4.6	3.6	7.3	2.8	0.9	1.8
AT	0.9	3.9	4.0	3.0	1.8	6.3	0.4	2.3
PL	8.1	4.3	2.3	-2.5	2.5	2.6	1.7	3.3
PT	1.0	3.3	4.9	4.6	2.9	4.5	9.3	4.9
RO	29.7	31.1	17.4	22.1	16.2	12.1	17.9	14.9
SI	4.2	7.1	13.5	11.8	5.2	4.0	4.0	6.8
SK	9.6	4.0	9.9	12.0	8.4	-0.7	3.1	4.4
FI	2.5	1.9	1.7	1.1	-10.7	-1.8	1.4	1.4
SE	1.7	1.3	1.0	1.6	0.7	0.5	1.2	7.2
UK	4.7	3.3	1.8	1.9	2.0	2.2	2.7	3.5
TR	88.7	61.7	53.1	45.4	19.0	13.5	20.8	9.9
IS	2.0	7.7	8.0	8.8	1.5	3.8	2.9	3.4
NO	6.9	3.5	-0.8	1.1	7.5	2.5	2.0	1.5
CH	:	:	:	:	:	:	1.1	2.1

Source: Eurostat, Harmonised indices of consumer prices (theme2/prc/prc_hicp_aind)

2.3.2 Price levels

In general terms, price level indices for 2006 show that alcoholic beverages and tobacco were much more expensive in the Nordic countries, the United Kingdom and Ireland than they were in eastern Member States, in particular the Baltic countries; note that these differences reflect to a large degree the differences in VAT rates, excise duties and other indirect taxies that may be levied by governments.

Price levels for alcoholic beverages and tobacco in Ireland and the United Kingdom were about 75 % higher than the EU-27 average and about three times as high as in Latvia, Bulgaria or Lithuania. The contrast between price levels was particularly marked for tobacco; as the price level index of tobacco in the United Kingdom was a little over twice the EU-27 average and about seven times as high as in Latvia or Lithuania (see Figure 2.3).

In the case of alcoholic drinks, much of the difference in price levels appears to be linked to national excise duties. In both the United Kingdom and Ireland, excise duties on still wine were about EUR 275 per hectolitre in 2008 and such duties were also relatively high in Finland and Sweden at about EUR 235 per hectolitre. In contrast, there was no excise duty on still wine in 11 of the remaining Member States, including Bulgaria and Slovakia, where the average price level of alcoholic drinks was at its lowest in the EU-27. All of the Member States applied minimum excise duties on cigarettes; these ranged from a little over one half of the retail price of cigarettes in Latvia to a little over three quarters of the retail price in Slovakia (see Table 2.7).

2.4 Safety

According to a WHO study – 'Global burden of disease study' – tobacco and harmful alcohol use constitute the first and third biggest causes of early death and illness in the EU. A number of steps have been taken within the EU to highlight the dangers of smoking and drinking excessive amounts of alcohol. The Tobacco Products Directive (2001/37/EC) of the European Parliament and of the Council introduced new health messages to be put on the packaging of tobacco products and increase the size of health warnings, and was supplemented by Commission Decision 2003/641/EC of 5 September 2003 to use colour photographs or other illustrations as health warnings on tobacco packages. In October 2006, the European Commission adopted a Communication (COM(2006) 625 final that sets out a strategy to support Member States in reducing alcohol-related harm, including the need to raise awareness as regards the consequences of harmful alcohol consumption and its impact on health.

A large majority (85 %) of EU-25 respondents to a Eurobarometer survey conducted in 2005 were aware of health warnings on cigarette packets. Awareness of these health warnings was highest in Luxembourg and Hungary (93 % of respondents) and lowest in Estonia (78 %). Awareness through various media of the risks associated with smoking was even higher (94 %), with a little over two thirds (69 %) of respondents having heard or read warnings within the media in the preceding month. An overwhelming majority (90 %) of individuals were also aware of the risks associated with alcohol consumption.

Figure 2.3: Price level indices, alcoholic beverages and tobacco, 2006 (1)
(EU-27=100)

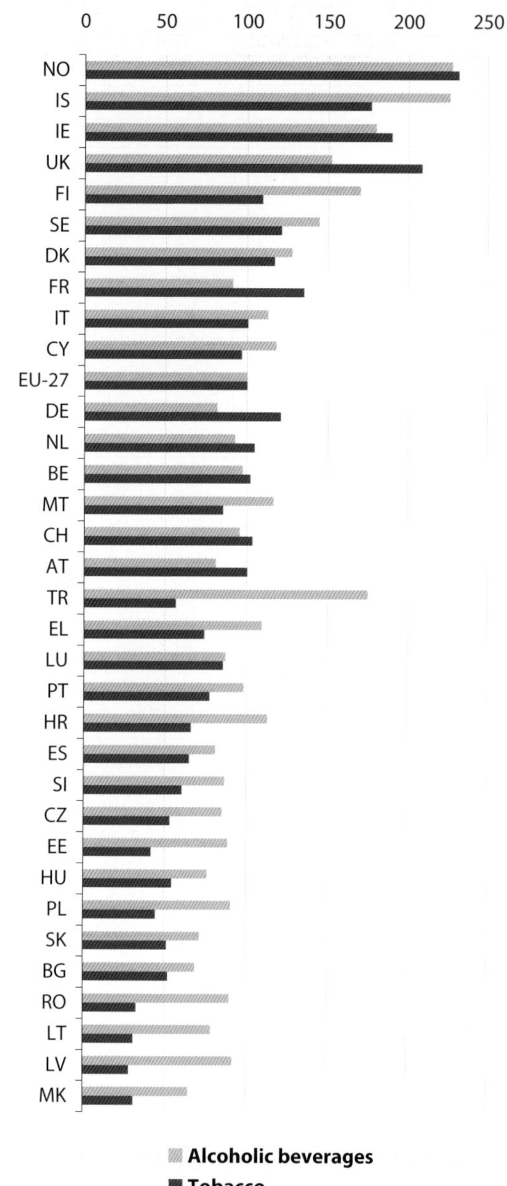

(1) Graph is ranked on overall price levels for alcoholic beverages and tobacco.

Source: Eurostat, Price level indices (theme2/prc/prc_ppp_ind)

Table 2.7: Excise duties and revenue

	Cigarettes		Still wine		Sparkling wine	
	Minimum excise duty, 2008 (% of retail price)	Revenue, 2006 (EUR million)	Excise duty, 2008 (EUR/hectolitre)	Revenue, 2006 (EUR million)	Excise duty, 2008 (EUR/hectolitre)	Revenue, 2006 (EUR million)
BE	60.1	1 459.0	47.1	113.7	161.1	33.2
BG	64.9	:	0.0	:	0.0	:
CZ	64.5	1 097.3	0.0	-	85.0	8.3
DK (1)	53.4	918.3	82.4	128.6	123.4	4.0
DE	59.8	12 973.8	66.5	0.0	136.0	420.8
EE	60.6	76.1	0.0	12.9	66.5	0.0
IE	61.0	1 089.4	273.0	194.0	546.0	11.0
EL	57.6	2 415.5	0.0	0.0	0.0	0.0
ES	63.8	6 414.6	0.0	-	0.0	-
FR	64.0	9 437.0	3.4	90.0	8.4	24.0
IT	58.5	9 624.0	0.0	0.0	0.0	0.0
CY	59.0	175.0	0.0	0.0	0.0	0.0
LV	74.6	81.7	42.6	6.9	42.6	3.4
LT	51.6	101.6	52.1	10.2	52.1	-
LU	57.9	421.2	0.0	0.0	0.0	0.0
HU	56.3	829.8	0.0	1.2	48.5	9.3
MT	60.8	62.7	0.0	0.0	0.0	0.0
NL	57.0	1 681.1	68.5	192.6	233.7	12.6
AT	58.3	1 408.5	0.0	0.0	0.0	0.0
PL	75.5	2 909.1	36.1	130.2	36.1	-
PT	62.2	1 410.5	0.0	0.0	0.0	0.0
RO	52.5	:	0.0	:	34.1	:
SI	58.2	290.1	0.0	0.0	0.0	0.0
SK	77.6	301.9	0.0	0.0	70.8	3.1
FI	57.0	562.8	233.0	194.0	233.0	-
SE	52.3	741.6	234.7	387.9	234.7	-
UK	61.6	10 930.8	278.6	3 206.1	356.9	225.8

(1) Excise duty rate for still wine in Denmark relates to wine with an alcoholic content of 6-15 % vol.

Source: European Commission, Directorate General for Taxation and Customs Union

Table 2.8: Awareness of health warnings/risks associated with tobacco and alcohol, EU-25, 2005 (1)
(% of respondents)

		of which:				
	Yes	During past week	During past month	During past 6 months	Over 6 months ago	No
Health warnings on cigarette packets - aware	85					15
Aware of smoking risks from the media (last read/heard)	94	*37*	*32*	*16*	*9*	3
Aware of alcohol risks from the media (last read/heard)	90	*24*	*32*	*21*	*13*	5

(1) A small percentage of respondents gave no response.

Source: 'Risk issues', Special Eurobarometer 238, European Commission

2.5 Externalities

(8) See, http://ec.europa.eu/health/ph_determinants/life_style/alcohol/keydoc_alcohol_en.htm.

An alcohol factsheet released by the Directorate-General for Health and Consumers [8] reports that the tangible cost of excess alcohol consumption in the EU was EUR 125 billion in 2003, equivalent to about 1.3 % of GDP. A little more than half (about 53 %) of this total was spent on alcohol-related problems (such as the costs of crime, healthcare and damage), while the rest related to productivity losses associated with foregone production, as a result of absenteeism, unemployment or premature mortality – see Figure 2.4.

A similar study (carried out by the ASPECT Consortium 2004 for the European Commission) produced a comparative estimate of the tangible cost of tobacco, which was situated between EUR 98 and EUR 130 billion in 2000 (corresponding to between 1.1 % and 1.4 % of GDP).

Across the EU-27, the standardised death rate from cancer of the trachea, bronchus and lung, a key disease associated with smoking, was 67 per 100 000 inhabitants among men and about 18 per 100 000 for women in 2006, although in Hungary these rates were closer to double the EU-27 average – see Table 2.9. The standardised death rate from alcohol abuse across the EU-27 was between 4 and 5 cases per 100 000 persons for men, although this figure rose to nearer 17 in Estonia.

An analysis over time shows that standardised death rates for men were generally falling at a faster pace than those for women, where death rates were in some countries rising or stationary, thus resulting in a closing of the gender gap.

Figure 2.4: The tangible cost of alcohol in Europe, 2003 (1)

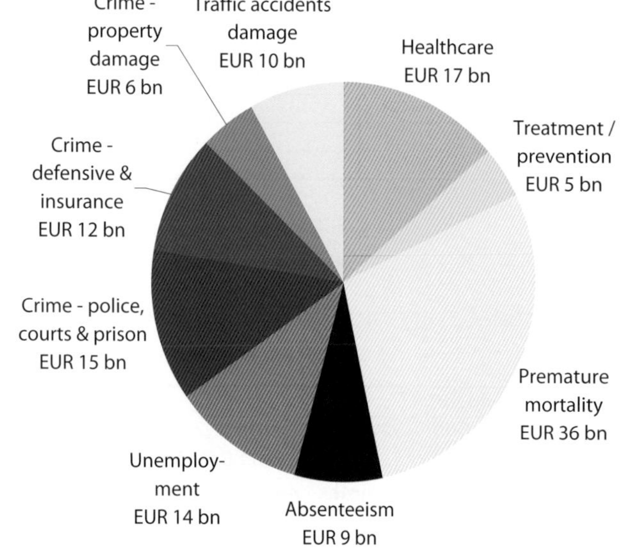

(1) Based on studies from Belgium, Denmark, Germany, Ireland, Spain, France, Italy, Latvia, the Netherlands, Portugal, Slovenia, Slovakia, Finland, Sweden, Great Britain and Norway.

Source: 'Alcohol-related harm in Europe', Anderson and Baumberg for Directorate-General for Health and Consumers, European Commission

Table 2.9: Deaths from smoking and drinking, 2006
(standardised death rates, per 100 000 persons)

	Malignant neoplasm of larynx and trachea, bronchus, lung (1)		Alcoholic abuse (including psychosis) (2)	
	Male	Female	Male	Female
EU-27	67.0	17.8	4.5	1.0
BE	:	:	:	:
BG	71.9	11.8	1.2	0.1
CZ	78.1	20.0	2.9	0.8
DK	:	:	:	:
DE	56.3	18.4	7.5	2.0
EE	91.4	13.2	16.8	4.5
IE	53.8	27.9	2.7	1.6
EL	73.5	11.3	0.4	0.0
ES	71.0	8.9	1.2	0.1
FR	67.3	14.0	7.9	1.8
IT	:	:	:	:
CY	33.8	7.2	0.8	:
LV	91.7	10.6	5.9	1.3
LT	87.5	9.2	1.9	0.1
LU	64.0	20.4	6.5	2.3
HU	112.6	32.8	8.5	1.2
MT	52.9	6.8	1.0	0.0
NL	70.4	30.4	1.8	0.4
AT	52.2	17.4	6.2	1.2
PL	102.7	21.7	8.6	1.0
PT	48.4	8.3	1.7	0.2
RO	75.6	13.3	3.8	0.7
SK	83.4	11.9	:	:
SI	77.6	18.0	5.2	1.0
FI	47.2	12.7	4.9	1.0
SE	32.8	23.4	5.2	1.1
UK	57.8	29.6	2.2	0.8

(1) Belgium, Denmark and Italy, not available; Bulgaria, France, Luxembourg, Malta, Portugal, Slovakia, Sweden and the United Kingdom, 2005.
(2) Belgium, Denmark, Italy, Cyprus (females) and Slovakia, not available; Bulgaria, France, Luxembourg, Malta, Portugal, Sweden and the United Kingdom, 2005.

Source: Eurostat, Population and social conditions (theme3/hlth/hlth_cd_asdr)

For more information

Directorate-General for Health and Consumers:
http://ec.europa.eu/health

3

Clothing and footwear

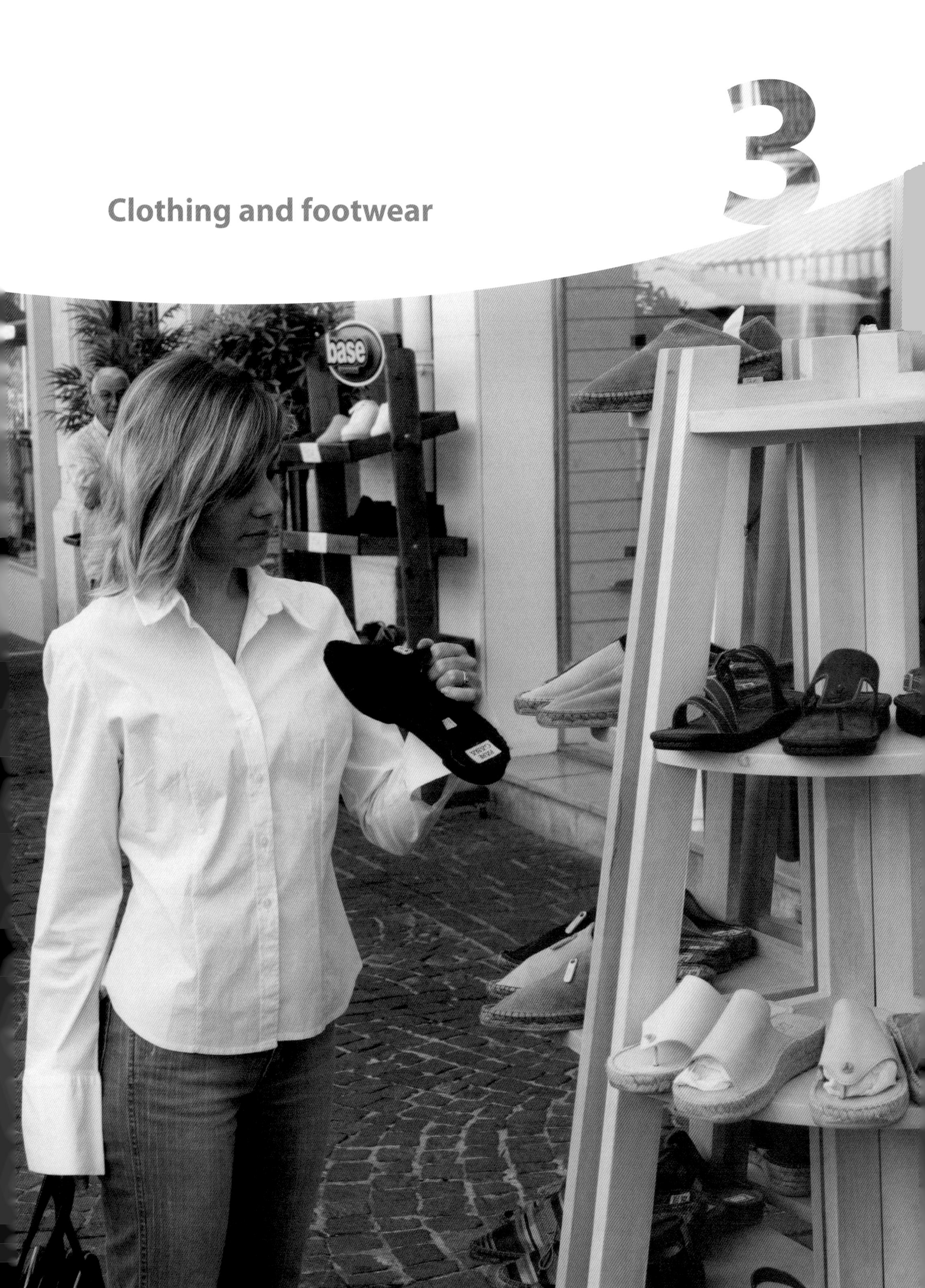

The consumer market for clothing and footwear in the EU has undergone important changes in recent years. Arguably, the greatest impact has come from market forces; under the auspices of the World Trade Organisation (WTO), as a ten-year transitional Agreement on Textiles and Clothing (ATC) came to an end with the abolition of textile and clothing import quotas on 31 December 2004. With the removal of quotas, there was an initial increase in relatively cheap imports of clothing and footwear into the EU, mainly originating from China. For example, in the first 40 days after the end of the ATC, imports of trousers from China were 3.3 times higher than during the whole of 2004 and imports of pullovers 4.5 times higher. A bilateral agreement between the EU and China (the so-called Shanghai Agreement) on a further, transitional period during which the growth of imports of clothing could be managed through until the end of 2007 was agreed in June 2005.

In addition to trade developments, consumer groups and other bodies are increasingly holding manufacturers and retailers accountable for ensuring that social standards and working conditions of their suppliers meet international labour standards. There are examples of retailers responding to this pressure: for example, in October 2007 the EU's INDITEX group signed an International Framework Agreement on corporate social responsibility with the International Textile, Garment and Leather Workers' Federation (ITGLWF), which expresses the company's commitment to respect fundamental rights at work throughout their entire production chain. Fair trade garment initiatives have also been taken, generally to ensure that a fair price is paid to producers who meet minimum social, and in some cases environmental, standards and that trading relationships between producers and buyers are more equal, rather than guaranteeing core labour standards (see the clean clothing campaign website – www.cleanclothes.org).

There has also been a response within the EU to concerns about environmental and safety issues. These concerns have predominantly focused on the use of chemicals (such as dyes, pigments or bleaches in the clothing manufacturing process) and on waste water discharge. On 1 June 2007, new legislation on chemicals and their safe use [9] came into force across the EU. REACH (Registration, Evaluation and Authorisation of Chemicals) aims to improve the protection of human health and the environment through the better and earlier identification of the intrinsic properties of chemical substances.

(9) Regulation (EC) No 1907/2006 of the European Parliament and of the Council.

3.1 Access and choice

Consumers in Europe are able to purchase clothing and footwear from a wide variety and large number of retailers, specialised and non-specialised. Specialist clothing and footwear retailers comprise chains (such as H&M, C&A or Zara) and independent clothes stores. Non-specialist retailers include department stores (that have clothing and footwear departments), hypermarkets and supermarkets, as well as mail-order retailers.

According to the Institut Français de la Mode, almost two thirds (62 %) of clothing expenditure in the EU-25 was carried out within specialist clothing stores (chain stores or independents) in 2004 (see Figure 3.1). One striking difference between the data for the EU-25 and the United States was the relative popularity of independent clothing stores in the EU-25; these accounted for the second highest proportion of clothing expenditure (28 %) among the categories shown, behind specialist clothing multiples/chain stores. In contrast, these independent clothing stores accounted for just 3 % of the retail clothing market in the United States. Sales of clothing in the United States were relatively high, compared with the EU-25, in non-specialist stores (department stores, supermarkets and hypermarkets).

There are generally higher levels of retail concentration in northern Europe. The overwhelming majority of clothing and footwear sales in Germany, France and particularly the United Kingdom are made in non-specialist stores (see Figure 3.2). The popularity of independent clothing and footwear retailers is considerably higher in southern Europe. For example, in Italy and Spain, the highest proportion of clothing sales was among independent retailers (65 % and 53 % respectively in 2004), and this tendency was even stronger in terms of footwear (76 % and 88 % respectively in 2003). Despite these differences, clothing markets in Europe are generally becoming more concentrated, as clothing chains, department stores and supermarkets/hypermarkets selling clothing and footwear open additional outlets in many of the countries that have joined the EU since 2004.

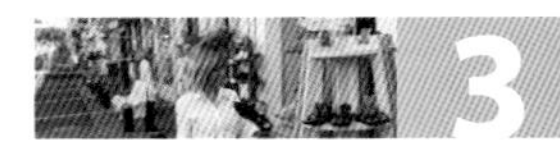

Figure 3.1: Clothing distribution channels, 2004
(% share of clothing sales)

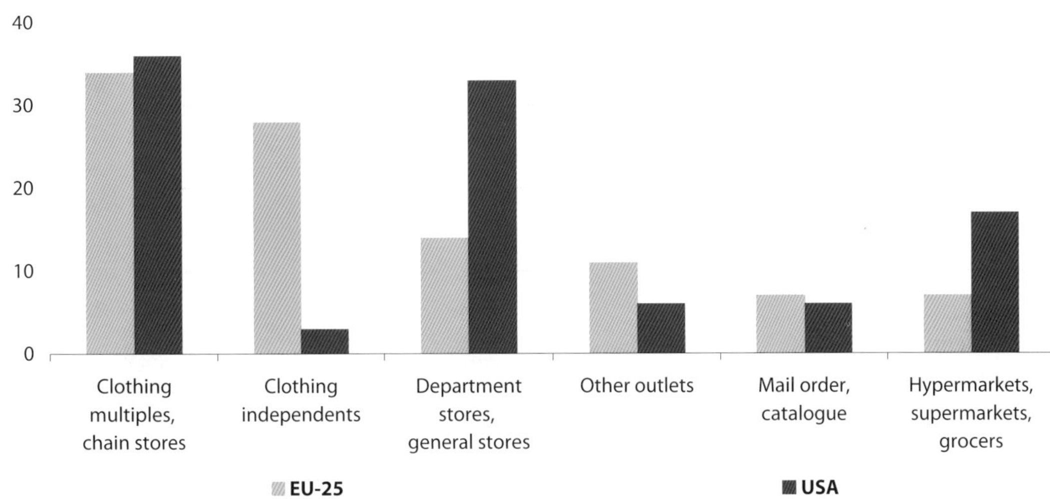

Source: Institut Français de la Mode

Figure 3.2: Concentrated distribution channels for clothing and footwear in selected Member States, 2004 and 2003 respectively (1)
(% share of clothing/footwear sales)

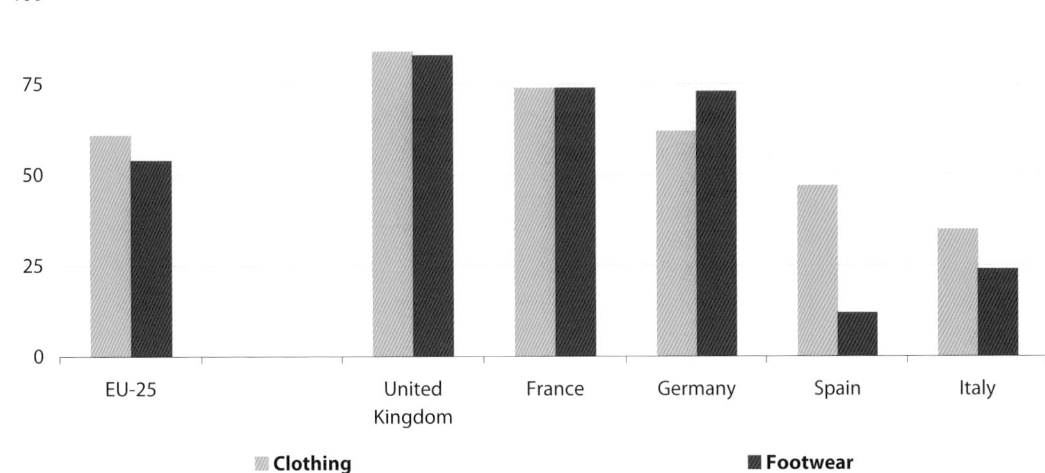

(1) Concentrated distribution comprises department stores, general stores, mail order, chain stores incl. discounters, hypermarkets and supermarkets - in contrast to independent clothing retailers.

Source: Institut Français de la Mode

Indeed, the structural make-up of clothing retailers in the EU has changed considerably over the past 15 years, according to a 2007 report on 'Business relations in the EU clothing chain' carried out for and funded by the European Commission [10]. The market share of independent retailers in the five largest EU markets (Italy, Spain, France, Germany and the United Kingdom, that together account for almost three quarters of the EU-25's clothing market) declined from 46.8 % of total clothing sales to 27.1 % by 2007. In contrast, there was steady growth in the share of speciality chains (from 18.7 % to 25.1 %), hypermarkets and supermarkets (5.1 % to 6.8 %) and emerging formats such as variety stores and large sports chains (whose share of clothing sales collectively rose from 14.0 % to 27.2 %).

[10] Bocconi University, ESSEC Business School and Baker and McKenzie.

A recent survey on consumer satisfaction provides further information on the shopping habits of European consumers for clothing and footwear; note that these figures relate to trips made by consumers purchasing clothing and footwear, and they do not reflect the average expenditure or value of sales made in each retail format (see Figure 3.3). More than half (55.7 %) of those surveyed in the EU-27 in 2008 replied that they themselves or a member of their household had bought clothing and footwear in a retail chain store, a somewhat higher proportion than for small, independent clothing retailers (50.2 %). Department stores (30.7 %), supermarkets/hypermarkets (23.0 %) and street markets (16.3 %) were also popular places for buying clothes and footwear. Furthermore, compared with a number of other products, a relatively high proportion of European consumers used mail or phone order (8.0 %) or the Internet (6.1 %) to purchase clothing and footwear.

This recent survey also reflects the dichotomy in the structure of clothing and footwear retailing across the EU. Retail chain stores specialising in clothing and footwear were the most common format for shopping in 13 of the Member States in 2008, while consumers in 12 of the Member States preferred small, independent shops. Denmark, Ireland, France and the Netherlands had a relatively high proportion of consumers who preferred shopping in retail chains specialising in clothes and footwear, while consumers in the vast majority of southern and eastern Member States chose small, independent stores. Among those surveyed in Denmark and the United Kingdom, a relatively large share made purchases of clothing and footwear in supermarkets and hypermarkets, whereas department stores were a popular retail format for clothes and footwear purchases in Germany, Ireland and Luxembourg.

Figure 3.3: In which of the following places have you or has a member of your household bought clothing and footwear most, EU-27, 2008?
(%)

Source: 'Retail satisfaction survey', IPSOS for the European Commission, August/September 2008

3.2 Consumption

Annual expenditure on clothing and footwear averaged EUR 800 per person in the EU-27 in 2006, with national averages ranging from EUR 100 per person in Romania to EUR 1 200 per person in Italy. For the majority of Member States, average expenditure in 2006 did not change much compared with 2000. However, there was a marked rise in expenditure devoted to clothing and footwear in Lithuania (up from an average of EUR 100 per person to EUR 400 per person) and relatively large increases in Estonia, Slovakia and Hungary.

A breakdown of the final consumption expenditure of households on clothing and footwear reveals some considerable changes in price and volume components over the period 2000 to 2006 (see Figure 3.4). The volume of clothing and footwear bought rose in most of the Member States for which data are available. This was particularly the case in the Czech Republic and the United Kingdom, where volumes increased by about 50 %, and in Estonia they more than doubled. Germany and particularly Italy reported declines in the volume of clothing and footwear bought (the only Member States to do so). The biggest price decreases were recorded in Ireland, Malta and the United Kingdom (between 20 % and 25 %). In contrast, high price increases between 2000 and 2006 were recorded in Estonia, Greece, Italy, Hungary and Spain (between 14 % and 18 %) and particularly Slovakia (up 37 %).

Average household expenditure on clothing and footwear in terms of comparable price levels (PPS rather than euro) was PPS 1 412 per household for the EU-27 in 2005, ranging from PPS 333 per household in Romania to PPS 3 343 per household in Luxembourg (see Table 3.2). Relatively high levels of spending on clothing and footwear in PPS terms were also recorded in Cyprus, Malta, Greece and Italy.

Table 3.1: Final consumption expenditure of households, clothing and footwear: consumption per head
(EUR)

	2000	2006
EU-27	700	800
BE	700	800
BG	0	:
CZ	200	300
DK	800	:
DE	800	800
EE	200	400
IE	900	900
EL	600	800
ES	600	700
FR	700	700
IT	1 100	1 200
CY	800	900
LV	200	:
LT	100	400
LU	1 100	1 100
HU	100	200
MT	500	400
NL	800	800
AT	1 100	1 100
PL	200	200
PT	600	:
RO (1)	0	100
SI	400	500
SK	100	200
FI	600	800
SE	700	:
UK	1 000	1 100
TR (1)	300	300
IS	1 100	1 100
NO	900	:
CH	900	900

(1) 2006, forecast.

Source: Eurostat, Final consumption expenditure of households by consumption purpose (theme2/nama/nama_co2_c)

Figure 3.4: Final consumption expenditure of households, clothing and footwear: price and volume changes between 2000 and 2006 (1)
(%)

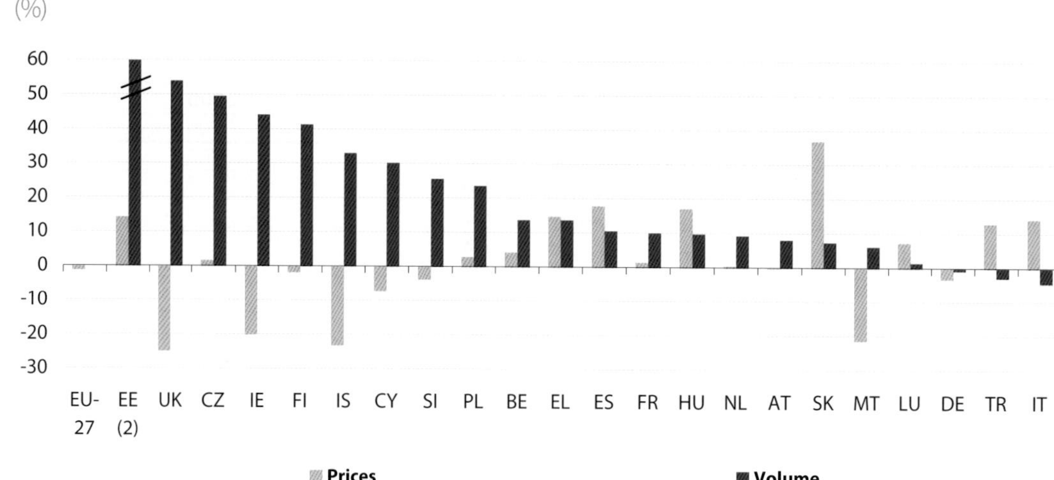

(1) Bulgaria, Denmark, Latvia, Lithuania, Portugal, Romania and Sweden, not available; EU-27, volume, not available.
(2) The volume of clothing and footwear purchased in Estonia increased by 106.4 % between 2000 and 2006.

Source: Eurostat, Final consumption expenditure of households by consumption purpose (theme2/nama/nama_co2_k and nama_co2_p)

Household expenditure on clothing and footwear accounted for an estimated 5.7 % of total household consumption expenditure across the EU-27 in 2005 (see Figure 3.5). The vast majority of this, almost three quarters, was spent on clothing garments. Among the Member States, the relative importance of clothing and footwear in total household consumption expenditure ranged from 3.1 % in Bulgaria to 8.3 % in Malta, with France, Spain and Italy well above the EU-27 average, and the United Kingdom and Germany well below. In each of the Member States, the majority of household spending was on clothing garments, proportions ranging from 59.7 % in Romania to 79.7 % in Luxembourg.

The relative importance of clothing and footwear expenditure also varied considerably among different subgroups of households. Spending on clothing and footwear tended to rise as a function of income, with the upper income quintile in the EU-27 devoting 6.1 % of their total household budget to these products, while those in the lowest income quintile spent 5 %. Spending on clothing and footwear was relatively high among non-manual workers (6.4 % of their total budget) and the self-employed (6.1 %), as compared the unemployed (5.3 %) or the retired (4.2 %). Perhaps unsurprisingly, the share of total expenditure spent on clothing and footwear was generally much higher among households with dependent children, rising to 7.0 % of the household budget for those households comprising two adults with dependent children, compared with 4.6 % of the budget for single persons.

Table 3.2: Mean consumption expenditure per household, clothing and footwear, 2005
(PPS)

EU-27 (1)	1 412
BE	1 425
BG	218
CZ	679
DK	1 168
DE	1 355
EE	601
IE	1 851
EL	2 154
ES	1 786
FR	1 853
IT	2 013
CY	2 649
LV	778
LT	743
LU	3 343
HU	537
MT	2 387
NL	1 694
AT	1 682
PL	489
PT	861
RO	333
SI	1 678
SK	661
FI	934
SE	1 270
UK	1 585
HR	1 059
NO	1 618

(1) Estimate.

Source: Eurostat, Household Budget Survey (theme3/hbs/hbs_exp_t121)

Figure 3.5: Structure of consumption expenditure: share of clothing and footwear in total expenditure, 2005 (1)
(%)

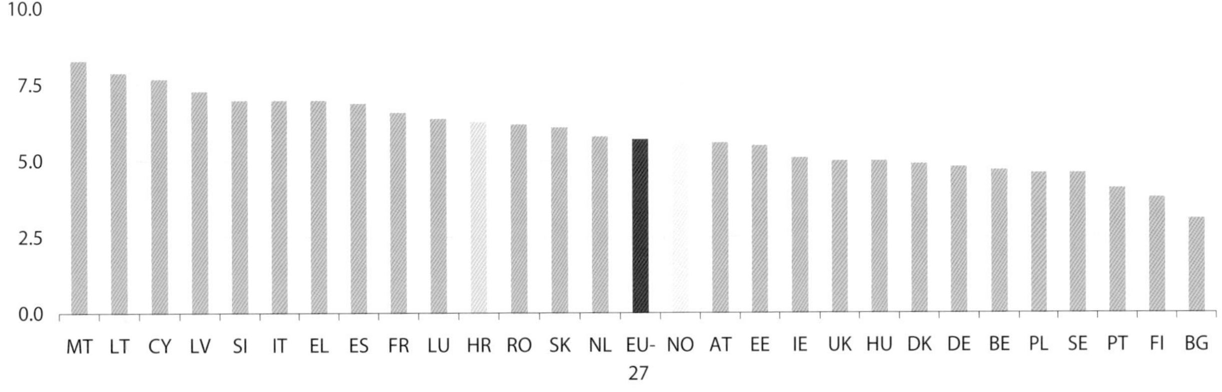

(1) EU-27, estimate; Czech Republic, not available.

Source: Eurostat, Household Budget Survey (theme3/hbs/hbs_str_t211)

Table 3.3: Structure of consumption expenditure: share in total expenditure, EU-27, 2005 (1)
(%)

	Clothing and footwear	Clothing	Footwear (including repair)
Socio-economic category (1)			
Manual workers	5.8	4.7	1.3
Non-manual workers	6.4	5.3	1.3
Self-employed	6.1	5.0	1.3
Unemployed	5.3	4.2	1.2
Retired	4.2	3.3	0.9
Other inactive	5.4	4.3	1.2
Income quintile			
Lowest	5.0	3.2	1.3
Second	5.1	3.3	1.2
Third	5.5	3.5	1.3
Fourth	5.8	3.8	1.3
Highest	6.1	4.3	1.2
Household type (1)			
Single person	4.6	3.4	1.2
Single parent with dependent children	6.7	5.0	1.7
Two adults	4.9	3.8	1.1
Two adults with dependent children	7.0	5.3	1.7
Three or more adults	5.7	4.3	1.3
Three or more adults with dependent children	6.3	4.7	1.7
Age of the reference person			
Less than 30	5.6	3.6	1.2
30-44	5.6	3.6	1.3
45-59	4.9	3.2	1.1
60 and over	3.6	2.3	0.8
Degree of urbanisation (1)			
Dense	5.5	3.6	1.2
Intermediate	5.7	3.8	1.2
Sparse	5.8	3.9	1.2

(1) Unreliable.

Source: Eurostat, Household Budget Survey (theme3/hbs/hbs_str_t221, hbs_str_t223, hbs_str_t224, hbs_str_t225, hbs_str_t226)

3.3 Prices

3.3.1 Price inflation

Data for 2000 and 2007 show no change in the harmonised index of consumer prices for clothing and footwear for the EU-27, with little evolution during the intervening years. This trend was in contrast to an average annual increase of 2.4 % for the all-items consumer price index during the same period. Among the Member States, there were sharp contrasts in the evolution of consumer prices for clothing and footwear (see Table 3.4); with consistent and sizeable price decreases in the Czech Republic, Ireland, Lithuania, Poland (after 2001) and the United Kingdom, but relatively steady price increases in Estonia, Greece, Spain, Italy, Luxembourg, Hungary and Romania. This varied pattern across Member States continued in 2007, with strong price growth in Estonia (4.1 %) and Bulgaria (7.0 %) but sharp decreases in the United Kingdom (-3.7 %), Lithuania (-4.9 %) and Poland (-7.2 %).

The overall stability of the EU-27's harmonised index of consumer prices for clothing and footwear fails to reflect two distinct periods: firstly, between 2000 and 2004, when falling prices for garments were largely compensated by rising prices of clothing materials, clothing accessories and footwear. In the period after 2004, the price of other articles of clothing and clothing accessories and footwear stabilised, in contrast to a continued reduction in the price of garments and a steep rise in the price of cleaning and repair services and the hire of clothing (see Figure 3.6).

Table 3.4: Harmonised indices of consumer prices, clothing and footwear, annual rate of change
(%)

	2000	2001	2002	2003	2004	2005	2006	2007
EU-27	0.7	0.1	1.0	0.3	-0.2	-0.8	-0.5	0.0
BE	-2.4	0.7	1.1	1.0	0.6	-0.1	-0.3	0.4
BG	-4.0	0.3	-0.2	-2.2	0.5	1.1	3.8	7.0
CZ	-2.0	-1.7	-2.6	-4.9	-4.1	-5.5	-6.3	-0.6
DK	-4.3	-1.5	2.3	1.0	0.0	-0.7	-1.9	-1.7
DE	0.1	0.8	0.7	-0.8	-0.7	-1.9	-0.8	0.9
EE	3.4	3.8	4.1	1.0	-0.1	1.9	3.5	4.1
IE	-4.8	-2.8	-4.2	-4.1	-3.5	-2.8	-1.9	-3.3
EL	2.0	3.2	3.5	2.0	4.1	4.7	2.3	3.2
ES	2.1	-0.6	5.1	3.8	1.8	1.4	1.2	1.1
FR	0.2	0.5	0.9	-0.3	0.3	0.2	0.2	0.7
IT	2.2	0.6	2.9	2.2	1.9	1.2	1.2	0.7
CY	-0.6	-7.1	-3.6	1.3	-0.8	-0.9	-4.3	-0.6
LV	1.2	0.9	-0.8	3.7	2.5	-0.2	0.0	2.3
LT	-0.8	-4.2	-3.5	-2.7	-0.9	-1.8	-2.4	-4.9
LU	0.9	2.1	1.7	1.5	0.5	0.5	0.1	0.5
HU	6.1	5.6	4.2	3.2	3.5	0.3	-0.7	1.0
MT	0.3	-1.3	-0.7	-6.8	-2.5	-0.5	-1.8	0.4
NL	-0.9	1.8	3.2	-3.1	-1.9	-2.6	0.5	1.4
AT	-0.7	-0.3	0.3	-0.1	-0.6	-1.2	-0.2	2.2
PL	5.5	1.5	-0.8	-2.5	-3.5	-5.3	-6.9	-7.2
PT	0.7	1.5	2.5	1.2	-1.1	-1.2	0.5	2.2
RO	29.8	28.0	15.6	11.8	7.6	4.8	3.9	3.3
SI	7.0	1.7	3.1	6.3	1.6	-1.0	-0.5	1.6
SK	3.1	2.4	3.3	2.7	0.5	-0.8	-0.1	0.8
FI	0.2	1.0	-1.1	-0.2	0.3	-0.6	-2.0	0.3
SE	0.9	2.1	1.6	-0.7	-2.6	-0.8	2.0	2.4
UK	-7.3	-7.5	-7.2	-3.8	-4.8	-5.1	-4.0	-3.7
TR	41.4	50.4	51.4	25.7	7.5	4.4	1.4	4.5
IS	-1.2	1.0	-0.9	-1.8	-0.3	-1.1	0.1	1.0
NO	-2.6	-1.4	-5.4	-10.0	-6.9	-4.7	-3.2	-4.6
CH	:	:	:	:	:	:	1.9	0.3

Source: Eurostat, Harmonised indices of consumer prices (theme2/prc/prc_hicp_aind)

Figure 3.6: Harmonised indices of consumer prices, EU-27
(2005=100)

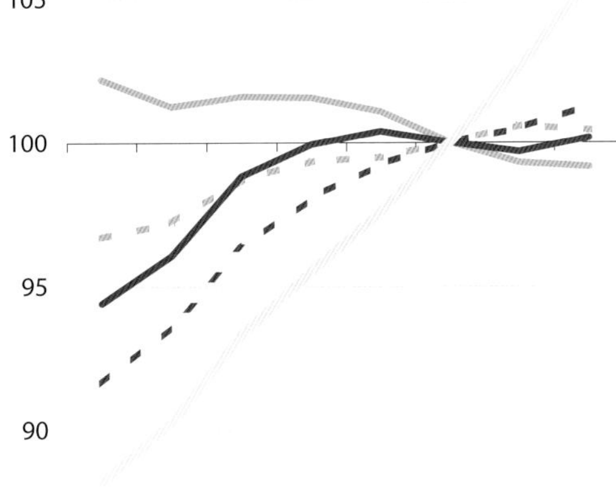

Source: Eurostat, Harmonised indices of consumer prices (theme2/prc/prc_hicp_aind)

3.3.2 Price levels

In 2007 clothing and footwear price level indices in most Member States were within a relatively narrow range of +/-10 % of the EU-27 average. Clothing and footwear was particularly expensive in the Nordic countries; in Denmark, Finland and Sweden prices were about 15-20 % higher than the EU-27 average, in Norway about one third higher, and in Iceland about 50 % higher. In contrast, prices for clothing and footwear were about 30 % lower than the EU-27 average in Bulgaria (see Figure 3.7).

Figure 3.7: Price level indices, clothing and footwear, 2007
(EU-27=100)

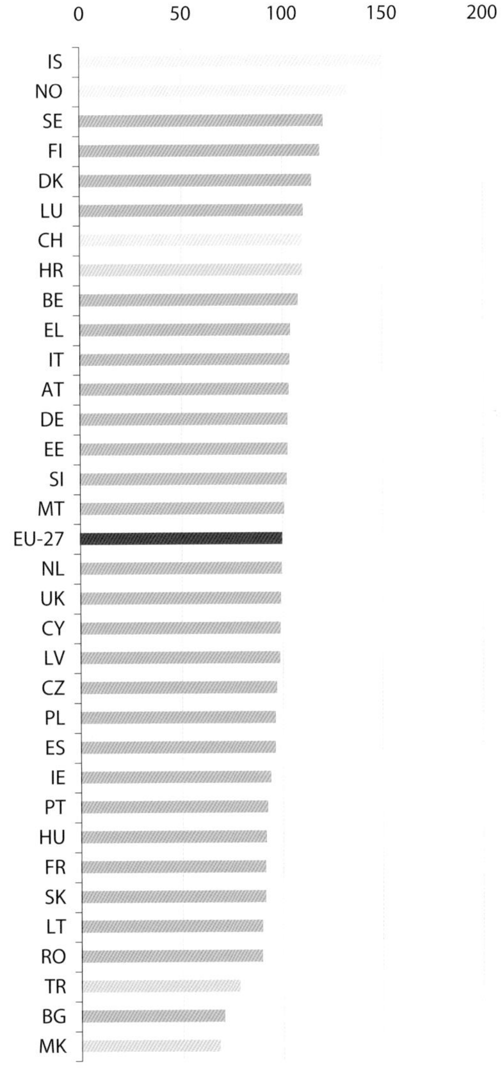

Source: Eurostat, Price level indices (theme2/prc/prc_ppp_ind)

3.4 Consumer satisfaction and complaints

A 2008 survey on satisfaction shows that the majority of consumers in the EU-27 are relatively satisfied with their clothing and footwear retailers: on a scale of 1-10, with 1 being not at all satisfied and 10 being fully satisfied, an average of 8.3 was recorded in the EU-27. Among the Member States, satisfaction was highest in Germany, Luxembourg, Austria and the United Kingdom, while Italian and Latvian consumers were the least satisfied.

The same survey shows that of the 10.9 % of EU-27 consumers who faced problems when buying clothing or footwear in the 12 months prior to the survey in mid-2008, more than two thirds (68.9 %) cited product quality as their complaint. The proportion of consumers complaining about other problems never rose into double figures (see Figure 3.9): with the next highest shares recorded for problems returning unwanted goods (9.2 % of unsatisfied consumers) and the quality of service provided (8.8 %).

Figure 3.8: Overall, to what extent are you satisfied with your regular retailer for clothing and footwear, 2008? (1)
(average, 1-10)

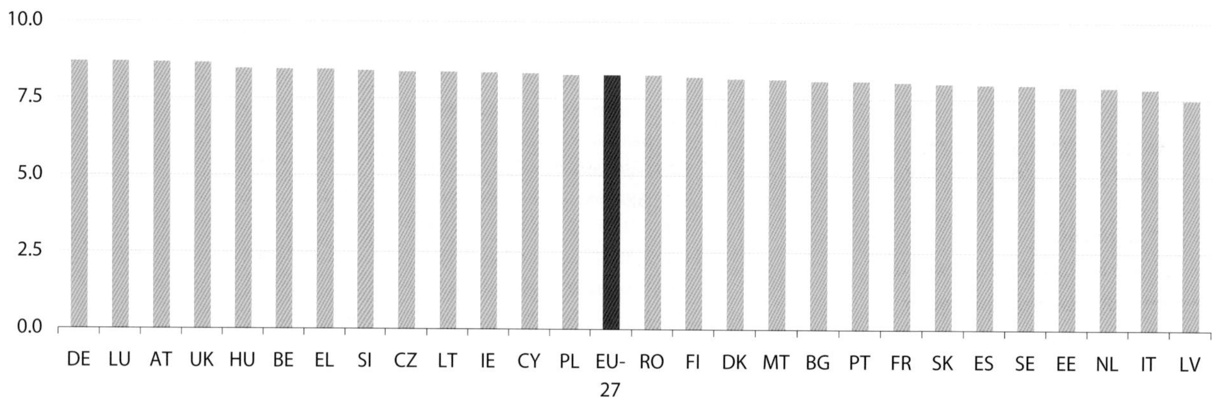

(1) Average on a scale of 1 (not at all satisfied) to 10 (fully satisfied).

Source: 'Retail satisfaction survey', IPSOS for the European Commission, August/September 2008

Figure 3.9: Problems faced by consumers when purchasing clothing or footwear in the past 12 months, EU-27, 2008 (1)
(% share of those experiencing problems, multiple answers allowed)

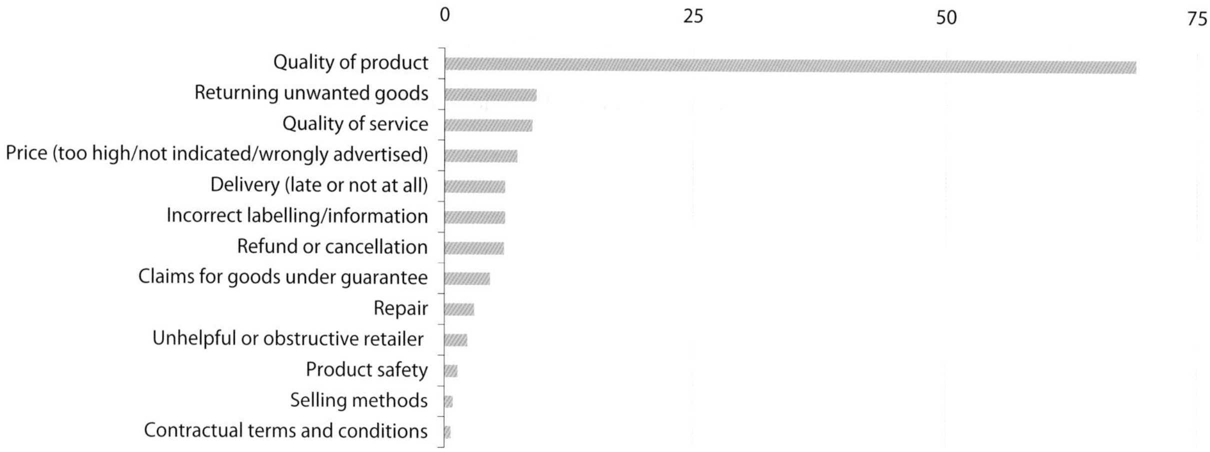

(1) When purchasing clothing and/or footwear in 2008, 10.9 % of EU-27 consumers reported facing at least one problem; note that consumers may have faced more than one problem.

Source: 'Retail satisfaction survey', IPSOS for the European Commission, August/September 2008

Figure 3.10: Do you agree that your regular retailer would replace, repair, reduce the price or give you your money back if clothing or footwear you had bought was defective or not fit for purpose, 2008? (1)
(average, 1-10)

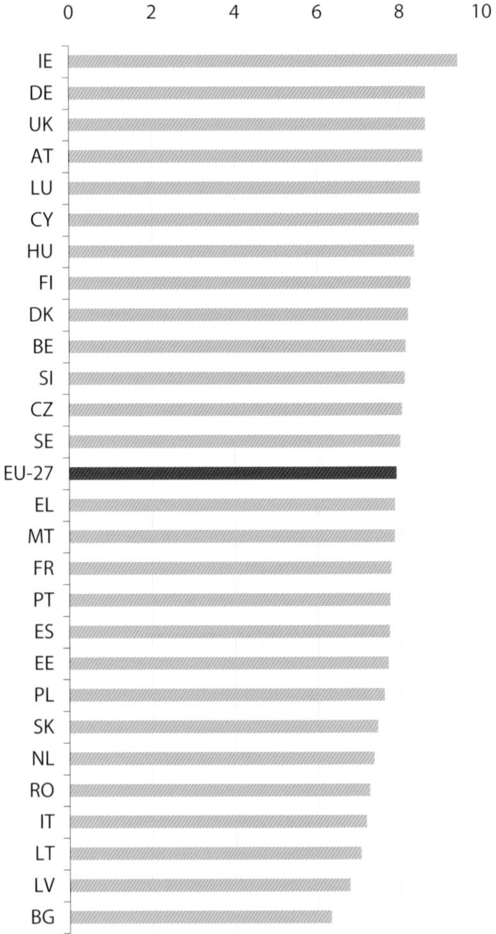

(1) Average on a scale of 1 (totally disagree) to 10 (totally agree).

Source: 'Retail satisfaction survey', IPSOS for the European Commission, August/September 2008

A majority of EU-27 consumers were of the opinion that clothing and footwear retailers would replace, repair, reduce the price or give them their money back if they had bought defective goods – see Figure 3.10. Using a scale from 1-10, the average for the EU-27 was 7.9, with a high of 9.4 in Ireland (considerably above the other countries) and a low of 6.3 in Bulgaria (well below the other Member States).

3.5 Quality

The same survey on consumer satisfaction also looked into the area of quality. With respect to clothing and footwear products this concerned two areas: the extent to which consumers felt goods were reliable (in other words, they did not fall apart, rip at the seams, tear or break when worn); and whether retailers provided enough choice regarding goods that were produced to high ethical standards (for example, without the use of child labour).

The results show that on a scale of 1-10 (with 10 being in total agreement) EU-27 consumers generally agreed that the clothing and footwear they purchased was reliable, with an average of 7.9. The highest scores were recorded in Ireland, Austria, the United Kingdom, Luxembourg and Germany – the same five countries that gave the most favourable replies when questioned on the likelihood of retailers replacing, repairing, reducing the price or giving them their money back in the event they had bought defective goods.

Regarding the supply of clothing and footwear products made to high ethical standards, there was a quite different picture. For the EU-27 as a whole, an average index of 7.5 was recorded (with higher scores reflecting agreement that there was enough choice when trying to buy ethically sourced clothes and footwear). Among the Member States, consumers from the Nordic countries, as well as those from Luxembourg, Latvia, France and Bulgaria were least satisfied with their choice of ethically produced goods.

Figure 3.11: To what extent do you agree that clothing and footwear products sold by your regular retailer are reliable (i.e. they do not fall apart, rip at the seams, tear or break), 2008? (1)
(average, 1-10)

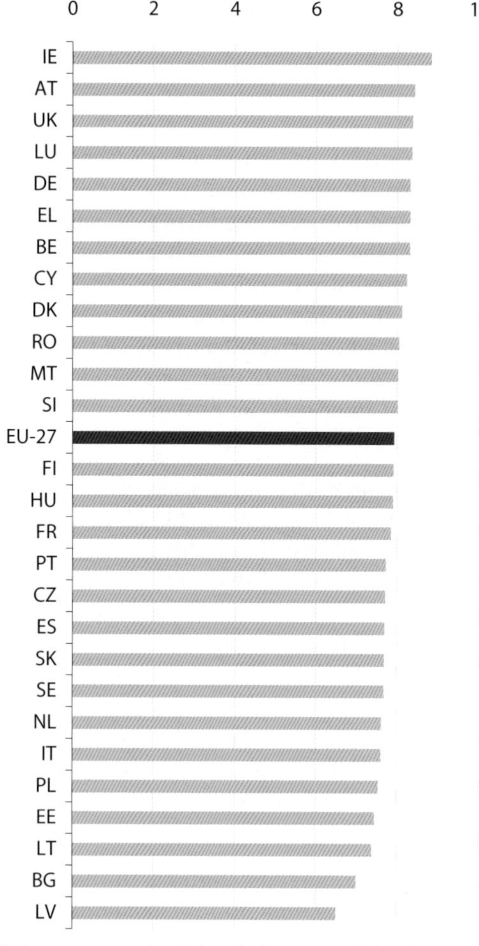

(1) Average on a scale of 1 (totally disagree) to 10 (totally agree).

Source: 'Retail satisfaction survey', IPSOS for the European Commission, August/September 2008

Figure 3.12: Do you agree that your regular retailer offers a wide enough choice of clothing and footwear that has been produced according to specific ethical standards (e.g. produced without the use of child labour, etc.), 2008? (1)
(average, 1-10)

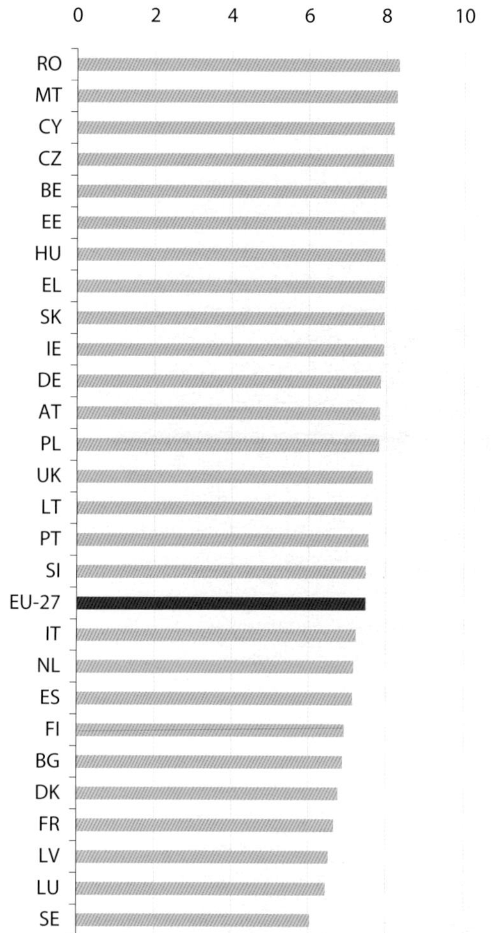

(1) Varies by region.

Source: World Health Organisation (www.who.int) and the Alcohol Policy Network co-financed by the European Commission

4

Housing, water, electricity, gas and other fuels

Housing, water supply, and fuel (such as electricity and gas) for use in the home (not for transport needs) are basic requirements for individuals. The provision of water, electricity and gas are among several services of general interest covered in this publication; others, such as transport and communications services are covered in Chapters 7 and 8, while retail banking is included as part of Chapter 12. Services of general interest can be defined as collective or social goods insofar as public authorities may consider that they need to be provided even where the market may not have sufficient incentive to do so. Services of general interest make an important contribution to economic, social and territorial cohesion, and users expect high quality services at affordable prices.

Consumption expenditure and price data presented in this chapter concerns housing, water, electricity, gas and other fuels, while furnishings, household equipment and routine maintenance of the house are covered in Chapter 5. Payments for housing, water and fuel are very important for consumers as they represent a large share of household consumption expenditure: EU households, on average, devoted more than one fifth of their total household consumption expenditure to housing (including maintenance and repair), water and household energy.

The gas and electricity markets in the EU have been changing through the requirements of the second electricity and gas directives adopted in 2003. The aim of this legislation was to have gas and electricity markets open for all customers by July 2007, as well as further unbundling the sector's supply and distribution/transmission enterprises. In January 2007, the European Commission published a communication on the prospects for the internal gas and electricity market [11]. Whilst recognising progress in these markets, the Commission noted the improper implementation of the current legal framework by several Member States, and outlined its planned actions to: ensure non-discriminatory access to well developed networks; improve regulation of network access at national and EU level; reduce the scope for unfair competition; provide a clear framework for investment; and resolve issues relating to households and smaller commercial customers. In September 2007 the European Commission proposed a third package of proposals with the objective to separate the operation of electricity and gas transmission networks from supply and generation.

Water is a limited natural resource on which human health and development depends, and in return human activities have an impact on this resource. European water policies place great attention on water quality, whether for drinking or other purposes. To guarantee drinking water quality, a 1998 Council Directive set standards for the most common substances that can be found in drinking water, and a total of 48 microbiological and chemical parameters must be monitored and tested regularly. In 2000, a long-term framework for Community action in the field of water policy was established with broader aims, including the promotion of sustainable water use. Notably this framework promotes a gradual implementation of the use of pricing, alongside other measures, as incentives for consumers to modify their consumption patterns towards a sustainable level with the aim of recovering the full costs of water services. These water pricing policies should be implemented by 2010.

(11) COM(2006) 841.

Table 4.1: Connection rates
(%)

	Urban waste water collecting system with treatment, 2005	Urban waste water collecting system, 2005	Municipal waste collection services, 2003	Public water supply Latest year
BE	55	86	100	96
BG	41	69	82	99
CZ	75	79	100	90
DK	:	:	100	97
DE (1)	94	96	:	99
EE (1)	73	73	79	72
IE	89	100	:	90
EL	:	:	100	:
ES	92	100	:	:
FR	:	:	:	99
IT	:	:	:	100
CY	30	30	:	100
LV	67	:	60	:
LT	70	70	:	76
LU	:	:	:	:
HU	:	:	:	93
MT	13	100	100	:
NL	99	99	100	100
AT (1)	89	89	:	90
PL	60	:	:	85
PT	65	74	100	85
RO	28	40	:	54
SI	45	63	:	91
SK	55	57	:	84
FI	:	:	100	:
SE	86	86	:	86
UK	:	:	:	:
TR (1)	36	68	:	:
IS	57	90	100	95
NO	77	82	:	89
CH	97	97	:	:

(1) Urban waste water, 2004.

Source: Eurostat, National population connected to waste water treatment plants, Generation and collection of municipal waste, Water use by supply category per capita (theme8/envir/env)

4.1 Access, choice and switching

Household use of water generates waste water which may or may not be collected through an urban wastewater system. Table 4.1 shows that in most EU Member States (for which data are available) around two thirds of dwellings are connected to such collecting systems, with only Cyprus, Romania, Slovenia and Slovakia falling below this level. In several countries, notably the Netherlands, Austria, Sweden, Estonia and Lithuania, there were high rates of connection to water collection systems which all involved treatment.

Electricity and water supply are widely available within the EU: the results of a 2006 Eurobarometer survey indicate that more than 90 % of respondents within the EU-25 had easy access to these, compared with less than three quarters of respondents for gas networks. Easy access to electricity exceeded 90 % in all EU-25 Member States except for Italy, while easy access to water supply exceeded 80 % everywhere, except for Italy and Latvia. In contrast, easy access to gas networks was much more varied, ranging from no access in the island Member States of Cyprus and Malta, though a low proportion in the sparsely populated countries of Finland and Sweden, to the highest rates in the natural gas producing countries of the Netherlands and the United Kingdom, as well as several central European countries (notably Hungary and Slovakia).

Table 4.2: Access to utilities: proportion of respondents having easy access, May–June 2006
(%)

	Electricity	Gas	Water
EU-25	93	72	93
BE	96	75	97
BG	:	:	:
CZ	93	80	93
DK	98	38	98
DE	97	74	96
EE	93	40	82
IE	97	51	95
EL	99	29	99
ES	95	77	94
FR	96	76	96
IT	76	74	77
CY	98	0	98
LV	98	56	78
LT	96	70	82
LU	93	58	96
HU	95	90	96
MT	97	0	97
NL	91	89	92
AT	93	69	92
PL	97	68	95
PT	98	43	96
RO	:	:	:
SI	98	46	97
SK	95	88	93
FI	99	11	98
SE	96	9	86
UK	97	89	97

Source: 'Services of General Interest', Special Eurobarometer 260, European Commission

Table 4.3: Electricity infrastructure: net installed capacity
(Megawatts)

	2006
EU-27	761 363
BE	16 258
BG	12 015
CZ	17 507
DK	13 012
DE	125 001
EE	2 288
IE	6 443
EL	13 566
ES	78 426
FR	115 916
IT	89 137
CY	1 134
LV	2 150
LT	4 562
LU	1 638
HU	8 620
MT	571
NL	22 853
AT	19 166
PL	32 360
PT	14 456
RO	19 224
SI	3 039
SK	8 210
FI	16 557
SE	34 122
UK	83 132
HR	3 879
TR	40 565
IS	1 725
NO (1)	28 896
CH (1)	19 097

(1) 2005.

Source: Eurostat, Infrastructure - electricity - annual data (theme8/nrg/nrg_113a)

The lack of integration between national markets, suggested by the absence of price convergence and the low but growing level of cross-border trade (see Figure 4.1), is generally attributed to barriers to entry, inadequate use of existing infrastructure and – in the case of electricity – insufficient interconnection between many Member States. In recent years initiatives have been taken in these areas, for example Belgium, Germany, France, Luxembourg and the Netherlands developed a single 'North-West European' market for electricity and started work on a similar market for gas.

In July 2007 full market liberalisation was completed in the gas and electricity market in the EU. Nevertheless, in its report on 'Progress in creating the internal gas and electricity market' the European Commission noted persisting restrictions to free and fair competition. The report also noted that market structures on a national scale are still very concentrated, and that incumbents control essential infrastructure facilities, further increasing their market power. Table 4.4 shows the extent to which the largest generator dominated each market. The two small island economies of Cyprus and Malta have only one generator, and the share of the largest generator exceeded 50 % in more than half of the remaining Member States with data available. Only in Poland, the United Kingdom and Finland was the share of the largest generator below one quarter.

Figure 4.1: Cross-border electricity flows between EU Member States, Norway and Switzerland as a share of gross electricity consumption
(%)

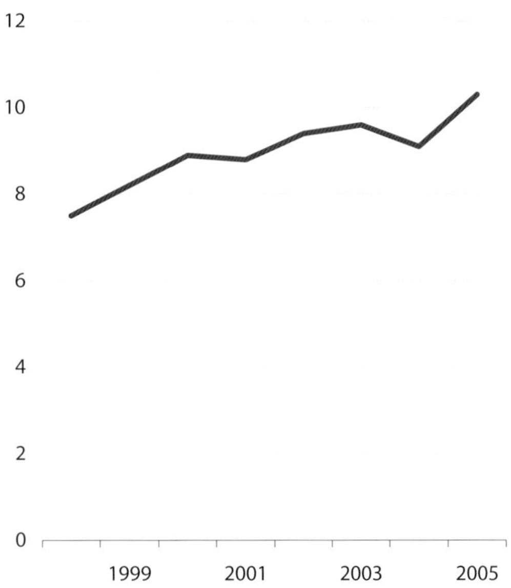

Source: Communication from the Commission to the Council and the European Parliament, COM(2007) 250.

Table 4.4: Market share of the largest generator in the electricity market: percentage of total generation
(%)

	2006
BE (1)	85
BG	:
CZ	74
DK	54
DE (2)	28
EE	91
IE	51
EL	95
ES	31
FR	89
IT	35
CY	100
LV	95
LT	70
LU (2)	81
HU	42
MT	100
NL	:
AT (3)	34
PL	17
PT (1)	54
RO	31
SI	51
SK	70
FI (1)	23
SE	45
UK	22
HR	83
TR (1)	38
NO (1)	30

(1) 2005.
(2) 2004.
(3) 2001.

Source: Eurostat, Market share of the largest generator in the electricity market (theme8/envir/nrg/nrg_indic/nrg_ind_331a)

Despite this relatively high dominance of the largest generators, a large majority of the population in each Member State regarded it as important to have a choice of electricity and gas supplier, with this view being shared by almost the entire population in Ireland according to a 2007 Eurobarometer survey. The same source reported that 18 % of respondents across the EU thought that choice was important just because of price issues, while 15 % responded that better customer care was an additional factor alongside price, and 44 % thought that the option to choose a cleaner energy supplier was also an additional factor; 21 % thought that price, customer care and cleaner energy sources were all reasons for favouring a choice of energy suppliers.

Figure 4.2: Importance of having a choice of electricity and gas supplier, February 2007 (% of respondents)

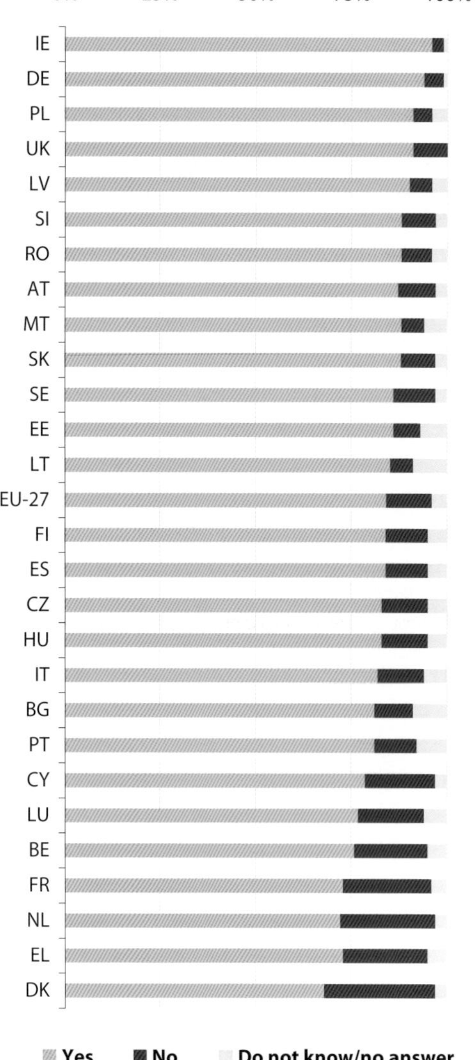

Source: 'Attitudes on issues related to EU Energy Policy', Flash Eurobarometer 206a, European Commission

Figure 4.3: Reasons for favouring a choice of energy suppliers, February 2007 (% of respondents)

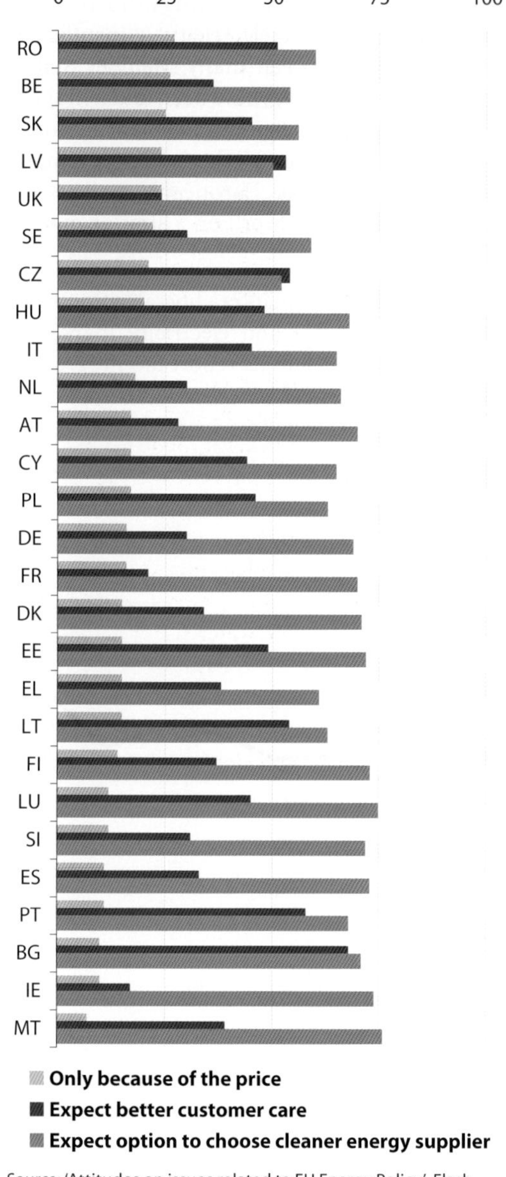

Source: 'Attitudes on issues related to EU Energy Policy', Flash Eurobarometer 206a, European Commission

4.2 Consumption

4.2.1 Ownership and consumption volume

Higher standards of living are changing water demand patterns. This is reflected mainly in increased domestic water use, especially for personal hygiene. Virtually the entire EU population has indoor toilets, showers and/or baths for daily use. Aside from personal hygiene, water use has increased as a result of the increased penetration of appliances such as washing machines and dishwashers, as well as other uses such as swimming pools and the watering of gardens. The amount that is used for cooking or for drinking is minimal in comparison with the other household uses. The pressure on the use of water is offset, to some extent, by technological/design improvements that have led to greater water efficiency in some appliances. Increased urbanisation concentrates water demand and can lead to the over-exploitation of local water resources. In most Member States (for which data are available), the public water supply accounted for less than 40 % of freshwater abstraction (taking water from any source, be it on the surface or underground), with the share around 60 % in the United Kingdom and Denmark, and 100 % in Malta.

Table 4.5: Households: water supply and waste generated

	Public water supply to households, 2005 (m^3/capita)	Waste generated by households, 2004 (thousand tonnes)
EU-27 (1)	17 406	211 666
BE (1)	:	5 325
BG	33	2 634
CZ	:	2 841
DK (2)	45	2 016
DE	:	38 008
EE	:	402
IE	:	1 702
EL (1)	:	4 213
ES (1, 2)	64	24 410
FR (1)	:	26 432
IT	:	31 150
CY	:	367
LV	:	543
LT	:	602
LU	:	221
HU (1)	:	4 442
MT	28	100
NL	44	9 440
AT	:	3 441
PL	32	6 768
PT (1)	:	4 583
RO	25	3 638
SI	:	661
SK	:	1 475
FI	:	1 164
SE (2)	59	4 079
UK	:	31 007
HR	41	:
TR (1)	:	29 225
IS	102	141
CH	84	1 934

(1) Includes estimates or provisional data for waste generated.
(2) Water supply, 2004.

Source: Eurostat, Water use by supply category per capita, Generation of waste (theme8/envir/env)

Table 4.6: Final energy consumption, households, 2006 (thousand TOE)

	Total	Solid fuels	Petroleum products	Gas	Electrical energy	Heat	Renewable energies
EU-27	304 372	9 765	53 191	119 315	68 987	20 282	32 832
BE	8 932	145	3 151	3 457	1 954	14	213
BG	2 180	276	25	24	800	420	635
CZ	6 509	820	33	2 275	1 307	1 113	961
DK	4 419	0	558	682	910	1 526	743
DE	69 124	608	18 187	28 813	12 167	3 630	5 720
EE	881	18	10	46	144	374	289
IE	3 060	498	1 218	631	695	0	18
EL	5 491	1	2 958	139	1 520	56	817
ES	14 753	195	3 785	3 043	5 650	0	2 080
FR	44 658	356	9 321	14 614	12 636	0	7 731
IT	29 919	7	5 342	17 047	5 816	0	1 707
CY	347	0	175	0	129	0	42
LV	1 492	19	39	103	149	426	756
LT	1 429	51	55	140	202	549	432
LU	610	0	243	247	71	32	16
HU	6 182	259	181	3 644	985	664	450
MT	81	0	24	0	57	0	0
NL	10 013	6	88	7 371	2 135	164	248
AT	6 631	121	1 587	1 295	1 358	684	1 586
PL	19 178	5 781	800	3 315	2 237	4 538	2 506
PT	3 201	0	664	203	1 153	6	1 175
RO	7 839	10	452	2 548	860	1 393	2 577
SI	1 158	0	377	93	263	101	324
SK	2 315	47	16	1 283	394	544	31
FI	4 947	15	625	34	1 818	1 470	986
SE	7 003	0	249	56	3 567	2 528	602
UK	42 018	528	3 026	28 211	10 013	52	188
HR	1 857	7	304	539	561	146	301
TR	20 077	2 488	1 956	6 183	2 964	0	6 488
IS	622	0	3	0	69	184	367
NO	3 800	1	239	3	2 878	43	636
CH (1)	6 217	31	3 078	1 018	1 515	140	435

(1) 2005.

Source: Eurostat, Supply, transformation, consumption (theme8/nrg)

Households accounted for 25.9 % of all final energy consumption in the EU-27 in 2006, making them one of the largest energy consumers: note that this does not include fuel for personal transport which is recorded under transport rather than household consumption. Rising energy prices and increasing awareness of climate change encourage energy conserving investment in homes (such as insulation), particularly as space and water heating are the two main uses of energy in households, far ahead of energy use for cooking, lighting and running appliances. Energy consumption within the home is, in the short-term, a relatively inelastic expenditure item, as reactions to price fluctuations can often only be made through investment in new equipment. Households in the EU relied primarily on gas for their energy needs: 39.2 % of the energy consumption was gas, 22.7 % electrical energy, 17.2 % petroleum products and 10.8 % renewable energy. Heat (district heating, for example) accounted for 6.7 % and solid fuels 3.2 %. Solid fuels were most used in Poland, Ireland, Bulgaria, and the Czech Republic, where their share was over 10 %. Petroleum products were most used in Greece and Cyprus where they accounted for just over half of the consumption. Gas accounted for around two thirds or more of consumption in the North Sea gas producing countries of the Netherlands and the United Kingdom. Electricity was by far the main type of energy used by households in Malta (70 %) and also exceeded 50 % in Sweden. Heat was an important energy source in the Nordic and Baltic Member States, and to a lesser extent in Poland and Slovakia. In Latvia renewable energy sources reached 50 % of consumption, and these sources were also important in the other Baltic States, Portugal, Romania and Bulgaria.

Table 4.7: Type and ownership of dwellings, 2003-2006
(number of households)

	Living in houses	Living in apartments	Owning their own dwelling	Social housing	Private rented housing
Berlin	:	:	:	232 449	1 265 551
Tallinn	14 436	154 701	130 452	831	28 615
Dublin	:	:	:	:	:
Athina	24 250	264 812	159 358	:	131 693
Riga	13	272	211	46	29
Vilnius	:	:	:	4 284	:
Budapest	300 567	97 583	682 860	11 563	10 147
Amsterdam	41 623	325 207	71 459	201 479	93 892
Lisboa	:	:	:	22 939	:
Ljubljana	39 601	64 037	85 492	5 959	4 424
Bratislava	20 973	165 446	119 680	2 084	16 461
Helsinki	288 215	245 766	129 843	66 415	79 255
Stockholm	43 394	370 012	195 680	0	217 725
London	:	:	2 359 774	787 336	:

(1) Those capital cities not presented, not available.

Source: Eurostat, Data collected for core cities (theme1/urb/urb_vcity)

When analysing housing statistics it is important to keep in mind that international comparisons in this area should be made with great caution because of the different traditions between countries in terms of the type of accommodation, mainly houses and flats, but also institutions and other types of accommodation, and the type of ownership, mainly owner-occupied or rented, but also social housing. Although incomplete, Table 4.7 provides some information on such differences for the capital cities of the Member States.

Table 4.8 provides information on plans to build or buy a house or undertake home improvements as reported in a consumer confidence survey in the second quarter of 2008. The figures are the balance between those that do not have such plans (negative) and those that do (positive) and, unsurprisingly given the infrequent nature of such events, the overall balance was negative in every country. The balance was highest in Cyprus, Romania, the Netherlands and Sweden, just above -80 indicating that around 10 % of respondents expected to purchase or build a home in the next 12 months. In every country the balance was higher for home improvements, and was above -20 in Sweden and the Czech Republic. For both variables Italy recorded the lowest balances.

Table 4.8: Plans to purchase, build or maintain accommodation, seasonally adjusted, second quarter 2008
(balance of percentage of respondents giving negative and positive replies)

	Purchase or build a home within the next 12 months	Home improvements over the next 12 months
EU-27	-89	-58
BE	-90	-52
BG	-89	-58
CZ	-85	-19
DK	-82	-57
DE	-94	-52
EE	-84	-36
IE	-89	-62
EL	-82	-68
ES	-87	-83
FR	-87	-58
IT	-97	-88
CY	-78	-66
LV	-81	-25
LT	-91	-57
LU	-81	-33
HU	-89	-80
MT	-92	-59
NL	-78	-49
AT	-90	-33
PL	-83	-40
PT	-94	-86
RO	-78	-42
SI	-82	-53
SK	-86	-47
FI	-86	-45
SE	-79	-16
UK	-88	-50

Source: Eurostat, Consumers - quarterly data (theme1/euroind/bs/bsco_q)

Table 4.9: Final consumption expenditure of households, housing, water, electricity, gas and other fuels: consumption per head
(EUR)

	2000	2006
EU-27	2 200	2 900
BE	2 900	3 500
BG	300	:
CZ	700	1 300
DK	4 100	:
DE	3 200	3 800
EE	600	1 000
IE	2 300	3 500
EL	1 600	2 300
ES	1 500	2 200
FR	3 000	4 000
IT	2 400	3 100
CY	1 500	1 800
LV	500	:
LT	400	600
LU	4 700	6 000
HU	500	900
MT	800	1 000
NL	2 600	3 500
AT	2 800	3 600
PL	600	1 000
PT	1 000	:
RO (1)	300	700
SI	1 200	1 600
SK	500	1 200
FI	3 000	3 900
SE	3 900	:
UK	3 000	3 800
TR (1)	500	800
IS	3 200	5 000
NO	3 300	:
CH	5 000	5 500

(1) 2006, forecast.

Source: Eurostat, Final consumption expenditure of households by consumption purpose (theme2/nama/nama_co2_c)

4.2.2 Consumption expenditure

When studying expenditure related to accommodation it is important to distinguish consumption expenditure from investment: the purchase of a dwelling is regarded as gross fixed capital formation (investment) as are major improvements to housing (for example, building, rebuilding, modernisation and extensions), and these should not be included in the consumption expenditure of households. For households renting a dwelling, the consumption expenditure on occupation is simply the rental cost, but in the case of owner-occupation no such expenditure is directly made, and an estimation (referred to as an imputed rent) is calculated in order to facilitate comparisons independently of the different types of occupation.

Table 4.10: Mean consumption expenditure per household, housing, water, electricity, gas and other fuels, 2005
(PPS)

EU-27 (1)	6 936
BE	7 610
BG	2 461
CZ	2 444
DK	7 194
DE	8 445
EE	3 240
IE	8 520
EL	7 442
ES	7 874
FR	7 339
IT	8 512
CY	7 381
LV	1 810
LT	1 776
LU	15 611
HU	2 073
MT	2 596
NL	7 513
AT	6 732
PL	3 341
PT	5 560
RO	832
SI	5 483
SK	2 517
FI	6 614
SE	8 250
UK	9 458
HR	4 983
NO	7 633

(1) Estimate.

Source: Eurostat, Household Budget Survey (theme3/hbs/hbs_exp_t121)

In 2006 annual expenditure on housing, water, electricity, gas and other fuels averaged EUR 2 900 per person within the EU-27, with national averages ranging from less than EUR 1 000 per person in Lithuania, Romania and Hungary, up to EUR 4 000 per person in France and EUR 6 000 in Luxembourg.

Table 4.10 provides a comparison of expenditure on the same items, based on household budget survey (HBS) data for 2005. The HBS data is presented in purchasing power standard (PPS) terms rather than in euro and show that, at comparable price levels, expenditure on housing, water, electricity, gas and other fuels within the EU-27 ranged from PPS 1 776 per household in Lithuania to PPS 9 458 in the United Kingdom, with Luxembourg above this range at PPS 15 611 and Romania below this range at PPS 832.

Expenditure on housing, water, electricity, gas and other fuels represented around 28 % of total household consumption expenditure in the EU-27 in 2005. In Bulgaria and Poland, the share of these items exceeded 30 %, while only Hungary, Lithuania, Latvia and Romania reported shares below 20 %, and Malta less than 10 % (see Figure 4.4).

The proportion of expenditure dedicated to housing, water, electricity, gas and other fuels varied greatly depending on the type of household (number of persons, with or without dependent children), with the share generally decreasing as the size of the household increased (see Figure 4.5). Equally, the share was around a third higher for households in the lowest income quintile than for those in the highest quintile. The share of total household consumption expenditure accounted for by these items was also higher for households headed by persons aged 60 or over, and also for households in densely urbanised areas.

Just over half of household consumption expenditure on housing, water, electricity, gas and other fuels in the EU-27 concerned imputed rent, in other words an estimate of the equivalent rent for owner occupied housing. Adding actual rents and repairs to this brought the total to around three quarters, with water, waste and similar services making up 7.9 % and all fuels and heat just under 20 %.

Figure 4.4: Structure of consumption expenditure: share of housing, water, electricity, gas and other fuels in total expenditure, 2005 (1)
(%)

(1) EU-27, estimate; Czech Republic, not available.

Source: Eurostat, Household Budget Survey (theme3/hbs/hbs_str_t211)

Figure 4.5: Structure of consumption expenditure: share of housing, water, electricity, gas and other fuels in total expenditure, EU-27, 2005
(%)

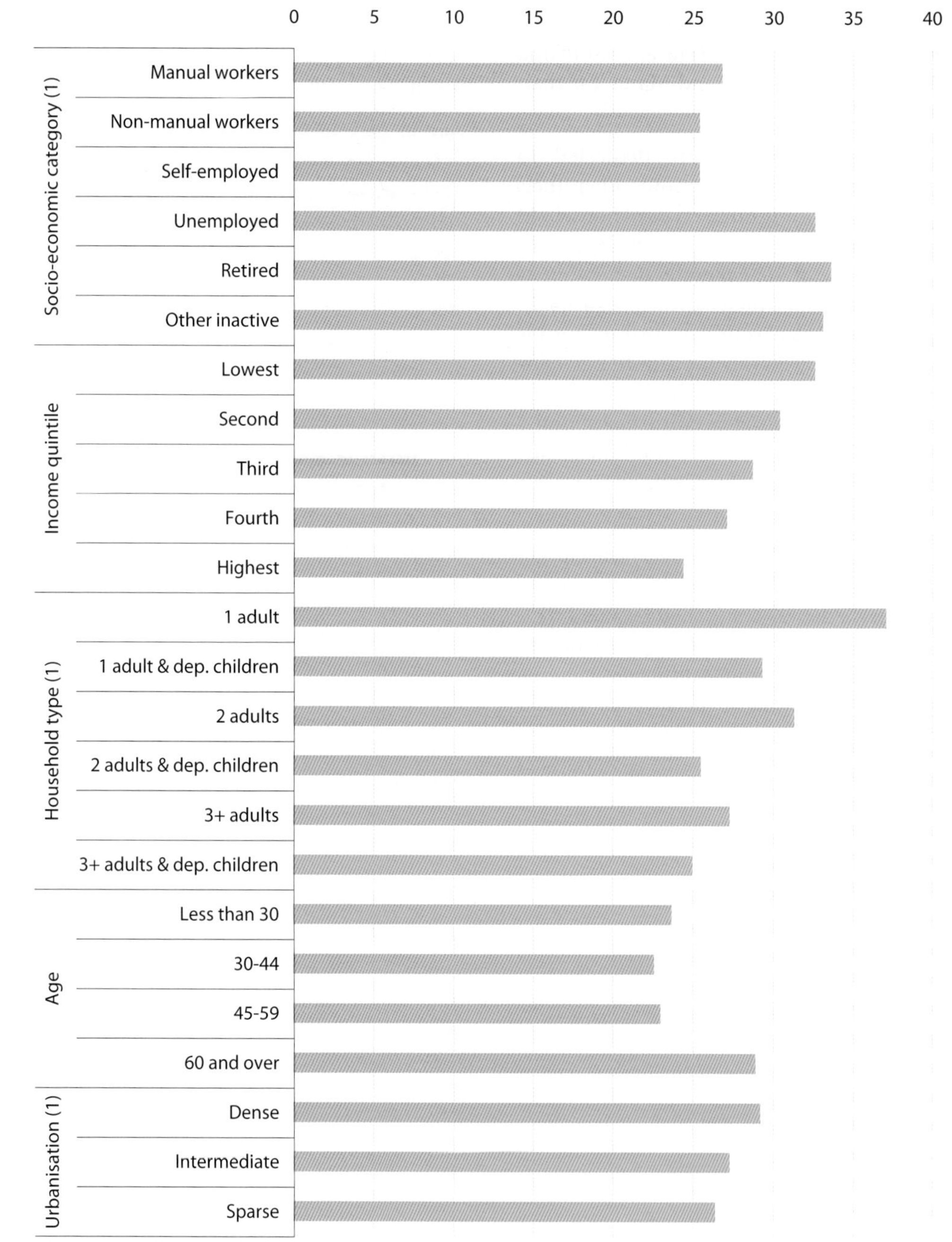

(1) Unreliable.

Source: Eurostat, Household Budget Survey (theme3/hbs/hbs_str_t221, hbs_str_t223, hbs_str_t224, hbs_str_t225, hbs_str_t226)

Table 4.11A: Structure of consumption expenditure on housing and water, 2005 (1)
(%)

	Actual rentals for housing	Imputed rentals for housing	Maintenance and repair of the dwelling	Water supply	Refuse collection	Sewerage	Other housing services
EU-27	16.2	54.2	5.4	3.2	0.7	0.7	3.2
BE	19.0	53.0	4.7	2.0	0.8	0.0	1.6
BG	0.9	63.1	3.7	3.7	0.6	0.6	0.6
CZ	:	:	:	:	:	:	:
DK	26.4	34.8	6.0	2.0	2.3	2.0	2.0
DE	28.7	39.2	8.8	<————	————	6.1 ————	————>
EE	0.0	57.2	9.4	0.0	1.0	0.0	4.0
IE	10.7	58.5	12.8	0.0	1.7	:	1.7
EL	11.7	59.2	6.7	1.7	1.7	0.4	2.1
ES	5.6	75.6	2.3	2.0	0.3	0.0	4.3
FR	25.5	45.6	2.3	2.7	0.0	0.0	4.6
IT	8.8	61.8	3.0	1.7	:	:	3.0
CY	11.1	63.4	5.1	1.9	0.9	0.9	0.5
LV	5.8	33.3	12.9	3.5	1.8	2.3	1.2
LT	3.2	41.3	4.8	<————	————	9.5 ————	————>
LU	13.0	65.4	5.3	1.3	1.0	0.3	1.3
HU	4.6	:	10.8	8.8	2.6	5.7	7.7
MT	7.7	:	65.9	5.5	0.0	0.0	0.0
NL	27.7	39.8	4.7	2.0	5.5	:	3.1
AT	18.4	36.8	9.0	<————	————	14.8 ————	————>
PL	1.6	43.5	8.9	3.2	1.3	2.5	7.3
PT	7.5	69.9	1.1	3.4	0.4	0.4	1.5
RO	2.6	:	7.1	<————	————	16.0 ————	————>
SI	3.5	54.3	4.3	4.3	2.2	0.4	1.7
SK	8.1	43.2	13.7	3.8	1.7	1.7	2.1
FI	18.8	65.8	0.0	<————	————	2.9 ————	————>
SE	32.4	45.3	6.4	<————	————	4.1 ————	————>
UK	20.3	59.1	5.7	3.7	0.0	0.3	0.7
HR	1.7	62.5	3.7	3.7	1.7	1.7	1.4
NO	11.8	43.9	22.9	1.1	1.5	1.5	0.4

(1) EU-27, unreliable; imputed rentals, Ireland and United Kingdom, estimates.

Source: Eurostat, Household Budget Survey (theme3/hbs/hbs_str_t211)

Table 4.11B: Structure of consumption expenditure on electricity, gas and other fuels, 2005 (1)
(%)

	Fuels & heat: total	Electricity	Gas	Liquid fuels	Solid fuels	Heat energy
EU-27	19.9	9.0	5.4	1.8	1.8	2.5
BE	19.0	8.3	5.9	4.7	0.4	:
BG	26.5	16.4	0.6	0.0	5.8	3.5
CZ	:	:	:	:	:	:
DK	24.7	8.7	2.0	2.0	1.0	11.0
DE	17.2	:	3.7	:	:	:
EE	21.4	9.0	1.0	0.3	3.0	7.7
IE	15.0	6.4	2.6	3.4	2.1	:
EL	12.9	5.4	0.4	6.3	0.8	0.0
ES	9.9	5.3	3.0	1.3	0.3	0.0
FR	19.8	11.8	2.3	4.9	0.8	0.0
IT	16.9	5.7	8.1	1.0	0.7	1.4
CY	15.7	9.7	1.9	3.2	0.9	0.0
LV	39.8	12.3	5.8	0.0	3.5	18.1
LT	41.8	13.2	5.8	0.0	4.2	18.5
LU	12.0	4.7	3.0	4.3	0.0	:
HU	59.8	24.2	21.6	0.0	5.7	7.7
MT	19.8	16.5	2.2	0.0	0.0	0.0
NL	17.2	8.6	10.5	0.0	0.0	0.8
AT	20.6	8.5	3.1	3.6	2.7	1.3
PL	31.7	10.8	6.0	0.3	6.7	8.3
PT	15.8	9.8	4.5	:	0.8	:
RO	74.4	28.8	23.7	0.0	12.2	9.6
SI	28.7	10.9	2.6	8.3	3.9	3.0
SK	67.9	23.1	22.2	0.0	2.6	20.1
FI	12.5	7.7	0.0	1.8	1.1	1.5
SE	11.8	9.8	0.0	0.7	0.3	0.7
UK	10.1	5.1	4.4	0.7	0.0	0.0
HR	24.0	11.1	5.7	1.7	4.1	1.0
NO	16.8	14.1	0.0	1.1	1.5	:

(1) EU-27, unreliable.

Source: Eurostat, Household Budget Survey (theme3/hbs/hbs_str_t211)

4.2.3 Mortgage debt and payment of bills

The extent to which homeowners resort to home loans varies greatly between Member States, as does the extent to which the level of debt is changing. The highest debt burdens per capita in 2006 were in Denmark, the Netherlands, Ireland, the United Kingdom and Luxembourg, all in excess of EUR 20 000. The lowest debt burdens were in Romania and Bulgaria with average mortgage debt of around EUR 100 to EUR 200 per capita, while all of the Member States that joined the EU in 2004 recorded an average mortgage debt per capita lower than those in the EU-15 Member States. In contrast, the ten Member States with the greatest percentage increase in mortgage debt in 2006 were all among the 12 that joined the EU in either 2004 or 2007, with Hungary and Malta recording slower growth. Among the EU-15 Member States, the fastest growth in mortgage debt was recorded in Greece, Ireland and Spain, and the slowest, by far, in Germany.

The results of the survey on income and living conditions (SILC) show that generally only a small proportion of households were in arrears on mortgage or rent payments during the 12 months period prior to the 2006 survey, the highest proportion being 7 % in Cyprus (see Table 4.13). In contrast, in nearly every Member State a larger proportion of households had been in arrears for payments of utility bills, with Greece reporting by far the highest proportion.

Table 4.12: Residential mortgage markets, 2006

	Value of mortgage debt (EUR million)	Growth in mortgage debt, relative to 2005 (%)	Ratio of residential debt to GDP (%)	Mortgage debt per capita (EUR thousand)
EU-27	5 713 615	11.1	49.0	11.6
BE	114 105	12.9	36.3	10.9
BG	1 745	73.5	7.0	0.2
CZ	8 055	33.9	7.1	0.8
DK	221 970	13.4	100.8	40.9
DE	1 183 834	1.8	51.3	14.4
EE	4 278	63.4	32.7	3.2
IE	123 288	24.6	70.1	29.3
EL	57 145	25.8	29.3	5.1
ES	571 746	20.2	58.6	13.1
FR	577 800	14.7	32.2	9.2
IT	276 102	13.3	18.7	4.7
CY	3 077	43.5	21.2	4.0
LV	4 680	86.5	28.9	2.0
LT	2 997	32.1	12.6	0.9
LU	11 345	13.4	34.3	24.7
HU	10 215	11.0	11.4	1.0
MT	1 770	16.5	34.7	4.4
NL	525 874	7.9	98.4	32.2
AT	60 669	12.7	23.5	7.3
PL	22 514	53.7	8.3	0.6
PT	91 895	15.7	59.2	8.7
RO	2 276	57.2	2.3	0.1
SI	1 956	43.0	6.6	1.0
SK	4 209	36.7	9.6	0.8
FI	73 200	11.0	43.8	13.9
SE	173 499	9.1	56.7	19.2
UK	1 583 372	11.9	83.1	26.2
HR	5 219	37.2	15.3	1.2
TR	12 237	65.7	3.8	0.2
IS (1)	9 828	4.5	75.5	32.8
CH	307 348	3.4	101.9	41.2

(1) Growth rate for Iceland was calculated based on data in national currency, not euro.

Source: European Mortgage federation (http://www.hypo.org), using data from Eurostat, national Central Banks and own sources

Table 4.13: Proportion of households that have been in arrears on payments/bills in the 12 months prior to the survey, 2006
(%)

	Mortgage or rent payments			Utility bills		
	Yes	No	No answer/ not relevant	Yes	No	No answer/ not relevant
BE	3	59	38	4	93	3
BG	:	:	:	:	:	:
CZ	4	56	40	5	94	1
DK	2	98	0	3	97	0
DE	2	95	3	5	94	1
EE	1	15	84	6	94	0
IE	4	44	52	6	91	4
EL	5	24	71	26	73	1
ES	2	35	63	3	74	23
FR	5	60	35	6	94	0
IT	3	28	69	9	91	0
CY	7	28	66	9	89	2
LV	3	29	68	13	85	2
LT	1	5	94	13	87	0
LU	1	62	37	2	96	3
HU	2	18	80	13	86	1
MT	1	34	65	6	94	0
NL	3	97	1	3	97	0
AT	1	58	41	2	98	0
PL	2	8	90	18	78	4
PT	2	40	58	4	91	5
RO	:	:	:	:	:	:
SI	2	6	92	10	89	1
SK	5	58	38	6	93	1
FI	5	59	36	4	96	0
SE	4	85	11	4	92	4
UK	4	64	32	0	100	0
IS	6	73	21	5	93	2
NO	6	73	21	6	84	9

Source: Eurostat, EU-SILC

4.3 Prices

4.3.1 Price inflation

Households' investment in energy using equipment, particularly for water and space heating, is based upon expectations of future prices, as well as affordability (which is related to income) and access (whether the chosen fuel network is established locally). When energy prices rise, consumers may become more aware of their everyday consumption and try to avoid consuming excessive amounts of energy. Alternatively, consumers may look for energy-saving measures.

The harmonised index of consumer prices for housing, water, electricity, gas and other fuels rose in the EU-27 by 31.5 % between 2000 and 2007, equivalent to an average of more than 4.0 % per annum. This was notably higher than the rate of increase recorded for the all-items consumer price index, which gained on average 2.4 % per annum between 2000 and 2007. Price increases decelerated from 6.0 % in 2000 to 2.8 % in 2002, after which the increases accelerated each year to 5.6 % by 2006: 2007 marked a slowdown as price increases of 3.5 % were recorded. All Member States except for Malta recorded price increases for housing, water, electricity, gas and other fuels in 2007, with the fastest increases recorded in Hungary, the Baltic Member States and Romania.

Table 4.14: Harmonised indices of consumer prices, housing, water, electricity, gas and other fuels, annual rate of change
(%)

	2000	2001	2002	2003	2004	2005	2006	2007
EU-27	6.0	4.5	2.8	3.1	3.3	5.2	5.6	3.5
BE	6.9	3.7	0.2	1.4	3.0	5.6	4.9	1.4
BG	13.7	7.4	14.7	11.6	7.6	5.7	4.6	5.4
CZ	9.1	11.9	5.6	0.7	2.3	4.7	8.3	3.9
DK	5.9	3.1	3.1	2.3	2.1	3.7	3.6	2.2
DE	3.6	3.2	0.7	1.8	1.9	4.0	3.9	2.2
EE	2.6	9.7	8.5	3.2	4.3	7.2	10.5	15.0
IE	9.1	5.8	4.1	4.2	3.8	9.6	7.3	7.6
EL	6.4	2.7	3.8	4.5	4.9	9.2	7.2	2.8
ES	4.4	2.9	2.3	2.9	3.5	5.3	6.5	3.7
FR	1.9	1.1	1.7	2.7	2.9	4.7	4.7	3.0
IT	6.0	3.0	0.4	3.4	2.0	5.0	5.7	2.7
CY	16.3	0.4	5.0	11.0	5.0	8.7	7.7	1.9
LV	4.4	2.7	1.2	4.6	8.1	5.8	13.7	16.4
LT	12.4	2.3	2.7	0.3	0.6	5.0	6.9	11.5
LU	7.7	1.7	0.2	2.8	3.1	6.8	5.8	3.4
HU	10.0	10.7	6.5	7.6	12.9	7.2	6.8	17.5
MT	0.9	2.2	2.3	1.9	2.8	9.3	10.6	-0.1
NL	5.7	6.5	4.0	4.3	3.2	5.9	4.8	3.0
AT	3.4	3.0	0.6	1.6	4.2	6.2	5.4	4.3
PL	11.1	10.2	5.9	3.3	4.0	3.8	4.4	4.6
PT	3.7	4.1	3.0	4.2	3.0	4.4	3.9	3.6
RO	63.6	34.2	36.5	19.8	21.5	19.1	14.4	10.0
SI	18.3	10.9	5.6	5.7	6.7	9.2	5.4	3.5
SK	37.7	17.7	3.9	21.6	15.9	8.2	12.1	2.3
FI	4.2	2.8	2.7	4.0	2.1	3.2	2.9	2.7
SE	0.9	5.0	3.2	8.4	2.6	2.2	4.6	1.1
UK	1.4	2.3	2.5	1.9	3.7	6.3	9.2	5.0
TR	63.1	70.9	41.9	22.3	10.9	11.0	12.9	11.2
IS	7.7	4.6	6.3	5.8	5.6	5.7	5.0	7.9
NO	5.2	9.7	2.2	11.1	1.5	1.7	8.9	-2.4
CH	:	:	:	:	:	:	3.2	2.1

Source: Eurostat, Harmonised indices of consumer prices (theme2/prc/prc_hicp_aind)

Between 2000 and 2007 the EU-27's index of consumer prices rose more quickly for electricity, gas and other fuels (6.0 % per annum on average) than for water supply and other services (4.0 %), or maintenance and repair (3.2 %), with the slowest increases (2.2 % per annum on average) recorded for actual rentals for housing (see Figure 4.6 and Table 4.15).

Figure 4.6: Harmonised indices of consumer prices, EU-27 (2005=100)

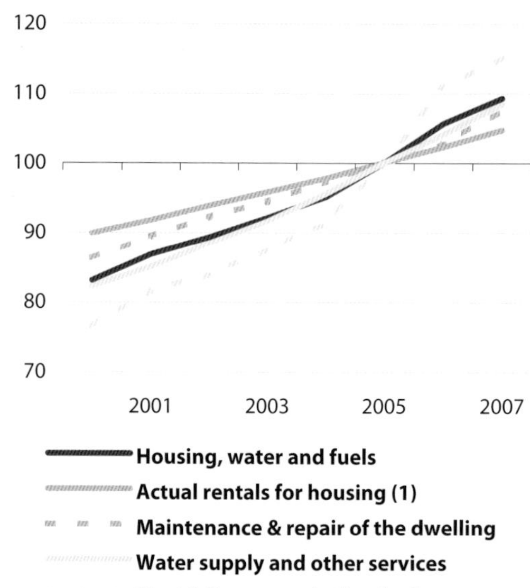

(1) Estimates.

Source: Eurostat, Harmonised indices of consumer prices (theme2/prc/prc_hicp_aind)

Table 4.15: Harmonised indices of consumer prices, annual rate of change, EU-27 (%)

	2000	2001	2002	2003	2004	2005	2006	2007
Housing, water, electricity, gas and other fuels	6.0	4.5	2.8	3.1	3.3	5.2	5.6	3.5
Actual rentals for housing (1)	2.0	2.1	2.3	2.1	2.1	2.3	2.2	2.4
Maintenance and repair of the dwelling	1.7	3.6	3.1	2.4	3.1	2.8	2.7	4.7
Materials for maintenance and repair	1.8	3.3	2.0	1.4	2.6	1.9	1.7	4.4
Services for maintenance and repair	1.7	4.0	4.1	3.3	3.5	3.6	3.7	5.0
Water supply and miscellaneous services	2.7	3.4	4.0	3.6	4.3	4.7	4.0	4.2
Water supply	2.9	3.9	4.9	3.9	4.8	5.1	4.0	3.9
Refuse collection	3.3	3.0	3.1	3.8	3.6	4.4	3.9	4.7
Sewerage collection	0.7	3.2	3.9	4.0	4.9	4.5	4.2	4.5
Other services relating to the dwelling n.e.c.	3.1	3.0	3.2	2.7	3.8	4.3	4.1	4.0
Electricity, gas and other fuels	9.3	6.8	2.7	4.4	4.4	9.4	10.9	3.9
Electricity	0.6	3.9	4.0	4.3	3.6	4.0	6.6	4.8
Gas	10.2	13.9	1.3	5.0	3.6	11.7	17.7	3.6
Liquid fuels	42.5	-5.7	-5.2	4.9	11.5	27.9	10.6	-0.6
Solid fuels	5.8	7.6	7.4	4.7	6.0	5.4	5.1	6.7
Heat energy	11.1	12.4	6.7	3.2	2.4	8.4	11.0	5.2

(1) Estimates.

Source: Eurostat, Harmonised indices of consumer prices (theme2/prc/prc_hicp_aind)

4.3.2 Affordability and price levels

A 2006 Eurobarometer survey of services of general interest investigated the affordability of electricity, gas and water across the then 25 EU Member States: the results presented in Table 4.16 are based only on the answers of the part of the population that had indicated that they used the specified services. Across the EU as a whole, two thirds of respondents said that electricity and gas were affordable, and three quarters that water was affordable. In Malta, Finland, Sweden, Poland and Cyprus more than half of the respondents regarded electricity as not affordable or the price as excessive. For gas, Poland (49 %) recorded the highest proportion of the population that regarded the price as not affordable or excessive, followed by France (46 %) and Germany (44 %). Concerning water the situation of Malta stood out, with a majority (60 %) of respondents regarding the price as not affordable or excessive.

Table 4.16: Affordability of utilities: proportion of respondents using the service, May–June 2006
(%)

	Electricity		Gas		Water	
	Affordable	Not affordable or excessive	Affordable	Not affordable or excessive	Affordable	Not affordable or excessive
EU-25	66	31	65	33	75	23
BE	75	23	76	22	78	21
BG	:	:	:	:	:	:
CZ	71	28	68	31	80	19
DK	81	17	77	20	86	10
DE	63	36	55	44	71	27
EE	70	29	78	19	79	20
IE	63	30	62	31	88	7
EL	83	16	90	10	96	4
ES	73	25	74	24	80	19
FR	62	34	49	46	61	36
IT	66	32	65	34	74	24
CY	44	52	:	:	76	21
LV	68	30	74	25	73	25
LT	92	7	92	7	94	5
LU	73	23	77	19	82	14
HU	68	31	59	41	73	26
MT	26	69	:	:	35	60
NL	68	29	69	27	86	11
AT	83	16	79	17	94	4
PL	42	55	48	49	59	38
PT	52	42	66	29	71	27
RO	:	:	:	:	:	:
SI	85	14	88	10	88	11
SK	80	17	80	20	85	14
FI	37	60	47	7	67	29
SE	40	56	55	30	82	8
UK	83	16	78	20	85	13

Source: 'Services of General Interest', Special Eurobarometer 260, European Commission

The 2006 survey on income and living condition (SILC) asked a more general question, indirectly linked to affordability, and identified that in most Member States at least 90 % of households could afford to keep their homes adequately warm. The highest proportions were recorded in more northerly Member States, while the lowest proportion by far was in Portugal (58 %).

Price level indices for 2006 show that housing, water, electricity, gas and other fuels were cheaper in the Member States that joined the EU in 2004 and 2007. Cyprus, which had the highest price level index for these products among the newer Member States, had an index level just under 70 % of the EU-27 average; Slovenia and Estonia were the only other newer Member States that had price level indices above 50 % of the EU-27 average, with the lowest relative price levels reported in Bulgaria. In contrast, Denmark and Ireland reported the highest price level indices, in the case of the former approximately 50 % above the EU-27 average and more than five times as high as in Bulgaria.

Table 4.17: Proportion of households that are able to keep their home adequately warm, 2006
(%)

	Yes	No	No answer
BE	85	15.2	0.1
BG	:	:	:
CZ	90	9.5	0.0
DK	89	10.2	1.0
DE	94	5.8	0.3
EE	97	3.1	0.0
IE	95	4.6	0.1
EL	86	13.6	0.0
ES	91	9.3	0.0
FR	93	6.7	0.1
IT	90	10.4	0.0
CY	65	35.0	0.0
LV	73	27.3	0.0
LT	69	31.3	0.0
LU	99	0.6	0.1
HU	84	16.5	0.0
MT	89	11.3	0.0
NL	97	2.6	0.2
AT	96	3.7	0.1
PL	70	30.3	0.0
PT	58	41.6	0.0
RO	:	:	:
SI	96	3.6	0.0
SK	90	10.0	0.1
FI	97	2.6	0.1
SE	97	2.8	0.6
UK	95	4.9	0.2
IS	88	11.1	0.4
NO	98	2.0	0.4

Source: Eurostat, EU-SILC

Figure 4.7: Price level indices, housing, water, electricity, gas and other fuels, 2006
(EU-27=100)

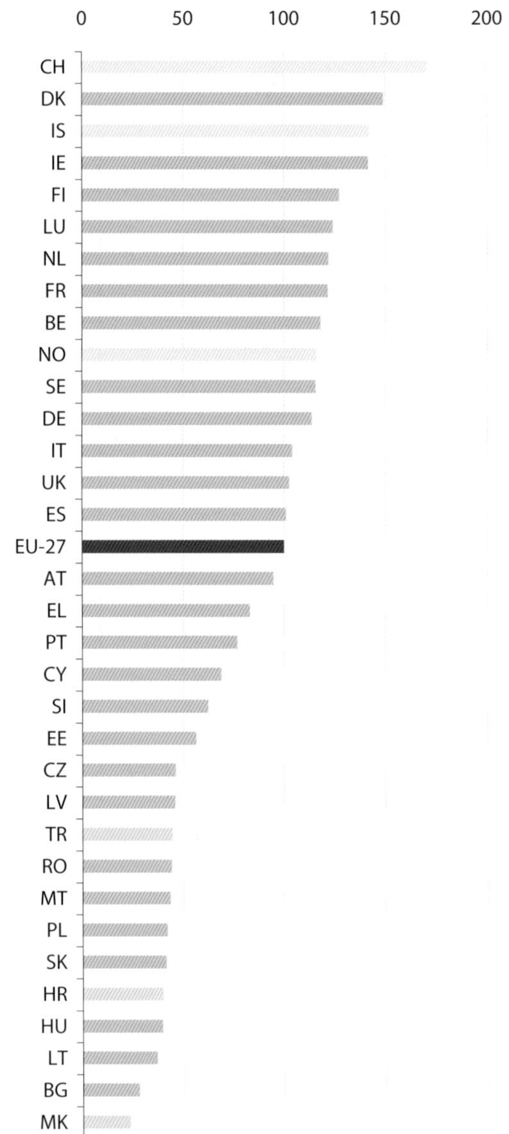

Source: Eurostat, Price level indices (theme2/prc/prc_ppp_ind)

4.3.3 Indirect taxes

Fuel is normally burdened with VAT, excise duties and sometimes other indirect environmental taxes. Table 4.18 provides information on the excise duty on heating fuel (which can be compared with similar duties on automotive fuel in Chapter 7), as well as VAT rates on electricity and gas. Excise duties applied to heating fuel ranged from EUR 403 per 1 000 litres in Italy to nothing in Luxembourg with 16 other Member States reporting duties less than EUR 100 per 1 000 litres.

Several Member States applied reduced VAT rates to electricity and natural gas, namely Ireland, Luxembourg, Hungary (only for gas), Portugal and the United Kingdom, with the two latter Member States applying the minimum 5 % required under the relevant Council Directives. Most Member States applied the standard rates, and Malta actually applied a slightly higher than standard rate for electricity.

4.3.4 Fuel and accommodation prices

Table 4.19 shows the electricity and gas prices households faced in 2007, excluding taxes. Generally in any given country prices were high for both products or low for both products, with a few exceptions: Hungary had particularly low gas prices relative to its fairly average electricity prices, whereas Sweden had the highest gas prices despite slightly lower than average electricity prices. Figure 4.8 shows how the average gas and electricity price have developed within the EU-15 during the last ten years. Electricity prices have been relatively stable, falling from 1996 to a period of stability between 2001 and 2004, since when prices have risen relatively quickly. In contrast gas prices have followed an overall upward path, with periods of relatively fast price growth interrupted by periods of price stability or relatively smaller price reductions.

The price of housing is very difficult to establish, not just because of the varying quality of different buildings as structures, but also because the precise location of each dwelling has an important impact on its valuation. Generally there are large differences in prices between regions within a country, as well as within regions and cities. The Urban Audit provides an indication of average prices for dwellings in some European capital cities (see Table 4.20).

Table 4.18: Taxation of energy products, July 2006

	Excise (EUR/thousand litres)	VAT rates (%)		
	Heating fuel (non-business use)	Standard rate	Electricity (non-business use)	Natural gas
EU (1)	21	15.0	5.0	5.0
BE	18	21.0	21.0	21.0
BG	:	:	:	:
CZ	336	19.0	19.0	19.0
DK	364	25.0	25.0	25.0
DE	61	16.0	16.0	16.0
EE	44	18.0	18.0	18.0
IE	47	21.0	13.5	13.5
EL	260	19.0	19.0	19.0
ES	85	16.0	16.0	16.0
FR	57	19.6	19.6	19.6
IT	403	20.0	20.0	20.0
CY	197	15.0	15.0	15.0
LV	20	18.0	18.0	18.0
LT	21	18.0	18.0	18.0
LU	0	15.0	6.0	6.0
HU	339	20.0	20.0	15.0
MT	97	18.0	19.0	18.0
NL	47	19.0	19.0	19.0
AT	98	20.0	20.0	20.0
PL	59	22.0	22.0	22.0
PT	91	21.0	5.0	5.0
RO	:	:	:	:
SI	53	20.0	20.0	20.0
SK	175	19.0	19.0	19.0
FI	71	22.0	22.0	22.0
SE	361	25.0	25.0	25.0
UK	95	17.5	5.0	5.0

(1) Minimum in accordance with Council Directives 2003/96/EC for excises, 2001/41/EC for VAT.

Source: Energy & transport in figures, Directorate-General for Energy and Transport, European Commission

Figure 4.8: Electricity and natural gas prices (excluding taxes) for final domestic consumers, EU-15

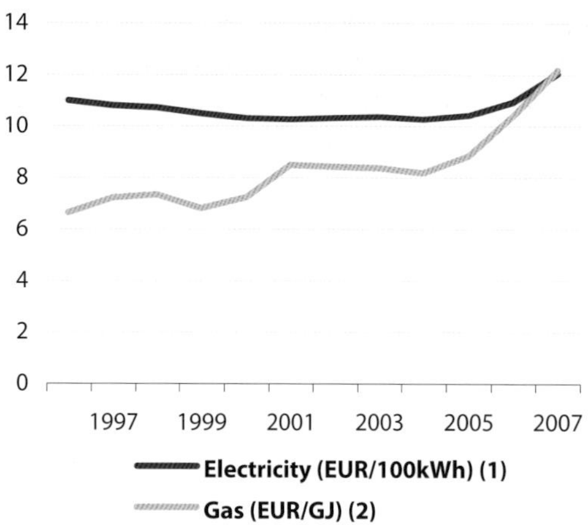

(1) Annual consumption of 3 500 kWh of which 1 300 kWh is overnight; standard dwelling of 90m².
(2) Annual consumption of 83.7 GJ; cooking, water heating and central heating.

Source: Eurostat, Electricity prices - households, Gas prices - households (theme0/strind/strind_t)

Table 4.20: Average accommodation prices - purchase or rent, 2003-2006
(EUR/m^2)

	Apartment	House	Annual rent
Bruxelles / Brussel	:	1 008	:
Sofia	:	:	:
Praha	827	1 563	:
København	:	:	:
Berlin	1 450	1 770	:
Tallinn	959	805	78
Dublin	:	:	:
Athina	:	:	:
Madrid	:	:	:
Paris	:	:	:
Roma	2 647	:	:
Lefkosia	:	:	:
Riga	341	896	6
Vilnius	638	409	:
Luxembourg	3 679	2 967	10
Budapest	942	811	:
Valletta	:	:	:
Amsterdam	1 921	2 044	63
Wien	2 317	1 863	85
Warszawa	:	:	:
Lisboa	1 846	1 774	:
București	624	546	:
Ljubljana	1 850	1 400	250
Bratislava	1 237	1 289	99
Helsinki	:	:	:
Stockholm	3 102	2 730	100
London	4 486	3 815	:
Oslo	2 998	2 700	:

Source: Eurostat, Derived Indicators for core cities (theme1/urb/urb_icity)

Table 4.19: Prices (excluding taxes) for final domestic consumers, 2007

	Electricity (1) (EUR/100kWh)	Gas (2) (EUR/GJ)
EU	12	12
BE	12	10.3
BG	5	7.4
CZ	9	7.9
DK	12	13.6
DE	14	14.0
EE	6	5.0
IE	15	14.7
EL	7	:
ES	10	12.3
FR	9	11.4
IT	17	11.8
CY	12	:
LV	6	6.4
LT	7	6.0
LU	15	10.9
HU	10	6.0
MT	9	:
NL	14	12.3
AT	11	11.0
PL	9	8.8
PT	14	13.2
RO	9	7.6
SI	9	10.8
SK	13	9.6
FI	9	:
SE	11	15.1
UK	13	11.2
HR	8	6.4
NO	14	:

(1) Annual consumption of 3 500 kWh of which 1 300 kWh is overnight; standard dwelling of 90m².
(2) Annual consumption of 83.7 GJ; cooking, water heating and central heating.

Source: Eurostat, Electricity prices - households, Gas prices - households (theme0/strind/strind_t)

4.4 Consumer satisfaction and complaints

In 2006 a survey of consumers' satisfaction with a range of services of general interest was undertaken on behalf of the European Commission. It surveyed persons aged 18 and over that had used the specified services during the 12 months prior to the survey. Consumers' satisfaction was calculated as a score out of 10, with consumers giving scores of 8 or higher classified as satisfied, 4 or less as dissatisfied, and 5 to 7 as neutral. Figure 4.9 provides an overview of the results, indicating that for electricity, gas and water services a majority of respondents were satisfied, and most of the remainder were neutral, leaving just 4 % or 5 % dissatisfied. The most dissatisfied were the Maltese, where 17 % of consumers were dissatisfied with their electricity supply and 14 % with their water supply (there is no network gas supply in Malta). Other Member States that were relatively dissatisfied with these three services included Slovakia (particularly gas supply), Portugal and Greece (particularly electricity and water), and the Czech Republic and Hungary. Some Member States reported relatively high dissatisfaction with just one of the three services, for example, electricity in Sweden, or water in all of the Baltic Member States. In contrast very few respondents in Belgium, Denmark, Austria and Luxembourg reported that they were dissatisfied with any of these three services.

Figure 4.9: Satisfaction rates for utilities, EU-25, 2006

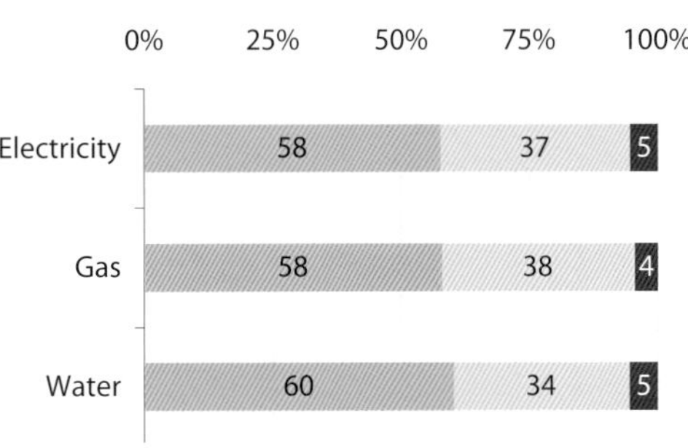

Source: Consumer satisfaction survey, IPSOS INRA for the European Commission Directorate-General for Health and Consumers, May 2007

Table 4.21: Satisfaction rates for utilities, 2006

	Electricity			Gas			Water		
	Dissatisfied	Satisfied	Neutral	Dissatisfied	Satisfied	Neutral	Dissatisfied	Satisfied	Neutral
EU-25	5	58	37	4	58	38	5	60	34
BE	2	65	33	3	65	32	0	64	35
BG	:	:	:	:	:	:	:	:	:
CZ	9	58	33	10	65	25	9	59	32
DK	2	79	19	3	78	20	1	85	14
DE	2	73	25	4	70	27	2	84	14
EE	4	72	24	2	68	30	12	52	36
IE	4	73	23	2	82	16	8	72	21
EL	10	48	42	2	87	11	10	59	31
ES	4	43	53	4	48	49	6	47	47
FR	3	60	37	5	58	37	4	52	44
IT	8	35	57	4	36	60	9	40	51
CY	6	70	24	-	-	-	2	83	15
LV	3	73	24	5	68	28	12	51	38
LT	2	82	17	1	85	15	9	60	32
LU	2	72	26	2	69	29	3	74	23
HU	9	73	19	9	65	26	7	71	22
MT	17	47	36	-	-	-	14	53	33
NL	6	41	53	4	48	49	1	53	46
AT	2	80	19	3	76	21	2	87	12
PL	6	60	34	5	59	36	8	57	36
PT	13	36	51	4	50	46	9	52	39
RO	:	:	:	:	:	:	:	:	:
SI	3	74	24	1	77	22	5	72	23
SK	9	53	39	15	43	42	9	53	38
FI	6	63	31	1	77	22	3	80	18
SE	12	53	35	2	74	24	2	81	18
UK	7	58	35	5	58	37	6	60	35

Source: Consumer satisfaction survey, IPSOS INRA for the European Commission Directorate-General for Health and Consumers, May 2007

Figure 4.10: Satisfaction rates for electricity supply, EU-25, 2006
(%)

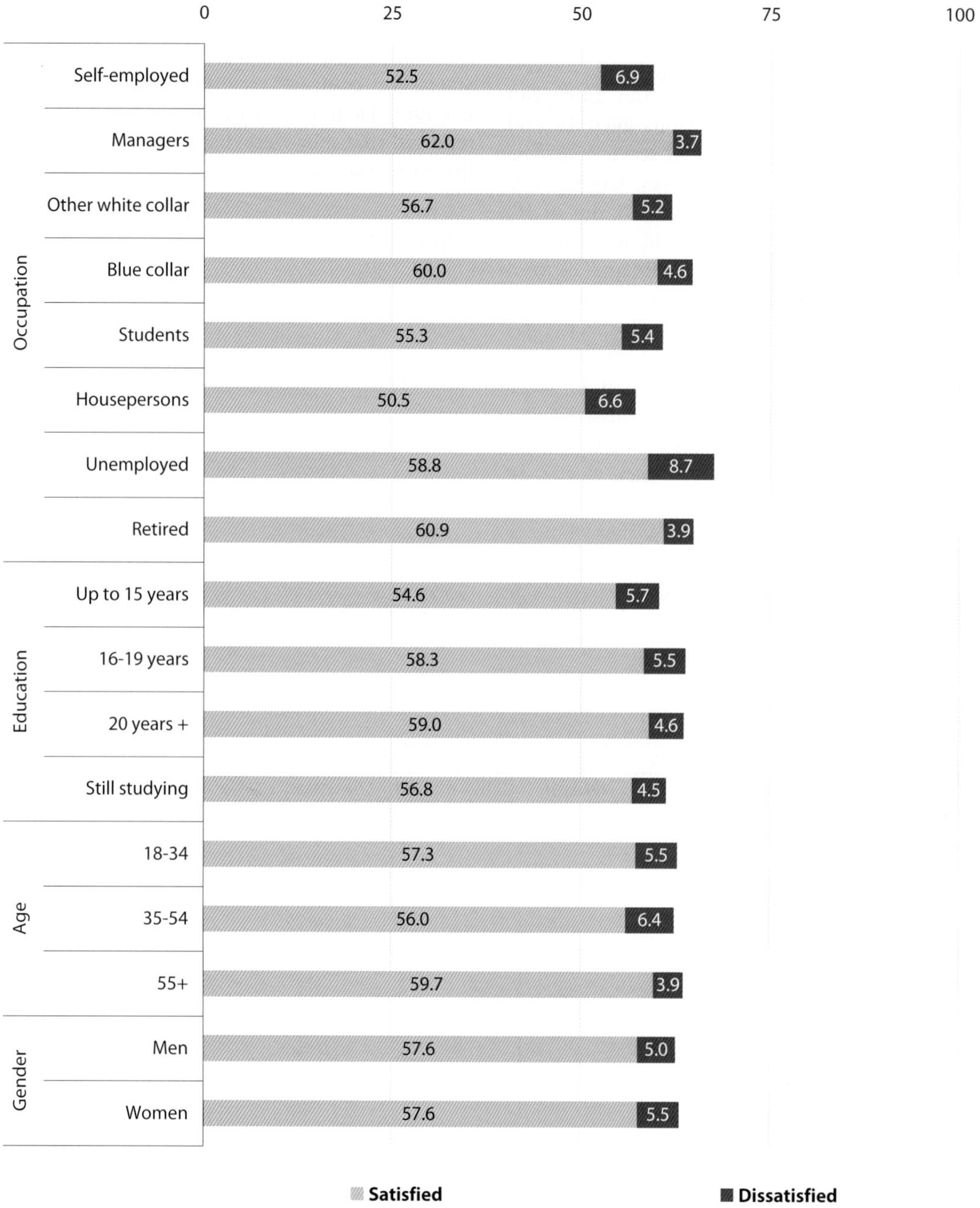

		Satisfied	Dissatisfied
Occupation	Self-employed	52.5	6.9
	Managers	62.0	3.7
	Other white collar	56.7	5.2
	Blue collar	60.0	4.6
	Students	55.3	5.4
	Housepersons	50.5	6.6
	Unemployed	58.8	8.7
	Retired	60.9	3.9
Education	Up to 15 years	54.6	5.7
	16-19 years	58.3	5.5
	20 years +	59.0	4.6
	Still studying	56.8	4.5
Age	18-34	57.3	5.5
	35-54	56.0	6.4
	55+	59.7	3.9
Gender	Men	57.6	5.0
	Women	57.6	5.5

Source: Consumer satisfaction survey, IPSOS INRA for the European Commission Directorate-General for Health and Consumers, May 2007

Socio-economic analyses of the overall results for the EU-25 are presented in Figures 4.10 to 4.13. For electricity an occupational analysis shows that dissatisfaction was highest among the unemployed and lowest among managers and retired persons. For gas, a similar analysis showed that dissatisfaction was lowest among other (than managers) white collar workers and house-persons, and highest for the unemployed and students. For water the self-employed were clearly the most dissatisfied, while rates of dissatisfaction were generally low for white collar workers, blue collar workers and students.

Figure 4.11: Satisfaction rates for gas supply, EU-25, 2006
(%)

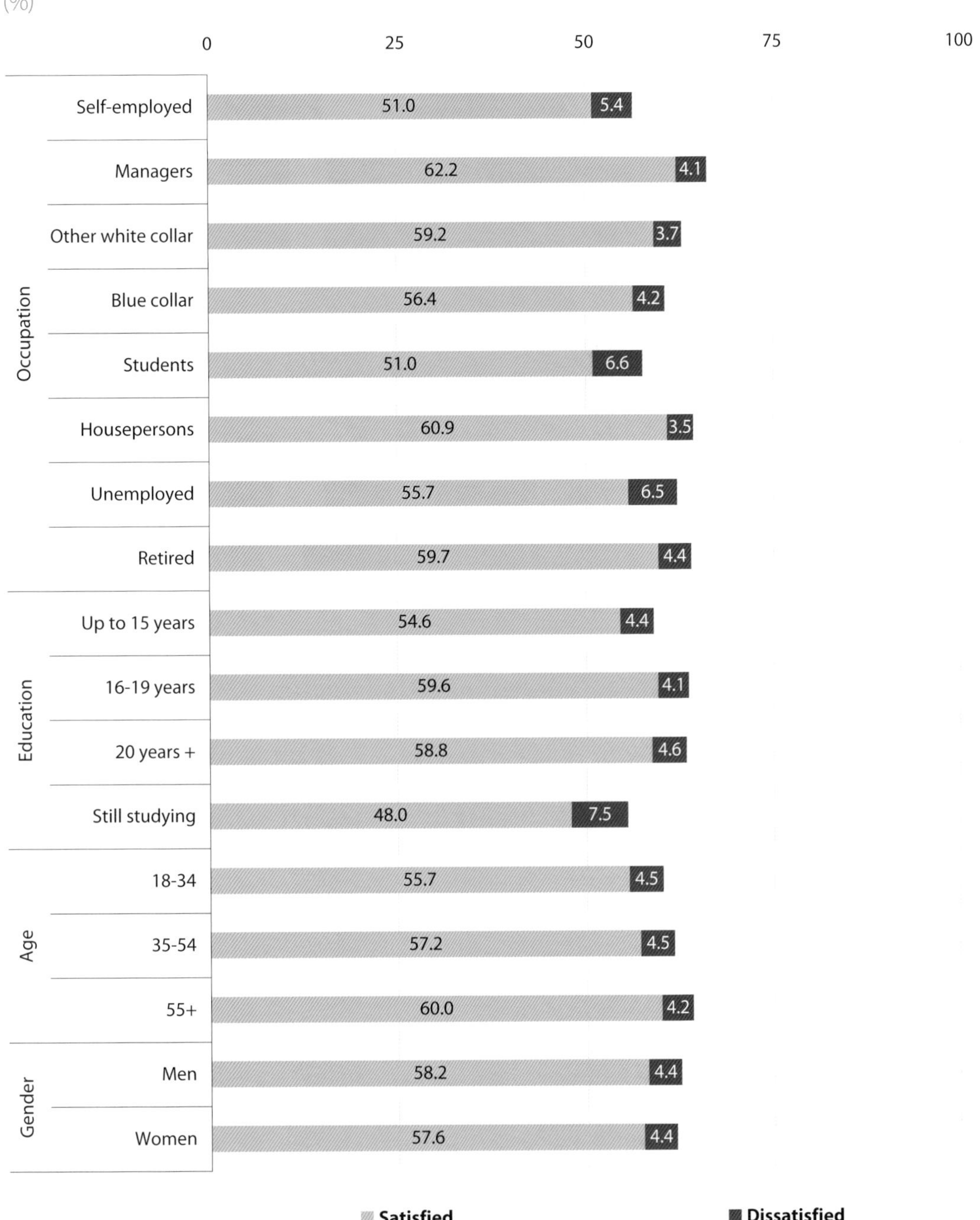

Source: Consumer satisfaction survey, IPSOS INRA for the European Commission Directorate-General for Health and Consumers, May 2007

Figure 4.12: Satisfaction rates for water supply, EU-25, 2006
(%)

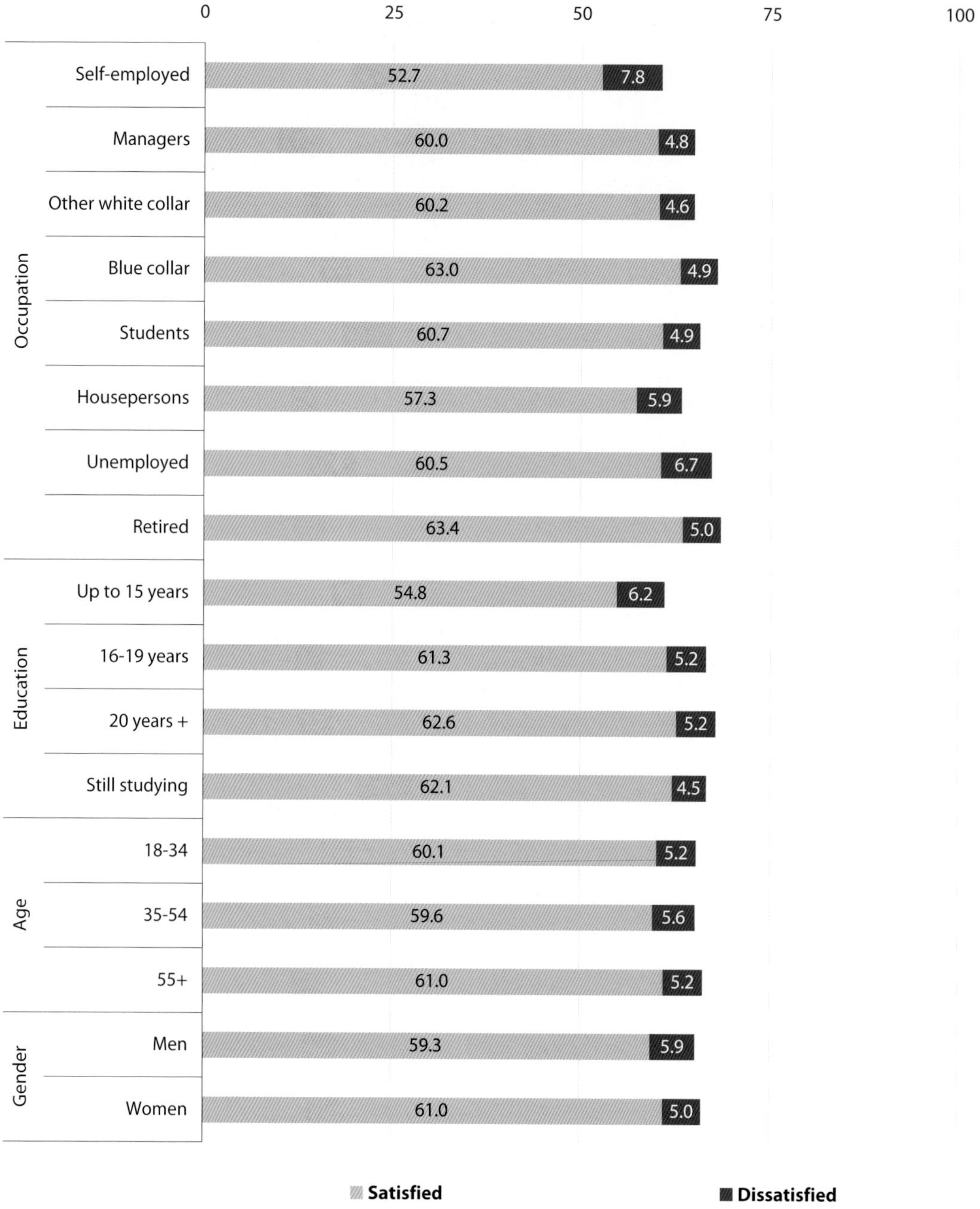

		Satisfied	Dissatisfied
Occupation	Self-employed	52.7	7.8
	Managers	60.0	4.8
	Other white collar	60.2	4.6
	Blue collar	63.0	4.9
	Students	60.7	4.9
	Housepersons	57.3	5.9
	Unemployed	60.5	6.7
	Retired	63.4	5.0
Education	Up to 15 years	54.8	6.2
	16-19 years	61.3	5.2
	20 years +	62.6	5.2
	Still studying	62.1	4.5
Age	18-34	60.1	5.2
	35-54	59.6	5.6
	55+	61.0	5.2
Gender	Men	59.3	5.9
	Women	61.0	5.0

Source: Consumer satisfaction survey, IPSOS INRA for the European Commission Directorate-General for Health and Consumers, May 2007

Table 4.22A: Satisfaction and importance for electricity, 2006

	Lower satisfaction	Higher satisfaction
Higher importance	**Priority actions** Transparency (7.05) Overall price (6.56) Commercial offer (6.41) Price level (5.81) Environmentally friendly actions (7.22) Familiarity (7.15) Ease (7.07) Customer service mentality (6.83) Uniqueness (6.74)	**Ideal situation** Payment process (7.92) Accuracy (7.37) Popularity (7.75) State of the art technology (7.49) Overall image (7.43) Relationship (7.38) Reputation (7.27)
Lower importance	**Lower importance** Points of sale (6.64) Information (6.56)	**Long term actions** Safety (8.11) Reliability (7.96) Offer relevance (7.89) Overall quality (7.71) Confidentiality (7.69) Order ease (7.58) Staff professionalism (7.55) Infrastructure (7.53) Technical support (7.34) Availability (7.29) Questions/problem handling (7.29)

Source: Consumer satisfaction survey, IPSOS INRA for the European Commission Directorate-General for Health and Consumers, May 2007

The report on this consumer satisfaction survey also provided a so-called two dimensional analysis, contrasting indicators of satisfaction and importance, in order to identify which quality aspects are regarded as important and having high or low satisfaction, and so indicating where service providers could try to maintain or improve satisfaction levels. These two-dimensional analyses are presented in Tables 4.22a to 4.22c for electricity, gas and water. Among the aspects that were regarded as important but with low satisfaction, ease, familiarity, customer service mentality, and biuniqueness were identified for all three of these services.

Table 4.22B: Satisfaction and importance for gas, 2006

	Lower satisfaction	Higher satisfaction
Higher importance	**Priority actions** Points of sale (6.79) Information (6.48) Environment friendly (7.24) Reputation (7.2) Familiarity (7.14) Ease (7.1) Customer service mentality (6.91) Uniqueness (6.67)	**Ideal situation** Safety (8.11) Reliability (8.07) Offer relevance (7.87) Order ease (7.85) Overall quality (7.76) Confidentiality (7.7) Staff professionalism (7.69) Infrastructure (7.5) Technical support (7.42) Questions/problem handling (7.38) Availability (7.31) Popularity (7.58) Relationship (7.45) State of the art (technology) (7.42) Overall image (7.34)
Lower importance	**Lower importance** Transparency (6.98) Overall price (6.41) Commercial offer (5.91) Price level (5.74)	**Long term actions** Payment process (7.93) Accuracy (7.37)

Source: Consumer satisfaction survey, IPSOS INRA for the European Commission Directorate-General for Health and Consumers, May 2007

Table 4.22C: Satisfaction and importance for water, 2006

	Lower satisfaction	Higher satisfaction
Higher importance	**Priority actions** Overall price (6.77) Price levels (6.21) Commercial offer (5.78) State of the art (technology) (7.19) Ease (7.13) Familiarity (7.12) Customer service mentality (6.97) Uniqueness (6.58)	**Ideal situation** Payment process (7.97) Accuracy (7.47) Transparency (7.23) Environment friendly (7.55) Popularity (7.48) Relationship (7.42) Overall image (7.37) Reputation (7.32)
Lower importance	**Lower importance** Availability (7.19) Technical support (7.19) Points of sale (6.88) Information (5.92)	**Long term actions** Reliability (7.94) Safety (7.86) Offer relevance (7.82) Order ease (7.78) Confidentiality (7.69) Overall quality (7.64) Staff professionalism (7.52) Infrastructure (7.38) Questions/problem handling (7.27)

Source: Consumer satisfaction survey, IPSOS INRA for the European Commission Directorate-General for Health and Consumers, May 2007

Information on households' satisfaction with accommodation is available from two sources, the Urban Audit which looked at the ease with which it is possible to find good housing at a reasonable price, and the survey on income and living conditions (SILC) which targeted specific problems with accommodation, such as noise or pollution – some of these parameters concern subjective feelings connected to individual preferences. Berlin was the only capital city were more than half of respondents thought that it was possible to find good housing at a reasonable price, the 53 % of respondents giving this view was far ahead of the 25 % in Madrid, which had the next highest share; in many capital cities less than 10 % agreed that it was possible to find good housing at a reasonable price. Turning to the five accommodation problems listed in Table 4.24, respondents in Latvia and Cyprus recorded generally high dissatisfaction levels, while the Nordic Member States of Finland, Denmark and Sweden were the least likely to respond that they suffered from these problems. Portugal reported the most problems with a lack of light, Cyprus with noise, Malta with pollution, the United Kingdom and Latvia with crime/vandalism, and Poland with damp or rot.

Table 4.23: Perceptions concerning accommodation availability and value for money, 2006
(%)

	Easy-to-find-good-housing:		
	at reasonable price (synthetic index 0-100)	agree (strongly & somewhat)	disagree (strongly & somewhat)
Bruxelles / Brussel	25	24	71
Sofia	22	19	70
Praha	16	15	77
København	12	12	87
Berlin	57	53	40
Tallinn	19	17	70
Dublin	6	6	94
Athina	28	25	65
Madrid	32	25	54
Paris	3	3	96
Roma	9	9	84
Lefkosia	14	13	83
Riga	11	10	78
Vilnius	18	16	70
Luxembourg	5	5	90
Budapest	26	22	63
Valletta	18	15	71
Amsterdam	12	12	85
Wien	25	22	67
Warszawa	14	13	80
Lisboa	12	11	83
Bucureşti	7	7	87
Ljubljana	16	15	78
Bratislava	8	8	85
Helsinki	9	9	87
Stockholm	8	8	88
London	12	11	83
Zagreb	10	10	82
Ankara	27	27	71

Source: Eurostat, Perception survey results (theme1/urb/urb_percep)

Table 4.24: Proportion of households that have problems with their accommodation, 2006
(%)

	Too dark, not enough light			Noise (from neighbours or street)			Pollution, grime (or other environmental problem)			Crime, violence or vandalism in the area			Leaking roof, damp (walls, floors, foundations), or rot (in windows or floor)		
	Yes	No	No answer	Yes	No	No answer	Yes	No	No answer	Yes	No	No answer	Yes	No	No answer
BE	10.1	89.9	0.0	22.9	77.1	0.0	15.6	84.4	0.0	18.2	81.8	0.0	14.3	85.7	0.0
BG	:	:	:	:	:	:	:	:	:	:	:	:	:	:	:
CZ	4.7	95.3	0.0	18.7	81.3	0.0	18.5	81.5	0.0	14.5	85.5	0.0	20.2	79.8	0.0
DK	3.7	95.1	1.1	20.1	79.1	0.8	7.9	91.0	1.1	14.3	84.8	0.9	8.5	90.5	1.0
DE	4.9	93.9	1.2	29.4	70.0	0.5	24.9	74.4	0.7	13.3	85.4	1.3	14.4	84.6	1.0
EE	6.6	93.4	0.0	22.7	77.3	0.0	20.8	79.2	0.0	20.3	79.7	0.0	24.6	75.4	0.0
IE	6.3	93.7	0.0	14.6	85.4	0.0	8.8	91.1	0.0	16.1	83.8	0.0	15.0	85.0	0.0
EL	8.6	91.4	0.0	20.7	79.3	0.0	17.4	82.6	0.0	9.1	90.9	0.0	20.8	79.2	0.0
ES	11.8	88.2	0.0	26.7	73.3	0.0	16.5	83.5	0.0	19.3	80.7	0.0	17.3	82.7	0.0
FR	8.1	91.9	0.0	20.2	79.8	0.0	16.0	83.9	0.1	16.2	83.6	0.2	11.7	88.3	0.0
IT	8.8	91.2	0.0	25.2	74.8	0.0	21.6	78.4	0.0	14.9	85.1	0.0	21.9	78.1	0.0
CY	6.0	94.0	0.0	35.8	64.2	0.0	23.9	76.1	0.0	12.1	87.9	0.0	33.8	66.2	0.0
LV	13.2	86.8	0.0	21.3	78.7	0.0	31.4	68.6	0.0	25.5	74.5	0.0	31.3	68.7	0.0
LT	11.4	88.6	0.0	20.0	80.0	0.0	14.0	86.0	0.0	8.0	92.0	0.0	28.0	72.0	0.0
LU	5.8	94.2	0.0	23.9	76.0	0.1	17.6	82.4	0.0	12.0	88.0	0.0	14.7	85.2	0.1
HU	7.6	92.2	0.2	17.7	82.3	0.0	13.4	86.6	0.0	10.0	89.8	0.2	27.8	72.2	0.0
MT	6.8	93.2	0.0	26.9	73.1	0.0	38.8	61.2	0.0	12.1	87.9	0.0	8.1	91.9	0.0
NL	5.5	94.4	0.0	32.2	67.8	0.0	14.5	85.5	0.0	16.9	83.1	0.0	16.4	83.4	0.3
AT	7.5	92.5	0.0	19.8	80.2	0.0	8.2	91.8	0.0	13.6	86.4	0.0	10.0	90.0	0.0
PL	10.5	89.5	0.0	20.4	79.6	0.0	13.4	86.6	0.0	9.8	90.2	0.0	40.0	60.0	0.0
PT	19.3	80.7	0.0	25.6	74.4	0.0	20.5	79.5	0.0	12.1	87.9	0.0	20.0	80.0	0.0
RO	:	:	:	:	:	:	:	:	:	:	:	:	:	:	:
SI	9.8	90.2	0.0	18.7	81.3	0.0	21.1	78.9	0.0	10.0	90.0	0.0	22.3	77.7	0.0
SK	4.0	95.9	0.1	19.9	80.1	0.0	19.8	80.2	0.1	8.1	91.9	0.1	6.7	93.2	0.0
FI	5.0	94.9	0.1	17.8	82.0	0.1	13.5	86.4	0.1	16.7	83.0	0.3	4.5	95.2	0.3
SE	5.0	95.0	0.1	13.6	86.3	0.0	7.0	92.9	0.1	13.8	85.9	0.4	6.5	93.3	0.1
UK	9.6	90.4	0.0	22.1	77.8	0.1	12.8	87.2	0.1	27.4	72.5	0.1	13.3	86.7	0.0
IS	2.0	97.6	0.5	13.2	86.5	0.4	8.6	91.0	0.4	2.6	97.0	0.4	12.5	87.0	0.5
NO	4.2	95.5	0.2	13.3	86.4	0.3	8.3	91.4	0.3	4.6	95.2	0.3	8.1	91.7	0.3

Source: Eurostat, EU-SILC

4.5 Quality

As well as studying problems leading to dissatisfaction with accommodation the SILC also studied the availability of certain amenities, including having an indoor bath or shower, and an indoor flushing toilet for the sole use of the household. For both of these types of amenities the Baltic Member States all reported the lowest rates of availability, between 76 % and 79 % for baths/showers, and between 75 % and 83 % for indoor flushing toilets.

Table 4.25: Proportion of households that have specified facilities, 2006
(%)

	Bath or shower in dwelling			Indoor flushing toilet for sole use of household		
	Yes	**No**	**No answer**	**Yes**	**No**	**No answer**
BE	98.4	1.6	0.0	98.4	1.6	0.0
BG	:	:	:	:	:	:
CZ	98.6	1.4	0.0	98.2	1.8	0.0
DK	99.0	1.0	0.0	100.0	0.0	0.0
DE	99.4	0.5	0.1	97.6	1.5	0.9
EE	79.1	20.9	0.0	83.3	16.7	0.0
IE	99.2	0.8	0.0	99.5	0.5	0.0
EL	98.2	1.8	0.0	96.5	3.5	0.0
ES	99.5	0.5	0.0	99.7	0.3	0.0
FR	98.8	1.2	0.0	98.7	1.3	0.0
IT	99.3	0.7	0.0	99.6	0.4	0.0
CY	97.3	2.7	0.0	97.3	2.7	0.0
LV	77.9	22.1	0.0	79.1	20.9	0.0
LT	76.4	23.6	0.0	75.4	24.6	0.0
LU	99.0	0.9	0.1	99.0	0.9	0.1
HU	94.4	5.6	0.0	93.0	7.0	0.0
MT	98.5	1.5	0.0	99.8	0.2	0.0
NL	0.0	0.0	100.0	0.0	0.0	100.0
AT	98.8	1.2	0.0	98.6	1.4	0.0
PL	90.0	10.0	0.0	91.2	8.8	0.0
PT	94.9	5.1	0.0	95.4	4.6	0.0
RO	:	:	:	:	:	:
SI	98.2	1.8	0.0	98.2	1.8	0.0
SK	98.0	1.9	0.1	95.8	4.1	0.1
FI	98.0	1.9	0.1	98.8	1.1	0.1
SE	98.2	0.3	1.5	100.0	0.0	0.0
UK	99.7	0.3	0.0	99.2	0.8	0.0
IS	100.0	0.0	0.0	98.8	1.2	0.0
NO	99.6	0.2	0.2	99.5	0.3	0.2

Source: Eurostat, EU-SILC

4.6 Externalities: environment

The construction and demolition of housing, the consumption of energy and water, and the disposal of waste and waste water impact in several ways on the environment. Buildings themselves require construction materials, which in many cases affect the landscape when extracted, and whose extraction and manufacture consumes energy; households directly consume energy which has a greater or lesser environmental impact depending on the choice of fuel. Water consumption can strain water reserves, and its use generates waste water. Hard surfacing around housing can reduce groundwater absorption affecting the level of water tables on the one hand and increasing pressure on sewerage systems on the other. Households generate large amounts, of often unsorted, municipal waste that needs to be processed for reuse, recycling or disposal. The combination of concerns about climate change and the rising cost of energy have raised awareness about energy consumption by households, and on the type of energy consumed. Table 4.26 shows the ratio of electricity generated from renewable sources relative to the total gross electricity consumption. The highest ratio in the EU was in Austria which generated much of its electricity from hydro power, as did Iceland and Norway. Several other Member States generate a large proportion of their electricity from hydro power, in particular Latvia and Sweden, while Denmark had the largest share of electricity generation from wind power, and Finland from biomass.

A Eurobarometer survey in 2007 looked at attitudes towards issues related to EU energy policy. Half of respondents within the EU-27 indicated that they were very concerned about climate change and global warming, and a similar but slightly lower proportion reported that energy efficiency influenced very much their choice of household appliances. Around 30 % of respondents thought that nuclear energy should be used more because of climate change and global warming concerns, equivalent to around half the proportion that felt that it should be used less because of safety concerns.

Table 4.26: Electricity generated from renewable sources as a share of gross electricity consumption
(%)

	2004	2005	2006	2010 target
EU-27	13.9	14.0	:	21.0
BE	2.1	2.8	:	6.0
BG	8.9	11.8	11.2	11.0
CZ	4.0	4.5	4.9	8.0
DK	27.1	28.2	:	29.0
DE	9.5	10.5	:	12.5
EE	0.7	1.1	1.4	5.1
IE	5.1	6.8	8.5	13.2
EL	9.5	10.0	:	20.1
ES	18.5	15.0	:	29.4
FR	12.9	11.3	12.4	21.0
IT	15.9	14.1	14.5	25.0
CY	0.0	0.0	0.0	6.0
LV	47.1	48.4	37.7	49.3
LT	3.5	3.9	3.6	7.0
LU	3.2	3.2	3.5	5.7
HU	2.3	4.6	:	3.6
MT	0.0	0.0	:	5.0
NL	5.7	7.5	7.9	9.0
AT	58.7	57.4	56.6	78.1
PL	2.1	2.9	2.9	7.5
PT	24.4	16.0	:	39.0
RO	29.9	35.8	31.4	33.0
SI	29.1	24.2	24.4	33.6
SK	14.3	16.5	:	31.0
FI	28.3	26.9	:	31.5
SE	46.1	54.3	48.2	60.0
UK	3.7	4.3	4.6	10.0
HR	41.0	36.2	33.4	:
TR	30.9	24.7	:	:
IS	100.0	99.9	:	:
NO	89.7	108.4	:	:

Source: Eurostat, Electricity generated from renewable sources - % of gross energy consumption (theme8/nrg/nrg_105a)

Table 4.27: Issues related to energy policy, February 2007
(% of respondents)

	Concern for climate change and global warming				Influence of energy efficiency concerns when buying household appliances				How should the share of nuclear energy change		
	Yes, very much	Yes, to some degree	No	Do not know/ no answer	Yes, very much	Yes, to some degree	No	Do not know/ no answer	Increase as it does not contribute to climate change and global warming	Decrease as it poses safety problems, like waste and danger of accidents	Do not know/ no answer
EU-27	50	37	12	1	48	32	19	2	30	61	10
BE	40	44	17	0	46	31	21	2	28	54	18
BG	40	39	20	1	49	30	17	5	51	33	16
CZ	48	36	16	1	50	33	16	2	48	40	12
DK	37	49	14	0	53	32	14	1	26	67	7
DE	47	42	10	1	52	32	14	2	28	66	6
EE	20	52	25	4	40	38	18	4	21	64	14
EL	68	27	5	0	29	35	32	3	13	83	5
ES	70	23	7	0	48	30	20	2	18	72	10
FR	55	35	10	1	48	28	23	1	28	59	13
IE	51	39	10	1	35	39	25	1	27	68	5
IT	58	32	10	1	66	22	10	2	29	58	13
CY	70	23	7	0	34	32	33	1	19	76	5
LV	24	48	27	1	32	37	30	2	21	69	10
LT	34	46	17	2	28	47	20	5	30	55	15
LU	53	38	9	0	46	31	20	2	20	67	13
HU	51	34	15	1	60	29	11	1	27	61	11
MT	68	24	7	1	63	20	15	2	27	58	15
NL	28	52	19	0	35	47	18	0	35	57	8
AT	45	40	14	0	52	30	17	2	15	78	7
PL	32	39	27	2	52	29	16	3	35	57	8
PT	65	24	9	3	43	31	22	4	23	57	20
RO	64	22	12	1	54	22	19	5	25	64	12
SI	53	34	13	0	42	36	21	1	29	65	6
SK	41	42	16	1	48	35	15	2	42	47	11
FI	24	57	19	1	35	47	18	1	42	47	11
SE	30	51	19	0	22	45	31	3	44	48	8
UK	48	42	10	1	33	41	25	1	36	57	7

Source: 'Attitudes on issues related to EU Energy Policy', Flash Eurobarometer 206a, European Commission

For more information

Directorate-General for Health and Consumers:
http://ec.europa.eu/consumers/citizen/my_rights/energy_en.htm

Directorate-General for the Environment:
http://ec.europa.eu/environment/water/index_en.htm

Directorate-General for Energy and Transport:
http://ec.europa.eu/energy/index_en.html

5

Furnishings, household equipment and maintenance

As for other manufactured goods, the supply of furnishings and household equipment is becoming increasingly global and competitive in nature. For consumers, greater competition offers potential for more choice, more competitive prices, and higher quality, through a wider range of outlets, but it also raises concerns about safety and environmental standards.

Safety and environmental legislation on furnishings and household equipment has become a key benchmark for consumer confidence in manufactured goods. A number of relevant policies have been implemented in both domains. The main environmental directives which directly affect the furniture industry are the Integrated Pollution Prevention and Control (IPPC) Directive [12], the Volatile Organic Compounds (VOC) Directive [13] and waste framework Directive [14]. Moreover, the furniture industry is a downstream user of chemicals and, as such, has obligations under the REACH Regulation [15]. As far as the VOC Directive is concerned, a best practice guide has been established by the Federation of European Furniture Manufacturers (UEA) to help manufacturers comply with the legal requirements; a growing number of firms in the furniture manufacturing sector are also implementing environmental management systems such as the EU's Eco-Management and Audit Scheme (EMAS) in order to evaluate, report and improve their environmental performance. Furthermore, a Community eco-label is also being considered for wooden furniture.

Domestic electrical appliances and lighting equipment mainly contain the risk of electric shock, often combined with the risk of fire. There are a range of legislative measures designed to ensure consumer safety in this domain. These often take the form of specific sectoral legislation, such as household electrical appliances that are covered by the Low Voltage Directive 2006/95/EC [16]. Any products that are not covered by sector specific legislation fall within the remit of the General Product Safety Directive (GPSD) [17], which aims to ensure that manufacturers and distributors only place safe products on the market, informing consumers of the risks associated with the products they supply, taking appropriate measures to prevent such risks and being able to trace dangerous products. The RAPEX system [18] ensures that the relevant authorities in each Member State are rapidly informed of any dangerous products. Its latest annual report contains information on the breakdown of product notifications for 2007, 12 % of which were electrical appliances and 6 % lighting equipment (behind toys and motor vehicles). In addition, the European Commission also carries out a range of market surveillance actions in an attempt to safeguard consumer safety. During the course of 2008, results of tests on lamps and electric cord extension sets were published (http://europa.eu/rapid/pressReleasesAction.do?reference=IP/08/615).

5.1 Access and choice

5.1.1 Furniture

Home furnishings reflect a mixture of function and form. Given the diversity of geographic and socio-demographic circumstances, there is a broad diversity in home furnishings and household equipment.

Furniture is a typical consumer durable good and was traditionally, to a very large extent, solid wood-based. Over time, however, new techniques, materials (such as wood-based panels – like chipboard and medium density fibreboard, as well as glass, plastics and metals) and designs have led to a broader range of goods, available through a larger spectrum of distribution channels (such as mail order, DIY stores, furniture stores selling flat-pack furniture).

According to the Institut de Promotion et Etudes de l'Ameublement, a little under three quarters (73 %) of furniture expenditure in the EU-25 was in specialist furniture stores (chain stores or independents) in 2004. About two fifths (41 %) of all furniture expenditure was spent in independent furniture stores, a significantly higher proportion than in the United States (see Figure 5.1). Another notable difference between the EU and the United States markets was the mail order and catalogue segment of the furniture market; this accounted for a tenth of furniture expenditure in the United States but only 1 % in Europe.

Within the EU, however, there are considerable differences in the way that people shop for their furniture. In Italy and Spain, a majority of furniture purchases were made with independent furniture retailers (see Figure 5.2), as was the case in a number of the Member States that joined the EU in 2004 or 2007 (such as Poland where 67 % of furniture expenditure was accounted for by independent stores). In contrast, spending in independent furniture stores in France only accounted for 13 % of total furniture expenditure. The situation in France was broadly similar to that in the United Kingdom and Germany.

(12) For more information: http://europa.eu/scadplus/leg/en/lvb/l28045.htm.

(13) For more information: http://europa.eu/scadplus/leg/en/lvb/l28029b.htm.

(14) For more information: http://ec.europa.eu/environment/waste/legislation/a.htm.

(15) For more information: http://ec.europa.eu/enterprise/reach/reach_more_info_en.htm.

(16) For more information: http://eur-lex.europa.eu/LexUriServ/LexUriServ.do?uri=OJ:L:2006:374:0010:0019:EN:PDF.

(17) For more information: http://eur-lex.europa.eu/LexUriServ/LexUriServ.do?uri=CELEX:32001L0095:EN:NOT.

(18) For more information: http://ec.europa.eu/consumers/safety/rapex/index_en.htm.

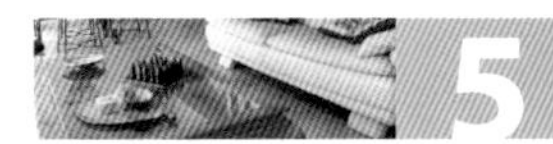

Nevertheless, these differences appear to be narrowing with a change in consumer behaviour in southern Europe, following the arrival of international retailers (such as IKEA); between 1995 and 2004, the proportion of expenditure accounted for by independent furniture retailers fell by 10 percentage points in Spain and 5 percentage points in Italy.

Figure 5.1: Furniture distribution channels, 2004
(% of furniture expenditure)

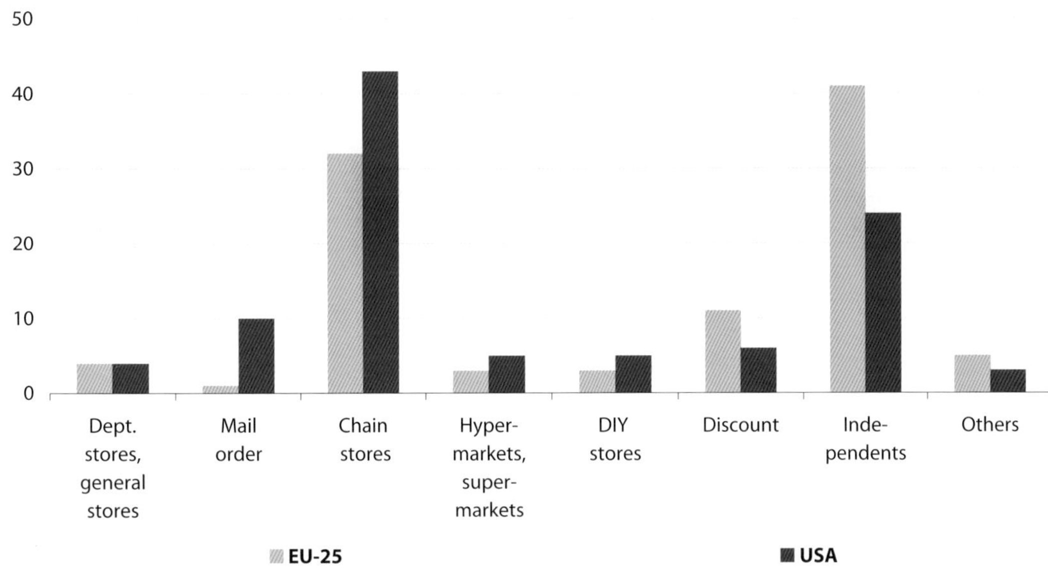

Source: Institut de Promotion et Etudes de l'Ameublement

Figure 5.2: Concentrated distribution channels for furniture, selected Member States, 2004 (1)
(% of furniture expenditure)

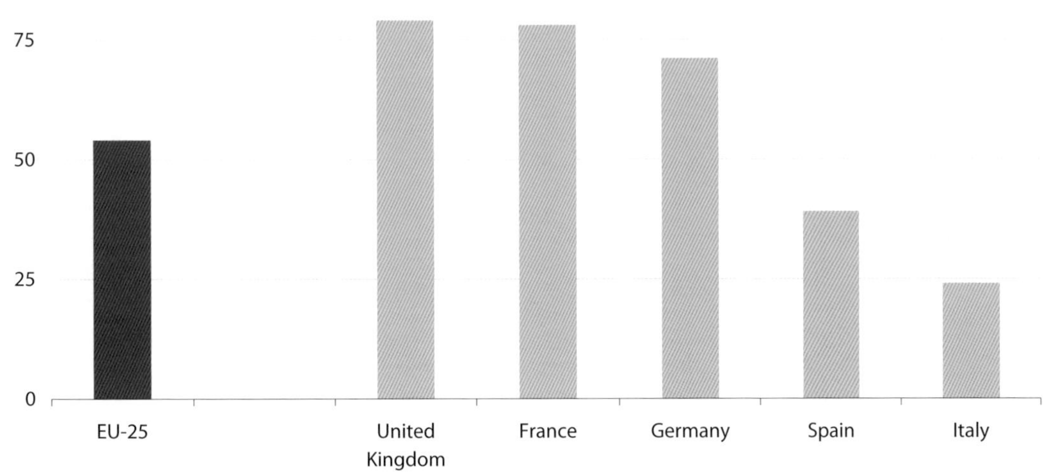

(1) Concentrated distribution comprises department stores, general stores, mail order, chain stores incl. discounters, DIY stores, hypermarkets and supermarkets; furniture expenditure excluding furnishings and carpets.

Source: Institut de Promotion et Etudes de l'Ameublement

5.1.2 Household electrical equipment

A consumer satisfaction survey in 2008 shows that specialised chain stores were by far the most popular place for EU-27 consumers to make purchases of household electrical equipment (see Figure 5.3) – note these figures relate to the most popular places for making purchases and not to the share of total expenditure. Just over two thirds (67.3 %) of consumers in the EU-27 in 2008 preferred to shop for household electrical equipment in a chain store specialising in these products. The next most popular retail formats were supermarkets/hypermarkets (28.5 %), while independent retailers (19.3 %) and department stores (11.8 %) were the only other types of sales channel to record shares in double digits.

There was a wide range of preferences across the Member States, with supermarkets and hypermarkets particularly favoured by consumers in Bulgaria, France and Romania, whereas department stores were relatively popular in Ireland, Luxembourg, Germany or Spain. Consumers in Ireland and Germany also reported a relatively high propensity to shop for household electrical goods in retail chain stores, alongside those from Greece, Lithuania, the Netherlands or the United Kingdom. Independent retailers were generally favoured in some of the smaller markets, in particular Malta and Cyprus.

Figure 5.3: In which of the following places have you or has a member of your household bought household electrical equipment most, EU-27, 2008? (%)

Source: 'Retail satisfaction survey', IPSOS for the European Commission, August/September 2008

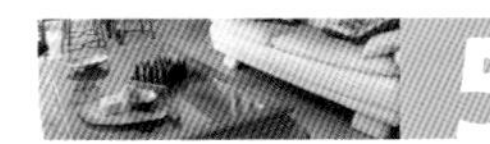

5.2 Consumption

5.2.1 Frequency and time spent on household activities

The economic, family and social commitments that come with owning or renting a home mean that a significant proportion of an adult's (aged 20 to 74 years old) day is spent on household activities. This information on time use may be used as a proxy for the consumption of domestic appliances, although for some of the headings it is not sure whether a machine is being used or not.

Among those Member States for which time use surveys have been carried out, women spent, on average, much more time on selected domestic household activities than men; this varied from at least twice as much time as men in Sweden, Finland and Lithuania, to as much as six to eight times as much time in Spain and Italy for activities like dishwashing, cleaning, laundry, ironing and other household upkeep (see Table 5.1). Women in Italy spent an average of two and a half hours on these activities, and a little under two hours in Spain and France, in stark contrast to women in Sweden and Latvia, where the time spent on these tasks averaged about one and a quarter hours. In Sweden and Latvia, however, men spent the longest time on these household activities, suggesting perhaps that in some households there was a more equitable share of chores between partners. Note however that these figures also reflect, at least to some degree, the structure of households, or more specifically, the proportion of adults living alone. By definition, a single adult (male or female) has to do all of these tasks, and hence, those countries (usually in northern Europe) where there is a higher propensity for living alone will likely show a more equitable balance in the use of time, than those countries where it is more common for children to remain with their families into adulthood up until the time they find an established partner.

Table 5.1: Average time spent per day on household activities, selected Member States (1) (hours:minutes per day)

	Dish-washing		Cleaning dwelling		Other household		Laundry		Ironing	
	Men	Women	Men	Women	Men	Women	Men	Women	Men	Women
BE	00:10	00:20	00:08	00:26	00:18	00:28	00:01	00:09	00:01	00:19
BG	00:05	00:36	00:06	00:31	00:22	00:13	00:01	00:19	00:00	00:06
DE	00:08	00:21	00:11	00:39	00:14	00:15	00:02	00:13	00:01	00:10
EE	00:06	00:25	00:09	00:34	00:22	00:14	00:01	00:14	00:00	00:07
ES	00:04	00:29	00:07	00:50	00:06	00:11	00:01	00:11	00:00	00:12
FR	00:08	00:25	00:11	00:58	00:08	00:07	00:01	00:07	00:01	00:15
IT	00:05	00:35	00:09	01:24	00:06	00:06	00:00	00:10	00:00	00:20
LV	00:04	00:22	00:06	00:27	00:21	00:15	00:01	00:09	00:00	00:03
LT	00:04	00:22	00:10	00:38	00:29	00:21	00:01	00:11	00:00	00:04
PL	00:06	00:29	00:09	00:34	00:20	00:14	00:01	00:14	00:01	00:07
SI	00:04	00:28	00:08	00:39	00:24	00:16	00:00	00:09	00:00	00:16
FI	00:04	00:15	00:08	00:26	00:26	00:23	00:02	00:13	00:00	00:05
SE	00:10	00:21	00:15	00:30	00:05	00:02	00:03	00:12	00:01	00:05
UK	00:09	00:18	00:11	00:38	00:09	00:12	00:02	00:11	00:02	00:11
NO	00:08	00:21	00:14	00:33	00:04	00:02	00:02	00:11	00:00	00:04

(1) Data are taken from national time use surveys (TUS) conducted between 1998 and 2004 and refer to men and women aged 20 to 74 years; data only shown for those countries participating in the survey; all remaining Member States, not available.

Source: Harmonised European Time Use Survey [online database version 2.0]; created 2005-2007 by Statistics Finland and Statistics Sweden [reference date 2007-10-01]; (https://www.testh2.scb.se/tus/tus/)

5.2.2 Consumption expenditure

The average household consumption expenditure on furnishings, household equipment and routine household maintenance in the EU-27 was EUR 800 per person in 2006, although national averages ranged from EUR 300 per person or less in the Czech Republic, Estonia, Lithuania, Hungary, Poland, Romania and Slovakia to EUR 2 100 per person in Luxembourg. Compared with average expenditure in 2000, the sharpest rises were recorded in Estonia, Lithuania and Slovakia, albeit from some of the lowest levels.

Developments in the price and volume components of the final consumption expenditure of households on furnishings, household equipment and routine household maintenance, point to the more than doubling of volumes between 2000 and 2006 as the principal reason for the sharp rise in average expenditure in Estonia and Lithuania. Indeed, in a majority of the Member States that joined the EU since 2004, the volume of consumption expenditure on furnishings, household equipment and maintenance items rose relatively sharply, and at a quicker pace than among the EU-15 Member States. This pattern of 'catch-up' was assisted by the relatively static nature of expenditure in volume terms in countries such as Italy and Austria, as well as slight reductions in the Netherlands and Germany.

Table 5.2: Final consumption expenditure of households, furnishings, household equipment and routine maintenance of the house: consumption per head
(EUR)

	2000	2006
EU-27	700	800
BE	700	800
BG	0	:
CZ	200	300
DK	900	:
DE	1 100	1 100
EE	100	300
IE	900	1 200
EL	500	700
ES	600	700
FR	800	1 000
IT	1 100	1 100
CY	800	1 000
LV	100	:
LT	100	300
LU	1 800	2 100
HU	200	300
MT	700	700
NL	1 000	1 000
AT	1 300	1 300
PL	100	200
PT	600	:
RO (1)	100	100
SI	400	500
SK	100	300
FI	600	900
SE	700	:
UK	1 000	1 100
TR (1)	300	300
IS	1 300	1 500
NO	1 000	:
CH	1 000	1 000

(1) 2006, forecast.

Source: Eurostat, Final consumption expenditure of households by consumption purpose (theme2/nama/nama_co2_c)

Figure 5.4: Final consumption expenditure of households, furnishings, household equipment and routine maintenance of the house: price and volume changes between 2000 and 2006 (1)
(%)

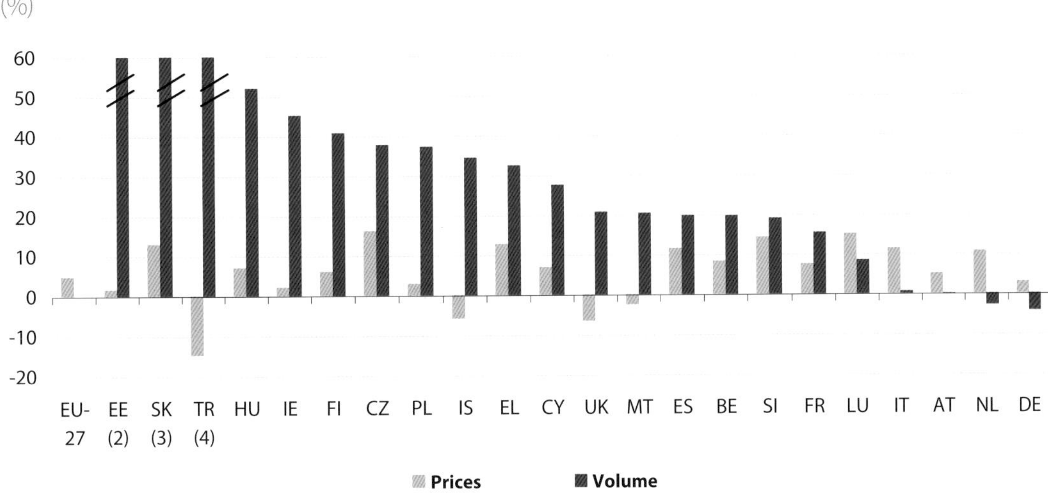

(1) Bulgaria, Denmark, Latvia, Lithuania, Portugal, Romania and Sweden, not available; EU-27, volume, not available.
(2) The volume of furnishings, household equipment and routine maintenance of the house purchased in Estonia increased by 141.7 % between 2000 and 2006.
(3) The volume of furnishings, household equipment and routine maintenance of the house purchased in Slovakia increased by 106.6 % between 2000 and 2006.
(4) The volume of furnishings, household equipment and routine maintenance of the house purchased in Turkey increased by 64.4 % between 2000 and 2006.

Source: Eurostat, Final consumption expenditure of households by consumption purpose (theme2/nama/nama_co2_k and nama_co2_p)

Using data in purchasing power standards (PPS) from the 2005 household budget survey, in order to provide an analysis at comparable price levels, consumption expenditure on furnishings, household equipment and the routine maintenance of the house within the EU-27 ranged from an average of PPS 201 per household in Romania and PPS 213 in Bulgaria to PPS 3 702 in Luxembourg (see Table 5.3).

Overall furnishings, household equipment and routine maintenance items together accounted for 5.5 % of total household consumption expenditure in the EU-27 in 2005, with comparatively little variation between Member States; the share ranged from about 4 % in Lithuania and Romania to a little over 7 % in Luxembourg and Ireland for all the Member States except Malta, where the relative importance of these items in household expenditure was highest (10.7 %).

Table 5.3: Mean consumption expenditure per household, furnishings, household equipment and routine maintenance of the house, 2005
(PPS)

EU-27 (1)	1 416
BE	1 687
BG	213
CZ	815
DK	1 459
DE	1 543
EE	568
IE	2 613
EL	1 929
ES	1 211
FR	1 693
IT	1 670
CY	2 008
LV	546
LT	392
LU	3 702
HU	498
MT	3 070
NL	1 888
AT	1 868
PL	478
PT	994
RO	201
SI	1 389
SK	494
FI	1 238
SE	1 640
UK	2 092
HR	697
NO	1 892

(1) Estimate.

Source: Eurostat, Household Budget Survey (theme3/hbs/hbs_exp_t121)

Figure 5.5: Structure of consumption expenditure: share of furnishings, household equipment and routine maintenance of the house in total expenditure, 2005 (1)
(%)

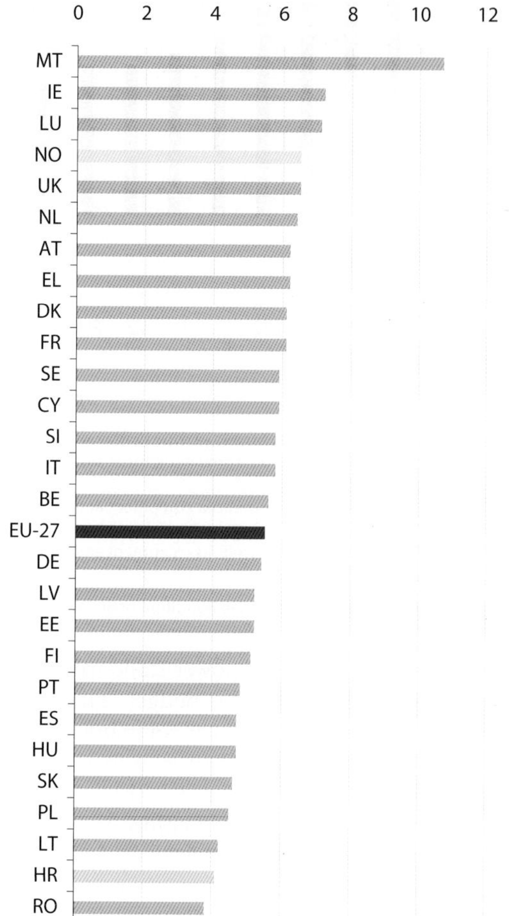

(1) EU-27, estimate; Czech Republic, not available.

Source: Eurostat, Household Budget Survey (theme3/hbs/hbs_str_t211)

Figure 5.6 shows the importance of expenditure on furnishings, household equipment and routine maintenance items for a number of different subgroups of households. Some of these items cannot be considered as a necessity, and this may help explain why expenditure tends to rise with income, as those persons with more money can afford to pay for domestic and household services, and to buy more furniture, gadgets, tools and appliances that make their lives more comfortable, while those persons with less money continue to do household chores by hand, rather than with the aid of a machine. As such, the share of these items in total expenditure rose relatively steadily through the income quintiles, to a high of 6.7 % for the highest income quintile. Similarly, the share varied from 4.1 % for those households headed by someone who was unemployed to 6.0 % for non-manual workers.

Figure 5.6: Structure of consumption expenditure: share of furnishings, household equipment and routine maintenance of the house in total expenditure, EU-27, 2005 (%)

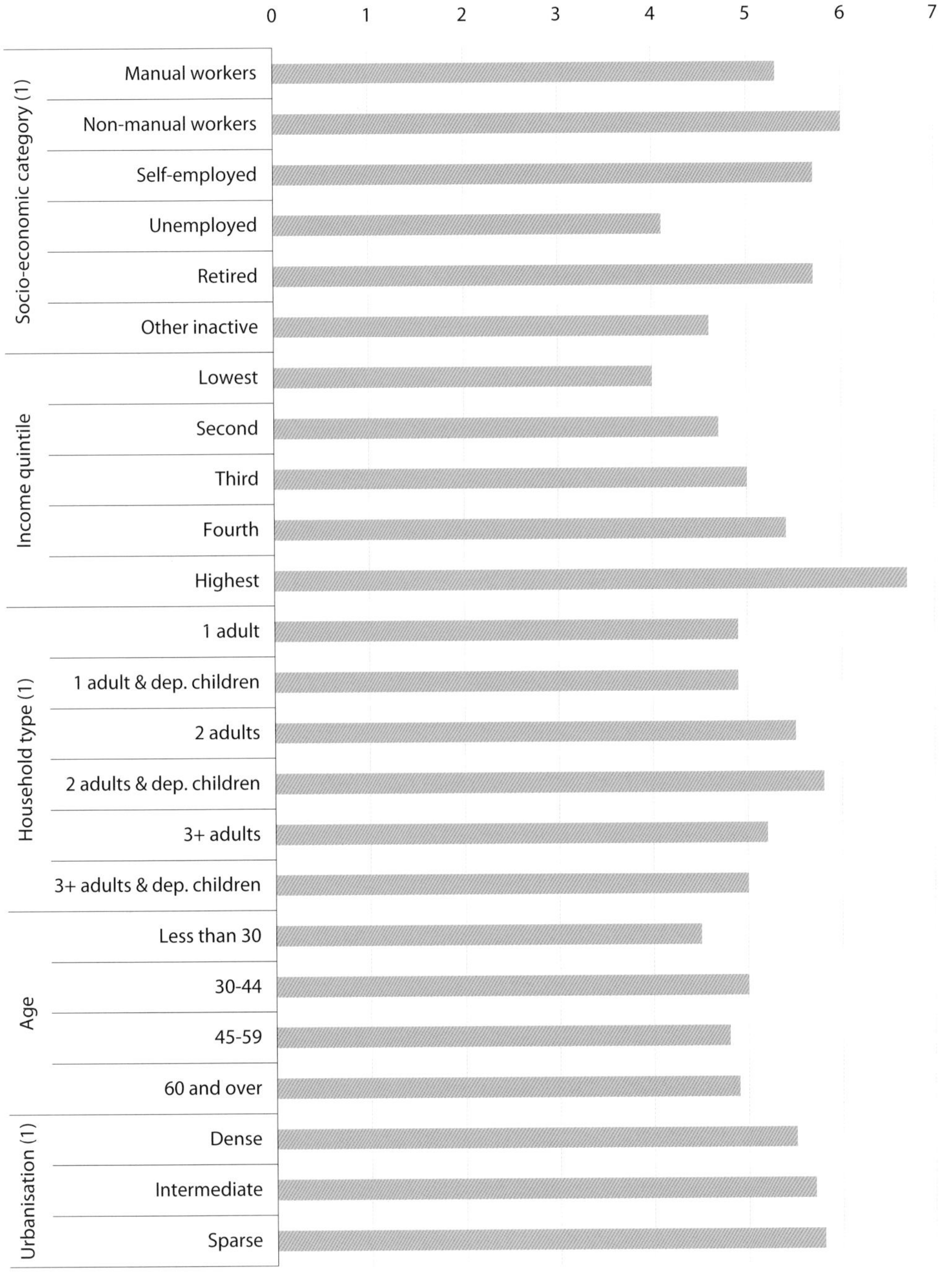

(1) Unreliable.

Source: Eurostat, Household Budget Survey (theme3/hbs/hbs_str_t221, hbs_str_t223, hbs_str_t224, hbs_str_t225, hbs_str_t226)

Figure 5.7: Mean consumption expenditure per household, furnishings, household equipment and routine maintenance of the house, 2005
(PPS, minimum and maximum (vertical lines at end of horizontal line), inter-quartile range containing half of the Member States (box), median (vertical line within box))

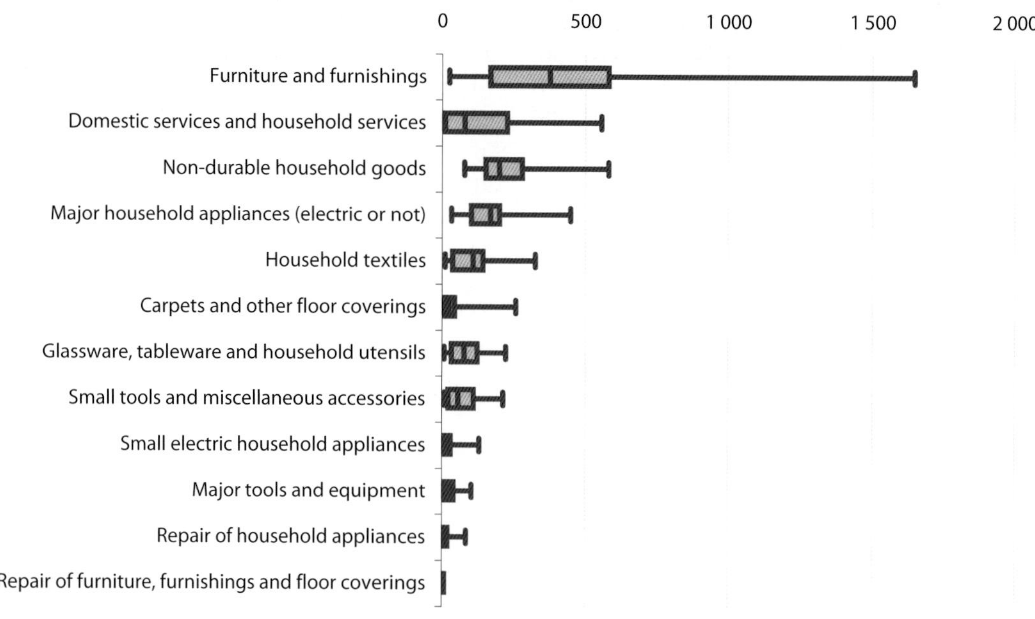

Source: Eurostat, Household Budget Survey (theme3/hbs/hbs_exp_t121)

Average consumption expenditure per household on different items of furnishings, household equipment and routine maintenance items varied considerably across the Member States. The range was greatest for furniture and furnishings, which also accounted for the largest proportion of expenditure (see Figure 5.7). Average consumption expenditure per household on furniture and furnishings was PPS 384 in the EU-27 in 2005, almost twice the level recorded for any of the other categories, as expenditure on non-durable household goods averaged PPS 201.

The differences in expenditure between the other categories reflect a range of factors, such as necessity (most Europeans believe they have to have a washing machine), the ability to pay, or cultural differences (which may influence the take-up of domestic and household services). For example, while average household expenditure on domestic and household services in the EU-27 was relatively low (PPS 135 in 2005), its range across Member States was the second highest among the categories covered in this chapter, with relatively high levels of expenditure in Luxembourg and several southern Member States.

5.3 Prices

5.3.1 Price inflation

During the period between 2000 and 2007, the EU-27's harmonised index of consumer prices for furnishings, household equipment and routine maintenance of the house rose steadily, at an average rate of 1.2 % per annum, which was about half the rate of increase recorded for the all-items consumer price index during the same period.

Prices increased in the vast majority of Member States, strongly in the case of Romania (particularly up to 2006) and Slovenia. In contrast, there were price reductions, albeit uneven in nature, in Ireland (concentrated in the period after 2002), Slovakia, the Czech Republic and Lithuania. The contrasting evolution of consumer prices continued in 2007, with strong price growth in Latvia, Bulgaria and Slovenia, but a further reduction in Ireland.

Table 5.4: Harmonised indices of consumer prices, furnishings, household equipment and routine maintenance of the house, annual rate of change
(%)

	2000	2001	2002	2003	2004	2005	2006	2007
EU-27	1.2	1.9	1.7	1.0	0.7	0.6	0.6	1.6
BE	0.7	2.6	1.9	1.2	0.9	0.9	1.1	2.1
BG	-0.5	2.3	0.2	-1.0	-1.2	0.4	1.7	4.2
CZ	0.2	0.1	0.0	-1.7	-2.2	-2.2	-1.5	-0.3
DK	1.8	1.9	1.9	1.0	2.7	0.7	0.9	1.3
DE	0.0	0.9	1.1	0.3	-0.2	-0.1	-0.1	1.1
EE	-0.2	1.3	1.1	-0.4	-0.7	0.6	2.3	3.8
IE	4.0	3.2	1.4	-0.7	-1.8	-1.5	-1.3	-1.8
EL	1.5	2.5	1.6	1.8	1.5	2.1	1.8	2.2
ES	2.5	2.0	2.0	2.0	1.6	2.1	2.6	2.6
FR	0.5	1.9	1.4	1.3	1.2	0.9	0.9	1.1
IT	1.9	2.0	1.9	2.0	2.1	1.6	1.6	2.5
CY	1.4	0.1	1.1	3.7	-0.3	0.4	0.3	0.3
LV	1.3	0.4	1.5	1.9	1.9	3.3	2.8	4.6
LT	-2.1	-2.3	-2.1	-2.9	-3.0	-2.0	0.4	2.1
LU	2.4	2.1	1.6	1.5	1.7	1.5	1.7	2.1
HU	5.5	4.9	3.1	0.8	1.0	-0.2	-1.5	1.5
MT	-1.2	0.3	0.5	-0.3	2.8	2.4	2.0	0.8
NL	1.8	5.2	3.9	1.7	-0.9	-0.3	0.0	1.3
AT	0.7	1.3	1.6	1.2	-0.1	-0.3	0.6	1.2
PL	5.5	3.8	1.8	0.5	1.7	1.2	0.1	1.1
PT	2.0	3.2	3.0	2.4	1.6	1.3	1.0	1.6
RO	31.8	27.7	18.3	10.6	7.5	5.6	2.6	1.9
SI	5.8	7.8	5.9	4.8	2.4	3.5	3.6	4.0
SK	4.0	-0.9	0.7	0.8	-2.2	-3.2	-0.5	0.1
FI	0.7	2.2	1.5	0.4	0.6	0.6	0.6	1.3
SE	0.4	2.5	2.2	1.3	-1.0	-1.5	-2.4	0.5
UK	-1.7	-0.1	0.1	-0.6	-0.1	-0.3	-0.4	1.8
TR	52.6	60.6	43.9	16.7	6.4	7.3	5.7	7.6
IS	0.9	5.7	7.9	-0.8	0.5	-0.7	2.4	4.4
NO	0.5	1.0	0.3	-0.8	-1.8	-0.4	-1.3	1.9
CH	:	:	:	:	:	:	0.1	0.3

Source: Eurostat, Harmonised indices of consumer prices (theme2/prc/prc_hicp_aind)

Growth in the EU-27's harmonised index of consumer prices for furnishings, household equipment and routine maintenance of the house was driven by price increases for labour-intensive services, such as the repair of furniture and furnishings (on average, 2.7 % per annum between 2000 and 2007), the repair of household appliances (2.8 % per annum), or domestic and household services (3.6 % per annum). In contrast, there was modest price growth for most consumer durables covered in this chapter, well below the inflation rate, with a reduction in the price index for household appliances (-1.1 % per annum).

5.3.2 Price levels

There were considerable differences in price levels for furnishings, household equipment and maintenance among the Member States. In 2007, these items were 20 % more expensive than the EU-27 average in Denmark. Price levels in all of the Member States that joined the EU since 2004 were below the EU-27 average, which was also the case in Greece, Germany, the Netherlands and Portugal.

Nevertheless, disparities in price levels for furnishings, household equipment and maintenance among the Member States narrowed during the period from 2000 to 2007. The coefficient of variation (a measure that indicates relative price dispersion) declined from 24.4 % to 18.2 % over the period considered. Price disparities for furnishings, household equipment and maintenance were considerably narrower among the EU-15 Member States, with a coefficient of variation in 2007 of 7.5 %.

Figure 5.8: Harmonised indices of consumer prices, EU-27
(2005=100)

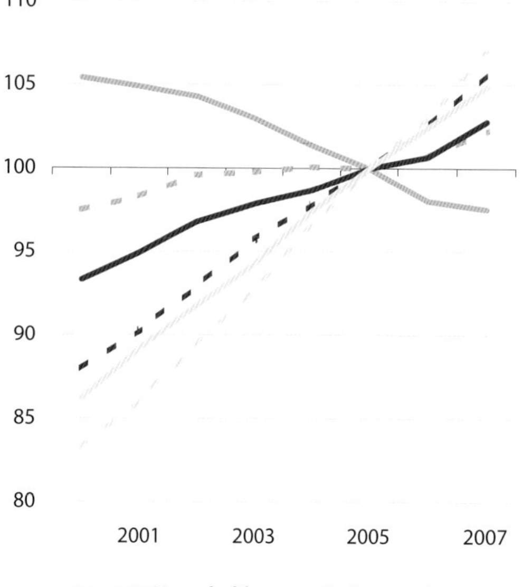

Source: Eurostat, Harmonised indices of consumer prices (theme2/prc/prc_hicp_aind)

Figure 5.9: Price level indices, furnishings, household equipment and routine maintenance of the house, 2007
(EU-27=100)

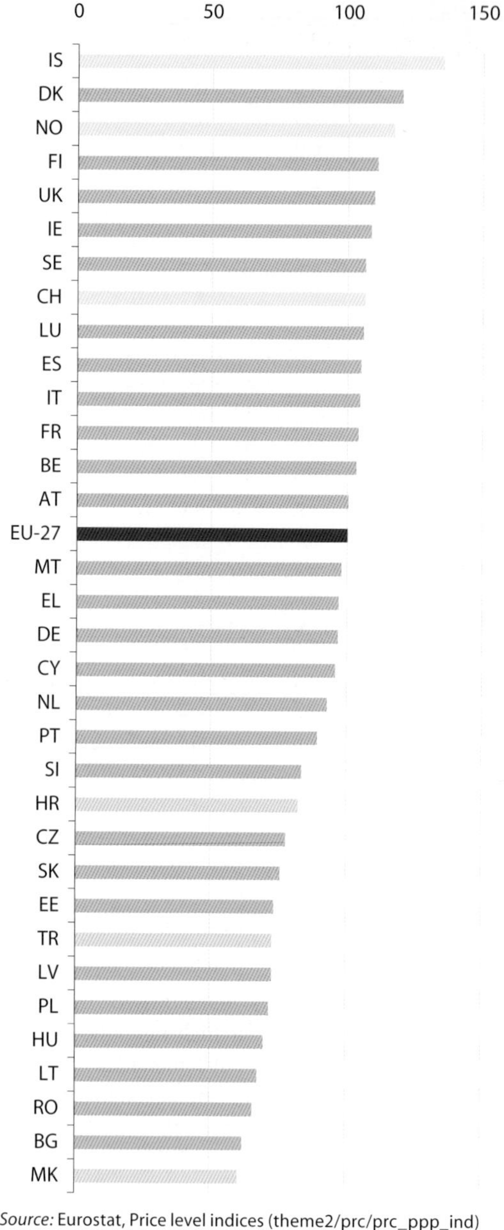

Source: Eurostat, Price level indices (theme2/prc/prc_ppp_ind)

Table 5.5: Coefficient of variation for price level indices, furnishings, household equipment and routine maintenance of the house
(%)

	EU-15		EU-27	
	2000	2007	2000	2007
Household furnishings, equipment & maintenance	11.7	7.5	24.4	18.2

Source: Eurostat, Price level indices (theme2/prc/prc_ppp_ind)

5.4 Consumer satisfaction and complaints

A 2008 consumer satisfaction survey included one section on buying household electrical equipment. In the EU-27, on a scale of 1-10 (higher scores reveal greater satisfaction), the average consumer rated their overall satisfaction with retailers in this domain at 8.3. The highest levels of satisfaction were recorded in Lithuania, Bulgaria, the Czech Republic and Romania, while the least satisfied consumers were in Italy, France, Sweden and the Netherlands.

The same survey reveals that 9.7 % of consumers in the EU-27 experienced problems when purchasing household electrical equipment in 2008. The most problems were reported in Finland, the Netherlands and Sweden, at just over 15 % of all consumers. Among those who faced problems in the EU-27 in 2008, the majority complained about product quality (51.9 %), while the other categories cited by at least 10 % of consumers included problems associated with delivery, the quality of service, or repairs. When asked if they thought their regular retailer would replace, repair, reduce the price or give them their money back if household electrical equipment that they had bought was defective or not fit for purpose, a majority of EU-27 consumers agreed (an average of 8.1 on a scale of 1-10).

Figure 5.10: Overall, to what extent are you satisfied with your regular retailer when it comes to buying household electrical equipment, 2008? (1)
(average, 1-10)

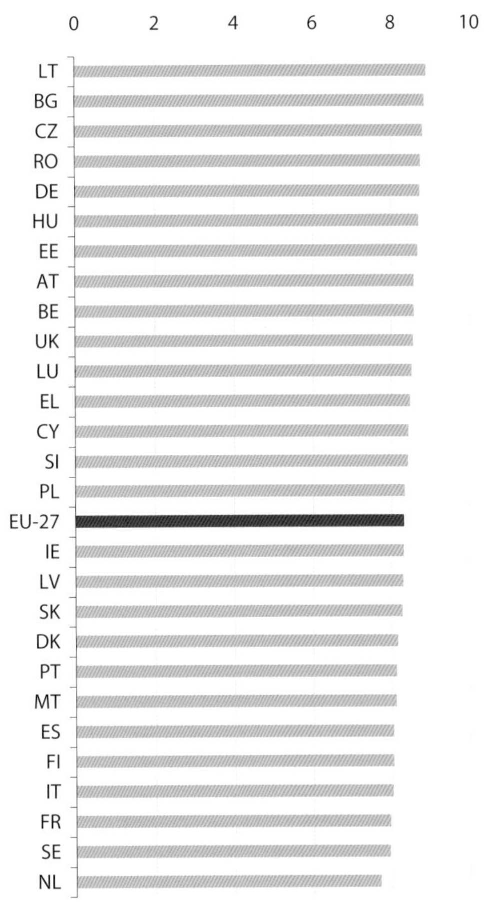

(1) Average on a scale of 1 (not at all satisfied) to 10 (fully satisfied).

Source: 'Retail satisfaction survey', IPSOS for the European Commission, August/September 2008

Figure 5.11: Do you agree that your regular retailer would replace, repair, reduce the price or give you your money back if household electrical equipment you had bought was defective or not fit for purpose, 2008? (1)
(average, 1-10)

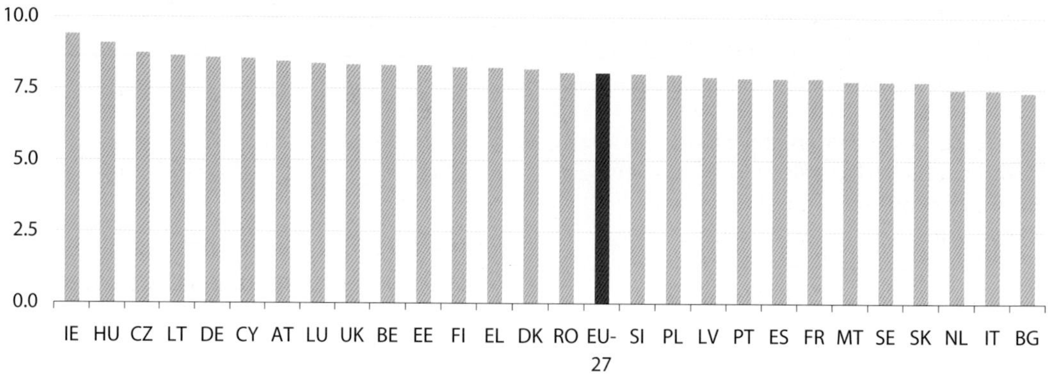

(1) Average on a scale of 1 (totally disagree) to 10 (totally agree).

Source: 'Retail satisfaction survey', IPSOS for the European Commission, August/September 2008

Figure 5.12: Problems faced by consumers when purchasing household electrical equipment in the past 12 months, EU-27, 2008 (1)
(% share of those experiencing problems, multiple answers allowed)

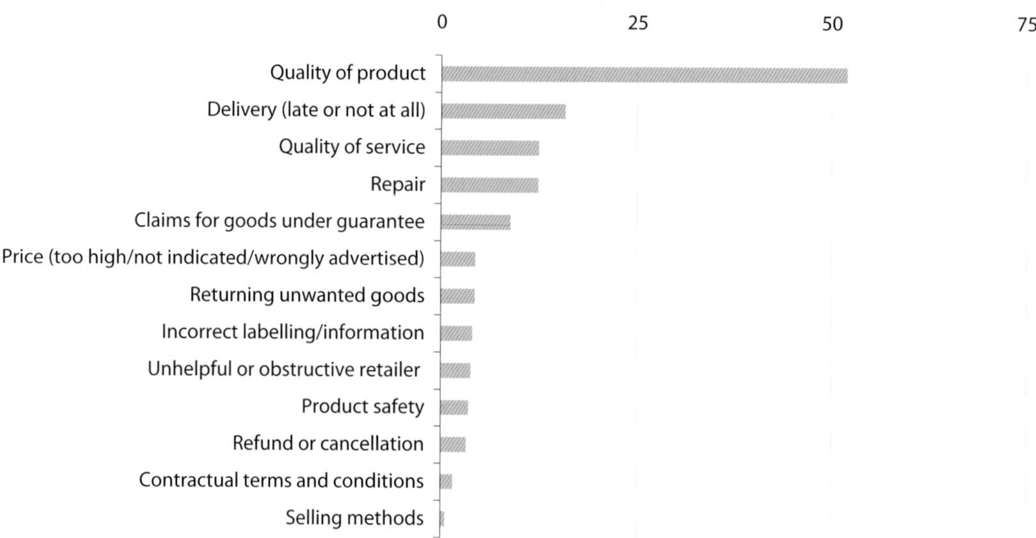

(1) When purchasing household electrical equipment in 2008, 9.7 % of EU-27 consumers reported facing at least one problem; note that consumers may have faced more than one problem.

Source: 'Retail satisfaction survey', IPSOS for the European Commission, August/September 2008

5.5 Quality

The same consumer satisfaction survey also asked respondents to what extent they agreed that household electrical equipment sold by their regular retailer was reliable (in other words, it worked well and without failure for a reasonable period of time) and to what extent it was safe. On a scale of 1-10 (with 10 for total agreement), the average score across the EU-27 was 8.2 for reliability and 8.4 for safety (see Figure 5.13). This pattern of consumers alluding to products being slightly safer than they were reliable was repeated in the vast majority of Member States, with the exception of Greece and Ireland.

Figure 5.13: To what extent do you agree that household electrical equipment sold by your regular retailer is reliable (i.e. it works well and without failure for a reasonable period of time) and safe, 2008? (1)
(average, 1-10)

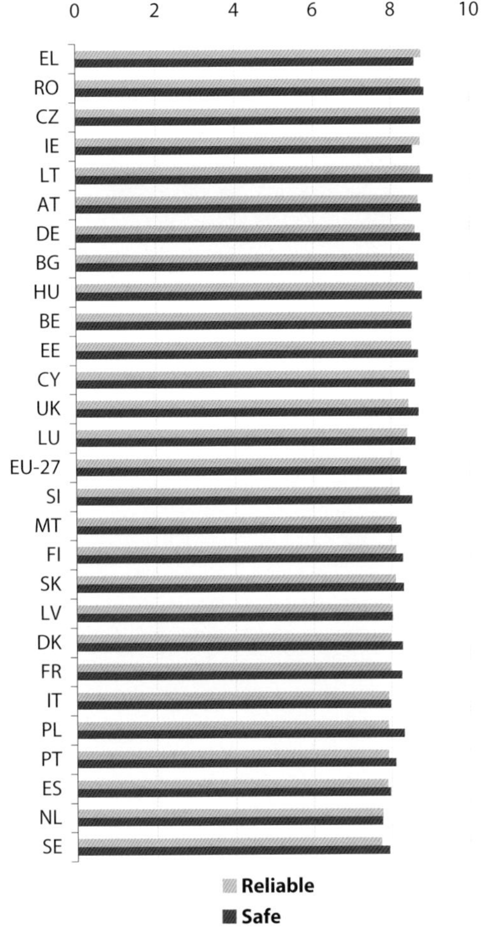

(1) Average on a scale of 1 (totally disagree) to 10 (totally agree).

Source: 'Retail satisfaction survey', IPSOS for the European Commission, August/September 2008

6 Health

Table 6.1: Availability of practising doctors, dentists, pharmacists and physiotherapists, 2006
(inhabitants per specified worker)

	Doctors	Dentists	Pharmacists	Physio-therapists
BE	250	1 214	874	417
BG	273	1 179	:	17 817
CZ	281	1 484	1 761	1 450
DK (1)	324	1 192	4 786	701
DE	289	1 313	1 753	968
EE	304	1 122	1 545	6 746
IE (2)	354	1 787	1 050	1 695
EL (1, 3)	203	828	:	:
ES (5)	278	1 908	1 096	1 688
FR (3)	296	1 489	876	981
IT (3)	273	1 588	1 335	816
CY	399	1 089	4 867	12 559
LV	343	1 479	1 697	8 626
LT	274	1 568	1 649	1 230
LU (4)	305	1 336	1 188	1 036
HU	329	2 014	1 253	4 421
MT (2)	261	2 146	827	1 545
NL (7)	270	2 016	5 790	474
AT	274	1 858	1 598	3 016
PL	459	3 034	1 690	2 112
PT (6, 8)	373	1 719	1 062	9 140
RO	463	2 036	2 177	:
SI	424	1 672	2 136	1 986
SK	316	1 987	1 779	:
FI (1, 8)	409	1 154	621	445
SE	280	1 208	1 380	835
UK	422	2 110	1 541	2 415
HR (12)	419	1 466	1 939	2 349
MK (9)	395	1 738	2 249	7 824
TR (10)	718	3 944	2 969	81 123
IS (11)	275	1 076	892	724
NO (11)	265	1 141	1 498	483
CH (12)	504	2 264	4 403	:

(1) 2005.
(2) Licensed instead of practising for doctors and dentists.
(3) Professionally active instead of practising for doctors, dentists and pharmacists.
(4) 2004 data for doctors, dentists and physiotherapists.
(5) Licensed instead of practising for dentists and professionally active for pharmacist.
(6) 2004.
(7) Licensed instead of practising for doctors and professionally active for dentists.
(8) Licensed instead of practising for pharmacists.
(9) Licensed instead of practising for doctors; professionally active instead of practising for dentists and pharmacists.
(10) 2003.
(11) Professionally active instead of practising for pharmacists.
(12) 2002.

Source: Eurostat, Health personnel (excluding nursing and caring professionals) - Absolute numbers and rate per 100 000 inhabitants (theme3/hlth/hlth_rs_prs)

The European Commission's activities in the area of health aim to complement those in the Member States, for example in relation to cross border health threats, patient mobility, and reducing health inequalities. In October 2007 the European Commission adopted a new Health Strategy, 'Together for Health: A Strategic Approach for the EU 2008-2013'. The strategy focuses on four principles and three strategic themes for improving health. The principles involve taking a value-driven approach, recognising the links between health and economic prosperity, integrating health in all policies, and strengthening the EU's voice in global health. The strategic themes are based on fostering good health in an ageing Europe, protecting citizens from health threats, and dynamic health systems and new technologies.

The analysis presented in this chapter focuses on healthcare, looking at the resources provided and levels of consumer satisfaction. The chapter concludes with a brief analysis of consumer's perceptions of their own health. The information on resources and patients are largely based on administrative data sources and therefore reflect country-specific ways of organising healthcare and may not always be completely comparable. In particular the types of tasks performed by some categories of professionals or health carers vary between Member States. The European Observatory on Health Systems and Policies (http://www.euro.who.int/observatory) supports and promotes evidence-based health policy-making through comprehensive and rigorous analysis of the dynamics of healthcare systems in Europe, and it provides an explanation of the national healthcare systems in a large number of countries.

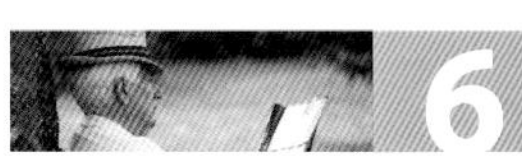

6.1 Access and choice

Data on healthcare form a major element of public health information as they describe the capacities available for different types of healthcare provision as well as potential 'bottlenecks' observed. The data on resources presented in Tables 6.1 to 6.3 refer to both human and technical resources, in other words staff and facilities. In most Member States there is an average of one doctor for every 250 to 500 inhabitants, and one dentist for every 1 000 to 3 000 inhabitants. On average, there was one hospital bed for every 173 inhabitants in the EU-27 in 2006, ranging from the highest availability of one bed for 121 inhabitants in Germany to the lowest availability of one bed for 348 inhabitants in Sweden.

Table 6.2: Availability of practising nurses and carers, 2006
(inhabitants per specified worker)

	Midwives	Qualified nurses	Qualified nurses and midwives (total)	Associate nurses	All nurses (qualified & associate nurses)	Nursing pro-fessionals (total)	Caring personnel
BE	1 936	:	:	:	160	148	:
BG	2 240	243	219	0	243	219	:
CZ	2 434	:	:	:	124	118	2 882
DK (1)	4 109	104	101	216	70	69	101
DE	4 842	131	128	460	102	100	:
EE (1)	3 171	160	152	0	160	152	1 952
IE (6)	:	:	66	:	:	:	:
EL	:	:	:	:	:	:	:
ES	:		243	308		136	:
FR (6, 7)	3 492	126	121	0	126	121	130
IT (6)	:	:	:	:	:	142	511
CY	:	:	:	:	:	:	:
LV	4 572	183	176	0	183	176	1 072
LT	3 497	140	135	0	140	135	567
LU	:	:	:	:	:	:	:
HU	5 157	218	209	709	166	161	380
MT	3 087	177	168	0	177	168	:
NL	7 446	391	372	166	116	115	:
AT	6 709	163	160	889	138	135	1 788
PL	1 810	196	177	:	196	177	:
PT (2)	0	2 181	2 181	314	274	274	2 660
RO	:	:	:	:	:	170	365
SI	27 539	545	534	174	132	131	826
SK (6)	3 475	:	:	:	166	158	592
FI (1, 6)	2 796	139	133	282	93	90	:
SE	1 385	93	87	:	:	:	:
UK (1)	1 923	137	128	446	105	99	591
HR (5)	2 979	214	199	:	:	:	:
MK (6)	1 585	:	:	:	349	286	4 993
TR (3)	1 464	886	1 447	:	:	:	:
IS	1 538	120	111	192	74	70	:
NO (6)	2 040	72	70	92	40	40	:
CH	:	:	:	:	:	:	:

(1) 2005.
(2) 2004.
(3) 2004, except 2005 for midwives.
(4) 2003.
(5) 2002.
(6) Professionally active instead of practising.
(7) France Métropolitaine.

Source: Eurostat, Nursing and caring professionals - Absolute numbers and rate per 100,000 inhabitants (theme3/hlth/hlth_rs_prsns)

Table 6.3: Availability of hospital beds, 2006
(inhabitants per specified category of beds)

	Available beds	Curative care beds	Psychiatric care beds	Long-term care beds (excluding psychiatric)	Other beds
EU-27	173	:	:	:	:
BE	149	230	547	5 535	2 792
BG	161	210	1 491	7 026	1 556
CZ	122	186	1 054	710	2 294
DK (3)	251	305	1 425	:	:
DE	121	161	:	:	477
EE	177	254	1 807	1 042	4 972
IE	191	375	1 107	653	7 004
EL (1)	211	258	1 151	:	:
ES	299	392	2 165	3 050	0
FR	139	274	1 079	870	686
IT	253	308	7 655	5 704	2 485
CY	268	288	3 720	:	:
LV	132	190	731	20 306	1 117
LT	125	196	974	674	2 600
LU	176	222	1 086	:	3 694
HU	126	181	2 610	1 282	815
MT	133	1 162	1 957	1 178	15 430
NL	228	352	764	0	4 309
AT (1)	130	165	1 620	974	:
PL	154	215	1 470	2 682	1 303
PT (2)	274	:	:	:	:
RO	152	219	1 255	817	:
SI	209	260	1 401	22 510	5 773
SK	149	205	1 194	1 216	5 782
FI	144	456	1 086	:	260
SE	348	473	2 036	3 836	77 231
UK (1)	257	323	1 357	21 745	145 877
HR (1)	184	294	1 060	906	:
MK	216	313	1 709	2 647	2 097
TR (2)	414	433	8 276	4 329	:
IS	:	:	:	897	:
NO	248	349	978	:	7 117
CH (1)	180	273	943	-	1 196

(1) 2005.
(2) 2004.
(3) 2003.
(4) 2002.

Source: Eurostat, Hospital beds (HP.1) - Absolute numbers and rate per 100,000 inhabitants (theme3/hlth/hlth_rs_bds)

Figure 6.1: People with self-perceived unmet needs for examination, 2006 (1)
(%)

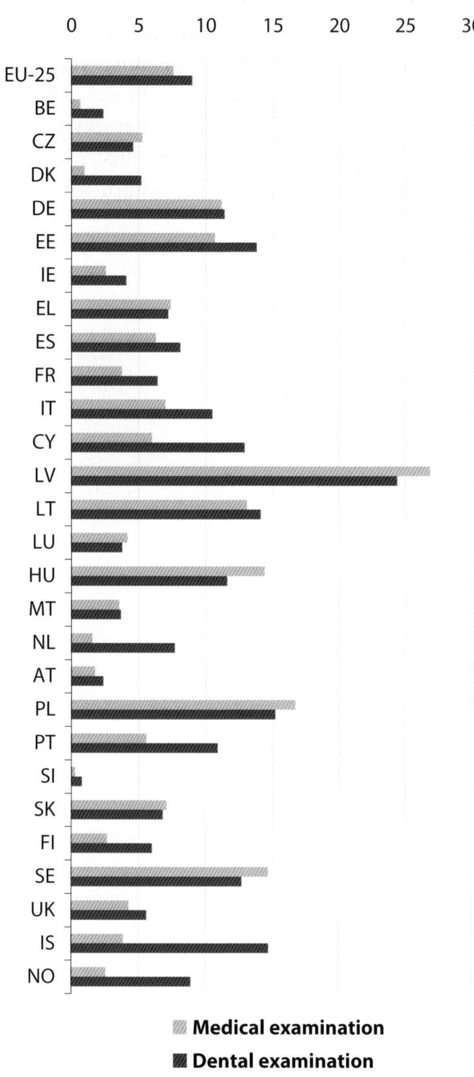

(1) Bulgaria and Romania, not available.

Source: Eurostat, People with unmet needs for medical/dental examination by sex, age, reason and income quintile (theme3/hlth/hlth_silc_08 and hlth_silc_09)

Just under one tenth of the population in the EU-25 in 2006 perceived unmet needs for health examinations, 8 % for medical examinations and 9 % for dental examinations. Slovenia had by far the lowest proportion of people with unmet needs for health examinations, and very low rates were also recorded in Belgium and Austria. In contrast, around one quarter of people in Latvia had unmet needs for either medical or dental examinations (see Figure 6.1).

From the perspective of individuals (as opposed to health professionals), the use of the Internet for health issues is almost entirely focused on seeking information related to injuries, diseases and nutrition, activities carried out by approximately one quarter of the population (aged 16 or over) in the EU-27. Direct contacts with health professionals through use of the Internet, such as making an appointment, getting advice, or requesting a prescription, was much less common, averaging less than 2 % of the population across the EU-27 (see Table 6.4 overleaf).

Figure 6.2: Organ donation rate, 2005 (1)
(%)

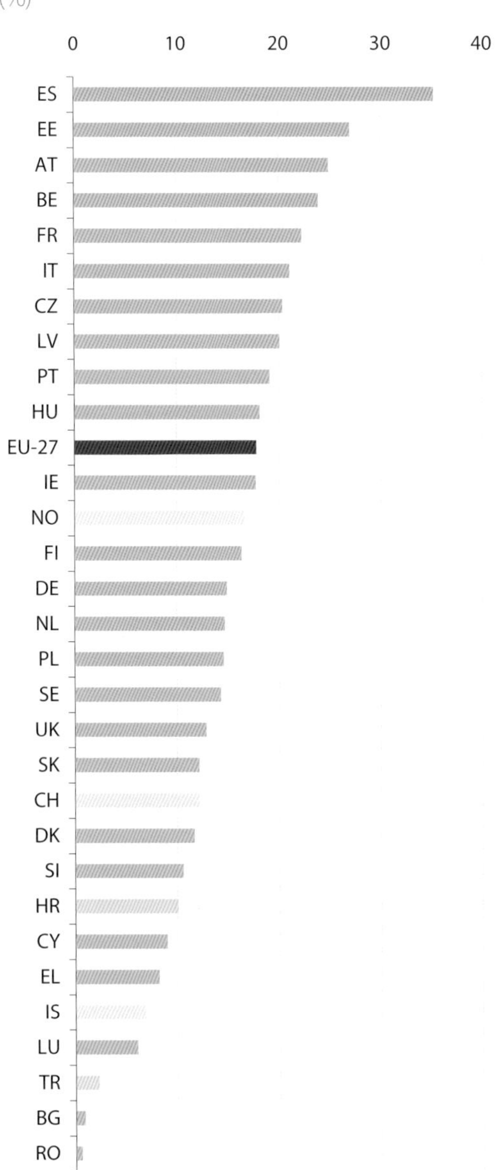

(1) Lithuania and Malta, not available.

Source: Council of Europe, Newsletter Transplant, September 2006, Vol. 11. N° 1

Table 6.4: Use of the Internet for health related information and prescriptions
(%)

	Percentage of individuals (aged 16 and over) who used Internet for:			
	Seeking health information on injury, disease or nutrition, 2007	Seeking medical advice with a practitioner, 2005	Making an appointment with a practitioner, 2005	Requesting a prescription from a practitioner, 2005
EU-27	23.8	1.7	0.5	0.4
BE	25.1	:	:	:
BG	5.0	:	:	:
CZ	10.7	0.3	0.4	:
DK	38.0	2.5	1.7	0.7
DE	40.9	:	:	:
EE	25.6	10.9	8.4	4.9
IE	12.2	0.6	0.1	0.1
EL	7.7	0.4	0.1	0.0
ES	21.4	2.4	0.4	0.1
FR	28.8	:	:	:
IT	15.7	1.6	0.4	0.2
CY	14.3	0.3	0.1	0.2
LV	11.2	0.5	0.1	0.1
LT	19.2	1.2	0.3	0.0
LU	48.4	1.6	0.7	0.8
HU	22.6	0.8	0.4	0.2
MT	20.3	0.4	0.3	0.1
NL	45.5	1.7	0.7	1.4
AT	27.4	0.5	0.8	0.3
PL	12.8	0.4	0.1	0.1
PT	17.8	0.4	:	:
RO	6.3	:	:	:
SI	26.1	:	:	0.0
SK	16.5	0.0	0.2	0.0
FI	47.1	2.7	3.4	:
SE	25.4	4.2	0.0	1.0
UK	19.8	4.4	:	:
MK (1)	3.1	:	:	:
TR (2)	3.1	0.3	0.1	0.0
IS	43.7	2.7	1.3	0.8
NO	36.8	1.1	0.9	0.3

(1) 2006.
(2) 2005.

Source: Eurostat, Percentage of population (aged 16 and over) using Internet to seek health information whether for themselves or others (theme9/science/isoc/isoc_pi/isoc_pi_f/)

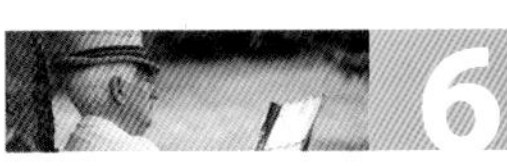

6.2 Consumption

6.2.1 Consumption volume

The output-related data of hospital activity refer to contacts between patients and the healthcare system. Hospitals comprise licensed establishments primarily engaged in providing medical, diagnostic, and treatment services that include physician, nursing, and other health services to in-patients and the specialised accommodation services required by in-patients. Hospitals may also provide out-patient services as a secondary activity. Measuring the output of healthcare in hospitals can be difficult, with comparisons between Member States complicated by differences in healthcare systems. This is further complicated as out-patient services (day care and day-surgery) expand as alternatives to in-patient services, with recourse to out-patient services varying within and between Member States.

Discharge rates of in-patients are often expressed as a number per 100 000 inhabitants, and among the Member States with data shown in Table 6.5 these rates were generally between 10 000 and 20 000 in 2006, in other words between 1 and 2 discharges for every 10 inhabitants over the course of a year. The average length of stay of in-patients is calculated from the number of hospital days of in-patients divided by the number of discharges (whether discharged or died). The average length of stay has fallen in recent decades, and was generally below ten days for the majority of the Member States shown in Table 6.5, with the exception of the Czech Republic, Germany, Lithuania and Finland.

Table 6.5: Indicators of hospital activity, 2006

	Discharges (per 100 000 inhabitants)	Hospital days of in-patients (number)	In-patient average length of stay (days)
BE	15 687	11 343 884	6.9
BG	21 474	12 450 927	7.5
CZ	20 799	22 785 822	10.7
DK (1)	15 936	5 031 080	5.9
DE	21 481	180 888 694	10.2
EE	18 307	1 881 689	7.7
IE	13 656	3 672 978	6.3
EL	:	:	:
ES	10 712	33 194 442	7.0
FR	16 367	59 783 332	5.8
IT (2)	15 347	66 714 349	7.4
CY	6 536	297 435	5.9
LV	20 970	4 126 345	8.6
LT	21 866	7 449 081	10.0
LU	16 720	581 456	7.4
HU	23 750	17 513 924	7.3
MT (3)	7 359	144 388	4.8
NL (2)	10 135	11 483 856	6.9
AT	27 119	19 997 560	8.9
PL	18 425	42 457 580	6.0
PT (2)	9 127	6 403 190	6.7
RO	22 954	38 959 920	7.9
SI	16 045	2 482 359	7.7
SK	19 941	8 830 222	8.2
FI	19 620	13 092 484	12.7
SE (1)	14 751	8 633 893	6.5
UK (1)	13 064	72 658 083	9.3
HR	14 151	6 709 117	10.7
MK	9 884	1 772 343	8.8
IS	16 416	267 339	5.5
NO	17 689	4 145 467	5.0
CH (2)	15 656	12 646 773	10.9

(1) 2003.
(2) 2005.
(3) 2007.

Source: Eurostat, Hospital discharges by diagnoses (ISHMT), in-patients, per 100,000 inhabitants, Hospital days of in-patients (ISHMT), In-patient average length of stay (ISHMT, in days) by region - Total (theme3/hlth/hlth_inpat/)

6.2.2 Consumption expenditure

In most European countries a large proportion of the population has statutory health cover either financed by taxes or compulsory contributions through non-profit insurance funds. Alternatively, or additionally, some consumers may pay for healthcare through the market, either by paying directly (out of their own pocket) or through private healthcare insurance schemes with premiums paid by individuals directly or provided as an employment benefit. Figure 6.3 gives an indication of the relative importance of out-of-pocket and private health insurance within current healthcare expenditure, with the situation in Cyprus (provisional data) standing out, as this was the only Member State (with data available) where such expenditure exceeded half of total current healthcare expenditure.

As noted, the level of healthcare expenditure recorded in household budget survey (HBS) depends heavily on the healthcare system in each country, as taxes and social security contributions are not considered as part of household consumption expenditure, and payments for health insurance made directly by households are considered as expenditure on insurance (see Chapter 12) rather than healthcare expenditure. HBS health expenditure may be high in countries where the cost of healthcare is paid by patients and then reimbursed, or to a lesser extent where the patient bears part or all of the cost of healthcare through cost-sharing arrangements or partly non-reimbursable costs. In contrast, low levels of expenditure on healthcare are recorded in the HBS for those countries where healthcare is free at the point of provision. HBS also records market payments for healthcare where people pay privately for their own care (as detailed in Figure 6.3).

Figure 6.3: Out-of-pocket and private health insurance spending: share of current health expenditure, 2005 (1)
(%)

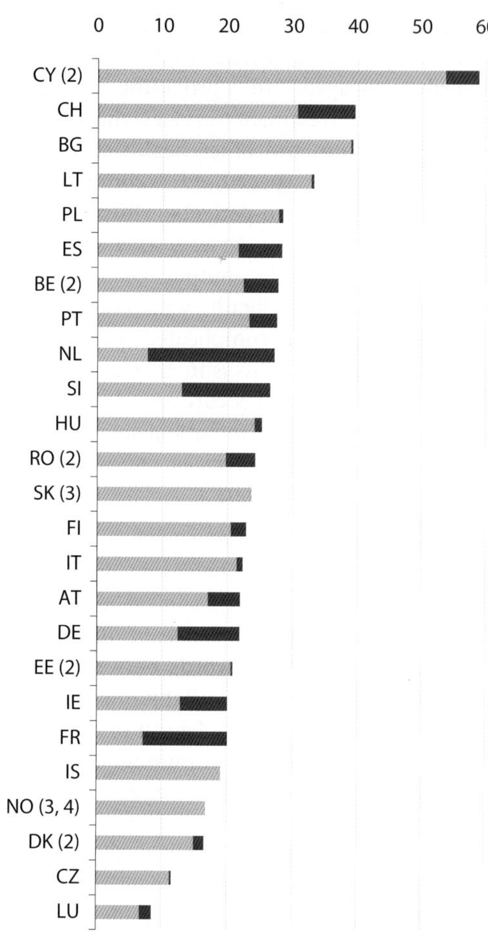

(1) Greece, Latvia, Malta, Sweden and the United Kingdom, not available.
(2) Provisional.
(3) Private health insurance, not available.
(4) 2004.

Source: Eurostat, Healthcare expenditure by financing agent (HF) (theme3/hlth/hlth_shat/hlth_sha_hf); OECD, Health at a Glance 2008: OECD Indicators, OECD

Table 6.6: Mean consumption expenditure per household, health, 2005
(PPS)

EU-27 (1)	796
BE	1 400
BG	305
CZ	239
DK	639
DE	1 024
EE	282
IE	904
EL	1 824
ES	577
FR	1 167
IT	1 132
CY	1 624
LV	394
LT	445
LU	1 351
HU	440
MT	869
NL	371
AT	946
PL	485
PT	1 264
RO	205
SI	356
SK	330
FI	852
SE	638
UK	383
HR	315
NO	872

(1) Estimate.

Source: Eurostat, Household Budget Survey (theme3/hbs/hbs_exp_t121)

Figure 6.4: Structure of consumption expenditure: share of health in total expenditure, 2005 (1)
(%)

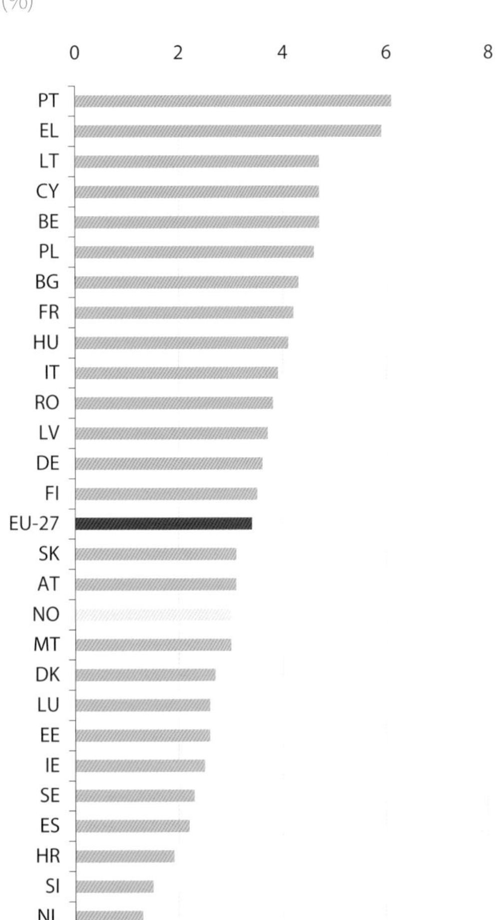

(1) EU-27, estimate; Czech Republic, not available.

Source: Eurostat, Household Budget Survey (theme3/hbs/hbs_str_t211)

HBS data from 2005 presented in purchasing power standards (PPS) shows that at comparable price levels, household expenditure on health within the EU-27 ranged from PPS 205 per household in Romania to PPS 1 400 in Belgium, with Greece (PPS 1 824) and Cyprus (PPS 1 624) above this level: as such, the level of household consumption expenditure on health was 8.9 times as high in Greece as it was in Romania (see Table 6.6).

Expenditure on health represented 3.4 % of total household consumption expenditure in the EU-27 in 2005, with the proportion of spending on health falling as low as 1.2 % and 1.3 % of the total in the United Kingdom and the Netherlands, while rising as high as 6.1 % and 5.9 % in Portugal and Greece (see Figure 6.4).

Figure 6.5: Structure of consumption expenditure: share of health in total expenditure, EU-27, 2005
(%)

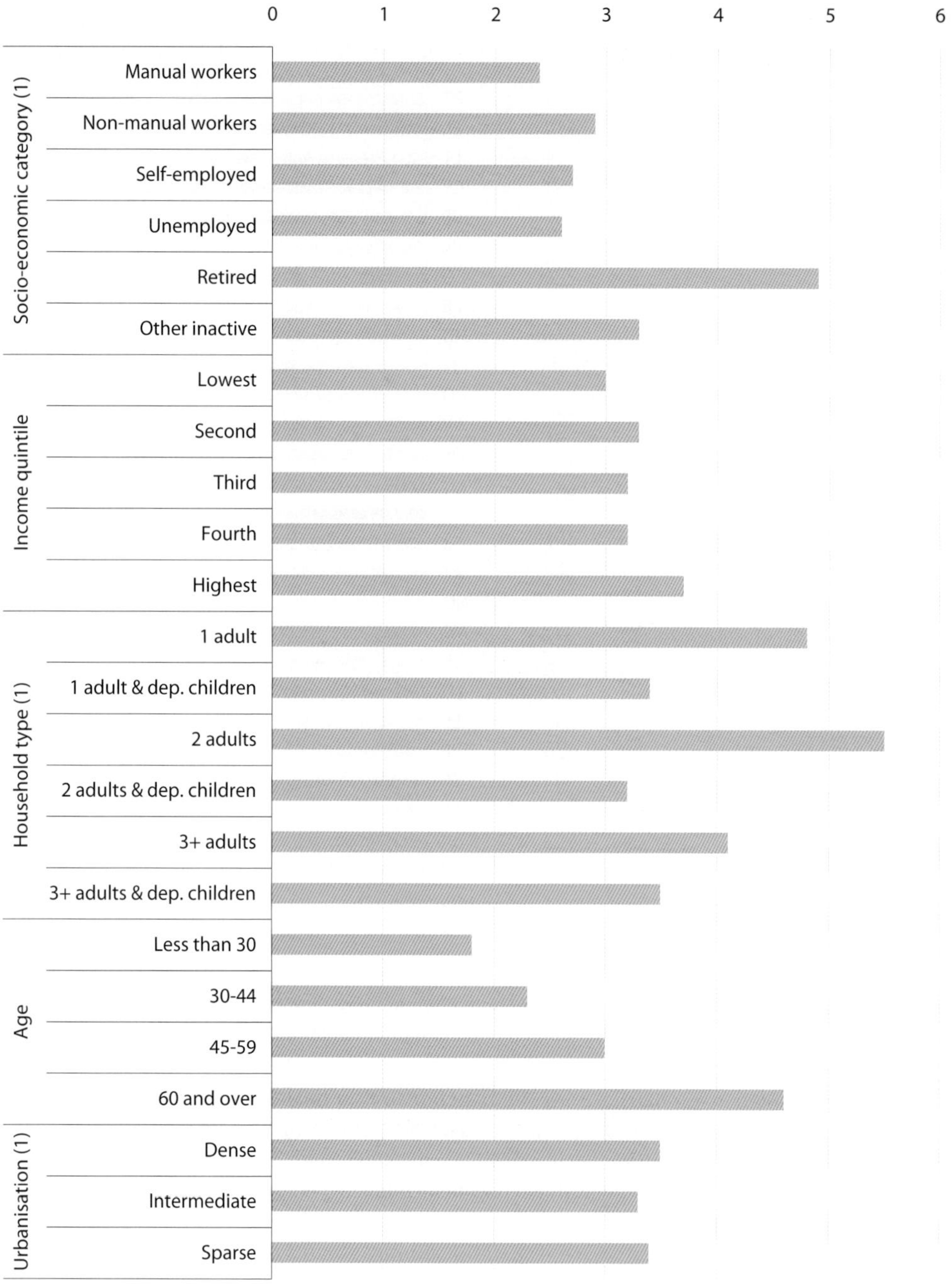

0 1 2 3 4 5 6

Socio-economic category (1)
Manual workers
Non-manual workers
Self-employed
Unemployed
Retired
Other inactive

Income quintile
Lowest
Second
Third
Fourth
Highest

Household type (1)
1 adult
1 adult & dep. children
2 adults
2 adults & dep. children
3+ adults
3+ adults & dep. children

Age
Less than 30
30-44
45-59
60 and over

Urbanisation (1)
Dense
Intermediate
Sparse

(1) Unreliable.

Source: Eurostat, Household Budget Survey (theme3/hbs/hbs_str_t221, hbs_str_t223, hbs_str_t224, hbs_str_t225, hbs_str_t226)

The share of total household consumption expenditure dedicated to health varies greatly depending on the type of household (number of persons, with or without dependent children), with shares generally lower for those households with children compared with those without. In this context, it should be noted that analyses by socio-economic category and age show the highest shares of health in total household expenditure recorded for retired persons and households where the head of the household was aged 60 or over, and it is likely that the particularly high shares recorded for households with one or two adults and no dependent children may be strongly influenced by the inclusion of retired, single persons and retired couples. An analysis by income quintile shows that the share of total household consumption expenditure dedicated to health was lowest for households in the lowest income quintile and highest for those in the highest quintile, suggesting an increased willingness of households with higher income to pay for out-of-pocket healthcare.

Just over half (55.6 %) of household consumption expenditure on health in the EU-27 concerned the direct purchase of pharmaceutical products, therapeutic appliances and equipment, while the remainder (44.4 %) was devoted to treatment services: 16.7 % for dental services, 13.9 % for medical services, 8.3 % for paramedical services and 5.6 % for hospital services.

Table 6.7: Structure of consumption expenditure on health, 2005
(%)

	Pharma-ceutical products	Other medical products	Therapeutic appliances and equipment	Medical services	Dental services	Paramedical services	Hospital services
EU-27 (1)	42	3	11	14	17	8	6
BE	30	0	9	26	11	13	11
BG	79	0	5	5	7	2	2
CZ	:	:	:	:	:	:	:
DK	30	0	19	0	30	19	4
DE	0	0	0	0	0	0	100
EE	67	0	8	4	17	0	4
IE	38	8	8	21	13	8	4
EL	17	2	2	23	30	12	15
ES	36	0	18	9	27	5	5
FR	31	2	19	24	12	10	2
IT	44	3	8	13	23	10	0
CY	30	0	4	23	9	17	17
LV	62	0	5	8	11	5	8
LT	83	0	4	2	6	2	2
LU	23	0	35	15	15	4	8
HU	66	0	10	7	10	2	5
MT	45	0	16	23	6	3	6
NL	23	0	31	15	23	8	0
AT	32	3	29	13	10	6	6
PL	67	0	4	11	13	2	2
PT	47	2	10	15	13	8	5
RO	79	0	3	5	5	3	5
SI	36	0	21	7	29	7	0
SK	63	3	9	6	13	3	3
FI	41	0	15	15	18	9	3
SE	32	0	18	0	36	14	0
UK	25	0	25	8	25	8	8
HR	58	0	11	5	16	5	5
NO	27	3	13	10	40	3	3

(1) Unreliable.

Source: Eurostat, Household Budget Survey (theme3/hbs/hbs_str_t211)

6.3 Prices

6.3.1 Price inflation

The EU-27 harmonised index of consumer prices for health rose by 24.1 % between 2000 and 2007, equivalent to an average of 3.1 % per annum. This was higher than the rate of increase recorded for the all-items consumer price index, which gained an average of 2.4 % per annum between 2000 and 2007. Annual price increases for health ranged between 1.7 % (2006) and 3.4 % (2002) for most of these years, with the 5.7 % increase in 2000 and 6.6 % increase in 2004 above this range. Several Member States recorded price decreases for health in 2007, with the largest price reductions recorded in Romania (-2.3 %) and Spain (-1.5 %). Price increases were generally less than 5 % in the other Member States, with increases between 7 % and 8 % in Portugal and the Baltic Member States, and an increase of 20.2 % in Hungary.

Between 2000 and 2007 the EU-27's index of consumer prices rose more quickly for hospital services (4.5 % per annum on average) than for out-patient services (3.6 %), or medical products, appliances and equipment (2.2 %) — see Figure 6.6.

Table 6.8: Harmonised indices of consumer prices, health, annual rate of change (%)

	2000	2001	2002	2003	2004	2005	2006	2007
EU-27	5.7	3.0	3.4	2.6	6.6	2.4	1.7	2.2
BE	0.5	1.1	1.5	2.4	1.4	2.2	2.8	-0.2
BG	18.3	28.9	28.5	5.2	0.7	9.6	5.9	4.5
CZ	1.6	4.0	6.1	4.6	2.3	6.9	4.7	3.7
DK	1.6	2.5	0.9	0.1	1.9	2.6	1.0	0.6
DE	0.8	1.2	0.6	0.4	19.2	1.9	0.8	1.4
EE	5.7	12.0	8.2	13.9	5.7	2.8	2.6	8.3
IE	6.1	6.7	10.1	7.7	6.0	6.2	4.4	3.0
EL	1.7	2.7	5.1	4.6	5.3	4.4	2.8	3.4
ES	3.0	1.8	2.7	2.1	0.4	0.9	1.3	-1.5
FR	1.0	-0.1	1.4	3.2	2.9	2.2	3.0	2.1
IT	2.9	-1.2	4.2	3.2	3.3	2.3	-0.5	2.8
CY	5.0	5.2	4.6	5.6	3.7	-0.5	1.9	4.6
LV	3.1	4.2	4.6	5.8	14.2	11.2	6.6	7.1
LT	-3.2	-1.6	1.1	4.2	8.4	8.0	6.7	7.1
LU	11.9	1.7	-5.1	-2.4	2.2	0.2	4.1	0.7
HU	27.6	11.8	8.5	7.3	7.1	8.2	4.4	20.2
MT	4.2	3.5	2.4	5.6	6.9	5.5	4.0	2.7
NL	2.9	6.8	6.5	2.7	9.6	1.2	3.6	1.3
AT	2.2	6.1	3.0	1.3	1.1	4.9	1.2	2.0
PL	10.5	6.5	4.6	2.0	2.0	2.7	1.2	1.9
PT	2.6	3.6	4.8	2.3	1.7	0.9	1.5	7.4
RO	59.0	37.6	19.5	13.9	-1.8	2.0	-1.2	-2.3
SI	15.4	12.3	6.7	5.8	1.5	-0.3	-1.7	1.7
SK	10.2	3.3	4.8	7.4	13.4	8.8	9.7	0.1
FI	2.7	2.6	5.0	3.1	2.1	1.9	0.7	-0.4
SE	4.5	5.0	3.9	3.0	4.0	1.8	1.0	2.6
UK	2.9	3.8	3.8	3.4	1.8	2.9	2.8	3.4
TR	58.3	49.3	38.3	26.9	11.2	4.9	4.3	4.8
IS	2.4	3.5	11.5	5.3	5.7	3.4	3.5	3.4
NO	3.4	3.1	4.2	4.1	4.9	2.9	3.5	2.3
CH	:	:	:	:	:	:	0.1	-0.2

Source: Eurostat, Harmonised indices of consumer prices (theme2/prc/prc_hicp_aind)

Figure 6.6: Harmonised indices of consumer prices, EU-27
(2005=100)

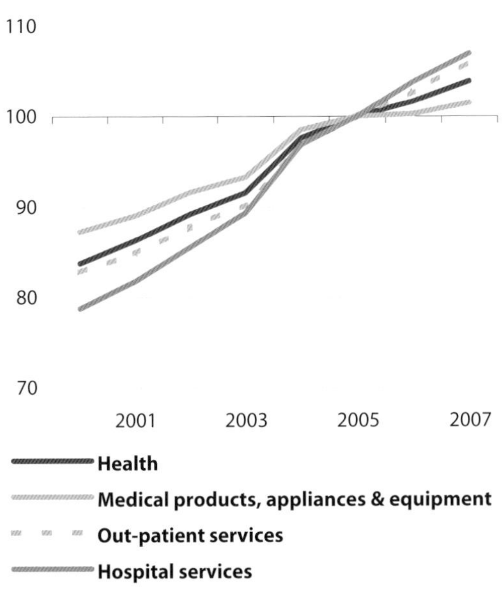

Source: Eurostat, Harmonised indices of consumer prices (theme2/prc/prc_hicp_aind)

Figure 6.7: Price level indices, health, 2006
(EU-27=100)

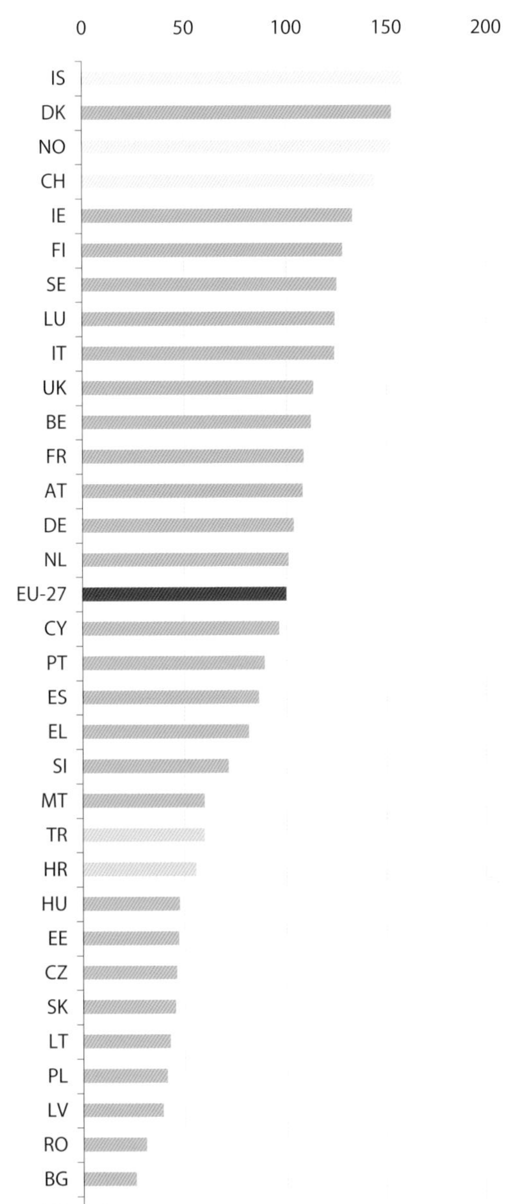

Source: Eurostat, Price level indices (theme2/prc/prc_ppp_ind)

6.3.2 Price levels

Price level indices for 2006 show that health goods and services were generally cheaper in the Member States that joined the EU in 2004 and 2007; Cyprus was the only exception to this general rule, having a price level index above that recorded for Portugal, Spain or Greece (see Figure 6.7). Among the Member States to join the EU since 2004, Cyprus, Slovenia and Malta were the only countries to report price level indices that were more than half the EU-27 average, while the lowest relative price levels were recorded in Bulgaria and Romania, 26 % and 31 % of the EU-27 average respectively. In contrast, Denmark and Ireland reported the highest price level indices for health, in the case of the former approximately 50 % above the EU-27 average and 5.9 times as high as in Bulgaria.

6.4 Consumer satisfaction

6.4.1 Consumer satisfaction with healthcare

Information on satisfaction with aspects of healthcare is available from two sources, the Urban Audit which can be used to present information on consumer satisfaction with hospitals and doctors in the capital cities of the EU's Member States, and a 2007 Eurobarometer survey on health and long-term care which looked at consumer attitudes towards hospitals and various types of healthcare.

More than half of the inhabitants in Bucharest, Vilnius, Sofia, Dublin and Athens were dissatisfied with their hospitals, in comparison with only about one tenth being dissatisfied in Brussels, Vienna or Amsterdam. Around half of the inhabitants of Vilnius, Bucharest, Sofia, Warsaw and Riga were also dissatisfied with their doctors. Among the capital cities of the Member States that joined the EU in 2004 or 2007 the lowest rates of dissatisfaction with hospitals and doctors were generally recorded in Valletta, Prague and Ljubljana, with Nicosia also recording relatively low rates of dissatisfaction with doctors.

Eurobarometer results, which are for Member States as a whole (rather than capital cities), show similar trends with respect to consumer satisfaction with hospitals, although there seemed to be less dissatisfaction in Ireland as a whole than in Dublin, and more in Hungary than in Budapest, although this could also be attributed

Table 6.9: Perceptions concerning hospitals and doctors, 2006
(%)

	Satisfaction with hospitals:			Satisfaction with doctors:		
	Synthetic index 0-100	Satisfied (rather & strong)	Dissatisfied (rather & strong)	Synthetic index 0-100	Satisfied (rather & strong)	Dissatisfied (rather & strong)
Bruxelles / Brussel	88	82	11	91	88	9
Sofia	36	30	53	48	45	49
Praha	73	56	21	79	71	20
København	83	72	15	88	85	11
Berlin	80	65	17	83	80	16
Tallinn	60	46	30	57	52	40
Dublin	47	45	52	74	73	26
Athina	45	42	51	58	55	39
Madrid	69	63	28	75	72	24
Paris	79	66	17	87	80	12
Roma	50	48	48	65	63	34
Lefkosia	57	52	39	78	73	20
Riga	47	39	44	49	46	47
Vilnius	36	31	56	40	38	56
Luxembourg	83	73	15	86	79	13
Budapest	49	40	41	71	67	27
Valletta	74	67	24	86	81	13
Amsterdam	90	80	9	92	88	8
Wien	90	81	9	89	86	11
Warszawa	41	32	47	47	42	47
Lisboa	56	47	37	67	58	28
Bucureşti	29	26	63	45	42	52
Ljubljana	72	64	25	73	70	26
Bratislava	51	38	36	69	65	29
Helsinki	72	64	25	73	68	25
Stockholm	83	71	15	84	74	14
London	68	63	30	78	75	21
Zagreb	53	49	44	68	66	31
Ankara	58	57	42	63	62	37

Source: Eurostat, Perception survey results (theme1/urb/urb_percep)

to methodological differences. An analysis of the results for the three other categories studied, namely dental care, medical or surgical care, and family doctors, showed some common features, notably the very low proportion of respondents in Malta and Belgium expressing the view that these healthcare services were bad, and the very high proportions who were dissatisfied in Portugal. The lowest shares of the population that thought that dental care was poor were recorded in Malta, Belgium and Sweden, while the highest shares were expressed in Portugal, Greece and Poland, where more than one third of respondents expressed dissatisfaction. Similar views were recorded for medical or surgical care, with Hungary joining Portugal, as one third of respondents in these two countries regarded medical and surgical healthcare as poor. The final category presented in Table 6.10 concerns family doctors, with Cyprus joining Malta and Belgium with a low proportion of respondents regarding family doctors as poor, and Bulgaria, Greece and Romania joining Portugal as the only countries where upwards of 25 % of respondents were dissatisfied with their family doctor.

Table 6.10: Attitudes towards healthcare, May-June 2007
(%)

	Hospitals			Dental care			Medical or surgical specialists			Family doctors		
	Good	Bad	Do not know	Good	Bad	Do not know	Good	Bad	Do not know	Good	Bad	Do not know
EU-27	71	25	4	74	21	5	74	15	11	84	14	2
BE	93	6	1	95	3	2	93	4	3	95	5	0
BG	43	49	8	62	29	9	58	29	13	69	28	3
CZ	80	18	2	88	11	1	86	8	6	82	18	0
DK	85	13	2	94	5	1	75	6	19	91	8	1
DE	79	16	5	89	10	1	77	12	11	88	11	1
EE	67	19	14	78	12	10	68	12	20	78	18	4
IE	64	30	6	77	13	10	66	17	17	90	8	2
EL	48	52	-	61	38	1	70	29	1	73	26	1
ES	82	15	3	62	32	6	81	13	6	89	10	1
FR	83	13	4	91	7	2	87	5	8	93	6	1
IT	63	35	2	61	32	7	75	22	3	77	22	1
CY	69	25	6	88	6	6	84	5	11	92	4	4
LV	55	32	13	78	11	11	61	16	23	72	21	7
LT	57	35	8	64	28	8	62	19	19	77	17	6
LU	82	14	4	91	6	3	80	8	12	90	7	3
HU	43	52	5	70	21	9	53	33	14	83	15	2
MT	84	13	3	90	2	8	83	3	14	96	1	3
NL	87	9	4	92	5	3	83	7	10	89	10	1
AT	92	6	2	91	8	1	87	8	5	93	6	1
PL	42	49	9	50	37	13	57	28	15	73	22	5
PT	58	40	2	51	44	5	59	33	8	62	36	2
RO	42	53	5	62	27	11	59	26	15	71	25	4
SI	76	19	5	71	26	3	75	12	13	84	14	2
SK	62	35	3	79	20	1	78	17	5	81	17	2
FI	88	9	3	82	14	4	85	5	10	81	17	2
SE	90	8	2	94	4	2	71	5	24	68	21	11
UK	77	18	5	70	23	7	71	8	21	88	10	2
HR	65	31	4	78	18	4	68	22	10	84	14	2
TR	68	30	2	60	24	16	69	17	14	53	18	29

Source: 'Health and long-term care in the European Union', Special Eurobarometer 283, European Commission

Figure 6.8: Attitudes towards own health, EU-25, 2006
(%)

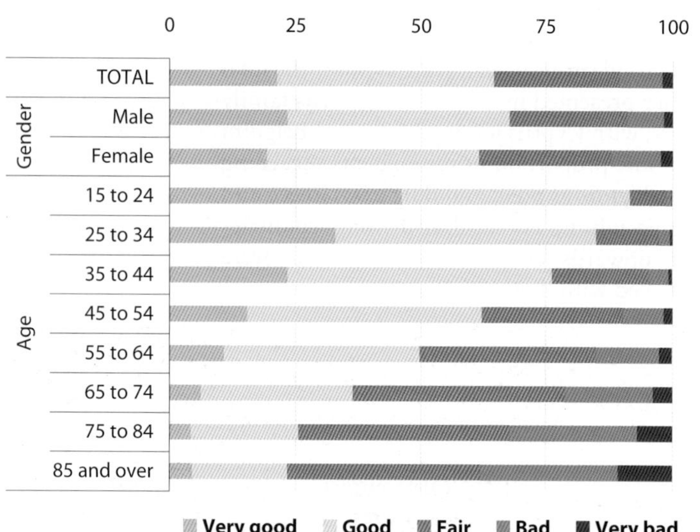

Source: Eurostat, Self-perceived health by sex, age and activity status (%) (theme3/hlth/hlth_silc_01)

Table 6.11: Attitudes towards own health, 2006
(%)

	Very good	Good	Fair	Bad	Very bad
EU-25	21.3	43.4	24.7	8.6	2.0
BE	28.5	45.8	17.3	6.8	1.6
BG	:	:	:	:	:
CZ	19.4	39.8	27.3	10.9	2.5
DK	41.4	33.6	17.2	5.7	2.0
DE	14.0	46.6	30.1	7.7	1.6
EE	7.5	45.9	31.6	12.3	2.8
IE	46.8	36.4	13.7	2.4	0.7
EL	51.6	25.2	14.0	6.3	2.9
ES	17.1	50.8	19.8	9.9	2.3
FR	25.2	44.2	21.1	8.1	1.4
IT	13.4	43.5	32.6	8.7	1.9
CY	48.7	27.5	14.5	7.7	1.6
LV	3.3	37.9	39.4	14.9	4.5
LT	6.3	37.2	38.4	14.9	3.3
LU	32.1	42.1	18.5	5.8	1.5
HU	13.2	35.1	31.4	16.1	4.2
MT	31.5	43.5	20.6	3.8	0.6
NL	21.1	55.8	17.9	4.4	0.8
AT	36.6	35.3	20.2	6.4	1.5
PL	15.5	39.1	28.1	14.2	3.1
PT	7.2	40.9	31.9	15.1	5.0
RO	:	:	:	:	:
SI	15.9	40.5	27.9	12.7	3.0
SK	23.1	29.1	29.8	13.1	4.9
FI	44.0	24.7	21.4	7.0	2.9
SE	34.2	41.8	18.2	4.8	1.0
UK	33.5	43.1	16.9	5.3	1.2
IS	50.8	31.0	13.8	2.9	1.6
NO	28.0	46.5	16.2	8.0	1.4

Source: Eurostat, Self-perceived health by sex, age and activity status (%) (theme3/hlth/hlth_silc_01)

6.4.2 Satisfaction with own health

A number of lifestyle factors can influence the health of a person over their lifetime, notably their level of physical activity, their diet, consumption of alcohol, tobacco and drugs. Furthermore, some risks to health can be linked with a person's living or working environment, for example, in terms of air and water pollution and noise, free-time activities within and outside the home, as well as the risk of transport accidents. Some of these issues are dealt with elsewhere in this publication, notably diet in Chapter 1, consumption of alcohol and tobacco in Chapter 2, and transport safety in Chapter 7, with the issue of toy safety addressed in Chapter 9.

Health status is often assessed through self-perception: these surveys are by their nature subjective and may be influenced by cultural issues. Results for 2006 from a self-perception survey are presented in Figure 6.8 and Table 6.11. Across the EU-25 nearly nine out of every ten people (89.4 %) described their health as fair or better, with close to two thirds (64.7 %) describing it as good or very good. Men were generally somewhat more positive about their health status, with a higher proportion reporting good or very good health and a lower proportion reporting bad or very bad health. The proportion of persons reporting good and very good health declined as age increased; this may influence the analysis by gender, as there are more older women than men in the population.

In ten of the EU-25 Member States, the proportion of persons perceiving their health to be bad or very bad was greater than the EU-25 average (10.6 %); of these only Spain (12.2 %) and Portugal (20.1 %) were EU-15 Member States. In Malta and Cyprus the proportion reporting bad or very bad health was below the EU-25 average, at 4.4 % and 9.3 % respectively, with only Ireland (3.1 %) reporting a lower proportion of persons with bad or very bad health than Malta.

For more information

Directorate-General for Health and Consumers: http://ec.europa.eu/health/index_en.htm

7

Transport

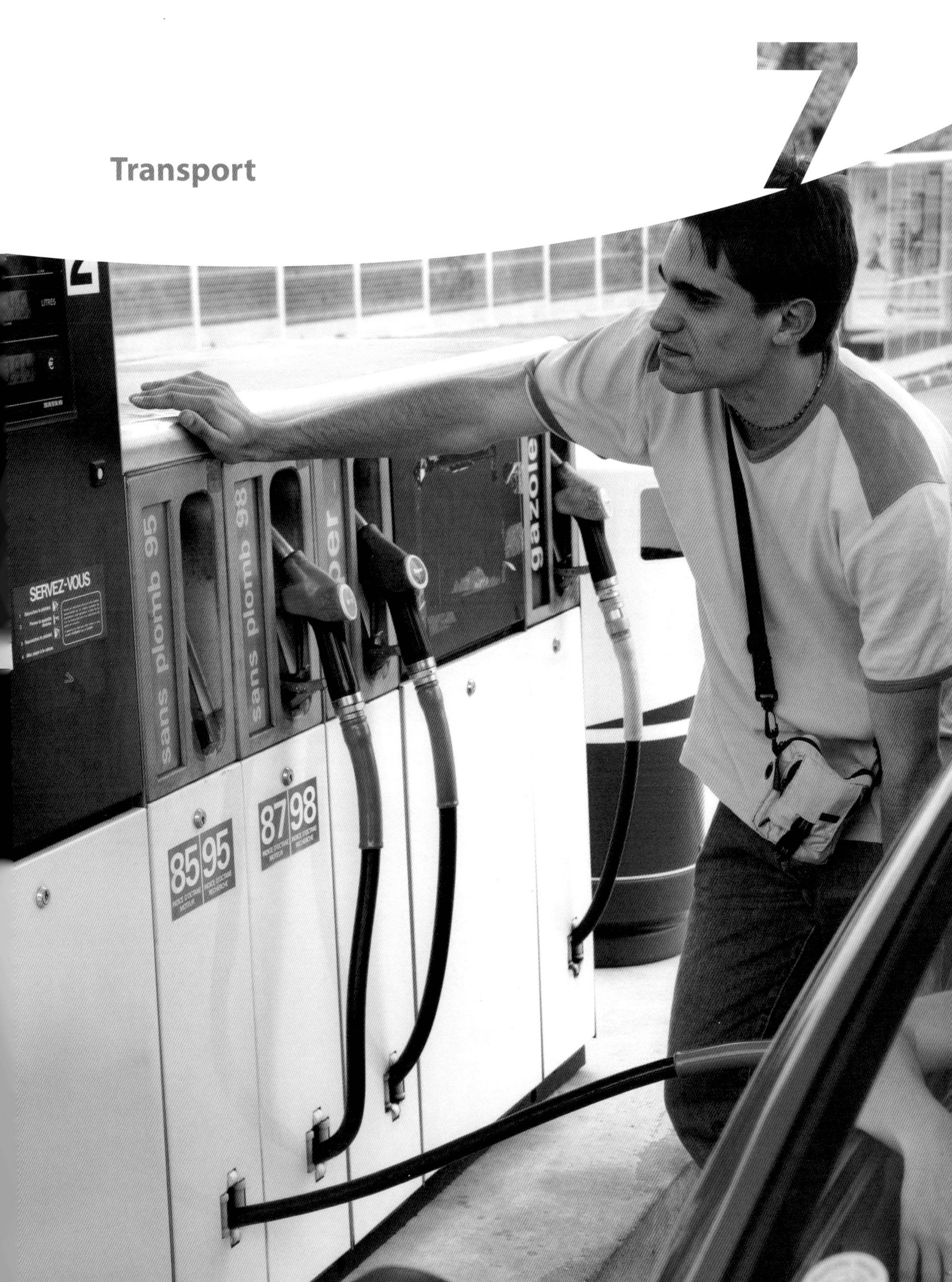
LITRES
SERVEZ-VOUS
sans plomb 95
sans plomb 98
gazole
85
95
87
98

In its Green paper 'towards a new culture for urban mobility' [19], the European Commission identifies towns and cities as a main driver of the European economy, as urban areas (with over 10 000 inhabitants) generate 85 % of the EU's gross domestic product; while more than 60 % of the population live in these areas. However, the Green paper states that an estimated 1 % of the EU's GDP or nearly EUR 100 billion is lost to congestion each year. It also suggests that urban traffic is responsible for 40 % of CO_2 emissions and 70 % of emissions of other pollutants arising from road transport. These delays and pollution that congestion entails are also reflected in higher accident levels in urban areas, increased health problems, more wide-reaching environmental problems (such as climate change), and negative economic losses both through bottlenecks in the logistics chain, as well as delays in getting staff to work.

(19) COM(2007) 551 final.

7.1 Access and choice

Transport therefore has an important impact on economic development, the environment and health, among other things through the transport networks in place, the interoperability of various modes of transport, and individuals' transport choices. Attitudes relating to EU transport policy were recorded in a Eurobarometer survey carried out in 2007. The survey revealed that a majority (53 %) of respondents across the EU-27 used individual motorised transport (car or motorcycle) as their main mode of transport (see Figure 7.1). A little over one in every five (21 %) respondents to the survey used public transport as their main mode of travel and a similar proportion (23 %) used bicycles or walked.

Figure 7.1: Main mode of mobility, May 2007
(% of respondents)

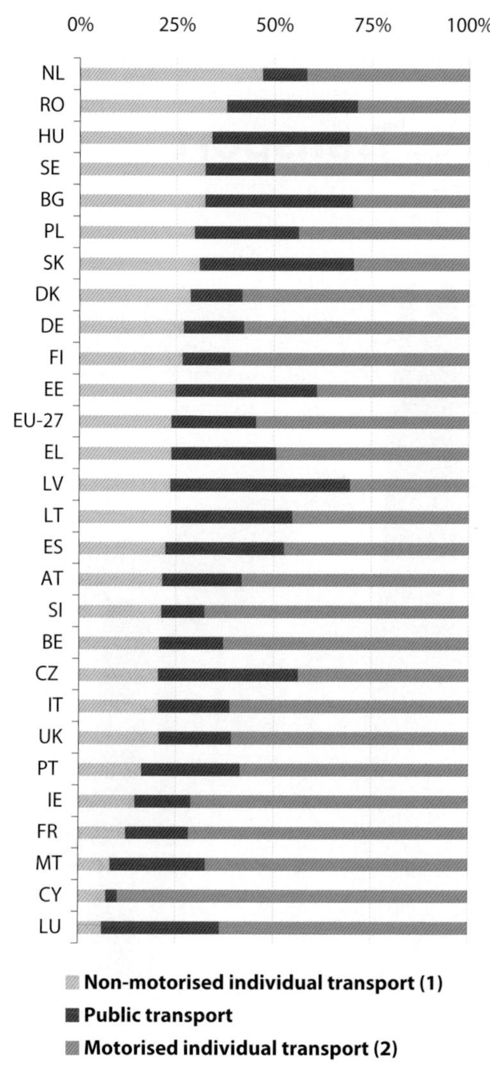

(1) Walking and cycling.
(2) Car and motorcycle.

Source: 'Attitudes on issues related to EU transport policy', Flash Eurobarometer 206b, European Commission

Among half of the Member States, the car or motorcycle was the main mode of transport for a majority of respondents. This proportion rose to about two thirds of respondents in Malta, Slovenia and France, and as many as nine out of every ten in Cyprus. Slightly less than half (46 %) of all respondents in the Netherlands declared that they walked or cycled as their main means of mobility. In Romania, Bulgaria, Slovakia and Latvia, between 26 % and 30 % of respondents used a car or motorcycle as their main form of transport, with a higher proportion of the population using either public transport or walking and cycling. Where car use (as a main means of transport) was lowest, it was relatively common to find that primary car users (those using cars as their main mode of transport) were the most resistant to the idea of switching to public transport; this was particularly the case in Romania, Bulgaria and Latvia (between 33 % and 41 %), as well as Hungary (44 %, the highest proportion). In contrast, primary car users in Cyprus, Spain and Slovenia were most open to change (see Figure 7.2). More generally, the receptiveness of primary car users to the idea of switching to public transport depended largely on the availability of better scheduling or better connections, although in some countries, such as France and Ireland, the issue of stops being closer to homes was also an important concern.

Figure 7.2: Receptiveness to a switch from car use to public transport use, May 2007 (% of respondents)

Source: 'Attitudes on issues related to EU transport policy', Flash Eurobarometer 206b, European Commission

The same Eurobarometer survey also revealed that the proportion of respondents across the EU-25 who felt access to local transport networks within towns was easy had risen from 68 % in 2002 to 80 % by 2006, and that just over two thirds (68 %) of respondents in the EU-27 thought that tax/price incentives and compulsory manufacturing changes would be the best measures to encourage the use of biofuels.

While the Eurobarometer survey looked at attitudes, the reality of access and choice can be analysed (to some extent) through network or passenger numbers for the main types of transport. An overview of the road network is given in Table 7.1, with a breakdown for the length of motorways and other types of road in 2005. The longest motorway networks were in Germany, France and Spain. Accessibility can be measured in terms of the length of the network compared with either the land area of a Member State or its population. Arguably, a consumer might be more interested in terms of the length of network per inhabitant – as this might give an indication of potential congestion. In Germany, France and Spain, the length of the motorway network was relatively high (between 0.15 and 0.25 metres) when expressed per inhabitant, compared with Member States like the United Kingdom (0.06 metres), Hungary (0.06 metres), the Czech Republic (0.05 metres), Poland or Romania (both 0.01 metres). In terms of all roads, more sparsely populated countries such as the Baltic Member States and Finland had relatively high levels of road accessibility per inhabitant (between 20 and 40 metres) compared with more densely populated Member States such as the Netherlands (8.3 metres) or Malta (5.2 metres). In contrast, the Netherlands, Belgium and Malta had the highest road density per square kilometre of land area (with between 4.0 and 6.6 metres).

A corresponding overview of the rail network is given in Table 7.2. France and Germany had by far the longest rail networks among the Member States in 2005, just over half of which was electrified. In terms of rail lines per inhabitant, the averages in France (0.47 metres) and Germany (0.42 metres) were much higher than, for example, the United Kingdom, Italy (both 0.28 metres) or the Netherlands (0.17 metres), this latter figure being the lowest density among the Member States. The highest rail network density levels (using the length of rail lines per inhabitant) were recorded in the Czech Republic (0.94 metres), Latvia (0.98 metres), Finland (1.1 metres) and Sweden (1.23 metres).

Table 7.1: Road networks, 2005 (1)
(kilometres)

	Motor-ways	Main & national roads	Secondary & regional roads	Other roads
BE	1 747	12 585	1 349	136 559
BG	331	2 969	4 012	11 976
CZ	564	6 154	48 792	72 300
DK	1 032	641	9 690	60 894
DE	12 363	40 983	178 134	:
EE	99	3 933	12 438	40 546
IE	247	5 168	11 645	79 447
EL	880	10 189	30 864	75 600
ES	11 432	13 983	140 231	:
FR	10 804	25 182	359 957	610 000
IT	6 542	21 524	147 364	:
CY	276	2 416	1 864	3 289
LV	-	6 949	13 233	49 647
LT	417	1 333	19 578	58 169
LU	147	837	1 891	:
HU	636	6 556	23 490	158 760
MT	-	184	0	2 043
NL	2 342	2 836	7 743	121 297
AT	1 677	10 566	23 685	71 059
PL	552	18 254	28 406	206 569
PT	2 341	8 161	4 500	63 880
RO	228	15 705	63 970	:
SI	569	972	4 853	32 091
SK	328	17 500	25 917	:
FI	693	12 580	13 480	51 436
SE	1 684	15 353	82 958	325 388
UK	3 634	48 927	122 228	238 144
HR	792	6 725	10 544	10 375
MK	208	698	3 806	8 566
TR	1 775	31 371	30 568	285 632
IS	-	4 265	3 965	4 799
NO	270	27 274	27 048	38 541
CH	1 361	398	18 094	51 446

(1) The definition of road types varies from country to country, the data are therefore not comparable; other roads sometimes include roads without a hard surface.

Source: International Road Federation, national statistics

Table 7.2: Rail transport capacity, 2005

	Seats (1) (thousand)	Stock of loco-motives (units)	Stock of coaches & railcars (units)	Length of lines		
				Total (km)	of which, electrified (%)	High-speed network (2) (km)
BE	287	1 518	3 251	3 544	84.0	120
BG	:	669	1 558	4 154	69.3	:
CZ	474	3 163	4 895	9 513	31.5	:
DK	127	464	1 473	2 644	24.1	:
DE	:	7 742	20 169	34 221	56.5	1 300
EE	2	170	183	959	13.7	:
IE	:	412	581	1 919	2.7	:
EL	25	289	564	2 576	3.2	:
ES	251	1 946	5 239	14 452	56.6	1 552
FR	1 279	7 354	15 879	29 286	50.4	1 893
IT	:	4 674	10 066	16 545	69.9	562
CY	-	-	-	-	-	-
LV	40	358	490	2 270	11.4	:
LT	36	365	467	1 771	6.9	:
LU	:	145	185	275	95.3	:
HU	200	1 385	2 787	7 950	35.8	:
MT	-	-	-	-	-	-
NL	242	2 078	852	2 811	73.4	:
AT	:	1 500	3 112	5 691	61.8	:
PL	586	4 723	7 725	19 507	60.8	:
PT	:	439	1 125	2 844	50.5	:
RO	:	2 186	3 310	10 948	36.3	:
SI	25	261	401	1 228	41.0	:
SK	88	466	1 808	3 626	42.9	:
FI	69	702	1 084	5 732	45.7	:
SE	122	622	791	11 017	70.2	:
UK	:	3 177	10 934	19 956	25.1	113
HR	:	377	579	2 726	36.1	:
MK	25	73	125	699	33.3	:
TR	88	735	1 312	8 697	22.1	:
IS	-	-	-	-	-	-
NO	122	289	191	4 087	61.9	:
CH	:	2 198	4 293	3 399	100.0	:

(1) Data are for 2004; the Czech Republic, Greece and Sweden, 2003; Denmark, 2002.
(2) Sections of lines on which trains can go faster than 250 km/h at some point during the journey in 2007.

Source: Union Internationale des Chemins de Fer, national statistics, Eurostat, Rail transport statistics

Table 7.3: Air passengers on board, 2007
(million)

	Total	National	International	
			Intra-EU	Extra-EU
EU-27	800.2	178.2	347.9	274.2
BE	21.0	0.1	15.1	5.8
BG	6.1	0.1	4.9	1.1
CZ	13.3	0.4	9.5	3.4
DK	24.2	2.0	15.9	6.3
DE	166.2	24.8	86.3	55.1
EE	1.7	0.0	1.4	0.3
IE	30.1	1.1	25.7	3.2
EL	34.8	6.7	23.8	4.3
ES	163.0	44.5	100.2	18.4
FR	120.3	27.4	51.0	41.9
IT	108.2	29.3	58.8	20.1
CY	7.3	0.1	5.9	1.3
LV	3.2	0.0	2.4	0.7
LT	2.2	0.0	1.8	0.4
LU	1.6	0.0	1.3	0.3
HU	8.6	0.0	6.5	2.0
MT	3.0	:	2.8	0.2
NL	50.8	0.1	30.2	20.4
AT	23.1	0.8	15.4	6.9
PL	17.2	1.1	13.0	3.0
PT	24.1	2.5	17.6	4.0
RO	7.0	0.6	5.4	1.1
SI	1.5	0.0	0.9	0.6
SK	2.3	0.2	1.8	0.3
FI	14.4	2.9	9.0	2.5
SE	27.3	7.1	16.0	4.2
UK	218.6	26.6	125.8	66.2

Source: Eurostat, Air transport statistics (theme7/transp/avia/avia_paoc)

There was a relatively high growth rate in air passenger transport during the ten years through until 2007 compared with other transport modes. According to estimates from the Directorate-General for Energy and Transport, the number of passenger-kilometres grew by about 50 % overall. There were 800 million air passengers carried on board planes in the EU-27 in 2007, more than a quarter of whom went from, to, or through the United Kingdom (see Table 7.3). Spain had a relatively high number of air passengers, almost as many as Germany, the vast majority of which were on intra-EU flights.

London's Heathrow airport had the highest number of air passengers (arriving, departing, or in transit) in 2007, the majority (56 %) of whom were on non-EU destination/origin flights (see Table 7.4). Amsterdam's Schiphol airport and Paris' Charles de Gaulle airport both counted a higher number of intra-EU passengers in 2007 than Heathrow. All the top 15 EU-27 airports (in terms of passenger numbers) recorded higher numbers of passengers in 2007 compared with 2003. The fastest rates of growth (around 45 %) were recorded at Dublin airport, Barcelona's Transoceania airport and Madrid's Barajas airport. Growth of between 30% and 40% was registered at Munich's F.J. Strauss airport, Milan's Malpenso airport and Rome's Fiumcino airport. Growth was relatively limited in comparison at Europe's largest airport, with a 7 % increase recorded for London Heathrow.

Table 7.4: Air passengers arriving, departing and in transit by top airport, 2007
(million)

	Total	National	International	
			Intra-EU	Extra-EU
London Heathrow	68.3	5.8	24.2	38.3
Paris Charles De Gaulle	59.5	5.2	25.7	28.7
Frankfurt	54.5	6.7	20.7	27.1
Madrid Barajas	51.4	22.6	17.5	11.3
Amsterdam Schiphol	47.8	0.1	27.5	20.2
London Gatwick	35.3	4.1	18.8	12.4
Munchen F.J. Strauss	34.1	10.0	15.1	8.9
Roma Fiumcino	33.6	13.8	12.6	7.2
Barcelona Transoceanico	32.8	15.1	14.4	3.3
Paris Orly	26.4	15.3	5.6	5.4
Milano Malpensa	24.0	4.0	11.6	8.3
London Stansted	23.8	2.6	19.6	1.6
Dublin	23.3	1.1	19.9	2.3
Palma de Mallorca	23.1	6.6	15.7	0.9
Manchester	22.3	3.5	12.4	6.5

(1) The Czech Republic, Ireland, Greece, Italy, Malta, Austria, Poland and Romania, 2006.

Source: Eurostat, Air transport statistics (theme7/transp/avia/avia_tf)

Table 7.5: Top-15 ports in terms of passenger transport - numbers of passengers embarked and disembarked, 2006
(million)

		Total	Growth 2001-2006 (%)
Dover	UK	14.0	-12.3
Paloukia Salaminas	EL	12.0	230.6
Perama	EL	12.0	230.6
Piraeus	EL	11.5	40.1
Calais	FR	11.5	-20.3
Messina	IT	10.8	-6.7
Helsingborg	SE	10.8	-8.5
Helsingør	DK	10.7	-6.9
Reggio di Calabria	IT	10.7	-7.3
Helsinki	FI	8.5	-5.1
Stockholm	SE	8.1	15.0
Napoli	IT	6.8	-3.6
Rødby Færgehavn	DK	6.8	12.6
Puttgarden	DE	6.8	13.5
Tallinn	EE	6.4	12.3

Source: Eurostat, Maritime transport statistics (theme7/transp/mar/mar_tf)

Figure 7.3: In which of the following places have you or has a member of your household bought a new car/motorcycle last, EU-27, 2008?
(%)

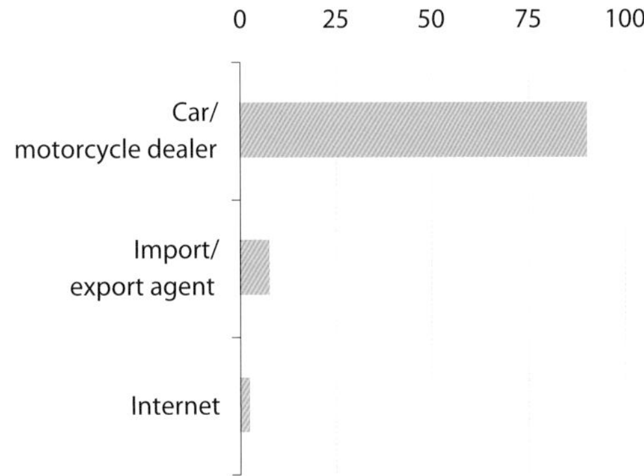

Source: 'Retail satisfaction survey', IPSOS for the European Commission, August/September 2008

On certain routes, consumers have the possibility to take a ferry as an alternative to road, rail or air transport. Among all the ports in the EU-27, Dover on the English Channel handled the greatest number of passengers in 2006; some 14 million passengers embarked or disembarked (see Table 7.5), although this was about one eighth (-12.3 %) less than the level recorded in 2001 and a third lower (-34.1 %) than in 1997. Passenger numbers through Dover's main connecting port of Calais in France were also down sharply (-42.9 %) between 1997 and 2006, in part reflecting the emergence of rail and air transport alternatives (such as the Channel tunnel and cheaper air flights). Indeed, passenger numbers were lower on a number of key sea routes in the period between 2001 and 2006 (such as between Helsingborg and Helsingør, in part due to the opening of the Øresund fixed link, or Reggio di Calabria and Messina). In contrast, there was relatively strong growth in passenger numbers through Stockholm, Rødby Færgehavvn, Puttgarden and Tallinn.

The vast majority of European consumers use car or motorcycle dealers to purchase a new vehicle. The EU-27 average in 2008, according to a consumer satisfaction survey, was close to 90 %, while almost 8 % of consumers used an import/export agent, and 2.5 % used the Internet.

Among the Member States there was a split between the EU-15 Member States and those Member States that joined the EU since 2004, as the latter reported a far higher recourse to making purchases through import/export agents (on average 27.3 % of consumers) compared with those living in the EU-15 Member States (4.2 %). This likely reflects, to some degree, a lack of showrooms for certain brands (smaller countries may lack the necessary critical mass of clients). However, as most consumers only buy a handful of new vehicles during a lifetime, it is also important to consider that the data likely reflect purchasing patterns over a lengthy period of time (maybe going back a couple of decades), and that considerable changes to the retail distribution of motor vehicles may have taken place in the meantime in many of the Member States that joined the EU since 2004.

7.2 Consumption

7.2.1 Ownership and consumption volume

With an estimated 230 million cars in use in the EU-27 in 2006 (see Table 7.6), it is perhaps unsurprising to find that cars accounted for the highest share of distance travelled using passenger transport. In total, cars accounted for a little under three quarters (74.5 %) of all passenger-kilometres [20] travelled in the EU-27 in 2006 (see Table 7.7). This was a lower proportion than in the United States (85.7 %), but considerably higher than in Japan (56.6 %) or China (53.2 %), where rail travel accounted for around a third of all passenger-kilometres.

([20]) Kilometres travelled by car, bus and coach, railway, tram and metro, waterborne means and aeroplane.

The number of passenger kilometres travelled by car within the EU-27 increased steadily during the period between 1995 and 2006 (up 19.4 % overall), and at a faster rate than any other form of land transport, except for motorcycles (24.6 % growth). By 2006, 82.3 % of all land transport passenger-kilometres were made by car, a share that rose to over 90 % in Lithuania and in Slovenia. The Czech Republic (69.4 %), Romania (69.3 %), Bulgaria (68.9 %) and Hungary (61.1 %) were the only Member States where the car accounted for less than 70 % of total land transport passenger-kilometres.

Table 7.6: Road vehicles, 2006
(thousand)

	New vehicle registrations					Stock		
		Goods vehicles						
	Cars (1)	Light (<3.5t)	Commercial (>3.5t-<16t)	Heavy (>16t)	Buses and coaches	Cars	Goods vehicles	Buses and coaches
EU-27	15 557	1 955	:	:	:	229 954	32 249	797.9
BE	524.8	60.2	3.0	7.8	1.1	4 976	670	15.3
BG	43.5	10.0	:	:	0.0	1 768	226	22.8
CZ	132.5	16.2	3.3	6.5	1.0	4 109	491	21.1
DK	162.6	62.8	0.8	5.2	3.2	2 020	509	14.6
DE	3 148.2	197.5	38.4	62.8	5.7	46 570	2 804	83.5
EE	30.9	3.7	0.1	1.4	0.2	554	93	5.4
IE	186.5	39.5	3.1	3.7	0.9	1 802	319	8.0
EL	279.8	23.7	1.2	1.0	0.5	4 543	1 220	26.9
ES	1 614.8	273.9	8.6	32.4	3.6	20 637	5 033	58.3
FR	2 064.5	439.2	9.7	43.6	5.9	31 002	5 345	92.2
IT	2 490.6	231.4	10.2	25.6	4.8	35 297	4 332	96.1
CY	22.9	<-------------3.7------------->			0.0	373	116	3.2
LV	32.5	2.5	0.2	1.9	0.2	822	121	10.6
LT	21.1	4.1	0.2	2.9	0.3	1 592	136	15.1
LU	52.6	3.1	0.2	1.3	0.2	315	31	1.4
HU	173.0	:	:	:	:	2 954	444	17.7
MT	6.2	<-------------0.6------------->			0.0	218	46	1.1
NL	504.2	63.9	3.3	16.7	0.8	7 230	996	10.8
AT	296.4	30.4	1.0	6.6	0.8	4 205	364	9.3
PL	293.3	38.6	5.2	10.7	1.5	13 384	2 393	83.5
PT	201.9	64.3	1.3	4.1	0.7	4 290	1 320	*15.0*
RO	312.5	30.5	3.6	4.2	2.5	3 603	545	40.4
SI	65.5	6.0	0.4	1.7	0.1	980	70	2.3
SK	59.7	19.5	0.9	3.5	0.5	1 334	189	8.8
FI	125.6	16.5	1.3	2.7	0.4	2 506	376	11.2
SE	306.8	39.6	0.9	5.4	1.3	4 202	480	13.6
UK	2 404.0	322.3	18.3	34.5	14.3	28 667	3 582	109.6
HR	114.4	:	:	:	:	1 436	170	4.9
MK	:	:	:	:	:	*260*	*18*	*2.3*
TR	540.0	:	:	:	:	6 141	2 405	533.5
IS	16.2	2.5	0.2	0.3	0.1	197	28	1.9
NO	129.2	42.6	1.8	4.0	0.8	2 084	489	27.0
CH	285.6	23.0	1.1	3.7	1.1	3 900	314	46.4

(1) Data are for 2007; Croatia, 2006; Turkey, 2005.

Source: national statistics, United Nations Economic Commission for Europe, Association des Constructeurs Européens d'Automobiles

Table 7.7: World passenger and freight transport, 2006

	Passenger transport (1) (billion pkm)						Freight transport (2) (billion tkm)				
	Car	Bus/ coach	Rail	Tram/ metro	Water-borne	Air (3)	Road	Rail	Inland waterway	Oil pipeline	Sea (3)
EU-27	4 602	523	384	84	40	*547*	*1 888*	435	138	*135*	*1 545*
US	7 254	227	23	18	1	939	1 888	2 531	468	835	385
Japan	738	88	391	:	4	83	335	23	:	:	212
China	929	:	606	:	7	205	869	2 073	1 112	109	3 855
Russia	:	139	177	55	1	94	201	1 951	58	2 499	48

(1) United States, 2005, except rail, tram/metro and waterborne, 2004; Japan and China, 2005; Japan, passenger cars includes light vehicles; China, passenger cars includes buses and coaches.
(2) United States, Japan and China, 2005.
(3) Domestic/intra EU-27.

Source: Eurostat, Japan Statistics Bureau, US Bureau of Transportation Statistics, Goskom STAT (Russia), National Bureau of Statistics of China, International Transport Forum

Table 7.8: Average time spent per day travelling (1)
(minutes)

	Walking		Travel to work		Travel for shopping		Transporting a child		Travel for leisure activities	
	Men	Women	Men	Women	Men	Women	Men	Women	Men	Women
BE	12	11	25	15	16	18	3	4	15	16
BG	16	14	23	17	12	14	1	1	21	13
DE	13	15	27	13	16	19	2	4	34	33
EE	10	10	28	20	13	16	1	3	22	18
ES	39	32	31	18	7	12	2	6	28	24
FR	20	17	24	15	-	-	2	5	-	-
IT	23	17	32	15	12	17	2	6	36	27
LV	12	15	37	24	12	20	1	3	26	23
LT	8	8	28	20	13	19	1	1	23	19
PL	17	12	23	14	14	19	1	3	27	25
SI	19	18	21	16	11	14	2	3	28	23
FI	12	13	18	14	11	14	2	3	33	31
SE	9	13	23	17	16	17	3	5	37	35
UK	4	3	29	17	16	22	3	9	36	34
NO	13	13	26	18	14	14	2	3	36	33

(1) Data are taken from national time use surveys (TUS) conducted between 1998 and 2004 and refer to men and women aged 20 to 74 years; data only shown for those countries participating in the survey; all remaining Member States, not available.

Source: Harmonised European Time Use Survey [online database version 2.0]; created 2005-2007 by Statistics Finland and Statistics Sweden [reference date 2007-10-01]; (https://www.testh2.scb.se/tus/tus/)

Road travel was much less dominant in terms of freight transport within the EU-27, reflecting the global nature of trade, geographical limitations, as well as the high cost of moving bulky, low valued items by road. Road transport accounted for 45.6 % of all freight transport-kilometres, somewhat higher than the share for sea transport (37.3 %). Indeed, among the trading partners presented in Table 7.7, Japan was the only country to report that road transport (58.8 %) accounted for more than half of all freight movements. In the United States, rail transport accounted for the highest proportion (41.4 %) of freight transport-kilometres. In China, both sea transport (48.1 %) and rail (25.8 %) accounted for a higher share of freight transport than road (10.8 %), while in Russia, oil pipelines (52.5 %) and rail (41.0 %) accounted the overwhelming majority of freight transport-kilometres in 2006.

7.2.2 Frequency and time spent in travel

Individuals may travel on a daily basis for a variety of reasons, including trips to and from work or school, shopping, or leisure activities. Time use surveys give an indication of the amount of time spent per day spent travelling by adults aged between 20 and 74 years old (see Table 7.8). The amount of time spent going to and from work each day was lowest in Finland for men (18 minutes on average) and in Germany for women (13 minutes on average), but highest in Latvia for both men (37 minutes) and women (24 minutes). Time spent by men travelling to leisure activities varied from 15 minutes (on average) in Belgium, to 37 minutes in Sweden, with a similar range (albeit from a low in Bulgaria) for women. Time spent travelling to the shops and in transporting children was generally higher among women than among men. Women in the United Kingdom spent almost twice as long travelling for shopping as women in Spain, and also spent longer than others transporting children.

7.2.3 Consumption expenditure

Average household consumption expenditure on transport in the EU-27 was EUR 1 800 per person in 2006. Among the Member States for which data are available, national averages varied widely, from EUR 400 per person in Poland and Slovakia to EUR 5 400 per person in Luxembourg (see Table 7.9). Compared with average expenditure in 2000, the sharpest rises were recorded in Estonia, Lithuania, Hungary, Romania and Slovakia, albeit from among the lowest levels. Where detailed data are available, these strong rises appeared to result from both sharp increases in the volume component of final consumption expenditure on transport, particularly in Estonia where the volume of consumption more than doubled, as well as from price increases (see Figure 7.4). Apart from the United Kingdom, where the price component remained almost unchanged, both the price and volume components of final consumption of transport increased during the period between 2000 and 2006 across all of the Member States for which data are available.

Table 7.9: Final consumption expenditure of households, transport: consumption per head
(EUR)

	2000	2006
EU-27	1 500	1 800
BE	1 800	2 300
BG	200	:
CZ	400	600
DK	1 900	:
DE	1 900	2 200
EE	300	800
IE	1 700	2 300
EL	900	1 500
ES	1 200	1 600
FR	2 000	2 300
IT	1 800	2 000
CY	1 700	2 000
LV	200	:
LT	300	800
LU	4 100	5 400
HU	400	800
MT	1 200	1 200
NL	1 500	1 800
AT	1 900	2 300
PL	300	400
PT	1 200	:
RO (1)	100	500
SI	1 000	1 400
SK	200	400
FI	1 600	2 000
SE	1 900	:
UK	2 600	2 800
TR (1)	600	800
IS	3 000	4 000
NO	2 500	:
CH	1 800	1 900

(1) 2006, forecast.

Source: Eurostat, Final consumption expenditure of households by consumption purpose (theme2/nama/nama_co2_c)

Figure 7.4: Final consumption expenditure of households, transport: price and volume changes between 2000 and 2006 (1)
(%)

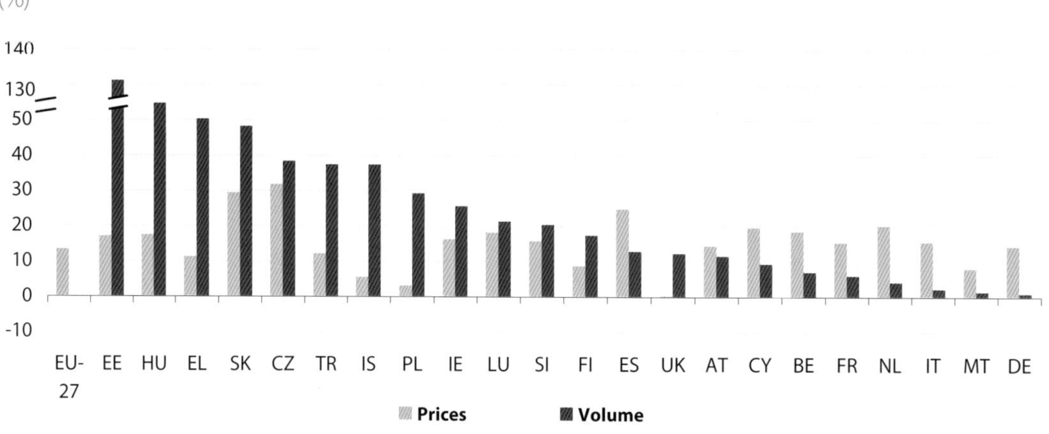

(1) Bulgaria, Denmark, Latvia, Lithuania, Portugal, Romania, Sweden and Norway, not available; EU-27, volume, not available.
Source: Eurostat, Final consumption expenditure of households by consumption purpose (theme2/nama/nama_co2_k and nama_co2_p)

In terms of comparable price levels, the 2005 HBS data shows that consumption expenditure on transport in purchasing power standard (PPS) terms was, on average, PPS 3 078 across the EU-27 as a whole. There were considerable variations among the Member States, from lows of about PPS 350 in Bulgaria and Romania to a high of PPS 8 403 in Luxembourg (see Table 7.10). The highest proportion of EU-27 transport consumption expenditure in 2005 was spent on the purchase of new motor cars, although this was relatively closely followed by purchases of fuel and lubricants. The variation between Member States in expenditure on new motor cars was particularly large (see Figure 7.5).

Table 7.10: Mean consumption expenditure per household, transport, 2005
(PPS)

EU-27 (1)	3 078
BE	3 863
BG	355
CZ	1 351
DK	3 331
DE	3 790
EE	1 087
IE	4 203
EL	3 222
ES	2 743
FR	3 777
IT	3 420
CY	4 980
LV	1 155
LT	762
LU	8 403
HU	1 511
MT	4 758
NL	3 196
AT	4 863
PL	862
PT	2 693
RO	344
SI	3 717
SK	986
FI	3 818
SE	3 623
UK	4 305
HR	1 484
NO	5 270

(1) Estimate.

Source: Eurostat, Household Budget Survey (theme3/hbs/hbs_exp_t121)

Figure 7.5: Mean consumption expenditure per household, transport, 2005
(PPS, minimum and maximum (vertical lines at end of horizontal line), inter-quartile range containing half of the Member States (box), median (vertical line within box))

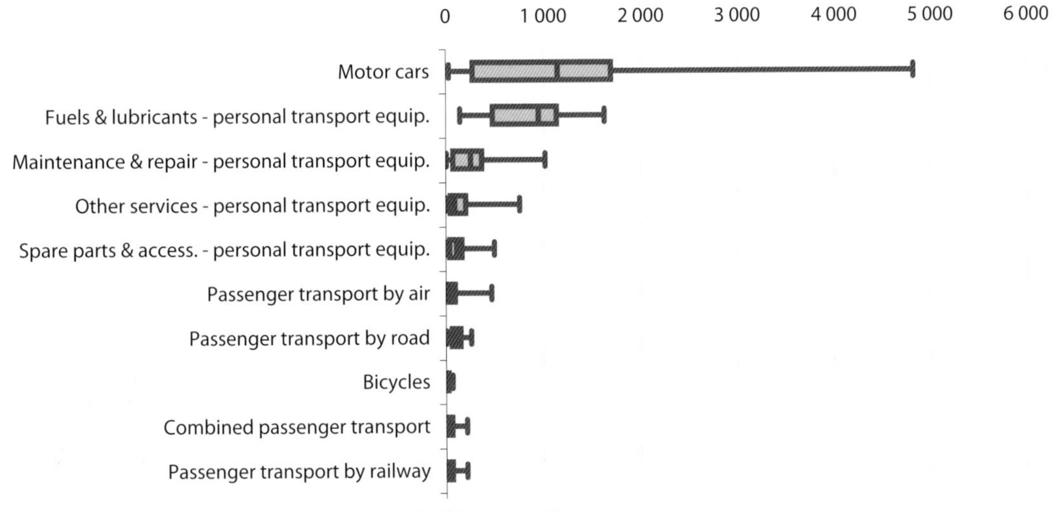

Source: Eurostat, Household Budget Survey (theme3/hbs/hbs_exp_t121)

Expenditure on transport accounted for an average 11.9 % of total household consumption expenditure across the EU-27 in 2005. Among the Member States, this share was highest (between 15 % and 17 %) in Slovenia, Finland, Austria, Luxembourg and Malta and lowest in Romania (6.5 %) and Bulgaria (5.0 %) – see Figure 7.6.

There was also a wide variation in the relative weight of transport in total expenditure among various socio-economic groups; the average share of expenditure on transport rising steadily for those with higher incomes (up to 14.4 % of total expenditure for the highest income quintile in the EU-27). A similar pattern was seen in terms of average household size, as the share of total expenditure on transport rose steadily up to 13.0 % for those households with at least three adults and dependent children. In contrast, the proportion of household budgets spent on transport was generally seen to fall as a function of age.

Figure 7.6: Structure of consumption expenditure: share of transport in total expenditure, 2005 (1)
(%)

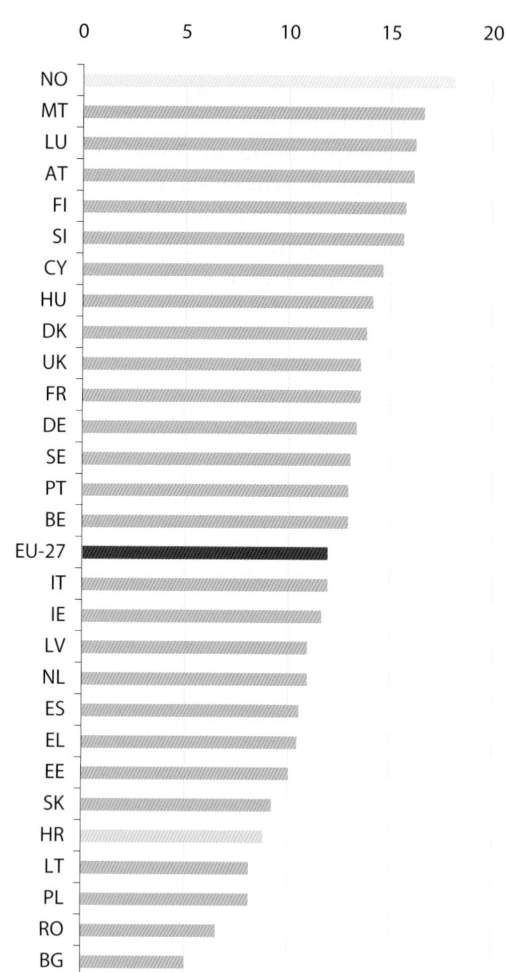

(1) EU-27, estimate; Czech Republic, not available.

Source: Eurostat, Household Budget Survey (theme3/hbs/hbs_str_t211)

7.3 Prices

A relatively high proportion of the price paid by consumers for fuels and lubricants may be attributed to taxes and duties. The data presented in this section include these taxes and duties, which, to some degree, explain some of the wide-ranging differences in price levels and the evolution of prices over time. Most Member States also impose some form of sales tax or vehicle registration tax, which may change as a function of engine-power or some other criteria; such taxes may be used to encourage consumers to purchase more environmentally-friendly vehicles.

7.3.1 Price inflation

There was a continuous and relatively steady rise in the EU-27's harmonised index of consumer prices for transport in the period between 2000 and 2007 (see Figure 7.7), at an average rate of 2.8 % per annum, which was slightly above the rate of increase recorded for the all-items consumer price index during the same period (2.4 %). Within transport, the highest price increases across the EU-27 were for fuels and lubricants, for passenger transport services (other than by air), and for the maintenance and repair of personal transport (an average of 4.1 % per annum, the highest increase).

In the period between 2000 and 2007, the consumer price index for transport rose for each of the Member States, relatively slowly in Finland (an average of 1.1 % per annum) and the Czech Republic (1.0 % per annum) and relatively sharply in Romania (an average of 17.0 %), despite slowing progressively and substantially to 1.7 % in 2007.

7.3.2 Price levels

A Eurobarometer survey on consumers' opinions of services of general interest, carried out in May and June 2006, revealed that an overwhelming majority (78 %) of respondents across the EU-25 found that urban transport services (transport within rather than between urban areas) were affordable. This proportion was considerably higher than the 68 % recorded in 2004, with the share of respondents finding prices unaffordable halving from 20 % to 10 % over the same period.

There was little variation in the perception of affordability when viewed in terms of age, gender or education of respondents, although there were notable differences across a few of the Member States; the share of respondents that found urban transport services affordable ranged from 55 % in Finland to 98 % in Greece. Over one third (37 %) of respondents in Finland found prices for these services unaffordable, while over one fifth (22 %) of respondents in the Netherlands found them excessive (see Figure 7.8).

Figure 7.7: Harmonised indices of consumer prices, EU-27 (2005=100)

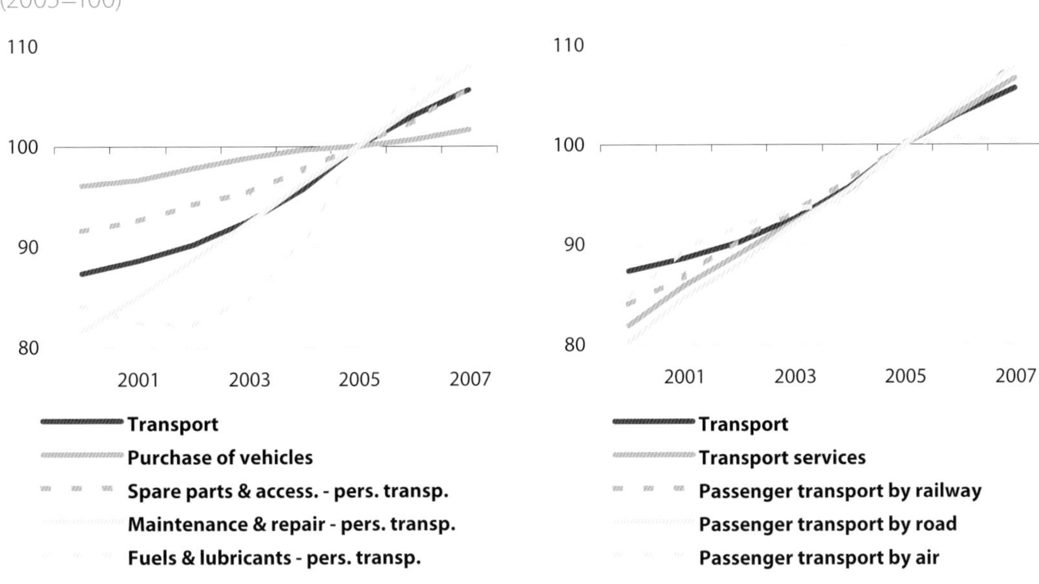

Source: Eurostat, Harmonised indices of consumer prices (theme2/prc/prc_hicp_aind)

The same Eurobarometer survey found that a similar proportion (74 %) of respondents across the EU-25 found rail services between towns and cities affordable. Again, the highest share was in Greece (97 %) and the lowest share in Finland (53 %), where about one third (36 %) of respondents found prices for rail services unaffordable.

Based on an analysis of price level indices among the Member States, the average price of transport was highest in Denmark, almost 50 % more than the average for the EU-27 (see Figure 7.9), and at least double the level in the Czech Republic, Latvia, Lithuania, Romania and Bulgaria. The lowest price levels for transport were recorded in the Member States that joined the EU since 2004, with only the average price level in Greece breaking this trend. Nevertheless, disparities in price levels for transport between the EU-27 Member States narrowed considerably during the period from 2000 to 2007.

Figure 7.8: The affordability of transport services within towns and cities, 2007
(%)

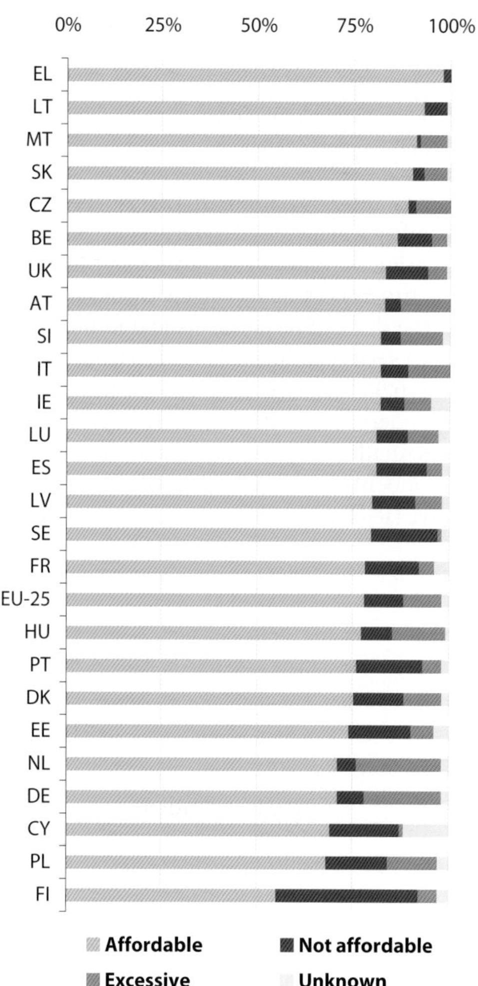

(1) Bulgaria and Romania, not available.

Source: 'Attitudes on issues related to EU transport policy', Flash Eurobarometer 206b, European Commission

Figure 7.9: Price level indices, transport, 2007
(EU-27=100)

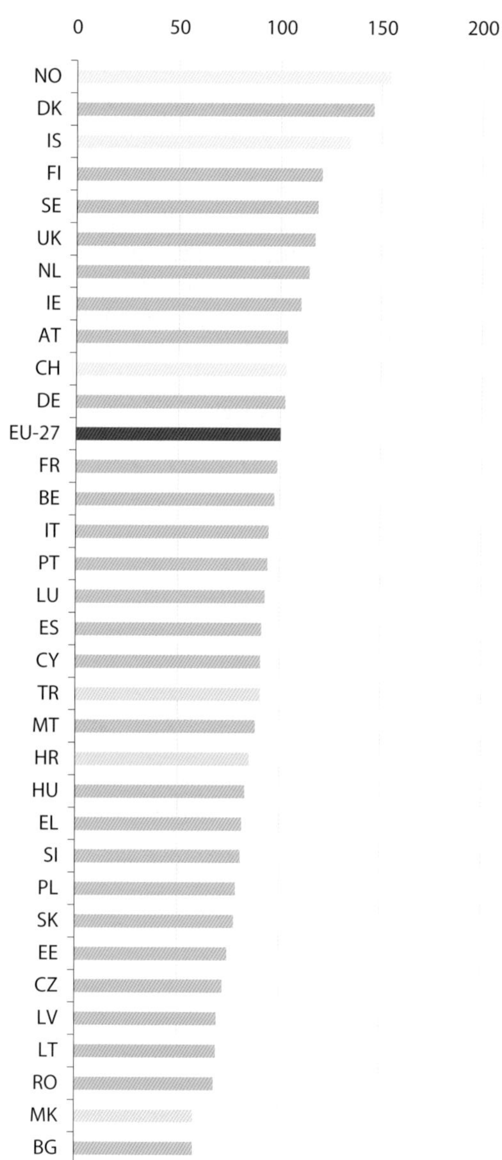

Source: Eurostat, Price level indices (theme2/prc/prc_ppp_ind)

There are considerable variations in the price of particular models of cars across the EU-27. Table 7.11 presents an overview of the pre-tax price differences for a selection of models across different market segments, with the lowest pre-tax price among the euro area Member States benchmarked to 100 (note that variations between Member States in after-tax prices can be notably different).

By way of example, the cost of a Fiat Panda varied by a little over one third (35.3 %) between the lowest price in the Netherlands and the highest in Slovakia. The price spread on the Peugeot 207 was almost the same, the price in France being nearly a third higher than the lowest pre-tax price which was offered in Malta.

In comparison to price variations observed for mini, small, medium and multi-purpose models, the variations in price for large, executive and luxury car models (BMW, Mercedes and Audi models in the table) was much narrower, while lower prices were more frequently observed in non-euro area countries.

Overall, the lowest car prices within the euro area tended to be in Finland (around a quarter of the 87 models covered by the European Commission's car price report for 2008), followed by Greece and Slovenia. However, among all of the Member States, pre-tax prices in Denmark tended to be even lower. Within the euro area, pre-tax car prices in Germany tended to be most expensive (for 27 of the 87 models), although outside the euro area, prices in the Czech Republic were generally higher than in Germany.

Table 7.11: Price differences, 1 January 2008
(lowest price among euro area Member States=100)

	FIAT Panda	PEUGEOT 207	RENAULT Mégane	BMW 320d	MERCEDES E220	AUDI A8	VOLVO XC90
BE	130.0	129.9	109.0	104.3	107.8	102.3	103.0
BG	107.4	113.9	87.5	98.2	106.2	99.0	95.9
CZ	129.0	124.1	120.2	114.0	112.9	111.8	117.0
DK	110.2	102.8	114.4	103.3	107.9	93.6	94.7
DE	133.2	132.0	113.0	109.1	108.0	103.0	100.7
EE	115.0	119.7	:	104.2	101.6	99.8	102.1
IE	130.9	127.1	110.3	106.7	108.0	101.5	107.1
EL	119.6	113.3	:	106.6	108.0	103.2	109.1
ES	116.6	126.0	102.7	108.4	107.7	104.0	104.0
FR	122.7	132.6	117.3	108.1	108.2	102.3	101.7
IT	119.7	118.3	105.9	108.4	109.3	102.5	104.0
CY	127.5	109.7	:	104.0	105.4	102.9	102.5
LV	123.8	130.0	95.4	104.9	106.0	99.8	101.9
LT	108.4	120.9	98.6	105.4	101.7	99.8	102.7
LU	130.0	129.9	109.0	104.5	108.0	101.3	103.6
HU	106.1	102.6	96.4	101.8	105.0	102.8	99.1
MT	108.9	100.0	:	112.0	106.7	:	102.6
NL	100.0	122.4	106.4	104.4	105.0	102.7	108.8
AT	132.2	125.4	107.8	107.5	107.3	102.9	100.0
PL	125.8	115.4	104.3	112.5	110.1	103.4	111.3
PT	114.5	114.1	100.0	108.7	102.3	104.8	104.4
RO	115.4	105.1	89.9	101.9	110.9	101.5	102.8
SI	115.9	109.1	106.3	100.0	105.8	100.0	110.1
SK	135.3	117.8	106.3	107.7	112.2	106.7	107.5
FI	120.6	114.0	116.7	103.9	100.0	107.4	100.8
SE	116.6	107.5	97.0	97.2	99.4	93.3	95.7
UK	113.0	113.8	104.7	98.6	94.9	81.6	94.1

Source: Car price report April 2008, European Commission

Table 7.12: Excise duty, VAT and tax revenues, 2008

	Leaded petrol			Unleaded petrol (1)		
	Excise duty (EUR per 1 000 litres)	Tax revenues other than VAT, 2007 (EUR million)	VAT (%)	Excise duty (EUR per 1 000 litres)	Tax revenues other than VAT, 2007 (EUR million)	VAT (%)
BE	637.7	2.3	21.0	555.1-611.9	1 260.8	21.0
BG (2)	(424.4)	0.0	(20.0)	350.2	529.9	20.0
CZ	497.9	0.3	19.0	430.0	1 186.2	19.0
DK	635.3	0.0	25.0	547.4	1 234.9	25.0
DE	721.0	9.7	19.0	654.5-669.8	18 805.2	19.0
EE	421.7	0.0	18.0	359.2	131.5	18.0
IE	553.0	0.0	21.0	442.7 & 547.8	1 079.4	21.0
EL (3)	409.0	:	19.0	349.0-352.0	1 776.4	19.0
ES	428.8	0.2	16.0	395.7 & 426.9	3 245.5	16.0
FR	639.6	15.0	19.6	606.9 & 639.6	16 302.0	19.6
IT (4)	564.0	:	20.0	564.0	:	20.0
CY (4)	421.0	:	15.0	298.7	:	15.0
LV (2)	(421.9)	0.0	(18.0)	323.9	150.7	18.0
LT	421.1	0.0	18.0	323.2	161.8	18.0
LU (2)	(516.7)	0.1	(15.0)	462.1 & 464.6	265.8	15.0
HU	444.7	22.9	20.0	411.7-462.57	848.6	20.0
MT (2)	(523.2)	0.0	(18.0)	404.4	40.0	18.0
NL	767.2	0.0	19.0	689.0	4 017.8	19.0
AT (4)	514.0 & 547.0	:	20.0	442.0 & 475.0	:	20.0
PL (3)	485.4	:	22.0	437.1	5 552.1	22.0
PT	650.0	:	21.0	583.0	1 165.1	21.0
RO	421.2	2.0	19.0	327.3	721.2	19.0
SI	421.6	0.2	20.0	359.0	298.9	20.0
SK (4)	530.6	:	19.0	458.4	:	19.0
FI (2)	(653.5)	0.0	(22.0)	627.0	1 440.6	22.0
SE	654.8	0.0	25.0	398.1-578.6	2 781.0	25.0
UK (3)	861.4	0.0	17.5	722.0	17 360.7	17.5

(1) Variations in excise duty reflect the octane rating (such as Oct. 95, 97 or 98), differences in sulphur content (such as < or > 10mg/kg) or comparisons with unleaded petrol substitutes.
(2) Leaded petrol no longer sold.
(3) No distinction in revenues between leaded and unleaded petrol.
(4) No distinction made between leaded and unleaded petrol, diesel, LPG and methane, heavy fuel oil; the total revenue from these streams was EUR 22 857.3 million in Italy, EUR 272.9 million in Cyprus, EUR 3 688.8 million in Austria and EUR 1 902.5 million in Slovakia.
(5) Aviation gasoline excluded.

Source: Directorate-General Taxation and Customs Union, European Commission

Aside from differences in the price of vehicles, there are also considerable differences in the costs of running vehicles once they have been purchased. Part of the aggregate price of the running costs associated with personal transport is comprised of fuel: in this respect Table 7.12 shows the differences in excise duties and VAT on petrol: in broad terms, excise duties were lowest among the Member States that joined the EU since 2004. The lowest excise duty rate for unleaded petrol (leaded petrol not being sold or barely sold in most EU countries) on 1 July 2008 was in Cyprus (EUR 0.30 per litre) and highest in the United Kingdom (EUR 0.72 per litre). VAT rates on petrol also varied from a low of 15 % in Luxembourg to highs of 25 % in Denmark and Sweden.

7.4 Consumer satisfaction and complaints

There are many indicators that may be used to cover consumer satisfaction with transport services: these include punctuality, comfort, safety and scheduling. While some can be measured objectively, others are more subjective. The first part of this section focuses on subjective opinions concerning how passengers are treated and whether they are satisfied with the quality of their transport services. The second half also uses subjective information from a consumer satisfaction survey that provides details of consumers' opinions of the retail network for the sale of motor vehicles.

In its December 2006 report for the European Commission on 'evaluating and monitoring trends with regard to passenger needs on the level of service and treatment of passengers', the Nexus Institute ranked EU-25 Member States according to their level of passenger treatment, taking into consideration factors such as the handling of complaints, guarantees and passengers' perceptions. Among the Member States, the United Kingdom achieved the highest overall score (see Figure 7.10), with wide-ranging customer charters and guarantee schemes and high standards for handling customer complaints. Sweden, France and then Germany were the next highest ranked Member States, generally lagging behind the United Kingdom in the handling of complaints. The Member States that joined the EU since 2004 tended to have among the lowest score in terms of passenger treatment, generally reflecting a low use of charters and guarantees, and a low or moderate perception of the schemes in place; Austria and Luxembourg were also near the bottom of the ranking for the same reasons.

Among the EU-27's capital cities, Eurostat's perception survey for 2006 indicates that passengers were most satisfied with their urban transport systems in Vienna (91 %) and Helsinki (93 %). In contrast, a majority of passengers in Rome (56 %), Bratislava (57 %), Sofia (67 %) and Nicosia (73 %) were rather or strongly dissatisfied with their public transport systems (see Table 7.13).

Figure 7.10: Ranking of the level of transport treatment, 2006
(points)

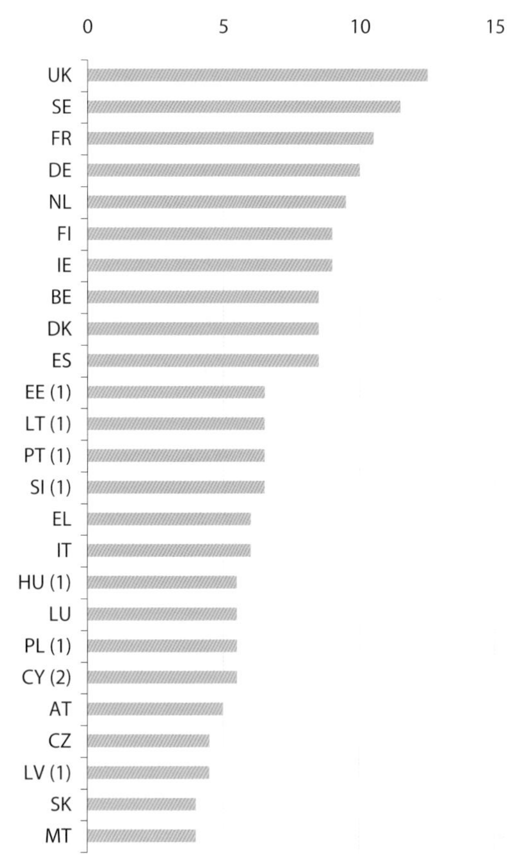

(1) Evaluation based on limited information.
(2) Evaluation based on very limited information.
(3) Bulgaria and Romania, not available.

Source: Nexus Institute for the European Commission, final report on 'Evaluating and monitoring trends with regard to passenger needs on the level of service and treatment of passengers', December 2006.

Table 7.13: Satisfaction with public transport in capital cities, 2006
(% of respondents)

	Satisfied with public transport (synthetic index 0-100)	Satisfied (rather+ strong)	Unsatisfied (rather+ strong)
Bruxelles / Brussel	67.5	61.6	29.6
Sofia	25.8	23.5	67.3
Praha	78.6	71.6	19.5
København	68.9	64.9	29.3
Berlin	86.7	81.0	12.4
Tallinn	60.3	52.6	34.6
Dublin	67.7	64.9	30.9
Athina	77.6	70.2	20.2
Madrid	67.2	64.9	31.7
Paris	76.6	74.8	22.8
Roma	40.0	37.5	56.2
Lefkosia	18.4	16.4	72.5
Riga	69.3	63.8	28.3
Vilnius	69.0	58.9	26.4
Luxembourg	79.1	72.6	19.2
Budapest	50.6	46.9	45.7
Valletta	53.6	41.6	36.0
Amsterdam	83.7	81.5	15.8
Wien	91.9	90.8	8.0
Warszawa	74.8	66.9	22.6
Lisboa	62.7	55.4	32.9
Bucureşti	42.7	39.3	52.7
Ljubljana	70.8	62.0	25.5
Bratislava	34.0	29.5	57.2
Helsinki	94.9	93.1	5.0
Stockholm	76.7	75.2	22.8
London	72.7	67.9	25.5

Source: Eurostat, Perception surveys (theme1/urb/urb_percep)

Whereas consumer dissatisfaction with urban transport may be city specific, an IPSOS consumer satisfaction survey for the European Commission suggests that a majority (53.8 %) of consumers in Cyprus were dissatisfied with their urban transport suppliers in 2006, while almost a third were dissatisfied in Slovakia. The countries where urban transport satisfaction rates were highest included Ireland, Finland, Latvia and Austria (all between 60 % and 66 %).

The same survey by IPSOS also measured the satisfaction of consumers with extra-urban transport suppliers (Figure 7.11) and air transport suppliers (Figure 7.12). About three quarters (72.4 %) of passengers in Ireland were satisfied with their bus and rail transport services outside of urban areas (in between towns and cities), the highest proportion among the Member States in 2006, while almost two thirds of passengers in Finland, Lithuania and Latvia were also satisfied. In contrast, only about one quarter of the passengers living in Italy and the Netherlands expressed their satisfaction with extra-urban transport services.

Among the EU-25 Member States, there was generally a much higher rate of satisfaction with air transport suppliers, with a little over 80 % of respondents in Germany, Cyprus, Hungary and Austria expressing satisfaction. In contrast, only about half of all respondents in the Netherlands (52.9 %) and Italy (51.1 %) expressed satisfaction, with an even lower proportion (45.0 %) in Spain expressing their satisfaction.

Figure 7.11: Satisfaction with extra-urban transport suppliers, 2006 (1)
(% of respondents)

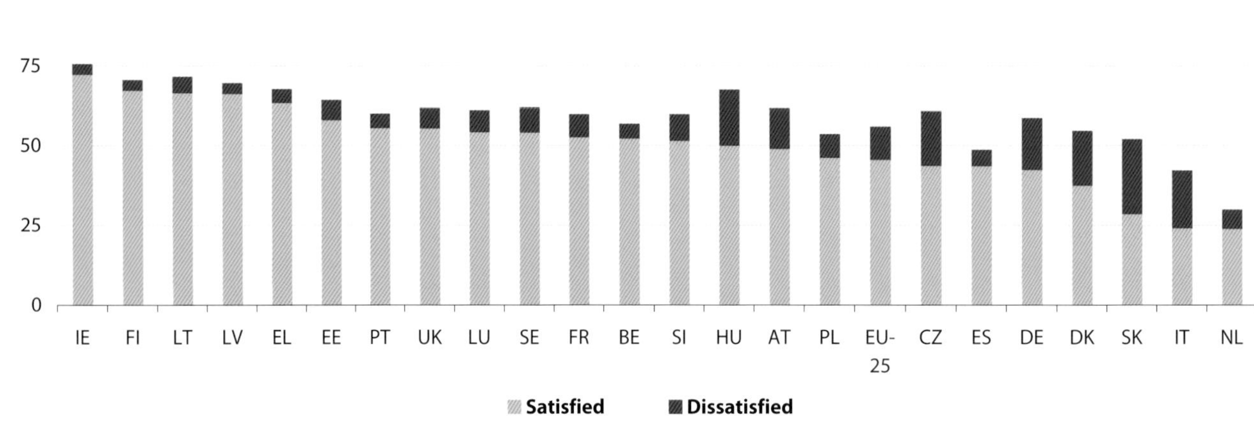

(1) Bulgaria, Cyprus, Malta and Romania, not available.

Source: IPSOS INRA for the European Commission, Consumer satisfaction survey, May 2007

Figures collected by the Directorate-General for Health and Consumers show that when averaged across all EU airlines, the principal complaints by passengers in 2007 related to cancellations (24 %), delays (21 %), poor customer assistance (17 %) and lost or delayed luggage (11 %) – see Figure 7.13 – with other complaints (20 %) comprising problems associated with information requests, ticketing, national enforcement bodies and issues of a general nature. The figures collected show a large decline (40 %) in complaints between 2006 and 2007, with large reductions in the number of complaints concerning cancellations and delays. The highest proportions of air passenger complaints among EU airlines in 2007 were received by Iberia (12.9 %), Ryanair (8.3 %) and Alitalia (6.2 %).

Figure 7.12: Satisfaction with air transport suppliers, 2006 (1)
(% of respondents)

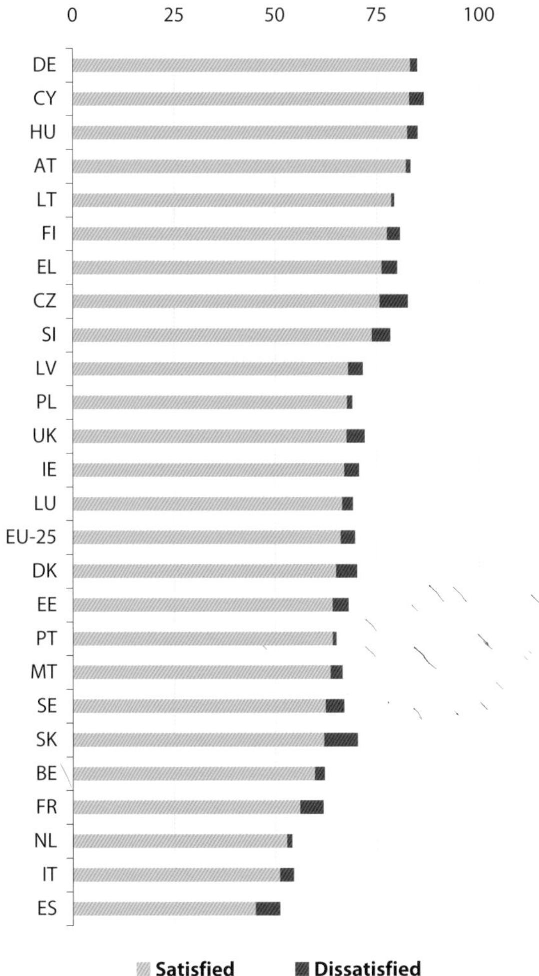

(1) Bulgaria and Romania, not available.

Source: IPSOS INRA for the European Commission, Consumer satisfaction survey, May 2007

Turning attention to motor vehicle retailers, a consumer satisfaction survey conducted in 2008 found that on a scale of 1 (not at all satisfied) to 10 (fully satisfied), an average of 8.4 was recorded for satisfaction with motor vehicle retailers – see Figure 7.14.

Figure 7.13: Airline customer complaints, 2007
(%)

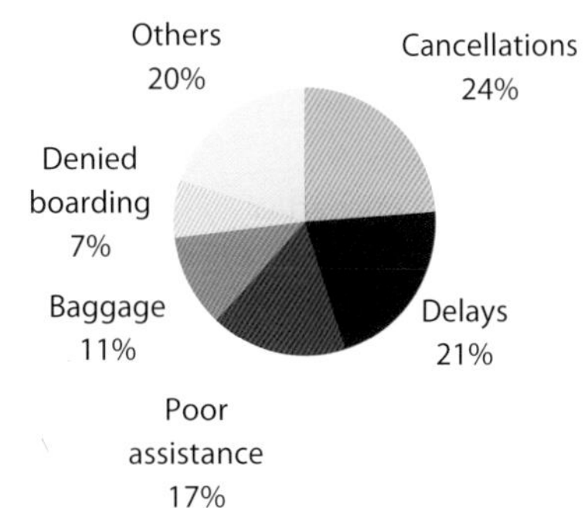

Source: Directorate-General Health and Consumers, European Commission

Figure 7.14: Overall, to what extent are you satisfied with your retailer when it comes to buying new motor vehicles, 2008? (1)
(average, 1-10)

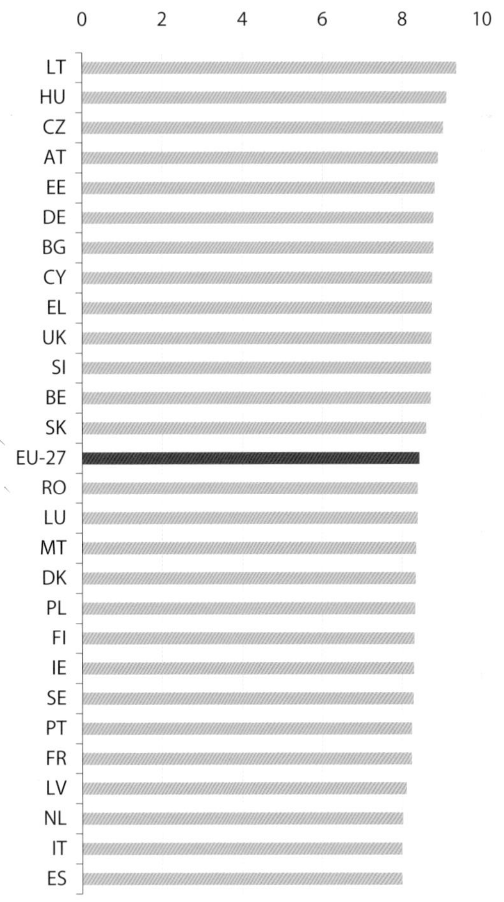

(1) Average on a scale of 1 (not at all satisfied) to 10 (fully satisfied).

Source: 'Retail satisfaction survey', IPSOS for the European Commission, August/September 2008

Figure 7.15: Problems faced by consumers when purchasing new motor vehicles in the past 12 months, EU-27, 2008 (1)
(% share of those experiencing problems, multiple answers allowed)

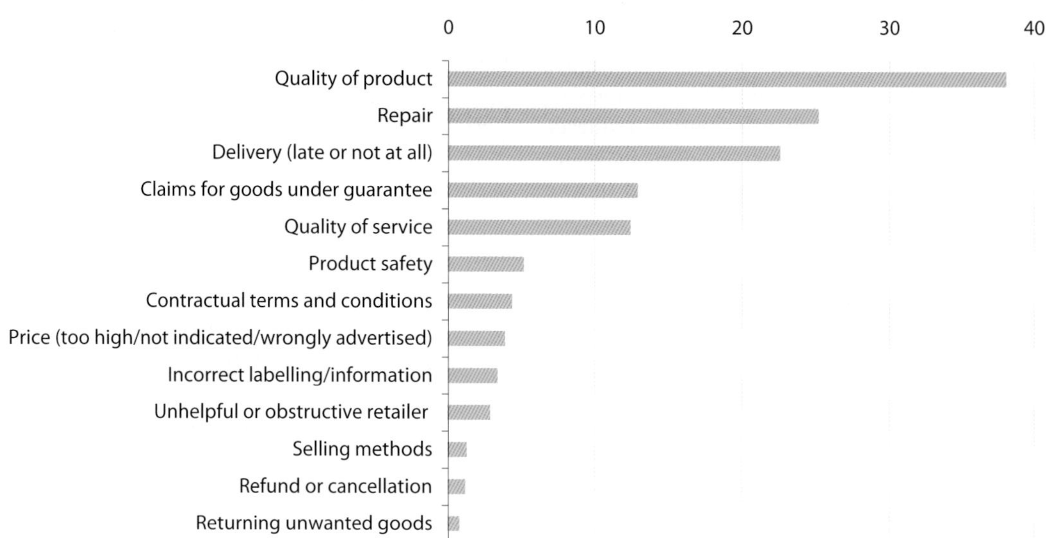

(1) When purchasing new motor vehicles in 2008, 15.3 % of EU-27 consumers reported facing at least one problem; note that consumers may have faced more than one problem.

Source: 'Retail satisfaction survey', IPSOS for the European Commission, August/September 2008

As with other products covered by the survey, the main problem faced by consumers who had purchased a new motor vehicle in the twelve months preceding the survey was product quality (cited by 38.1 % of respondents). In contrast, the relative importance of problems associated with repairs, late delivery and claims under guarantee were considerable higher than for many of the other products surveyed – see Figure 7.15.

When asked if they thought their retailer would replace, repair, reduce the price, or give them their money back for the purchase of a defective car, on a scale of 1 (totally disagree) to 10 (totally agree), the average score in the EU-27 was 7.8, with the lowest levels in Bulgaria (6.2) and the highest in Ireland (9.2) – see Figure 7.16.

Figure 7.16: Do you agree that your retailer would replace, repair, reduce the price or give you your money back if the new motor vehicle you had bought was defective or not fit for purpose, 2008? (1)
(average, 1-10)

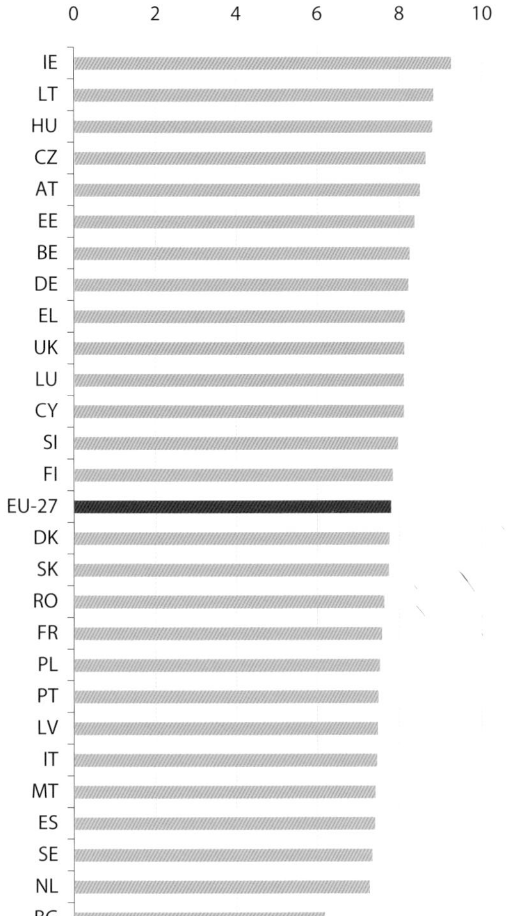

(1) Average on a scale of 1 (totally disagree) to 10 (totally agree).

Source: 'Retail satisfaction survey', IPSOS for the European Commission, August/September 2008

7.5 Quality and safety

One important measure of the quality of transport services concerns delays in getting from A to B. Regarding flight travel, Regulation (EC) No 261/2004 of the European Parliament and of the Council increased the level of compensation airlines must pay passengers denied boarding and introduced new compensation and assistance rights in the event of cancelled flights and long delays (depending on the length of the flight, this could be 2, 3 or 4 hours).

Records of airlines' delay rates on intra- and extra-European services are collected and published on a twice-yearly basis by the Association of European Airlines (AEA). In 2007 there was a marginal decline in punctuality; as 78.9 % of departures for intra-European services were within 15 minutes of schedule, compared with 79.4 % in 2006. All of the airlines covered by AEA reported that a majority of their short and medium haul flights arrived on time. The largest proportion of delayed (by at least 15 minutes) short and medium haul flights was recorded by TAP Portugal (40.5 %). For long haul destinations, only 36.6 % of Spanair flights arrived on time, while a majority of TAP Portugal flights were also delayed (see Table 7.14).

The AEA states that, on average, 85 % of delayed bags are traced and delivered to the passenger within 48 hours. The number of bags delayed (bags reported as delayed upon the passengers' arrival at their final destination) per thousand passengers was 16.6 in 2007 (slightly up on the average for the year before, 15.7). TAP Portugal recorded the highest rate of delayed baggage, at 27.8 bags per thousand passengers, slightly higher than the rate for British Airways (26.5); none of the remaining airlines reported baggage delays for more than 20 items per thousand passengers, with the lowest rates registered by Air Malta and Turkish Airlines (both below five bags per thousand passengers).

Table 7.14: Flight delays (of greater than 15 minutes) and lost baggage, 2007 (1)

Carrier	Short and medium haul			Long haul			Bags delayed per 1 000 persons
	Number of flights (unit)	On-time arrivals (%)	On-time departures (%)	Number of flights (unit)	On-time arrivals (%)	On-time departures (%)	
AF - Air France	501 477	82.1	81.5	55 528	63.7	61.6	17.6
AP - Air One	90 804	65.8	73.7	-	-	-	9.9
AY - Finnair	79 292	81.0	80.6	5 941	70.5	68.7	15.8
AZ - Alitalia	252 802	74.7	77.9	13 298	71.6	74.5	19.7
BA - British Airways plc	235 182	64.7	67.5	60 126	56.2	61.5	26.5
BD - bmi	121 085	79.4	81.5	1 732	73.8	76.2	17.0
CY - Cyprus Airways	15 606	64.3	70.6	-	-	-	8.8
FI - Icelandair	6 896	66.3	76.8	2 595	69.2	76.7	11.1
IB - Iberia	357 520	77.8	81.3	17 718	64.1	70.2	13.8
JK - Spanair	99 866	62.9	71.3	656	36.6	44.2	15.4
JP - Adria Airways	21 154	73.9	73.8	-	-	-	9.8
JU - JAT Airways	19 975	75.6	79.6	-	-	-	:
KL - KLM Royal Dutch Airlines	182 333	84.9	80.5	31 052	76.4	71.7	19.7
KM - Air Malta	16 668	68.6	67.5	-	-	-	4.5
LG - Luxair	11 655	86.6	88.1	-	-	-	17.2
LH - Deutsche Lufthansa AG	619 131	81.2	80.2	49 067	74.3	73.0	15.8
LO - LOT Polish Airlines	86 481	73.9	76.4	2 989	56.3	54.5	13.9
LX - Swiss International Airlines	116 874	79.3	78.2	13 428	75.6	73.5	11.4
MA - Malev Hungarian Airlines	49 606	84.0	83.1	1 085	64.4	71.5	9.5
OA - Olympic Airlines	86 447	68.9	68.9	1 779	62.8	59.6	:
OK - CSA Czech Airlines	72 982	81.8	88.6	1 392	73.9	86.4	12.4
OS - Austrian	155 248	84.1	83.7	6 761	82.1	79.5	12.9
OU - Croatia Airlines	22 244	72.8	77.5	-	-	-	9.3
RO - Tarom Romanian Airlines	13 568	82.2	88.8	-	-	-	9.5
SK - SAS Scandinavian Airlines	291 757	80.6	80.1	6 338	74.3	76.0	14.8
SN - Brussels Airlines	70 906	83.1	83.4	3 434	58.3	51.7	11.7
TK - Turkish Airlines	151 714	79.1	83.8	9 470	59.5	69.2	4.5
TP - TAP Portugal	75 153	59.5	62.5	11 200	40.3	42.5	27.8
Association of European Airlines	3 824 426	77.7	78.9	295 589	65.9	66.7	16.6

(1) Aer Lingus and Virgin Atlantic Airways are members of AEA, but no information was provided; information based on voluntary submissions from airlines; short/medium haul includes operations within Europe, cross border and domestic, to North Africa and the Middle East; all other services are included in long haul; bags reported delayed upon the passengers' arrival at their final destination (on average 85% of delayed bags are traced and delivered to the passenger within 48 hours).

Source: Association of European Airlines (www.aea.be)

For European [21] flights, a Eurocontrol report on trends in air traffic, 'A Place to Stand: Airports in the European Air Network' suggests that there is little to distinguish airports of different size as regards delays en route; as the average length of a delayed air traffic flow management (ATFM) flight in 2006 was 16 minutes for all sizes of airport. However, delays on arrival were up to 50 % longer for flights to medium or small airports [22] compared with flights to large airports; this may be due to small and medium-sized airports lacking developed infrastructure and therefore being less able to respond to peaks in demand.

According to a Eurobarometer survey on attitudes related to EU transport policy, the overwhelming majority (90 %) of respondents in May 2007 were of the belief that there was a need to improve the traffic situation in their cities and surrounding areas. In most of the EU-15 Member States, a majority of respondents felt that better public transport would improve the traffic situation, the highest rates being recorded in Portugal (59.7 %), the United Kingdom (59.8 %), Italy (62.4 %) and Ireland (67.0 %) – see Table 7.15. This share was considerably lower in most of the Member States that joined the EU since 2004, the lowest proportion being in Bulgaria (21.2 %). A higher proportion of respondents in Bulgaria (38.7 %) believed that speed limitations would improve the traffic situation in cities, relatively high shares also being recorded among respondents in Lithuania (25.8 %) and Poland (27.6 %). Limitations on traffic flows in city centres were considered by one third (33.0 %) of respondents in Greece as the most effective way for improving the traffic situation, the highest proportion among the Member States, while over a quarter of respondents in the Czech Republic, Latvia, Lithuania and Slovakia also took this view.

(21) EU-27 Member States and Albania, Armenia, Azerbaijan, Belarus, Bosnia-Herzegovina, Croatia, former Yugoslav Republic of Macedonia, Georgia, Moldova, Norway, Serbia and Montenegro, Switzerland, Turkey and the Ukraine.

(22) Small airports: 5 000 to 20 000 flights per year under instrument flight rules (IFR) and under the control of a (civilian) air traffic controller for some or all of the route; medium-sized airports: between 20 000 and 50 000 such flights; large airports: between 50 000 and 200 000 such flights; very large airports: between 200 000 and 500 000 such flights.

Table 7.15: Attitudes to improving city traffic situations, 2007
(% of respondents)

	Better public transport	City limitations	Speed limitations	Road charges	No need to improve	Other and do not know
EU-27	48.5	16.8	16.5	4.8	5.9	7.5
BE	46.9	17.1	18.8	5.1	6.3	5.8
BG	21.2	21.4	38.7	3.7	2.7	12.3
CZ	39.5	26.4	13.4	7.9	4.0	8.8
DK	46.3	12.0	17.3	8.4	9.0	7.0
DE	45.0	14.2	17.4	6.9	9.9	6.6
EE	38.8	16.1	18.9	3.1	12.3	10.8
IE	67.0	13.2	9.8	6.4	0.4	3.2
EL	41.2	33.0	13.0	5.4	1.9	5.5
ES	58.2	14.0	13.7	1.1	6.1	6.9
FR	46.1	18.8	20.0	4.5	5.0	5.6
IT	62.4	14.8	10.4	1.8	4.2	6.4
CY	57.3	9.7	22.0	4.5	1.6	4.9
LV	25.0	25.8	20.7	6.8	10.3	11.4
LT	24.4	25.7	25.8	5.8	7.9	10.4
LU	55.6	9.3	17.2	5.1	6.4	6.4
HU	33.9	24.0	20.6	2.9	10.1	8.5
MT	44.0	19.3	20.7	3.5	3.3	9.2
NL	53.1	14.4	13.7	5.3	6.8	6.7
AT	52.2	12.8	9.2	7.2	9.9	8.7
PL	27.1	21.8	27.6	3.5	6.4	13.6
PT	59.7	17.3	8.8	2.4	6.6	5.2
RO	39.1	14.7	17.0	9.5	6.2	13.5
SI	45.1	20.1	24.5	2.8	2.4	5.1
SK	36.7	26.9	21.2	4.0	4.5	6.7
FI	52.7	15.5	12.2	4.8	8.0	6.8
SE	52.0	14.5	14.2	6.6	5.0	7.7
UK	59.8	14.4	12.4	5.9	1.3	6.2

Source: 'Attitudes on issues related to EU transport policy', Flash Eurobarometer 206b, European Commission

Improving travel safety has been a long-standing area of EU policy: one of the main areas of focus has been to improve road safety, for example, through legislation on speed limits, maximum blood alcohol levels for drivers, or vehicle safety legislation. During the period between 1990 and 2006, the number of road fatalities in the EU-27 declined sharply, overall by 43.4 %, to some 42 953 deaths in 2006. Over the same period, the number of road fatalities more than halved in Portugal, France, Latvia, Spain, Germany, Estonia and Denmark.

Table 7.16: Road fatalities, 2006

(per million inhabitants)		(per 10 billion pkm)		(per million passenger cars)	
MT	24.6	SE	44.7	MT	46.4
NL	44.7	UK	47.6	NL	101.9
SE	49.0	NL	48.4	SE	106.5
UK	54.4	MT	48.8	DE	109.9
DK	56.3	FI	53.0	UK	115.7
DE	61.8	LU	54.1	LU	115.8
FI	63.8	DK	55.8	FI	136.1
LU	76.2	DE	57.3	FR	153.1
FR	76.8	FR	63.9	DK	153.6
IE	86.3	IT	73.8	IT	162.1
EU-27	87.3	EU-27	90.0	AT	174.6
AT	88.1	BE	96.2	EU-27	189.0
PT	91.6	AT	99.7	ES	200.7
ES	93.0	SI	112.7	IE	211.1
IT	96.2	ES	117.2	BE	216.1
BE	101.3	IE	129.6	PT	228.3
CZ	103.5	PT	130.8	CY	236.2
SK	107.4	CZ	145.8	CZ	263.5
CY	111.3	CY	167.5	SI	270.0
RO	114.8	EL	174.4	EL	374.6
HU	129.0	EE	175.3	EE	389.4
SI	130.6	LT	190.6	PL	407.6
BG	135.5	SK	215.0	SK	439.1
PL	137.5	PL	234.9	HU	446.0
EL	148.6	LV	256.5	BG	484.5
EE	151.8	HU	271.2	LT	498.1
LV	177.9	BG	328.0	LV	520.3
LT	223.6	RO	397.8	RO	711.3

Source: CARE database, Directorate-General Transport and Energy, European Commission, International Transport Forum, national statistics

Despite relatively sharp declines in road deaths in all Member States (with the exception of Malta) during a period of rising traffic volumes, there remain considerable differences between Member States. In terms of road fatalities per million inhabitants, the lowest rates of fatalities were recorded in Malta, the Netherlands, Sweden and the United Kingdom. The same four countries were also the safest in terms of fatalities per passenger-kilometre (see Table 7.16).

Among the EU-15 Member States, passenger fatalities in accidents involving railways also fell in recent decades. While almost 400 passengers were killed in road accidents in 1970, and more than 300 in 1980, by 1990 this figure had dropped to 165. The trend continued, such that by 2000 there were 117 passenger fatalities in railway accidents, and despite a rise to 121 deaths in 2002, the downward trend was thereafter re-established, as 51 deaths were registered in the EU-15 in 2005 (65 deaths for the EU-27).

The number of lives lost in aviation accidents over the territory of the EU-27 on flights made by any operator averaged between 200 and 300 deaths each year during the 1970s and 1980s. This value was considerably reduced in the 1990s when, on average, 57 lives were lost per annum. Despite a rapid increase in the volume of air transport in the last decade, the number of travellers whose lives were lost remained relatively stable, as between 2000 and 2007 there was an average of 63 persons killed each year over EU-27 territory, with 4 and 3 deaths respectively in 2006 and 2007.

Measures to improve airport security have been stepped up in recent years to counter the perceived threat from terrorism. In a Eurobarometer survey on attitudes relating to EU transport policy, respondents were asked whether they considered security controls at airports as being appropriate. Of the 57 % of respondents who were in a position to judge (infrequent flyers were excluded), about six out of every ten persons across the EU-27 thought security controls were appropriate (see Figure 7.17). A higher proportion of regular flyers thought that airport security was insufficient (24 %) when compared with the proportion that thought that it was excessive (15 %) – this position was strongest among regular flyers from Italy, Cyprus, Bulgaria and Poland. In contrast, about one third of regular flyers from Denmark (31 %), the Netherlands (32 %) and Austria (34 %) thought that airport security was excessive.

Figure 7.17: Opinion about airport security controls among regular flyers, 2007
(% of respondents)

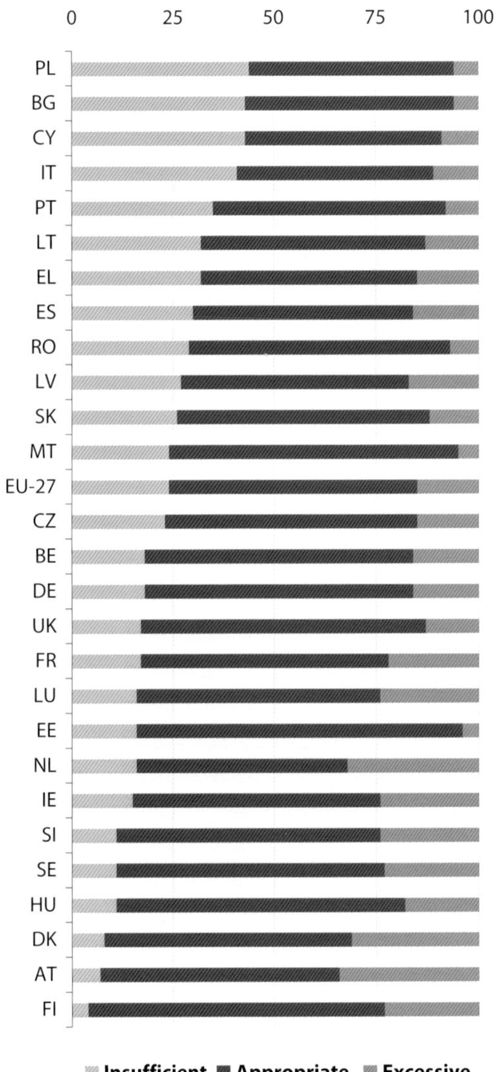

Source: 'Attitudes on issues related to EU transport policy', Flash Eurobarometer 206b, European Commission

Figure 7.18: To what extent do you agree that new motor vehicles sold by your retailer are reliable (i.e. they work well and without failure for a reasonable period of time) and safe, 2008? (1)
(average, 1-10)

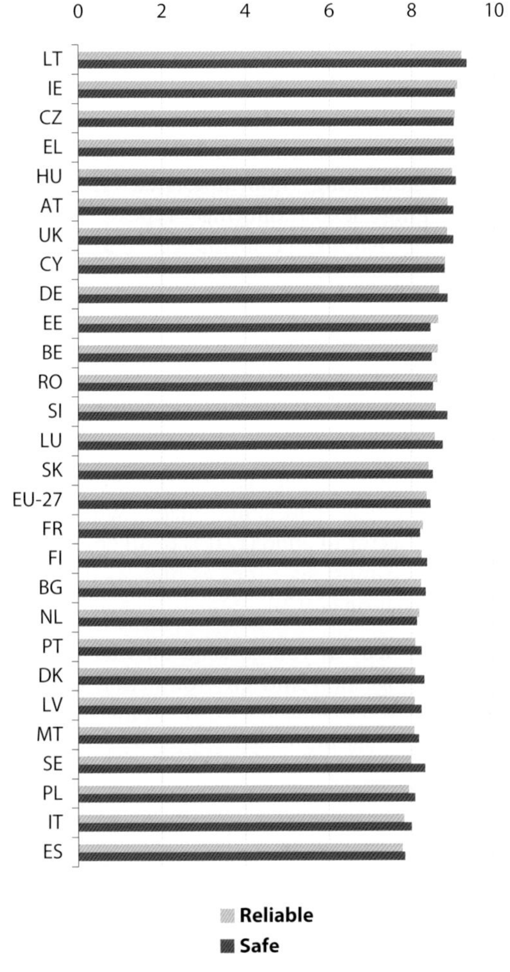

(1) Average on a scale of 1 (totally disagree) to 10 (totally agree).

Source: 'Retail satisfaction survey', IPSOS for the European Commission, August/September 2008

As regards the safety of personal transport equipment, a consumer satisfaction survey conducted in 2008 asked respondents to rate the extent to which they thought new motor vehicles were reliable and safe. On a scale of 1 (totally disagree) to 10 (totally agree), an average score of 8.4 was registered across the EU-27 for reliability and 8.5 for safety. There was generally a close relationship, as only Slovenia and Sweden reported differences of more than 0.2 points in average scores for the two indicators (in both cases a higher proportion of consumers agreed that new motor vehicles were safe, rather than reliable).

7.6 Externalities

The energy and fuel used in transport is one of the main contributors to greenhouse gas emissions; joint work by the European Environment Agency, the European Topic Centre on air and climate change and the United Nations estimates that fuel combustion from all transport sectors combined contributed close to a quarter (23.8 %) of all greenhouse gas emissions in 2006 in the EU-27, a higher proportion than the combustion from industry (19.9 %), but less than that associated with energy industries (29.2 %) – see Figure 7.19. Encouraging non-motorised transport, encouraging less polluting types of fuel, improving engine performance, encouraging car-sharing and promoting investment in various forms of passenger transport (predominantly train, trams and buses), as well as improving the fluidity of transport networks are all initiatives that could reduce greenhouse gas emissions and improve air quality.

Road transport accounted for the bulk of the greenhouse gas emissions made within the transport sector in 2006 (17.0 % of all emissions), which was almost six times as high as the value for civil aviation (2.9 %).

The idea of pay-as-you-go road tolls in order to pay for congestion and environmental damage was put to EU citizens in a Eurobarometer survey of attitudes relating to EU transport policy. Six out of every ten respondents in the EU-27 were opposed to such tolls. The greatest resistance to this idea was among those surveyed in France (71 %), while relatively high levels of opposition were also recorded in Hungary (67 %) and Italy (68 %). In contrast, a small majority of respondents in Latvia (51 %), Greece (51 %), Lithuania (52 %), as well as the Czech Republic (54 %) were in favour of pay-as-you-go road tolls to alleviate congestion and rectify environmental damage – see Figure 7.20.

Figure 7.19: Greenhouse gas emissions by sector, EU-27, 2006
(%, based on tonnes of CO_2 equivalents)

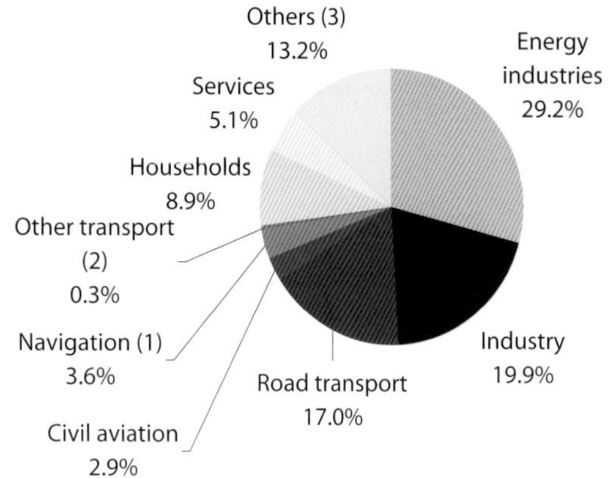

(1) Including international bunkers (international traffic departing from the EU).
(2) Including rail, pipeline transportation and ground activities in airports and harbours.
(3) Including solvent Use, fugitive, waste and agriculture.

Source: European Environment Agency

Figure 7.20: Opinion about paying for congestion and environmental damage through road tolls, 2007
(% of respondents)

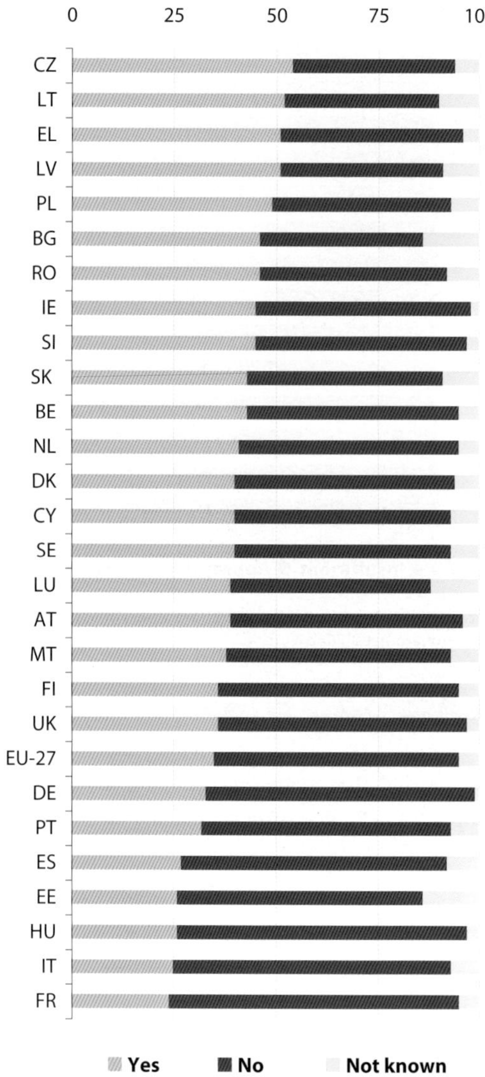

Source: 'Attitudes on issues related to EU transport policy', Flash Eurobarometer 206b, European Commission

8

Communications

For households, distance communication traditionally comprised postal services for written communication (and parcels), progressively complemented and substituted by fixed line telephone for spoken communications from the home or public payphones. Since the 1980's this mix of services has changed considerably, with courier services increasingly competing for the delivery of mail and parcels to households, while mobile telephony and Internet access have expanded rapidly and become commonplace: the use of telegrams has effectively disappeared, and the use of public payphones has withered. Although the use of the Internet goes beyond simple communications, and in many ways can be considered in the context of recreation (for example, on-line gaming or web radio services), it is covered in this chapter because it relies on the same infrastructure as telecommunications and is often used to substitute or complement other communication services, for example, the use of e-mail, and more recently Internet-based telephony services.

The striking changeover in the nature of communication services has occurred through technological developments allied to the provision of innovative, communications equipment and services. These services are offered by incumbents (often formerly state-controlled, monopoly providers) and new entrants whose market access has been facilitated by regulatory changes that opened-up the telecommunications and postal markets; this liberalisation is widely credited with encouraging the development of new products and services, increasing choice, and lowering prices.

In 2005 the European Commission launched 'i2010: European Information Society 2010', a five-year strategy to foster growth and jobs in the information society and media related activities. Among other objectives i2010 aims to promote high-speed and secure broadband networks. The Commission outlined three policy priorities:

- to create an open and competitive single market including an updating of the regulatory framework for electronic communications and a strategy for a secure information society;
- to increase EU investment in research on information and communication technologies;
- to promote an inclusive European information society.

Postal markets are dynamic and quickly evolving in conjunction with the ever-widening markets of communication, advertising and electronic commerce. While the use of e-mail and SMS messaging has increased remarkably and letter mail has declined as a percentage of overall message volumes, many activities, such as e-commerce, publishing, mail order, insurance, banking and advertising continue to depend on the postal infrastructure. The bulk of mail deliveries are no longer dominated by private, person to person communications, but instead by business to business and business to consumer communications. Improvements in the quality of service, in particular in terms of delivery performance and convenient access are fundamental aspects of the EU's postal policy.

The 'reserved area' for postal services is a segment of the postal services market reserved for those operators (regardless of type of ownership) that provide universal services (the provision of services at sufficient points so as to take account of the needs of users, meeting specified quality targets, and provided at affordable prices). In practice, letter mail/parcels under certain weight and cost limits can only be handled by operators bound by universal service obligations. The size of the reserved area has been progressively reduced, and will be abolished through the implementation of the latest Directive on postal services adopted by the European Parliament and the Council in February 2008. This Directive also confirmed the scope and standard of universal service, reinforced consumers' rights and upgraded the role of national regulatory authorities. Furthermore, it established a list of measures Member States may take to safeguard and finance, where necessary, a universal service. The final date for achieving full market opening is 31 December 2010, with the possibility for some Member States to postpone this by up to two more years.

8.1 Access, choice and switching

Tables 8.1 to 8.3 provide detailed information on the supply of various telecommunication services, and the level of penetration into households. The information on telecommunication services covers all lines and subscriptions, regardless of whether they are for business or household (residential) users, while in contrast the penetration rates come from a recent Eurobarometer household survey on e-communications and an ICT usage survey of households and individuals, and therefore focus on household/consumer use.

Table 8.1: Telecommunication services: access to networks, 2008 (1)
(thousand)

	Main telephone lines (1)	ISDN (2)	DSL lines (3)	Cellular mobile lines (4)	Fixed broadband lines (3)	Non-DSL broadband lines (3)
EU-27	233 556	:	80 173	553 462	99 846	19 673
BE	3 169	399	1 619	9 866	2 714	1 095
BG	2 427	853	164	9 431	580	416
CZ	2 888	161	613	12 373	1 497	884
DK	2 332	283	1 207	6 023	1 961	754
DE	54 960	12 808	18 548	93 292	19 579	1 031
EE	472	51	136	1 765	298	162
IE	1 728	111	550	4 937	753	203
EL	6 171	586	1 013	11 815	1 017	5
ES	18 227	1 129	6 394	49 087	8 155	1 761
FR	38 250	:	14 977	52 536	15 687	710
IT	26 890	:	9 755	87 724	10 122	367
CY	385	27	106	922	108	1
LV	657	:	152	3 193	343	191
LT	792	16	232	4 861	508	276
LU	247	78	109	696	121	12
HU	3 365	594	752	10 499	1 429	677
MT	202	47	38	369	69	31
NL	5 977	1 490	3 388	18 443	5 588	2 200
AT	2 468	413	1 018	9 421	1 656	638
PL	11 284	527	2 252	36 968	3 200	947
PT	4 234	774	975	12 941	1 597	622
RO	4 204	19	365	21 164	1 949	1 584
SI	561	231	247	1 892	347	101
SK	1 167	57	278	5 480	477	199
FI	1 909	105	1 273	5 720	1 619	346
SE	4 987	154	1 755	9 813	2 843	1 088
UK	33 603	:	12 259	72 233	15 630	3 372
HR	1 531	126	:	:	:	:
TR	18 832	15	:	:	:	:
IS	147	15	:	:	:	:
NO	1 177	514	:	:	:	:
CH	2 896	864	:	:	:	:

(1) All data refer to 2006; Switzerland, provisional.
(2) Greece, Malta, Romania and Slovakia, 2005; Hungary and the Netherlands, 2004.
(3) January 2008.
(4) October 2007.

Source: Eurostat, information society statistics (theme9/science/isoc/isoc_tc_ac1), Progress report on the single European electronic communications market 2007, European Commission.

Table 8.2: Penetration rates of telephony services in households, November-December 2007
(%)

	Telephone	Mobile telephone	Fixed telephone	Fixed and mobile	Mobile only	Fixed only
EU-27	95	83	70	57	24	14
BE	96	84	67	52	32	12
BG	89	68	61	41	25	21
CZ	96	92	31	27	64	4
DK	99	92	73	65	22	8
DE	95	78	81	64	11	20
EE	96	89	49	40	41	8
IE	99	90	78	69	20	9
EL	99	86	83	69	16	14
ES	93	80	65	52	25	16
FR	98	81	82	64	16	18
IT	96	91	59	53	37	6
CY	100	91	84	75	15	9
LV	94	88	44	37	45	7
LT	90	83	33	24	53	9
LU	100	92	95	87	5	8
HU	91	82	42	31	50	10
MT	99	88	96	85	3	12
NL	100	94	91	85	9	6
AT	97	86	54	41	38	13
PL	95	79	62	46	32	16
PT	90	82	40	30	48	9
RO	80	66	47	32	33	15
SI	98	91	84	75	14	12
SK	92	81	43	32	47	8
FI	98	93	41	28	61	5
SE	100	91	96	88	3	9
UK	97	87	82	71	15	11

Source: 'E-communications household survey', Special Eurobarometer 293, European Commission

In most Member States, 90 % or more of households had access to a telephone (either a fixed line or mobile), with only Romania below this level. Across the EU-27, an average of 83 % of households had a mobile phone connection and 70 % had a fixed line connection, while 57 % had both. In the vast majority of Member States, a higher proportion of households had a mobile phone connection than a fixed line connection, with fixed line telephony slightly more common than mobile telephony in Malta, Sweden, Luxembourg and Germany, and approximately the same in France. Around 24 % of households in the EU-27 only had a mobile phone (no fixed line), with this share over 50 % in the Czech Republic, Finland, Lithuania and Hungary. Figure 8.1 shows that there were slightly more households in the EU-27 using mobile phones with pre-paid cards than with contracts.

Figure 8.1: Households with and without mobile telephone access, EU-27, November-December 2007
(%)

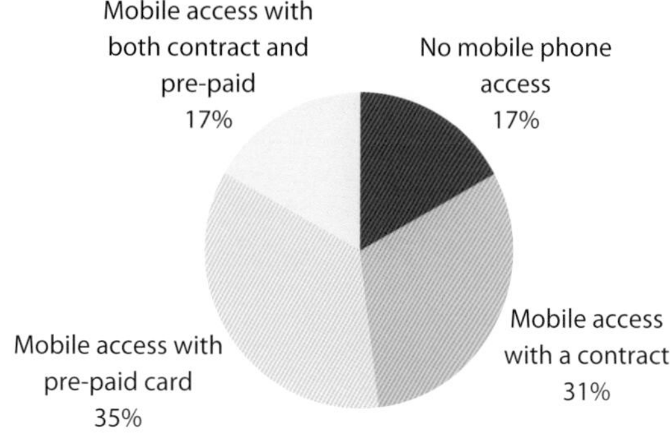

Source: 'E-communications household survey', Special Eurobarometer 293, European Commission

Figure 8.2: Rural access to DSL, December 2007 (1)
(%)

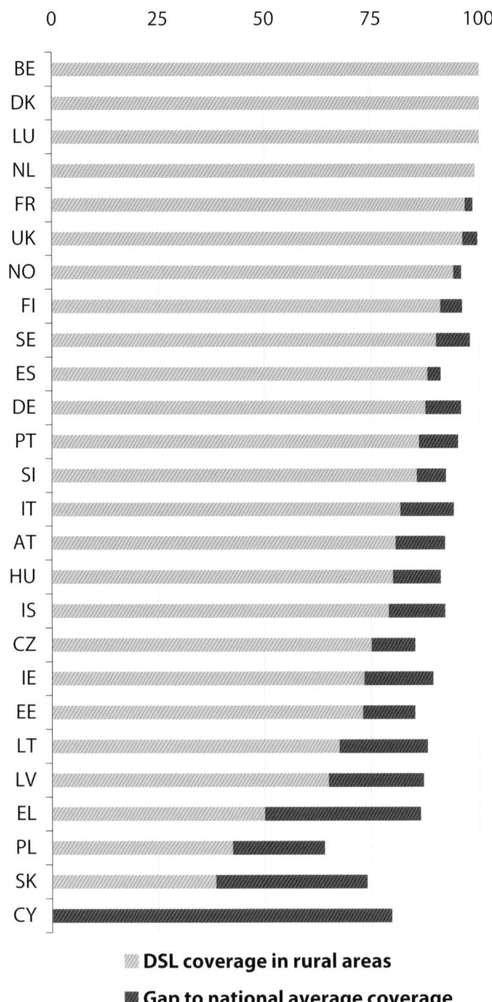

(1) Rural areas have a population density lower than 100 inhabitants/km²; Malta, definition of rural areas, not applicable; Bulgaria and Romania, not available.

Source: Broadband Coverage in Europe Final Report, 2008 Survey, IDATE

Table 8.3: Penetration rates of Internet access in households, 2007 (1)
(%)

	All households		Share of broadband access among households with access to the Internet at home
	All Internet access	Broadband access	
EU-27	54	42	77
BE	60	56	94
BG	19	15	81
CZ	35	28	80
DK	78	70	89
DE	71	50	70
EE	53	48	90
IE	57	31	54
EL	25	7	29
ES	45	39	88
FR	49	43	87
IT	43	25	58
CY	39	20	52
LV	51	32	63
LT	44	34	77
LU	75	58	77
HU	38	33	86
MT	54	44	82
NL	83	74	89
AT	60	46	77
PL	41	30	72
PT	40	30	77
RO	22	8	36
SI	58	44	76
SK	46	27	57
FI	69	63	91
SE	79	67	85
UK	67	57	85
MK	14	1	6
TR	8	2	23
IS	84	76	91
NO	78	67	86

(1) The former Yugoslav Republic of Macedonia, 2006; Turkey, 2005.

Source: Eurostat, information society statistics (theme9/science/isoc/isoc_ci_in_h and isoc_ci_it_h)

Close to half of all the households in the EU-27 had Internet access at home, a share that rose to over three quarters in the Netherlands, Sweden, Denmark and Luxembourg. A little over two fifths (42 %) of households had a broadband Internet connection at home. Digital subscriber lines (DSL), which along with cable modems are a popular way for consumers to have broadband Internet access, were available to the majority of the rural population in most Member States, but coverage was still low in a number of Member States (see Table 8.2). In most Member States a lower proportion of the rural population could potentially access DSL services; the only exceptions were Denmark and the Benelux countries, where the roll-out of DSL was effectively complete.

Two recent Eurobarometer household surveys (at the end of 2006 and end of 2007) on e-communications looked at the reasons for households not using certain services. Concerning fixed line telephony, just over two fifths (43 %) of households without a telephone line had never had one, and a similar proportion had previously had one but given it up.

Figure 8.3: Households without fixed line access, EU-27, November-December 2006
(%)

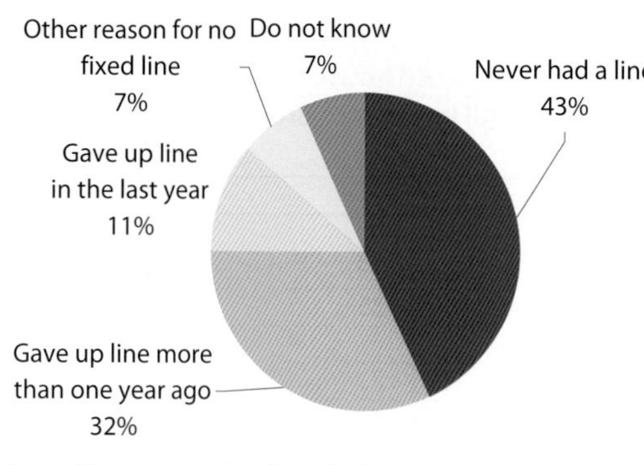

Source: 'E-communications household survey', Special Eurobarometer 274, European Commission

Figure 8.4: Households without mobile telephone access, EU-27, November-December 2006
(%, multiple answers possible)

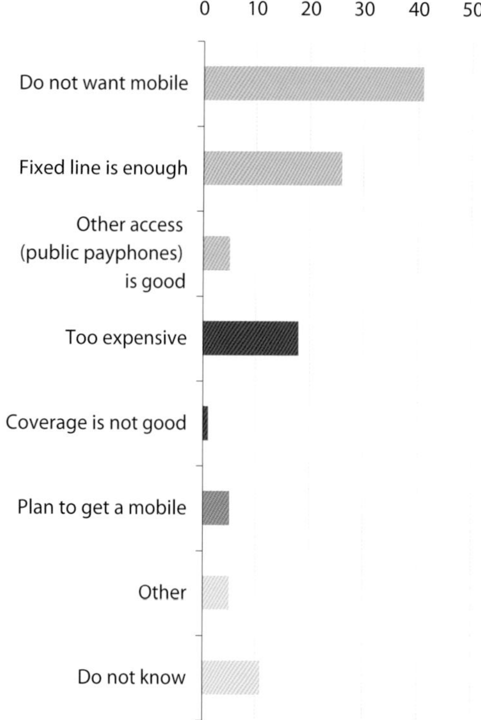

Source: 'E-communications household survey', Special Eurobarometer 274, European Commission

Figure 8.5: Households without Internet access at home, EU-27, November-December 2007
(%, multiple answers possible)

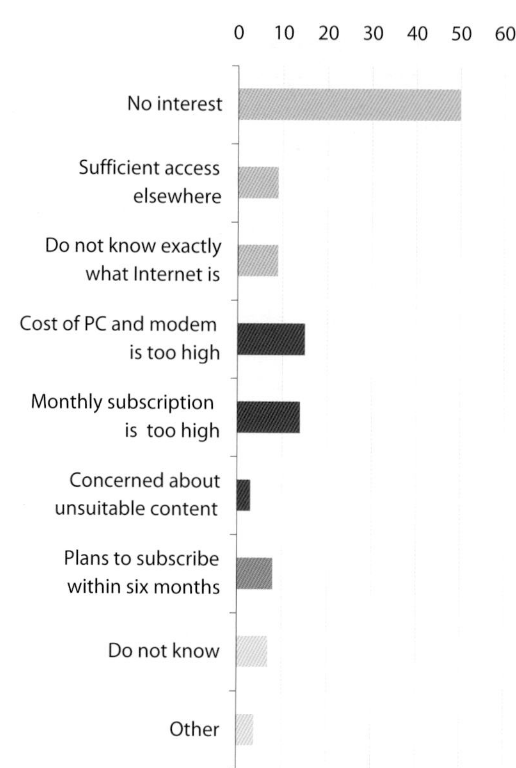

Source: 'E-communications household survey', Special Eurobarometer 293, European Commission

Concerning mobile telephony, the main reason for not having a subscription was simply that no one in the household wanted one (41 %) and the next most common reason (26 %) was that an existing fixed line was regarded as being sufficient. Less than one fifth (18 %) of households did not have a mobile phone because it was considered too expensive, and just over 5 % planned to get a mobile phone within the six months following the survey. Equally for Internet access, half of all households without Internet access simply did not want to have access, with around 15 % citing costs (hardware or subscription) as being too high.

Alongside the increase in the range of communication services available to consumers the choice of suppliers has also generally increased, leading to the possibility for users to switch suppliers. A 2006 Eurobarometer survey on services of general interest looked at the ease and appeal of switching suppliers: the results for mobile and fixed telephony, as well as for Internet access, show that for each of these three services up to one fifth of users had easily changed providers within the two years prior to the survey, and in each case some 4 % of users had given up trying to change provider because of the obstacles involved.

Figure 8.6: Switching providers in the previous two years, EU-25, May-June 2006
(% of users of the service)

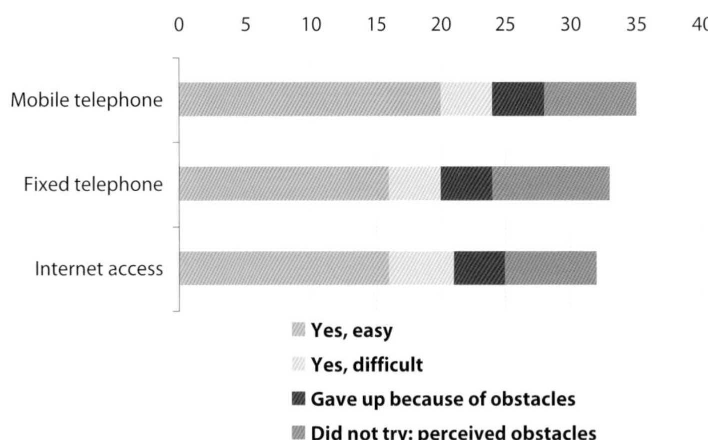

Source: 'Services of General Interest', Special Eurobarometer 260, European Commission

Table 8.4: Telephone calls, 2006 (1)
(million minutes)

	National calls (2)	Cellular mobile calls	Incoming international calls (3)	Outgoing international calls (4)
BE	13 388	9 612	:	1 599
BG	:	:	:	:
CZ	2 428	9 598	796	610
DK	11 799	7 566	1 020	595
DE	304 900	58 100	:	10 000
EE	919	1 742	86	102
IE	5 776	7 086	:	1 277
EL	18 408	11 309	1 102	1 435
ES	63 938	62 682	4 712	5 441
FR	85 633	94 026	7 802	6 070
IT	:	:	:	:
CY	1 264	2 160	152	253
LV	1 352	:	:	:
LT	1 547	3 777	284	112
LU	996	386	:	338
HU	6 305	11 904	583	475
MT	767	163	44	23
NL	20 633	16 075	811	2 179
AT	6 406	13 728	:	1 590
PL	25 394	25 714	1 936	931
PT	19 952	12 452	1 260	1 133
RO	6 130	2 811	1 750	603
SI	1 783	2 506	181	216
SK	1 543	4 708	535	308
FI	3 144	12 687	:	187
SE	23 693	12 642	:	1 430
UK	:	:	:	:
HR	3 991	4 744	840	390
TR	47 048	48 118	1 744	515
IS	575	450	32	40
NO	17 143	7 579	468	887
CH	12 392	5 812	:	2 687

(1) Greece, Malta and Slovakia, 2005; Latvia, 2003; Switzerland, including provisional data.
(2) Germany, 2005.
(3) Denmark, Germany, Spain and Romania, 2005; Greece, 2003.
(4) Germany, Finland, 2005.

Source: Eurostat, information society statistics (theme9/science/isoc/isoc_tc_tra and isoc_tc_cal)

8.2 Consumption

8.2.1 Consumption volume

As with data on the number of telephone lines and subscriptions to various services, data on the volume of voice and text messages services do not distinguish between business and residential use, with the relative importance of these two categories varying greatly between countries. Relative to the size of the population or the number of lines, the volume of national telephone calls was particularly large in Germany and Sweden, and to a lesser extent in Luxembourg, Malta and Portugal, while the lowest relative usage was in the Czech Republic, Romania and Slovakia; it should be noted that no recent data is available for three Member States including Italy (which traditionally had the highest number of minutes of national calls per head).

Among the countries with recent data available, Cyprus recorded the highest volume of mobile phone calls (in minutes) per inhabitant and per mobile phone subscription, ahead of Finland, with the lowest use of mobile phones in Romania.

In approximately half of the Member States the time spent making national calls exceeded the time spent making mobile phone calls, with the largest relative differences in Germany and Malta; in the other half of the Member States the reverse was true, with more time spent on mobile phone calls, most notably in Finland and the Czech Republic. The number of SMS messages per inhabitant and per mobile phone subscription was highest in Lithuania, Denmark and Cyprus.

Eurostat information society statistics provide a wide range of data on the use of communication services. Among these are information in relation to the use of the Internet for communications, including VoIP (Voice over Internet Protocol) calls. Among those countries for which data are available, by far the highest use of the Internet for making calls in 2006 was in Germany (some 60 000 million minutes in total, equivalent to an average of around 12 hours per person). There were wide ranging differences between countries as regards the take-up of Internet and VoIP calls, the former being far more common in Germany, whereas in France and Norway the relative importance of VoIP was considerably higher.

Table 8.5: Number of short and multimedia messages (SMS and MMS), 2006 (1)
(million)

	SMS	MMS (2)
BE	4 474	:
BG	538	1
CZ	6 230	39
DK	10 158	28
DE	22 200	153
EE	215	2
IE	5 745	31
EL	3 827	33
ES	8 761	216
FR	15 050	294
IT	:	:
CY	1 362	3
LV	:	:
LT	9 034	4
LU	248	:
HU	1 709	:
MT	410	1
NL	2 523	:
AT	2 059	29
PL	26 297	159
PT	12 458	50
RO	2 253	4
SI	538	9
SK	1 324	19
FI	3 088	22
SE	2 857	70
UK	:	:
HR	2 511	19
TR	25 088	:
IS	120	1
NO	5 225	99
CH	3 677	52

(1) Greece, Malta and Slovakia, 2005; the Netherlands, 2003.
(2) Romania, 2004.

Source: Eurostat, information society statistics (theme9/science/isoc/isoc_tc_sms)

Table 8.6: Internet telephony

	Internet and VoIP calls, 2006 (million minutes) (1)		Proportion of individuals having used the Internet (for private purposes) in the last 3 months, for telephoning over the Internet or for video-conferencing, November-December 2007 (%)
	Internet calls	VoIP (2)	
EU-27	:	:	9.8
BE	:	:	10.4
BG	:	:	11.1
CZ	1 237	92	16.1
DK	:	451	11.1
DE	60 000	9 000	12.6
EE	98	56	16.2
IE	5 378	:	7.4
EL	11 935	:	3.0
ES	13 505	:	8.2
FR	25 915	18 663	8.8
IT	:	:	5.6
CY	819	:	5.8
LV	94	:	18.1
LT	157	:	19.0
LU	231	:	23.1
HU	1 280	:	12.5
MT	:	129	7.0
NL	1 540	:	20.7
AT	3 901	:	11.8
PL	8 101	:	10.1
PT	997	:	8.6
RO	1 302	41	4.0
SI	806	149	8.8
SK	1 857	:	12.3
FI	:	:	17.7
SE	4 645	:	8.6
UK	:	:	8.5
HR	1 952	21	:
TR	4 242	:	:
NO	1 609	1 332	12.2
CH	:	*1 019*	:

(1) Greece, Malta and Slovakia, 2005; Ireland, 2004; Latvia and Poland, 2003.
(2) Romania, 2005; Switzerland, provisional.

Source: Eurostat, information society statistics (theme9/science/isoc/isoc_tc_tra); 'E-communications household survey', Special Eurobarometer 293, European Commission

These figures can be supplemented by data from a recent Eurobarometer survey that presents information on the proportion of households that used the Internet for telephoning or video-conferencing. At the end of 2007, the highest proportion of households using the Internet for these purposes was recorded in Luxembourg (23.1 %), while the Netherlands also reported a share of more than one in five households; the Czech Republic, Baltic Member States and Finland also had relatively high shares, with upwards of 16 % of households using the Internet for telephoning or video-conferencing. The EU-27 average stood at 9.8 %, while the lowest use of these technologies was reported in Cyprus, Italy, Romania and Greece.

A 2006 Eurobarometer survey focused on the use and cost of roaming services for mobile phones. A small majority (53 %) of mobile phone users in the EU-25 reported that they used mobile services when abroad, with the others either not travelling, switching off their mobile when abroad, or not taking it with them. Of those that did use mobile services abroad, 38 % only used voice services, 21 % only text message services, and 37 % both voice and text messages. The vast majority (90 %) of those using mobile services abroad did so with the same SIM (subscriber identification module) card as at home. Most consumers used their mobile phone abroad less than at home, with only a small proportion (3 % of all mobile telephone users using mobile services abroad) making more use of their phone. Only a small proportion (6 %) bought a SIM card in the country being visited, and so paid local mobile phone rates rather than roaming charges. More information may be found on roaming charges in the section on prices.

Figure 8.7: Use of roaming services, EU-25, September-October 2006
(% of mobile telephone users)

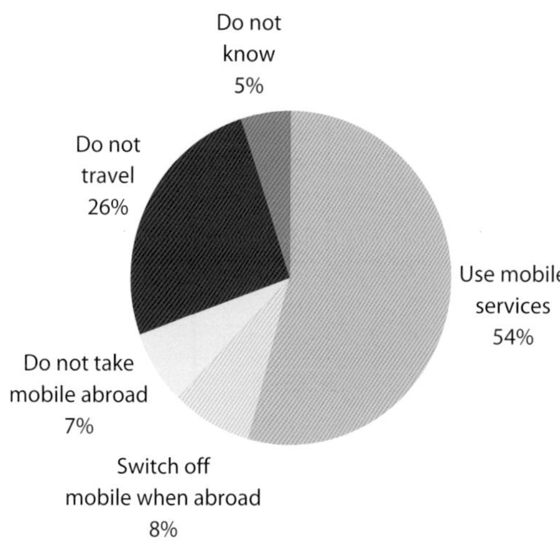

Source: 'Roaming', Special Eurobarometer 269, European Commission

Figure 8.8: Use of roaming services, EU-25, September-October 2006
(% of mobile telephone users using mobile services abroad)

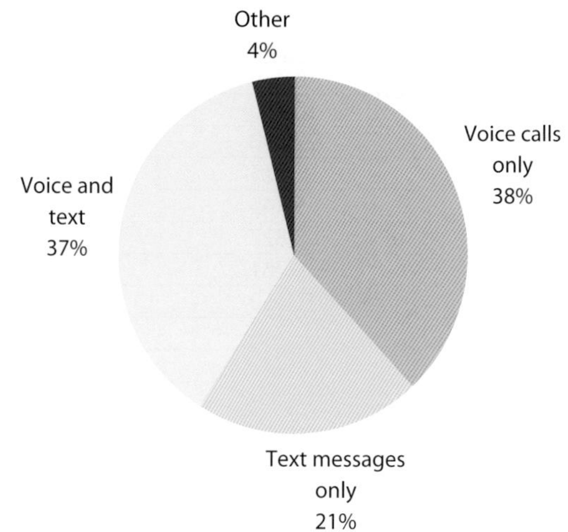

Source: 'Roaming', Special Eurobarometer 269, European Commission

Figure 8.9: Frequency of use of roaming services, EU-25, September-October 2006
(% of mobile telephone users using mobile services abroad)

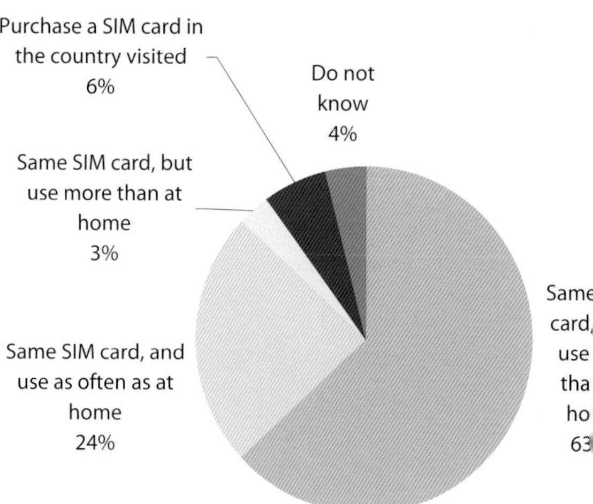

Source: 'Roaming', Special Eurobarometer 269, European Commission

As noted above, the Internet can be considered as a telecommunication service because of the shared technology and also because it is a competitor to more traditional communications channels. However, as can be clearly seen from Figure 8.10, the uses made of the Internet are far wider than simple communications, although e-mail, along with researching product information, was the most common Internet activity for EU-27 households in 2007. Overall 57 % of individuals (as opposed to households) aged 16 to 74 used the Internet in the three months prior to the 2007 ICT usage survey of households and individuals, with 38 % of individuals reporting using the Internet (nearly) every day. Many users accessed the Internet from a number of different places, the most common being at home or at work.

Figure 8.10: Percentage of individuals who, in the three months prior to the survey, used the Internet for specified activities, EU-27, 2007
(%)

(1) 2005.
(2) 2006.

Source: Eurostat, information society statistics (theme9/science/isoc/isoc_ci_ac_i)

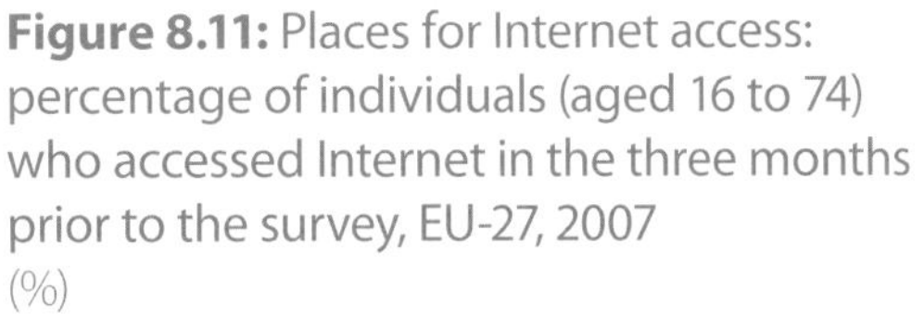

Figure 8.11: Places for Internet access: percentage of individuals (aged 16 to 74) who accessed Internet in the three months prior to the survey, EU-27, 2007
(%)

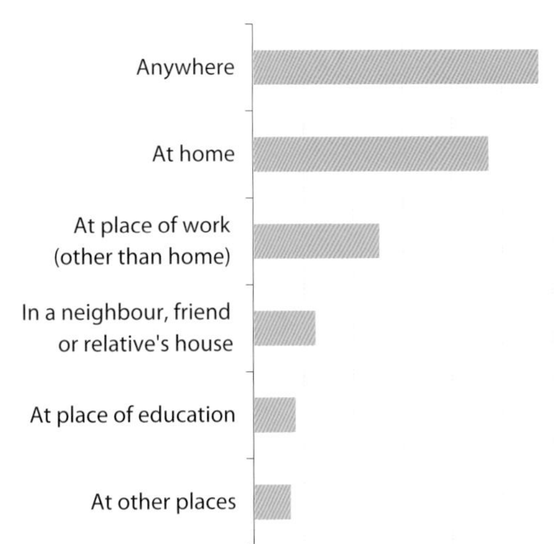

Source: Eurostat, information society statistics (theme9/science/isoc/isoc_ci_ifp_pu)

8.2.2 Consumption expenditure

Annual household consumption expenditure on communications averaged EUR 400 per person in the EU-27 in 2006. Household budget survey (HBS) data is presented in purchasing power standard (PPS) terms rather than in euro. This shows that, at comparable price levels, expenditure on communications within the EU-27 averaged PPS 738 per household. Among the Member States, expenditure generally ranged between PPS 400 and PPS 1 000 per household, with Ireland, Greece, Cyprus and Luxembourg above this range, and Romania and Bulgaria below it.

Expenditure on communications represented around 3.3 % of total household consumption expenditure in the EU-27 in 2005: telecommunications services accounted for nearly all of this, as postal services and telecommunications equipment each accounted for just over 4 % of the communications total. Figure 8.12 shows the share of communications in total household consumption expenditure for the EU-27 Member States, with the countries ranked by the average level of their total household consumption expenditure – this clearly shows that countries with lower overall expenditure spent a larger proportion of their budget on communications than those countries with higher overall expenditure, with a clear break between Portugal and Estonia in the graph. For the countries with higher levels of overall household expenditure, the share that communications accounted for ranged from 2.2 % in Luxembourg to 4.0 % in Slovenia, while among those with lower levels of total household consumption expenditure the share ranged from 4.6 % in Bulgaria and Lithuania to 6.5 % in Hungary.

The share of communications in household consumption expenditure ranged from 3.0 % among households in the highest income quintile to 3.7 % among those in the lowest income quintile for the EU-27 in 2005. There was also some variation in the proportion of total expenditure accounted for by communications according to age, as younger generations were more likely to use communication services. Expenditure peaked at 4.0 % for households with a head of household aged less than 30, falling to 2.5 % for those with a head of household aged 60 or over.

Figure 8.12: Structure of consumption expenditure: share of communications in total expenditure, 2005 (1)
(%)

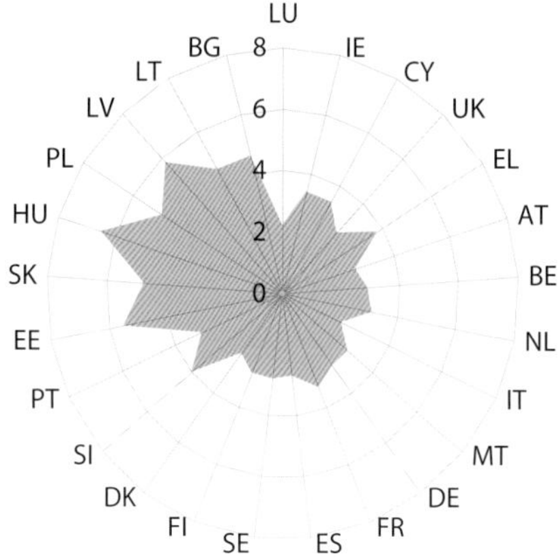

(1) Graph is ranked on overall household consumption per household (PPS); Czech Republic and Romania, not available.

Source: Eurostat, Household Budget Survey (theme3/hbs/hbs_str_t211 hbs_exp_t121)

Table 8.7: Mean consumption expenditure per household, communications, 2005
(PPS)

EU-27 (1)	738
BE	878
BG	325
CZ	555
DK	583
DE	828
EE	596
IE	1 255
EL	1 174
ES	701
FR	914
IT	621
CY	1 164
LV	610
LT	435
LU	1 139
HU	696
MT	837
NL	903
AT	793
PL	512
PT	616
RO	259
SI	950
SK	506
FI	693
SE	791
UK	852
HR	729
NO	770

(1) Estimate.

Source: Eurostat, Household Budget Survey (theme3/hbs/hbs_exp_t121)

8.3 Prices

8.3.1 Price inflation

Communications, particularly telecommunications, is one area where for many years prices have fallen, rather than increased. The harmonised index of consumer prices for communications fell in the EU-27 by 10.1 % between 2000 and 2007, equivalent to an average fall of 1.4 % per annum. Apart from a rise of 0.4 % in 2002, the communications consumer price index fell each year during this period.

The latest annual consumer price indices for communications show the greatest fall in 2007 was in Italy, the index dropping 8.4 %, while in Latvia and Lithuania the index fell by 6.0 % and 5.0 % respectively. Only two Member States recorded price increases in excess of 1 % in 2007, as prices rose by 7.1 % and 4.5 % respectively in Finland and Austria.

At a more detailed level, the price index for telecommunications equipment fell, on average, by 12.4 % per annum between 2000 and 2007 in the EU-27, while the index for telecommunications services fell much more sedately (1.0 % per annum on average). In contrast, the price index for postal services increased by an annual average of 2.4 %, in line with the increases witnessed for the all-items consumer price index.

Figure 8.13: Harmonised indices of consumer prices, EU-27
(2005=100)

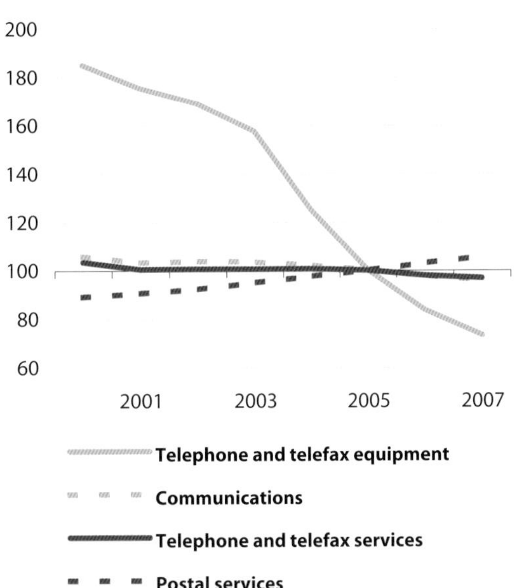

Source: Eurostat, Harmonised indices of consumer prices (theme2/prc/prc_hicp_aind)

8.3.2 Price transparency, affordability and price levels

The latest Eurobarometer household e-communications survey from 2007 provides information on households' opinions regarding various issues relating to price transparency. Figure 8.14 shows the vast majority of users felt that it was easy to check their fixed and their mobile telephony usage in a simple and user-friendly manner, around 80 % of all respondents in both cases. Around two thirds of respondents felt that it was easy to compare the tariff of their current provider with the tariff of competitors, with a slightly lower proportion for fixed telephony and slightly higher for Internet access. For each of these three telecommunications services around one third of respondents reported that they regularly read third-party price comparisons.

Figure 8.14: Households with specified services, EU-27, November-December 2007
(%)

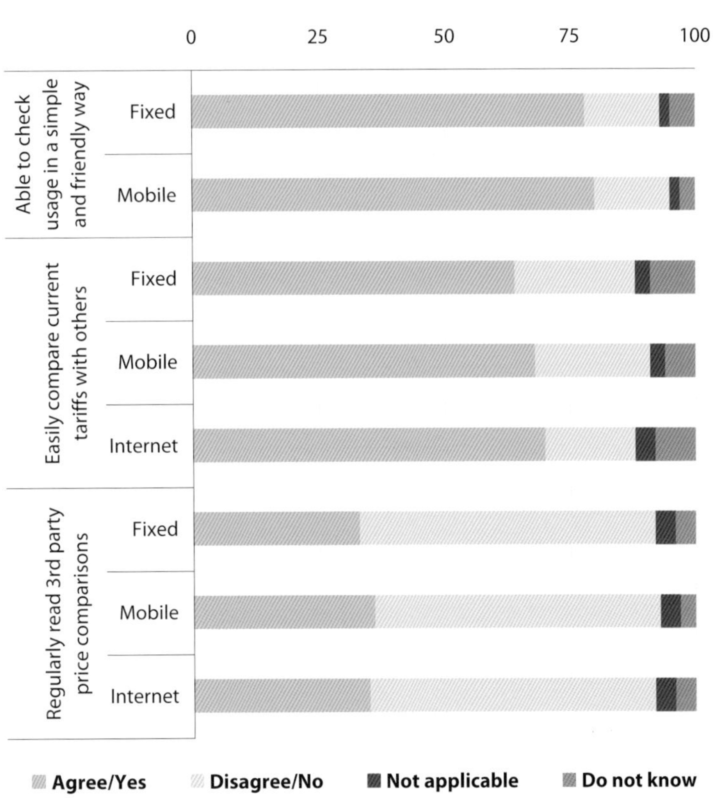

Source: 'E-communications household survey', Special Eurobarometer 293, European Commission

A 2006 Eurobarometer survey on services of general interest investigated the affordability of a range of services: the results are based only on the answers provided by the part of the population that indicated that they had used the specified services. Across the EU-25 as a whole, more than three quarters of respondents said that each of the three telecommunications services were affordable, 76 % for fixed and mobile telephony and 80 % for Internet access.

Information on households' opinions concerning the affordability of Internet access is also available from Eurostat's Urban Audit survey, which asked respondents in some of Europe's main cities whether communications' access was available at a reasonable price in public places and in the home. In several capital cities, mainly in northern Europe, more than half of all respondents agreed that public Internet access was available at a reasonable price, with the highest proportions being recorded in Dublin and London (although the proportion that disagreed with this view was also quite high in Dublin). In comparison, a large share of respondents in every capital city, except for Dublin, agreed that Internet access at home was available at a reasonable price; 80 % or more of respondents shared this view in Copenhagen, Helsinki and Amsterdam. The largest share that disagreed with this view was in Luxembourg (13 %), followed by Dublin (12 %) — see Table 8.8.

A Eurobarometer survey conducted in 2006 focused on roaming and the results indicate that just over two thirds of respondents agreed that the EU should ensure that tariffs for voice and text messages should not be a lot higher abroad than at home.

In June 2007, Regulation (EC) No 717/2007 of the European Parliament and of the Council on new rules concerning roaming came into force, setting maximum prices for phone calls made and received while abroad. A 'Eurotariff' set maximum prices for mobile phone calls made and received while abroad, and these maximum prices applied to all consumers unless they opted for special packages. Since the end of August 2008 making a roaming call cannot cost more than 46 cents and receiving one cannot cost more than 22 cents (excluding VAT). In September 2008, the Commission proposed to extend the scope and duration of this Roaming Regulation, limiting the Euro-SMS tariff for an SMS sent from abroad to no more than 11 cents (excluding VAT) and reducing further the tariff for voice calls from 43 cents on 1 July 2009, to 40 cents, 37 cents and 34 cents in each of the following years. The proposals also foresee the price of receiving a call decreasing from 19 cents on 1 July 2009 to 16 cents, 13 cents and 10 cents in each of the following years. Furthermore, users must receive an SMS when they are crossing borders within the EU to inform them of the price they are expected to pay for calls, while further information can be requested.

Figure 8.15: Affordability of communications, EU-25, May-June 2006
(% of respondents using the service)

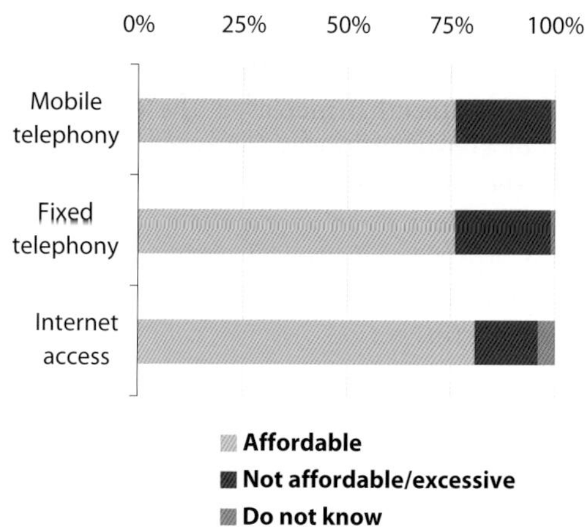

Source: 'Services of General Interest', Special Eurobarometer 260, European Commission

Table 8.8: Perceptions concerning Internet access, 2006
(%)

	Public Internet access			Internet access at home		
	At reasonable price (synthetic index 0-100)	Agree (strongly & somewhat)	Disagree (strongly & somewhat)	At reasonable price (synthetic index 0-100)	Agree (strongly & somewhat)	Disagree (strongly & somewhat)
Bruxelles / Brussel	82	41	9	86	59	10
Sofia	83	43	9	92	59	5
Praha	79	39	10	90	73	8
København	90	62	7	94	85	5
Berlin	91	55	6	92	69	6
Tallinn	92	51	5	94	69	4
Dublin	87	73	11	85	65	12
Athina	68	32	15	81	42	10
Madrid	81	39	9	84	51	10
Paris	80	38	9	92	71	6
Roma	72	35	14	88	57	8
Lefkosia	69	40	18	85	61	11
Riga	81	38	9	91	66	6
Vilnius	84	44	9	90	57	6
Luxembourg	66	29	15	82	61	13
Budapest	89	30	4	89	58	7
Valletta	87	46	7	96	64	3
Amsterdam	90	47	5	99	80	1
Wien	81	44	10	94	69	4
Warszawa	77	36	11	90	68	8
Lisboa	67	33	17	86	55	9
Bucureşti	83	43	9	89	53	7
Ljubljana	77	50	15	92	73	6
Bratislava	83	40	8	88	60	8
Helsinki	83	55	12	99	85	1
Stockholm	81	39	9	89	73	9
London	92	67	6	93	74	6
Zagreb	69	40	17	86	61	10
Ankara	57	39	30	61	38	24

Source: Eurostat, Perception survey results (theme1/urb/urb_percep)

Price level indices for 2007 show that communications were clearly cheapest in Cyprus (see Figure 8.17), where they were less than half the EU-27 average, and they were also relatively cheap in Lithuania, Sweden and Slovenia. The vast majority of Member States recorded price level indices within a relatively narrow range of 80 % to 110 % of the EU-27 average, with the Czech Republic, Ireland, Slovakia and Greece above this range. As such, the variation in price levels between Member States was lower for communications than for most of the other product headings covered in this publication, except for clothing and footwear (see Chapter 3).

Figure 8.16: Roaming charges, EU-25, September-October 2006
(%)

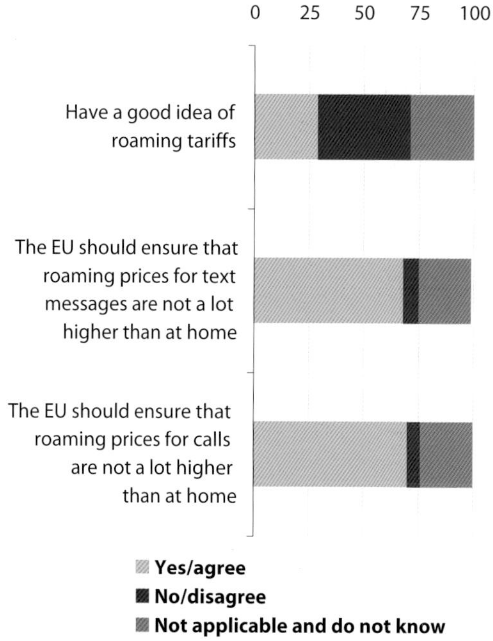

Source: 'Roaming', Special Eurobarometer 269, European Commission

Figure 8.17: Price level indices, communications, 2007
(EU-27=100)

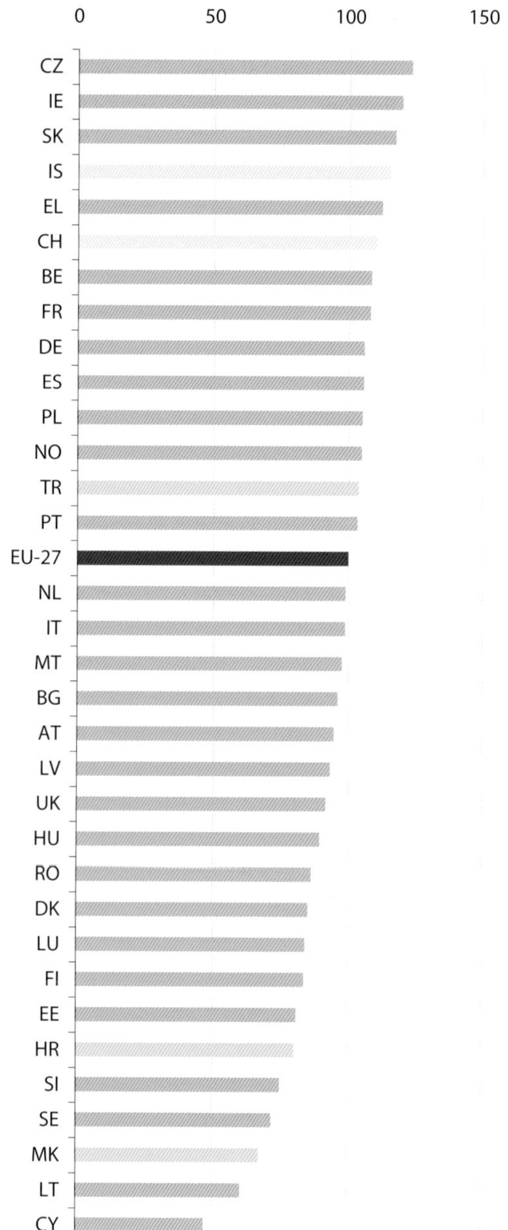

Source: Eurostat, Price level indices (theme2/prc/prc_ppp_ind)

8.3.3 Model and unit prices

Billing for telecommunications services is often, but not always, made up of a fixed (monthly) charge and a part related to the level of consumption. The fixed charge is therefore effectively the price of access to the service (the line rental), while the unit price (per second, per minute, per call or per megabyte, for example) is the cost of consumption. Not all packages are made up of both elements: there are many packages that are just a fixed charge, particularly common for broadband Internet access and some mobile telephony services, while others may focus on charges for usage, common for dial-up Internet access and pre-paid mobile services.

An overview of the relative importance of the two cost elements, namely the fixed charge and the usage charge, is provided in Figure 8.18 for fixed telephony; while these appear to be expenditure data they are more like a monthly price as they do not reflect actual levels of expenditure in each country, but are the cost for a fixed, identical basket of services in each country and so the data show how much, on average, consumers would pay in different countries for the same basket of services. The average share of fixed charges was particularly large in Cyprus, Ireland and Luxembourg, and it also accounted for more than half of total expenditure in the Netherlands and Austria. In contrast, the fixed charge share was lowest in Latvia, and was also less than one quarter of total expenditure in Lithuania. For the particular basket presented the total cost was notably higher in Finland and Ireland, and to a lesser extent in Belgium, while the lowest costs (for this basket) were recorded in Cyprus and Estonia.

Figure 8.18: Average monthly expenditure of standard residential user of fixed line telephony, September 2007 (1)
(EUR/line)

(1) Based on a basket of fixed national calls, international calls and calls to mobile networks.

Source: European Electronic Communication Regulation and Markets (13th report), European Commission, 2008

Table 8.9 shows example prices for three types of 10-minute telephone calls. Cyprus figures among the cheapest Member States for all three types of call, while Estonia is among the cheapest for both types of national call – although for international calls to the United States Estonia is above the EU-25 average. Slovakia is the most expensive Member State for both types of national call, while Latvia and Finland were the most expensive countries for making a call to the United States.

Figure 8.19 confirms the downward price trend noted for the harmonised index of consumer prices for telecommunications services, with the price of national long-distance calls declining faster between 2002 and 2006 than local calls. It also shows that across the EU-25 the average price of (national) incumbent operators in each Member State was slightly higher than the average price of (national) competitors: the difference was very small for local calls, but more substantial for national, long-distance calls.

Figure 8.19: Price (normal tariff, including VAT) of a 10 minute call at 11 am on a weekday, EU-25 (weighted average) (1)
(EUR)

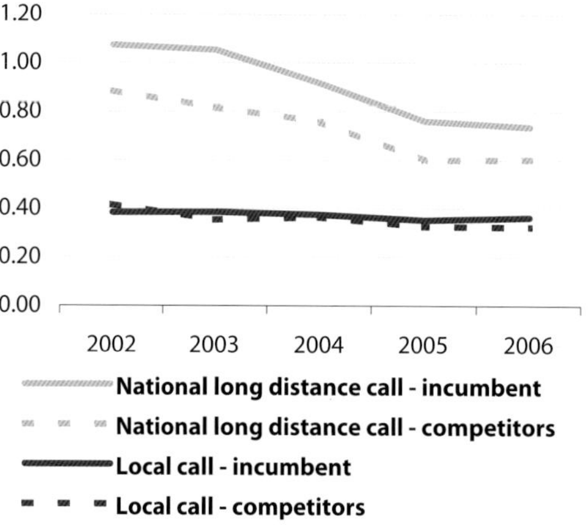

(1) Prices are for August or September each year.

Source: Telecoms price development, Teligen for the European Commission, December 2006

Table 8.9: Price (normal tariff, including VAT) of a 10 minute call at 11 am on a weekday, September 2006
(EUR)

	Local	National long distance	To United States
EU-25	0.36	0.74	1.79
BE	0.57	0.57	1.98
BG	:	:	:
CZ	0.56	0.56	2.02
DK	0.37	0.37	2.38
DE	0.39	0.49	0.46
EE	0.23	0.23	2.13
IE	0.49	0.82	1.91
EL	0.31	0.74	3.49
ES	0.19	0.85	1.53
FR	0.36	0.89	2.32
IT	0.22	1.15	2.12
CY	0.22	0.22	0.66
LV	0.36	1.03	5.94
LT	0.39	0.79	4.07
LU	0.31	:	1.37
HU	0.40	1.04	2.88
MT	0.25	:	1.64
NL	0.33	0.49	0.85
AT	0.49	0.59	1.90
PL	0.50	1.00	1.23
PT	0.37	0.65	3.11
RO	:	:	:
SI	0.26	0.26	1.40
SK	0.60	1.29	1.23
FI	0.24	0.94	4.90
SE	0.29	0.29	1.18
UK	0.44	0.44	2.23

Source: Teligen in Eurostat, structural indicators (theme0/strind/strind_t)

8.4 Consumer satisfaction and complaints

In 2006 a survey of consumers' satisfaction with a range of services of general interest was undertaken on behalf of the European Commission. It surveyed persons aged 18 and over that had used the specified services during the 12 months prior to the survey. Table 8.10 provides an overview of the levels of satisfaction and dissatisfaction for mobile and fixed telephony, as well as postal services. This indicates that a majority of respondents were satisfied with each of these services, and most of the remainder were neutral, leaving less than 10 % of respondents dissatisfied.

The most dissatisfied consumers were the Czechs, 23 % dissatisfied with their fixed telephone supply, 11 % with postal services, and 6 % with mobile telephony services – among the highest rates of dissatisfaction for each of these services. Some Member States reported relatively high dissatisfaction with just one or two of the three services covered, for example, postal services in Sweden and Denmark, fixed telephony and postal services in Italy, and fixed telephony in Portugal and Poland. In contrast, very few respondents in Ireland, Estonia or the Netherlands reported that they were dissatisfied with any of the three services.

Table 8.10: Satisfaction rates for communications services providers, 2006

	Mobile telephony		Fixed telephony		Postal services	
	Satisfied	Dissatisfied	Satisfied	Dissatisfied	Satisfied	Dissatisfied
EU-25	66	4	52	8	53	7
BE	74	1	62	3	44	6
BG	:	:	:	:	:	:
CZ	74	6	41	23	52	11
DK	71	6	61	8	53	12
DE	84	3	71	6	59	5
EE	78	2	71	4	72	3
IE	73	3	78	2	82	2
EL	71	3	45	9	70	4
ES	42	9	36	8	48	4
FR	55	6	49	8	46	7
IT	50	3	27	15	29	10
CY	84	1	69	7	77	6
LV	80	3	65	4	68	4
LT	79	4	72	5	80	1
LU	69	3	69	4	68	3
HU	83	2	65	10	71	8
MT	80	2	73	3	62	8
NL	51	3	40	3	48	3
AT	76	2	70	3	58	8
PL	67	4	45	13	61	8
PT	69	3	30	20	65	4
RO	:	:	:	:	:	:
SI	77	3	69	6	74	4
SK	73	4	53	9	59	6
FI	73	3	61	5	66	5
SE	72	5	63	7	45	22
UK	68	3	60	5	56	9

Source: Consumer satisfaction survey, IPSOS INRA for the European Commission Directorate-General for health and consumer protection, May 2007

A 2006 Eurobarometer survey on services of general interest looked at views concerning the fairness of terms and conditions of contracts with various telecommunication service providers. More than a quarter (28 %) of EU-25 respondents regarded such terms and conditions as unfair in the case of both mobile and fixed telephony, with one fifth (20 %) also finding Internet access terms and conditions unfair (see Figure 8.20).

For mobile telephony, the lowest proportions of respondents regarding their terms and conditions as fair were in France (42 %), Italy (45 %), Poland (48 %) and Spain (51 %), with all other Member States reporting rates well over 60 %. For fixed telephony, Poland (33 %) and Italy (36 %) again recorded a low proportion of consumers regarding their terms and conditions as fair, as was the case for Internet access (both just under 50 %).

The same survey looked at complaints concerning the three telecommunications services, as well as postal services, and found that the proportion of respondents having made a complaint to their service provider within the previous two years was notably higher for the three telecommunications services than for postal services, and also higher than for the other services surveyed (mainly energy, water and transport service providers). The proportion having made a complaint to their service provider peaked at an EU-25 average of 12 % for Internet access, and was particularly high for this service in Sweden (25 %), the Netherlands (19 %) and Finland (17 %) — see Figure 8.21.

Figure 8.20: Proportion of respondents regarding the terms and conditions of their contracts to be fair, EU-25, May-June 2006 (1)
(% of users of the specified services)

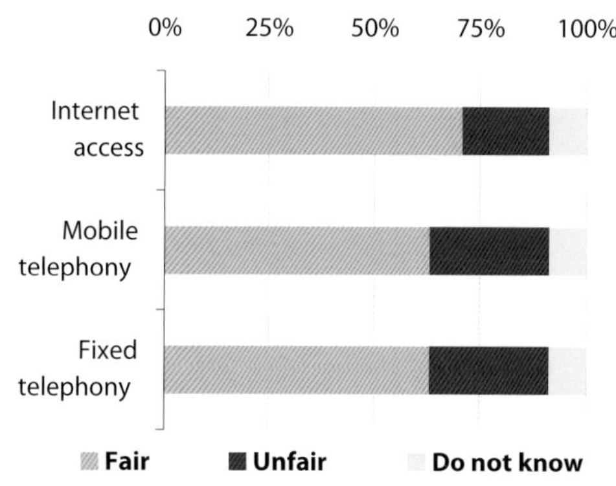

Source: 'Services of General Interest', Special Eurobarometer 260, European Commission

Figure 8.21: Proportion of respondents having personally made a complaint about any aspect of specified services, EU-25, May-June 2006
(%)

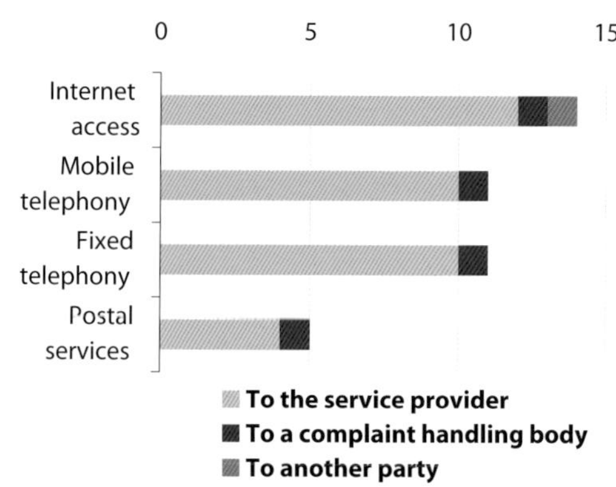

Source: 'Services of General Interest', Special Eurobarometer 260, European Commission

Table 8.11: Lack of satisfaction: reasons for not using the Internet more intensively (multiple answers allowed), EU-27

General Internet use, 2008 (% of households without Internet access at home)	
Access not needed (content is not useful, not interesting, etc.)	37
Equipment costs are too high	25
Lack of skills	23
Access costs are too high (telephone, etc.)	21
Access elsewhere	14
Access not wanted (content is harmful, etc.)	14
Privacy or security concerns	5
Physical disability	2
Other reasons	11
Broadband use, 2007 (% of households without broadband access)	
Do not need it	37
Too expensive	25
Not available in the area	20
Some members can access broadband somewhere else (e.g. at work)	12
Other reasons	13

Source: Consumer satisfaction survey, IPSOS INRA for the European Commission Directorate-General for health and consumer protection, May 2007

8.5 Quality

Targets have been set regarding delivery speed for postal services: 85 % delivery within three days and 98 % delivery within five days. According to the International Post Corporation, the actual performance of postal operators surpasses these objectives. In 2007, an average of 94.9 % of cross-border priority letter mail was delivered within three days of posting for the EU-15 plus Iceland, Norway and Switzerland, up from 69.1 % in 1994; when expanded to cover all but one of the EU-27 countries the average was 94.1 % within three days.

At least half of the EU-25 respondents to a 2006 Eurobarometer survey on services of general interest reported that their interests were well protected concerning fixed and mobile telephony, with around 30 % reporting that they were badly protected. For Internet services both shares were much lower, reflecting the relatively high proportion of respondents who did not know whether they were well protected or not. For postal services the proportion regarding their interests as badly protected (19 %) was the lowest of the ten services covered by the survey, while the share regarding their interest as well protected (70 %) was the highest.

A 2005 survey gives some indication of the problems EU-27 consumers face regarding security issues linked to computer and Internet use. By far the most common problem was the loss of time and information from computer viruses, reported by one third of respondents having used the Internet in the previous year.

Figure 8.22: Cumulative proportion of European international first class/priority letter mail delivered within specified number of days after the day-of-posting (1)
(%)

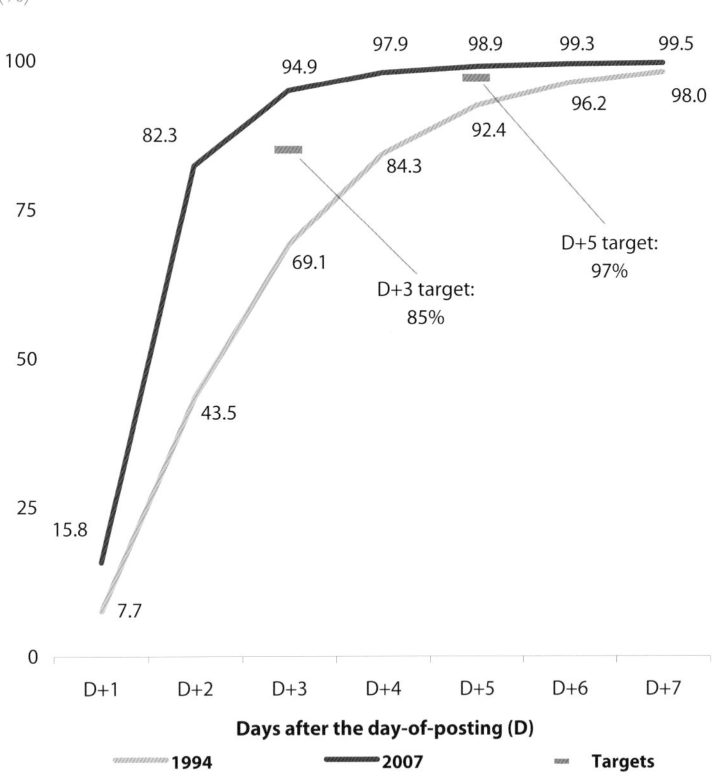

(1) UNEX-18 includes EU-15, Iceland, Norway and Switzerland; D is the day of posting, and the number of days after the day of posting is calculated on a five day working week, also excluding public holidays in the recipient country.

Source: UNEX Quality of Service Monitoring, International Post Corporation, 2007 (www.ipc.be)

Figure 8.23: Proportion of respondents who feel that consumers' interest are well protected, EU-25, May-June 2006
(%)

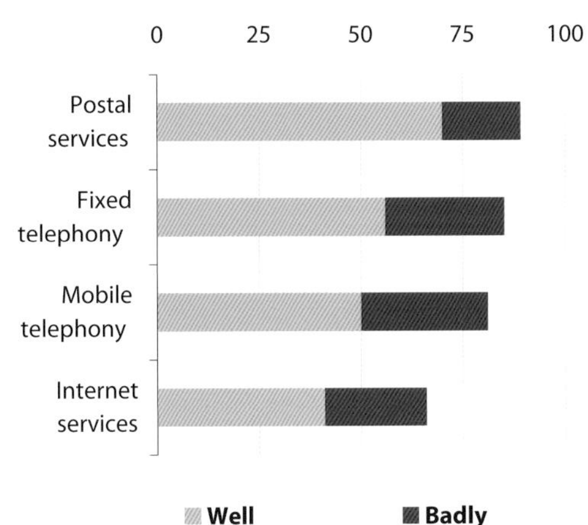

Source: 'Services of General Interest', Special Eurobarometer 260, European Commission

Figure 8.24: Percentage of individuals who have, in the 12 months prior to the survey, experienced the following security problems, EU-27, 2005
(%)

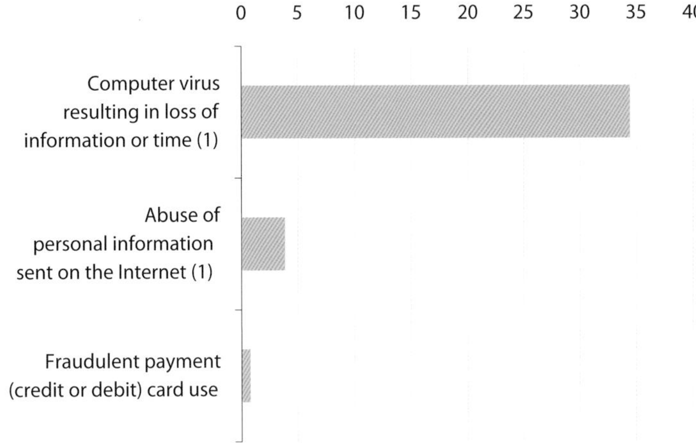

(1) Percentage among individuals who used Internet within the last year.

Source: Eurostat, information society statistics (theme9/science/isoc/isoc_pi_i1)

8.6 Externalities: health

Electromagnetic fields (EMF) occur in nature; exposure to man-made sources has increased due to increased electricity demand, and the development of various electrical appliances that rely on electromagnetic fields. Exposure comes, for example, from high-voltage power lines, household electrical appliances, radio and television broadcast facilities, mobile telephones and their base stations. Research has so far produced no conclusive evidence one way or the other concerning the health effects from exposure to these fields.

In 2006, a Eurobarometer survey looked at opinions concerning EMF, and asked whether respondents felt that various EMF producing appliances affected their health or not. Figure 8.25 shows the results for mobile phones and mobile phone masts for the EU-27, with around three quarters of respondents expressing the opinion that these two types of equipment affect their health to at least some extent.

Figure 8.25: Proportion of respondents who feel that the selected items affect their health, EU-27, October-November 2006 (%)

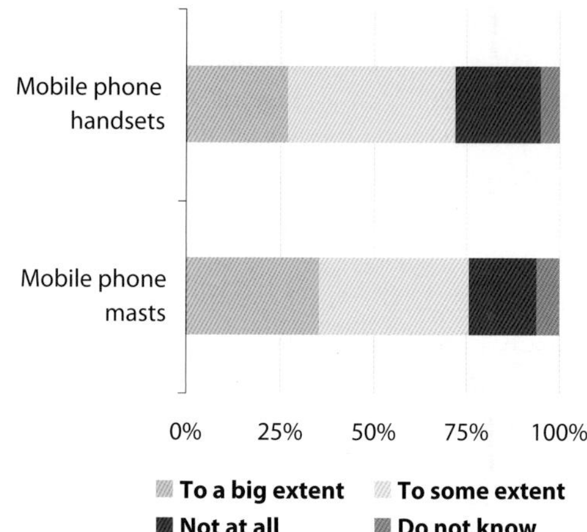

Source: 'Electromagnetic fields', Special Eurobarometer 272, European Commission

For more information

Directorate-General for the Information Society and Media:
http://ec.europa.eu/dgs/information_society/index_en.htm

Directorate-General for the Internal Market and Services:
http://ec.europa.eu/internal_market/post/index_en.htm

Directorate-General for Enterprise and Industry:
http://ec.europa.eu/enterprise/ict/index_en.htm

9

Recreation and culture

Recreational and cultural activities play a key role in promoting social cohesion, improving health, and providing education. Expressing and sharing cultural ideas and traditions (for example, through exhibitions, theatre, food and music) can be an important asset for strengthening and promoting diversity, and breaking down prejudices, as was illustrated during the 2008 European Year of Intercultural Dialogue.

Reading books and magazines can also be an important form of information and education. Indeed, cultural exposure can stimulate skills, such as openness to inter-cultural ideas, styles, teamwork, creativity and imagination, which may be particularly useful for citizens and workers in the knowledge-based economy. This will be a constant message during the 2009 European Year of Creativity and Innovation.

Table 9.1: Availability of entertainment venues in capital cities, 2003-2006
(per million inhabitants)

	Cinema seats (1)	Museums (2)	Theatres (3)	Public libraries (4)
Bruxelles/Brussel	15 283	81	112	81
Sofia	9 371	24	22	109
Praha	20 546	75	47	83
København	23 039	54	100	46
Berlin	17 267	49	18	19
Tallinn	8 776	107	28	61
Dublin	:	40	65	117
Athina	24 732	35	44	86
Madrid	23 178	4	21	:
Paris	34 376	20	80	31
Roma	19 146	20	:	17
Lefkosia	19 932	65	35	23
Riga	6 367	45	8	69
Vilnius	8 130	47	11	54
Luxembourg	42 547	120	72	409
Budapest	14 418	59	14	:
Valletta	:	111	30	:
Amsterdam	14 682	:	:	:
Wien	19 499	65	28	96
Warszawa	18 007	29	18	174
Lisboa	37 387	76	60	672
Bucureşti	5 916	16	15	27
Ljubljana	19 500	:	:	:
Bratislava	22 961	35	47	42
Helsinki	16 274	71	16	89
Stockholm	24 974	67	53	96
London	15 153	22	19	52

(1) Sofia, Copenhagen, Rome, Nicosia, Amsterdam and London, 1999-2002; Ljubljana, 1994-1998.
(2) Sofia, Prague, Copenhagen, Berlin, Dublin, Athens, Madrid, Nicosia, Bucharest and London, 1999-2002.
(3) Sofia, Prague, Copenhagen, Berlin, Dublin, Madrid, Nicosia and London, 1999-2002.
(4) Sofia, Prague, Copenhagen, Dublin, Athens, Paris and Bucharest, 1999-2002.

Source: Eurostat, Urban Audit (theme1/urb/urb_vcity)

As well as these key roles, recreational and cultural activities are a primary source of entertainment and well-being, in which a growing proportion of Europe's population are participating. Furthermore, sport and leisure activities can bring health benefits, reducing the risk of disease and weight problems.

9.1 Access and choice

Eurostat's Urban Audit survey provides information about the numbers of cinema seats, museums, theatres and public libraries in a range of European cities and towns. In order to express the concept of availability, numbers are expressed per million inhabitants in the resident population. However, the relative size of cities should also be borne in mind: for example, with 83 000 residents, Luxembourg's population was by far the smallest among the EU-27 capitals, dwarfed by the 7.4 million inhabitants of London. Furthermore, for some of the cities, it should be borne in mind that data relate to the survey period through until 2002 or in the case of Ljubljana even earlier (see the footnotes to the table) and there are likely to have been changes in the intervening period.

In broad terms, the city of Luxembourg scored relatively highly as regards the availability of a range of cultural amenities (see Table 9.1). Elsewhere, the availability of cinema seats per million residents was relatively high in Paris and Lisbon, the number of museums was relatively high in Tallinn and Valletta (also two of the EU-27's smaller capital cities), the number of theatres was relatively high in Brussels and Copenhagen, while the number of libraries was relatively high in Sofia, Dublin, Warsaw and Lisbon.

While the number of libraries may be used as a proxy for availability and access, it should be noted that different libraries will offer a range of different titles and media. Furthermore, while some libraries are rich in terms the number of titles and different media that they offer, the uptake of renting/borrowing by citizens may also be quite different from one city to the next (with others choosing to consult books in the library rather than take them home). Each resident in Helsinki borrowed an average of more than 18 titles per year, compared with less than one title per resident per year in Vilnius.

Table 9.2: Density of screens in multiplexes (1)
(%)

	1996 (2)	2001 (3)	2006
BE	37.1	48.7	59.0
BG	:	11.1	41.1
CZ	1.1	10.0	18.5
DK	7.8	15.5	20.0
DE	:	25.2	26.2
EE	:	13.6	16.4
IE	27.4	30.8	45.1
EL	5.6	10.4	29.6
ES	10.5	40.9	61.3
FR	12.4	26.3	32.5
IT	0.4	12.0	27.9
CY	:	:	:
LV	:	12.7	28.6
LT	:	10.1	28.8
LU	38.5	40.0	41.7
HU	1.6	17.7	27.9
MT	:	38.1	41.5
NL	3.5	12.4	20.0
AT	12.1	38.9	39.9
PL	1.1	22.0	39.1
PT	12.1	18.9	35.3
RO	:	3.6	19.4
SI	:	13.0	36.5
SK	:	2.8	8.1
FI	3.0	12.7	15.5
SE	12.7	13.9	15.5
UK	30.9	56.2	64.8

(1) The screens situated in multiplexes (i.e. theatres with at least 8 screens), as a percentage of the total number of screens.
(2) Greece and Luxembourg, 1997; Poland and Finland, 1998.
(3) Lithuania, 2002; Bulgaria, Latvia and Malta, 2003.

Source: Cinema d'Europa, Media Salles (http://www.mediasalles.it/ybk07adv/)

Table 9.3: Market share of films, by origin of film, 2006 (1)
(%)

	Domestic (2)	Other Europe (3)	US (4)
BE	6.3	15.9	77.1
DK	22.3	15.4	60.8
DE	25.4	7.5	66.0
EL	16.7	:	:
ES	15.6	11.8	71.0
FR	44.6	8.8	44.7
IT	22.9	10.8	64.2
LU	1.8	24.8	72.7
NL	11.3	9.9	76.9
AT	2.0	15.9	:
PT	2.2	26.9	69.4
FI	23.7	14.4	60.8
SE	21.4	15.8	59.8
UK	19.1	0.9	76.2

(1) Those Member States for which no information is shown, not available.
(2) Austria and Sweden, 2005; Greece, 1999.
(3) Portugal and Sweden, 2005; United Kingdom, 2000.
(4) Portugal and Sweden, 2005.

Source: Cinema d'Europa, Media Salles (http://www.mediasalles.it/ybk07adv/)

While the number of seats per million inhabitants might be regarded as a broad indicator of accessibility to cinemas, it says nothing about their distribution, nor the choice of films shown. The cinema market has changed rapidly in the EU-27 in recent years, as multiplexes (in other words, theatres with at least eight screens) account for an increasing share. In Belgium, Spain and the United Kingdom about six out of every ten screens are now found in a multiplex (see Table 9.2), up from about three out of ten a decade before in Belgium and the United Kingdom and one out of every ten in Spain. The increase in multiplex cinemas in the ten years to 2006 was particularly fast in a number of the Member States that joined the EU since 2004 (for example, Poland and Hungary). Among the Member States for which data are available for 2006, only Slovakia had fewer than 10 % of its cinema screens in multiplexes.

In most of the EU-15 Member States, US films dominated the cinema market in 2006 – although this was not the case in France, where there was an almost equal number of French and US films being shown (see Table 9.3). Figures from Media Salles suggest a renaissance in domestic and other European films in some of the Member States, as about one quarter of the films being shown in Luxembourg (2006) and Portugal (2005) came from other Member States, in contrast to only 1 % of films being shown in the United Kingdom (2000).

Consumers across the EU-27 tend to make most of their purchases of information and communication equipment, as well as entertainment and leisure goods, in specialised chain stores (see Figure 9.1). According to a retail satisfaction survey in 2008, almost two thirds (65.5 %) of consumers in the EU-27 preferred to shop for information and communication equipment in a chain store specialising in these products, while 53.7 % of EU-27 consumers shopped for entertainment and leisure goods in chain stores specialising in these products. The next most popular retail formats were independent retailers and supermarkets/ hypermarkets for both groups of products. While the Internet was a more popular retail format than department stores for information and communication equipment, this was not the case for entertainment and leisure goods.

There was a wide range of shopping preferences across the Member States. For example, the purchase of information and leisure goods from independent stores was the favoured retail format for consumers in Hungary and Slovenia, whereas supermarkets and hypermarkets were favoured by consumers in Bulgaria. About half of all consumers in Denmark bought information and communication equipment as well as entertainment and leisure goods through the Internet in 2008.

Figure 9.1: In which of the following places have you or has a member of your household bought information or communication equipment and entertainment and leisure goods most, EU-27, 2008?
(%)

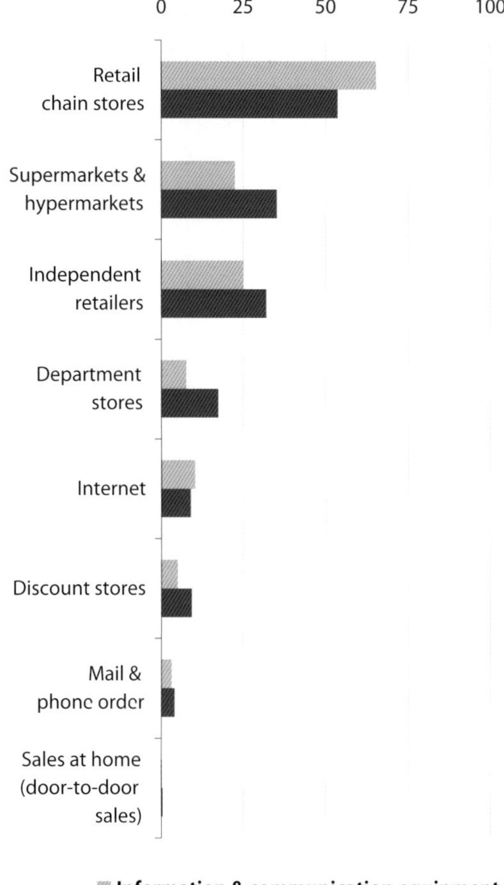

Source: 'Retail satisfaction survey', IPSOS for the European Commission, August/September 2008

9.2 Consumption

9.2.1 Consumption volume

Television

Watching television is a recreational activity enjoyed by millions of Europeans. Hungarians watched an average of about four and three quarter hours per week in 2004, the highest figure among the Member States; each individual in Greece, Poland and Italy also watched over four hours of television on average per week. In contrast, those living in Cyprus, Denmark, Finland, Austria, Sweden and Luxembourg watched between two and a half and three hours of television per week, the lowest levels in the EU – note that the age range of the population covered in Figure 9.2 varies greatly between Member States and this may to some extent influence the results shown.

Figure 9.2: Average viewing time per adult, 2004 (1)
(minutes per week)

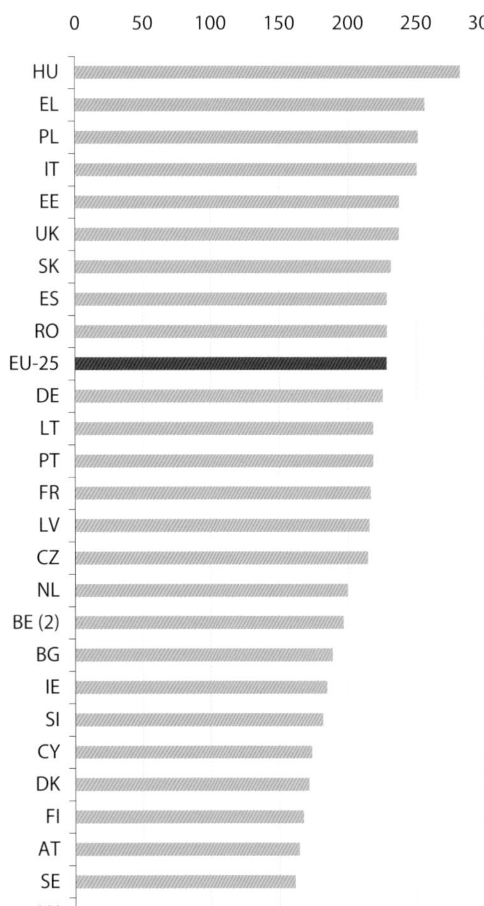

(1) Adult individuals aged 15 years and over (with the following exceptions): Estonia, Cyprus, Hungary and Latvia, 18 years and over; Poland, Spain and the United Kingdom, 16 years and over; Germany, 14 years and over; the Netherlands, 13 years and over; Denmark, Luxembourg, Austria and Slovakia, 12 years and over; Finland, 10 years and over; Malta, not available.
(2) Simple average of the figures for northern (172) and southern Belgium (220).

Source: Television 2005, International key facts, IP International Marketing Committee (CMI)

Figure 9.3: Television, cable and home satellite usage, third quarter 2005
(% of households)

Source: Dataxis for the European Commission

Technological innovation has resulted in audio-visual content being made available on a variety of devices (such as mobile phones, laptop computers, MP3 players), and through a variety of different platforms. These innovations have triggered new entrants to the market (such as Internet protocol television and network operators offering online video services) and resulted in ever-increasing audience fragmentation.

The European Commission recommended [23] that Member States switch-off analogue, terrestrial television transmission by 2012, citing consumer benefits of improved picture quality, better sound, better portable and mobile reception, more TV and radio channels and enhanced information services. Most of the Member States have started running digital, terrestrial television and as the switch-off gathers pace, more and more households have switched to cable and satellite systems (with terrestrial freeview options becoming available). An OECD and International Telecommunication Union (ITU) report on the 'Communications outlook, 2007' suggested that in September 2006, Luxembourg was the first Member State to complete the switch-off process (with more than 95 % of households having cable access).

(23) COM(2005) 204 final.

According to Dataxis (see Figure 9.3), in the third quarter of 2005, Austria was the only Member State where satellite television was the most common means of household access to television. Although the number of terrestrial-only households fell sharply from 1995, there remain some Member States where such households continue to be in the majority, such as Greece and Cyprus, where they accounted for over 90 %, or Latvia, Lithuania, Spain and Italy (between two thirds and three quarters of all households); to some degree, these patterns may also reflect the degree to which different access possibilities are available.

Table 9.4: Cinema, theatre and museum admissions in capital cities, 2003-2006
(thousand)

	Cinema (1)	Museums (2)	Theatres (3)
Bruxelles/Brussel	4 606	1 992	:
Sofia	1 062	825	430
Praha	4 372	2 793	3 000
København	3 973	2 237	1 121
Berlin	11 488	8 740	3 100
Tallinn	981	662	506
Dublin	:	1 033	:
Athina	2 456	938	1 038
Madrid	13 160	4 484	2 843
Paris	30 209	17 272	:
Roma	11 857	847	1 361
Lefkosia	523	511	:
Riga	1 390	826	560
Vilnius	966	500	322
Luxembourg	1 300	160	74
Budapest	7 793	4 033	2 457
Valletta	266	1 240	118
Amsterdam	3 218	:	:
Wien	5 348	8 853	2 456
Warszawa	7 180	2 235	1 478
Lisboa	4 714	3 451	347
București	1 751	:	:
Ljubljana	370	922	242
Bratislava	1 310	469	452
Helsinki	2 460	1 488	719
Stockholm	3 968	5 078	1 730
London	:	26 885	:

(1) Sofia, Copenhagen, Rome, Nicossia and Amsterdam, 1999-2002; Valletta, 1989-1993.
(2) Sofia, Prague, Copenhagen, Berlin, Dublin, Madrid, Nicossia and London, 1999-2002.
(3) Sofia, Prague, Copenhagen, Berlin, Madrid, Rome, Lisbon and Ljubljana, 1999-2002.

Source: Eurostat, Urban Audit (theme1/urb/urb_vcity)

Cinemas, theatres and museums

According to Media Salles, there were about 930 million admissions to cinemas in the EU-27 in 2006, of which about 855 million were in EU-15 Member States. France (22.1 %), the United Kingdom (18.3 %), Germany (16.0 %) and Spain (14.4 %) collectively contributed over two thirds (70.8 %) of cinema admissions in the EU-27 in 2006.

Among most of the EU-27's capital cities, admissions to cinemas were higher than for either museums or theatres (see Table 9.4), although of these three types of cultural venues, theatres proved the most visited venues in Valletta, Vienna, Ljubljana and Stockholm. Note that admissions data (in particular for museums) are likely to be affected by the number of tourists visiting each city.

Internet

The use of computers is widespread: computers are used on a daily basis for work, study, shopping and communications (in particular e-mail), as well as other recreational activities such as playing games, or accessing information.

According to Eurostat's survey on ICT usage, almost six out of every ten (57 %) individuals in the EU-27 aged between 16 and 74 years old [24] used the Internet in the three months preceding the 2007 survey, a proportion that has grown steadily (up from 44 % in 2004). Of these, the most common recreational use (31.0 %) was for services related to travel and accommodation (see Table 9.5). A little more than one fifth of Internet users played or downloaded music or games (22.0 %), as well as reading or downloading online newspapers or journals (21 %), while about one in seven Internet users across the EU-27 used the Internet to listen to or watch radio or television.

Among the Member States, nearly four out of every five individuals in the Netherlands (84 %), Denmark (81 %), Sweden (80 %), Finland (79 %) and Luxembourg (78 %) used the Internet in the three months preceding the 2007 survey, and these were generally the Member States where Internet use for the various recreational activities was also highest.

([24]) There are some Member States where the age range is different: for example, in Slovenia and Finland the data covers individuals aged 10 to 74; see http://epp.eurostat.ec.europa.eu/cache/ITY_SDDS/EN/isoc_ci_base.htm for more information.

Table 9.5: Internet use for recreational and cultural activities in the three months preceding the survey, 2007
(% of individuals)

	Internet use	of which, used for: Music & games	Travel & accomm.	Papers & journals	VOIP & video conf. (1)	Selling goods & services (2)	Web radio or T.V.
EU-27	57	22	31	21	10	10	15
BE	67	23	34	17	10	8	13
BG	31	16	5	10	11	1	10
CZ	49	20	25	22	16	5	8
DK	81	33	51	47	20	22	34
DE	72	21	45	21	13	21	15
EE	64	29	21	50	16	5	21
IE	57	13	39	10	7	3	10
EL	33	15	16	16	3	0	8
ES	52	25	33	24	8	3	17
FR	64	22	30	18	9	7	17
IT	38	14	18	17	6	4	8
CY	38	20	23	22	6	1	13
LV	55	27	18	18	18	2	20
LT	49	27	14	32	19	1	20
LU	78	33	55	42	23	12	29
HU	52	27	24	28	13	4	16
MT	45	19	21	20	7	7	14
NL	84	45	48	40	21	20	35
AT	67	17	28	24	12	7	7
PL	44	17	11	15	10	5	13
PT	40	21	14	15	9	1	14
RO	24	12	5	9	4	1	6
SI	53	25	26	23	9	9	23
SK	56	23	26	25	12	2	11
FI	79	34	57	50	18	13	24
SE	80	35	41	43	9	13	33
UK	72	26	46	22	8	13	18

(1) Voice-over-Internet Protocol.
(2) Czech Republic, Greece and Portugal, 2006.

Source: Eurostat, Urban Audit (theme1/urb/urb_vcity)

9.2.2 Consumption expenditure

Annual household consumption expenditure on recreation and culture averaged EUR 1 300 per person across the EU-27 as a whole in 2006. Between 2000 and 2006, particularly sharp increases in household consumption expenditure on recreation and culture were noted in Lithuania, Estonia, Hungary and Slovakia, where expenditure more than doubled from relatively low levels of between EUR 100 and EUR 200 per person. There were also notable increases in the Czech Republic, the United Kingdom, Cyprus and Ireland, generally resulting from increases in the volume component of final consumption expenditure rather than price increases.

In terms of comparable price levels between countries, the 2005 HBS shows that consumption expenditure on recreation and culture in purchasing power standard (PPS) terms was, on average, PPS 2 187 for the EU-27. There were considerable variations among the Member States, from lows of a little over PPS 200 in Bulgaria and Romania, to a high of PPS 3 943 in the United Kingdom (see Table 9.6).

Expenditure on recreation and culture accounted for an average 8.3 % of total household consumption expenditure across the EU-27 in 2005. This share was highest in Austria (12.6 %), closely followed by the United Kingdom and Sweden, and lowest in Greece, Romania (at about half of the EU-27 average) and particularly in Bulgaria (2.9 %) – see Figure 9.4.

Table 9.6: Mean consumption expenditure per household, recreation and culture, 2005 (PPS)

EU-27 (1)	2 187
BE	2 868
BG	204
CZ	1 289
DK	2 738
DE	3 168
EE	691
IE	3 670
EL	1 285
ES	1 659
FR	1 926
IT	1 680
CY	2 044
LV	667
LT	402
LU	3 869
HU	909
MT	2 879
NL	3 193
AT	3 809
PL	662
PT	1 182
RO	224
SI	2 234
SK	712
FI	2 731
SE	3 398
UK	3 943
HR	853
NO	3 593

(1) Estimate.

Source: Eurostat, Household Budget Survey (theme3/hbs/hbs_exp_t121)

Figure 9.4: Structure of consumption expenditure: share of recreation and culture in total expenditure, 2005 (1)
(%)

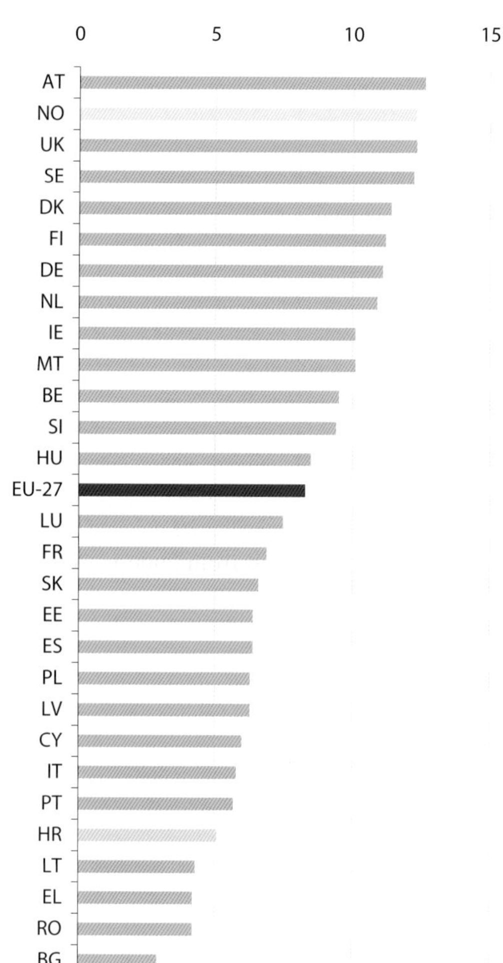

(1) EU-27, estimate; Czech Republic, not available.

Source: Eurostat, Household Budget Survey (theme3/hbs/hbs_str_t211)

Many recreational and cultural goods cannot be considered as essential consumer goods, but rather as luxury purchases (holidays, cultural services, recreational and sporting services). It is perhaps unsurprising, therefore, that a steadily increasing proportion of household consumption expenditure was spent on recreation and cultural activities as household income rose; this expenditure represented 6.4 % of the household expenditure for the lowest income quintile within the EU-27 in 2005, rising to a 9.4 % share among those households in the highest income quintile. There was also a wide disparity in the proportion of expenditure on recreation and culture between various socio-economic groups, the highest share (9.6 %) being recorded for non-manual workers, well above the 6.9 % share for the unemployed.

9.3 Prices

9.3.1 Price inflation

The EU-27's harmonised index of consumer prices for recreation and culture rose moderately in the period between 2000 and 2002 (up by 1.2 % per annum), and then remained largely unchanged (-0.1 % per annum) through to 2007. However, there were contrasting price developments for many of the items that make-up the aggregate for recreation and culture (see Figure 9.5). For example, there was a strong and steady decline in the price of audio-visual, photographic and information processing equipment during the period 2000 to 2007 (on average by 7.6 % per annum), in contrast to price increases for recreational and cultural services (3.1 % per annum), package holidays (2.7 %), or newspapers, books and stationery (2.5 %).

Among the Member States, the consumer price index for recreation and culture rose relatively quickly during the period from 2000 to 2007 in Hungary and Slovenia (4.0 % per annum), with the highest price increases being recorded in Romania (10.1 % per annum). In contrast, there were relatively moderate price reductions in Sweden (-0.2 % per annum), the United Kingdom (-0.4 %), France (-0.6 %) and Lithuania (-0.7 %).

Figure 9.5: Harmonised indices of consumer prices, EU-27
(2005=100)

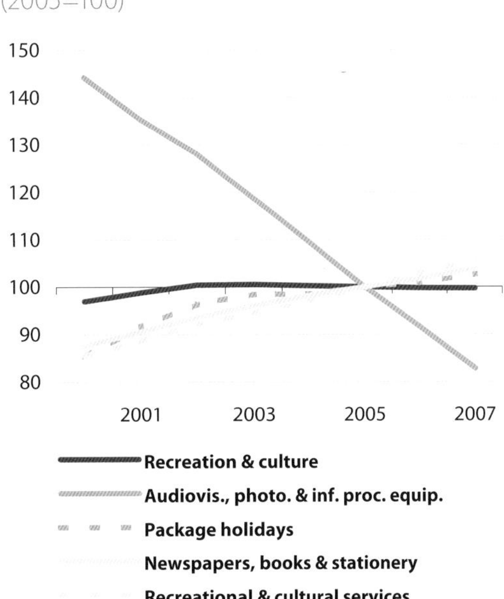

Source: Eurostat, Harmonised indices of consumer prices (theme2/prc/prc_hicp_aind)

9.3.2 Price levels

In comparison with the average price level across the EU-27, prices for recreation and culture in 2006 were highest in the Scandinavian countries (see Figure 9.6); in particular in Denmark, about one third (34.4 %) above the EU-27 average. In contrast, price level indices in all of the Member States that joined the EU since 2004 were below the EU-27 average; the lowest levels were recorded in Bulgaria (at a little less than half the EU-27 average), Romania, Lithuania, Slovakia, Latvia and the Czech Republic.

The average price paid for a cinema ticket was above EUR 7.00 in Finland, the United Kingdom and Denmark in 2006, but was closer to EUR 9.00 in Sweden (see Table 9.7). In contrast, the lowest average entry prices to see a film at the cinema were recorded in Slovakia and Bulgaria (both about EUR 2.50 a ticket).

Between 1996 and 2006, there was a broad and widespread increase in average cinema ticket prices. The strongest price increases were recorded among many of the Member States that joined the EU since 2004, but there were also relatively substantial increases in Spain and the United Kingdom.

Figure 9.6: Price level indices, recreation and culture, 2006
(EU-27=100)

Source: Eurostat, Price level indices (theme2/prc/prc_ppp_ind)

Table 9.7: Average ticket price for the cinema
(EUR)

	1996 (1)	2001	2006 (2)
BE	4.99	5.50	5.88
BG	0.72	2.16	2.59
CZ	1.00	2.37	3.26
DK	5.99	7.29	7.18
DE	5.11	5.55	5.96
EE	1.66	3.70	4.28
IE	4.66	5.21	6.43
EL	4.20	5.60	:
ES	3.18	4.20	5.22
FR	5.30	5.46	5.94
IT	4.81	5.32	5.76
CY	3.99	6.47	6.44
LV	1.15	2.85	3.53
LT	:	2.31	2.88
LU	5.12	6.20	6.60
HU	0.96	2.54	3.26
MT	:	:	4.59
NL	5.54	6.24	6.66
AT	5.38	6.29	6.01
PL	1.63	3.65	3.73
PT	2.60	3.80	4.17
RO	0.39	0.96	2.98
SI	2.67	3.20	3.77
SK	0.81	1.63	2.45
FI	6.17	7.08	7.53
SE	7.17	7.49	8.68
UK	4.34	6.63	7.23

(1) Bulgaria, 1997; Greece, 1995.
(2) Belgium and Luxembourg, 2005

Source: Cinema d'Europa, Media Salles (http://www.mediasalles.it/ybk07adv/)

9.4 Consumer satisfaction

Residents of the EU-27's capitals vary considerably in how they feel about the recreational and cultural aspects of their city. Table 9.8 shows public perception about a range of characteristics in capital cities. In terms of green space, sports facilities, cinemas and cultural facilities, a large majority of residents in Amsterdam and Helsinki seemed to be satisfied (rather or strongly) with the amenities their city offered. In Copenhagen, Paris, Luxembourg, Stockholm and London, a high proportion of respondents were also satisfied, although the share fell considerably for those satisfied with sports facilities (which was notably lower than for the other amenities).

There was dissatisfaction with green space areas in Budapest (50 %), Bratislava (62 %), Athens (68 %) and Sofia (74 %), while a majority of respondents were dissatisfied with sports facilities in Bratislava (51 %) and Sofia (55 %). A relatively high proportion of residents in Athens (26 %), Nicosia (28 %) and Sofia (31 %) were dissatisfied with their cities' cultural facilities.

A consumer satisfaction survey in 2008 covered purchases of information and communication equipment, as well as entertainment and leisure goods. On a scale of 1-10 (higher scores reveal greater satisfaction), the average EU-27 consumer rated their overall satisfaction with retailers as 9.0 for information and communication equipment and 8.9 for entertainment and leisure goods. The highest levels of satisfaction were recorded in Lithuania, Bulgaria and Hungary, with the lowest levels of satisfaction being recorded among consumers in Italy, Spain and the Netherlands (see Figure 9.7).

Table 9.8: Perception of satisfaction with recreational facilities in capital cities, 2006 (1)
(% of resident population)

	Green space	Sports facilities	Cinemas	Cultural facilities
Bruxelles/Brussel	85.4	60.4	68.8	81.3
Sofia	25.6	25.8	56.8	46.4
Praha	65.8	61.0	67.8	83.5
København	88.2	59.9	87.7	93.6
Berlin	82.0	61.2	80.8	88.6
Tallinn	67.8	58.7	53.2	84.7
Dublin	78.7	55.5	83.3	86.4
Athina	32.0	53.5	65.3	63.2
Madrid	65.7	51.6	68.7	70.7
Paris	77.6	48.9	81.0	89.0
Roma	73.4	54.5	76.1	71.6
Lefkosia	52.5	55.4	69.0	63.4
Riga	75.0	43.0	59.0	74.8
Vilnius	66.7	36.5	58.7	77.1
Luxembourg	84.2	64.8	73.6	78.3
Budapest	49.7	34.7	50.2	78.5
Valletta	51.9	52.7	54.7	61.8
Amsterdam	80.6	74.4	80.8	91.4
Wien	83.6	62.0	77.8	92.6
Warszawa	79.1	30.3	76.0	76.2
Lisboa	50.9	44.5	69.3	69.4
București	52.0	35.0	38.8	62.2
Ljubljana	67.1	44.3	74.0	81.2
Bratislava	36.6	31.7	58.2	69.3
Helsinki	88.2	87.9	84.4	94.8
Stockholm	92.3	62.0	83.9	89.5
London	86.9	55.8	73.5	81.7

(1) Ratings are given for 'rather' and 'strong' satisfaction.

Source: Eurostat, Perception surveys (theme1/urb/urb_percep)

Figure 9.7: Overall, to what extent are you satisfied with your regular retailer when it comes to buying information and communication equipment and entertainment and leisure goods, 2008? (1)
(average, 1-10)

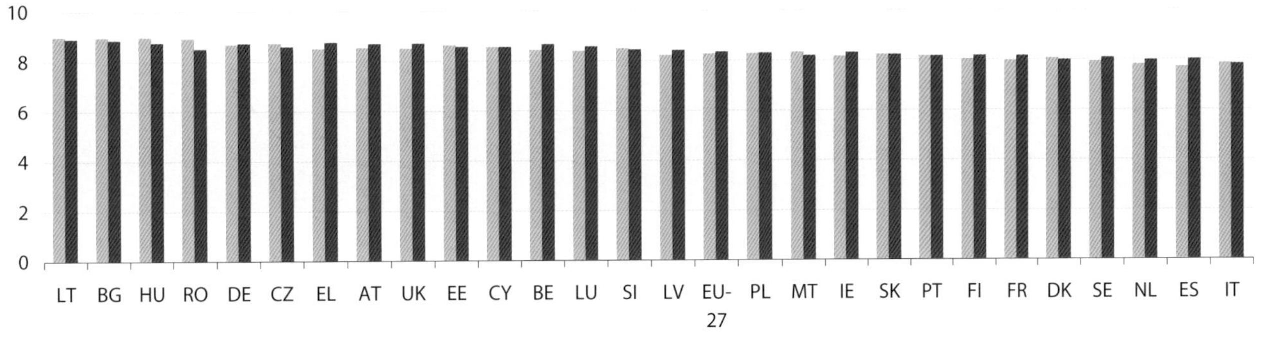

(1) Average on a scale of 1 (not at all satisfied) to 10 (fully satisfied).

Source: 'Retail satisfaction survey', IPSOS for the European Commission, August/September 2008

The same survey reveals that 12.5 % of consumers in the EU-27 experienced problems when purchasing information and communication equipment in 2008, the share for entertainment and leisure goods being 8.9 %. Among those who faced problems, about half complained about product quality (see Figure 9.8), with between 10 % and 16 % complaining about problems associated with the quality of service, repairs, or delivery.

When asked if they thought their regular retailer would replace, repair, reduce the price or give them their money back if the information and communication equipment or the entertainment and leisure goods that they had bought were defective or not fit for purpose, a majority of EU-27 consumers agreed (in both cases an average of 8.0 was recorded – see Figure 9.9).

Figure 9.8: Problems faced by consumers when purchasing information and communication equipment and entertainment and leisure goods in the past 12 months, EU-27, 2008 (1)
(% share of those experiencing problems, multiple answers allowed)

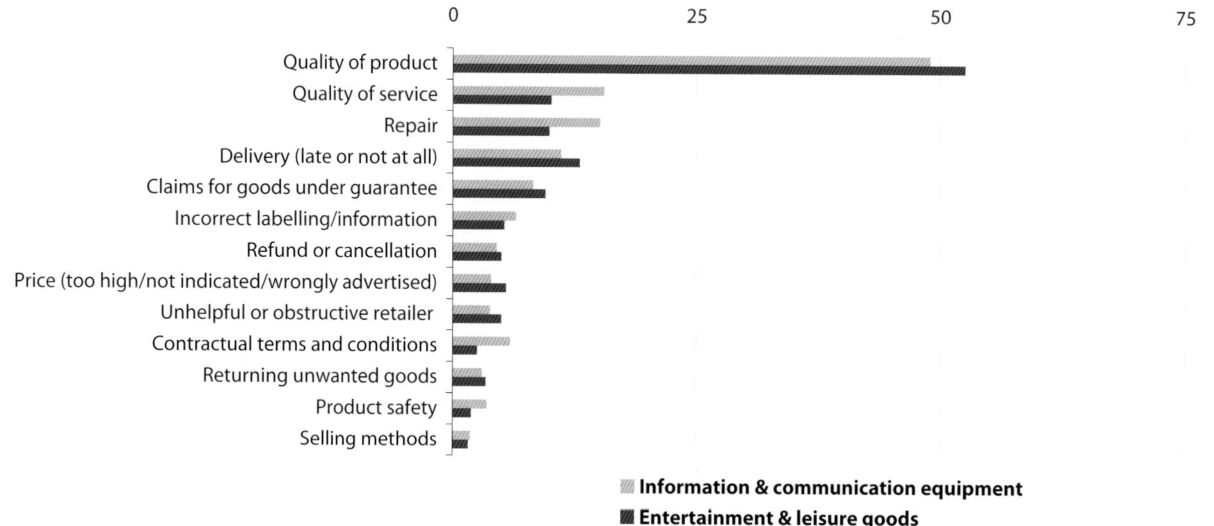

(1) When purchasing information and communication equipment in 2008, 12.5 % of EU-27 consumers reported facing at least one problem, the corresponding share for entertainment and leisure goods being 8.9 %; note that consumers may have faced more than one problem.

Source: 'Retail satisfaction survey', IPSOS for the European Commission, August/September 2008

Figure 9.9: Do you agree that your regular retailer would replace, repair, reduce the price or give you your money back if information and communication equipment and entertainment and leisure goods you had bought were defective or not fit for purpose, 2008? (1)
(average, 1-10)

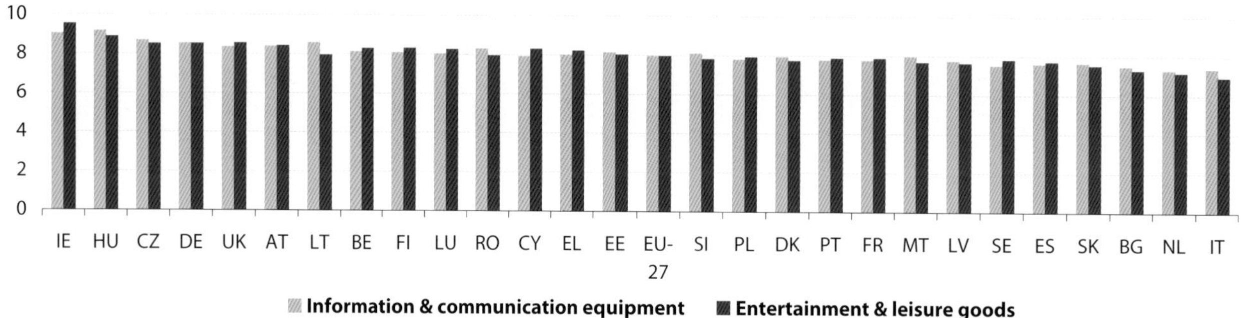

(1) Average on a scale of 1 (totally disagree) to 10 (totally agree).

Source: 'Retail satisfaction survey', IPSOS for the European Commission, August/September 2008

9.5 Quality

The same consumer satisfaction survey also asked respondents to what extent they agreed that information and communication equipment as well as entertainment and leisure goods sold by their regular retailer were reliable (in other words, they worked well and without failure for a reasonable period of time) and to what extent they were safe. On a scale of 1-10 (with 10 for total agreement), the average score across the EU-27 was, in both cases, 8.2 for reliability, while scores of 8.2 and 8.3 were recorded for safety (see Figure 9.10).

Figure 9.10: To what extent do you agree that information and communication equipment and entertainment and leisure goods sold by your regular retailer are reliable (i.e. it works well and without failure for a reasonable period of time) and safe, 2008? (1)
(average, 1-10)

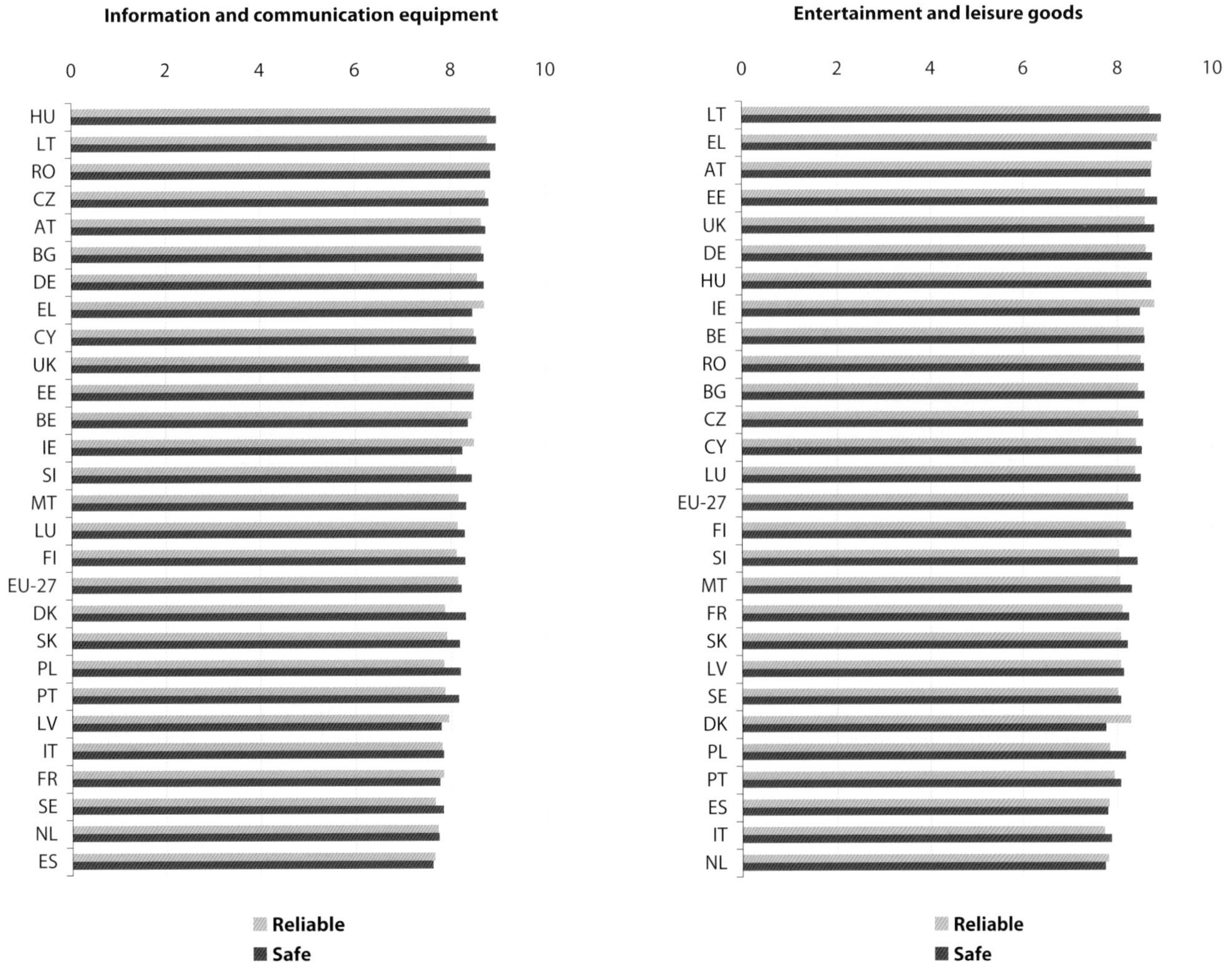

(1) Average on a scale of 1 (totally disagree) to 10 (totally agree).

Source: 'Retail satisfaction survey', IPSOS for the European Commission, August/September 2008

10

Education

The majority of pupils in the EU spend around a decade or more at school – it is where they gain the basic knowledge, skills and competences that will serve them throughout their lives. The importance of education and training are widely recognised for the development and success of a knowledge-based society and economy. The EU's education and training policy has been given added impetus since the adoption of the Lisbon strategy in 2000, the EU's overarching programme focusing on growth, productivity and jobs, which underlined the importance of knowledge and innovation.

EU Member States and the European Commission have in recent years strengthened their cooperation through the Education and Training 2010 work programme. The programme integrates previous actions in the fields of education including vocational education and training under the Copenhagen process, and links up with the Bologna process. There are three overall objectives:

- improving the quality and effectiveness of education and training systems;
- facilitating access to education and training systems;
- opening up EU education and training systems to the wider world.

The European Commission has set-out number of lifelong learning programmes:

- Comenius, which focuses on pre-school and primary to secondary school education and seeks to develop knowledge and understanding of European cultures, languages and values;
- Erasmus, which seeks to enhance the quality and reinforce the European dimension of higher education by encouraging transnational cooperation between universities;
- Leonardo de Vinci, which plays a role in preparing EU citizens for entering the labour market;
- Grundtvig, which addresses the teaching and learning needs of institutions and individuals involved in adult education;
- Jean Monnet, which aims to promote knowledge on European integration on a world-level.

The European Commission has published a modernisation agenda for universities and other reforms have been promoted through the Bologna process, working towards establishing a European higher education area by 2010. Key programmes in this context include:

- Tempus, which funds co-operation projects in the areas of curriculum development, innovation, teacher training, university management and structural reforms in higher education, and;
- Erasmus Mundus, which is a co-operation and mobility programme in the field of higher education that promotes the European Union as a centre of excellence in learning around the world.

Vocational education and training (VET) are considered important activities to assist the population to meet current (and future) challenges in society and the labour market. The basis for European cooperation in VET was laid out in the Copenhagen declaration which was endorsed in November 2002, and signified the starting point of the Copenhagen process. A central part of the process is the development of common frameworks and tools to enhance the transparency, recognition and quality of competences and qualifications, making the mobility of learners and workers easier. The most important of these tools are the European qualifications framework (EQF), Europass, the European credit system for VET (ECVET) and the common quality assurance reference framework for VET (CQARF). The Copenhagen process was developed within the perspective of lifelong learning, which should enable people to connect up and build-on learning acquired at various times, and in both formal and non-formal contexts. The Leonardo da Vinci strand of the lifelong learning programme 2007-2013 provides financial support for the implementation of VET policies.

Table 10.1: ISCED 97 codes used in this chapter

ISCED 97 level code	Education level
0	Pre-primary education
1-4	Primary, secondary and non-tertiary post-secondary education
1-3	Primary and secondary education
1	Primary education or first stage of basic education
2	Lower secondary or second stage of basic education
3	Upper secondary education (including some vocational or technical orientation)
3A	Upper secondary programmes with academic orientation
3B	Upper secondary programmes with occupation orientation
3C	Upper secondary programmes with labour market orientation
4	Post-secondary non-tertiary education
5-6	Tertiary education
5A	Tertiary programmes with academic orientation
5B	Tertiary programmes with occupation orientation
6	Second stage of tertiary education leading to an advanced research qualification

Classification of education: ISCED

Throughout this chapter tables and figures frequently make reference to particular levels of education based on the 1997 version of the international standard classification of education (ISCED). Empirically, ISCED assumes that several criteria exist which can help allocate education programmes to different levels of education. Depending on the level and type of education concerned there is a need to establish a hierarchical ranking system between main and subsidiary criteria (typical entrance qualification, minimum entrance requirement, minimum age, staff qualification, etc.). Table 10.1 provides a description of the levels 0 to 6 and the main aggregates thereof that are used throughout this chapter. It should be noted that there is ongoing work to revise the current ISCED classification.

10.1 Access and choice

In the EU-27, there were in excess of 8.2 million teachers (ISCED levels 0-4) and academic staff (ISCED levels 5-6) in 2006. In primary and secondary education (ISECD levels 1-3) the number of teachers per 1 000 inhabitants ranged from 9.6 in Bulgaria to 15.7 in Sweden, with Belgium above this range with a ratio of 17.9. In tertiary education (ISCED levels 5-6), the number of academic staff per 1 000 inhabitants ranged from 2.1 in Malta and the United Kingdom to 4.0 in Sweden, with Romania (1.5), France and Italy (both 1.7) recording ratios below this range and Austria (4.9) above; note that further information on average class sizes, and pupil/teacher ratios are given in Subchapter 10.5 which covers the quality of education.

One of the main choices concerning primary and secondary education is between private and public education institutions: there are essentially two types of private institutions, those that are independent and those that are Government-dependent (in other words, they receive half or more of their funds from public authorities). In nearly every Member State most primary and secondary education students were enrolled in public institutions in 2006, the only exception [25] being Belgium where 57 % of the students were enrolled in private institutions. In terms of student numbers, private institutions were also relatively common in Malta, Spain, France and the United Kingdom. In contrast, very nearly all students in the Baltic Member States, Ireland, Romania, Slovenia and Bulgaria were enrolled in public institutions.

(25) No recent data available for the Netherlands, which traditionally has a very high proportion of students in private institutions.

One factor that can assist access to education is financial support for students. Such support varies between Member States in nature, eligibility criteria and levels of education (examples being child care expenditure, scholarships or student loans). Financial aid may provide support during compulsory education or be designed to encourage greater participation in education beyond what is required by law. Across the EU-27 some 6.0 % of public expenditure on education was used to provide financial aid to pupils and students in 2005. The importance of this aid is much higher in the tertiary education sector, where it accounted for 16.0 % of all public expenditure: Bulgaria and Poland were the only Member States where financial aid as a share of public expenditure on education was greater for primary and secondary education than for tertiary education. Focusing on tertiary education, financial aid accounted for 58 % of public expenditure on tertiary education in Cyprus, explained to a large extent by the fact that a very large proportion of Cypriots study abroad. Over one quarter of public expenditure on tertiary education was used this way in Denmark, Malta, the Netherlands, Sweden and the United Kingdom, while this ratio was below 5 % in Greece and Poland.

Table 10.2: Availability of teachers by ISCED 97 level, 2006
(number per thousand inhabitants)

			of which:				
	Level 0	Levels 1-3	Level 1	Level 2	Level 3	Level 4	Levels 5-6
BE	2.8	17.9	6.2	4.1	7.6	:	2.5
BG	2.3	9.6	2.3	3.2	4.1	0.0	2.9
CZ	2.4	11.9	2.9	4.2	4.7	0.3	2.2
DK	:	:	:	10.7	:	:	:
DE	2.5	10.1	2.9	5.0	2.2	0.3	3.5
EE	4.5	11.8	5.6	3.8	2.3	:	:
IE	0.0	13.4	6.4	:	7.1	:	2.9
EL	1.0	13.2	5.5	3.8	3.9	1.2	2.6
ES	2.5	10.7	4.2	6.4	:	-	3.3
FR	2.2	11.3	3.4	3.9	3.9	:	1.7
IT	2.3	11.8	4.5	3.0	4.2	:	1.7
CY	1.4	12.4	4.7	3.7	3.9	-	2.2
LV	2.7	13.9	2.9	6.6	4.4	0.2	2.7
LT	3.2	15.7	3.2	11.5	:	0.2	3.9
LU	2.6	14.6	6.8	:	7.8	:	:
HU	3.0	13.6	4.0	4.9	4.7	0.8	2.5
MT	1.7	14.6	5.4	7.5	1.7	:	2.1
NL	:	14.9	8.3	:	6.5	:	2.7
AT	1.9	12.2	3.5	5.2	3.5	0.8	4.9
PL	1.3	13.7	6.1	3.4	4.2	0.7	2.6
PT	1.7	15.6	6.7	4.5	4.4	:	3.5
RO	1.7	9.8	2.6	4.1	3.2	0.1	1.5
SI	2.4	11.3	3.1	4.0	4.2	0.0	2.6
SK	2.0	11.8	2.5	4.9	4.3	0.1	2.4
FI (1)	2.2	12.7	4.7	4.0	4.0	:	3.6
SE	3.8	15.7	7.0	4.4	4.3	0.1	4.0
UK	0.7	12.5	4.1	2.4	5.9	:	2.1
HR	1.4	11.9	2.6	4.1	5.3	-	2.1
MK	1.6	9.9	2.7	4.3	3.0	:	1.4
TR	0.3	7.9	5.4	-	2.6	-	1.2
IS	6.3	20.2	:	14.5	5.7	:	6.2
LI	2.4	17.8	7.7	8.6	1.5	0.5	0.0
NO	:	19.3	9.6	4.5	5.1	:	3.9
CH	1.5	11.1	5.5	4.3	1.3	:	4.4

(1) 2005.

Source: Eurostat, Teachers (ISCED 0-4) and academic staff (ISCED 5-6) by age and sex (theme3/educ/educ_pers1d)

Figure 10.1: Private and public institutions: students in levels 1-4, 2006 (1)
(%)

(1) The Netherlands, not available.

Source: Eurostat, Participation/enrolment in education (ISCED 0-4) (theme3/educ/educ_ipart)

Table 10.3: Financial aid to pupils and students as % of total public expenditure on education by ISCED 97 level, 2005 (1)
(%)

	All levels	Levels 1-4	Levels 5-6
EU-27	6.0	3.4	16.0
BE	4.6	2.0	15.2
BG	15.2	17.0	10.8
CZ	4.3	4.6	5.9
DK	17.5	11.5	30.8
DE	7.9	4.8	19.1
EE	4.5	4.0	8.2
IE	10.7	9.4	14.8
EL	0.6	0.2	1.4
ES	3.0	1.6	8.2
FR	3.9	3.3	7.9
IT	4.5	1.7	16.8
CY	13.2	:	57.6
LV	6.3	6.6	9.4
LT	8.4	7.1	17.0
LU	2.2	2.2	:
HU	6.0	4.6	15.7
MT	9.3	8.1	30.2
NL	11.6	6.3	27.7
AT	5.1	0.7	16.8
PL	1.3	1.6	1.1
PT	2.6	1.4	8.9
RO	4.6	5.2	5.6
SI	8.3	4.5	23.7
SK	4.8	3.0	13.7
FI	7.2	3.0	16.6
SE	11.2	5.9	27.1
UK	5.8	0.1	25.8
HR	0.7	:	4.0
MK	2.6	0.6	13.8
TR	5.8	0.6	19.3
IS	5.2	1.1	23.1
LI	5.1	:	:
NO	19.3	7.1	42.6
CH	1.6	1.3	2.4

(1) EU-27, estimates, 2004; Malta and the former Yugoslav Republic of Macedonia, 2003; Turkey, 2004. In many countries student loans from public sources are not applicable; for country specific methodological notes, refer to Internet metadata file (http://europa.eu.int/estatref/info/sdds/en/educ/educ_base.htm).

Source: Eurostat, Financial aid to students (theme3/educ/educ_fiaid)

10.2 Consumption

10.2.1 Consumption volume: education and vocational training

In 2006 the total number of pupils and students in the EU-27 was 108.0 million, of which 13 % were in pre-primary education (ISCED level 0), 69 % in primary, secondary and non-tertiary post-secondary education (ISCED levels 1 to 4), and 17 % in tertiary education (ISCED levels 5 to 6).

Education is compulsory in all EU Member States and generally starts with the beginning of primary education, although there are exceptions where some pre-primary education may also be compulsory, or where primary education may be offered for children not yet required to attend school. Compulsory education therefore generally starts when children are aged between four and seven years old. Compulsory education normally ends at the end of lower secondary (ISCED level 2) education, with age limits within the EU mainly set at 15 or 16, or exceptionally based on a minimum number of years (generally between 9 and 12) of schooling. There are special cases specific to many Member States, for example, to allow children to go on to a vocational education at an earlier age, or with more emphasis on the completion of a specific level of education rather than the actual age of the pupil.

Table 10.4: Number of students and distribution by ISCED 97 level, 2006
(%)

	Total (thousand)	ISCED level 0	1	2	3	4	5-6	5A	5B	6	Un-known
EU-27	107 967	13	26	21	21	1	17	15	2	:	0
BE	2 821	15	26	15	28	2	14	6	7	0	0
BG	1 399	15	20	21	27	0	17	15	2	0	0
CZ	2 153	13	22	23	23	4	16	13	1	1	0
DK	1 395	18	30	17	19	0	16	14	2	0	0
DE	16 837	15	20	31	17	3	14	12	2	:	0
EE	325	14	24	18	19	3	21	13	7	1	0
IE	1 037	0	44	17	14	7	18	12	5	0	0
EL	2 185	7	30	16	17	2	30	18	11	1	0
ES	9 019	17	29	22	12	0	20	16	3	1	0
FR	14 948	18	27	22	18	0	15	11	4	0	0
IT	11 127	15	25	16	25	0	18	18	0	0	0
CY	166	12	36	20	20	0	12	3	10	0	0
LV	537	12	15	28	20	1	24	21	3	0	0
LT	873	10	17	35	13	1	23	16	7	0	0
LU	92	16	39	20	21	1	3	2	:	:	0
HU	2 279	14	18	21	24	3	19	18	1	0	0
MT	86	10	34	32	12	1	10	9	1	0	0
NL	3 673	10	35	21	18	0	16	16	0	0	0
AT	1 688	13	21	23	23	5	15	13	1	1	0
PL	9 503	9	27	17	21	3	23	22	0	0	0
PT	2 124	12	35	19	16	0	17	16	0	1	0
RO	4 479	14	21	21	23	1	19	18	1	0	0
SI	447	10	21	17	26	0	26	14	12	0	0
SK	1 234	12	19	28	25	0	16	15	0	1	0
FI	1 386	10	27	15	25	1	22	21	0	2	0
SE	2 429	14	28	17	23	0	17	16	1	1	0
UK	13 725	7	33	17	26	:	17	13	4	1	0
HR	822	11	24	25	24	0	17	11	5	0	0
MK	401	9	26	29	24	0	12	11	1	:	0
TR	16 825	3	63	0	19	0	14	10	4	0	0
IS	96	12	32	14	24	1	16	16	0	0	0
LI	7	11	32	23	22	2	9	9	0	0	0
NO	1 227	13	35	16	18	1	17	17	0	0	0
CH	1 496	10	35	20	19	2	14	10	2	1	1

Source: Eurostat, Students by ISCED level, age and sex (theme3/educ/educ_enrl1tl)

Table 10.5: Participation rates, 2006
(%)

	4-year olds in education (levels 0-1)	Students aged 15-24 years (as a share of all 15-24 year olds) Total	Male	Female
EU-27	86.8	59.3	57.3	61.5
BE	100.0	69.4	66.7	72.2
BG	68.4	51.5	50.8	52.3
CZ	86.5	60.9	58.9	62.9
DK	93.4	66.7	64.1	69.4
DE	93.1	65.4	65.6	65.3
EE	86.1	63.0	58.6	67.5
IE	46.9	57.4	56.7	58.1
EL	56.1	66.8	63.6	70.2
ES	97.1	55.1	51.4	58.9
FR	100.0	59.4	57.4	61.4
IT	100.0	56.2	52.9	59.7
CY	70.4	39.8	38.6	40.9
LV	73.5	64.4	60.4	68.5
LT	59.7	69.5	66.1	73.1
LU	94.0	44.5	43.3	45.7
HU	92.8	62.6	60.5	64.8
MT	95.5	43.4	42.3	44.5
NL	74.2	66.3	66.4	66.3
AT	83.2	53.7	52.0	55.5
PL	41.2	70.0	68.1	72.0
PT	80.6	51.0	47.1	55.1
RO	75.8	51.7	48.8	54.7
SI	79.3	69.7	63.8	76.0
SK	73.1	55.0	53.0	57.2
FI	48.5	71.0	68.2	74.0
SE	86.5	68.1	64.6	71.9
UK	91.3	46.8	44.6	49.1
HR	48.2	49.9	47.1	52.8
MK	15.9	39.8	38.9	40.8
TR	7.0	31.1	34.8	27.2
IS	94.8	67.0	63.8	70.4
LI	52.7	54.0	62.5	45.1
NO	91.8	65.3	63.1	67.6
CH	38.0	57.3	58.9	55.6

Source: Eurostat, Participation/ Enrolment in education (theme3/educ/educ_ipart; theme3/educ/educ_ipart_s)

Education participation rates indicate the proportion of a sub-population (for example, within a specified age range) that is in education. Table 10.5 gives an idea of the proportion of children in education at the age of four when compulsory education may or may not have started, and also between the ages of 15 and 24, an age range during which students generally move out of compulsory education.

The vast majority of four-year olds within the EU are in education, with the proportion only below half in Finland, Ireland and Poland. Looking at the other end of compulsory education, three fifths of people aged between 15 and 24 in the EU-27 were in education in 2006, a share that only dropped below half in Cyprus, Malta, Luxembourg and the United Kingdom, while exceeding two thirds in Finland, Poland, Slovenia, Lithuania, Belgium, Sweden, Greece and Denmark. In nearly every Member State, participation rates among females between the ages of 15 and 24 were higher than among males, with only Germany and the Netherlands recording slightly higher participation rates for men. In the EU-27 as a whole the participation rate of females was 4.2 percentage points higher than for males, with the largest percentage point difference recorded in Slovenia where the rate for females was 12.2 percentage points higher.

An insight into participation in education can also be achieved from an analysis of the education level of the post-school age population. One common indicator is the proportion of persons aged 25 to 64 (all of whom can confidently be assumed to have finished their initial school education) having completed at least upper secondary education. Across the EU-27, the average proportion was 71 %, with the rate slightly higher for males than females. Figure 10.2 shows the proportion of men and women having completed at least upper secondary education, with countries ranked on the overall proportion of men and women combined. The top of the ranking is headed by six of the countries that joined the EU in 2004. In contrast, the five countries at the bottom of the ranking are all southern Member States, with particularly low shares in Malta (27 %) and Portugal (28 %).

Figure 10.2: Education completion: proportion of the population aged 25 to 64 having completed at least upper secondary education, 2007
(%)

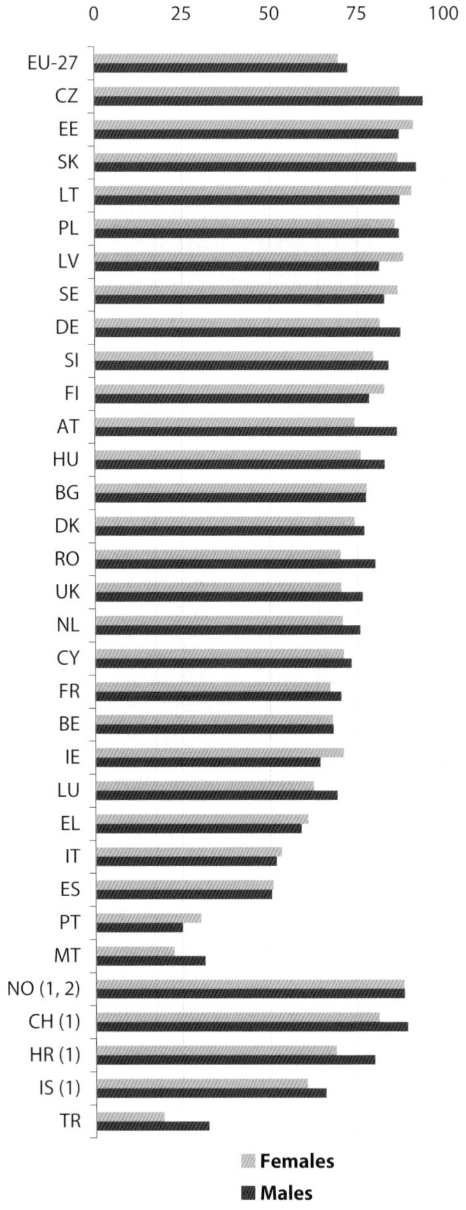

(1) 2006.
(2) Provisional.

Source: Eurostat, Educational attainment by sex (theme3/educ/educ_iatt)

Table 10.6: Tertiary education by age and gender: students (ISCED levels 5-6) of the specified age as a proportion of population of the same age, 2006
(%)

	Aged 18		Aged 20		Aged 22		Aged 24	
	Male	Female	Male	Female	Male	Female	Male	Female
EU-27	12.5	18.6	29.5	40.7	26.2	32.8	18.1	19.8
BE	28.8	43.7	41.8	56.0	29.6	34.4	13.6	14.6
BG	2.4	3.2	30.5	38.3	26.5	32.2	15.4	17.4
CZ	0.5	0.6	30.0	40.0	26.3	34.6	17.5	18.9
DK	0.2	0.4	11.1	16.8	25.5	39.5	29.7	41.0
DE	0.9	4.4	13.8	23.8	23.0	25.8	23.8	22.0
EE	6.6	13.2	31.3	50.4	28.1	37.3	15.2	21.3
IE	29.1	39.7	35.6	47.5	19.9	23.3	9.1	10.0
EL	59.3	80.1	65.0	82.8	33.1	36.9	12.9	14.1
ES	22.0	34.1	31.0	44.9	26.1	34.3	18.5	20.8
FR	22.5	32.6	36.5	46.2	27.6	33.7	13.9	16.3
IT	9.4	14.0	30.1	44.3	26.5	36.2	17.9	22.8
CY	5.8	29.4	19.8	26.6	19.5	12.7	16.0	7.0
LV	3.2	5.3	33.8	51.1	27.0	40.3	16.9	24.5
LT	6.7	12.5	43.0	59.0	34.7	47.0	18.5	24.6
LU	0.7	1.2	4.9	8.9	6.1	6.4	4.0	3.0
HU	9.5	15.0	30.5	42.6	29.2	37.5	17.7	21.8
MT	0.2	0.1	14.9	25.6	17.1	27.9	10.0	11.3
NL	18.1	23.9	30.9	39.3	32.5	34.1	23.7	19.9
AT	2.0	8.4	16.3	26.7	21.6	26.1	19.6	19.8
PL	0.7	1.1	37.8	51.5	36.9	48.8	24.0	24.9
PT	14.8	25.1	22.7	36.5	23.5	32.8	16.2	17.5
RO	10.9	16.0	27.0	37.1	24.0	32.0	16.9	18.8
SI	3.3	5.8	42.7	62.1	36.1	56.6	26.3	41.8
SK	2.5	3.4	29.0	38.3	24.2	31.3	12.5	14.4
FI	0.4	0.6	27.3	38.8	38.1	49.8	38.0	41.2
SE	0.8	1.2	19.8	26.6	28.8	39.1	27.6	34.5
UK	21.0	27.9	28.8	37.0	16.2	18.5	10.0	12.2
HR	11.5	15.4	33.6	45.9	23.2	29.1	11.9	11.8
MK	6.6	9.8	19.7	27.5	15.7	24.0	8.9	10.0
TR	18.4	17.0	26.4	22.5	20.5	15.1	12.1	8.4
IS	0.5	0.3	15.2	19.0	24.2	38.1	23.7	33.6
LI	-	2.0	9.2	8.2	18.2	11.8	13.6	9.7
NO	0.2	0.5	22.7	38.1	29.5	40.9	25.1	30.7
CH	1.8	2.4	14.0	18.2	23.1	22.7	22.6	18.3

Source: Eurostat, Participation/ Enrolment in education by sex (theme3/educ/educ_ipart_s)

Tables 10.6 to 10.8 focus on tertiary education. In the EU-27 as a whole participation rates in tertiary education for 2006 were higher for women than for men, and this was true in almost every Member State. Participation rates generally peaked (among the four ages specified in Table 10.6) for persons aged 20 or 22: the most notable exception was Denmark where the highest rates were recorded among persons aged 24, while in Germany the participation rate for men was also highest among those aged 24, while in Cyprus the rate for women was highest among those aged 18.

These differences can be attributed to a number of factors including the proportion of secondary education pupils that become tertiary education students, the age at which this move from secondary to tertiary education takes place, and the length of time students stay in tertiary education. Furthermore, in some countries the move into tertiary education may be delayed because of compulsory military or civil service, and where this is only applicable to men this can sometimes explain in part the large differences in the participation rates between men and women of a particular age (Cyprus or Germany).

Table 10.7: Number of ISCED level 5-6 students and distribution by field, 2006
(%)

	Number of students (thousand)	Edu- cation	Humanities & arts	Social sciences, business & law	Science, maths & computing	Engineering, manufact. & construction	Agri- culture & veterinary	Health & welfare	Services
EU-27	18 783	8.8	13.2	34.2	10.6	14.6	1.9	12.9	3.7
BE	394	11.1	11.5	29.9	7.5	11.5	2.7	24.1	1.7
BG	244	7.0	7.9	42.5	5.0	21.0	2.5	6.4	7.6
CZ	337	14.4	9.1	29.5	9.1	15.4	3.9	12.9	5.6
DK	229	11.4	15.0	29.5	8.0	10.1	1.5	22.2	2.3
DE	2 290	7.3	15.6	27.4	15.2	15.8	1.4	14.7	2.5
EE	68	7.6	11.6	39.0	10.0	12.3	2.5	8.5	8.5
IE	186	6.3	18.5	27.3	13.7	12.3	1.4	15.1	5.3
EL (1)	647	6.5	11.6	31.9	15.7	16.5	5.9	6.9	5.0
ES	1 789	9.2	10.4	32.0	11.4	17.9	3.4	9.9	5.6
FR	2 201	3.2	17.1	35.8	12.7	11.9	1.0	14.7	3.6
IT	2 029	6.4	15.6	36.8	7.9	15.7	2.3	12.6	2.6
CY	21	9.4	8.5	47.4	12.7	6.1	0.1	6.6	9.2
LV	131	12.2	7.1	54.2	5.2	10.0	1.2	5.2	4.9
LT	199	12.3	7.0	41.8	6.1	18.0	2.3	9.2	3.4
LU	3	22.7	8.2	45.2	8.4	15.0	:	0.4	:
HU	439	13.4	8.0	41.6	5.2	12.4	2.9	8.2	8.3
MT	9	9.9	14.0	37.4	8.4	7.6	0.2	20.3	2.2
NL	580	14.9	8.4	38.1	6.7	8.3	1.2	16.5	6.0
AT	253	12.8	14.9	35.0	12.4	11.8	1.6	9.4	2.1
PL	2 146	14.5	9.2	40.9	9.7	12.6	2.2	5.7	5.4
PT	367	7.2	8.6	31.5	7.3	21.9	1.9	16.0	5.6
RO	835	2.3	10.8	51.4	4.8	18.7	2.9	5.8	3.1
SI	115	8.8	7.5	43.5	5.4	15.6	3.1	7.4	8.7
SK	198	16.5	6.0	28.3	9.0	16.4	2.8	15.2	5.8
FI	309	5.3	14.5	22.5	11.4	25.9	2.2	13.3	4.8
SE	423	15.2	12.6	26.2	9.7	16.3	0.9	17.3	1.8
UK	2 336	9.3	17.9	28.4	14.4	8.6	1.0	19.7	0.7
HR	137	4.3	9.9	40.5	7.4	16.3	3.8	7.5	10.2
MK	48	12.8	10.7	32.6	7.2	18.3	3.6	10.2	4.5
TR	2 343	12.3	6.9	47.4	7.5	13.3	3.5	5.6	3.5
IS	16	17.4	14.8	38.0	8.0	7.3	0.5	12.4	1.5
LI	1	-	1.4	71.4	-	25.0	-	2.2	-
NO	215	14.4	12.3	32.7	9.0	6.8	0.8	19.6	4.3
CH	205	10.3	13.0	37.2	10.8	13.4	1.2	10.2	3.9

(1) 2005.

Source: Eurostat, Tertiary education participation (theme3/educ/educ_iterp)

Among the 18.8 million tertiary education students in the EU-27 in 2006 just over one third were studying in social science, business and law fields – in Latvia and Romania over half of all tertiary education students were concentrated in these fields. Science, mathematics and computing accounted for a relatively large share of tertiary education students in Greece, Germany, the United Kingdom and Ireland, while a relatively high proportion of students were studying engineering, manufacturing and construction in Finland, Portugal and Bulgaria.

In several Member States, particularly the smaller ones, it is very common for students to travel abroad for tertiary education, reflecting the restricted (but sometimes increasing) tertiary education offered nationally: 81 % of students from Luxembourg studied in another EU-27 Member State, while the corresponding share in Cyprus was 53 %.

Studying abroad was much less common in the larger Member States, for example 0.6 % of students from the United Kingdom studied in another EU-27 Member State, 1.3 % from Spain, 1.6 % from Poland, and 1.7 % from Italy. It should be noted that statistics on student mobility may be based on the registration of the nationality of students rather than actual mobility, and as such a non-national who is resident in a country (and may have gone through the national school system) may be recorded as an inflow.

Developing skills through continuing vocational training (CVT) at work is a part of lifelong learning. Statistics on this subject show how enterprises contribute to the development of the labour force's skills. The main forms of CVT are internal or external courses, although other forms exist, such as self-learning, conferences, workshops, job rotation or exchanges.

Table 10.8: Students (ISCED levels 5-6) studying abroad, 2006
(%)

	Studying in another EU-27 country, as a % of all students	Inflow of students from EU-27, EEA & candidate countries, as a % of all students in the country
EU-27	2.6	2.9
BE	2.5	8.1
BG	8.4	2.8
CZ	2.0	5.0
DK	2.2	4.5
DE	2.7	5.6
EE	4.0	1.1
IE	13.7	2.5
EL	5.3	1.6
ES	1.3	0.8
FR	2.3	2.3
IT	1.7	0.8
CY	53.2	4.6
LV	2.1	0.6
LT	2.9	0.3
LU	80.8	38.5
HU	1.6	2.1
MT	10.0	2.2
NL	2.0	3.9
AT	4.4	12.1
PL	1.6	0.1
PT	3.7	0.8
RO	2.2	0.2
SI	2.1	0.8
SK	10.2	0.5
FI	2.9	1.1
SE	2.4	4.8
UK	0.6	8.4
HR	-	0.1
MK	-	0.2
TR	-	0.1
IS	-	3.3
LI	-	86.7
NO	-	2.6

Source: Eurostat, Tertiary education participation (theme3/educ/educ_itertp)

Table 10.9: Continuous vocational training: percentage of employees participating in CVT, 2005 (1)
(%)

	Total	Male	Female	Age		
				<25	25-54	55+
EU-27	33	34	31	29	33	24
BE	40	40	39	35	41	28
BG	15	16	13	15	16	8
CZ	59	63	52	54	60	54
DK	35	32	39	29	35	36
DE	30	32	27	25	32	21
EE	24	23	26	25	26	15
IE	:	:	:	:	:	:
EL	14	13	15	13	14	7
ES	33	33	35	30	35	25
FR	46	47	43	:	:	:
IT	29	29	28	22	30	22
CY	30	30	30	22	31	15
LV	15	14	15	16	15	8
LT	15	15	14	17	15	9
LU	49	48	51	42	51	31
HU	16	16	15	12	17	9
MT	32	30	36	29	34	24
NL	34	36	31	26	38	23
AT	33	36	30	36	34	21
PL	21	21	20	16	22	13
PT	28	29	27	26	29	18
RO	17	18	17	17	18	12
SI	50	48	55	54	51	44
SK	38	42	31	32	40	32
FI	39	38	41	25	43	34
SE	46	47	45	39	50	37
UK	33	32	34	34	34	26
NO	29	30	28	23	31	24

(1) Enterprises with 10 or more persons employed, within NACE Sections C to K and O.

Source: Eurostat, Percentage of employees (all enterprises) participating in CVT courses (theme3/trng/trng_cvts3_41; theme3/trng/trng_cvts3_43)

Overall one third of employees in the EU-27 participated in CVT in 2005, ranging from 14 % in Greece to 50 % in Slovenia, with the Czech Republic (59 %) above this range. Overall, the CVT participation rate was slightly higher for men (34 %) than for women (31 %), with the Czech Republic and Slovakia recording the largest differences in rates.

It should be noted, however, that CVT rates for the EU-27 have fallen relative to 1999, when the share of employees engaged in CVT was 39 % (which was split 40 % for men and 36 % for women). There were particularly sharp declines in the share of total employees in CVT between 1999 and 2005 in Denmark (down from 53 %), the United Kingdom (from 49 %), Sweden (from 61 %) and Finland (50 %), in contrast to relatively sharp rises in many of the Member States that joined the EU since 2004.

10.2.2 Frequency

Table 10.10 provides information on the average time spent on three different aspects of education: a person's own initial education at school or university; other studying in a person's own free time; and teaching children (including reading and talking with children).

The time spent at school and university and doing homework should be interpreted with particular care, bearing in mind that the data concerns the population aged 20 to 24, and as was noted in Table 10.6 the participation in tertiary education varies greatly between countries and in some countries between men and women depending on the precise age group studied.

Table 10.10: Time use, persons aged 20 to 74, latest available year (1)
(minutes per day)

	School and university; homework			Free time study			Teaching, reading, talking with child		
	Total	Male	Female	Total	Male	Female	Total	Male	Female
BE	11	8	12	3	3	4	6	4	7
BG	5	3	6	0	0	0	8	5	10
DE	9	11	8	4	4	4	7	5	9
EE	5	5	5	2	2	2	7	4	10
ES	13	13	13	5	4	6	5	4	5
FR	13	14	13	1	1	1	6	4	8
IT	12	10	13	1	1	1	8	7	10
LV	9	7	11	1	2	1	5	2	7
LT	9	9	8	1	1	2	7	4	9
PL	12	13	12	1	1	1	14	10	17
SI	16	14	17	1	1	1	9	7	11
FI	12	10	14	2	3	2	6	5	8
SE	15	12	18	2	2	2	7	6	8
UK	6	7	7	2	2	2	8	5	10
NO	14	12	15	:	:	:	7	5	9

(1) No data available for those Member States not shown; mixed reference years.

Source: harmonised European time use surveys (https://www.testh2.scb.se/tus/tus/StatMeanMact2.html)

10.2.3 Consumption expenditure

As with health (see Chapter 6), education accounts for a seemingly small proportion of total household consumption expenditure; this reflects the fact that the vast majority of education services are provided by governments free at their point of use. The interpretation of data concerning household consumption expenditure on education is therefore limited by the extent to which this is provided free (or at a greatly reduced price).

According to household budget survey (HBS) data, in 2005 annual household consumption expenditure on education within the EU-27 averaged PPS 238 per household. A wide range of expenditure on education was observed among the Member States, from PPS 34 per household in Bulgaria to PPS 356 in Portugal, with Sweden below this range at PPS 8 and Cyprus (PPS 1 354), Greece (PPS 738), Ireland (PPS 687) and the United Kingdom (PPS 457) above.

Table 10.11: Mean consumption expenditure per household, education, 2005
(PPS)

EU-27 (1)	238
BE	136
BG	34
CZ	66
DK	100
DE	236
EE	145
IE	687
EL	738
ES	292
FR	165
IT	202
CY	1 354
LV	145
LT	102
LU	223
HU	90
MT	352
NL	306
AT	242
PL	138
PT	356
RO	45
SI	202
SK	92
FI	51
SE	8
UK	457
HR	105
NO	95

(1) Estimate.

Source: Eurostat, Household Budget Survey (theme3/hbs/hbs_exp_t121)

Figure 10.3: Structure of consumption expenditure: share of education in total expenditure, 2005 (1)
(%)

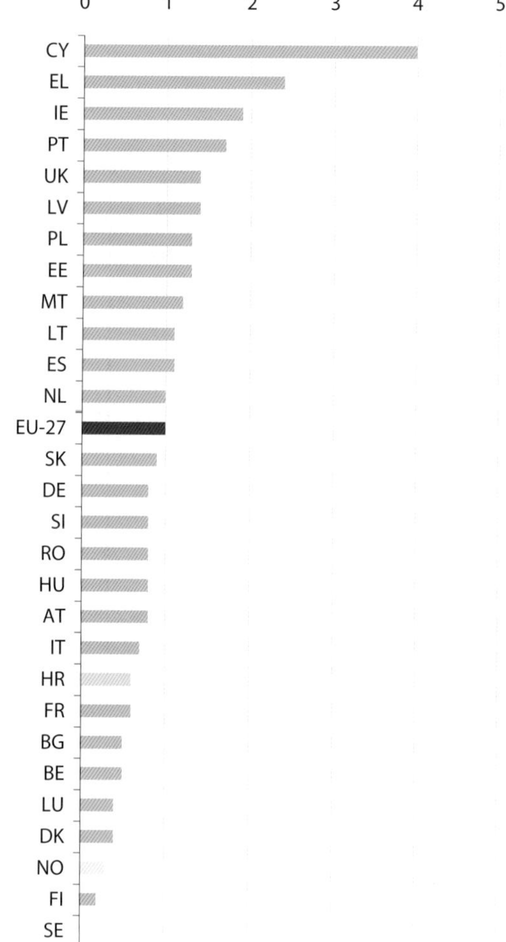

(1) EU-27, estimate; Czech Republic, not available.

Source: Eurostat, Household Budget Survey (theme3/hbs/hbs_str_t211)

Expenditure on education represented around 1 % of total household consumption expenditure in the EU-27 (see Figure 10.3), and was only over 2 % in Cyprus (4.0%) and Greece (2.4 %).

The share of total household consumption expenditure dedicated to education varied greatly depending on the type of household (number of persons, with or without dependent children), with the proportion unsurprisingly higher among households with dependent children, and those with more than two adults (see Figure 10.4). Equally the share was lower for households in the lowest income quintile than for those in the highest quintile. The share was particularly low for households where the head of the household was retired and/or aged 60 or over. The share also decreased as the degree of urbanisation fell.

Figure 10.4: Structure of consumption expenditure: share of education in total expenditure, EU-27, 2005
(%)

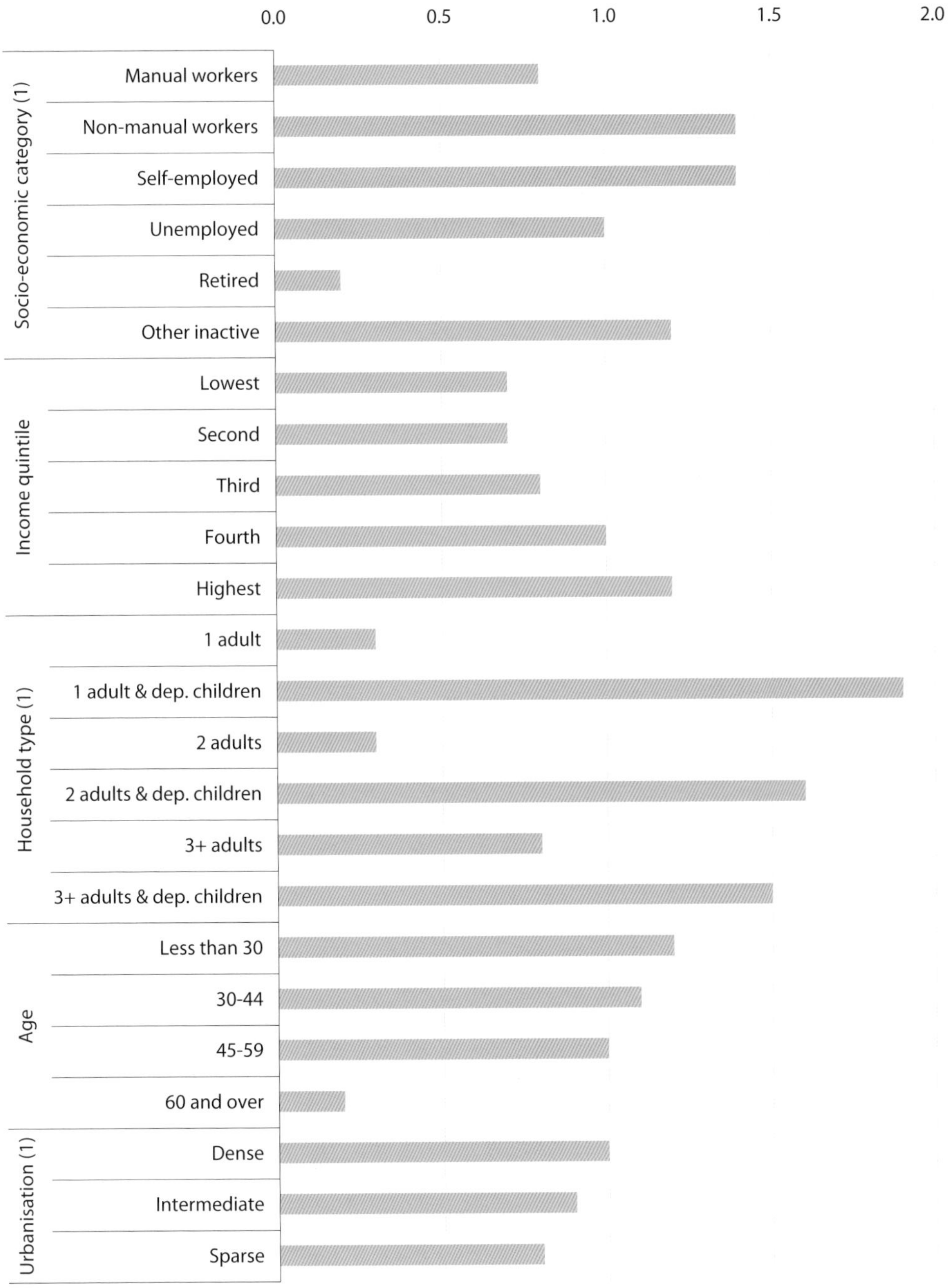

(1) Unreliable.

Source: Eurostat, Household Budget Survey (theme3/hbs/hbs_str_t221, hbs_str_t223, hbs_str_t224, hbs_str_t225, hbs_str_t226)

Table 10.12: Expenditure on educational institutions relative to GDP, 2005 (1)
(%)

	Public sources	Private sources
EU-27	4.7	0.7
BE	5.7	0.4
BG	3.8	0.6
CZ	4.1	0.6
DK	6.8	0.6
DE	4.2	0.9
EE	4.6	0.4
IE	4.3	0.3
EL	4.0	0.3
ES	4.1	0.5
FR	5.4	0.6
IT	4.2	0.4
CY	6.0	1.2
LV	4.7	0.8
LT	4.5	0.5
LU	3.7	:
HU	5.1	0.5
MT	2.9	0.2
NL	4.6	0.4
AT	5.0	0.5
PL	5.4	0.6
PT	5.3	0.4
RO	3.3	0.4
SI	5.3	0.8
SK	3.7	0.7
FI	5.8	0.1
SE	6.2	0.2
UK	5.0	1.3
HR	4.6	:
MK	3.3	:
TR	3.8	0.1
IS	7.2	0.7
LI	2.1	:
NO	6.1	0.1
CH	5.5	0.6

(1) EU-27, estimates; the former Yugoslav Republic of Macedonia, 2003; Turkey and Norway, 2004 ; for country specific metyhodological notes, refer to Internet metadata file (http://europa.eu.int/estatref/info/sdds/en/educ/educ_base.htm).

Source: Eurostat, Expenditure on education as % of GDP or public expenditure (theme3/educ/educ_figdp)

Although expenditure on education accounts for a relatively low share of household consumption expenditure, the total expenditure (from all sources) on educational institutions made up a relatively large share of GDP.

Table 10.12 shows that expenditure from public sources was equivalent to 4.7 % of GDP in the EU-27 in 2005, and expenditure from private sources was 0.7 %: private expenditure includes tuition fees and other payments, and is mainly undertaken by households, enterprises and non-profit institutions. The highest combined shares of public and private expenditure on education institutions were recorded in Denmark and Cyprus with GDP shares of 7.4 % and 7.2 % respectively. In the United Kingdom private sources accounted for around 20 % of total expenditure on educational institutions compared with a 12 % average for the EU-27, while in Finland, Sweden and Malta public sources accounted for 95 % or more of total expenditure.

Total public expenditure on education (as opposed to just educational institutions) was equivalent to 5.0 % of GDP in the EU-27 in 2005. Nearly half of this was directed to secondary and post-secondary non-tertiary education, while just less than one quarter was for primary education and the same share for tertiary education.

Average expenditure per pupil/student in public educational institutions was highest for tertiary education, averaging close to PPS 8 000 per student in the EU-27 in 2005. The highest average expenditure per pupil/student among the Member States, for all levels of education combined, was PPS 12 024 in Luxembourg, more than double the EU-27 average of PPS 5 344. Generally the Member States that joined the EU since 2004 spent less on average per pupil/student than the EU-15 Member States, with Cyprus the main exception to this pattern (and Slovenia to a lesser extent).

Table 10.13: Public expenditure on education relative to GDP by ISCED 97 levels, 2005 (1)
(%)

	Total	ISCED level			
		1	2-4	5-6	0 or unallocated
EU-27	5.0	1.2	2.3	1.2	0.5
BE	6.0	1.4	2.6	1.3	0.7
BG	4.5	0.9	2.1	0.8	0.8
CZ	4.3	0.6	2.2	0.9	0.5
DK	8.3	1.9	3.0	2.4	1.0
DE	4.5	0.7	2.3	1.1	0.5
EE	4.9	1.2	2.3	0.9	0.4
IE	4.8	1.6	2.1	1.1	0.0
EL	4.0	1.1	1.4	1.4	:
ES	4.2	1.1	1.7	1.0	0.5
FR	5.7	1.1	2.7	1.2	0.6
IT	4.4	1.1	2.1	0.8	0.5
CY	6.9	1.9	3.1	1.6	0.3
LV	5.1	0.8	2.8	0.9	0.6
LT	5.0	0.7	2.6	1.0	0.6
LU	3.8	2.1	1.8	:	:
HU	5.5	1.1	2.4	1.0	1.0
MT	2.9	0.6	1.3	0.5	0.6
NL	5.2	1.4	2.1	1.4	0.4
AT	5.4	1.0	2.5	1.5	0.4
PL	5.5	1.7	2.0	1.2	0.5
PT	5.4	1.7	2.2	1.0	0.6
RO	3.5	1.3	0.8	0.8	0.7
SI	5.8	2.7	1.4	1.3	0.5
SK	3.9	0.7	1.9	0.8	0.5
FI	6.3	1.3	2.6	2.0	0.4
SE	7.0	1.8	2.7	1.9	0.5
UK	5.5	1.4	2.5	1.2	0.3
HR	4.6	2.1	1.0	0.8	0.7
MK	3.4	2.1	0.8	0.5	:
TR	4.1	2.0	0.9	1.1	0.0
IS	7.6	2.7	2.6	1.5	0.9
LI	2.3	0.7	1.1	0.2	0.3
NO	7.0	1.8	2.3	2.3	0.7
CH	5.7	1.7	2.2	1.5	0.3

(1) EU-27, Estimates; the former Yugoslav Republic of Macedonia, 2003; Turkey, 2004; for country specific methodological notes, refer to Internet metadata file (http://europa.eu.int/estatref/info/sdds/en/educ/educ_base.htm).

Source: Eurostat, Expenditure on education as % of GDP or public expenditure (theme3/educ/educ_figdp)

Table 10.14: Expenditure on public educational institutions by ISCED 97 levels, 2005 (1)
(PPS per pupil/student in full time equivalents)

	Total	ISCED level		
		1	2-4	5-6
EU-27	5 344	4 325	5 420	7 992
BE	6 889	6 302	6 886	9 766
BG	1 964	1 685	1 575	3 669
CZ	3 853	2 351	4 061	5 960
DK	8 151	7 530	8 140	12 654
DE	5 744	4 222	4 887	10 806
EE	2 813	2 729	3 260	4 410
IE	6 066	4 861	6 114	9 312
EL	4 605	3 824	4 897	5 186
ES	6 514	5 230	7 052	8 843
FR	6 588	4 719	8 022	9 472
IT	6 241	5 782	6 470	6 790
CY	7 389	5 272	8 715	17 329
LV	2 512	2 453	2 511	2 484
LT	2 474	1 788	:	3 847
LU	12 024	9 878	16 151	:
HU	3 944	3 651	3 229	5 926
MT	2 588	1 331	2 157	3 898
NL	:	:	:	:
AT	:	:	:	:
PL	3 212	2 802	2 583	5 546
PT	4 997	4 121	5 473	7 434
RO	1 467	1 134	1 293	2 696
SI	6 099	6 636	4 631	7 320
SK	2 700	2 324	2 277	4 893
FI	6 222	4 696	6 200	10 686
SE	7 202	6 336	6 778	13 701
UK	5 845	5 075	6 797	:
HR	3 030	2 611	2 686	4 238
TR	1 325	966	1 559	3 650
IS	8 117	7 848	7 157	8 785
LI	7 167	7 203	7 867	:
NO	9 322	7 717	9 166	14 441
CH	8 551	7 164	7 934	18 386

(1) EU-27, estimates; Turkey, 2004; for country specific methodological notes, refer to Internet metadata file (http://europa.eu.int/estatref/info/sdds/en/educ/educ_base.htm).

Source: Eurostat, Expenditure on public educational institutions (theme3/educ/educ_fipubin)

10.3 Prices

10.3.1 Price inflation

The harmonised index of consumer prices for education rose in the EU-27 by 39.1 % between 2000 and 2007, equivalent to an average of 4.8 % per annum. This was double the rate of increase recorded for the all-items consumer price index, which gained, on average, 2.4 % per annum. Year on year price increases generally ranged between 3.8 % and 4.7 % from 2001 to 2006, with prices rising by 6.7 % and 8.6 % in 2000 and 2007.

In 2007 nearly all of the Member States recorded price increases for education below the EU-27 average, as prices rose at a rapid pace in two of the largest Member States, increasing by 22.2 % in Germany and 13.7 % in the United Kingdom (compared with 2006), with Latvia (14.2 %) the only other Member State recording an above average increase.

10.3.2 Price levels

Price level indices for 2006 show prices for education below the EU-27 average in all of the Member States that joined the EU since 2004, as well as in Greece and Spain. In fact most of the newer Member States recorded price levels for education that were less than half the EU-27 average, with Cyprus, Slovenia and Malta the

Table 10.15: Harmonised indices of consumer prices, education, annual rate of change
(%)

	2000	2001	2002	2003	2004	2005	2006	2007
EU-27	6.7	4.3	4.4	4.7	4.0	3.8	4.1	8.6
BE	:	2.1	3.0	1.3	0.9	2.1	1.8	2.3
BG	20.6	26.5	6.4	5.7	4.8	6.2	7.0	7.3
CZ	4.4	2.9	3.7	3.4	3.5	3.1	3.4	2.3
DK	2.8	3.7	6.5	21.5	3.3	2.4	2.9	4.5
DE	2.3	1.3	2.6	2.1	3.3	2.2	2.5	22.2
EE	7.8	7.4	4.8	3.9	2.8	3.7	3.9	5.8
IE	12.6	7.2	10.3	9.1	5.9	6.0	4.9	5.1
EL	3.7	3.7	4.0	4.5	4.4	4.1	3.8	4.0
ES	4.6	4.1	3.8	4.9	4.0	4.2	4.0	4.5
FR	1.6	2.4	2.6	2.8	2.8	2.6	3.4	3.3
IT	2.5	3.2	3.0	2.7	2.2	3.3	2.8	2.4
CY	3.6	3.7	5.1	3.7	4.3	5.3	5.2	4.9
LV	2.5	4.8	6.8	4.3	5.2	8.7	9.7	14.2
LT	10.5	5.9	-0.7	-3.4	0.7	-0.5	-0.7	4.9
LU	1.4	2.0	8.5	7.5	1.0	1.8	4.1	2.1
HU	11.0	7.9	10.2	13.6	12.5	8.3	7.8	6.4
MT	4.2	6.7	10.1	3.2	3.0	1.6	2.6	4.2
NL	2.9	2.9	4.4	4.1	2.8	-3.7	-10.8	0.8
AT	4.3	10.0	21.9	3.3	1.9	1.9	7.2	1.9
PL	11.2	6.9	3.9	2.3	2.6	3.1	1.4	1.4
PT	3.0	5.2	5.8	6.6	9.4	7.0	5.2	3.7
RO	53.4	40.7	21.8	11.8	12.0	6.1	9.5	5.2
SI	8.9	9.8	9.9	4.4	7.9	5.7	2.6	2.1
SK	8.2	5.3	3.7	6.8	11.4	30.1	5.9	3.7
FI	2.2	3.5	3.2	6.0	5.5	4.0	2.3	3.7
SE	5.8	2.1	-26.6	-2.5	7.8	3.1	3.2	3.7
UK	5.8	6.0	5.7	7.5	4.8	4.9	7.3	13.7
TR	51.7	43.9	56.1	36.9	20.7	13.0	7.8	7.2
IS	5.2	7.1	11.9	7.8	4.2	7.0	8.0	5.6
NO	4.0	6.7	8.2	5.9	4.8	1.3	2.3	2.0
CH	:	:	:	:	:	:	1.6	1.5

Source: Eurostat, Harmonised indices of consumer prices (theme2/prc/prc_hicp_aind)

Figure 10.5: Price level indices, education, 2006
(EU-27=100)

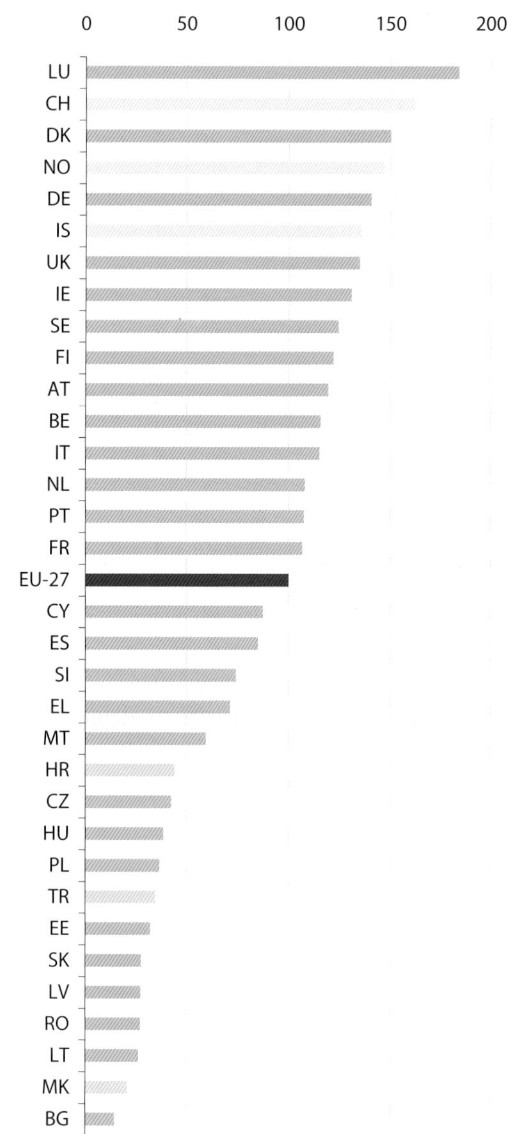

Source: Eurostat, Price level indices (theme2/prc/prc_ppp_ind)

only exceptions. Among all of the Member States, price levels were highest, by far, in Luxembourg (84 % above the EU-27 average), with Denmark the only other Member State to report price levels for education at least 50 % above the EU-27 average.

10.4 Consumer satisfaction

Information on satisfaction with schools (not education in general) is available from the Urban Audit. In all of the EU-27 capital cities except Athens, Sofia and Bucharest a greater proportion of respondents reported satisfaction compared with dissatisfaction in terms of their perception of schools. In most capital cities there was a clear majority of people satisfied with schools, upwards of two thirds of those questioned in Prague, Lefkosia and Dublin, and more than three quarters of those questioned in Ljubljana and Helsinki.

An alternative perspective on satisfaction can be drawn from indicators on early school leavers, which is based on Labour Force Survey (LFS) data and calculated as the share of the population aged 18 to 24 years whose highest completed education level was lower secondary or less, and who had not received education or training in the four weeks prior to the survey. The proportion of early school leavers in the EU-27 in 2007 was 12.7 % for females and 16.9 % for males: in every Member State, except for Bulgaria, this ratio was higher for males than for females, with the difference increasing to more than ten percentage points in Cyprus, Portugal, Spain and Estonia. Overall, the highest rates of early school leavers were recorded in Malta, Portugal and Spain, with all three recording early school leaver rates in excess of 25 % for both males and females. In contrast, the lowest rates of early school leavers were recorded in Slovenia, Poland and the Czech Republic, at less than 7 % for both males and females.

Table 10.16: Perception of satisfaction concerning schools, 2006
(%)

	Synthetic index 0-100	Satisfied (rather & strong)	Unsatisfied (rather & strong)
Bruxelles/Brussel	76	64	20
Sofia	47	36	41
Praha	84	69	13
København	65	48	26
Berlin	52	36	33
Tallinn	78	52	15
Dublin	85	68	12
Athina	40	36	53
Madrid	71	48	19
Paris	83	56	11
Roma	67	56	27
Lefkosia	78	68	19
Riga	83	62	13
Vilnius	55	39	31
Luxembourg	79	54	14
Budapest	65	43	23
Valletta	87	66	10
Amsterdam	86	58	9
Wien	78	59	17
Warszawa	75	55	18
Lisboa	69	51	23
Bucureşti	49	40	41
Ljubljana	88	77	11
Bratislava	76	60	19
Helsinki	94	76	5
Stockholm	80	53	14
London	75	54	18
Zagreb	71	62	26
Ankara	66	61	32

Source: Eurostat, Perception survey results (theme1/urb/urb_percep)

Figure 10.6: Early school leavers: percentage of people aged 18-24 with only lower secondary education who are not in education, 2007 (1)
(%)

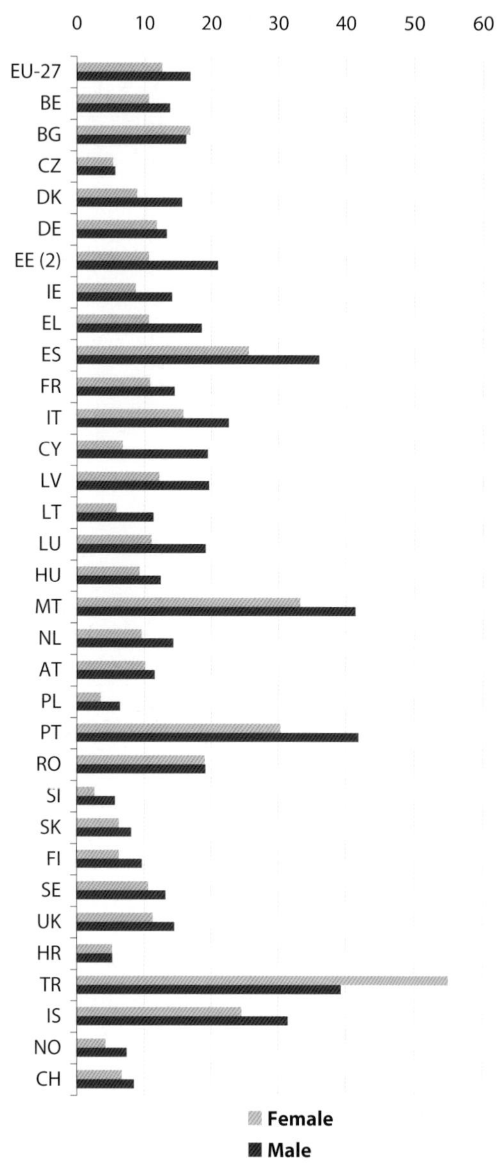

(1) Czech Republic, Sweden, the United Kingdom, Croatia, Iceland and Norway, 2006; Latvia, Portugal, Finland and Iceland, provisional; Lithuania, Luxembourg, Slovenia and Croatia, include unreliable data.
(2) Females, 2005, unreliable data.

Source: Eurostat, Educational attainment by sex (theme3/educ/educ_iatt)

10.5 Quality

Table 10.17 and Figure 10.7 provide information on the ratio of pupils to teachers and average class sizes. The pupil/teacher ratio is calculated by dividing the number of pupils by the number of teachers (normally excluding non-teaching staff) measured as full-time equivalents. In contrast, average class sizes are calculated by simply averaging the number of pupils in each class. In all Member States average class sizes are higher than pupil/teacher ratios. Some of the reasons for this include the sharing of a class among several teachers and the use of specialised teachers for pupils with special needs, both of which increase the number of teachers and therefore reduce the pupil/teacher ratio without directly affecting the average class size. In every Member State with data available, other than Poland, the ratio of pupils to teachers within lower secondary education is inferior to that within primary education. In more than two thirds of the Member States (with available data) the ratio was higher for upper secondary education than for lower secondary education; the most notable exception was the United Kingdom where the ratio for upper secondary education was less than half that for lower secondary education. Some, but not all Member States have limits on primary education class sizes: maximum class sizes are more common and often in the range of 25 to 30 pupils; while minimum class sizes are less common, and are generally between 10 and 15. In practice, average primary class sizes were between 14.8 pupils in Lithuania and 24.3 pupils in Ireland. For secondary education the average class size ranged from 18.0 pupils in Latvia to 24.9 pupils in Poland.

Table 10.17: Pupil/teacher ratios by ISCED 97 levels, 2005

	ISCED level			
	1-3	1	2	3
BE	10.8	12.8	9.4	9.9
BG	13.2	16.3	12.6	11.9
CZ	14.4	17.5	13.5	12.8
DK	11.9	:	11.9	:
DE	17.2	18.8	15.5	19.2
EE	:	:	:	:
IE	16.8	17.9	:	15.6
EL	9.4	11.1	7.9	8.8
ES	12.1	14.3	12.5	8.1
FR	14.3	19.4	14.2	10.3
IT	10.6	10.6	10.1	11.0
CY	14.1	17.9	11.9	11.5
LV	11.7	12.2	11.2	12.1
LT	9.4	11.3	8.8	:
LU	9.8	10.7	:	9.0
HU	11.0	10.6	10.4	12.2
MT	10.6	12.1	8.4	17.4
NL	16.1	15.9	:	16.2
AT	11.8	14.1	10.6	11.3
PL	12.3	11.7	12.7	12.9
PT	7.0	10.8	8.2	7.3
RO	14.9	17.4	12.4	16.0
SI	13.5	15.0	11.1	14.5
SK	15.2	18.9	14.1	14.3
FI	14.7	15.9	10.0	18.0
SE	12.6	12.2	12.0	14.0
UK	14.5	20.7	17.0	7.9
HR	13.2	18.1	12.8	10.7
MK	16.9	:	:	17.5
TR	23.0	25.8	-	16.2
IS	11.3	:	11.4	11.1
LI	8.8	10.3	7.0	9.8
NO	11.0	11.9	10.5	9.6

(1) Luxembourg, Iceland and Norway, 2004; Portugal for level 3, 2004; for country specific metyhodological notes, refer to Internet metadata file (http://europa.eu.int/estatref/info/sdds/en/educ/educ_base.htm).

Source: Eurostat, Pupil/ Student - teacher ratio and average class size (ISCED 1-3) (theme3/educ/educ_iste)

Figure 10.7: Class size by ISCED 97 levels (ranked on level 2), 2005 (1)
(number)

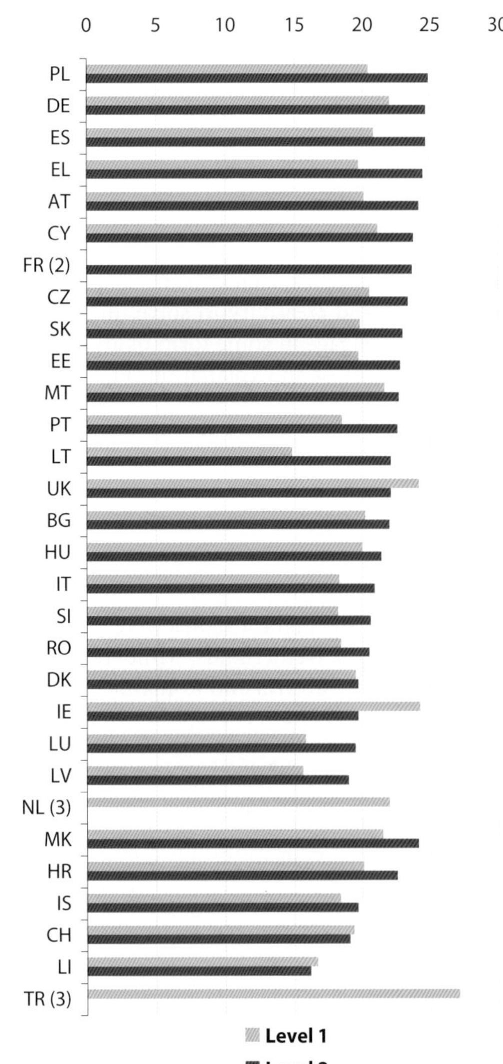

(1) Belgium, Finland and Sweden, not available.
(2) Level 1, not available.
(3) Level 2, not available.

Source: Eurostat, Pupil/ Student - teacher ratio and average class size (ISCED 1-3) (theme3/educ/educ_iste)

The Programme for International Student Assessment (PISA) is a triennial survey of the knowledge and skills of 15-year-olds. It is the product of collaboration between participating countries and economies through the Organisation for Economic Co-operation and Development (OECD). More than 400 000 students from 57 countries took part in PISA 2006. Mathematics was studied in detail in PISA 2003, and a simpler study of this subject was included in PISA 2006. In order to perform the hardest mathematics tasks in PISA, students must put together complex elements of a question, use reflection and creativity to solve unfamiliar problems and engage in some form of argument, often in the form of an explanation. Figure 10.8 shows an overall ranking based on the proficiency of the surveyed students, with countries presented in three categories related to the OECD average, those significantly above the average, below the average, or close to the average. Eight Member States were significantly above the OECD average and 11 significantly below, with six around the OECD average. The highest scores were recorded by Finland and the Netherlands, while the lowest were recorded by Bulgaria and Romania.

For more information

Directorate-General for Education and Culture: http://ec.europa.eu/education/index_en.htm

Figure 10.8: PISA study: ranking on mathematics score, 2006 (1)

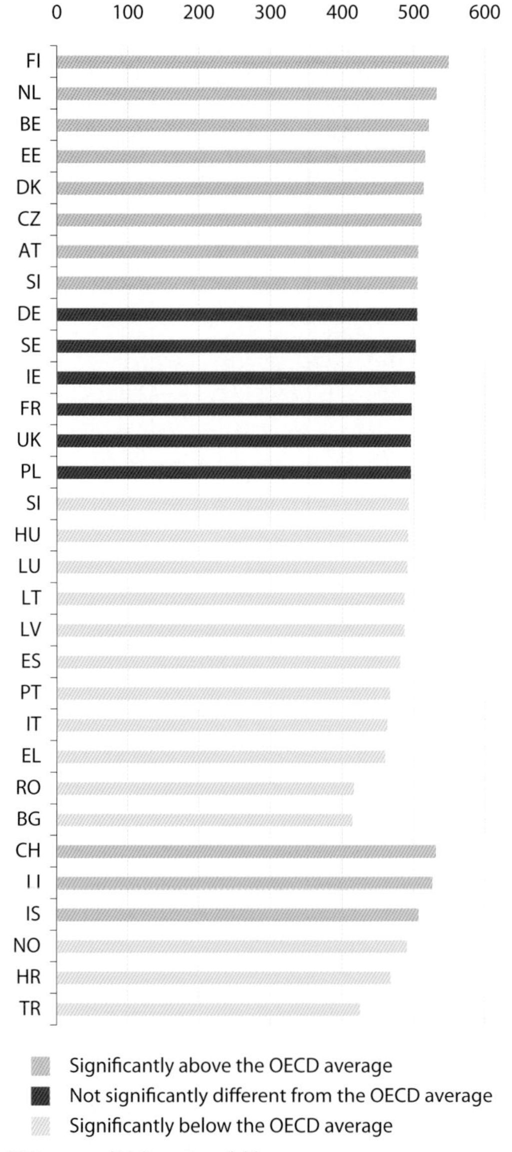

(1) Cyprus and Malta, not available.

Source: OECD, The Programme for International Student Assessment (PISA)

11 Restaurants and hotels

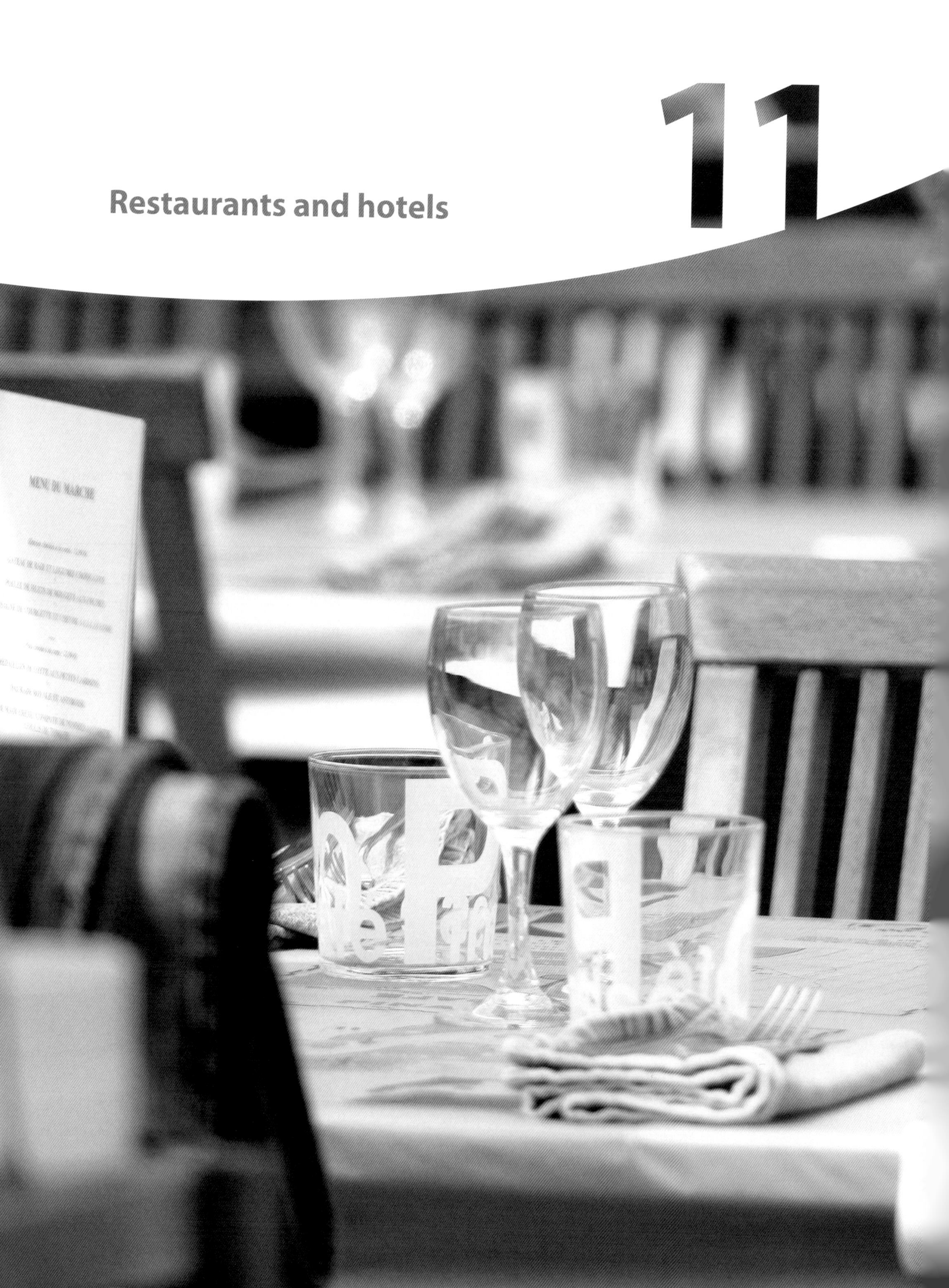

Whether for business or leisure, there is a wide range of accommodation for both short-stay breaks and longer holidays within the EU. Various factors contributed to make travel more accessible for a wider range of consumers: the growth of so-called 'low-cost airlines'; increased levels of car ownership and higher disposable incomes (particularly in the Member States that joined the EU since 2004); the completion of new stretches of high-speed rail networks; and an expanding motorway network.

11.1 Access and choice

There is little data on the actual number of restaurants (local units) that exist in the EU-27, although Eurostat's structural business statistics do provide information on enterprise numbers. There were about 1.4 million enterprises operating with the restaurants, bars, canteens and catering sector across the EU-27 in 2005, offering a wide choice of places to eat and drink. A little under one in five (18.8 %) of all restaurants, bars, canteens and catering enterprises was found in Spain (see Table 11.1).

Between 2000 and 2005 there was a relatively sharp rise in the number of enterprises in the restaurants, bars, canteens and catering sector in the EU-27 (up 10.6 % overall), with increases recorded for most of the Member States. Among the exceptions, there were relatively steep declines in Slovenia (-20.9 %) and Germany (-13.9 %). Relative to the size of their populations, there were few restaurants, bars, canteens and catering enterprises in Slovakia and the Baltic Member States, but a relatively high number in Luxembourg, as well as Cyprus, Portugal, Greece, and Spain (all of which cater for high numbers of tourists).

Table 11.1: Number of enterprises: restaurants, bars, canteens and catering (unit)

	2000	2002 (1)	2005 (2)
EU-27	*1 258 952*	*1 311 353*	1 392 298
BE	39 107	38 018	39 952
BG	21 297	21 903	20 932
CZ	35 079	38 904	41 748
DK	11 886	11 835	12 077
DE	139 907	125 893	120 514
EE	1 020	1 220	1 152
IE	8 965	10 999	9 738
EL	73 252	:	79 660
ES	244 299	245 650	261 997
FR	158 381	165 300	179 674
IT	210 138	214 618	224 379
CY	6 162	6 451	6 237
LV	1 793	1 816	2 255
LT	2 410	2 686	2 713
LU	2 100	2 212	2 341
HU	:	29 826	29 593
MT	1 809	2 545	:
NL	34 555	32 170	31 870
AT	22 626	27 239	30 307
PL	39 392	45 485	45 321
PT	56 357	58 401	78 532
RO	9 038	12 219	16 651
SI	7 615	6 683	6 021
SK	509	493	954
FI	9 121	9 078	8 675
SE	17 642	18 718	20 816
UK	101 374	107 739	115 083

(1) Belgium, 2001.
(2) Czech Republic, 2006.

Source: Eurostat, Structural business statistics (theme4/sbs/sbs_na_1a_se)

Table 11.2: Infrastructure for hotels and similar establishments, 2007 (1) (unit)

	Establishments	Bedrooms	Bed places
EU-27	*203 244*	*5 855 777*	*11 719 904*
BE	2 013	56 693	124 811
BG	1 526	103 841	231 303
CZ	4 559	106 907	248 077
DK	477	37 098	73 384
DE	35 941	899 068	1 643 748
EE	346	13 875	28 634
IE	4 087	67 355	156 775
EL	9 207	367 992	700 933
ES	18 426	825 220	1 639 009
FR	18 135	626 981	1 253 962
IT	34 037	1 058 543	2 141 952
CY	735	43 799	87 804
LV	318	11 457	20 685
LT	348	10 973	21 871
LU	273	7 639	14 559
HU	2 032	66 873	158 762
MT	173	18 533	39 518
NL	3 196	98 966	200 254
AT	14 204	285 558	573 726
PL	2 443	93 944	190 387
PT	2 028	117 565	264 037
RO	4 163	112 177	228 123
SI	396	17 251	33 040
SK	1 249	32 766	67 178
FI	909	54 924	119 397
SE	1 893	103 793	207 439
UK	40 130	615 986	1 250 536

(1) Hungary, Malta and Portugal, 2006.

Source: Eurostat, Tourism statistics (theme4/tour/tour_cap_nuts3)

There were about 200 thousand hotels or similar establishments in the EU-27 in 2007, with 5.9 million bedrooms and 11.7 million bed places (see Table 11.2). The United Kingdom had more hotels or similar establishments than any other Member State (19.7 % of the EU-27 total) in 2007, although a relatively high proportion of these establishments were quite small in size; they had an average of 31 bed places, among the lowest in any of the Member States, in part reflecting the high number of bed and breakfast establishments. The largest hotels and similar establishments (based on average numbers of bed places) were found in Malta (228), followed by Denmark (154) and Bulgaria (152). A little under half (46.3 %) of all bed places in the EU-27 were located in three of the Member States, namely, Italy (18.3 %), Germany (14.0 %) and Spain (14.0 %).

11.2 Consumption

11.2.1 Consumption volume

Tourism is a key sector for the European economy, as well as an important leisure activity for its population. The number of nights spent by tourists in the EU-27 was estimated at 2 309 million in 2007, a little over two thirds of which were spent in hotels or similar establishments (see Table 11.3). More nights were spent in hotels in Spain (17.3 % of the total for the EU-27) than in any other Member State, with the combined nights in hotels in Italy, Germany, France and the United Kingdom accounting for about one half (53.5 %) of the EU-27 total.

Table 11.3: Number of tourist nights, by type of accommodation, 2007 (1)
(thousand)

				Other collective accommodation		
	Total	(% share of EU-27)	Hotels	Tourist campsites	Holiday campsites	Other n.e.c.
EU-27	*2 309 250*	100.0	*1 575 613*	*352 984*	*201 200*	*179 453*
BE	29 849	1.3	16 197	2 925	4 884	5 844
BG	17 977	0.8	16 736	77	458	706
CZ	40 831	1.8	27 044	2 781	733	10 273
DK	28 068	1.2	11 080	11 684	4 007	1 297
DE	317 306	13.7	214 675	21 921	29 757	50 953
EE	4 675	0.2	3 843	222	138	472
IE	35 993	1.6	28 282	3 160	*1 491*	3 060
EL	65 420	2.8	64 086	1 335	:	:
ES	383 300	16.6	272 733	31 676	70 922	7 969
FR	301 963	13.1	204 269	97 694	:	:
IT	374 628	16.2	254 076	61 404	34 328	24 820
CY	14 378	0.6	14 298	18	62	:
LV	3 325	0.1	2 759	166	108	292
LT	3 264	0.1	2 591	73	429	171
LU	2 528	0.1	1 438	803	101	186
HU	19 652	0.9	15 808	1 456	932	1 456
MT	7 424	0.3	7 307	:	:	*117*
NL	88 267	3.8	34 159	20 824	29 283	4 002
AT	100 645	4.4	79 153	4 924	7 019	9 549
PL	54 954	2.4	24 307	696	949	29 001
PT	45 522	2.0	37 566	6 832	:	1 124
RO	20 593	0.9	19 756	224	:	613
SI	7 993	0.3	5 546	1 107	666	674
SK	11 423	0.5	7 233	386	353	3 450
FI	19 037	0.8	15 817	2 241	830	149
SE	48 605	2.1	25 416	17 012	3 467	2 710
UK	261 633	11.3	169 440	61 344	10 283	20 565

(1) Hungary, Malta and Portugal, 2006.

Source: Eurostat, Tourism statistics (theme3/tour/tour_occ_ninat)

Table 11.4: Number of holiday trips (at least 1 night) by residents aged 15 and over, 2006

	Trips (thousand)		Average annual growth rate of trips, 2000-2006 (%)	
	1-3 nights	=>4 nights (1)	1-3 nights	=>4 nights
BE	3 189	6 647	1.7	0.7
BG	:	:	:	:
CZ	17 821	8 934	-1.0	-3.5
DK	4 735	5 896	6.6	4.4
DE	47 845	105 431	13.5	0.0
EE	585	279	-14.7	6.3
IE	5 007	4 790	22.1	14.7
EL	7 305	8 578	28.7	10.3
ES	81 302	39 599	-2.1	6.0
FR	105 020	83 137	4.3	1.6
IT	36 920	41 135	4.1	2.5
CY	:	719	:	:
LV	3 792	909	0.6	19.6
LT	2 386	1 090	4.4	8.4
LU	420	679	9.0	3.0
HU	17 973	6 711	23.4	10.9
MT	:	:	:	:
NL	9 881	18 384	0.1	2.9
AT	7 026	8 745	-5.6	7.4
PL	20 475	17 808	-7.0	3.5
PT	6 602	3 663	-0.8	-0.1
RO	3 505	3 387	-24.4	-10.7
SI	2 958	1 807	10.0	:
SK	1 865	4 555	0.1	:
FI	21 541	6 620	4.8	5.9
SE	:	:	:	:
UK	50 874	61 821	-6.2	-3.8

(1) Cyprus, 2004.

Source: Eurostat, Tourism statistics (2008 pocketbook)

Figure 11.1: Evolution of the number of tourist nights spent by residents and non-residents in hotels or similar establishments (2000=100)

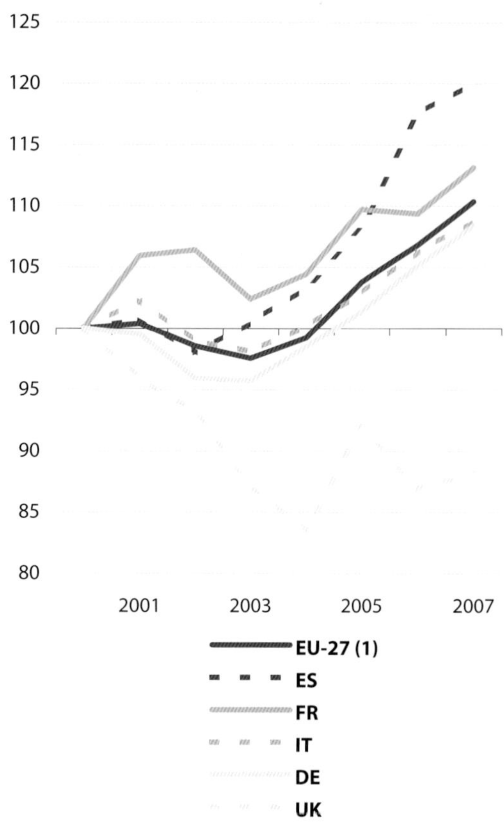

(1) Includes estimates for Romania during the period 2002 to 2005 and for Malta during the period 2000 to 2002.

Source: Eurostat, Tourism statistics (theme3/tour/tour_occ_ninat)

In the period between 2000 and 2007, there were some contrasting developments in terms of the number of nights spent by residents and non-residents in hotels or similar establishments. There was moderate growth (an average of 2.6 % per annum) in Spain, but a sharp fall in the United Kingdom through until 2004, after which there was a partial recovery (see Figure 11.1). Apart from the United Kingdom, Cyprus was the only other Member State in which there was a confirmed decline (an average of -2.8 % per annum) in nights spent. In contrast, there was strong growth, albeit from relatively low levels, in Lithuania (16.6 % per annum), Estonia (12.2 % per annum), Latvia (10.6 % per annum) and Bulgaria (10.8 % per annum), as well as in Poland (7.9 % per annum). Across the EU-27 as a whole, the number of nights spent in hotels or similar establishments increased steadily from a relative low in 2003.

In the period between 2000 and 2006, the number of trips by residents increased in the majority of Member States – the United Kingdom and Romania were the most notable exceptions (see Table 11.4). There tended to be a higher number of short trips (of 1-3 nights) made by residents than long trip (4 or more nights) in the majority of Member States in 2006, in particular in the Baltic States, Spain, Hungary and the Czech Republic. Among the exceptions, short trips by residents from the Benelux group of Member States, Germany and Slovakia represented closer to one third of all trips made. In the case of Germany, the number of short trips more than doubled between 2000 and 2006, although this rate of increase was lower than those recorded for Ireland, Hungary and, particularly, Greece.

11.2.2 Consumption expenditure

The average annual household consumption expenditure on restaurants and hotels across the EU-27 rose by about 20 % between 2000 and 2006 to an average of EUR 1 200 per person; note these figures do not include package holidays that, following the COICOP classification, are included as part of Chapter 9. The rise in expenditure on restaurants and hotels appears to have been driven by both higher prices (noted for all of the Member States for which data are available, but particularly Slovakia, Hungary and the Czech Republic), as well as widespread increases in the volume component of final consumption expenditure (where growth in Estonia was particularly strong).

Expressed in purchasing power standard (PPS) terms, average consumption expenditure on restaurants and hotels across the EU-27 was an estimated PPS 1 417 in 2005 (see Table 11.5). In comparison to many other goods and services, there was a particularly wide spread in mean household consumption expenditure on restaurants and hotels; by far the highest level was in Luxembourg (a little over PPS 4 000), followed some way behind by Cyprus, Greece and the United Kingdom, while the lowest levels of expenditure were registered in Romania (PPS 58).

Expenditure on restaurants and hotels represented an average of 5.3 % of total household consumption expenditure across the EU-27 in 2005. The share of these items in the total budget was highest in Portugal (at a little more than double the EU-27 average), Spain and Greece, and was lowest (at less than 2 % of total expenditure) in Romania and Poland (see Figure 11.2); there were also relatively low shares among the Scandinavian countries.

Table 11.5: Mean consumption expenditure per household, restaurants and hotels, 2005
(PPS)

EU-27 (1)	1 417
BE	1 894
BG	255
CZ	619
DK	960
DE	1 212
EE	339
IE	2 190
EL	2 661
ES	2 414
FR	1 277
IT	1 428
CY	2 830
LV	557
LT	429
LU	4 098
HU	343
MT	2 030
NL	1 647
AT	1 660
PL	180
PT	2 263
RO	58
SI	1 035
SK	520
FI	1 021
SE	981
UK	2 558
HR	465
NO	1 111

(1) Estimate.

Source: Eurostat, Household Budget Survey (theme3/hbs/hbs_exp_t121)

Figure 11.2: Structure of consumption expenditure: share of restaurants and hotels in total expenditure, 2005 (1)
(%)

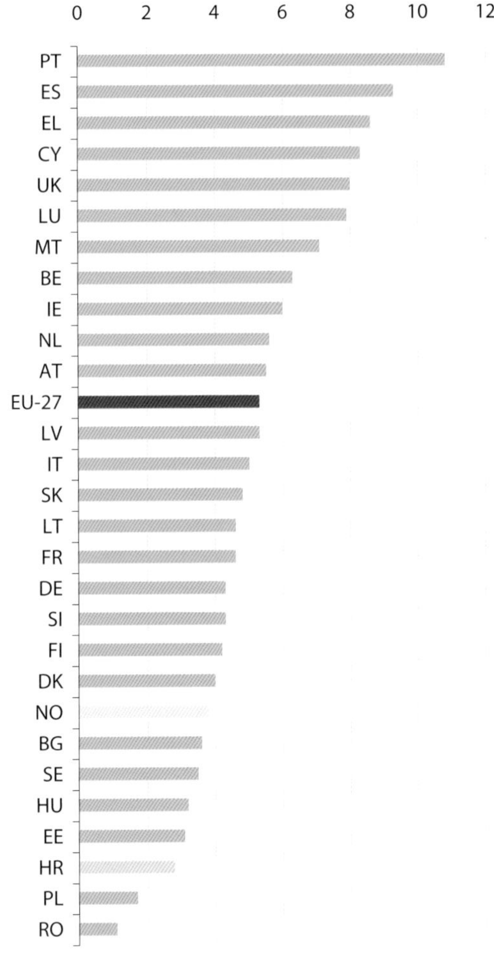

(1) EU-27, estimate; Czech Republic, not available.

Source: Eurostat, Household Budget Survey (theme3/hbs/hbs_str_t211)

Most expenditure on restaurants and hotels can be considered as luxury spending, in the sense that it is not a necessity to eat out or to go on holiday. As such, it is perhaps not surprising that spending on these items accounted for a progressively higher share of total household expenditure as incomes rose; the share for households in the highest income quintile across the EU-27 was 6.2 % in 2005, compared with 4.0 % for those households in the lowest income quintile. In contrast, the proportion of expenditure devoted to restaurants and hotels declined with age; the average share among households headed by someone under 30 years being 5.8 %, which was notably higher than for households headed by someone aged 60 years or more (3.6 %).

11.3 Prices

11.3.1 Price inflation

There was a relatively steep and sustained rise in the EU-27's harmonised index of consumer prices for restaurants and hotels in the period between 2000 and 2007 (increasing on average by 3.4 % per annum), with almost identical developments for the sub-indices of catering services, canteens and accommodation services. Progressively higher prices for restaurants and hotels were a general feature across all of the Member States during the period between 2000 and 2007 (see Table 11.6). The highest price increases in 2007 were noted in Latvia (14.3 %) and Bulgaria (11.8 %), continuing the trend of accelerating prices in both of these countries. In contrast, there was a slowdown in the rate of price increases in Romania (to 5.1 % in 2007). The price index for restaurants and hotels in Malta declined slightly in 2007 (-0.6 %), the only fall noted for any of the Member States in any of the years between 2000 and 2007.

Table 11.6: Harmonised indices of consumer prices, restaurants and hotels, annual rate of change (%)

	2000	2001	2002	2003	2004	2005	2006	2007
EU-27	3.4	3.9	4.4	3.2	3.0	2.8	2.8	3.4
BE	3.0	2.4	4.4	3.2	2.6	2.8	2.9	2.2
BG	11.8	8.4	4.3	3.4	4.2	4.9	8.5	11.8
CZ	2.6	3.3	3.7	2.3	5.0	3.8	3.4	4.0
DK	3.0	3.0	2.2	2.3	2.5	2.4	2.5	2.6
DE	1.4	1.9	3.7	0.8	0.7	1.0	1.3	2.6
EE	5.7	7.3	5.5	3.7	2.7	3.0	3.2	8.6
IE	5.6	5.9	7.1	6.3	4.0	3.3	3.9	4.2
EL	4.6	5.2	6.7	4.8	4.3	3.1	2.6	4.0
ES	4.2	4.4	5.5	4.3	4.1	4.2	4.5	4.8
FR	1.9	2.5	3.9	2.6	2.8	2.5	2.3	2.8
IT	3.2	4.0	4.5	4.0	3.0	2.5	2.3	2.6
CY	8.0	6.1	4.4	5.8	4.7	2.8	0.2	3.8
LV	2.1	2.4	2.6	2.6	7.3	11.2	11.3	14.3
LT	0.0	1.8	1.9	0.0	1.0	2.4	3.4	8.0
LU	2.6	3.1	4.2	3.3	3.2	3.5	3.0	3.3
HU	10.9	13.8	10.2	8.9	10.2	5.7	5.3	7.9
MT	7.6	4.0	4.5	7.4	2.6	0.0	1.9	-0.6
NL	3.6	6.1	6.9	1.9	2.0	1.8	2.0	3.6
AT	2.1	2.6	2.8	2.7	2.5	2.4	1.8	2.2
PL	8.3	6.1	2.9	1.1	2.6	3.5	1.8	3.4
PT	3.7	4.4	5.6	5.1	5.0	1.4	2.0	2.4
RO	52.1	43.9	27.4	16.6	14.1	13.1	7.9	5.1
SI	4.6	7.3	9.0	8.6	6.1	4.6	4.4	7.3
SK	7.7	9.8	4.7	8.5	10.3	5.3	2.6	3.0
FI	3.0	2.5	3.3	2.9	1.0	1.8	2.2	2.5
SE	1.5	3.2	4.1	2.7	2.1	2.3	2.5	3.2
UK	3.3	3.8	3.4	3.1	2.9	3.3	3.2	3.5
TR	52.1	42.6	38.2	34.2	19.9	13.7	13.9	11.2
IS	5.7	6.5	6.9	2.9	2.3	2.6	5.7	4.5
NO	2.9	4.4	4.1	2.9	2.3	1.6	3.0	4.1
CH	:	:	:	:	:	:	1.3	1.3

Source: Eurostat, Harmonised indices of consumer prices (theme2/prc/prc_hicp_aind)

11.3.2 Price levels

The average price level of restaurants and hotels in Denmark was about 45 % above the EU-27 average (see Figure 11.3) and higher than in any of the other Member States. In contrast, the average price level in Bulgaria was about ne third (34.4 %) of the EU-27 average. These ative price levels were very similar to those for sumer services as a whole. However, this was the case in Cyprus, where the average price l of hotels and restaurants was similar to the -27 average (2.4 % lower), while price levels for nsumer services in general were some 22.6 % wer than the EU-27 average. Similarly, the price vel of restaurants and hotels in Poland was one uarter (27.2 %) less than the EU-27 average, hereas the average price of consumer services s a whole was closer to half (52.1 %) the EU-27 verage.

Between 2000 and 2007, the extent to which verage price levels of restaurants and hotels differed among the EU-27 Member States arrowed slightly, although it remained relatively high (with a coefficient of variation of 30.3 %). In contrast, the diversity in price levels between the EU-15 Member States increased during the same period (the coefficient of variation rising from 14.0 % to 17.6 %).

Figure 11.3: Price level indices, restaurants and hotels, 2007
(EU-27=100)

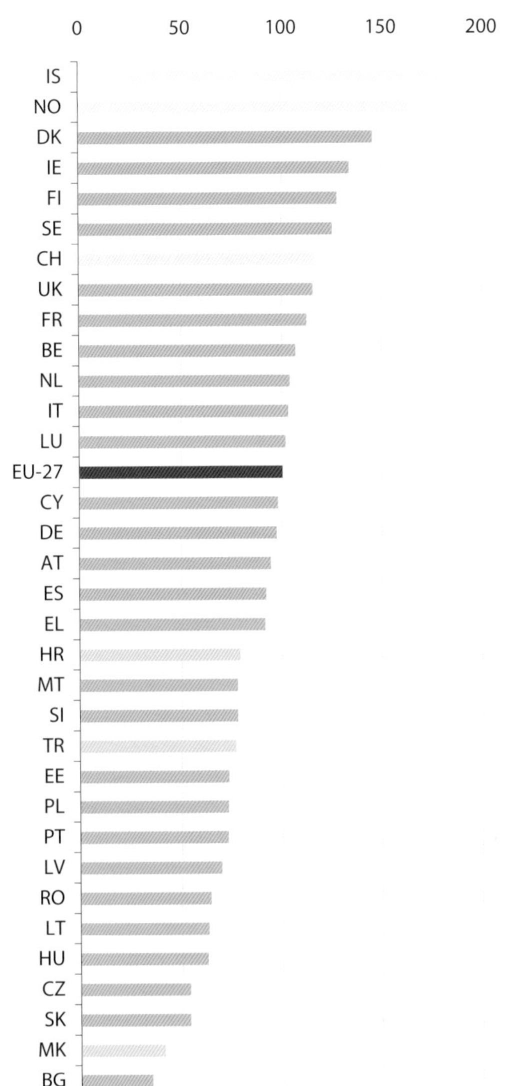

Source: Eurostat, Price level indices (theme2/prc/prc_ppp_ind)

11.4 Quality

Since 2007, the European Commission has made awards to 'European Destinations of Excellence' (EDEN) at its annual European Tourism Forum. The EDEN programme was launched in 2006 to promote the specific characteristics of European destinations and to offer particular support to those where competitive tourism is developed to take into account social, cultural and environmental sustainability. It aims to provide a platform for the exchange of good practices at the European level, while rewarding sustainable forms of tourism and successful business models.

In 2007, ten destinations were awarded the title of 'Best Emerging Rural Destinations of Excellence': the Pielachtal (Austria), Durbuy (Belgium), Sveti Martin na Muri (Croatia), Troodos (Cyprus), Florina (Greece), Őrség (Hungary), Clonakilty district (Ireland), Commune di Specchia (Italy), Kuldiga (Latvia), and Nadur (Malta).

Table 11.7: Restaurants with one, two or three Michelin stars, 2005 (unit)

	*	**	***	Total no. of stars	Number of stars per million inhabitants
BE	79	12	3	112	11.0
DK	9	1	0	11	2.1
DE	166	14	6	212	2.6
IE	1	2	0	5	1.4
EL	3	0	0	3	0.3
ES	91	10	4	123	3.1
FR	402	70	26	620	10.5
IT	197	23	4	255	4.5
LU	10	2	0	14	32.6
NL	64	7	2	84	5.3
AT	48	4	0	56	6.9
PT	6	1	0	8	0.8
FI	2	1	0	4	0.8
SE	7	1	0	9	1.0
UK	201	10	3	230	3.9

Source: Andy Hayler's Michelin Restaurants' Guide

In 2008, twenty destinations of excellence were awarded the title of the '2008 European Tourist Destination of Excellence in Intangible Heritage': Steirisches Vulkanland (Austria), La Ville d'Ath (Belgium), Belogradchik Municipality (Bulgaria), Djurdjevac – the Rooster Town (Croatia), Agros (Cyprus), Viljandi (Estonia), Wild Taiga (Finland), the tourist wine rou of the Jura (France), the prefecture of Gre (Greece), Hortobágy (Hungary), Carling and the Cooley Peninsula (Ireland), Comun Corinaldo (Italy), Latgalian potters, master clay (Latvia), Plateliai (Lithuania), Echtern (Luxembourg), the hamlet of Santa Lucija Kercem (Malta), Horezu Depression (Romania the Soca Valley (Slovenia), Sierra de las Nieve (Spain), and Edirne (Turkey).

'Le Guide Michelin' is a well-known Frenc review of hotels and restaurants, in particula the section devoted to restaurant excellenc (that awards up to three stars in its classificatio system). Collated data for 2005 show that Franc held the most Michelin stars among the Membe States, although the quality of restaurants (usin this measure) was also relatively high in Italy, the United Kingdom, Germany and Spain (see Table 11.7). Relative to population size, there were more restaurants with stars in Luxembourg and Belgium than in France, while Austria and the Netherlands came fourth and fifth using this ranking. The most recent awards for 2008 suggest that the quality of top-end restaurants in Germany has risen, with nine restaurants attaining three star status and fifteen restaurants attaining two stars. A first Michelin star was also awarded, in 2008, to a restaurant in the Czech Republic, making this the first star given to a restaurant in any of the Member States that joined the EU since 2004.

12

Miscellaneous goods and services

This chapter focuses on products related to Section 12 of COICOP, which covers miscellaneous goods and services. These are quite diverse in nature and so, unlike the other chapters in this publication, this one has been split into two parts:

- Part 12A focuses on COICOP headings 12.1, 12.3, 12.4 and 12.7, covering personal care, personal effects, social protection, and other services;
- Part 12B focuses on COICOP headings 12.5 and 12.6, covering insurance and financial services.

12A. PERSONAL PRODUCTS, SOCIAL CARE AND OTHER SERVICES

This part of Chapter 12 covers a wide range of goods and services. Personal care includes: services from hairdressers, beauticians, saunas and solariums; personal care appliances, such as razors, hair dryers and tooth brushes; as well as toiletries, cosmetics, and other beauty products. Personal effects include: jewellery, clocks and watches, travel goods, bags and wallets, cigarette lighters, sunglasses and umbrellas, as well as items for transporting babies such as push-chairs, car seats and harnesses. Social protection services include: care for infants, disabled persons and the elderly, as well as family counselling services. The heading 'other services not elsewhere classified' includes: legal services, services of employment agencies, estate agents and undertakers, payments for issuing of certificates, copying documents, as well as advertisements; this heading also includes payments to astrologers, bodyguards and marriage guidance counsellors.

For households, personal care (goods and services) are the most important of these four categories in terms of expenditure, accounting for around three fifths of total household expenditure on personal products, social care and other services.

12A.1 Consumption

12A.1.1 Consumption volume: childcare

Table 12A.1 gives an indication of the number of children in childcare in the capital cities of the Member States. In all cities there are more children aged three and four in childcare than those aged from birth to two years old, although the difference is quite small in Stockholm. Of the cities with data available, Bratislava stands out from the others in that there are very few children under the age of three in childcare, in contrast to a relatively large number aged three or four.

Table 12A.1: Number of children in childcare, 2003-2006
(number)

	Aged 0-4	Aged 0-2	Aged 3-4
Bruxelles / Brussel	17 670	:	:
Sofia	:	:	:
Praha	:	:	:
København	:	:	:
Berlin	:	:	:
Tallinn	10 043	3 273	6 770
Dublin	:	:	:
Athina	3 794	991	:
Madrid	69 691	18 882	50 809
Paris	:	:	:
Roma	8 906	:	:
Lefkosia	:	:	:
Riga	12 787	3 579	9 208
Lithuania	46 447	11 592	34 855
Luxembourg	:	:	:
Budapest	57 525	9 712	47 813
Valletta	:	:	:
Amsterdam	14 500	:	:
Wien	35 419	10 662	24 757
Warszawa	21 963	2 402	19 561
Lisboa	:	:	:
București	:	:	:
Ljubljana	7 570	2 933	4 637
Bratislava	11 063	215	10 848
Helsinki	9 334	2 927	6 407
Stockholm	28 113	13 004	15 109
London	:	:	:
Bern	1 391	:	:
Oslo	18 737	8 069	10 668

Source: Eurostat, Data collected for core cities (theme1/urb/urb_vcity)

12A.1.2 Consumption expenditure

When studying expenditure related to personal products, social care and other services it is important to note that the methods of provision for social protection services varies considerably between countries. The interpretation of data oncerning household expenditure on social tection services is therefore limited by the nt to which this is provided free (or at a tly reduced price) at the point of use.

ure 12A.1 provides a comparison of household sumption expenditure on various items of ial and personal care and other services, based n 2005 household budget survey (HBS) data. he HBS data are presented in PPS terms and how that at comparable price levels, expenditure r some of these items varied enormously: for xample, expenditure on hairdressing salons and ersonal grooming establishments ranged from PPS 7 per household in Bulgaria to PPS 497 in yprus, with expenditure in Luxembourg double his level at PPS 1 006. A similar situation was bserved for expenditure on jewellery, clocks and watches, ranging from PPS 6 in Romania to PPS 163 in Malta, with again Luxembourg recording an exceptional value of PPS 620 per household. The miscellaneous category of other services not elsewhere classified ranged from PPS 10 in Romania to over PPS 1 300 in Finland and Belgium.

Figure 12A.2: Structure of consumption expenditure: share of personal care, effects, social protection, and other services in total expenditure, 2005 (1)
(%)

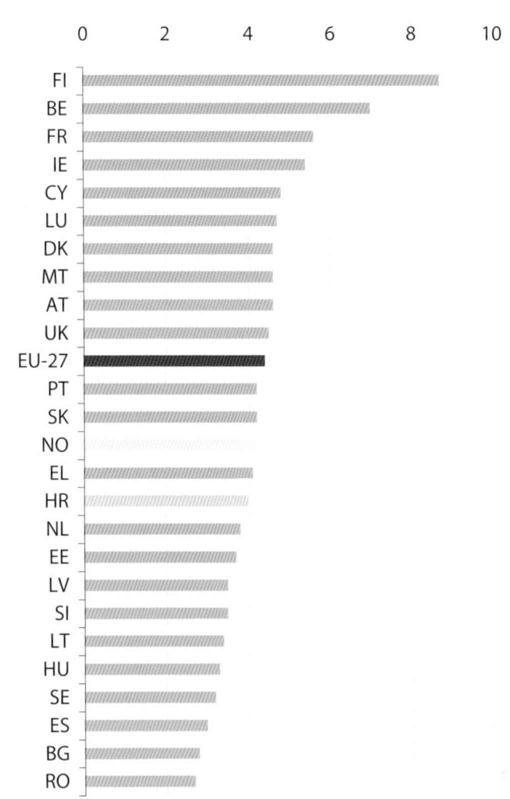

(1) EU-27, estimate; Czech Republic, Germany, Italy and Poland, not available.

Source: Eurostat, Household Budget Survey (theme3/hbs/hbs_str_t211)

Figure 12A.1: Mean consumption expenditure per household, personal care, effects, social protection, and other services, 2005
(PPS, minimum and maximum (vertical lines at end of horizontal line), inter-quartile range containing half of the Member States (box), median (vertical line within box))

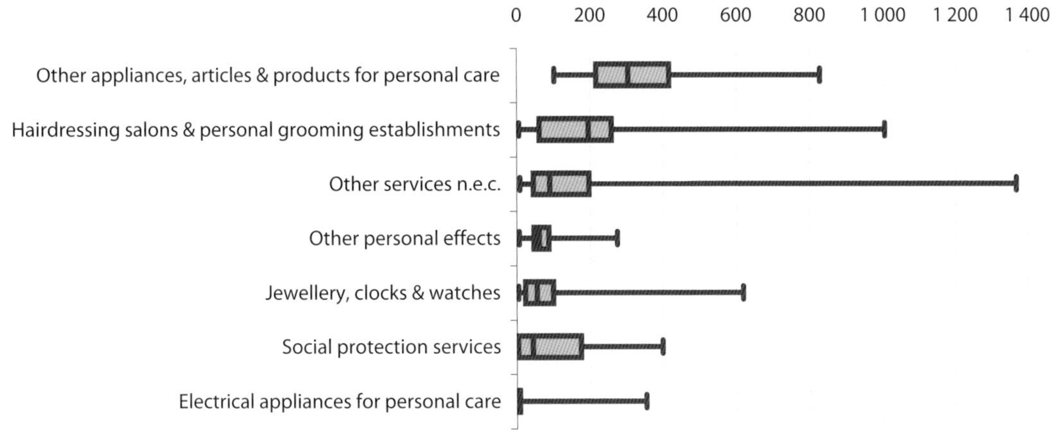

Source: Eurostat, Household Budget Survey (theme3/hbs/hbs_exp_t121)

Figure 12A.3: Structure of consumption expenditure: share of personal care, effects, social protection, and other services in total expenditure, EU-27, 2005
(%)

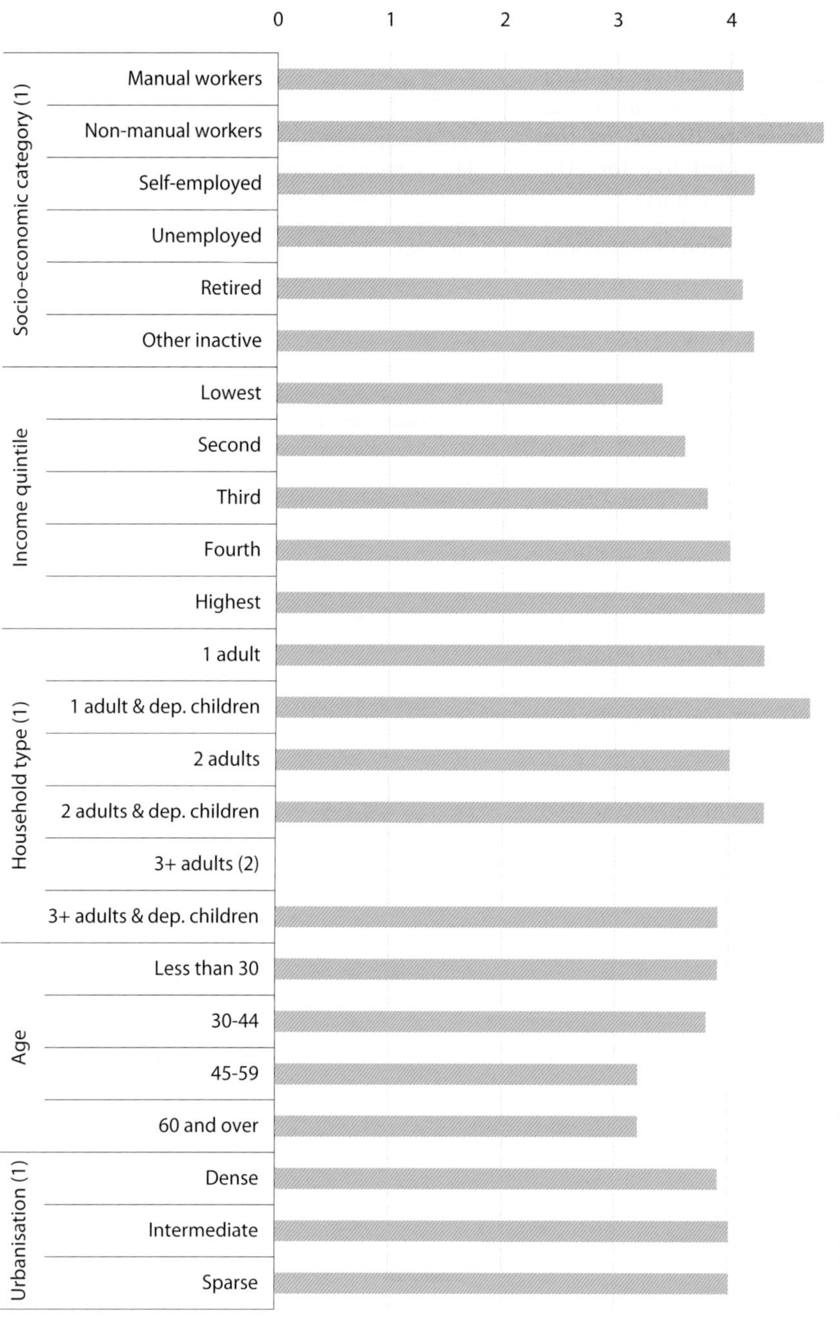

(1) Unreliable.
(2) Not available.

Source: Eurostat, Household Budget Survey (theme3/hbs/hbs_str_t221, hbs_str_t223, hbs_str_t224, hbs_str_t225, hbs_str_t226)

Collectively, personal products, social care and other services accounted for 4.4 % of total household consumption expenditure in the EU-27 in 2005, and their share was typically between 2.7 % and 5.6 % in each Member State, although it reached 8.7 % in Finland and 7.0 % in Belgium. The relative importance of these oducts and services was particularly high for -manual workers, where they accounted .8 % of total expenditure in the EU-27, and erally increased with income, the share for highest income quintile being approximately quarter higher than the share recorded for se within the lowest income quintile.

Figure 12A.4: Structure of consumption expenditure on personal care, effects, social protection, and other services, EU-27, 2005 (1)
(%)

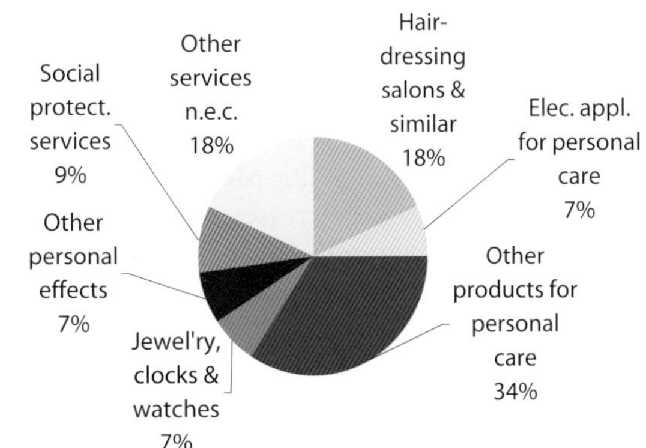

(1) Unreliable data.

Source: Eurostat, Household Budget Survey (theme3/hbs/hbs_str_t211)

able 12A.2: Structure of consumption expenditure on personal care, effects, social protection, and other ervices, 2005 (1)
%)

	Hairdressing salons & similar	Electrical appliances for personal care	Other appliances, articles & products for personal care	Jewellery, clocks & watches	Other personal effects	Social protection services	Other services n.e.c.
EU-27	18	7	34	7	7	9	20
BE	13	0	14	3	3	4	63
BG	4	0	61	4	4	7	21
CZ	:	:	:	:	:	:	:
DK	17	0	28	9	7	28	9
DE	:	:	:	:	:	:	:
EE	14	0	41	5	11	8	16
IE	17	0	43	6	7	20	6
EL	12	0	51	5	10	2	20
ES	37	0	33	10	7	7	10
FR	14	23	21	4	4	9	23
IT	:	:	:	:	:	:	:
CY	31	0	38	6	6	6	15
LV	17	0	60	6	11	0	9
LT	15	0	62	6	12	0	6
LU	40	2	6	26	11	9	4
HU	12	0	58	3	6	3	18
MT	15	0	57	13	9	0	7
NL	21	3	34	11	5	21	5
AT	24	2	30	7	9	4	26
PL	:	:	:	:	:	:	:
PT	24	0	33	2	5	19	14
RO	11	0	70	4	7	0	7
SI	17	:	46	3	11	3	20
SK	14	0	52	7	19	0	10
FI	9	0	14	2	2	8	64
SE	25	0	34	9	9	16	6
UK	16	2	31	9	7	13	24
HR	23	3	48	3	5	5	15
NO	21	0	31	10	7	26	2

(1) EU-27, unreliable. Note that shares do not always sum to 100 %.

Source: Eurostat, Household Budget Survey (theme3/hbs/hbs_str_t211)

12A.2 Prices

The EU-27's harmonised indices of consumer prices rose between 2000 and 2007 by an average of 3.9 % per annum for other services not elsewhere classified, and 3.5 % for social protection services, while for personal effects and for personal care the average rates of growth were 2.1 % and 1.9 % per annum respectively. Generally, the Baltic Member States recorded the highest price increases for these items in 2007, with Latvia and Lithuania both recording double digit increases for social protection and for other services.

Figure 12A.5: Harmonised indices of consumer prices, EU-27
(2005=100)

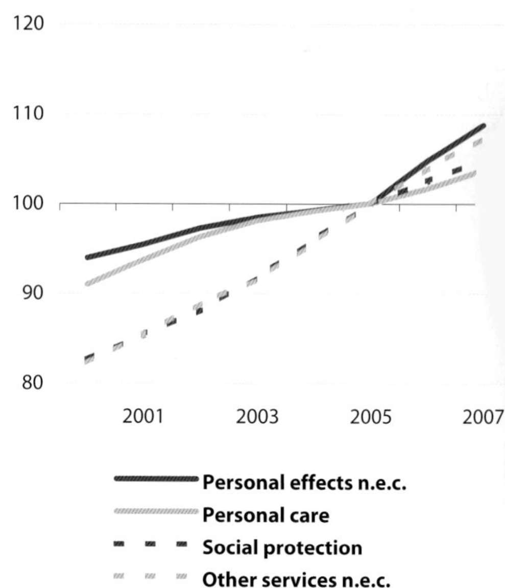

Source: Eurostat, Harmonised indices of consumer prices (theme2/prc/prc_hicp_aind)

Table 12A.3: Harmonised indices of consumer prices, annual rate of change, EU-27
(%)

	2000	2001	2002	2003	2004	2005	2006	2007
Personal care	1.6	3.1	2.8	1.9	1.1	0.8	1.6	2.0
Hairdressing salons and personal grooming	2.6	3.2	4.3	2.9	2.8	2.7	2.6	3.0
Electrical appliances for personal care; other appliances, articles and products for personal care	0.9	3.0	1.8	1.3	0.0	-0.3	1.0	1.4
Personal effects n.e.c.	1.0	1.6	1.9	1.2	0.8	0.8	4.7	3.8
Jewellery, clocks and watches	1.0	1.7	2.3	1.8	1.3	1.1	8.8	5.4
Other personal effects	0.9	1.5	1.5	0.6	0.2	0.5	0.7	1.9
Social protection	7.3	3.4	3.2	4.2	4.7	4.1	2.5	2.3
Other services n.e.c.	2.4	3.9	4.0	3.0	4.6	4.5	3.9	3.2

Source: Eurostat, Harmonised indices of consumer prices (theme2/prc/prc_hicp_aind)

Table 12A.4: Harmonised indices of consumer prices, annual rate of change
(%)

	Personal care		Personal effects n.e.c.		Social protection		Other services n.e.c.	
	2006	2007	2006	2007	2006	2007	2006	2007
EU-27	1.6	2.0	4.7	3.8	2.5	2.3	3.9	3.2
BE	1.9	2.4	5.3	5.1	2.0	2.1	2.1	2.5
BG	4.0	5.9	12.0	4.9	9.6	2.6	1.3	7.5
[illegible]	1.4	1.4	0.1	0.3	4.3	15.6	4.3	3.0
[illegible]	1.8	2.7	2.7	3.5	-0.4	-2.6	3.9	3.8
[illegible]	0.6	2.1	1.8	2.4	1.2	1.2	5.1	2.3
[illegible]	4.2	6.7	5.4	7.2	18.3	17.0	2.8	-1.2
[illegible]	1.3	2.6	-1.5	-2.1	4.0	3.8	1.0	3.0
EL	2.2	1.9	5.7	3.0	3.9	3.9	2.3	4.2
ES	3.1	3.1	10.2	6.0	5.3	5.2	2.2	2.2
FR	1.5	1.2	6.5	4.6	4.1	2.9	1.6	0.9
IT	1.3	1.8	6.5	5.2	2.3	2.0	1.3	3.8
CY	2.7	2.9	5.2	-2.4	3.1	4.9	-0.2	0.1
LV	5.6	8.7	2.0	7.5	18.7	15.8	16.6	22.1
LT	1.1	3.4	4.4	6.7	12.3	17.0	6.3	12.1
LU	1.7	2.6	6.6	4.2	4.2	5.6	1.6	5.7
HU	1.3	4.4	3.4	4.8	:	3.9	5.7	6.5
MT	2.1	1.2	6.4	0.6	4.2	2.6	-0.7	1.5
NL	1.1	2.0	7.9	4.5	-6.2	-9.1	3.3	4.4
AT	1.9	2.0	8.6	3.6	4.3	4.4	2.9	3.4
PL	0.1	0.6	-0.1	0.7	2.8	3.3	7.3	4.8
PT	2.6	1.6	10.0	7.7	4.4	3.5	4.2	4.8
RO	3.4	2.9	6.3	4.7	:	:	2.4	2.1
SI	1.5	3.7	8.3	5.0	3.7	3.3	1.1	1.5
SK	2.3	1.9	2.3	2.2	3.0	5.4	1.6	1.0
FI	0.8	-0.2	4.0	2.2	3.5	5.1	5.6	7.9
SE	1.5	2.0	9.6	4.2	1.9	2.8	15.9	2.1
UK	2.0	2.5	2.4	3.0	5.4	5.6	6.1	3.7
TR	4.3	3.9	33.1	5.1	12.0	10.1	11.2	8.4
IS	6.3	9.8	2.8	7.6	-15.9	-5.0	9.7	10.6
NO	2.3	4.1	2.4	1.2	-11.7	2.0	2.4	0.6
CH	0.3	0.2	0.5	1.0	0.5	3.1	1.2	0.8

Source: Eurostat, Harmonised indices of consumer prices (theme2/prc/prc_hicp_aind)

12B INSURANCE AND FINANCIAL SERVICES

This part of Chapter 12 focuses on consumption related to banking and non-life insurance. Some information is also provided on savings and borrowing products (which are not consumption) such as financial investments, pensions, life insurance, and loans – more information on the levels of savings, credit and indebtedness, as well as on interest rates can be found in parts A5 and A6 of the overview at the start of the publication.

Retail financial services are essential for the everyday lives of EU citizens and small businesses. They facilitate their full participation in the economy, enable them to plan for the long-term and protect them through unforeseen circumstances. They include services such as current accounts, payments, personal loans, mortgages, pensions, investments and insurance products, all of which can be provided to individual customers.

The desire to promote competitive retail financial services markets stimulated the European Commission's decision in June 2005 to open sector inquiries into two important areas of the financial services sector, one of which was retail banking. In its sector inquiry, the European Commission examined two complementary aspects of retail banking: firstly, the markets for payment cards and payment systems; and secondly, the markets for current accounts and related services.

In December 2005, following extensive consultation with stakeholders, the European Commission set out its future strategy on financial services in a White Paper titled 'financial services policy 2005-2010'.

In April 2007, following the publication of the results of the sector inquiry into retail banking, the European Commission adopted a Green Paper on retail financial services in the single market. The publication of the Green Paper launched a public debate on the European Commission's future retail financial services strategy. The results of this debate were subsequently incorporated into the single market review which was adopted on the 20 November 2007. This review identified four areas where the competitiveness and efficiency of retail financial services markets could be enhanced: improving customer choice and mobility; making retail insurance markets wo better; moving towards adequate and consis rules for the distribution of retail investm products; and promoting financial educa inclusion and adequate redress for consumers

In the context of payments, two related initiati are of interest. In November 2007, the Europe Parliament and Council Directive on payme services in the internal market was adopted which aims to provide the legal foundation fo the creation of an EU-wide single market fo payments. The target is to make cross-bord payments as easy, efficient and secure as 'nationa payments within a Member State, bringing majo benefits to consumers as well as businesses. Fo example, funds transferred in euro to an accoun must be available for use by the end of the ne business day, regardless of whether these are from domestic or cross-border sources. More broadly, the legislation also seeks to improve competition by opening up payment markets to new entrants, thus fostering greater efficiency and cost-reduction, for example, allowing mobile phone operators and retailers to become payment service providers.

At the same time the Directive provides the necessary legal platform for the single euro payments area (SEPA).Although euro coins and notes can be used in the same way for cash payments throughout the euro area this has not been true for other types of payments; only with the launch of the SEPA at the beginning of 2008, was it possible to use the same format for credit transfers in euro throughout the European Union; for technical and legal reasons, cross-border direct debits are only likely to become widely available after October 2009. Another stage, further into the future, could be the implementation of common standards for credit cards.

Figure 12B.1: Market integration in retail banking: ownership of the five largest (gross total retail income) banks, 2004 (1)
(number)

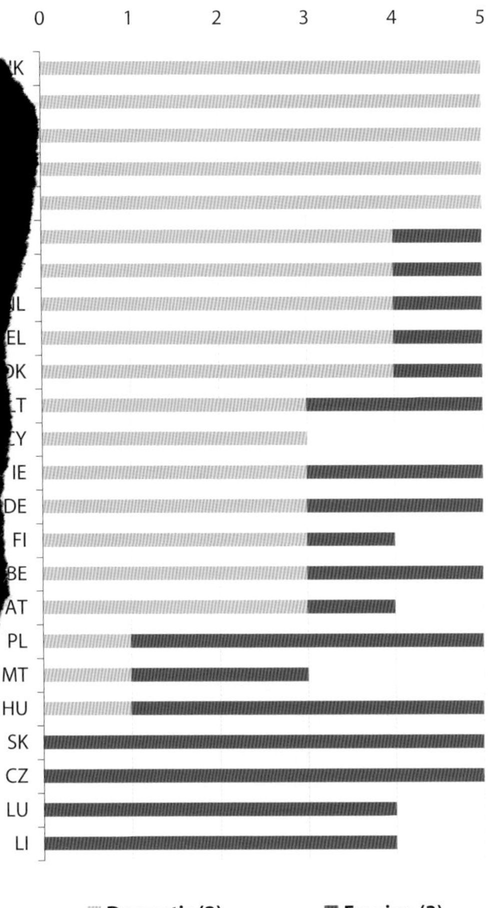

(1) In some countries less than five banks were surveyed.
(2) Banks where a controlling interest is held by a domestic institution.
(3) Banks where a controlling interest is held by an institution domiciled in another Member State.

Source: Report on the retail banking sector inquiry; Commission Staff Working Document accompanying the Communication from the Commission - Sector Inquiry under Art 17 of Regulation 1/2003 on retail banking (Final Report) [COM(2007) 33 final] SEC(2007) 106

12B.1 Access, choice and switching

On the demand side, the sector inquiry concluded that two factors may weaken the operation of a competitive marketplace. Firstly, consumers lack, or are unable to act on full information, so reducing the intensity of price competition. Secondly, consumers often face switching costs (informational and transactional costs) that discourage them from leaving their current provider.

Figure 12B.1 contains data from the final report of the sector inquiry, illustrating the extent to which foreign banks are among the largest retail banks in each Member State. In several Member States all of the largest banks in 2004 were domestically owned, notably Cyprus, the United Kingdom, Sweden, Spain, Italy and France.

The issue of buying financial services in another EU Member State was raised in a Eurobarometer survey conducted in 2008 (results are presented in Table 12B.1). The single biggest barrier (among those consumers surveyed) preventing people from signing-up to financial services was the difficulty of communicating in another language (37 %), followed by concerns over risks related to fraud (30 %). Issues relating to information also figured highly among the perceived barriers, with 29 % of respondents reporting incomprehensible information, 26 % insufficient information and 13 % reporting misleading or deceptive information.

Table 12B.1: Barriers to purchasing or signing up for financial services from sellers/providers in another EU Member State, EU-27, February-March 2008
(% of respondents; maximum of three answers per respondent)

	(%)
Having to communicate in another language	37
Risks related to fraud	30
Incomprehensible information	29
Insufficient information	26
Extra costs	24
Lack of personal contact when purchasing/signing-up at a distance	23
Misleading/deceptive information	18
Lower level of consumer protection	13
Information presented in too many ways	12
No answer/do not know	11
Different currencies	8
Refused by seller/provider as customer lives in another	5
No different risks in purchasing from companies located in other EU countries	2
Other	1

Source: 'Consumer protection in the Internal Market', Special Eurobarometer 298, European Commission

Figure 12B.2: Ease of access to the banking system, May-June 2006 (1)
(% of respondents)

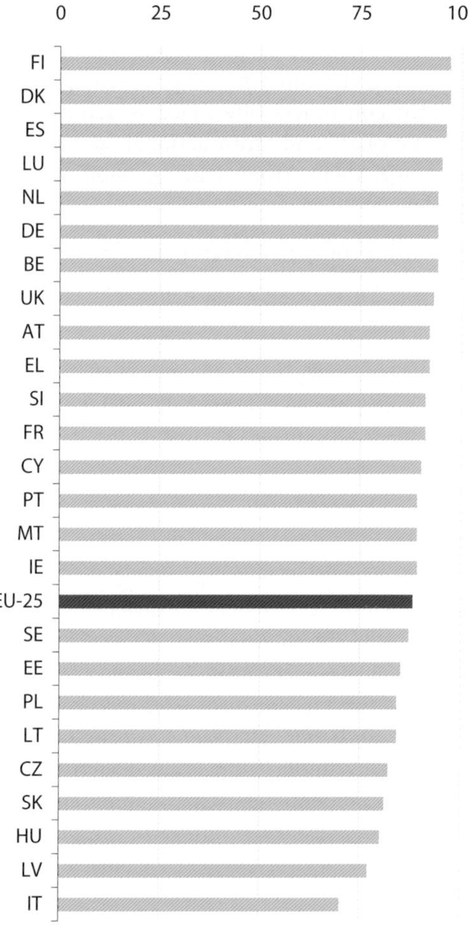

(1) Bulgaria and Romania, not available.

Source: 'Services of General Interest', Special Eurobarometer 260, European Commission

Figure 12B.3: Current account switching in the previous two years, May-June 2006 (1)
(% of respondents)

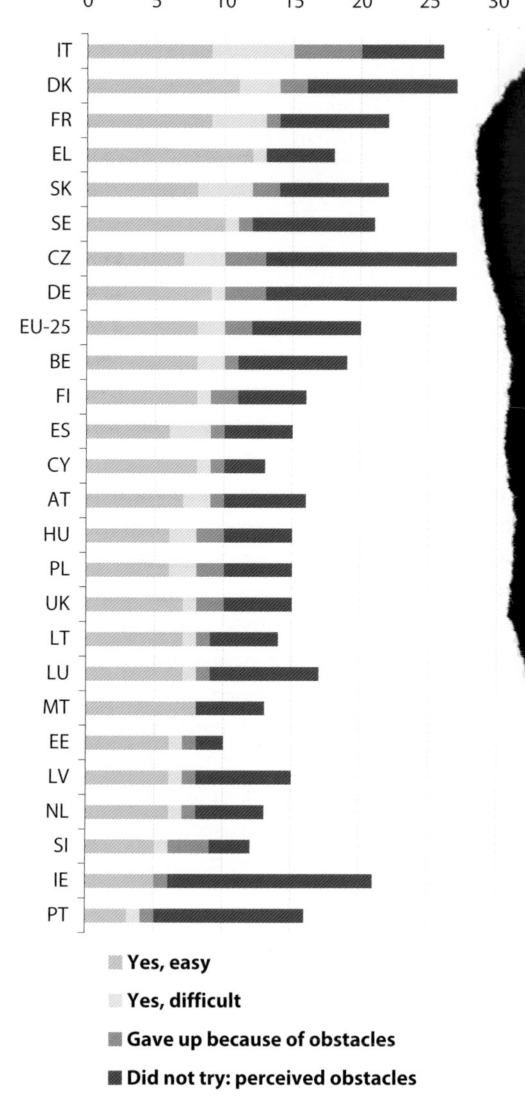

(1) Bulgaria and Romania, not available.

Source: 'Services of General Interest', Special Eurobarometer 260, European Commission

The results of another Eurobarometer survey that was also conducted in 2006 (see Figure 12B.2) indicate that the vast majority of respondents regard access to the banking system as easy, some 88 % across the EU-25 as a whole. At least 80 % of respondents regarded access as easy in all Member States except in Latvia (77 %) and Italy (70 %). The same survey looked at the ease of switching current accounts (between banks). Figure 12B.3 shows the proportion of all respondents that did switch, or did not switch either because they perceived the obstacles to be too great to try, or who tried but gave up because of the obstacles met. Overall 10 % of respondents did switch accounts, the vast majority without any problem. A similar proportion of account holders wanted to switch but did not do so, the vast majority because they had the impression that the obstacles would be too great (although they did not get as far as trying to switch). In this sense the most pessimistic respondents were in Ireland, with 15 % of respondents not trying to switch accounts because of perceived obstacles.

12B.2 Consumption

12B.2.1 Frequency

Insurance, savings and borrowing may be contracted for a relatively long, fixed period (in the case of a pension plan, life insurance, house ꞏn, or regular savings plan), while other services ꞏis area are provided on an open-ended basis, ꞏ as a current account. As such, the frequency ꞏ which customers sign-up for new financial ꞏices or purchase them is relatively low.

ꞏ006 Eurobarometer survey noted that around ꞏ% of respondents in the EU-25 had not ꞏmmitted to any of a list of ten insurance, saving ꞏr borrowing products during the 12-month ꞏeriod prior to the survey. Among the remaining ꞏ % who had signed-up or purchased a financial ꞏroduct, the most common products included ꞏon-life insurance, current or savings accounts, or ꞏome form of credit, debit, payment or other bank ꞏard. A follow-up question from a Eurobarometer ꞏurvey conducted in early 2008 shows that 12 % of ꞏespondents made a distance purchase of financial products (either over the Internet, by post or by phone) during the 12-month period prior to the survey. Of these, the vast majority (10 %) purchased products from sellers/providers in their own country, while 1 % of respondents said they purchased from another EU Member States, the same proportion (1 %) that said they had purchased a financial product from a country located outside of the EU. Across the Member States the highest proportion of consumers making distance purchases of financial products was in Sweden (32 %), followed by Estonia, Latvia, the United Kingdom and the Netherlands, where upwards of one in five persons made such purchases.

12B.2.2 Consumption expenditure

The household budget survey (HBS) covers non-life insurance and other financial services related to consumption: payments for life insurance, as well as other savings/investments are not considered as consumption expenditure, nor are interest payments. The vast majority, around 95 %, of the PPS 814 average household consumption expenditure on insurance and financial services concerned insurance, while the remainder was for financial services such as bank charges, and agents and brokers' fees.

Table 12B.2: Proportion of respondents having purchased or signed up to specified products in the 12 months prior to the survey, EU-25, February–March 2006
(% of respondents)

	(%)
None	70
Non-life insurance (health, home, travel, car etc.)	9
A current or savings account	8
A debit/credit/payment/bank card	7
Life insurance	4
A mortgage (house loan)	4
A loan other than a mortgage	4
A private pension plan	3
Stocks/shares	3
Shares in an investment fund	2
Other	1
Do not know	2

Source: 'Consumer protection in the Internal Market', Special Eurobarometer 252, European Commission

Figure 12B.4: Mean consumption expenditure per household, non-life insurance and financial services, 2005
(PPS, minimum and maximum (vertical lines at end of horizontal line), inter-quartile range containing half of the Member States (box), median (vertical line within box))

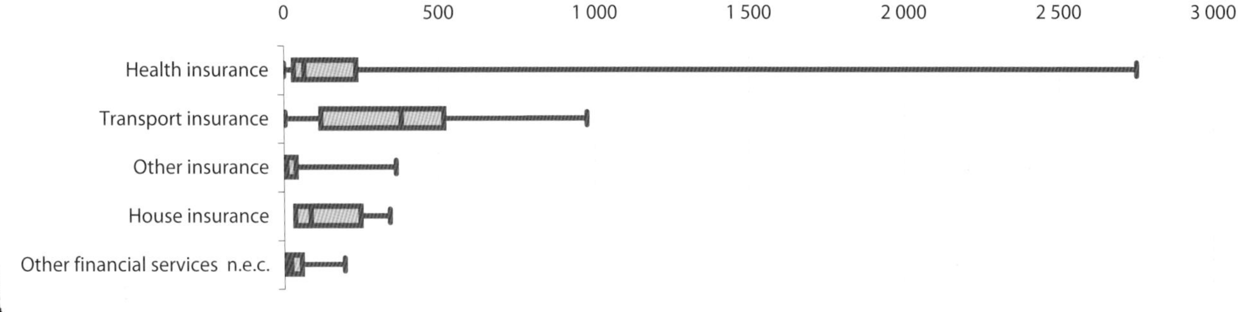

Source: Eurostat, Household Budget Survey (theme3/hbs/hbs_exp_t121)

Table 12B.3: Structure of consumption expenditure on non-life insurance and financial services, 2005 (1)
(%)

	Insurance connected with the dwelling	Insurance connected with health	Insurance connected with transport	Other insurance	Other financial services n.e.c.
EU-27	16	32	44	4	4
BE	24	19	42	9	6
BG	0	6	61	17	11
CZ	17	13	43	2	25
DK	29	23	40	4	5
DE	:	:	:	:	:
EE	39	1	55	3	3
IE	15	50	30	2	2
EL	4	14	79	0	2
ES	18	22	58	1	1
FR	14	42	31	8	5
IT	:	:	:	:	:
CY	14	10	68	7	1
LV	8	25	46	:	20
LT	22	12	61	:	7
LU	17	11	49	18	5
HU	33	13	50	0	3
MT	9	17	62	2	10
NL	4	74	14	3	5
AT	22	34	37	6	1
PL	19	18	57	0	6
PT	15	8	76	0	1
RO	5	5	25	20	45
SI	8	45	42	1	4
SK	14	12	49	8	18
FI	16	10	56	:	18
SE	29	17	48	2	3
UK	34	11	51	1	2
HR	5	25	64	0	6
NO	40	3	48	:	9

(1) EU-27, unreliable.

Source: Eurostat, Household Budget Survey (theme3/hbs/hbs_str_t211)

Figure 12B.5: Structure of consumption expenditure on non-life insurance and financial services, EU-27, 2005 (1)
(%)

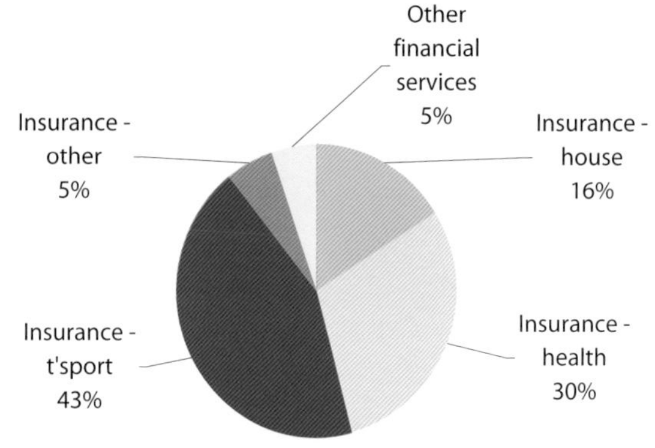

(1) Unreliable data.

Source: Eurostat, Household Budget Survey (theme3/hbs/hbs_str_t211)

There was a very wide range of average household consumption expenditure on these products, from PPS 20 or below in Bulgaria and Romania, to PPS 2 007 in Ireland, with the Netherlands recording average expenditure of PPS 3 730 per household.

Household consumption expenditure o insurance and other financial services represen 3.7 % of total household consumption expendi in the EU-27, with this share below 1 % Bulgaria, Romania and Lithuania, and as hig 12.8 % in the Netherlands; the high share in Netherlands is mainly attributed to a particula high level of expenditure on health insurance.

Figure 12B.6: Structure of consumption expenditure: share of non-life insurance and financial services in total expenditure, 2005 (
(%)

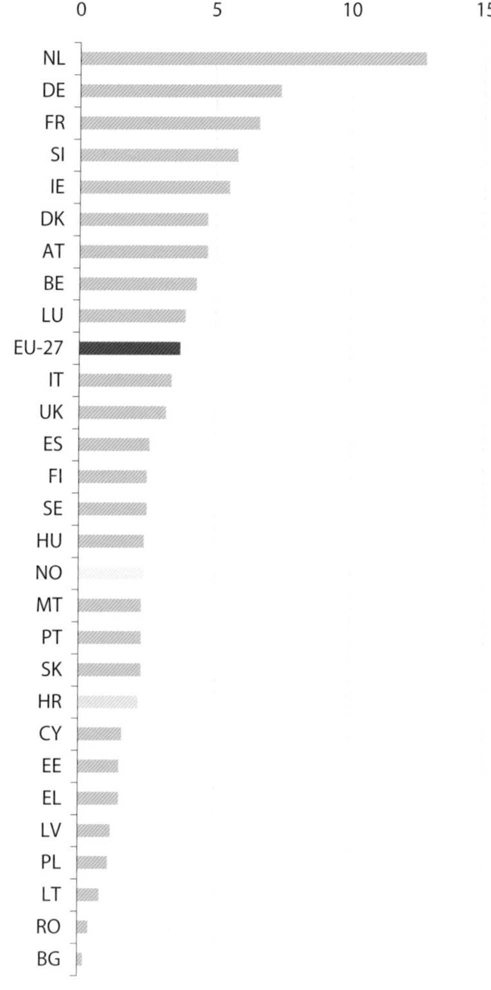

(1) EU-27, estimate; Czech Republic, not available; Germany and Italy, insurance only.

Source: Eurostat, Household Budget Survey (theme3/hbs/hbs_str_t211)

12B.3 Prices

12B.3.1 Price inflation

The harmonised index of consumer prices for insurance covers non-life insurance such as that related to dwellings, transport, health, civil bility and travel. In the EU-27 this index rose 21.9 % between 2000 and 2007, equivalent to verage of 2.9 % per annum, slightly above rate of increase recorded for the all-items sumer price index (2.4 % per annum). Price reases for non-life insurance slowed each year om a 6.3 % increase in 2000 to a 1.4 % increase 2006, with 2007 marking a reversal in this attern as the rate of change accelerated to 2.7 %. Non-life insurance prices rose particularly fast 2007 in Romania, Bulgaria, and Latvia, while ortugal was the only Member State to record a all in prices.

The price index for financial services increased, on average, by 3.4 % per annum between 2000 nd 2007, therefore at a quicker pace than that ecorded for non-life insurance. In contrast to non-life insurance, price developments during this period were irregular, fluctuating between a low of 2.6 % and a high of 5.4 % growth (2000 and 2001 respectively), with no change in prices in 2007. Among the Member States, Bulgaria was the only one to record double-digit price increases for financial services in 2007 (20.1 %). Luxembourg, Malta and Denmark recorded price reductions of between 2 % and 3 %, while the United Kingdom recorded a reduction of 1.3 %; Germany and Estonia recorded no change in their respective indices, and several of the remaining Member States recorded price increases below 1 %.

Table 12B.4: Harmonised indices of consumer prices, annual rate of change
(%)

	Non-life insurance			Financial services		
	2005	2006	2007	2005	2006	2007
EU-27	1.8	1.4	2.7	4.6	3.5	0.0
BE	2.4	2.6	4.8	0.1	3.9	8.4
BG	34.4	3.0	29.6	-1.0	-2.5	20.1
CZ	-0.8	-0.5	1.7	6.3	4.4	0.5
DK	3.5	4.8	1.0	2.7	-1.2	-2.3
DE	1.1	-0.2	2.9	0.0	1.3	0.0
EE	3.2	1.2	4.6	-0.3	0.0	0.0
IE	2.6	6.8	3.2	1.2	-1.4	1.1
EL	2.7	1.0	0.6	3.8	1.4	2.1
ES	3.7	3.4	2.9	5.1	3.5	7.8
FR	1.8	2.8	2.0	1.8	2.0	0.7
IT	1.7	2.2	1.5	6.4	1.7	0.1
CY	6.5	2.9	2.1	3.2	0.9	0.3
LV	11.1	-0.5	25.7	18.1	12.6	8.7
LT	3.3	16.8	2.0	1.0	8.1	6.4
LU	1.8	0.7	0.7	1.1	2.2	-2.9
HU	6.1	1.3	7.4	2.1	5.8	3.3
MT	3.7	0.1	0.7	2.3	1.1	-2.8
NL	5.4	1.2	1.8	1.6	-4.2	2.9
AT	3.1	-0.6	1.2	4.9	2.8	1.6
PL	2.2	-1.7	0.8	0.5	10.6	2.2
PT	2.9	0.7	-1.3	1.0	2.4	2.4
RO	18.5	13.3	45.6	4.1	11.9	7.2
SI	4.1	7.0	3.6	4.6	9.2	7.3
SK	6.1	15.1	3.5	4.5	3.5	4.4
FI	3.2	2.0	3.4	1.8	1.8	1.0
SE	4.2	3.5	6.9	1.6	1.6	2.1
UK	-0.3	1.6	3.9	7.5	4.4	-1.3
TR	16.5	11.6	10.2	13.7	15.1	4.6
IS	-1.0	8.1	15.7	10.1	6.5	5.1
NO	2.0	0.2	0.8	4.5	-0.1	-0.6
CH	:	2.0	-1.6	:	0.1	5.7

Source: Eurostat, Harmonised indices of consumer prices (theme2/prc/prc_hicp_aind)

Table 12B.5: Harmonised indices of consumer prices, annual rate of change, EU-27
(%)

	2000	2001	2002	2003	2004	2005	2006	2007
Non-life insurance	6.3	5.1	3.5	3.2	2.4	1.8	1.4	2.7
Connected with the dwelling	2.6	1.5	3.9	3.2	3.6	2.6	1.6	1.9
Connected with health	11.4	4.8	4.3	4.7	3.7	3.6	3.7	3.7
Connected with transport	7.8	7.7	2.9	2.0	1.4	-0.6	0.1	1.6
Other insurance	4.0	2.2	2.7	3.1	1.7	5.2	0.3	4.9
Financial services n.e.c.	2.6	5.4	3.7	2.9	4.0	4.6	3.5	0.0

Source: Eurostat, Harmonised indices of consumer prices (theme2/prc/prc_hicp_aind)

Figure 12B.7: Harmonised indices of consumer prices, EU-27
(2005=100)

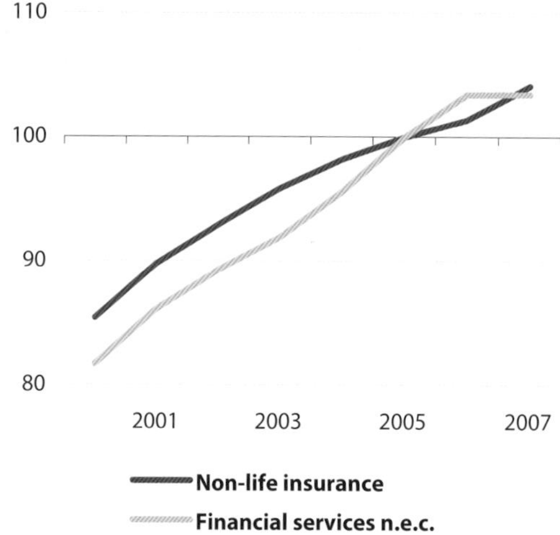

Source: Eurostat, Harmonised indices of consumer prices (theme2/prc/prc_hicp_aind)

Figure 12B.8: Affordability of bank current account, May-June 2006 (1)
(% of respondents)

(1) Bulgaria and Romania, not available.

Source: 'Services of General Interest', Special Eurobarometer 260, European Commission

12B.3.2 Price levels

Comparing actual prices between banks can be difficult: charges and interest paid or received are often bundled and high charges for one aspect of service may be offset by low charges elsewhere or a higher savings interest rate. Furthermore, special low charges may be offered to new customers or to other particular target groups (such as students/young persons or those willing to deposit considerable sums of money).

The report on the sector inquiry into retail banking looked at several types of charges, notably fees for account management, account closing, excess borrowing, automated teller machine (ATM) withdrawals, and credit transfers. Figure 12B.9 is based on the average account management fees in each of a selection of banks, analysed in terms of the dispersion of the charges. A high dispersion of average account management fees was recorded in the Czech Republic, Germany, Italy and Luxembourg, with these same Member States and the United Kingdom recording the highest maximum averages.

ATM withdrawals and credit transfer fees may be charged at a fixed amount per transaction, as a percentage of the transacted amount (often with a minimum amount), or as a combination of these two methods. For ATM withdrawals, the level and pricing structure of the fees may ary depending on whether a debit or credit d is used. The sector inquiry used a model drawal of EUR 100 with a debit card from an belonging to a different payment network. report focused on the euro area countries, noted a high variability in fees in Belgium, many, Spain, the Netherlands and Finland. Ireland, Luxembourg, the Netherlands, stria, Portugal and Finland, the weighted (by e number of current accounts) average fee was wer than half of the euro area average (EUR 4), whereas Germany and Spain reported erages higher than EUR 2.80 per transaction. e report also stated that a further analysis of e data suggests that larger banks (in terms of umbers of current accounts) tended to charge wer ATM fees than smaller banks.

r credit transfers a sum of EUR 100 was also sed, with separate analyses for domestic transfers within the same payment network and domestic transfers to a different payment network. The euro area average fees were EUR 1.30 within the same payment network and EUR 2.00 for a different network. Large differences in the average fees were observed between Member States for both types of transfer, ranging from zero to EUR 9.77 within the same payment network and from zero to EUR 10.85 to a different network. In seven of the Member States, the majority of surveyed banks did not charge fees for credit transfers within the same network, while the most expensive (on average) such transfers were reported in Greece. For transfers to a different payment network, banks in five Member States (Belgium, Germany, the Netherlands, Austria and Finland) reported zero or very low weighted average fees, with the highest weighted average fees in Greece and Luxembourg.

A 2006 Eurobarometer survey on services of general interest looked at a number of aspects concerning banking, including the affordability of current accounts. Some 82 % of respondents in the EU-25 reported that current accounts were affordable, while 8 % said that they were not and a further 8 % that costs were excessive. Less than 75 % of respondents regarded current accounts as affordable in Italy, Finland, France and Poland, while in Lithuania some 96 % of respondents agreed that they were affordable.

Figure 12B.9: Bank-average account management fees: minimum, inter-quartile range and maximum, 2004 (1)
(EUR/account)

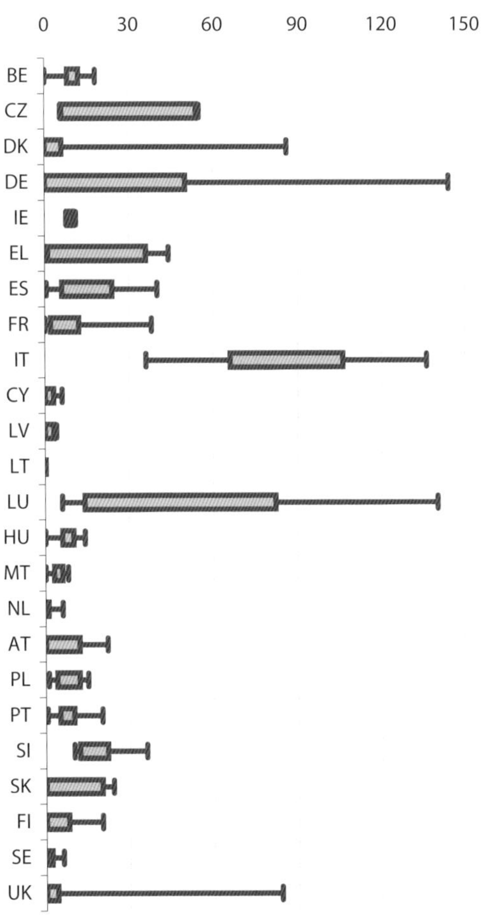

(1) The shaded box shows the range of average account management charges which the middle half (50%) of banks charge: the horizontal lines lead to the average charges of the banks with the lowest and highest account management charges; Bulgaria and Romania, not available.

Source: Report on the retail banking sector inquiry; Commission Staff Working Document accompanying the Communication from the Commission - Sector Inquiry under Art 17 of Regulation 1/2003 on retail banking (Final Report) [COM(2007) 33 final] SEC(2007) 106

12B.4 Consumer satisfaction and complaints

In 2006, a survey of consumers' satisfaction with a range of services of general interest was undertaken on behalf of the European Commission. It surveyed persons aged 18 and over that had used the specified services during the 12 months prior to the survey. Consumer satisfaction was calculated as a score out of 10, with consumers giving scores of 8 or higher classified as satisfied, 4 or less as dissatisfied, and 5 to 7 as neutral. More than three fifths of respondents were satisfied with retail banking, and most of the remainder were neutral leaving just 5 % of respondents dissatisfied. The highest proportions of persons dissatisfied with their retail bank were located in France, Italy, the Czech Republic and Hungary. Satisfaction with retail banking was lowest among students, the self-employed and unemployed, and was also lower among men (61 %) than women (65 %).

More than three fifths of respondents were also satisfied with their insurance services, with just 3 % dissatisfied; insurance services provoked the most dissatisfaction in the Czech Republic, Slovakia, Hungary and Malta. As with retail banking, students were the group least satisfied with insurance services, and the proportion o[illegible] respondents that were satisfied was (as with re[illegible] banking) low for the self-employed.

The 2006 Eurobarometer survey on servic[illegible] general interest also looked at views conce[illegible] the fairness of terms and conditions of cont[illegible] with financial institutions. Two thirds (67 %[illegible] respondents regarded them as fair, a share t[illegible] fell below half in Italy (36 %) and Poland (47 [illegible] and reached 85 % or more in Denmark, Finla[illegible] and the United Kingdom.

The same survey looked at complaints concerni[illegible] bank accounts, and found that some 6 % [illegible] respondents within the EU-25 had personal[illegible] made a complaint to their bank concerni[illegible] their current account within the previous tw[illegible] years. This proportion peaked at 9 % in Cypr[illegible] and the United Kingdom, followed by Italy an[illegible] Austria at 7 %. Hardly any other channels were used for complaining about current accounts, the most significant being 2 % of Italian respondents having made a complaint through a complaint handling body.

Table 12B.6: Satisfaction rates for financial institutions, 2006

	Retail banking		Insurance	
	Satisfied	Dissatisfied	Satisfied	Dissatisfied
EU-25	63	5	64	3
BE	76	1	74	1
BG	:	:	:	:
CZ	67	7	65	9
DK	72	5	74	3
DE	79	3	81	2
EE	84	1	71	3
IE	68	4	81	1
EL	65	2	68	2
ES	51	5	55	3
FR	56	8	65	2
IT	37	7	42	5
CY	86	3	79	4
LV	81	1	71	3
LT	80	2	76	2
LU	75	2	75	4
HU	74	6	71	7
MT	77	3	67	6
NL	51	2	47	1
AT	77	3	76	2
PL	62	4	56	4
PT	65	3	50	4
RO	:	:	:	:
SI	75	4	74	3
SK	65	5	58	9
FI	87	1	75	2
SE	80	2	67	4
UK	67	4	68	3

Source: Consumer satisfaction survey, IPSOS INRA for the European Commission Directorate-General for Health and Consumers, May 2007

Figure 12B.10: Satisfaction rates for retail banking, EU-25, 2006
(%)

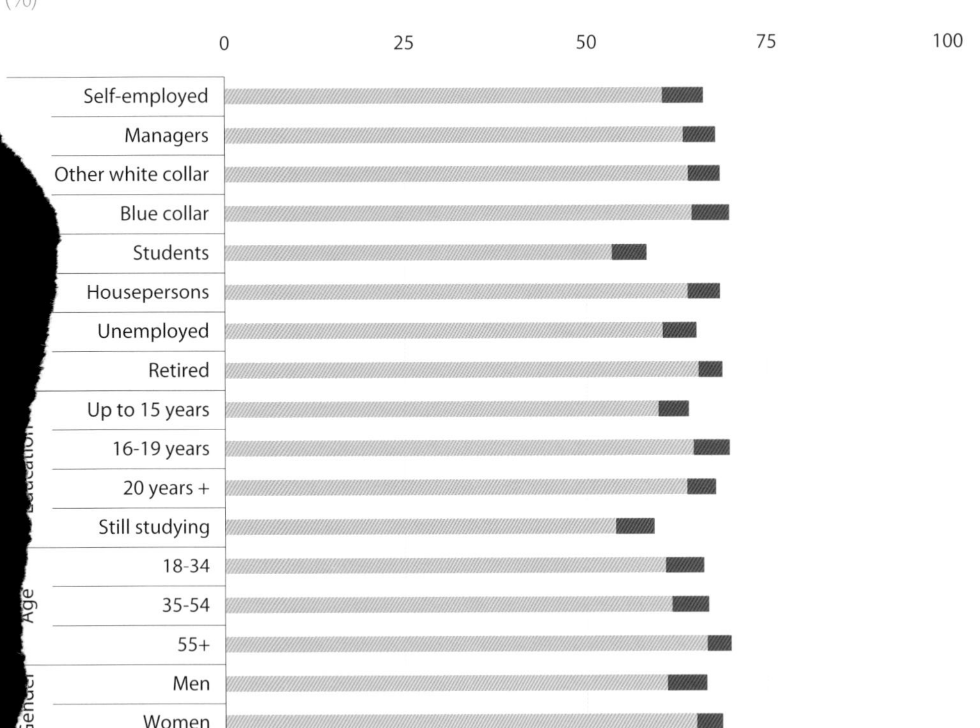

Source: Consumer satisfaction survey, IPSOS INRA for the European Commission Directorate-General for Health and Consumers, May 2007

Figure 12B.11: Satisfaction rates for insurance services, EU-25, 2006
(%)

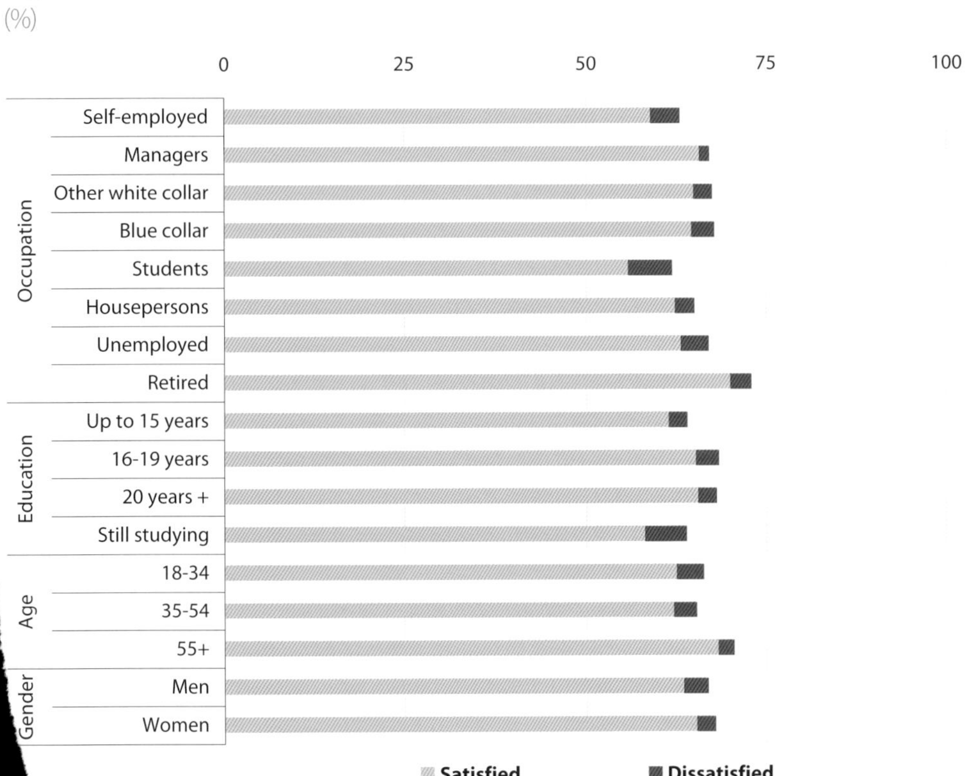

rce: Consumer satisfaction survey, IPSOS INRA for the European Commission Directorate-General for Health and Consumers, May 2007

Table 12B.7: Did you personally make a complaint about any aspect of a bank current account in the previous 12 months?, May-June 2006
(% of respondents)

	To the bank	To complaint handling body	To another party	No	Do not know
EU-25	6	0	0	93	0
BE	3	0	0	97	-
BG	:	:	:	:	:
CZ	6	0	0	93	0
DK	5	0	0	94	0
DE	6	0	0	92	1
EE	3	-	0	97	0
IE	5	0	0	92	3
EL	3	0	0	96	-
ES	3	0	0	96	1
FR	5	0	0	94	0
IT	8	2	0	90	1
CY	9	0	1	89	1
LV	1	0	-	98	0
LT	1	-	0	99	-
LU	1	-	-	98	1
HU	6	0	0	93	-
MT	7	-	-	93	-
NL	7	0	-	93	0
AT	8	1	1	90	1
PL	3	1	-	95	0
PT	2	-	0	97	1
RO	:	:	:	:	:
SI	3	0	0	97	-
SK	5	1	0	92	2
FI	5	-	-	94	0
SE	5	-	0	94	0
UK	9	0	0	91	-

Source: 'Services of General Interest', Special Eurobarometer 260, European Commission

Figure 12B.12: Fairness of terms and condition of contracts with bank/financial institutions, May-June 2006 (1)
(% of respondents)

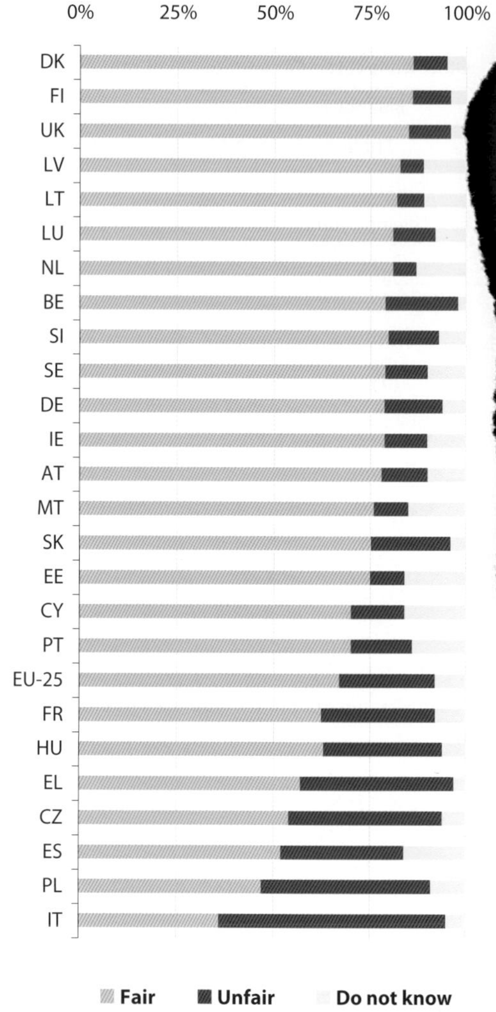

(1) Bulgaria and Romania, not available.

Source: 'Services of General Interest', Special Eurobarometer 260, European Commission

For more information

Directorate-General for the Internal Market and Services:
http://ec.europa.eu/internal_market/top_layer/index_24_en.htm

Annex

13

Data sources

Several data sources have been used across many of the chapters in this publication; an overview of these is provided here. Five Eurostat sources are presented, as well as information on the Eurobarometer surveys, a 2008 consumer satisfaction survey, as well as information on the consumer markets scoreboard. The Eurostat sources are:

- the household budget survey (HBS);
- the survey on income and living conditions (EU-SILC);
- national accounts final household consumption expenditure;
- the harmonised index of consumer prices (HICP);
- purchasing power parities and price level indices (PLI).

Household budget survey (HBS)

The household budget survey (HBS) describes the level and the structure of household expenditure. HBS are national surveys that focus on consumption expenditure, and nationally are used to calculate weights for consumer price indices; they may also be used in the compilation of national accounts.

HBS provide a picture of the total consumption expenditure of private households, analysed by a variety of socio-economic household characteristics such as the employment status of the main reference person, their income, their age, the number of active persons living in the household, the type of household, the location of the household (rural or urban), or the main source of income. Information is available at a detailed level using the classification of individual consumption by purpose (COICOP), with over 230 headings for different goods and services (including aggregates).

HBS data are confined to the population residing in private households. In other words, the survey excludes collective or institutional households (such as hospitals, old persons' homes, prisons, or military barracks), as well as persons without a fixed place of residence.

The basic unit for the collection of information is the household (defined as a social unit which shares household expenses or daily needs, in addition to having a common residence) – in other words, the household is seen as a housekeeping unit. Nevertheless, it is also important to identify the head of the household, as their personal characteristics are often used as the basis to classify information on socio-economic characteristics. The head of the household is defined, for the purpose of the HBS, as the person who contributes the most to the income of the household (the main earner).

To take economies of scale into accou household expenditures can be expre per adult equivalent. This allows househ expenditures to be compared between househ of different sizes. Adult equivalents are comp by assigning a coefficient of 1 to the first adult i household, 0.5 to other persons aged 14 and ov and 0.3 to children aged less than 14; the sum o these coefficients gives the overall household siz in terms of adult equivalents.

The expenditure effected by households t acquire goods and services is recorded at th price actually paid, which includes indirect taxe (VAT and excise duties) borne by the purchaser A household's own production for consumptio (internal production) constitutes a non-monetar component of consumption. Eurostat guidelines encourage this to be included within the survey results, with internal production valued at retail prices, as if the product had been bought in a shop. Examples of internal production include own production of food (either by a farming household or by a family that have a different professional activity but grow their own food in a vegetable garden or allotment), or withdrawals from stocks for own-use in the case of tradesmen or retailers. HBS data should also reflect benefits in kind provided by employers in exchange for work done. Notional rents are imputed to owner-occupiers and households accommodated free of charge.

HBS are carried out by means of combinations of interviews, questionnaires and diaries over variable periods of time depending on the countries and on the type of products. The intensive recording period can vary between a quarter of a month and 30 days. Interviews are used to obtain retrospective data, and their frequency can range from a month when asking about frequent purchases (for example, food) to a whole year for items that are purchased on an infrequent basis (for example, a car or other consumer durables).

The table below shows some details relating to the data collection exercise for the last round of the HBS, which was generally for the reference year of 2005. The table shows the size of the sample and the dates during which the surveys were conducted. When the reference period was not in line with the standard reporting year then data ...re inflated/deflated using the general consumer ...e index of the country concerned. Note the ... of the samples varies considerably across ...ntries, partly as a function of country size, but ... due to factors such as budget constraints and ... accuracy of the estimates being produced.

...e Member States generally supplied Eurostat ...ith micro-data files (with records for individual ...ouseholds and household members) which were ...hen treated for confidentiality, harmonised, ...ggregated and tabulated.

HBS are conducted in all 27 EU Member States, as well as Croatia, the former Yugoslav of Republic of Macedonia, Turkey, Norway and Switzerland. The data are collected on the basis of a gentleman's agreement between Eurostat and the National Statistics Institutes (NSIs). As there is no legal basis, each country has, to some degree its own methodology and survey techniques. Eurostat issues recommendations for harmonising the survey and produces a methodological document describing methodological and technical aspects of the national surveys, as well as a consolidated EU quality report. Despite this work, some differences remain in terms of the frequency, timing, content or structure of national surveys. Furthermore, the on-going work of harmonising the data collection exercise between successive rounds of the survey means that comparisons over time should be conducted with caution. Generally, cross-country comparisons made on the basis of more recent data are more robust than those made on the basis of historical data.

...iming and survey details for household budget surveys
...%)

	Reference year	Sampling unit	Gross sample	Eligible units	Actual sample	Response rate (before substitution)
BE	2005	Household	35 000	33 723	3 550	10.5%
BG	2005	Household	3 000	-	2 870	57.0%
CZ	2005	Household/person	2 966	-	2 965	-
DK	2003-2005	Address	4 500	4 457	2 449	55.0%
DE	2003	Household	59 713	53 432	52 217	97.7%
EE	2005	Household/person	7 803	7 187	3 432	44.0%
IE	2004		-	-	6 884	-
EL	2004	Dwelling	6 801	6 720	6 555	74.5%
ES	2004	Dwelling	15 000	-	8 881	59.2%
FR	2006	Household	20 000	10 240	10 240	51.0%
IT	2005	Household	28 296	-	24 107	-
CY	2003	Dwelling	3 599	3 364	2 990	88.9%
LV	2005	Household	7 429	7 275	3 774	50.8%
LT	2005	Household	10 866	7 586	7 586	69.8%
LU			-	-	3 202	-
HU	2005	Dwelling/household	17 995	-	9 058	-
MT			-	-	2 586	-
NL	2004		-	-	1 570	-
AT	20.09.2004-25.09.2005	Dwelling	20 087	20 045	8 400	41.9%
PL	2005	Household	34 992	-	34 767	-
PT		Dwelling	16 700	-	10 403	62.3%
RO	2005	Dwelling	37 440	36 607	33 066	90.3%
SI	2003-2005		-	-	3 725	-
SK	2005	Household	6 447	6 305	4 710	74.7%
FI	2006		-	-	4 007	-
SE	2005	Household	4 000	-	2 079	52.0%
UK	2005		-	-	6 785	-
HR	2005	Dwelling	4 056	2 727	2 727	67.2%
NO	2005	Person	6 601	6 496	3 376	52.0%

...urce: Eurostat, Household Budget Survey

Quality checks suggest that some of the main areas of concern as regards the comparability of data include health, education and housing. Otherwise, some expenditure items can be under-reported, for example, COICOP headings that are linked to activities that might not be considered as socially correct, such as the consumption/use of alcoholic beverages, narcotics or prostitution.

Survey on income and living conditions (SILC)

Data on income and living conditions is derived from a number of statistical sources, although the most important of these is the survey of Community Statistics on Income and Living Conditions (EU-SILC), which has largely superseded the European Community Household Panel (ECHP).

EU-SILC mainly focuses on income, collecting detailed income components for individuals, as well as a few components for households. In addition, information on social exclusion, housing conditions, labour, education and health is obtained.

EU-SILC is based on the idea of a common framework: this defines harmonised lists of target primary (annual) and secondary (every four years or less frequently) variables to be transmitted to Eurostat; guidelines and procedures; concepts (household and income) and classifications aimed at maximising comparability of the information produced. Minimum sample sizes are specified with the aim of ensuring representativeness.

EU-SILC collects annual micro-data on income, poverty, social exclusion and living conditions. Cross-sectional data pertaining to a given time or a certain time period are collected, as well as longitudinal data pertaining to individual-level changes over time, observed periodically over, typically, a four-year period.

EU-SILC was launched with limited geographical coverage in 2003 and was extended to all EU-25 Member States in 2005, and to Bulgaria and Romania in 2006; several non-member countries also participate. To compile the data most countries launched a new survey with integrated cross-sectional and longitudinal elements.

The EU-SILC target population consists of all persons living in private households. The data may be analysed by household type, activity status, level of education (according to the International Standard classification of Education – ISCED) and occupation (according to the International Standard Classification of Occupations – ISCO).

National accounts consumption expenditure

National accounts are compiled in accordance with the European system of national and regional accounts (ESA 1995). Households, as consumers, may be defined as small groups of persons who share the same living accommodation, who po[illegible] some, or all, of their income and wealth and [illegible] consume certain types of goods and ser[illegible] collectively, mainly housing and food; the cri[illegible] of the existence of family or emotional ties [illegible] also be added.

Two concepts of final consumption are us[illegible] in national accounts: final consumpti[illegible] expenditure and actual final consumption. Fin[illegible] consumption expenditure refers to expenditu[illegible] on consumption goods and services. In contras[illegible] actual final consumption refers to the acquisiti[illegible] of consumption goods and services. The differen[illegible] between these concepts lies in the treatmen[illegible] of certain goods and services financed by th[illegible] government or non-profit institutions servin[illegible] households (NPISHs) but supplied to household[illegible] as social transfers in kind.

Final consumption expenditure of households is primarily made up of goods and services purchased in the market, but also includes consumption of household production for own final use, such as the services of owner-occupied dwellings, and goods or services received as income in kind. It does not include social transfers in kind, intermediate consumption or gross capital formation, acquisitions of non-produced assets, payments to NPISHs, taxes other than taxes on products, or voluntary transfers. Final consumption expenditure may take place on the domestic territory or abroad. Goods and services should in general be recorded when the purchaser incurs a liability to the seller, implying that expenditure on a good is to be recorded at the time its ownership changes; expenditure on a service is recorded when the delivery of the service is completed. Expenditure on a good acquired under a hire purchase or similar credit agreement (and also under a financial lease) should be recorded at the time the good is delivered, even if there is no legal change of ownership at this point. Own-account consumption should be recorded when the output retained for own final consumption is produced. The final consumption expenditure of households is recorded at the purchaser's price. This is the price the purchaser actually pays for the products at the time of the purchase. Goods and services supplied as compensation of employee[illegible] in kind are valued at basic prices if produced b[illegible] the employer and at the purchaser's prices of the employer if bought in by the employer. Goods and services retained for own consumption are valued at basic prices.

Harmonised indices of onsumer prices (HICPs)

increase in the overall price of consumer ds and services is usually referred to as ation, and when expressed as a percentage nge, as the inflation rate. The inflation rate icates the loss of living standards due to price lation, and is one of the most well-known onomic statistics among the general public. is used as a leading indicator to determine onetary policy management, with price stability efined by the ECB as an annual increase in the armonised index of consumer prices (HICP) for e euro area of close to, but below, 2 % (over the edium-term). HICPs give comparable measures f inflation for individual countries, as well as or aggregates such as the euro area, the EU, or e European Economic Area (EEA). HICPs are alculated according to a harmonised approach and a single set of definitions, providing an official measure of consumer price inflation for the purposes of monetary policy and assessing inflation convergence.

HICPs are economic indicators constructed to measure the changes over time in the prices of consumer goods and services acquired by households; they aim to measure pure price changes, unaffected by changes in the quality of items which people buy. The prices included in HICPs are therefore adjusted for changes in the quality of goods and services to which they relate. Conceptually, HICPs are Laspeyres-type price indices and are computed as annual chain-indices allowing for weights changing each year. HICPs are presented with a common reference year, which is currently 2005=100.

The prices used in the HICP are the prices paid by households to purchase individual goods and services in monetary transactions. The purchaser's price is the price the purchaser actually pays and is net of reimbursements, subsidies, and discounts. Prices for goods are entered into the HICP for the month in which they are observed. Prices for services are entered into the HICP for the month in which the consumption can commence. HICPs are based on appropriate sampling procedures, taking into account the national diversity of products and prices. The weights of the HICP are based upon aggregate expenditures by households on any set of goods and services covered by the HICP. The relative distribution of consumers' expenditure on individual products varies from country to country, hence there is no uniform basket applying to all Member States. HICPs cover practically every good and service that may be purchased by households in the form of final monetary consumption expenditure. Owner occupied housing is, however, not yet reflected in the HICPs.

The different goods and services are classified according to the classification of individual consumption by purpose (COICOP). At its most disaggregated level, Eurostat publishes close to 100 sub-indices, which can be aggregated to broad categories of goods and services, and up to a total index referred to as the all-items index.

Price levels, price level indices and price convergence

Purchasing power parities (PPPs) can be considered as currency conversion rates (similar to exchange rates) that convert expenditures expressed in national currencies into an artificial common currency, the purchasing power standard (PPS). PPPs are indicators of price level differences across countries: they indicate how many currency units a given quantity of goods and services will cost in different countries; the conversion of expenditure using PPPs therefore eliminates price level differences across countries. The use of PPPs ensures that the GDP of all countries is valued at a uniform price level and thus reflects only volume differences in the economy, as opposed to price level differences. When PPPs are applied to economic expenditure aggregates, the resulting figures are expressed in PPS.

PPPs are aggregated price ratios calculated from price comparisons over a large number of goods and services. To compile the price ratios detailed price level surveys are conducted, generally over a three-year cycle. The full range of products is split into six groups, and the survey for each group has three phases: i) the selection of products and the preparation of the final product list; ii) the collection and validation of prices; iii) the calculation and publication of survey results. The surveys can take between 18 and 20 months to complete.

Individual consumption expenditure by households is broken down into 148 basic headings; prices are collected for 126 of these. As well as reflecting the expenditures on the basic headings, the products priced must be comparable across all participating countries pricing them, and at all outlets at which the products are priced; for PPPs spatial comparability is crucial, rather than the HICPs focus on comparability over time.

Eurostat produces indices of comparative price levels using PPPs – these price level indices (PLIs) provide a comparison of a country's price levels with respect to the EU average. If the price level index is higher than 100, the country concerned is relatively expensive compared with the EU average and vice versa.

An analysis of the PLIs for a range of countries gives an indication of the dispersion in price levels, and this can be quantified by calculating the coefficient of variation for the national PLIs. The coefficient of variation is calculated as the ratio of the standard deviation to the arithmetic mean of the PLIs. An analysis of the coefficient of variation over time indicates whether prices levels are converging or diverging: if the coefficient of variation for the EU decreases over time, the national price levels in the Member States are converging.

Eurobarometer

Eurobarometer surveys cover the population aged 15 years and over, resident in each of the Member States. The basic design is a multi-stage, random (probability) sample at level 2 of the geographical classification, NUTS. All interviews are conducted face-to-face for standard and special Eurobarometers, with telephone interviewing used for Flash Eurobarometers. The results of Eurobarometer surveys are analysed and made available through the 'Public Opinion Analysis' sector of the Directorate-General for Communication of the European Commission: http://ec.europa.eu/public_opinion/index_en.htm.

Eurobarometer surveys are not conducted within the European Statistical System (ESS). Nevertheless, they are an important source of information as they provide rapid information on topics of high political interest within the EU.

Satisfaction survey

This survey was carried out in 2007 and focused on services of general interest (SGI). The main focus of the survey is to help understand consumers' perceptions and the problems they have experienced. The survey is financed and co-ordinated by the Directorate-General for Heal and Consumers.

For the purposes of the survey, 'consum were defined as people aged 18 or more ha used a particular service or good in the previ 12 months. Satisfaction was defined as ' consumer's assessment of a product or serv in terms of the extent to which that product service has met his/her needs or expectations Consumer satisfaction was measured bot directly (observed satisfaction) and after th responses to specific questions were statistical processed (calculated satisfaction).

For each service and country, 500 interview were carried out (250 for services with low level of usage). Data was collected through face-to-fac interviews lasting an average of 55 minutes. A representative random sample was drawn based on stratification by region, degree of urbanisation, gender, age and occupation. A complete report on the survey is available from: http://ec.europa.eu/consumers/cons_int/serv_gen/cons_satisf/consumer_service_finrep_en.pdf.

In 2008, a similar survey was conducted for the Directorate-General for Health and Consumers, but focusing on consumer retail satisfaction. The results of this are presented in a number of chapters, with a focus on specific product groups (such as fresh fruit and vegetables, motor vehicles, or information and communications equipment).

Consumer markets scoreboard

In January 2008 the European Commission adopted a Communication (COM(2008) 31) on 'Monitoring consumer outcomes in the single market: the consumer markets scoreboard'. This noted that better monitoring and evaluation f outcomes for citizens is a priority for the ropean Commission to move to the next stage he single market. While better monitoring is portant because it will help drive better policy king and regulation, it is also essential in itself a way of demonstrating to citizens that their ncerns are taken into account. Evidence on the erformance of the single market for consumers s however largely absent at present. Developing ndicators to better monitor this demand-side spect of the single market is, therefore, key to his new approach. The scoreboard is intended to ontribute to the general monitoring exercise by rying to detect those cases where signs of market malfunctioning are linked to unsatisfactory conditions of the consumer environment. The data gathered will not only help deliver a better consumer policy, but will feed through to all policies that affect consumers, ensuring the better integration of consumer interests into all EU policies.

The first consumer markets scoreboard set out the indicators needed for screening consumer markets and the institutional framework in which markets and consumers operate. It presented existing data and suggested ways of filling the extensive gaps. The following objectives were identified.

- Identify which markets are malfunctioning in terms of consumer outcomes and need further in-depth market analysis. This analysis could generate policy-specific recommendations (competition policy, consumer policy, sectoral regulation, etc.).
- Show which horizontal consumer issues need further analysis, especially in terms of European and/or national consumer legislation.
- Show progress towards the Commission's consumer policy goals of an integrated retail internal market with confident consumers.
- Allow benchmarking of Member States' performance across the national consumer environment.

For more information: http://ec.europa.eu/consumers/strategy/facts_en.htm.

Classifications

The classification of individual consumption by purpose (COICOP) is a classification used to classify household consumption expenditure, harmonised consumer price indices and price level indices. Only COICOP Divsions 01-12 are shown as the consumption expenditure of non-profit institutions serving households (COICOP Division 13) and of general government (COICOP Division 14) are generally excluded from this publication.

01-12 Individual consumption expenditure of households

01 Food and non-alcoholic beverages

- 01.1 Food
- 01.2 Non-alcoholic beverages

02 Alcoholic beverages, tobacco and narcotics

- 02.1 Alcoholic beverages
- 02.2 Tobacco
- 02.3 Narcotics

03 Clothing and footwear

- 03.1 Clothing
- 03.2 Footwear

04 Housing, water, electricity, gas and other fuels

- 04.1 Actual rentals for housing
- 04.2 Imputed rentals for housing
- 04.3 Maintenance and repair of the dwelling
- 04.4 Water supply and miscellaneous services relating to the dwelling
- 04.5 Electricity, gas and other fuels

05 Furnishings, household equipment and routine household maintenance

- 05.1 Furniture and furnishings, carpets and other floor coverings
- 05.2 Household textiles
- 05.3 Household appliances
- 05.4 Glassware, tableware and household utensils
- 05.5 Tools and equipment for house and garden
- 05.6 Goods and services for routine household maintenance

06 Health

- 06.1 Medical products, appliances and equipment
- 06.2 Outpatient services
- 06.3 Hospital services

07 Transport

- 07.1 Purchase of vehicles
- 07.2 Operation of personal transport equipment
- 07.3 Transport services

08 Communication

08.1 Postal services

08.2 Telephone and telefax equipment

08.3 Telephone and telefax services

09 Recreation and culture

09.1 Audio-visual, photographic and information processing equipment

09.2 Other major durables for recreation and culture

09.3 Other recreational items and equipment, gardens and pets

09.4 Recreational and cultural services

09.5 Newspapers, books and stationery

09.6 Package holidays

10 Education

10.1 Pre-primary and primary education

10.2 Secondary education

10.3 Post-secondary non-tertiary education

10.4 Tertiary education

10.5 Education not definable by level

11 Restaurants and hotels

11.1 Catering services

11.2 Accommodation services

12 Miscellaneous goods and services

12.1 Personal care

12.2 Prostitution

12.3 Personal effects n.e.c.

12.4 Social protection

12.5 Insurance

12.6 Financial services n.e.c.

12.7 Other services n.e.c.

14.3 Recreation and culture

14.4 Education

14.5 Social protection

The classification shown is for COICOP Groups. There is one further level of detail within COICOP for Classes. In order to obtain a more detailed listing of the COICOP and further information realting to the classification, refer to: http://unstats.un.org/unsd/cr/registry/regcst.asp?Cl=5.

Abbreviations

ADR	Alternative dispute resolution
AEA	Association of European airlines
ANEC	European association for the coordination of consumer representation in standardisation
ATC	Agreement on textiles and clothing
ATFM	Air traffic flow management
ATM	Automated teller machine
B2B	Business-to-business
B2C	Business-to-consumer
BEUC	European consumers' organisation
BSE	Bovine spongiform encephalopathy
CARE	Community database on road accidents resulting in death or injury
CD	Compact disc
CEN	European committee for standardisation which deals with all sectors except the electro-technology and telecommunications sectors
CENELEC	European committee for electro technical standardisation
CIAA	Confederation of the food and drink industries of the EU
CMI	International marketing committee
CO_2	Carbon dioxide
COICOP	Classification of individual consumption by purpose
CPI	Consumer price index
CPC	Consumer protection co-operation
CQARF	Common quality assurance reference framework for VET
CVT	Continuing vocational training
DG	Directorate-General (of the European Commission)
DIY	Do-it-yourself
DSL	Digital subscriber line
ECB	European Central Bank
ECC-Net	European consumer centres network
ECDC	European centre for disease prevention and control
ECVET	European credit system for VET
EDEN	European destinations of excellence
EEA	European Economic Area (27 Member States of the European Union, Iceland, Liechtenstein and Norway)
EEAICP	European economic area index of consumer prices
EFSA	European food safety authority
EFTA	European free trade association
EICP	European index of consumer pri
EMAS	Eco-management and audit sche
EMF	Electromagnetic field
EMU	Economic and monetary union
EQF	European qualifications framewor
ESA 1995	European system of accounts (199
ETSI	European telecommunications standards institute
EUFIC	European food information counci
Eurostat	Statistical office of the European Communities
FEDSA	Federation of European direct selling associations
GDA	Guideline daily amounts
GDP	Gross domestic product
GMO	Genetically modified organism
GPSD	General product safety directive
HBS	Household budget survey
HD DVD	High-definition digital versatile disc
HICP	Harmonised indices of consumer prices
ICT	Information and communication technology
IPPC	Integrated pollution prevention and control
ISCED	International standard classification of education
ISDN	Integrated services digital network
ISHMT	International shortlist for hospital morbidity tabulation
ITGLWF	International textile, garment and leather workers' federation
ITU	International telecommunication union
LFS	Labour force survey
LPG	Liquefied petroleum gas

Ltd	Private limited company
MP3	Mpeg audio layer 3
MMS	Multimedia messaging service
MUICP	Monetary union index of consumer prices
CE	Classification of economic activities in the European Community
.	Not elsewhere classified
O(s)	Non-governmental organisation(s)
ISH	Non-profit institutions serving households
ECD	Organisation for economic co-operation and development
J	Official Journal
TE	Organisation for timeshare in Europe
C	Personal computer
DA	Personal digital assistant
DF	Portable document format
PDO	Protected designations of origin
PGI	Protected geographical indications
PISA	Programme for international student assessment
PLI	Price level indices
PPP	Purchasing power parities
PPS	Purchasing power standard
PSP	PlayStation portable
RAPEX	Rapid alert system for non-food products
RASFF	Rapid alert system for food and feed
RDA	Recommended daily allowances
REACH	Registration, evaluation and authorisation of chemicals
R&D	Research and development
SANCO	Health and consumers (Directorate-General of the European Commission)
SDDS	Special data dissemination standard
SEPA	Single euro payments area
SGI(s)	Service(s) of general interest
SILC	Survey on income and living conditions
SIM	Subscriber identification module
SME(s)	Small and medium-sized enterprise(s)
SMS	Short message service
TSG	Traditional speciality guaranteed
TUS	Time use survey
TV	Television
UCP	Unfair commercial practices
UEA	Federation of European furniture manufacturers
UN	United Nations
VAT	Value added tax
VET	Vocational education and training
VOC	Volatile organic compounds
VoIP	Voice over Internet protocol
WHO	World Health Organisation
WTO	World Trade Organisation

Geographical aggregates and countries

EU	European Union
EU-27	European Union of 27 Member States from 1 January 2007 (BE, BG, CZ, DK, DE, EE, IE, EL, ES, FR, IT, CY, LV, LT, LU, HU, MT, NL, AT, PL, PT, RO, SI, SK, FI, SE, UK)
EU-25	European Union of 25 Member States from 1 May 2004 to 31 December 2006 (BE, CZ, DK, DE, EE, IE, EL, ES, FR, IT, CY, LV, LT, LU, HU, MT, NL, AT, PL, PT, SI, SK, FI, SE, UK)
EU-15	European Union of 15 Member States from 1 January 1995 to 30 April 2004 (BE, DK, DE, IE, EL, ES, FR, IT, LU, NL, AT, PT, FI, SE, UK)
Euro area	At the time of writing the euro area is composed of BE, DE, IE, EL, ES, FR, IT, CY, LU, MT, NL, AT, PT, SI, FI. The euro area was initially composed of 11 Member States (BE, DE, IE, ES, FR, IT, LU, NL, AT, PT, FI) – as of 1 January 2001 Greece joined, and as of 1 January 2007 Slovenia joined, and as of 1 January 2008 Cyprus and Malta joined.

BE	Belgium
BG	Bulgaria
CZ	Czech Republic
DK	Denmark
DE	Germany
EE	Estonia
IE	Ireland
EL	Greece
ES	Spain
FR	France
IT	Italy
CY	Cyprus
LV	Latvia
LT	Lithuania
LU	Luxembourg
HU	Hungary
MT	Malta
NL	Netherlands
AT	Austria
PL	Poland
PT	Portugal
RO	Romania
SI	Slovenia
SK	Slovakia
FI	Finland
SE	Sweden
UK	United Kingdom
HR	Croatia
MK	former Yugoslav Republic of Macedonia
TR	Turkey
IS	Iceland
LI	Liechtenstein
NO	Norway
CH	Switzerland
US	United States of America

Units of measurement

bn	billion = 1 000 million
EUR	euro
g	gram
GJ	gigajoule
[illegible]l	kilocalorie
[illegible]	kilogram(s)
[illegible]	kilometre
[illegible]	square kilometre
[illegible]h	kilowatt hour
[illegible]	square metre
[illegible]	cubic metre
[illegible]g	milligram=1/1 000 of a gram
[illegible]m	passenger-kilometre
[illegible]	tonne
[illegible]m	tonne-kilometre
[illegible]OE	tonne of oil equivalent
[illegible]l.	alcohol expressed as a percentage of total liquid volume
[illegible]g	microgram=1/1 000 000 of a gram

European Commission

Consumers in Europe

Luxembourg: Office for Official Publications of the European Communities

2009 — 375 pp. — 21 x 29.7 cm

SBN 978-92-79-11362-8
SSN 1831-4023

Price (excluding VAT) in Luxembourg: EUR 25